The Discourse Reader

Third Edition

In this bestselling Reader, Jaworski and Coupland have collected in one volume the most important and influential articles on discourse analysis. Designed as a structured sourcebook and divided into clear sections, *The Discourse Reader* covers the foundations of modern discourse analysis and represents all of its contemporary methods and traditions.

The third edition:

*   Has been revised and updated throughout to ensure a selection of up-to-date and accessible readings
*   Includes new readings by Jan Blommaert, Norman Fairclough, James Paul Gee, Barbara Johnstone, Ron Scollon and Don H. Zimmerman, among others.
*   Features papers by leading researchers commissioned especially for the new edition.

The general introduction serves as an essential introduction to the field of discourse analysis, while the section introductions provide a useful overview and further insight into the readings.

The third edition of *The Discourse Reader* is a key resource for all students of discourse analysis in a wide range of disciplines from linguistics to communication studies, anthropology and psychology.

Authors:

J.L. Austin, Paul Baker, M.M. Bakhtin, Jan Blommaert, Pierre Bourdieu, Penelope Brown, Wolfram Bublitz, Deborah Cameron, Derek Edwards, Norman Fairclough, Elizabeth Frazer, James Paul Gee, Erving Goffman, H.P. Grice, Penelope Harvey, Ian Hutchby, Roman Jakobson, Barbara Johnstone, William Labov, Stephen C. Levinson, David Machin, Bronislaw Malinowski, Gerlinde Mautner, Tony McEnery, Hugh Mehan, Ben Rampton, Geoffrey Raymond, Kay Richardson, Harvey Sacks, Emanuel A. Schegloff, Deborah Schiffrin, Ron Scollon, Jack Sidnell, Deborah Tannen, Jenny Thomas, Crispin Thurlow, Teun A. Van Dijk, Theo Van Leeuwen, Cynthia Wallat and Don H.

Adam Jaworski is Professor at the University of Hong Kong. He is co-editor of *Semiotic Landscapes: Language, Image, Space* (2010) and co-author of *Tourism Discourse: The Language of Global Mobility* (2010).

Nikolas Coupland is Research Professor at the University of Copenhagen and Distinguished Professor of Sociolinguistics at the University of Technology Sydney. He is editor of *The Handbook of Language and Globalization* (2010) and co-editor of *Standard Languages and Language Standards in a Changing Europe* (2011) with Tore Kristiansen.

The Discourse Reader

Third Edition

Edited by

Adam Jaworski and
Nikolas Coupland

Routledge
Taylor & Francis Group

LONDON AND NEW YORK

Third edition published 2014
by Routledge
2 Park Square, Milton Park, Abingdon, Oxon OX14 4RN

and by Routledge
711 Third Avenue, New York, NY 10017

*Routledge is an imprint of the Taylor & Francis Group,
an informa business*

First edition published 1999 by Routledge
Second edition published 2006 by Routledge

British Library Cataloguing in Publication Data
A catalogue record for this book is available from the British Library

Library of Congress Cataloging in Publication Data
The discourse reader/edited by Adam Jaworski and
Nikolas Coupland. – 3rd edition.
    pages cm
    Includes index.
    1. Discourse analysis. I. Jaworski, Adam, 1957– editor of
    compilation. II. Coupland, Nikolas, 1950– editor of compilation.
    P302.D564 2014
    401'.41–dc23   2013040528

ISBN: 978-0-415-62948-5 (hbk)
ISBN: 978-0-415-62949-2 (pbk)

Typeset in Perpetua and Bell Gothic
by Florence Production Ltd, Stoodleigh, Devon

Printed and bound in Great Britain by
TJ International Ltd, Padstow, Cornwall

CONTENTS

LIST OF FIGURES

PREFACE

IN THIS NEW EDITION of *The Discourse Reader* we provide the reader with an up-to-date, integrated and structured collection of original writings, representing the interdisciplinary and fast-changing field of discourse studies. The book focuses principally on the linguistic, interactional, textual, social, cultural and ideological issues that have motivated the analysis of discourse. The book is planned for use as a beginners/intermediate degree-level teaching text, either on its own or as a secondary sourcebook. The readings are organized to provide a wide-ranging introduction to discourse theory and practice, but also to bring the reader into contact with much of the best contemporary scholarship in discourse analysis. For this reason, we have included several different sorts of text, some of which appeared in the two previous editions of the *Reader*, some of which are new, including five chapters specially written for the present edition. This edition consists of:

- influential early papers that laid the ground for the concept of discourse and defined the main priorities for what has come to be called discourse analysis;
- discussions of key research methods and resources;
- reflexive commentaries by leading theorists, highlighting key differences between sub-traditions of discourse studies;
- papers by contemporary specialists showing what discourse analysis is able to achieve, applied to a wide range of social issues and social settings.

Since so many disciplines nowadays claim the term 'discourse' as their own, it is inevitably true that we have emphasized some traditions and schools more than others. Whatever discourse is, and however concretely or abstractly the term is used, there will at least be agreement that it has focally to do with language, meaning and context. For this reason we have started with a substantial section of readings (in Part One) on this theme. It is certainly true that discourse is not the privileged domain of linguists and linguists alone. But some appreciation of early ideas in functional linguistics and linguistic philosophy is essential for all students of discourse. Similarly, and although we would resist the idea that discourse analysis is 'a research method' in the conventional sense (see our Introduction to Part Two), it is important to see the broader research enterprise to which discourse analysis contributes. Part Two is therefore a collection of readings on methods and resources for doing discourse analysis. It introduces different traditions of social research and questions of research ethics, linked to practical issues of representing and analysing discourse data, and to forms of language analysis.

Parts Three to Six of the *Reader* then reproduce many of the key articles and book chapters that, over two decades and more, have made decisive contributions to discourse studies. Despite the need to be selective, a large proportion of the most influential issues, writers and texts are represented. Part Three introduces those approaches most concerned with sequence and discourse structure, tracing links back to ethnomethodology and carried forward in modern conversation analysis and related research. Part Four deals with social and relational aspects of discourse; Five with identity and subjectivity, as mediated by language; and Six with critical approaches to discourse with the main emphasis on ideology, power and control.

One problem for us as editors has been to establish a boundary between discourse analysis and those approaches to language and society referred to as 'interactional sociolinguistics'. In many people's view, including our own, there is no meaningful distinction between interactional work in sociolinguistics and discourse analysis applied to social settings and themes. Several of the readings we include in the present volume would be considered important contributions to interactional sociolinguistics, and indeed to sociolinguistics generally. Therefore, the reader might find it useful to consult, in parallel, the collection of readings titled *The New Sociolinguistics Reader*, edited by Nikolas Coupland and Adam Jaworski, published by Palgrave Macmillan, 2009.

We have reproduced all original papers and chapters as faithfully as we have been able to, given the inevitable restrictions of space and the need to produce a coherent and readable collection. We have, for example, maintained authors' original writing styles and conventions, whether they wrote according to British or USA norms. In several cases this policy results in maintaining what is thought of as sexist pronoun usage (for example, Grice's and many others' use of 'man' for non-specific gender, where 'person' would be more usual and acceptable today). Where we have had to shorten texts, '. . .' shows that we have omitted an amount of original material (usually several sentences or whole sections). Sometimes we have added a short summary of the topic or main points of omitted sections. Our own editorial comments are contained in square brackets.

ACKNOWLEDGEMENTS

The editors and publishers would like to thank the following copyright holders for permission to reprint material:

Roman Jakobson, 'Closing statement: linguistics and poetics', pp. 350–77 in Thomas A. Sebeok (ed.) *Style in Language*, 1966. Reproduced by permission of MIT Press.

J.L. Austin, pp. 63–75, Chapter 2 from *How To Do Things with Words*, 2nd edition, Oxford University Press, 1962. Reprinted by permission of the publisher from *How To Do Things With Words* by John L. Austin, edited by J.O. Urmson and Marina Sbisa, Cambridge, MA: Harvard University Press. Copyright © 1962, 1975 by the President and Fellows of Harvard College.

H.P. Grice, 'Logic and conversation', from *Syntax and Semantics*, volume 3, Peter Cole and Jerry L. Morgan (eds.) 'Logic and conversation', pp. 41–58. Copyright © 1975, with permission from Elsevier.

M.M. Bakhtin, 'The problem of speech genres', from *Speech Genres and Other Late Essays*, translated by Vern W. McGee, edited by Caryl Emerson and Michael Holquist. Copyright © 1986. By permission of the University of Texas Press.

Norman Fairclough (2003) *Analysing Discourse: Textual Analysis for Social Research* (Abingdon: Routledge).

Ron Scollon (2007) *Analyzing Public Discourse: Discourse Analysis in the Making of Public Policy* (Abingdon: Routledge).

Deborah Cameron, Elizabeth Frazer, Penelope Harvey, Ben Rampton and Kay Richardson, 'Ethics, advocacy and empowerment', in Cameron et al (eds.) *Researching Language: Issues of Power and Method*, 1992, Routledge. Reproduced by permission of the publisher and the authors.

James Paul Gee (2011) *An Introduction to Discourse Analysis: Theory and Method*, 3rd edition (Abingdon: Routledge).

Wolfram Bublitz, 'Cohesion and Coherence' in Jan Zienkowski, Prof. Dr. Jan-Ola Östman and Prof. Dr. Jef Verschueren (eds.) *Discursive Pragmatics*, 2001, pp 37–49. With kind permission by John Benjamins Publishing Company, Amsterdam/Philadelphia. www.benjamins.com

Jenny Thomas (1995) *Meaning in Interaction: An Introduction to Pragmatics* (Abingdon: Routledge).

William Labov, 'The transformation of experience in narrative', in *Language in the Inner City*. Copyright © 1972 by the University of Pennsylvania Press. Reprinted by permission of the University of Pennsylvania Press and Blackwell Publishing.

Derek Edwards, 'Narrative analysis', from Widdicombe and Woolfit (eds.) *Discourse and Cognition*. Copyright © 1996. Reprinted by permission of Sage Publications Ltd.

Harvey Sacks. 1986 [1972] 'On the analyzability of stories by children', in John J. Gumperz and Dell Hymes (eds.) *Directions in Sociolinguistics: The Ethnography of Communication*. Oxford: Basil Blackwell. Originally published by Holt, Rinehart and Winston. 325–345.

Emanuel A. Schegloff and Harvey Sacks, 'Opening up closings', *Semiotica* 8, 1973. Reproduced by permission of Emmanuel A. Schegloff and Mouton de Gruyter.

Deborah Schiffrin, 'Oh as a marker of information management', in Schiffrin, *Discourse Markers*, 1988, Cambridge University Press. Reproduced with permission of the publisher.

Bronislaw Malinowski, 'On phatic communion', in Ogden and Richards (eds.) *The Meaning of Meaning*, 1946, Routledge. Reproduced by permission of the publisher.

Excerpt from *Interaction Ritual* by Erving Goffman, Copyright © 1967 by Erving Goffman. Used by permission of Pantheon Books, an imprint of the Knopf Doubleday Publishing Group, a division of Random House LLC. All rights reserved.

Penelope Brown and Stephen C. Levinson, 'Strategies for doing face threatening acts', in Brown and Levinson (eds.) *Politeness: Some Universal in Language Usage*, 1987, Cambridge University Press. Reproduced with permission of the authors and the publishers.

Interactive Frames and Knowledge Schemas in Interaction: Examples from a Medical Examination/Interview', by Deborah Tannen and Cynthia Wallat in *Social Psychology Quarterly*, Vol. 50, No. 2, Special Issue: Language and Social Interaction (Jun., 1987), pp. 205–216.

Deborah Cameron, 'Performing gender', in Johnson and Meinhof (eds.) *Language and Masculinity*, Blackwell Publishing, 1997. Reproduced by permission of the author and publisher.

Don Zimmerman, 'Identity, Context and Interaction', extracted from D. H. Zimmermann. 1998. In Charles Antaki and Sue Widdicombe (eds.) *Identities in Talk*. London: Sage. 87–106.

Barbara Johnstone, "Pittsburghese Shirts: Commodification and the Enregisterment of an Urban Dialect," in *American Speech*, Volume 84, no. 2, pp. 157–175. Copyright, 2009, the American Dialect Society. All rights reserved. Republished by permission of the copyright holder, and the present publisher, Duke University Press. *www.dukeupress.edu*.

Pierre Bourdieu, pp. 66–89 from *Language and Symbolic Power*, edited and introduced by John B. Thompson, translated by Gino Raymond and Matthew Adamson, Cambridge, MA: Harvard University Press. English translation Copyright © 1991 by Polity Press. Reprinted by permission of Harvard University Press and Polity Press.

Teun Van Dijk, 'Discourse and the denial of racism', from *Discourse and Society*, 3(1), Copyright © 1992. Reprinted by permission of Sage Publications Ltd.

Ian Hutchby, 'Power in discourse' from *Discourse and Society*, 7(4), Copyright © 1996. Reprinted by permission of Sage Publications Ltd.

Hugh Mehan, 'Oracular reasoning in a psychiatric exam: the resolution of conflict in language', in A. Grimshaw (ed.) *Conflict Talk*, 1990, Cambridge University Press. Reproduced with permission of the author and publisher.

Jan Blommaert, Orders of Indexicality and Polycentricity. Extracted from J. Blommaert. 2007. Sociolinguistics and discourse analysis: Orders of indexicality and polycentricity. *Journal of Multicultural Discourse* 2: 115–130.

Extract from 'Texting more popular than face-to-face conversation', p.491 of this volume © Telegraph Media Group Limited 2012.

Extract from 'OMG! Texting ruins kids' grammar' by Michelle Maltais, p.492 of this volume. Copyright © 2012. *Los Angeles Times*. Reprinted with Permission.

We are very grateful to Justine Coupland for editorial advice and input in preparing this edition.

Introduction

PERSPECTIVES ON DISCOURSE ANALYSIS

Adam Jaworski and Nikolas Coupland

Discourse: an interdisciplinary movement

DEBORAH SCHIFFRIN'S (1994) BOOK, *Approaches to Discourse*, compiles and discusses various definitions of 'discourse'. Here are three of them (Schiffrin 1994: 23–43):

> Discourse is: 'language above the sentence or above the clause'.
>
> > (Stubbs 1983: 1)

> The study of discourse is the study of *any* aspect of language use.
>
> > (Fasold 1990: 65)

> [T]he analysis of discourse is, necessarily, the analysis of language in use. As such, it cannot be restricted to the description of linguistic forms independent of the purposes or functions which these forms are designed to serve in human affairs.
>
> > (Brown and Yule 1983: 1)

Here are some others:

> [W]ith the sentence we leave the domain of language as a system of signs and enter into another universe, that of language as an instrument of communication, whose expression is discourse.
>
> > (Benveniste 1971: 110, cited in Mills 1997: 4–5)

> Instead of gradually reducing the rather fluctuating meaning of the word 'discourse', I believe I have in fact added to its meanings: treating it

> sometimes as the general domain of all statements, sometimes as an individualizable group of statements, and sometimes as a regulated practice that accounts for a number of statements.
>
> (Foucault 1972: 80, cited in Mills 1997: 6)

Roger Fowler says that his programme for literary studies has the aim

> to change or even deconstruct the notion of literature so that a very wide range of discourses is actively used by individuals in their conscious engagements with ideology, experience and social organization.
>
> (Fowler 1981: 199)

> 'Discourse' is for me more than *just* language use: it is language use, whether speech or writing, seen as a type of social practice.
>
> (Fairclough 1992: 28)

> Discourse *constitutes* the social. Three dimensions of the social are distinguished – knowledge, social relations, and social identity – and these correspond respectively to three major functions of language . . . Discourse is shaped by relations of power, and invested with ideologies.
>
> (Fairclough 1992: 8)

According to David Lee, it is an

> uncomfortable fact that the term 'discourse' is used to cover a wide range of phenomena . . . to cover a wide range of practices from such well documented phenomena as sexist discourse to ways of speaking that are easy to recognise in particular texts but difficult to describe in general terms (competitive discourse, discourse of solidarity, etc.).
>
> (Lee 1992: 97)

> 'Discourse' . . . refers to language in use, as a process which is socially situated. However . . . we may go on to discuss the constructive and dynamic role of either spoken or written discourse in structuring areas of knowledge and the social and institutional practices which are associated with them. In this sense, discourse is a means of talking and writing about and acting upon worlds, a means which both constructs and is constructed by a set of social practices within these worlds, and in so doing both reproduces and constructs afresh particular social-discursive practices, constrained or encouraged by more macro movements in the overarching social formation
>
> (Candlin 1997: iix)

Other definitions of discourse will appear in the chapters to follow. Taken together, they clearly span a considerable range, although a core set of concerns also emerges.

It is this core, and the best-established deviations from it, that we intend to unpack in the pages of the *Reader*. The quotations above consistently emphasize 'language in use'. But there is a large body of opinion (see the later quotations) that stresses what discourse is *beyond* language in use. Discourse is language use relative to social, political and cultural formations – it is language reflecting social order but also language shaping social order, and shaping individuals' interaction with society. This is the key factor explaining why so many academic disciplines entertain the notion of discourse with such commitment. Discourse falls squarely within the interests not only of linguists, literary critics, critical theorists and communication scientists, but also of geographers, philosophers, political scientists, sociologists, anthropologists, social psychologists and many others. Despite important differences of emphasis, discourse is an inescapably important concept for understanding society and human responses to it, as well as for understanding language itself.

Part of the explanation for the upsurge of interest in discourse lies in a fundamental realignment that has taken place, over the past four decades or so, in how academic knowledge, and perhaps all knowledge, is assumed to be constituted. To put the negative side of this change, we might describe it as a weakening of confidence in traditional ways of explaining phenomena and processes, a radical questioning of how people, including academics, come to appreciate and interpret their social and cultural environments. The rise in importance of discourse has coincided with a falling off of intellectual security in what we know and what it means to know – that is, a shift in epistemology, in the theorizing of knowledge (see Cameron et al, Chapter 7; Gee, Chapter 8). The question of *how* we build knowledge has come more to the fore, and this is where issues to do with language and linguistic representation come into focus.

Academic study, but in fact all aspects of experience, are based on acts of classification, and the building of knowledge and of interpretations is very largely a process of defining boundaries between conceptual classes, and of labelling those classes and the relationships between them. This is one central reason why all intellectual endeavour, and all routine social living, needs to examine language, because it is through language that classification becomes possible (Lee 1992). Seen this way, language ceases to be a neutral medium for the transmission and reception of pre-existing knowledge. It is the key ingredient in the very constitution of knowledge. Many disciplines, more or less simultaneously, have come to see the need for an awareness of language, and discourse more broadly, and of the structuring potential of language, as part of their own investigations. This is the shift often referred to as the 'linguistic turn' in the social sciences, but it has been experienced in academic study more generally.

All the same, it is not as if linguistics, 'the scientific study of language', has always provided the most appropriate means of studying knowledge-making processes and their social implications. Linguistics has tended to be an inward-looking discipline. It has not always appreciated the relevance of language and discourse to people other than linguists. The dominant traditions in linguistics, one could say until at least the 1970s, were particularly narrow, focusing on providing good descriptions of the grammar and pronunciation of utterances at the level of the sentence. Considerations of meaning in general, and particularly of how language, meaning and society interrelate, are still quite recent concerns. Discourse analysis is therefore a relatively new area of importance to linguistics too, which is moving beyond its earliest ambition. That was, to put it simplistically, to describe sentences and to gain autonomy for itself as a 'scientific' area of academic study. Under the heading of discourse, studies of language have come to be concerned with far wider issues. Discourse linguists analyse, for example, the structure of conversations, stories and various forms of written text, the subtleties of implied meanings, and how language in the form of speech interacts with non-linguistic (e.g., visual or spatial) communication. Under the headings of cohesion and coherence (see Chapter 9 by Wolfram Bublitz) they study how one communicative act depends on previous acts, and how people creatively interact in the task of making and inferring meaning. We consider some of these main developments, in linguistics and in other disciplines, in more detail in Parts One and Two of the *Reader*.

So discourse has gained importance through at least two different, concurrent developments – a shift in the general theorizing of knowledge and a broadening of perspective in linguistics. The *Reader* includes extracts from many of the most influential original writings on discourse, both theoretical and applied, which have brought about and benefited from this confluence of ideas. As individual chapters show, language studied as discourse opens up countless new areas for the critical investigation of social and cultural life – the composition of cultural groups, the management of social relations, the constitution of social institutions, the perpetuation of social prejudices, and so on.

Other general trends too have promoted interest in discourse. One is the growing recognition that contemporary life, at least in the world's most affluent and 'developed' societies, has qualities that distinguish it quite markedly from the 'modern' industrial, pre-World War Two period. One of the most obvious manifestations of what Anthony Giddens and many others have called 'Late Modernity' or 'High Modernity' (Giddens 1991), and what is more generally referred to as *postmodernity*, is the shift in advanced capitalist economies from manufacturing to service industries. Norman Fairclough (1992, 1995) refers to one part of this phenomenon as the *technologization* of discourse in post-Fordist societies (since the beginning of mass production of motor cars and similar industrial developments). Manufacturing and assembly workers working on production lines, isolated from consumers of the items they are producing, have been largely replaced by teams of workers, networked together, involved in communication tasks of different sorts or representing their companies in different kinds of service encounters with clients. Language takes on greater significance in the worlds of knowledge and service economies such as marketing, education, banking, insurance, telesales, tourism, and so on.

Rapid growth in communications media, such as cable, satellite and digital television and radio, desktop publishing, telecommunications (mobile phone networks, video-conferencing), email, online social and content sharing networks, internet-mediated sales and services, information provision and entertainment, has created new markets for language use. It is not surprising that language is being more and more closely scrutinized, for example within school curricula and by self-styled experts and guardians of so-called 'linguistic standards' (Cameron 1995; Milroy and Milroy 1999; Thurlow, Chapter 31). At the same time language is being shaped and honed, for example by advertisers, journalists and broadcasters, in a drive to generate ever-more attention and persuasive impact. Under these circumstances, language itself becomes marketable and a sort of commodity (Cameron 2000; Heller 2003, 2011), and its purveyors can market themselves through their skills of linguistic and textual manipulation (see Bourdieu, Chapter 26). Discourse ceases to be 'merely' a function of work. It *becomes* work, just as it defines various forms of leisure and, for that matter, academic study. The analysis of discourse becomes correspondingly more important – in the first instance for those with direct commercial involvement in the language economies, and secondly for those who need to deconstruct these new trends, to understand their force and even to oppose them (Cameron 2000).

This *critical* or socially engaged perspective on analysing discourse is apparent in several of the quotations above – most obviously those from Christopher Candlin, Norman Fairclough and Roger Fowler. (Part Six of the *Reader* contains several texts that are critically oriented in this sense, but see also Chapters 6, 7, 11 and 25.) If we ask what is the purpose of doing discourse analysis, the answer from critical discourse analysts would go well beyond the description of language in use. Discourse analysis offers a means of exposing or deconstructing the social practices that constitute 'social structure' and what we might call the conventional meaning structures of social life. It is a sort of forensic activity, with a libertarian political slant. The motivation for doing discourse analysis is very often a concern about social inequality and the perpetuation of power relationships, either between individuals or between social groups, difficult though it is to pre-judge moral correctness in many cases.

As this implies, the focus for a particular analysis can be either very local – analysing a particular conversation between two people or a single diary entry – or very global and abstract. In this latter tradition, the theoretical work of Michel Foucault (1980) and that of Michel Pêcheux (1982) has been very influential in introducing the link between discourse and ideology. Foucault prefers the term 'regimes of truth' rather than 'ideology', by which he means different types of discourses that are accepted and made to function as true. Pêcheux stresses how any one particular discourse or 'discursive formation' stands, at the level of social organization, in conflict with other discourses. He gives us a theory of how societies are organized through their ideological struggles, and how particular groups (e.g., social class groups or gender groups) will be either more or less privileged in their access to particular discourse networks. Local and global perspectives come together when some type of discourse analysis can show how the pressure of broad social or institutional norms are brought to bear on the identity and classification of individuals (see, for example, Mehan's analysis of a psychiatric interview in Chapter 29; Baker and McEnery's analysis of the construction of the category 'foreign doctor' by the British press in Chapter 30; and Thurlow's analysis of the print media positioning of young people as semi-illiterate and obsessed by text messaging in Chapter 31).

Let us recap briefly. At the most basic level, discourse is definable as language in use, but many definitions incorporate significantly more than this. Discourse is implicated in expressing people's points of view and value systems, many of which are 'pre-structured' in terms of what is 'normal' or 'appropriate' in particular social and institutional settings. Discourse practices can therefore be seen as the deployment of, and indeed sometimes as acts of resistance to, dominant ideologies. The focus of discourse analysis will usually be the study of particular texts (e.g., conversations, interviews, speeches, etc., or various written documents), although discourses are sometimes held to be abstract value systems which will never surface directly as texts (see Gee's distinction in Chapter 8 between the small 'd' and big 'D' discourses, respectively). Texts are specific products, or 'sediments' of meaning, which, to varying degrees, will reflect global as well as local discourse practices relevant to their production and reception. Discourse analysis can range from the description and interpretation of meaning-making and meaning-understanding in specific situations through to the critical analysis of ideology and access to meaning-systems and discourse networks. Language and discourse seem to have a particular salience in contemporary, *late-modern* social arrangements.

From this preliminary overview it is already apparent why the study of discourse is an interdisciplinary project. Most disciplines, and certainly all of the human and social sciences, need to deal with the interrelations between discourse and concepts such as social structure, social relations, conflict, ideology, selfhood, postmodernity and social change.

Multi-modal and multi-voiced discourses

It is worth emphasizing that discourse reaches out further than language itself in the forms as well as the meanings that can be the focus of analysis. When we think of discourse in the wider context of communication, we can extend its analysis to include non-linguistic *semiotic systems* (systems for signalling meaning), those of non-verbal and non-vocal communication which accompany or replace speech or writing (see Hodge and Kress 1991 for an overview of social semiotics, and Van Leeuwen 2005 for a wide-ranging introduction). Discourse practices include the 'embodied' or more obviously physical systems of representation, for example performance art, sign language or, more generally, what Pierre Bourdieu has called the 'bodily hexis'; see Chapter 26. Other non-verbal discourse modes (although often incorporating aspects of speech or writing) include painting, sculpture, photography, dance, music and film. In this sense, all texts are multi-modal (Kress and Van Leeuwen 1996, 2001; Scollon, Chapter 6); speech involves not only words but also intonation, stress and voice quality (prosodic and paralinguistic features), and is normally accompanied by gestures, facial expressions and so on (non-verbal features). Considerations of written words increasingly involve typography, page layout, the materiality of signs, colour, relation to accompanying images, and so on (see Machin and Van Leeuwen, Chapter 11; Mautner, Chapter 25).

The idea that discourse is multiply structured has been a dominant one since the earliest days of discourse analysis and its predecessor in functional linguistics (see our Introduction to Part One). Roman Jakobson (Chapter 1), Michael Halliday (1978) and others stressed that language-in-use realizes many functions simultaneously, for example an informational function alongside relational/interpersonal and aesthetic functions. The focus on multi-modal discourse is in one sense a continuation of this traditional view, especially when it can be shown that different semiotic resources or dimensions (e.g., visual images and linguistic text in a school textbook or in a newspaper) fulfil different communicative functions. But texts can be multiply structured in other ways, if they show *multiple voicing* or *heteroglossia* (Bakhtin 1981, 1986; Chapter 4). Texts often reflect and recycle different voices, which may be realized through different modalities or indeed a single modality, and addressing one or many audiences. For example, Ron Scollon's (Chapter 6) study of texts from the domain of public discourse illustrates how different *modes* (e.g., textual or visual) produce different effects with regards to the texts' truth claims (*modality*). He also draws our attention to how texts can be constructed and interpreted against background awareness of other texts – the phenomenon of *intertextuality*. A text whose meaning is achieved relative to other texts may include, blend or erase other salient points of view or voices.

Take another example, a hypothetical TV advertisement promoting a new car, which may embody a number of 'real' or 'implied' voices, addressing viewers in a multitude of roles – as drivers, passengers, car experts, status-seekers, parents concerned over their children's safety, overseers of family budgets, etc. Some of the different voices in this context may be ones we actually hear, realized via spoken language – perhaps a matter-of-fact commentary on the merits of the car, such as its safety, its comfort or its favourable price. But alternatively, they may be 'heard' in a less direct sense, through written/visual signs, e.g., the company's logo or the advertisement's on-screen small print. Cinematic and musical elements will also be present, perhaps photographs representing selected features of the car's design or its appearance and performance on the road, or a well-known tune with 'fitting' lyrics and so on.

Some of these voices may be competing with each other, representing conflicting interests or ideologies (e.g., safety vs. speeding). For Mikhail Bakhtin all discourse is multi-voiced, as all words and utterances echo other words and utterances derived from the historical, cultural and genetic heritage of a community and from the ways these words and utterances have been previously interpreted. In a broader sense then, 'voices' can be interpreted as discourses – positions, ideologies or stances that speakers and listeners take in particular instances of co-constructed interaction. Following Dell Hymes (1996), Jan Blommaert (2005) defines 'voice' as one's capacity to be heard and understood, or not. The concept of voice becomes particularly salient under globalization, where social actors with increasingly *non*-overlapping systems of knowledge, divergent goals and competing interests face the task of negotiating meaning (see Blommaert, Chapter 32). Since many and even *most* texts do not represent 'pure' discourses, genres and styles, analysis will have to incorporate a significant element of text-to-text comparison, tracing the influence of one sort or genre of text upon another. The forensic task of the discourse analysis will be to track how various forms of discourse, and their associated values and assumptions, are incorporated into a particular text, why and with what effects.

The layering of social meaning in discourse

Discourse analysis is an interdisciplinary project for many reasons. Most obviously, as we suggested above, many disciplines are fundamentally engaged with discourse as social and cultural practice. But let us accept, for the moment, the least ambitious definition of discourse analysis from the set at the head of this chapter, 'the analysis of language in use'. Even at this level, it is easy enough to demonstrate that discourse is, for example, a thoroughly linguistic *and* social *and* cognitive affair. Consider the following simple instance, reconstructed from a real social event, but with the names of the participants changed. The person called 'Mother' is the mother of the eight-year-old child, called 'Rebecca'. The person called 'Mrs Thomson' is employed as a domestic cleaner by the family in which 'Mother' is the mother; Mrs Thomson's first name is Margaret. Mrs Thomson has just come in through the front door, having rung the doorbell first, and Mother speaks first, calling downstairs to her daughter. (These brief notes are of course a remarkably sparse account of 'the context' for the talk exchange below, but they will allow us to make some first-level observations on the discourse construction of meanings of various sorts in this episode.)

> **Extract 1**
> (*The front door bell rings.*)
> *Mother*:   Open the door, darling. Who is it?
> *Rebecca*:   It's only Maggie.
> *Mother*:   (*looking sheepish*) Oh hello, Mrs Thomson.
> *Mrs Thomson*:   (*smiles*) Hello.

Even this short sequence alerts us to the complexities of meaning-making and the range of resources that both we, as observers or analysts, but also the participants themselves, have to draw on to 'make sense' of what is happening in the sequence as a piece of situated social interaction. It seems obvious that there is a measure of discomfort in the conversational exchanges here, signalled in our representation of Mother's facial expression as 'sheepish'. 'Sheepish' is, of course, already an interpretation (ours). It is based on a linguistic classification of a possibly complex emotional state. In glossing Mother's expression as 'sheepish', we are appealing to a type of emotional state that we assume is both recognizable to others (in this case, you, the readers of this text), and reasonably applicable to the facial and perhaps postural configurations that we remember as being adopted by Mother. A video-taped recording would in fact be important in justifying our use of the term 'sheepish', if we needed to. But even then, our interpretation that these face and body features properly represent the category 'sheepishness' would depend on others (such as you) making the same or a similar inference.

So far, we have pointed to one small aspect of the linguistic work of classification that is built into the written record of Extract 1. But of course there are very many other classification processes at work here, for us and for the participants themselves. As readers, you may be asking *why* Mother is uncomfortable, and how the discourse – the totality of meaning-making and meaning-inferring generated through this interaction – produces an impression that this is the probable emotional effect. A likely explanation (and the one that led us to choose this bit of talk as an example) is that Mother is embarrassed by her daughter referring to Mrs Thomson as 'Maggie'. She is probably embarrassed further by the expression *only Maggie*, especially (or maybe *only*?) because Mrs Thompson has overheard Rebecca's utterance referring to her.

A linguistic analysis of the usual circumstances under which we use the word 'only' will get us some distance here, when we realize that 'only' often projects an event as being unimportant or unexceptional. Mother may well be embarrassed that Rebecca considers Mrs Thomson's arrival as an event of the sort that might be called an 'only' event. She may also be uncomfortable that her daughter, a child, is referring to an adult by an overly familiar expression – using her first name, all of that being witnessed by Mrs Thompson. In any event, precisely how the different participants are positioned and involved in the discourse is clearly a relevant concern.

On the whole, we have few problems making these or similar inferences. But it is interesting to consider just *how* we are able to make them. For example, they seem to rely, in part, on there being a social consensus about how children usually do talk, or ought to talk, to adults. But is this universally true or just a convention in one particular cultural situation? More particularly, some of the social sensitivity in the exchange hinges on the child using a first name not only to an adult, but to an adult employed as a cleaner. There are particularly strong reverberations of social class and economic power behind this exchange, and they certainly make up an element of its 'meaning'. However, bringing these underlying political and economic assumptions to the surface is a social taboo, and it is Rebecca's unwitting breaking of this taboo that probably also causes her mother's embarrassment.

In the other direction, there is an element of 'understanding' suggested in Mrs Thomson's smile, perhaps implying she appreciates that Rebecca is not fully able to judge the social conventions or rules for addressing adults. The smile may be an attempt to mitigate the discomfort Mother is feeling. On the other hand, Mrs Thompson's smile could also be an accommodating reaction to Rebecca's remark. For her to react in a different way and signal indignation would mean breaking another taboo. In any case, note how 'child' and 'cleaner', not to mention 'mother' and 'daughter', are linguistic labels for social categories with culturally meaningful and somewhat predictable social qualities and expectations attached to them. Note that our access to 'the meaning' of the interaction depends on how we hang these labels on individuals, and on particular people's labelling of other people. Note how we have to make inferences about people's intentions, and about how those intentions are perceived and evaluated by others (see Sacks, Chapter 14 on some cognitive processes of categorical work in organizing social actors into groups, or 'teams', and attributing specific actions to them).

Another part of what is achieved as meaning in the interaction depends on rather precise timing and placement, which are not at all captured in the written transcript of what was said. As we suggested, Mother's embarrassment may be exacerbated by the fact that, in our reconstruction of it, the *It's only Maggie* utterance is said when all three participants are present together, face-to-face. *Maggie* might well be the usual way the family has of referring to Mrs Thomson when she is not present. Changing the composition of the group by Mrs Thompson's joining the *participation framework* (the structure of who is participating in a given event) as an unratified recipient, or 'overhearer' (Goffman 1981: 132), of Rebecca's utterance certainly shifts expectations of what are the 'appropriate' forms of expression. In this regard, we might read a particular significance into Mother's *oh*, perhaps as a conventional way of expressing a 'change of state' in the discourse (Heritage 1984a; Schiffrin, Chapter 17). Mother's expectation that she was speaking with her daughter, and only her, is broken when she sees that Mrs Thomson has already entered the house, and Mother signals this in her talk when she uses the particle *oh*.

There are other, seemingly more mundane, observations to be made about how this interaction is structured, although they are still important from some perspectives. For example, we take it for granted that Mrs Thomson's *hello* is structurally linked to Mother's *hello* in the previous turn at talk. That is, it is not coincidental that both speakers do greeting, and do it through the use of the same greeting word. As conversation analysis has established (see Schegloff and Sacks, Chapter 15; Raymond and Sidnell, Chapter 16; Zimmerman, Chapter 23; Hutchby, Chapter 28, and our Introduction to Part Three), the second *hello* not only follows the first *hello*, but is 'occasioned by' it; it is the second part of a pair of utterances. Its absence would be a noticeable absence. In more cognitive terms, it is probable that Mrs Thomson feels something of an obligation, however subconsciously, to match Mother's *hello* which had been offered to her. This is part of what it means to call an exchange of greetings a cultural convention, or a *mini-ritual* of social interaction. Exchanging paired greetings is the predictable or 'unmarked' way of opening social encounters, between either strangers or (as here) people already familiar with each other (see our Introduction to Part Four).

The general point is that, in social interaction, speakers are achieving meaning at many levels. They are exchanging information between them (although very little of the extract under discussion is concerned with transmitting 'information' in the usual sense of 'facts' or 'data'), and negotiating particular relationships between them as individuals. But at the same time their talk is filling out and confirming wider patterns of social organization, for example in running through predictable patterns of turn-taking, and pairing of utterances. We can say that the structured nature of everyday talk (see Erving Goffman's 1983 concept of *the interaction order*) generates and confirms broader patterns of social organization (*the social order*). One important facet of discourse analysis is therefore, as we saw earlier, to show how micro-level social actions realize and give local form to macro-level social structures (see Fairclough, Chapter 5; Scollon, Chapter 6; Gee, Chapter 8; Machin and Van Leeuwen, Chapter 11).

Rather than pursue this particular example any further, we can at least summarize those dimensions of discourse that we need to attend to if we want to (begin to) understand how it functions as a discourse event. We have, directly or indirectly, already identified the following aspects:

1   The meaning of an event or of a single utterance is only partly accounted for by its formal features (that is, by the 'direct meaning' of the words used). The social significance of discourse, if we define it simply as language-in-use, lies in the relationship between linguistic meanings and the wider context (i.e., the social, cultural, economic, demographic and other characteristics of the communicative event) in which interaction takes place (see the notion of 'activity types' discussed by Jenny Thomas in Chapter 10).

2   Our interpretation of discourse therefore relates far more to what is done by participants than what is said (or written, or drawn, or pointed at) by them. That is, a functional analysis of language and other semiotic systems lies at the heart of analysing discourse.

3   It is important to distinguish between meanings (including goals and intentions) that are inferred by observers and, on the other hand, meanings (including goals and intentions) that are inferred by participants. Analysing discourse is often making inferences about inferences.

4   All aspects of meaning-making are acts of construction. Attributing meaning to discursive acts is never a neutral or value-free process.

5   Social categorization is central to these acts of construction. Our language presents us with many categories that seem 'natural' or 'obvious', although they are very probably so only at a given time and place: they may well be culture-specific or idiosyncratic (favoured by an individual).

6   We can only access discourse through the textual data that we collect by observation, audio or video recording. This means that the texts we analyse are always 'filtered' or 'mediated'; they are in themselves a form of social (re)construction. (This particular aspect of discourse is of central importance in the burgeoning new area of mediated discourse analysis, see Scollon and Scollon 2004; Jones and Norris 2005.)

7   Linguistic expression itself (as speech or writing) often needs to be interrelated with other physical, temporal and behavioural aspects of the social situation, such as body movement and the synchronization or sequencing of actions. Discourse is more than (verbal/vocal) language itself.

8   Paying close attention to and critical reading of particular instances of language-in-use, linked to other aspects of the social context, is a useful way of discovering the normal and often unwritten assumptions behind communication. Although interpretation will always have elements of subjectivity within it, communication is based on linked, subjective interaction (*inter-subjectivity*). A more formal approach is likely to miss the creative inter-subjectivity of social interaction. (In saying this we do not deny that language is a structured phenomenon, or deny the importance of this fact. Language and other semiotic systems have recognizable structures and the study of these structures as formal systems constitutes an entirely viable, but different, research programme.)

9   Discourse analysis provides a way of linking up the analysis of local characteristics of communication to the analysis of broader social characteristics. It can let us see how macro-structures are carried through micro-structures.

Traditions of discourse analysis

The *Reader* offers a broad and inclusive perspective on the concept of discourse, which is appropriate in view of how many academic disciplines (as we have explained) now see discourse as an important theoretical and empirical focus for them. At the same time, discourse, however we define it, has focally to do with language-use. Some approaches remain quite close to the central goals of linguistics, offering detailed linguistic descriptions of texts, spoken and written. At the other extreme, as we have seen, there are approaches to discourse that assume that the most significant sorts of linguistic organization are highly abstract, and not directly amenable to textual analysis.

We can use this approximate scale of directness–indirectness as a way to organize a discussion of several different traditions of discourse analysis. All of them are represented in the *Reader*, although the following sub-sections (as many taxonomic or listing frameworks do) probably overstate the degree of difference between approaches. In practice, discourse analysts and the analyses they produce do not fall quite so neatly into these types. It is also true that many researchers have taken an inclusive view of discourse studies, to the extent that their work spans most or all of the traditions we survey below. One clear instance is the work of Teun Van Dijk, who has been more responsible than any other person for integrating the field of discourse analysis (see, for example, Van Dijk 1977, 1984, 1985, 1988, 1997, 2008, 2009; also Chapter 27).

Despite these limitations, it should be helpful to approach the various Parts of the *Reader* armed with a mental map of the principal traditions of discourse studies and their main defining qualities. These general overviews should also be helpful in identifying sources for further reading for students new to any of these fields. We have included at the end of this chapter a list of the main academic journals that print new research in discourse and related fields.

Speech act theory and pragmatics

The study of meaning is at the heart of the discipline referred to as pragmatics. Closely related to semantics, which is primarily concerned with the study of word and sentence meaning, pragmatics concerns itself with the meaning of utterances in specific contexts of use. It is one thing to understand a phrase as far as the individual meanings of its words and its referential meaning is concerned, and quite another to know what its intended and achieved meanings may be in context. Charles Fillmore illustrates the pitfalls of relying on sentence meaning in interpreting talk and disregarding pragmatic meaning of an utterance by recounting two anecdotes concerning the fixed phrase *I thought you'd never ask*:

> It's a fairly innocent teasing expression in American English, but it could
> easily be taken as insulting by people who did not know its special status
> as a routine formula. In one case a European man asked an American

woman to join him in the dance, and she, being playful, said, 'I thought you'd never ask'. Her potential dancing partner withdrew his invitation in irritation. In another case a European hostess offered an American guest something to drink, when he, unilaterally assuming a teasing relationship, said, 'I thought you'd never ask'. He was asked to leave the party for having insulted his host.

(Fillmore 1984: 129–30)

Jenny Thomas (1995) distinguishes three types of meaning (illustrated here with our own examples):

- *abstract* meaning (the meaning of words and sentences in isolation, e.g., the various meanings of the word *grass*, or the ambiguity of the sentence *I saw her duck*);
- *contextual* or *utterance* meaning (e.g., when two intimate persons hold their faces very near each other and one whispers to the other *I hate you* while smiling, the utterance might *really* mean 'I love you'); and
- utterance *force* (i.e., how the speaker intends his/her utterance to be understood; e.g., when X says to Y *are you hungry?*, X might intend the question as a request for Y to make X a sandwich).

Thomas focuses on utterance meaning and force, which are central to pragmatics, which she defines as the study of 'meaning in interaction' (1995: 22) with the special emphasis on the interrelationship between the speaker, hearer, utterance and context.

The notion of *force* is borrowed directly from J.L. Austin's work on speech act theory (Chapter 2), and his threefold distinction into the *locution* of a speech act (the actual words used in an utterance), its *illocution* (the force or the intention of the speaker behind the utterance), and its *perlocution* (the effect of the utterance on the listener). Studying the effects of the speaker's utterances on the listener derived from Austin's view of language as a form of action. Austin observed that by saying something, we not only communicate ideas, but may also bring about a change in the social environment – a transformation, however small, of social reality. Speech acts that effect such a change through the action of being spoken are called *performative speech acts* (or *performatives*). For example, the act of joining two people in marriage is principally a (performative) speech act involving the formula: *I now pronounce you husband and wife*. Of course, in order for a performative to realize its perlocutionary force, it has to meet certain social and cultural criteria, or fulfil *felicity conditions*. It is clear, for example, that unauthorized individuals cannot pronounce anyone 'husband and wife'. Austin's work gained renewed significance with recent interest in the notions of 'performance' and 'performativity' in cultural criticism and discourse analysis (see Cameron, Chapter 22; our Introduction to Parts Five and Six).

Much of speech act theory has been concerned with taxonomizing speech acts and defining felicity conditions for different types of speech acts. For example, John Searle (1969, 1979) suggested the following typology of speech acts based on different types of conditions that need to be fulfilled for an act to 'work' or succeed: 'representatives (e.g., asserting), directives (e.g., requesting), commissives (e.g., promising), expressives (e.g., thanking), and declarations (e.g., appointing)' (quoted from Schiffrin 1994: 57). This taxonomy was one of many, and it soon became clear in speech act theory that a full and detailed classification would be unwieldy given the multitude of illocutionary verbs in English. Stipulating the felicity conditions for all of them appeared to be not only a complex procedure but also an 'essentializing' one – relying too heavily on factors assumed to be essential in each case, when reality shows us that they are variably determined by the precise social context.

An elaboration of speech act theory was offered by Labov and Fanshel (1977) in their examination of a psychiatric interview. Although their prime concern was with the identification of speech acts and specifying the rules governing their successful realization, they broadened the view that an utterance may only perform one type of speech act at a time. For example, the following utterance by a client in their data, reported to have been said to her mother, *well, when d'you plan to come home?*, may be a request for information, a challenge, or an expression of obligation (see also Taylor and Cameron 1987).

Like Austin and Searle, Labov and Fanshel explain communication in terms of hearers accurately identifying the intended meaning of the speaker's utterance and responding to it accordingly. However, given the multi-functionality of utterances, we cannot be sure that the hearers always pick up the 'right' interpretation of an utterance, i.e., the one that was intended by the speaker. At the same time, we might doubt whether speakers always have a clear and singular intention behind many of their own utterances. In general, the problem of intentionality and variability in people's discourse rules precluded developing a coherent framework for explaining communication, beyond producing an inventory of such rules and speech act types. A different way of explaining communication was proposed by H.P. Grice (Chapter 3), whose work was central in the development of inferential pragmatics and interactional sociolinguistics.

Grice, like Austin and Searle, was a philosopher, whose interest in language stemmed from the investigations of sense, reference, truth, falsity and logic. However, Grice argued that the logic of language (or conversation, as the title of his classic paper has it) is not based on the same principles as formal (mathematical) logic. Instead, he proposed a model of communication based on the notion of the Coopera- tive Principle, i.e., the collaborative efforts of rational participants in directing conversation towards attaining a broadly common goal. In following the Cooperative Principle the participants follow a number of specific maxims (called conversational maxims), such as be informative, be truthful, be relevant and be clear. When the maxims are adhered to, meaning is produced in an unambiguous, direct way. However, most meaning is implied, through two kinds of implicatures: 'conventional implica- tures', which follow from the conventional meanings of words used in utterances, and 'conversational implicatures', which result from the non-observance of one (or more) of the conversational maxims. When participants assume that the Cooperative Principle is being observed but one of the maxims is violated, they seek an indirect interpretation via conversational implicature. To use a well-known example from Grice (see p. 69), if a letter of recommendation appears to be under-informative (violating the maxim be informative) and concentrates wholly on, say, the candidate's punctuality and good manners (violating the maxim be relevant), then, assuming that the author is being in a general sense cooperative, the addressee may infer that the candidate is not suitable for the job.

Grice's impact on pragmatics and discourse analysis in general cannot be overestimated. Although he has been criticized for formulating his Cooperative Principle to suit the conversational conventions of middle-class English speakers, and for not attending to the idea of strategic *non*-cooperation, the guiding principle of inference as the principal means for generating meaning in interaction remains central in most current approaches to discourse. Two areas in which Grice's influence has been felt most strongly are in the theories of linguistic politeness (see Brown and Levinson, Chapter 20) and of relevance. We will introduce relevance theory in some detail because it is a significant independent model of discourse processing which we have been unable to incorporate as a discrete chapter.

The cognitively oriented approach to communication proposed by Dan Sperber and Deidre Wilson (1986, 1995) makes Grice's maxim of relevance central to explaining how information is processed in discourse. In sharp opposition to the code models of language, relevance theory assumes that linguistic communication is based on *ostension* and *inference*, which can be said to be the same process viewed from two different perspectives. The former belongs to the communicator, who is involved in a form of 'showing' (ostension), and the latter to the audience, who is/are involved in the process of interpretation (inference). Inferential comprehension of the communicator's ostensive behaviour relies on deductive processing of any new information presented in the context of old or already-known information. This derivation of new information is spontaneous, automatic and unconscious, and it gives rise to certain contextual effects in the cognitive environment of the audience. The occurrence of contextual effects, such as contextual implications, contradictions and strengthening, is a necessary condition for relevance. The relation between contextual effects and relevance is that, other things being equal, 'the greater the contextual effects, the greater the relevance' (Sperber and Wilson 1986: 119). In other words, an assumption which has no contextual effects at some particular moment of talk is irrelevant, because processing this assumption does not change the old context.

A second factor in assessing the degree of relevance of an assumption is the processing effort necessary for the achievement of contextual effects. It is a negative factor, which means that, other things being equal, 'the greater the processing effort, the lower the relevance' (Sperber and Wilson 1986: 124). The theory holds that, in communication, speaking partners first assume the relevance of an assumption behind an utterance and then select a context in which its relevance will be maximized (it is not the case that context is determined first and then the relevance of a stimulus assessed). Sperber and Wilson also say that, of all the assumptions that a phenomenon can make manifest to an individual, only some will actually catch his/her attention. Others will be filtered out at a sub-attentive level. These phenomena, which have some bearing on central thought processes, draw the attention of an individual and make assumptions and inferences appear at a conceptual level. Thus, they define the relevance of a phenomenon as follows:

> [A] phenomenon is relevant to an individual to the extent that the contextual effects achieved when it is optimally processed are large. . .

> [A] phenomenon is relevant to an individual to the extent that the effort required to process it optimally is small.
>
> (Sperber and Wilson 1986: 153)

Owing to its cognitive orientation and its initial interest in information processing, relevance theory has been largely concerned with the referential function of language. Due to this methodological and programmatic bias, it has been criticized for being inadequate to account for the socially relevant aspects of discourse, and for insufficient involvement with the interactional aspects of language use. Relevance theory has dismissed such criticisms as misguided, because its primary interest has explicitly *not* been social. Still, in more recent revisions, its authors have begun to explain the potential of relevance theory in accounting for social aspects of communication (see Sperber and Wilson 1997).

Conversation analysis

The origins and much of current practice in conversation analysis (commonly abbreviated to CA) reside in the sociological approach to language and communication known as *ethnomethodology* (Cicourel 1973; Garfinkel 1974). Ethnomethodology means studying the link between what social actors 'do' in interaction and what they 'know' about interaction. Social structure is a form of order, and that order is partly achieved through talk, which is itself structured and orderly. Social actors have common-sense knowledge about what it is they are doing interactionally in performing specific activities and in jointly achieving communicative coherence. Making this knowledge about ordinary, everyday affairs explicit, and in this way finding an under-standing of how society is organized and how it functions, is ethnomethodology's main concern (Garfinkel 1967; Turner 1974; Heritage 1984b).

Following this line of inquiry, CA views language as a form of social action and aims, in particular, to discover and describe how the organization of social inter-action makes manifest and reinforces the structures of social organization and social institutions (see, e.g., papers in Boden and Zimmerman 1991; Drew and Heritage 1992a; Hutchby and Wooffitt 1998; Chapters 14, 15, 17, 23, 28). Hutchby and Wooffitt, who point out that 'talk in interaction' is now commonly preferred to the designation 'conversation', define CA as follows:

> CA is the study of *recorded, naturally occurring talk-in-interaction* . . . Principally it is to discover how participants understand and respond to one another in their turns at talk, with a central focus being on how

sequences of interaction are generated. To put it another way, the objective of CA is to uncover the tacit reasoning procedures and sociolinguistic competencies underlying the production and interpretation of talk in organized sequences of interaction.

(Hutchby and Wooffitt 1998: 14)

As this statement implies, the emphasis in CA, in contrast to earlier ethnomethodological concerns, has shifted away from the patterns of 'knowing' *per se* towards discovering the *structures of talk* that produce and reproduce patterns of social order. At least, structures of talk are studied as the best evidence of social actors' practical knowledge about them. (Schegloff et al 1996 give an informative account of the early history of CA.) Key conversational features that CA has focused on include:

*   openings and closings of conversations (see Schegloff and Sacks, Chapter 15);
*   adjacency pairs (i.e., paired utterances of the type summons–answer, greeting–greeting, compliment–compliment response, etc.);
*   topic management and topic shift;
*   preference (favouring of certain types of responses over others, e.g., the socially preferred response to an invitation is acceptance, not rejection);
*   conversational repairs;
*   showing agreement and disagreement;
*   introducing bad news and processes of troubles-telling;
*   (probably most centrally) mechanisms of turn-taking.

Most of these concerns of CA are discussed in some detail by Raymond and Sidnell's Chapter 16. What we want to emphasize here is that CA's insights are valuable to understand patterns of individual relations between interactants, individuals' positions within larger institutional structures (e.g., Zimmerman, Chapter 23; Mehan, Chapter 29), and overall societal organization. Also and importantly, CA has taken the study of discourse firmly into a more dynamic and interactional realm of interaction away from the speaker-centredness of speech act theory (see above).

This is not to say that CA is without its critics. The most contested notion in relation to CA is that of 'context'. Indeed, what CA programmatically assumes to be the sole (and sufficient) source for analysing context is, as John Heritage points out, the organization of talk itself:

> The initial and most fundamental assumption of CA is that all aspects of social action and interaction can be examined in terms of the conventionalized or institutionalized structural organizations which analyzably inform their production. These organizations are to be treated as structures in their own right which, like other social institutions and conventions, stand independently of the psychological or other characteristic of particular participants.

(Heritage 1984b: 1–2)

The ethnographic critique of CA's disregard for the cultural and historical context of interactions is summarized by Alessandro Duranti (1997). Although he does not dismiss CA's methods and goals *a priori*, he also argues that some of the insights and observations about interaction cannot be accessed without attending to the fine detail of ethnographic analyses. (See Moerman 1988; Ochs 1988; Besnier 1989 for examples of studies that combine CA with attention to the cultural detail characteristic of the ethnographic approach. We return to aspects of this critique in our Introduction to Part Three.)

Discursive psychology

An interdisciplinary movement such as discourse analysis is likely to spawn new areas of specialist research, at first on the fringes of established disciplines. Discursive psychology (Edwards and Potter 1992 is an integrative overview) has established itself as a coherent, critical approach to some traditional research themes in psychology, such as the study of attitudes, strongly opposing the statistical and experimental methods that have come to dominate research in psychology (including social psychology). Jonathan Potter and Margaret Wetherell's (1987) book, *Discourse and Social Psychology: Beyond Attitudes and Behaviour*, was a groundbreaking critique of established methods and assumptions in social psychology.

Discourse analysts' hostility to the notion of linguistic 'behaviour' (referred to in the book title above) should already be clear from what we have said so far. No approach that treats language as behaviour can come to terms with the strategic complexity and the local and emergent contextualization of talk, with how talk is co-constructed by social actors, or with how meanings are generated by inference as much as by overt signalling. Potter and Wetherell's position on attitude research is similar. They stress the need to examine contextualized accounts of beliefs, rather than surveying (usually by questionnaire methods) large numbers of people's decontextualized and self-reported attitudes, as social psychologists have tended to do:

> Contextual information gives the researcher a much fuller understanding of the detailed and delicate organization of accounts. In addition, an understanding of this organization clarifies the action orientation of talk and its involvement in acts such as blaming and disclaiming.
>
> (Potter and Wetherell 1987: 54)

Accounts, they go on to argue, can and should focus on variability and even inconsistency, rather than trying to disguise variation in the hope of producing clear and stable patterns. Rather antagonistically, they suggest that variability in discursive accounts of beliefs amounts to 'a considerable embarrassment to traditional attitude theories' (Potter and Wetherell 1987: 54). They also argue that attitude research tends to reify the assumption that attitudes are held about 'an existing out-there-in-the-world group of people' (Potter and Wetherell 1987: 54) when most naturally occurring accounts are directed at specific cases rather than idealized 'objects'. A discursive approach to the psychology of attitudes will bring research back to investigating local and specific discourse representations, which are how we produce and experience 'attitudes' in everyday life.

These are powerful arguments, but we should also bear in mind the corresponding limitation of a discursive approach to social beliefs, attitudes and all subjective phenomena, especially regarding its inability to deal with social trends and distributions. It seems necessary to recognize the inherent weaknesses of *all* general approaches, and the most persuasive line of argument is that discourse analysis is able to complement other approaches (such as quantitative surveys) rather than take their place.

Discursive psychology is, however, more than the application of concepts and methods from discourse analysis and CA in the traditional realm of social psychology, even though this was its origin. Much of the most articulate and insistent theorizing of *social constructionism* has emerged from social psychology, for example in John Shotter's (1993) book, *Conversational Realities* (see also Billig 1991; Gergen 1982, 1991). Psychology, which studies the interface between individuals, cognition and society, needs to theorize 'reality' – arguably more urgently than other disciplines. Shotter's argument, like that of Potter and Wetherell, is that psychology and most social science has tended to seek out invariance, and ignore the processes (the 'ethnomethodological' processes) through which we come to see the world as stable:

> In our reflective thought, upon the nature of the world in which we live, we can either take what is invariant as its primary subject matter and treat change as problematic, or, activity and flux as primary and treat the achievement of stability as problematic. While almost all previous approaches to psychology and the other social sciences have taken the first of these stances, social constructionism takes the second.
>
> (Shotter 1993: 178)

Shotter and his colleagues are therefore keen to reintroduce a *relativist* perspective into social science (see Cameron et al, Chapter 7) and to take very seriously Edward Sapir and Benjamin Lee Whorf's early research on linguistic relativity – the so-called Sapir/Whorf hypothesis (e.g., Whorf 1956; Lucy 1992).

The principle of relativism followed from an early American anthropological tradition (developed mainly by Franz Boas at the beginning of the twentieth century), which argued that languages classify experience and that each language does so differently. The classification of experience through language was held to be automatic and beyond speakers' awareness. Sapir's and Whorf's comments on social reality are well worth pondering, many decades after publication:

> Language is a guide to 'social reality' . . . Human beings do not live in the objective world alone, nor alone in the world of social activity as ordinarily understood, but are very much at the mercy of the particular

language which has become the medium of expression for their society
. . . [T]he 'real world' is to a large extent unconsciously built up on the
language habits of the group. No two languages are ever sufficiently
similar to be considered as representing the same social reality. The
worlds in which different societies live are distinct worlds, not merely
the same world with different labels attached . . . We see and hear and
otherwise experience very largely as we do because the language habits
of our community predispose certain choices of interpretation . . .
From this standpoint we may think of language as the *symbolic guide to
culture*.

(Sapir, originally published in 1929, quoted in
Lucy 1992: 22)

That portion of the whole investigation here to be reported may be summed up
in two questions: (1) Are our own concepts of 'time', 'space', and 'matter' given in
substantially the same form by experience to all men, or are they in part conditioned
by the structure of particular languages? (2) Are there traceable affinities between
(a) cultural and behavioral norms and (b) large-scale linguistic patterns? (Whorf
1956: 138; see also Coupland and Jaworski 1997: 446). One of Whorf's key
observations, which transfers directly into the domain of discourse analysis, is that
a language or a particular form of utterance can unite demonstrably different aspects
of reality by giving them similar linguistic treatment, what Whorf calls the process
of *linguistic analogy*. Linguistic analogy allows or encourages us to treat diverse
experience as 'the same'. A famous example in the area of vocabulary is the word
'empty' in the expression *empty gasoline drums*. As Whorf pointed out, the word
'empty' commonly implies a void or absence, and conjures up associations of 'absence
of threat' and therefore 'safety'. It is as if this expression steers us into treating
'empty gasoline drums' as lacking danger, when they are in fact *unusually dangerous*.
Language used to shape cognitive structures can therefore be referred to as *the
cognitive appropriation of linguistic analogies*.

As Shotter (1993: 115) concludes: 'Whorf forces us to see that the basic
"being" of our world is not as basic as we had thought; it can be thought of and
talked of in other ways.' More recent studies in discursive psychology have elaborated
on this central point and supported Sapir's, Whorf's, Shotter's and other people's
theorizing with textual analysis. Potter (1996), for example, analyses how 'out-there-
ness' is discursively constructed in the writing styles of empiricist (experimental,
quantitative) scientific researchers (cf. Gilbert and Mulkay 1984). Derek Edwards's
book is a radical reworking of cognitive themes in psychology, for example research
on 'ape language' and child language acquisition, and on the psychology of emotions
(Edwards 1997; see also Chapter 13). He attends to the language in which psychologists represent and objectify cognition. It is perhaps the ultimate challenge for a
psychologist (even of the discursive kind) to undermine cognitivism, but Edwards
writes that 'one of the reasons for pursuing discursive psychology is the requirement
to re-conceptualize relations between language and mind, and to find alternative ways
of dealing empirically with that "constitutive" relationship' (Edwards 1997: 44).

The ethnography of communication

In the 1960s and 1970s, the Chomsky-inspired formalism in linguistics triggered a concerted reaction from function-oriented and action-oriented researchers of language. Most notably, Noam Chomsky (1965) contrasted the notion of *linguistic competence*, i.e., internalized knowledge of the rules of a language and the defined object of linguistic inquiry, with what he called *linguistic performance*, i.e., the realization of competence in actual speech. Dell Hymes (1972a) also viewed language as 'knowledge', but extended the object of (socio)linguistic inquiry, or what he called the ethnography of communication, to *communicative competence*. Hymes's definition of the term consisted of four elements:

- whether and to what degree something is grammatical (linguistic competence);
- whether and to what degree something is appropriate (social appropriateness);
- whether and to what degree something is feasible (psycholinguistic limitations);
- whether and to what degree something is done (observing actual language use).

This far broader conceptualization of competence in language, and indeed of the purpose of language study, imposed a radically different methodology from Chomsky's linguistics, which was based on introspection (thinking about one's own uses of language) and intuition. The object of inquiry for Hymes was no longer the structure of isolated sentences, but *rules of speaking* within a community. Consequently, the sentence was replaced as a basic unit of analysis with a threefold classification of speech communication (Hymes 1972b):

- **speech situations**, such as ceremonies, evenings out, sports events, plane trips, and so on; they are not purely communicative (i.e., not only governed by rules of speaking) but provide a wider context for speaking;
- **speech events** are activities that are *par excellence* communicative and governed by rules of speaking, e.g., conversations, lectures, political debates, ritual insults, and so on. As Duranti (1997: 289) comments, these are activities in which 'speech plays a crucial role in the definition of what is going on – that is, if we eliminate speech, the activity cannot take place';
- **speech acts** are the smallest units of the set, e.g., orders, jokes, greetings, summonses, compliments, etc.; a speech act may involve more than one turn from only one person, e.g., greetings usually involve a sequence of two turns.

Hymes's model was based on a set of *components of speech events*, which provided a descriptive framework for ethnography of communication. These components were arranged into an eight-part mnemonic based on the word *SPEAKING*:

situation (physical, temporal psychological setting defining the speech event);
participants (e.g., speaker, addressee, audience);
ends (outcomes and goals);
act sequence (form and content);

key (manner or spirit of speaking, e.g., mock, serious, perfunctory, painstaking);
instrumentalities (channels of communication, e.g., spoken, written, signed;
    forms of speech, e.g., dialects, codes, varieties, registers);
norms of interaction (e.g., organization of turn-taking and norms of
    interpretation, i.e., conventionalized ways of drawing inferences);
genres (e.g., casual speech, commercial messages, poems, myths, proverbs).

Although the *Reader* does not explicitly address the ethnographic tradition (we deal with it in greater detail in Coupland and Jaworski 2009, especially Chapters 10 and 39; see also Bauman and Scherzer 1974; Saville-Troike 1989), the impact of the ethnography of communication, its methodology and attendance to contextual, historical and cultural detail of interaction is felt across most discourse analytic traditions, especially in interactional sociolinguistics (e.g., Rampton 1995, 2005; and see the following section). In Chapter 10 of this book Jenny Thomas offers a critique of the SPEAKING acronym as a heuristic for the study of context in social interaction in favour of Stephen Levinson's concept of 'activity types'.

Interactional sociolinguistics

This approach to discourse is inextricably linked with the names of the sociologist Erving Goffman (e.g., 1959, 1967, 1974, 1981; Chapter 19) and Dell Hymes's close associate, the anthropological linguist John Gumperz (e.g., 1982a, 1982b). Gumperz aimed 'to develop interpretive sociolinguistic approaches to the analysis of real time processes in face to face encounters' (1982a: vii), and this aim has been taken up by various sociolinguists and discourse analysts in a wide range of approaches to social interaction, some of which are represented in this volume (see Schiffrin, Chapter 17; Zimmerman, Chapter 23).

Goffman summarizes his research programme in one of his later papers as being

> to promote acceptance of the . . . face-to-face domain as an analytically viable one – a domain which might be titled, for want of any happy name, the interaction order – a domain whose preferred method of study is microanalysis.
>
> (Goffman 1983: 2)

Although it is hard to find any contemporary approach to discourse that does *not* more or less explicitly refer to Goffman's work, we have included in the *Reader* several papers in which the affinity to Goffman's work is especially clear. (Apart from the chapters mentioned above, see Brown and Levinson, Chapter 20; Tannen and Wallat, Chapter 21; Cameron, Chapter 22.)

Much of Gumperz's research has concentrated on the mechanisms of *miscommunication*. He demonstrates how miscommunication can be associated with seemingly trivial signalling details, such as falling rather than rising intonation on a single word, that can trigger complex patterns of interpretation and misinterpretation between individuals. These patterns of (mis)interpretation, which he labels *conversational inferencing*, depend not only on the 'actual' contents of talk, but to a great extent on the processes of perception and evaluation of signalling mechanisms, once again based on details of intonation, tempo of speech, rhythm, pausing, phonetic shape, lexical and syntactic choices, non-verbal signals, and so on. Gumperz (2009) calls such features *contextualization cues*, and he showed that they

> relate what is said to the contextual knowledge (including knowledge of particular activity types: cf. frames; Goffman 1974) that contributes to the presuppositions necessary to the accurate inferencing of what is meant (including, but not limited to, the illocutionary force).
>
> (Schiffrin 1994: 99–100)

Gumperz adapts and extends Hymes's ethnographic framework by examining how interactants from different cultural groups apply different rules of speaking in face-to-face interaction. In his work, he draws heavily on the pragmatic notion of inferential meaning and the ethnomethodological understanding of conversation as joint action (see above).

We have already mentioned the link between Gumperz's contextualization cues and their role as markers signalling types of speech event, or in Goffman's terms *frames*, which participants engage in. Frames are part of the interpretive means by which participants understand or disambiguate utterances and other forms of communicative behaviour. For example, a person waving his or her arm may be stopping a car, greeting a friend, flicking flies or increasing blood circulation (Goffman 1974). There is a constant interplay between contextualization cues and what is being said. Framing devices usually form a part of the communicated message, but they are used to label or categorize the communicative process itself. Therefore, they also constitute the utterance's *metamessage* (Watzlawick et al 1967; Tannen 1986; Jaworski et al 2004), or its 'message about its own status as a message'. When we look for ways in which frames are constructed and changed or shifted, we try to identify how participants convey their metamessages through various verbal and non-verbal cues. Another concept that links Goffman's work with that of Gumperz is *footing*, 'the alignments we take up to ourselves and the others present as expressed in the way we manage the production or reception of an utterance' (Goffman 1981: 128). As Goffman notes, changes in footing depend in part on the use of specific contextualization cues, for example, switching between language codes or speech styles.

One of the most significant developments in interactional sociolinguistics was the formulation of politeness theory (Brown and Levinson 1987; Chapter 20). Penelope Brown and Stephen Levinson believe that the phenomenon of politeness is responsible for how people deviate from the maximally efficient modes of communication as these were outlined by Grice. In other words, politeness is the reason why people do not always 'say what they mean'. Politeness theory, which aims to provide a universal descriptive and explanatory framework of social relations, is built around Goffman's notion of *face* (Chapter 19), referring to a person's self-image and the image that we project onto other individuals. The theory also integrates Grice's model of inferential communication and the assumption that people communicating are rational when they do *facework* in social interaction. Brown and Levinson stress the strategic nature of human communication, which is a radical departure from earlier, rule-oriented approaches (e.g., Lakoff 1973).

The *Reader* carries Goffman's chapter on face (Chapter 19) and Brown and Levinson's chapter on politeness (Chapter 20), so we will not present an overview of these interconnected theories here. But it is worth pointing out that, apart from Lakoff's approach to politeness mentioned above, there have been several other alternative attempts to theorize politeness. The best-known example is Leech's (1983) approach, based on Grice's notion of the 'Politeness Principle' (analogous to the Cooperative Principle but never fully developed by Grice himself) and a set of corresponding politeness maxims, such as *tact*, *generosity*, *approbation*, *modesty* and so on. For another discussion and reformulation of politeness theory from a postmodern perspective, see Watts (2003).

Narrative analysis

Telling stories is a human universal of discourse. Stories or narratives are discursive accounts of factual or fictitious events that are taking place, have taken place or will take place at a particular time. We construct narratives as structured representations of events in a particular temporal order. Sometimes, the ordering of events is chronological (as it tends to be in most fairy stories) although some plays, novels or news stories (e.g., Bell 1998) may move backwards and forwards in time, for particular reasons and effects.

Narratives can be verbal (spoken or written), musical, mimed or pictorial, e.g., in children's picture books. Sometimes a story can be narrated in a single visual image, a painting or a photograph, implying a temporal succession of events (e.g., something has happened or is about to happen). Of course, narratives often combine different modalities and many voices in a single storytelling event. For example, recounting a family holiday may involve several family members presenting their versions of events, to which the participating audience may add questions and comments. It may involve showing souvenirs, photographs or a video, or even sampling foods brought home from the trip. This can turn the narrative into a multi-modal, multi-voiced text, including the gustatory (taste) and olfactory (smell) channels. Sometimes, different voices are introduced into a story by a single narrator, for example by introducing quotations as direct speech, perhaps marked by changes in pitch or body posture.

The functions of storytelling are quite varied. Some stories are primarily informative, others are mainly used for self-presentation, for entertainment, for strengthening in-group ties (e.g., gossip), in therapy or problem-solving (e.g., life-stories told in counselling sessions or in problem-sharing among friends), and so on. Although narratives vary greatly in their form (including their length) and function, all verbal narratives share a basic structure (Labov, Chapter 12). William Labov's study of oral narratives was based on data he collected in New York City, in response to the interview question 'Were you ever in a situation where you were in a serious danger of being killed?' (Labov 1972: 363; Chapter 12). He formulated the following structural features of narratives (as summarized by Ochs 1997: 195), although it is clear that some narratives do not display all of the following elements:

1   abstract (a summary of what is to be said, for example, 'My brother put a knife in my head');
2   orientation ('This was just a few days after my father died');
3   complicating action ('I twisted his arm up behind him. . .');
4   evaluation ('Ain't that a bitch?');
5   result or resolution ('After all a that I gave the dude the cigarette, after all that');
6   coda (a concluding element, such as 'And that was that').

One feature that is common to all narratives is of course the plot-line, or what the story 'is about'. Plot is most commonly associated with narratives found in various literary genres (e.g., novels, ballads, fairy tales) and its structure has indeed been extensively studied within literary stylistics (e.g., Propp 1968; Toolan 1988). One example of how this type of analysis may be applied to the study of non-literary texts is given by Vestergaard and Schroeder (1985) in their study of the language of advertising. Following Greimas's (1966) taxonomy of participants (or as Greimas called them 'actants') in narratives, Vestergaard and Schroeder distinguished the following six, paired roles:

subject – object
helper – opponent
giver – receiver.

The relationships between those roles can be presented diagramatically in the following way:

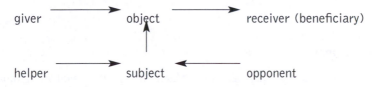

A realization of this model can be found in many fairy tales. Consider Michael Toolan's generic summary, where he explains how the classical roles interconnect with each other:

> The subject or hero, perhaps a young man of lowly origin, seeks marriage to a beautiful princess (object), in which case the man will also be beneficiary (possibly the princess and the country will too). In his quest he is helped generously but with limited success by a friend or relative (helper), but their combined efforts count for little in the struggle against some opponents (wicked uncle of the princess, some other eligible but

ignoble suitor), until a sender (better, a superhelper), such as the king or God, or some individual with magical powers for good, intervenes.

(Toolan 1988: 93–4)

Narratives are not inherently objective or impartial ways of representing events, even though they might be *objectifying devices* (ways of claiming or constructing an air of factuality). This is immediately clear with regard to narratives which are works of fiction (fairy tales, detective stories, etc.). But even 'factual' narratives are intimately tied to the narrator's point of view, and the events recounted in a narrative are his/her (re)constructions rather than some kind of objective mirror-image of reality. The first instance of the narrator's subjectivity is present in what s/he chooses to narrate, what s/he finds 'tellable' or 'reportable'. Furthermore, as Goffman explains, the meaning of the narrative is jointly constructed by the actions of both speaker and listener and how they selectively filter the account:

A tale or anecdote, that is, a replaying, is not merely any reporting of a past event. In the fullest sense, it is such a statement couched from the personal perspective of an actual or potential participant who is located so that some temporal, dramatic development of the reported event proceeds from that starting point. A replaying will therefore incidentally be something that listeners can empathetically insert themselves into, vicariously re-experiencing what took place. A replaying, in brief, recounts a personal experience, not merely reports on an event.

(Goffman 1974: 504; quoted in Ochs 1997: 193)

In sum, narrative analysis is an important tradition within discourse analysis. It deals with a pervasive genre of communication through which we enact important aspects of our identities and relations with others. It is partly through narrative discourse that we comprehend the world and present our understanding of it to others.

Critical discourse analysis

In all but its blandest forms, such as when it remains at the level of language description, discourse analysis adopts a 'critical' perspective on language in use. Roger Fowler (1981) is explicit about what 'critical' means for his own research, much of it related to literary texts. He says it does *not* mean 'the flood of writings about texts and authors which calls itself literary criticism', nor the sense of 'intolerant fault-finding' (1981: 25):

I mean a careful analytic interrogation of the ideological categories, and the roles and institutions and so on, through which a society constitutes and maintains itself and the consciousness of its members . . . All knowledge, all objects, are constructs: criticism analyses the processes of construction and, acknowledging the artificial quality of the categories concerned, offers the possibility that we might profitably conceive the world in some alternative way.

(Fowler 1981: 25)

Many elements in Fowler's definition of critical analysis have already come up as hallmarks of discourse analysis in our review – notably its questioning of objectivity and its interest in the practices that produce apparent objectivity, normality and factuality. What we called the forensic goals of discourse analysis resurface in Fowler's definition, probing texts and discourse practices in order to discover hidden meaning and value-structures. His view of society as a set of groups and institutions structured through discourse is closely reminiscent of Foucault's and Pêcheux's theoretical writings (see above).

There is a wealth of critical-theoretic writing behind these general perspectives, which we have decided not to represent directly in the *Reader*. Our thinking is that *critical theory*, while exerting considerable influence on discourse analysis, remains 'theory'. It is a diverse set of abstract and philosophical writing (for example by Louis Althusser, Emile Benveniste, Jacques Derrida, Umberto Eco and Jacques Lacan), which does not always impinge directly on the empirical analysis of discourse, but is definitely part of the same intellectual climate. (Belsey 1980 provides a useful overview of critical theory approaches; Cobley 1996 is an excellent collection of original writings by several of these theorists.) The 'theoretical' chapters (to use a more conventional sense of the word) that we have included – Bakhtin (Chapter 4), Fairclough (Chapter 5), Scollon (Chapter 6), Bourdieu (Chapter 26), Blommaert (Chapter 32) – are ones where theoretical concepts lead more naturally to forms of linguistic/textual/discourse analysis.

But if Fowler's *critical* perspective is established in all or most discourse analysis, why does critical discourse analysis (commonly referred to as CDA) need to be distinguished as a separate tradition? One reason is historical. Several early approaches to discourse, such as the work of the Birmingham school linguists who developed analyses of classroom discourse (Sinclair and Coulthard 1975), had mainly descriptive aims. They introduced an elaborate hierarchical framework for coding teachers' and pupils' discourse 'acts', 'moves' and 'transactions' in classroom talk. The intention was to provide an exhaustive structural model of discourse organization, from the (highest) category, 'the lesson', down to the (lowest) category of the individual speech act. CDA distances itself from descriptivism of this sort. It fore-grounds its concern with social constructionism and with the construction of *ideology* in particular. As Theo Van Leeuwen (1993: 193) says: 'Critical discourse analysis is, or should be, concerned with ... discourse as the instrument of the social construction of reality.' Ideological structures are necessarily concerned with the analysis of power relations and social discrimination, for example through demonstrating differential access to discourse networks (see above; Caldas-Coulthard and Coulthard 1996; Fairclough, Chapter 5).

Norman Fairclough gives the clearest account of critical discourse analysis as ideological analysis:

> I view social institutions as containing diverse 'ideological-discursive formations' (IDFs) associated with different groups within the institution. There is usually one IDF which is clearly dominant ... Institutional subjects are constructed, in accordance with the norms of an IDF, in subject positions whose ideological underpinnings they may be unaware of. A characteristic of a dominant IDF is the capacity to 'naturalise' ideologies, i.e., to win acceptance for them as non-ideological 'common sense'. It is argued that the orderliness of interactions depends in part upon such naturalised ideologies. To 'denaturalise' them is the objective of a discourse analysis which adopts 'critical' goals. I suggest that denaturalisation involves showing how social structures determine properties of discourse, and how discourse in turn determines social structures.
>
> (Fairclough 1995: 27)

The important point about concepts such as 'naturalization' and 'denaturalization' is that they are dynamic processes. They imply a continuing struggle over social arrangements and acts of imposition and resistance. In fact, the critical perspective of CDA is directly oriented to social change, in two different senses. First, and particularly in Fairclough's work, CDA sets out to understand social changes in the ideological use of language. We have briefly mentioned Fairclough's arguments about 'technologization'. Under this heading he identifies an ongoing cultural 'process of redesigning existing discursive practices and training institutional personnel in the redesigned practices' (Fairclough 1995: 102), brought about partly through so-called 'social skills training'. Fairclough suggests that social skills training is marked by the emergence of 'discourse technologists', the policing of discourse practices, designing context-free discourse techniques and attempts to standardize them (1995: 103). He finds examples in the instituting of 'staff development' and 'staff appraisal' schemes in British universities (and of course elsewhere). New forms of discourse (e.g., learning terminology that will impress supervisors or assessors, or learning how to appear efficient, friendly or resourceful) are normalized (made to appear unexceptional) and policed or monitored, with a system of status-related and financial rewards and penalties following on from them. Other discursive shifts that Fairclough has investigated are the conversationalization of public discourse and the marketization of public institutions (again, in particular, universities).

The second aspect of change is the critic's own attempt to resist social changes held to curtail liberty. Ideological critique is often characterized by some form of intervention. Notice how Fowler (in the quotation above) mentions 'profitably conceiv[ing] the world in some alternative way'. A critical orientation is not merely 'deconstructive'; it may aim to be 'reconstructive', reconstructing social arrangements. Fowler's use of the term 'profitable' is perhaps unfortunate, although he seems to mean 'more justifiable' or 'more fair'. Fairclough also writes that

> the problematic of language and power is fundamentally a question of democracy. Those affected need to take it on board as a political issue,

as feminists have around the issue of language and gender . . . Critical
linguists and discourse analysts have an important auxiliary role to play
here [i.e., secondary to the role of people directly affected] in providing
analyses and, importantly, in providing critical educators with resources
of what I and my colleagues have called 'critical language awareness'.

(Fairclough 1995: 221)

Critical discourse analysis in this view is a democratic resource to be made
available through the education system. Critical discourse analysts need to see
themselves as politically engaged, working alongside disenfranchised social groups.
This point returns us to issues of method and ethics, of the sort debated by Cameron
et al in Chapter 7.

Overview: what discourse analysis can and cannot do

It may be useful to end this overview chapter with a brief consideration of the
limitations inherent in the discourse perspective – what discourse analysis *cannot* do.
Understandably enough, the readings in this book actively construct the discipline of
discourse studies as a vibrant one, alert to social divisions and, in some cases, seeking
to resist them. Discourse promotes itself as being aware, liberated and liberating,
and to us this stance seems generally justified.

Yet there are some basic issues of research methods and interpretation that do
not and should not get overlooked in the rush to discourse. Discourse analysis is a
committedly *qualitative* orientation to linguistic and social understanding. As hinted
earlier, it inherits both the strengths and the weaknesses associated with qualitative
research. As weaknesses, there will always be problems in justifying the selection
of materials as research data. It is often difficult to say why a particular stretch of
conversation or a particular piece of written text has come under the spotlight of
discourse analysis, and why certain of its characteristics are attended to and not others.
If discourse analysis is able to generalize, it can normally only generalize about process
and not about distribution. This is a significant problem for research projects that
assert that there are broad social changes in discourse formations within a community,
e.g., Fairclough's claims about increasing technologization. A claim about change
over time – and Fairclough's claims are intuitively very convincing – needs, where
possible, to be substantiated with time-sequenced data, linked to some principled
method for analysing it, able to demonstrate significant differences. The point is that
qualitative, interpretive studies of particular fragments of discourse are not self-
sufficient. They need support from other traditions of research, even quantitative
surveying. Discourse analysis is therefore not a panacea, and is suited to some types
of research question and not others.

Discourse data tend not to lend themselves to distributional surveying. If we
emphasize the local contexting of language and the shared construction of meaning,
then it follows that we cannot confidently identify recurring instances of 'the same'
discourse phenomenon (such as a conversational interruption, a racist reference or

an intimate form of address). It is certainly true that a lot of quantitative research has been done – and sometimes inappropriately – on discourse data, through gross coding of language forms and expressions that hide significant functional/contextual/ inferential differences. But it is also true that discourse analysts often feel the *need* to make distributional claims (e.g., that men interrupt others in conversation more than women do, that racist discourse is rife in contemporary Britain or that some forms of signalled intimacy redress threats to a person's face) that their data, analysed qualitatively, may not directly support. One common weakness of discourse analysis is therefore that there is a potential mismatch between the analytic method and the interpretation of data in distributional terms. In-depth single-case analyses (e.g., of a particular conversation or written report) are entirely appropriate in discourse analytic research, and have full validity, relative to their aims and objectives (usually to demonstrate meaning-making processes and to build rich interpretations of local discourse events). But they cannot stand as straightforward alternatives to larger-scale projects based on sampled instances, designed to answer questions about social differences or social change. Such studies have their own limitations and (as we suggested above) they risk essentializing and glossing complex local processes. But research is inherently imperfect, and we would support the line of argument that multiple perspectives and methods increase the likelihood of reaching good explanations.

Several strands of discourse analysis, as we have seen, find their vigour in opposing other research trends and assumptions. This is evident in, for example, discursive psychology's antagonism to quantitative social psychology, and in ethnomethodology and CA's resistance to the 'conventional' sociology of social structure. In both these cases, discourse theorists argue for more tentativeness, more context-relatedness, more contingency and more tolerance of ambiguity. It is hard to avoid the conclusion that the discourse perspective requires us to scale back our ambition in some ways, again particularly in relation to generalizing, when it comes to linguistic and social explanation. The nature of research itself as a discourse practice needs to be questioned (see Cameron et al, Chapter 7; Gilbert and Mulkay 1984), but when we question we lose some of the security as well as the hegemony of the research institutions.

The corresponding power of the discourse analysis perspective is its explanatory and critical depth. Discourse studies offer the possibility of a greater clarity of vision, specifically of how language permeates human affairs, offering us opportunities but also constraints. Alessandro Duranti, as a linguistic anthropologist, has written lucidly about this:

> Having a language is like having access to a very large canvas and to hundreds or even thousands of colors. But the canvas and the colors come from the past. They are hand-me-downs. As we learn to use them, we find out that those around us have strong ideas about what can be drawn, in which proportions, in what combinations, and for what purposes. As any artist knows, there is an ethics of drawing and coloring as well as a market that will react sometimes capriciously, but many times quite predictably

to any individual attempts to place a mark in the history or representation or simply readjust the proportions of certain spaces at the margins . . . Just like art-works, our linguistic products are constantly evaluated, recycled or discarded.

(Duranti 1997: 334)

Duranti's metaphor captures many of the insights that we have anticipated in this Introduction, to be filled out and illustrated in the following chapters. But it also follows that if we can become more aware of the ethics of using language, and of the linguistic market and its practices, we should be better prepared to use language for the purposes we deem valuable. As the 'information revolution' continues to gain new ground, demands will increase on us to acquire new literacies and discourse competences. These competences will include 'technical' literacies, such as the ability to produce and read new media-generated texts (Snyder 1998; Thurlow et al 2004; Thurlow, Chapter 31). But they will also include being able to produce reasoned accounts and interpretations of complex discourse events and situations. The ability to reflect critically on and analyse discourse will increasingly become a basic skill for negotiating social life and for imposing a form of interpretive, critical order on the new discursive universe.

Journals

The following is a list of journals publishing discourse research.

Applied Linguistics (Oxford University Press)
American Anthropologist (American Anthropological Association)
Critical Approaches to Discourse Analysis across Disciplines
Discourse, Context and Media (Elsevier)
Critical Discourse Studies (Routledge)
Discourse & Society (Sage)
Discourse Processes (Routledge)
Discourse & Communication (Sage)
Discourse Analysis Online (Sheffield Hallam University)
Discourse Studies (Sage)
International Journal of Applied Linguistics (Wiley-Blackwell)
Journal of Communication (Oxford University Press for International Communication Association)
Journal of Language and Social Psychology (Sage)
Journal of Language and Politics (John Benjamins)
Journal of Linguistic Anthropology (American Anthropological Association)
Journal of Multicultural Discourses (Routledge)
Journal of Multilingual and Multicultural Development (Routledge)
Journal of Politeness Research (Mouton de Gruyter)
Journal of Pragmatics (Elsevier)
Journal of Sociolinguistics (Wiley-Blackwell)
Language Awareness (Routledge)
Language and Communication (Elsevier)
Language in Society (Cambridge University Press)

Multilingua (Mouton de Gruyter)
Narrative Inquiry (John Benjamins)
Pragmatics (International Pragmatics Association)
Pragmatics and Society (John Benjamins)
Research on Language and Social Interaction (Routledge)
Semiotica (Mouton de Gruyter)
Social Semiotics (Routledge)
Text & Talk (Mouton de Gruyter)
Visual Communication (Sage)
Written Communication (Sage)

References

Bakhtin, M.M. (1981) *The Dialogic Imagination: Four Essays*, edited by M. Holquist, translated by V.W. McGee, Austin, TX: University of Texas Press.
—— (1986) *Speech Genres and Other Late Essays*, translated by V.W. McGee, Austin, TX: University of Texas Press.
Bauman, R. and Scherzer, J. (eds.) (1974) *Explorations in the Ethnography of Speaking*, Cambridge: Cambridge University Press.
Bell, A. (1998) 'The discourse structure of news stories', in A. Bell and P. Garrett (eds.) *Approaches to Media Discourse*, Oxford: Blackwell, 64–104.
Belsey, C. (1980) *Critical Practice*, London: Methuen.
Benveniste, E. (1971) *Problems in General Linguistics*, Florida: University of Miami Press.
Besnier, N. (1989) 'Information withholding as a manipulative and collusive strategy in Nukulaelae gossip', *Language in Society* 18: 315–41.
Billig, M. (1991) *Ideologies and Beliefs*, London: Sage.
Blommaert, J. (2005) *Discourse: A Critical Introduction*, Cambridge: Cambridge University Press.
Boden, D. and Zimmerman, D.H. (eds.) (1991) *Talk and Social Structure: Studies in Ethnomethodology and Conversation Analysis*, Oxford: Polity Press.
Brown, P. and Levinson, S. (1987) *Politeness: Some Universals in Language Usage*, Cambridge: Cambridge University Press [originally published in 1978 as part of E.N. Goody (ed.) *Questions and Politeness*, Cambridge: Cambridge University Press].
Brown, G. and Yule, G. (1983) *Discourse Analysis*, Cambridge: Cambridge University Press.
Caldas-Coulthard , R. and Coulthard, M. (eds.) (1996) *Texts and Practices: Readings in Critical Discourse Analysis*, London: Routledge.
Cameron, D. (1995) *Verbal Hygiene*, London: Routledge.
—— (2000) *Good to Talk? Living and Working in a Communication Culture*, London: Sage.
Candlin, C.N. (1997) 'General editor's preface', in B-L. Gunnarsson, P. Linell and B. Nordberg (eds.) *The Construction of Professional Discourse*, London: Longman, x–xiv.
Chomsky, N. (1965) *Aspects of the Theory of Syntax*, Cambridge, MA: MIT Press.
Cicourel, A.V. (1973) *Cognitive Sociology: Language and Meaning in Social Interaction*, Harmondsworth: Penguin Education.
Cobley, P. (ed.) (1996) *The Communication Theory Reader*, London: Routledge.
Coupland, N. and Jaworski, A. (eds.) (1997) *Sociolinguistics: A Reader and Coursebook*, Basingstoke: Macmillan.
—— (2009) *The New Sociolinguistics Reader*, Basingstoke: Palgrave Macmillan.
Drew, P. and Heritage, J. (eds.) (1992a) *Talk at Work: Interaction in Institutional Settings*, Cambridge: Cambridge University Press.
Duranti, A. (1997) *Linguistic Anthropology*, Cambridge: Cambridge University Press.

Edwards, D. (1997) *Discourse and Cognition,* London: Sage.

Edwards, D. and Potter, J. (1992) *Discursive Psychology,* London: Sage.

Fairclough, N. (1992) 'Introduction', in N. Fairclough (ed.) *Critical Language Awareness,* London: Longman.

—— (1995) *Critical Discourse Analysis: The Critical Study of Language,* London: Longman.

Fasold, R. (1990) *Sociolinguistics of Language,* Oxford: Blackwell.

Fillmore, C. (1984) 'Remarks on contrastive pragmatics', in J. Fisiak (ed.) *Contrastive Linguistics: Prospects and Problems,* Berlin: Mouton, 119–41.

Foucault, M. (1972) *The Archaeology of Knowledge,* translated by S. Smith, London: Tavistock.

—— (1980) *Power/Knowledge: Selected Interviews and Writings,* New York: Pantheon Books.

Fowler, R. (1981) *Literature as Social Discourse: The Practice of Linguistic Criticism,* London: Batsford Academic.

Garfinkel, H. (1967) *Studies in Ethnomethodology,* Englewood Cliffs, NJ: Prentice Hall.

—— (1974) 'On the origins of the term "ethnomethodology"', in R. Turner (ed.) *Ethnomethodology,* Harmondsworth: Penguin.

Gergen, K.J. (1982) *Toward Transformation in Social Knowledge,* New York: Springer.

—— (1991) *The Saturated Self: Dilemmas of Identity in Contemporary Life,* New York: Basic Books.

Giddens, A. (1991) *Modernity and Self-identity: Self and Society in the Late Modern Age,* Cambridge: Polity Press.

Gilbert, G.N. and Mulkay, M. (1984) *Opening Pandora's Box: A Sociological Analysis of Scientists' Discourse,* Cambridge: Cambridge University Press.

Goffman, E. (1959) *The Presentation of Self in Everyday Life,* New York: Doubleday Anchor.

—— (1967) *Interaction Ritual: Essays on Face-to-Face Behavior,* New York: Doubleday Anchor.

—— (1974) *Frame Analysis: An Essay on the Organization of Experience,* New York: Harper and Row.

—— (1981) 'Footing', in E. Goffman, *Forms of Talk,* Philadelphia: University of Pennsylvania Press, 124–59 [first published in *Semiotica* 25 (1979): 1–29].

—— (1983) 'The interaction order', *American Sociological Review* 48: 1–17.

Greimas, A. (1966) *Semantique Structurale,* Paris: Larousse.

Gumperz, J.J. (1982a) *Discourse Strategies,* Cambridge: Cambridge University Press.

—— (1982b) *Language and Social Identity,* Cambridge: Cambridge University Press.

—— (2009) 'Contextualization conventions', in N. Coupland and A. Jaworski (eds.) *The New Sociolinguistics Reader,* Basingstoke: Palgrave Macmillan, 598–606.

Halliday, M.A.K. (1978) *Language as Social Semiotic,* London: Edward Arnold.

Heller, M. (2003) 'Globalization, the new economy, and the commodification of language and identity', *Journal of Sociolinguistics* 7: 473–92.

—— (2011) *Paths to Post-Nationalism: A Critical Ethnography of Language and Identity,* New York: Oxford University Press.

Heritage, J. (1984a) 'A change-of-state token and aspects of its sequential placement', in J. Atkinson and J. Heritage (eds.) *Structures of Social Action: Studies in Conversation Analysis,* Cambridge: Cambridge University Press, 299–345.

—— (1984b) *Garfinkel and Ethnomethodology,* Oxford: Blackwell.

Hodge, R. and Kress, G. (1991) *Social Semiotics,* Cambridge: Polity.

Hutchby, I. and Wooffitt, R. (1998) *Conversation Analysis,* Cambridge: Polity Press.

Hymes, D. (1972a) 'On communicative competence', in J.B. Pride and J. Holmes (eds.) *Sociolinguistics,* Harmondsworth: Penguin, 269–93 [originally published in 1971].

—— (1972b) 'Models of the interaction of language and social life', in J.J. Gumperz and D. Hymes (eds.) *Directions in Sociolinguistics,* New York: Holt, Rinehart & Winston and Oxford: Blackwell, 35–71.

—— (1996) *Ethnography, Linguistics, Narrative Inequality: Towards an Understanding of Voice*. London: Taylor & Francis.

Jaworski, A., Coupland, N. and Galasiński, D. (eds.) (2004) *Metalanguage: Social and Ideological Perspectives*, Berlin and New York: Mouton de Gruyter.

Jones, R.H. and Norris, S. (2005) 'Discourse as action/discourse in action', in S. Norris and R.H. Jones (eds.) *Discourse in Action: Introducing Mediated Discourse Analysis*, London: Routledge, 3–14.

Kress, G. and Van Leeuwen, T. (1996) *Reading Images: The Grammar of Visual Design*, London: Routledge.

—— (2001) *Multimodal Discourse: The Modes and Media of Contemporary Communication*, London: Arnold.

Labov, W. (1972) 'The transformation of experience in narrative syntax', in W. Labov *Language in the Inner City*, Philadelphia: University of Philadelphia Press and Oxford: Blackwell, 354–96.

Labov, W. and Fanshel, D. (1977) *Therapeutic Discourse: Psychotherapy as Conversation*, New York: Academic Press.

Lakoff, R.T. (1973) 'The logic of politeness; or, minding your *p*s and *q*s', *Papers from the Ninth Regional Meeting of the Chicago Linguistic Society 1973*, 292–305.

Lee, D. (1992) *Competing Discourses*, London: Longman.

Leech, G. (1983) *Principles of Pragmatics*, London: Longman.

Lucy, J. (1992) *Language Diversity and Thought: A Reformulation of the Linguistic Relativity Hypothesis*, Cambridge: Cambridge University Press.

Mills, S. (1997) *Discourse*, London: Routledge.

Milroy, J and Milroy, L. (1999) *Authority in Language: Investigating Language Prescription and Standardisation*, 3rd edition, London: Routledge.

Moerman, M. (1988) *Talking Culture: Ethnography and Conversation Analysis*, Philadelphia: University of Pennsylvania Press.

Ochs, E. (1988) *Culture and Language Development: Language Acquisition and Language Socialization in a Samoan Village*, Cambridge: Cambridge University Press.

—— (1997) 'Narrative', in T.A. van Dijk (ed.) *Discourse Studies: A Multidisciplinary Introduction. Vol. 1. Discourse as Structure and Process*, London: Sage, 185–207.

Ochs, E., Schegloff, E.A. and Thompson, S.A. (eds.) (1996) *Interaction and Grammar*, Cambridge: Cambridge University Press.

Pêcheux, M. (1982) *Language, Semantics and Ideology*, Basingstoke: Macmillan.

Potter, J. (1996) *Representing Reality*, London: Sage.

Potter, J. and Wetherell, M. (1987) *Discourse and Social Psychology: Beyond Attitudes and Behaviour*, London: Sage.

Propp, V. (1968) *Morphology of Folk Tale*, Austin, TX: University of Texas Press [first published in Russian, 1928].

Rampton, B. (1995) *Crossing: Language and Ethnicity among Adolescents*, London: Longman.

—— (2005) *Language in Late Modernity: Interaction in an Urban School*, Cambridge: Cambridge University Press.

Saville-Troike, M. (1989) *The Ethnography of Communication: An Introduction*, 3rd edition, Oxford: Blackwell Publishing.

Schegloff, E.A., Ochs, E. and Thompson, S.A. (1996) 'Introduction', in E. Ochs, E.A. Schegloff and S.A. Thompson (eds.) *Interaction and Grammar*, Cambridge: Cambridge University Press.

Schiffrin, D. (1994) *Approaches to Discourse*, Oxford: Blackwell.

Scollon, R. and Scollon, S.W. (2004) *Nexus Analysis: Discourse and the Emerging Internet*, London: Routledge.

Searle, J.R. (1969) *Speech Acts: An Essay in the Philosophy of Language*, Cambridge: Cambridge University Press.

—— (1979) 'The classification of illocutionary acts', *Language in Society* 8: 137–51.

Shotter, J. (1993) *Conversational Realities*, London: Sage.

Sinclair, J.M. and Coulthard, M. (1975) *Towards an Analysis of Discourse: The English Used by Teachers and Pupils*, London: Oxford University Press.

Snyder, I. (ed.) (1998) *Page to Screen: Taking Literacy into the Electronic Era*, London: Routledge.

Sperber, D. and Wilson, D. (1986) *Relevance: Communication & Cognition*, Oxford: Blackwell.

—— (1995) *Relevance: Communication & Cognition*, 2nd edition, Oxford: Blackwell.

—— (1997) 'Remarks on relevance theory and the social sciences', *Multilingua* 16: 145–52.

Stubbs, M. (1983) *Discourse Analysis*, Oxford: Blackwell.

Tannen, D. (1986) *That's Not What I Meant! How Conversational Style Makes or Breaks your Relations with Others*, New York: William Morrow, Ballantine.

Taylor, T. and Cameron, D. (1987) *Analysing Conversation: Rules and Units in the Structure of Talk*, Oxford: Pergamon.

Thomas, J. (1995) *Meaning in Interaction: An Introduction to Pragmatics*, London: Longman.

Thurlow, C., Lengel, L. and Tomic, A. (2004). *Computer Mediated Communication: Social Interaction and the Internet*, London: Sage.

Toolan, M.J. (1988) *Narrative: A Critical Linguistic Introduction*, London: Routledge.

Turner, R. (1974) *Ethnomethodology*, Harmondsworth, Middlesex: Penguin.

Van Dijk, T.A. (1977) *Text and Context*, London: Longman.

—— (1984) *Prejudice in Discourse*, Amsterdam: Benjamins.

—— (ed.) (1985) *Handbook of Discourse Analysis* (4 volumes), New York: Academic Press.

—— (1988) *News Analysis: Case Studies of International and National News in the Press*, Hillsdale, NJ: Lawrence Erlbaum.

—— (ed.) (1997) *Discourse Studies* (2 volumes), London: Sage.

—— (2008) *Discourse and Context: A Sociocognitive Approach*, Cambridge: Cambridge University Press.

—— (2009) *Society and Discourse: How Context Controls Text and Talk*, Cambridge: Cambridge University Press.

Van Leeuwen, T. (1993) 'Genre and field in critical discourse analysis', *Discourse & Society* 4: 193–225.

—— (2005) *Introducing Social Semiotics*. London: Routledge.

Vestergaard, T. and Schroeder, K. (1985) *The Language of Advertising*, Oxford: Blackwell.

Watts, R.J. (2003) *Politeness*, Cambridge: Cambridge University Press.

Watzlawick, P., Beavin-Bavelas, J. and Jackson, D. (1967) *The Pragmatics of Human Communication*, New York: Norton.

Whorf, B.L. (1956) *Language, Thought and Reality: Selected Writings of Benjamin Lee Whorf*, edited by J.B. Carroll, Cambridge, MA: MIT Press.

PART ONE

Discourse: meaning, function and context

Editors' introduction to Part One

IN THE GENERAL INTRODUCTION we characterized discourse analysis as a reaching out beyond the visible or audible forms of language into social context, and as exploring the interplay between language and social processes. Construing language as discourse involves orienting to language as a form of social action, as a functioning form of social action embedded in the totality of social processes. In this part of the *Reader* we represent several of the key writers and texts who, influentially, argued the case for a functional approach to language, initially within their various disciplines – linguistics (Jakobson), philosophy (Austin, Grice), literary criticism (Bakhtin) – alongside two more recent perspectives – Fairclough's critical discourse analysis (CDA) approach and Scollon's mediated discourse analysis. What is important here is not so much the disciplinary origins, even though these clearly influence individuals' ways of theorizing and writing. Rather, it is the cumulative perspective that develops out of their work – pressure towards a notion of discourse (whether so-labelled or not) and towards new theoretical frameworks for explaining meaning-making and sense-making as contextual processes. These six foundational, theoretical chapters do not make the easiest reading, but it should be helpful to keep referring back to them from later, more data-based chapters.

Roman Jakobson's text introduces what he saw as the six basic functions of verbal communication: *referential, emotive, conative, phatic, metalingual* and *poetic*. Although it focuses specifically on the link between linguistics and poetics, Jakobson's article clearly demonstrates how, as early as 1960, some European linguists were committed to a multi-functional view of language. Such a perspective was to become the foundation of Michael Halliday's functional linguistics, influenced heavily by the functionalism of J.R. Firth, which continues to influence social semiotic and critical linguistic approaches to discourse. But the mainstream of descriptive and theoretical linguistics did not follow this line. It came to be dominated by structural models, culminating in Chomsky's formal and cognitivist theory of language. We can therefore see modern discourse studies as a re-imposition of some early priorities in functional linguistics, and this is why Jakobson's work remains an important foundational source.

Jakobson challenges the view that using language is a simple exchange of factual information, and this is the case even in his 'referential' function. What he called the 'conative' function attends to relationships between speakers and what communication achieves in this social dimension. The 'phatic' function is realized in aspects of socially organized, ritualized communication; the 'emotive' function relates to the expressive and subjective dimension of talk; the 'metalinguistic' function identifies those ways in which language can be turned in on itself, used reflexively; the 'poetic' function pays particular attention to the aesthetic dimension of linguistic form. These concepts recur in the *Reader*. Many of them developed into major traditions of discourse analysis (reflected in the *Reader*'s division into parts). Exploring the poetic function of language, as much of this particular Jakobson reading does, is particularly stimulating for discourse analysis, for example Jakobson's suggestion that 'virtually any poetic message is a quasi-quoted discourse' (p. 49). Mikhail Bakhtin (Chapter 4) takes this idea even further, arguing that our speech is never fully 'our own'; it is also in one sense quotative, in recycling the voices of others. The poetic function of language, as Jakobson points out, is not restricted to poetry alone. It surfaces whenever discourse achieves playfulness, self-awareness or creativity, and when we respond to language in these terms. For example, Deborah Cameron (Chapter 22) demonstrates how five young men's informal talk, ranging between gossip about other men and verbal duelling, is full of imaginative and humorous, and sometimes offensive, language. Jan Blommaert (Chapter 32) cites an example of a South African DJ whose spoken routine includes intertextual references and quotations from Reggae song titles and lyrics as an important resource for identity construction. Crispin Thurlow (Chapter 31) observes how language use can be policed on the grounds of 'aesthetics'.

The same concern with communicative function dominates J.L. Austin's famous series of lectures, delivered at Harvard University in 1955, about 'How to do things with words' (Chapter 2). In this case, the backdrop is linguistic philosophy and his concern for a 'true' account of what utterances achieve. Austin's method, working with single instances of fabricated utterances, suggests little concern for social context. But his argument is precisely that the function of an utterance (e.g., making a promise or naming a ship) is partly constituted by the social circumstances in which it is uttered. He shows that utterances have to have 'felicitous' or well-suited conditions for their function to be fulfilled, and that utterance meaning lies in the interplay between social circumstances and utterances themselves.

There are some important questions for discourse analysis embedded in this reading. The question, 'Can saying something make it so?' is one of them. This is the social constructionist stance (Cameron et al, Chapter 7), developed in detail and with a much heavier theoretical loading in the ethnomethodological tradition (see our general Introduction), and in CDA (Fairclough, Chapter 5; Van Dijk, Chapter 27). In fact, many major approaches to discourse work from the assumption that what we understand as social reality is, at least in part, produced through language and social interaction (for example Edwards, Chapter 13, and Sacks, Chapter 14). The exploration of the nature of implied meaning is another central concern of Austin's text, and the distinction between the explicit and implicit functioning of utterances. This perspective again opens up a territory beyond mainstream linguistics, taken up, for example, in Ron Scollon's theorizing of modality (Chapter 6), and Fairclough's 'text relations' (Chapter 5). Another important early observation is Austin's insight that 'function' includes far more than what is achieved *in* the act of uttering, but also what is achieved *through* utterances. As he writes, 'saying something will often, or even normally, produce certain consequential effects upon the feelings, thoughts or actions of the audience, or of the speaker, or of other persons: and it may be done with design, intention or purpose of producing them' (p. 57). Language is aligned to social action generally, and to communicative goals and strategies, and their social effects.

H.P. Grice's perspective on language and implied meaning, very much in the same philosophical tradition as Austin, was also first developed in a series of lectures at Harvard, this time in 1967. Grice takes many of the emphases we see in Austin's work as his own starting point – that discourse is driven by speakers fulfilling specific goals and purposes, that much of the significant meaning of talk is implicit and needing to be reconstructed by inference, and that talk is essentially a form of collaborative social action. Grice points to the specific importance of the medium of conversation as a resource for making sense of what speakers say. Certain expectations follow from being able to assume, for example, that conversation is a cooperative medium – not in the sense that people are always supportive or compliant, but in that they jointly collaborate in the production of meanings and inferences. Talk is a matter of sharing in meaning-making procedures, the starting point for conversation analysis (CA) (e.g., Chapters 14, 15, 16, 23, 28). Austin wanted 'to see talking as a special case or variety of purposive, indeed rational, behavior' (p. 65). His approach to discourse therefore involves focusing in on social action and on the conditions under which human communicators can mutually generate meanings and interpret them. Grice's maxims are an attempt to specify some of these conditions. They amount to regular assumptions that we can make about communicative intention which allow us to draw inferences about what people mean. A set of principles guides the way in which conversation takes place (see our general Introduction).

Not surprisingly, many of the chapters in this first part of the *Reader* are attempts to generalize about 'normal' or 'unexceptional' discourse processes. Jakobson, Austin and Grice are mainly interested in detailing the character of talk between individuals in the most general terms. This reflects the fact that the earliest important contributions to discourse analysis needed to argue against the dominant traditions in linguistics, in linguistic semantics and in the philosophy of language. They needed to make the case that context is theoretically central to the understanding of language in use. Initially, this took priority over more local studies of discourse in particular settings.

The work we have discussed so far originated, as we have pointed out, in different disciplines, but none of these functional approaches to discourse came to be recognized as a fully independent tradition of research. A more distinct tradition, which has been (and rightly continues to be) highly influential in all fields of discourse analysis, originated in the USA in the 1960s as a branch of sociology. It consolidated around the label *ethnomethodology* (see the general Introduction p. 16; Raymond and Sidnell, Chapter 16). Aaron Cicourel offered a definition of ethnomethodology as 'the study of interpretive procedures and surface rules in everyday social practices and scientific activities' (Cicourel 1973: 51). Ethnomethodologists opposed what they saw as the glib and uncritical assumptions made by academics, including social scientists, about how society is structured. They embarked on a radical critique of the *methods* of social and scientific inquiry, and of how specific practices and assumptions are 'naturalized' (made to seem natural or ordinary) and rendered invisible (see Cameron et al, Chapter 7). Through a critique of language and discourse, ethnomethodology tried to show that social facts, and a sense of orderliness in social practices (including research), are generated within those practices themselves. Ethnomethodology is therefore the origin of radical social relativism (seeing truth as being relative to local practices, not absolute) and social constructionism (the social or discursive construction of reality), and its influence is still strongly apparent in many strands of discourse analysis, especially in CA and CDA.

In the rough historical time-ordering of Part One of the *Reader*, Mikhail Bakhtin's chapter (Chapter 4) on 'The problem of speech genres', written in the 1930s, is clearly out of sequence. However, the chronological placement of Bakhtin's chapter is of lesser importance because, in his highly unique way, Bakhtin manages to be highly contemporary. His work, whose origins and even precise authorship are still a little mysterious, is probably more widely cited now than at any previous time. The text tends to be repetitive, and we have edited it quite heavily. It is sometimes obscure, partly because of the difficulty in translating his terminology into English from Russian. For example, a key term such as 'utterances' seems to equate to all language use or discourse; 'the national language' sometimes appears to refer to the standard language code of a community, and at other times to any group-based variety of language. Bakhtin's arguments tend to be highly abstract, but they set an agenda for modern perspectives on discourse.

The view of all language use as organized into specific *genres* or discursive types is a case in point. Bakhtin presents a highly dynamic view of speech genres. He suggests that genres inter-penetrate and 're-accentuate' each other, being continually renewed as they are used. These claims are the basis for an *intertextual* perspective on discourse, seeing discourse as the recontextualizing of already-existing forms and meanings, one text echoing and partially replaying the forms, meanings and values of another (what Bakhtin calls 'the organized chain of other utterances'). Bakhtin stresses the active role of the listener and the co-construction of meaning ('the listener becomes the speaker', p. 76), which is now a standard assumption about conversational practice. He is interested in the shifting boundary between the individual and social structure, anticipating much recent research on selfhood and subjectivity (see Part Five). In a chapter where virtually every sentence is 'a quotable', Bakhtin's text invites us to reconsider what is new and what is actually of long-standing theoretical importance at the interface of language, society, ideology and selfhood.

Bakhtin's ideas about dialogicality, heteroglossia (or multiple voicing) and intertextuality are taken up by Norman Fairclough (Chapter 5). Fairclough 'concretizes' Bakhtin's work by adapting its principles to his own version of CDA, focusing on contemporary political discourse. Fairclough argues, for example, that different levels of dialogicality in the design of discourse open up possibilities for 'difference' of opinion and representation in discourse (see Blommaert's Chapter 32 on 'polycentricity'), while a lack of dialogicality and adherence to a 'common ground', or implicit 'assumptions', lead to a more uniform and hegemonic (politically dominant) set of representations.

In Chapter 6 Ron Scollon develops a different view of how meaning emerges in discourse. His work is closely aligned to the Bakhtinian tradition and to CDA, but there is a slight shift in emphasis away from the discourses of social and political issues to a broader view of discourse as constitutive of social action and as mediating the relationship between text and society. For example, Scollon argues that discourse needs to be examined as one of the physical objects in the world, particularly in terms of the material modes and media through which it is produced. This takes us into the realm of *multimodality* – the interaction of linguistic, non-verbal, pictorial/visual and other modes in meaning-making. One specific example presented in Chapter 6 involves a photographic, diagrammatic and textual (list of bullet points) representation of one geographic location. Scollon demonstrates how these different modes, embedded in specific discourses (e.g., touristic, scientific or commercial), convey information about the world with different orientations to the expression of 'truth' and 'reality'.

Reference

Cicourel, A.V. (1973) *Cognitive Sociology: Language and Meaning in Social Interaction*, Harmondsworth: Penguin Education.

Chapter 1

Roman Jakobson

LINGUISTICS AND POETICS

. . .

LANGUAGE MUST BE INVESTIGATED in all the variety of its functions. . . . An outline of these functions demands a concise survey of the constitutive factors in any speech event, in any act of verbal communication. The ADDRESSER sends a MESSAGE to the ADDRESSEE. To be operative the message requires a CONTEXT referred to, seizable by the addressee, and either verbal or capable of being verbalized; a CODE fully, or at least partially, common to the addresser and addressee (or in other words, to the encoder and decoder of the message); and, finally, a CONTACT, a physical channel and psychological connection between the addresser and the addressee, enabling both of them to enter and stay in communication. All these factors inalienably involved in verbal communication may be schematized as follows:

```
                            CONTEXT
                            MESSAGE
ADDRESSER ------------------------------------------------ ADDRESSEE
                            CONTACT
                             CODE
```

Each of these six factors determines a different function of language. Although we distinguish six basic aspects of language, we could, however, hardly find verbal messages that would fulfill only one function. The diversity lies not in a monopoly of some one of these several functions but in a different hierarchical order of functions. The verbal structure of a message depends primarily on the predominant function. But even though a set (*Einstellung*) toward the referent, an orientation toward the

Source: Roman Jakobson, 'Closing statement: linguistics and poetics', in Thomas A. Sebook (ed.) *Style in Language*, Cambridge, Mass: the MIT Press, 1960: 350–77.

CONTEXT – briefly the so-called REFERENTIAL, "denotative," "cognitive" function – is the leading task of numerous messages, the accessory participation of the other functions in such messages must be taken into account by the observant linguist.

The so-called EMOTIVE or "expressive" function, focused on the ADDRESSER, aims a direct expression of the speaker's attitude toward what he is speaking about. It tends to produce an impression of a certain emotion whether true or feigned; therefore, the term "emotive" . . . has proved to be preferable to "emotional." The purely emotive stratum of language is presented by the interjections. They differ from the means of referential language both by their sound pattern (peculiar sound sequences or even sounds elsewhere unusual) and by their syntactic role (they are not components but equivalents of sentences). "*Tut! Tut!* said McGinty*"*: the complete utterance of Conan Doyle's character consists of two suction clicks. The emotive function, laid bare in the interjections, flavors to some extent all our utterances, on their phonic, grammatical, and lexical level. If we analyze language from the standpoint of the information it carries, we cannot restrict the notion of information to the cognitive aspect of language. A man, using expressive features to indicate his angry or ironic attitude, conveys ostensible information, and evidently this verbal behavior cannot be likened to such nonsemiotic, nutritive activities as "eating grapefruit" . . . The difference between [big] and the emphatic prolongation of the vowel [bi:g] is a conventional, coded linguistic feature like the difference between the short and long vowel in such Czech pairs as [vi] 'you' and [vi:] 'knows,' but in the latter pair the differential information is phonemic and in the former emotive. As long as we are interested in phonemic invariants, the English /i/ and /i:/ appear to be mere variants of one and the same phoneme, but if we are concerned with emotive units, the relation between the invariant and variants is reversed: length and shortness are invariants implemented by variable phonemes. . . .

Orientation toward the ADDRESSEE, the CONATIVE function, finds its purest grammatical expression in the vocative and imperative, which syntactically, morphologically, and often even phonemically deviate from other nominal and verbal categories. Imperative sentences cardinally differ from declarative sentences: the latter are and the former are not liable to a truth test. When in O'Neill's play *The Fountain*, Nano, "(in a fierce tone of command)," says "Drink!" – the imperative cannot be challenged by the question "is it true or not?" which may be, however, perfectly well asked after such sentences as "one drank," "one will drink," "one would drink." In contradistinction to the imperative sentences, the declarative sentences are convertible into interrogative sentences: "did one drink?" "will one drink?" "would one drink?"

The traditional model of language as elucidated particularly by Bühler (1933) was confined to these three functions – emotive, conative, and referential – and the three apexes of this model – the first person of the addresser, the second person of the addressee, and the "third person," properly – someone or something spoken of. Certain additional verbal functions can be easily inferred from this triadic model. Thus the magic, incantatory function is chiefly some kind of conversion of an absent or inanimate "third person" into an addressee of a conative message. For example, "May this sty dry up, *tfu, tfu, tfu, tfu*" (Lithuanian spell); "Water queen river, daybreak! Send grief beyond the blue sea, to the sea-bottom, like a grey stone never to rise from the sea-bottom, may grief never come to burden the light heart of God's servant, may grief be removed and sink away." (North Russian incantation); "Sun, stand thou still upon Gibeon; and thou, Moon, in the valley of Aj-a-lon. And the sun stood still, and the moon stayed . . ." (Josh. 10.12). We observe, however, three further constitutive factors of verbal communication and three corresponding functions of language.

There are messages primarily serving to establish, to prolong, or to discontinue communication, to check whether the channel works ("Hello, do you hear me?"), to attract the attention of the interlocutor or to confirm his continued attention ("Are you listening?" or in Shakespearean diction, "Lend me your ears!" – and on the other end of the wire "Um-hum!"). This set for CONTACT, or in Malinowski's terms PHATIC function (1953; Chapter 20) may be displayed by a profuse exchange of ritualized formulas, by entire dialogues with the mere purport of prolonging communication. Dorothy Parker caught eloquent examples: " 'Well!' the young man said. 'Well!' she said. 'Well, here we are,' he said, 'Here we are,' she said, 'Aren't we?' 'I should say we were,' he said, 'Eeyop! Here we are.' 'Well!' she said. 'Well!' he said, 'well.'" The endeavor to start and sustain communication is typical of talking birds; thus the phatic function of language is the only one they share with human beings. It is also the first verbal function acquired by infants; they are prone to communicate before being able to send or receive informative communication.

A distinction has been made in modern logic between two levels of language, "object language" speaking of objects and "metalanguage" speaking of language. But metalanguage is not only a necessary scientific tool utilized by logicians and linguists; it plays also an important role in our everyday language. Like Molière's Jourdain who used prose without knowing it, we practice metalanguage without realizing the metalingual character of our operations. Whenever the addresser and/or the addressee need to check up whether they use the same code, speech is focused on the CODE: it performs a METALINGUAL (i.e., glossing) function. "I don't follow you – what do you mean?" asks the addressee, or in Shakespearean diction, "What is't thou say'st?" And the addresser in anticipation of such recapturing questions inquires: "Do you know what I mean?" Imagine such an exasperating dialogue: "The sophomore was plucked." "But what is *plucked?*" "*Plucked* means the same as *flunked.*" "And *flunked?*" "To be *flunked* is to *fail in an exam.*" "And what is *sophomore?*" persists the interrogator innocent of school vocabulary. "A *sophomore* is (or means) a *second-year student.*" All these equational sentences convey information merely about the lexical code of English; their function is strictly metalingual. Any process of language learning, in particular child acquisition of the mother tongue, makes wide use of such metalingual operations; and aphasia may often be defined as a loss of ability for metalingual operations.

We have brought up all the six factors involved in verbal communication except the message itself. The set (*Einstellung*) toward the MESSAGE as such, focus on the message for its own sake, is the POETIC function of language. This function cannot be productively studied out of touch with the general problems of language, and, on the other hand, the scrutiny of language requires a thorough consideration of its poetic function. Any attempt to reduce the sphere of poetic function to poetry or to confine poetry to poetic function would be a delusive oversimplification. Poetic function is not the sole function of verbal art but only its dominant, determining function, whereas in all other verbal activities it acts as a subsidiary, accessory constituent. This function, by promoting the palpability of signs, deepens the fundamental dichotomy of signs and objects. Hence, when dealing with poetic function, linguistics cannot limit itself to the field of poetry.

"Why do you always say *Joan and Margery*, yet never *Margery and Joan?* Do you prefer Joan to her twin sister?" "Not at all, it just sounds smoother." In a sequence of two coordinate names, as far as no rank problems interfere, the precedence of the shorter name suits the speaker, unaccountably for him, as a well-ordered shape of the message.

A girl used to talk about "the horrible Harry." "Why horrible?" "Because I hate him." "But why not *dreadful, terrible, frightful, disgusting?*" "I don't know why, but *horrible* fits him better." Without realizing it, she clung to the poetic device of paronomasia.

The political slogan "I like Ike" /ay layk ayk/, succinctly structured, consists of three monosyllables and counts three diphthongs /ay/, each of them symmetrically followed by one consonantal phoneme, /. . l . . k . . k/. The make-up of the three words presents a variation: no consonantal phonemes in the first word, two around the diphthong in the second, and one final consonant in the third. A similar dominant nucleus /ay/ was noticed by Hymes in some of the sonnets of Keats. Both coda of the trisyllabic formula "I like /Ike" rhyme with each other, and the second of the two rhyming words is fully included in the first one (echo rhyme), /layk/ – /ayk/, a paronomastic image of a feeling which totally envelops its object. Both cola alliterate with each other, and the first of the two alliterating words is included in the second: /ay/ – /ayk/, a paronomastic image of the loving subject enveloped by the beloved object. The secondary, poetic function of this electional catchphrase reinforces its impressiveness and efficacy.

As we said, the linguistic study of the poetic function must overstep the limits of poetry, and, on the other hand, the linguistic scrutiny of poetry cannot limit itself to the poetic function. The particularities of diverse poetic genres imply a differently ranked participation of the other verbal functions along with the dominant poetic function. Epic poetry, focused on the third, strongly involves the referential function of language; the lyric, oriented toward the first person, is intimately linked with the emotive function; poetry of the second person is imbued with the conative function and is either supplicatory or exhortative, depending on whether the first person is subordinated to the second one or the second to the first.

Now that our cursory description of the six basic functions of verbal communication is more or less complete, we may complement our scheme of the fundamental factors by a corresponding scheme of the functions:

	REFERENTIAL	
	POETIC	
EMOTIVE	PHATIC	CONATIVE
	METALINGUAL	

What is the empirical linguistic criterion of the poetic function? In particular, what is the indispensable feature inherent in any piece of poetry? To answer this question we must recall the two basic modes of arrangement used in verbal behavior, *selection* and *combination*. If "child" is the topic of the message, the speaker selects one among the extant, more or less similar, nouns like child, kid, youngster, tot, all of them equivalent in a certain respect, and then, to comment on this topic, he may select one of the semantically cognate verbs – sleeps, dozes, nods, naps. Both chosen words combine in the speech chain. The selection is produced on the base of equivalence, similarity and dissimilarity, synonymity and antonymity, while the combination, the build up of the sequence, is based on contiguity. *The poetic function projects the principle of equivalence from the axis of selection into the axis of combination.* Equivalence is promoted to the constitutive device of the sequence. In poetry one syllable is equalized with any other syllable of the same sequence; word stress is assumed to equal word stress, as unstress equals unstress; prosodic long is matched with long, and short with short; word boundary equals word boundary, no boundary equals no boundary; syntactic pause equals syntactic pause, no pause equals no pause. Syllables are converted into units of measure, and so are morae or stresses.

. . .

In poetry, and to a certain extent in latent manifestations of poetic function, sequences delimited by word boundaries become commensurable whether they are sensed as isochronic or graded. "Joan and Margery" showed us the poetic principle of syllable gradation, the same principle which in the closes of Serbian folk epics has been raised to a compulsory law. Without its two dactylic words the combination "*in*nocent by*stand*er" would hardly have become a hackneyed phrase. The symmetry of three disyllabic verbs with an identical initial consonant and identical final vowel added splendor to the laconic victory message of Caesar: "*Veni, vidi, vici.*"

Measure of sequences is a device which, outside of poetic function, finds no application in language. Only in poetry with its regular reiteration of equivalent units is the time of the speech flow experienced, as it is – to cite another semiotic pattern – with musical time. Gerard Manley Hopkins, an outstanding researcher in the science of poetic language, defined verse as "speech wholly or partially repeating the same figure of sound" (1959). Hopkins's subsequent question, "but is all verse poetry?" can be definitely answered as soon as poetic function ceases to be arbitrarily confined to the domain of poetry. Mnemonic lines cited by Hopkins (like "Thirty days hath September"), modern advertising jingles, and versified medieval laws, mentioned by Lotz, or finally Sanscrit scientific treatises in verse which in Indic tradition are strictly distinguished from true poetry (*kāvya*) – all these metrical texts make use of poetic function without, however, assigning to this function the coercing, determining role it carries in poetry. Thus verse actually exceeds the limits of poetry, but at the same time verse always implies poetic function. And apparently no human culture ignores verse-making, whereas there are many cultural patterns without "applied" verse; and even in such cultures which possess both pure and applied verses, the latter appear to be a secondary, unquestionably derived phenomenon. The adaptation of poetic means for some heterogeneous purpose does not conceal their primary essence, just as elements of emotive language, when utilized in poetry, still maintain their emotive tinge. A filibuster may recite *Hiawatha* because it is long, yet poeticalness still remains the primary intent of this text itself. Self-evidently, the existence of versified, musical, and pictorial commercials does not separate the questions of verse or of musical and pictorial form from the study of poetry, music, and fine arts.

To sum up, the analysis of verse is entirely within the competence of poetics, and the latter may be defined as that part of linguistics which treats the poetic function in its relationship to the other functions of language. Poetics in the wider sense of the word deals with the poetic function not only in poetry, where this function is superimposed upon the other functions of language, but also outside of poetry, when some other function is superimposed upon the poetic function.

. . .

Ambiguity is an intrinsic, inalienable character of any self-focused message, briefly a corollary feature of poetry. Let us repeat with Empson (1955): "The machinations of ambiguity are among the very roots of poetry." Not only the message itself but also its addresser and addressee become ambiguous. Besides the author and the reader, there is the "I" of the lyrical hero or of the fictitious storyteller and the "you" or "thou" of the alleged addressee of dramatic monologues, supplications, and epistles. For instance the poem "Wrestling Jacob" is addressed by its title hero to the Saviour and simultaneously acts as a subjective message of the poet Charles Wesley to his readers. Virtually any poetic message is a quasi-quoted discourse with all those peculiar, intricate problems which "speech within speech" offers to the linguist.

The supremacy of poetic function over referential function does not obliterate the reference but makes it ambiguous. The double-sensed message finds correspondence in a split addresser, in a split addressee, and besides in a split reference, as it is cogently exposed in the preambles to fairy tales of various peoples, for instance, in the usual exordium of the Majorca storytellers: "Aixo era y no era" (It was and it was not). The repetitiveness effected by imparting the equivalence principle to the sequence makes reiterable not only the constituent sequences of the poetic message but the whole message as well. This capacity for reiteration whether immediate or delayed, this reification of a poetic message and its constituents, this conversion of a message into an enduring thing, indeed all this represents an inherent and effective property of poetry.

. . .

In poetry the internal form of a name, that is, the semantic load of its constituents, regains its pertinence. The "Cocktails" may resume their obliterated kinship with plumage. Their colors are vivified in Mac Hammond's lines "The ghost of a Bronx pink lady // With orange blossoms afloat in her hair," and the etymological metaphor attains its realization: "O, Bloody Mary, // The cocktails have crowded not the cocks!" ("At an Old Fashion Bar in Manhattan"). Wallace Stevens's poem "An Ordinary Evening in New Haven" revives the head word of the city name first through a discreet allusion to heaven and then through a direct pun-like confrontation similar to Hopkins's "Heaven-Haven."

> The dry eucalyptus *seeks god in the rainy cloud.*
> Professor Eucalyptus of New Haven *seeks him in New Haven* . . .
> The instinct *for heaven* had its counterpart:
> The instinct for earth, *for New Haven*, for his room . . .

The adjective "New" of the city name is laid bare through the concatenation of opposites:

> The oldest-newest day is the newest alone.
> The oldest-newest night does not creak by . . .

When in 1919 the Moscow Linguistic Circle discussed how to define and delimit the range of *epitheta ornantia*, the poet Majakovskij rebuked us by saying that for him any adjective while in poetry was thereby a poetic epithet, even "great" in the *Great Bear* or "big" and "little" in such names of Moscow streets as *Bol'shaja Presnja* and *Malaja Presnja*. In other words, poeticalness is not a supplementation of discourse with rhetorical adornment but a total re-evaluation of the discourse and of all its components whatsoever.

A missionary blamed his African flock for walking undressed. "And what about yourself?" they pointed to his visage, "are not you, too, somewhere naked?" "Well, but that is my face." "Yet in us," retorted the natives, "everywhere it is face." So in poetry any verbal element is converted into a figure of poetic speech.

My attempt to vindicate the right and duty of linguistics to direct the investigation of verbal art in all its compass and extent can come to a conclusion with the same burden which summarized my report to the 1953 conference at Indiana University: "Linguista sum; linguistici nihil a me alienum puto." If the poet Ransom is right (and he is right) that "poetry is a kind of language," the linguist whose field is any kind of language may and must include poetry in his study. . . .

References

Bühler, K. (1933) "Die Axiomatik der Sprachwissenschaft," *Kant-Studien* 38: 19–90.

Empson, W. (1955) *Seven Types of Ambiguity*, New York: Chatto & Windus, 3rd edition.

Hopkins, G.M. (1959) *The Journals and Papers*, H. House (ed.), London: Oxford University Press.

Malinowski, B. (1953) "The problem of meaning in primitive languages," in C.K. Ogden and I.A. Richards, *The Meaning of Meaning*, 9th edition, New York and London: Routledge & Kegan Paul, 296–336. [See also Chapter 20 of this *Reader*.]

Chapter 2

J.L. Austin

HOW TO DO THINGS
WITH WORDS

WHAT I SHALL HAVE to say here is neither difficult nor contentious; the only merit I should like to claim for it is that of being true, at least in parts. The phenomenon to be discussed is very widespread and obvious, and it cannot fail to have been already noticed, at least here and there, by others. Yet I have not found attention paid to it specifically.

It was for too long the assumption of philosophers that the business of a 'statement' can only be to 'describe' some state of affairs, or to 'state some fact', which it must do either truly or falsely. Grammarians, indeed, have regularly pointed out that not all 'sentences' are (used in making) statements:[1] there are, traditionally, besides (grammarians') statements, also questions and exclamations, and sentences expressing commands or wishes or concessions. And doubtless philosophers have not intended to deny this, despite some loose use of 'sentence' for 'statement'. Doubtless, too, both grammarians and philosophers have been aware that it is by no means easy to distinguish even questions, commands, and so on from statements by means of the few and jejune grammatical marks available, such as word order, mood, and the like: though perhaps it has not been usual to dwell on the difficulties which this fact obviously raises. For how do we decide which is which? What are the limits and definitions of each?

But now in recent years, many things which would once have been accepted without question as 'statements' by both philosophers and grammarians have been scrutinized with new care. . . . It has come to be commonly held that many utterances which look like statements are either not intended at all, or only intended in part, to record or impart straightforward information about the facts: for example, 'ethical propositions' are perhaps intended, solely or partly, to evince emotion or to prescribe conduct or to influence it in special ways. . . . We very often also use utterances in ways beyond the scope at least of traditional grammar.

Source: J.L. Austin, *How to do Things with Words*, Oxford: Oxford University Press, 1962.

It has come to be seen that many specially perplexing words embedded in apparently descriptive statements do not serve to indicate some specially odd additional feature in the reality reported, but to indicate (not to report) the circumstances in which the statement is made or reservations to which it is subject or the way in which it is to be taken and the like. To overlook these possibilities in the way once common is called the 'descriptive' fallacy; but perhaps this is not a good name, as 'descriptive' itself is special. Not all true or false statements are descriptions, and for this reason I prefer to use the word 'Constative' . . .

Utterances can be found . . . such that:

A   they do not 'describe' or 'report' or constate anything at all, are not 'true or false'; and

B   the uttering of the sentence is, or is a part of, the doing of an action, which again would not *normally* be described as, or as 'just', saying something . . .

. . .

Examples:

(a)   'I do (sc. take this woman to be my lawful wedded wife)' – as uttered in the course of the marriage ceremony.

(b)   'I name this ship the *Queen Elizabeth*' – as uttered when smashing the bottle against the stern.

(c)   'I give and bequeath my watch to my brother' – as occurring in a will.

(d)   'I bet you sixpence it will rain tomorrow.'

In these examples it seems clear that to utter the sentence (in, of course, the appropriate circumstances) is not to *describe* my doing of what I should be said in so uttering to be doing or to state that I am doing it: it is to do it. None of the utterances cited is either true or false: I assert this as obvious and do not argue it. It needs argument no more than that 'damn' is not true or false: it may be that the utterance 'serves to inform you' – but that is quite different. To name the ship *is* to say (in the appropriate circumstances) the words 'I name, etc.'. When I say, before the registrar or altar, 'I do', I am not reporting on a marriage: I am indulging in it.

What are we to call a sentence or an utterance of this type? I propose to call it a *performative sentence* or a performative utterance, or, for short, 'a performative'. The term 'performative' will be used in a variety of cognate ways and constructions, much as the term 'imperative' is. The name is derived, of course, from 'perform', the usual verb with the noun 'action': it indicates that the issuing of the utterance is the performing of an action – it is not normally thought of as just saying something.

. . .

Are we then to say things like this:

'To marry is to say a few words', or
'Betting is simply saying something'?

Such a doctrine sounds odd or even flippant at first, but with sufficient safeguards it may become not odd at all.

. . .

The uttering of the words is, indeed, usually a, or even *the*, leading incident in the performance of the act (of betting or what not), the performance of which is also the object of the utterance, but it is far from being usually, even if it is ever, the *sole* thing necessary if the act is to be deemed to have been performed. Speaking generally, it is always necessary that the *circumstances* in which the words are uttered should be in some way, or ways, *appropriate*, and it is very commonly necessary that either the speaker himself or other persons should *also* perform certain *other* actions, whether 'physical' or 'mental' actions or even acts of uttering further words. Thus, for naming the ship, it is essential that I should be the person appointed to name her; for (Christian) marrying, it is essential that I should not be already married with a wife living, sane and undivorced, and so on; for a bet to have been made, it is generally necessary for the offer of the bet to have been accepted by a taker (who must have done something, such as to say 'Done'); and it is hardly a gift if I *say* 'I give it you' but never hand it over. . . .

But we may, in objecting, have something totally different, and this time quite mistaken, in mind, especially when we think of some of the more awe-inspiring performatives such as 'I promise to . . .'. Surely the words must be spoken 'seriously' and so as to be taken 'seriously'? This is, though vague, true enough in general – it is an important commonplace in discussing the purport of any utterance whatsoever. I must not be joking, for example, nor writing a poem. . . .

Well we shall next consider what we actually do say about the utterance concerned when one or another of its normal concomitants is *absent*. In no case do we say that the utterance was false but rather that the utterance – or rather the *act*, e.g., the promise – was void, or given in bad faith, or not implemented, or the like. In the particular case of promising, as with many other performatives, it is appropriate that the person uttering the promise should have a certain intention, viz. here to keep his word: and perhaps of all concomitants this looks the most suitable to be that which 'I promise' does describe or record. Do we not actually, when such intention is absent, speak of a 'false' promise? Yet so to speak is *not* to say that the utterance 'I promise that . . .' is false, in the sense that though he states that he does he doesn't, or that though he describes he misdescribes – misreports. For he *does* promise: the promise here is not even *void*, though it is given *in bad faith*. His utterance is perhaps misleading, probably deceitful and doubtless wrong, but it is not a lie or a misstatement. At most we might make out a case for saying that it implies or insinuates a falsehood or a misstatement (to the effect that he does intend to do something): but that is a very different matter. Moreover, we do not speak of a false bet or a false christening; and that we *do* speak of a false promise need commit us no more than the fact that we speak of a false move. 'False' is not necessarily used of statements only.

. . .

Besides the uttering of the words of so-called performative, a good many other things have as a general rule to be right and to go right if we are to be said to have happily brought off our action. What these are we may hope to discover by looking at and classifying types of case in which something *goes wrong* and the act – marrying, betting, bequeathing, christening, or what not – is therefore at least to some extent a failure: the utterance is then, we may say, not indeed false but in general *unhappy*. And for this reason we call the doctrine of *the things that can be and go wrong* on the occasion of such utterances, the doctrine of the *Infelicities*.

Suppose we try first to state schematically – and I do not wish to claim any sort of finality for this scheme – some at least of the things which are necessary for the smooth or 'happy' functioning of a performative (or at least of a highly developed explicit performative, such as we have hitherto been alone concerned with), and then give examples of infelicities and their effects. . . .

A.1 There must exist an accepted conventional procedure having a certain conventional effect, that procedure to include the uttering of certain words by certain persons in certain circumstances, and further,

A.2 the particular persons and circumstances in a given case must be appropriate for the invocation of the particular procedure invoked.

B.1 The procedure must be executed by all participants both correctly and

B.2 completely.

C.1 Where, as often, the procedure is designed for use by persons having certain thoughts or feelings, or for the inauguration of certain consequential conduct on the part of any participant, then a person participating in and so invoking the procedure must in fact have those thoughts or feelings, and the participants must intend so to conduct themselves, and further

C.2 must actually so conduct themselves subsequently.

Now if we sin against any one (or more) of these six rules, our performative utterance will be (in one way or another) unhappy. But, of course, there are considerable differences between these 'ways' of being unhappy – ways which are intended to be brought out by the letter–numerals selected for each heading.

The first big distinction is between all the four rules A and B taken together, as opposed to the two rules C . . . . If we offend against any of the former rules (As or Bs) – that is, if we, say, utter the formula incorrectly, or if, say, we are not in a position to do the act because we are, say, married already, or it is the purser and not the captain who is conducting the ceremony, then the act in question, e.g., marrying, is not successfully performed at all, does not come off, is not achieved. Whereas in the two C cases the act *is* achieved, although to achieve it in such circum-stances, as when we are, say, insincere, is an abuse of the procedure. Thus, when I say 'I promise' and have no intention of keeping it, I have promised but. . . . We need names for referring to this general distinction, so we shall call in general those infelicities A.1–B.2 which are such that the act for the performing of which, and in the performing of which, the verbal formula in question is designed, is not achieved, by the name MISFIRES: and on the other hand we may christen those infelicities where the act *is* achieved ABUSES. . . . When the utterance is a misfire, the procedure which we purport to invoke is disallowed or is botched: and our act (marrying, etc.) is void or without effect, etc. We speak of our act as a purported act, or perhaps an attempt – or we use such an expression as 'went through a form of marriage' by contrast with 'married'. On the other hand, in the C cases, we speak of our infelicitous act as 'professed' or 'hollow' rather than 'purported' or 'empty', and as not implemented, or not consummated, rather than as void or without effect. But let me hasten to add that these distinctions are not hard and fast, and more especially that such words as 'purported' and 'professed' will not bear very much stressing. Two final words about being void or without effect. This does not mean, of course, to say that we won't have done anything: lots of things will have been done – we shall most interestingly have committed the act of bigamy – but we shall *not* have done the purported act, viz. marrying. Because despite the name, you do not when bigamous marry twice. . . . Further, 'without effect' does not here mean 'without consequences, results, effects'.

. . .

The performative utterances I have taken as examples are all of them highly developed affairs, of the kind that we shall call *explicit* performatives, by contrast with merely *implicit* performatives. That is to say, they (all) begin with or include some highly significant and unambiguous expression such as 'I bet', 'I promise', 'I bequeath' – an expression very commonly also used in naming the act which, in making such an utterance, I am performing – for example betting, promising, bequeathing, etc. But, of course, it is both obvious and important that we can on occasion use the utterance 'go' to achieve practically the same as we achieve by the utterance 'I order you to go': and we should say cheerfully in either case, describing subsequently what someone did, that he ordered me to go. It may, however, be uncertain in fact, and, so far as the mere utterance is concerned, is always left uncertain when we use so inexplicit a formula as the mere imperative 'go', whether the utterer is ordering (or is purporting to order) me to go or merely advising, entreating, or what not me to go. Similarly 'There is a bull in the field' may or may not be a warning, for I *might* just be describing the scenery, and 'I shall be there' may or may not be a promise. Here we have primitive as distinct from explicit performatives; and there may be nothing in the circumstances by which we can decide whether or not the utterance is performative at all. Anyway, in a given situation it can be open to me to take it as *either* one or the other. It was a performative formula – *perhaps* – but the procedure in question was not sufficiently explicitly invoked. Perhaps I did not *take it as* an order or was not anyway *bound* to take it as an order. The person did not *take it as* a promise: i.e., in the particular circumstance he did not accept the procedure, on the ground that the ritual was incompletely carried out by the original speaker.

. . .

We shall next consider three of the many ways in which a statement implies the truth of certain other statements. One of those that I shall mention has been long known. The others have been discovered quite recently. We shall not put the matter too technically, though this can be done. I refer to the discovery that the ways we can do wrong, speak outrageously, in uttering conjunctions of 'factual' statements, are more numerous than merely by contradiction . . .

1   *Entails*: 'All men blush' entails 'some men blush'. We cannot say 'All men blush but not any men blush', or 'the cat is under the mat and the cat is on top of the mat' or 'the cat is on the mat and the cat is not on the mat', since in each case the first clause entails the contradictory of the second.

2   *Implies*: My saying 'the cat is on the mat' implies that I believe it is . . . We cannot say 'the cat is on the mat but I do not believe it is'. (This is actually not the ordinary use of 'implies': 'implies' is really weaker: as when we say 'He implied that I did not know it' or 'You implied you knew it' (as distinct from believing it.)

3   *Presupposes*: 'All Jack's children are bald' presupposes that Jack has some children. We cannot say 'All Jack's children are bald but Jack has no children', or 'Jack has no children and all his children are bald'.
      There is a common feeling of outrage in all these cases. But we must not use some blanket term, 'implies' or 'contradiction', because there are very great differences. There are more ways of killing a cat than drowning it in butter; but this is the sort of thing (as the proverb indicates) we overlook: there are more ways of outraging speech than contradiction merely . . .

The act of 'saying something' in the full normal sense I call, i.e., dub, the performance of a locutionary act, and the study of utterances thus far and in these respects the study of locutions, or of the full units of speech. Our interest in the locutionary act is, of course, principally to make quite plain what it is, in order to distinguish it from other acts with which we are primarily concerned . . .

To perform a locutionary act is in general, we may say, also and *eo ipso* to perform an *illocutionary* act, as I propose to call it. Thus in performing a locutionary act we shall also be performing such an act as:

   asking or answering a question;
   giving some information or an assurance or a warning;
   announcing a verdict or an intention;
   pronouncing sentence;
   making an appointment or an appeal or a criticism;
   making an identification or giving a description;

and the numerous like. (I am not suggesting that this is a clearly defined class by any means.) . . . When we perform a locutionary act, we use speech: but in what way precisely are we using it on this occasion? For there are very numerous functions of or ways in which we use speech and it makes a great difference to our act in some sense – in which way and which *sense* we were on this occasion 'using' it. It makes a great difference whether we were advising, or merely suggesting, or actually ordering, whether we were strictly promising or only announcing a vague intention, and so forth. These issues penetrate a little but not without confusion into grammar, but we constantly do debate them, in such terms as whether certain words (a certain locution) *had the force of* a question, or *ought to have been taken as* an estimate and so on.

I explained the performance of an act in this new and second sense as the performance of an 'illocutionary' act, i.e. performance of an act *in* saying something as opposed to performance of an act *of* saying something; I call the act performed an 'illocution' and shall refer to the doctrine of the different types of function of language here in question as the doctrine of 'illocutionary forces'.

. . .

There is yet a further sense in which to perform a locutionary act, and therein an illocutionary act, may also be to perform an act of another kind. Saying something will often, or even normally, produce certain consequential effects upon the feelings, thoughts, or actions of the audience, or of the speaker, or of other persons: and it may be done with the design, intention or purpose of producing them; and we may then say, thinking of this, that the speaker has performed an act in the nomenclature of which reference is made either (a), only obliquely, or even (b), not at all, to the performance of the locutionary or illocutionary act. We shall call the performance of an act of this kind the performance of a 'perlocutionary' act, and the act performed, where suitable – essentially in cases falling under (a) – a 'perlocution' . . .

Acts of all our three kinds [locutionary, illocutionary and perlocutionary] necessitate, since they are the performing of actions, allowance being made for the ills that all action is heir to. We must systematically be prepared to distinguish between 'the act of doing *x*', i.e., achieving *x*, and 'the act of attempting to do *x*'.

In the case of illocutions we must be ready to draw the necessary distinction, not noticed by ordinary language except in exceptional cases, between:

(a)   the act of attempting or purporting (or affecting or professing or claiming or setting up or setting out) to perform a certain illocutionary act, and
(b)   the act of successfully achieving or consummating or bringing off such an act.

This distinction is, or should be, a commonplace of the theory of our language about 'action' in general. But attention has been drawn earlier to its special importance in connexion with performatives: it is always possible, for example, to try to thank or inform somebody yet in different ways to fail, because he doesn't listen, or takes it as ironical, or wasn't responsible for whatever it was, and so on. This distinction will arise, as over any act, over locutionary acts too; but failures here will not be unhappiness as there, but rather failures to get the words out, to express ourselves clearly, etc.

Since our acts are actions, we must always remember the distinction between producing effects or consequences which are intended or unintended; and (i) when the speaker intends to produce an effect it may nevertheless not occur, and (ii) when he does not intend to produce it or intends not to produce it it may nevertheless occur. To cope with complication (i) we invoke as before the distinction between attempt and achievement; to cope with complication (ii) we invoke the normal linguistic devices of disclaiming (adverbs like 'unintentionally' and so on) which we hold ready for general use in all cases of doing actions.

. . .

The perlocutionary act may be either the achievement of a perlocutionary object (convince, persuade) or the production of a perlocutionary sequel. Thus the act of warning may achieve its perlocutionary object of alerting and also have the perlocutionary sequel of alarming, and an argument against a view may fail to achieve its object but have the perlocutionary sequel of convincing our opponent of its truth ('I only succeeded in convincing him'). What is the perlocutionary object of one illocution may be the sequel of another. For example, warning may produce the sequel of deterring and saying 'Don't', whose object is to deter, may produce the sequel of alerting or even alarming. Some perlocutionary acts are always the producing of a sequel, namely those where there is no illocutionary formula: thus I may surprise you or upset you or humiliate you by a locution, though there is no illocutionary formula 'I surprise you by . . .', 'I upset you by . . .', 'I humiliate you by . . .'

It is characteristic of perlocutionary acts that the response achieved, or the sequel, can be achieved additionally or entirely by non-locutionary means: thus intimidation may be achieved by waving a stick or pointing a gun. Even in the cases of convincing, persuading, getting to obey and getting to believe, we may achieve the response non-verbally; but if there is no illocutionary act, it is doubtful whether this language characteristic of perlocutionary objects should be used. Compare the use of 'got him to' with that of 'got him to obey'. However, this alone is not enough to distinguish illocutionary acts, since we can for example warn or order or appoint or give or protest or apologize by non-verbal means and these are illocutionary acts. Thus we may cock a snook or hurl a tomato by way of protest.

. . .

When we originally contrasted the performative with the constative utterance we said that

1   the performative should be doing something as opposed to just saying something; and
2   the performative is happy or unhappy as opposed to true or false.

Were these distinctions really sound? Our subsequent discussion of doing and saying certainly seems to point to the conclusion that whenever I 'say' anything (except perhaps a mere exclamation like 'damn' or 'ouch') I shall be performing both locutionary and illocutionary acts, and these two kinds of acts seem to be the very things which we tried to use, under the names of 'doing' and 'saying', as a means of distinguishing performatives from constatives. If we are in general always doing both things, how can our distinction survive?

Let us first reconsider the contrast from the side of constative utterances: of these, we were content to refer to 'statements' as the typical or paradigm case. Would it be correct to say that when we state something

1   we are doing something as well as and distinct from just saying something, and
2   our utterance is liable to be happy or unhappy (as well as, if you will, true or
     false)?

Surely to state is every bit as much to perform an illocutionary act as, say, to
want or to pronounce. Of course it is not to perform an act in some specially physically
way, other than in so far as it involves, when verbal, the making of movements of
vocal organs; but then nor, as we have seen, is to warn, to protest, to promise or to
name. 'Stating' seems to meet all the criteria we had for distinguishing the illocutionary
act. Consider such an unexceptionable remark as the following:

> In saying that it was raining, I was not betting or arguing or warning: I
> was simply stating it as a fact.

Here 'stating' is put absolutely on a level with arguing, betting, and warning. . . .
     Moreover, although the utterance 'He did not do it' is often issued as a statement,
and is then undoubtedly true or false (*this* is if anything is), it does not seem possible
to say that it differs from 'I state that he did not do it' in this respect.
If someone says 'I state that he did not do it', we investigate the truth of his statement
in just the same way as if he had said 'He did not do it' . . .
     Moreover, if we think of the alleged contrast, according to which performatives
are happy or unhappy and statements true or false, again from the side of supposed
constative utterances, notably statements, we find that statements *are* liable to
every kind of infelicity to which performatives are liable. Let us look back again
and consider whether statements are not liable to precisely the same disabilities
as, say, warnings by way of what we called 'infelicities' – that is various disabilities
which make an utterance unhappy without, however, making it true or false.
     We have already noted that sense in which saying, as equivalent to stating, 'The
cat is on the mat' implies that I believe that the cat is on the mat. This is parallel to
the sense – is the same sense – as that in which 'I promise to be there' implies that
I intend to be there and that I believe I shall be able to be there. So the statement is
liable to the *insincerity* form of infelicity; and even to the *breach* form of infelicity in
this sense, that saying or stating that the cat is on the mat commits me to saying or
stating 'The mat is underneath the cat' just as much as the performative 'I define X
as Y' (in the *fiat* sense, say) commits me to using those terms in special ways in future
discourse, and we can see how this is connected with such acts as promising. This
means that statements can give rise to infelicities of our two C kinds.
     Now what about infelicities of the A and B kinds, which rendered the
act – warning, undertaking, etc. – null and void? Can a thing that looks like a
statement be null and void just as much as a putative contract? The answer seems to
be Yes, importantly. The first cases are A.1 and A.2, where there is no convention
(or not an accepted convention) or where the circumstances are not appropriate
for its invocation by the speaker. Many infelicities of just this type do infect statements.
     We have already noticed the case of a putative statement *presupposing* (as it is
called) the existence of that which it refers to; if no such thing exists, 'the statement'
is not about anything. Now some say that in these circumstances, if, for example,

someone asserts that the present King of France is bald, 'the question whether he is bald does not arise'; but it is better to say that the putative statement is null and void, exactly as when I say that I sell you something but it is not mine or (having been burnt) is not any longer in existence. Contracts often are void because the objects they are about do not exist, which involves a breakdown of reference.

But it is important to notice also that 'statements' too are liable to infelicity of this kind in other ways also parallel to contracts, promises, warnings, etc. Just as we often say, for example, 'You cannot order me', in the sense 'You have not the right to order me', which is equivalent to saying that you are not in the appropriate position to do so: so often there are things you cannot state – have no right to state – are not in a position to state. You *cannot* now state how many people there are in the next room; if you say 'There are fifty people in the next room', I can only regard you as guessing or conjecturing (just as sometimes you are not ordering me, which would be inconceivable, but possibly asking me to rather impolitely, so here you are 'hazarding a guess' rather oddly). Here there is something you might, in other circumstances, be in a position to state; but what about statements about other persons' feelings or about the future? Is a forecast or even a prediction about, say, persons' behaviour really a statement? It is important to take the speech-situation as a whole.

. . .

Once we realize that what we have to study is *not* the sentence but the issuing of an utterance in a speech situation, there can hardly be any longer a possibility of not seeing that stating is performing an act . . .

What then finally is left of the distinction of the performative and constative utterance? Really we may say that what we had in mind here was this:

(a)   With the constative utterance, we abstract from the illocutionary (let alone the perlocutionary) aspects of the speech act, and we concentrate on the locutionary: moreover, we use an oversimplified notion of correspondence with the facts – oversimplified because essentially it brings in the illocutionary aspect. This is the ideal of what would be right to say in all circumstances, for any purpose, to any audience, etc. Perhaps it is sometimes realized.

(b)   With the performative utterance, we attend as much as possible to the illocutionary force of the utterance, and abstract from the dimension of correspondence with facts.

Perhaps neither of these abstractions is so very expedient: perhaps we have here not really two poles, but rather a historical development. Now in certain cases, perhaps with mathematical formulas in physics books as examples of constatives, or with the issuing of simple executive orders or the giving of simple names, say, as examples of performatives, we approximate in real life to finding such things. It was examples of this kind, like 'I apologize', and 'The cat is on the mat', said for no conceivable reason, extreme marginal cases, that gave rise to the idea of two distinct utterances. But the real conclusion must surely be that we need (1) to distinguish between locutionary and illocutionary acts, and (2) specially and critically to establish with respect to each kind of illocutionary act – warnings, estimates, verdicts, statements, and descriptions – what if any is the specific way in which they are intended, first to be in order or not in order, and second, to be 'right' or 'wrong'; what terms of appraisal and disappraisal are used for each and what they mean. This is a wide field and certainly will not lead to a simple distinction of 'true' and 'false'; nor will it lead to a distinction of statements from the rest, for stating is only one among very numerous speech acts of the illocutionary class.

Furthermore, in general the locutionary act as much as the illocutionary is an abstraction only: every genuine speech act is both.

. . .

Note

1   It is, of course, not really correct that a sentence ever *is* a statement: rather, it is *used* in *making a statement*, and the statement itself is a 'logical construction' out of the makings of statements.

Chapter 3

H.P. Grice

LOGIC AND CONVERSATION

. . .

Suppose that **A and B** are talking about a mutual friend, C, who is now working in a bank. A asks B how C is getting on in his job, and B replies, *Oh quite well, I think; he likes his colleagues, and he hasn't been to prison yet.* At this point, A might well inquire what B was implying, what he was suggesting, or even what he meant by saying that C had not yet been to prison. The answer might be any one of such things as that C is the sort of person likely to yield to the temptation provided by his occupation, that C's colleagues are really very unpleasant and treacherous people, and so forth. It might, of course, be quite unnecessary for A to make such an inquiry of B, the answer to it being, in the context, clear in advance. I think it is clear that whatever B implied, suggested, meant, etc., in this example, is distinct from what B said, which was simply that C had not been to prison yet. I wish to introduce, as terms of art, the verb *implicate* and the related nouns *implicature* (cf. *implying*) and *implicatum* (cf. *what is implied*). The point of this maneuver is to avoid having, on each occasion, to choose between this or that member of the family of verbs for which *implicate* is to do general duty. I shall, for the time being at least, have to assume to a considerable extent an intuitive understanding of the meaning of *say* in such contexts, and an ability to recognize particular verbs as members of the family with which *implicate* is associated. I can, however, make one or two remarks that may help to clarify the more problematic of these assumptions, namely, that connected with the meaning of the word *say*.

In the sense in which I am using the word *say*, I intend what someone has said to be closely related to the conventional meaning of the words (the sentence) he has uttered. Suppose someone to have uttered the sentence *He is in the grip of a*

Source: H.P. Grice, 'Logic and conversation', in Peter Cole and Jerry L. Morgan (eds) *Syntax and Semantics*, Volume 3: *Speech Arts*, New York: Academic Press, 1975, 41–58.

vice. Given a knowledge of the English language, but no knowledge of the circumstances of the utterance, one would know something about what the speaker had said, on the assumption that he was speaking standard English, and speaking literally. One would know that he had said, about some particular male person or animal x, that at the time of the utterance (whatever that was), either (1) x was unable to rid himself of a certain kind of bad character trait or (2) some part of x's person was caught in a certain kind of tool or instrument (approximate account, of course). But for a full identification of what the speaker had said, one would need to know (a) the identity of x, (b) the time of utterance, and (c) the meaning, on the particular occasion of utterance, of the phrase *in the grip of a vice* (a decision between (1) and (2)). This brief indication of my use of *say* leaves it open whether a man who says (today) *Harold Wilson is a great man* and another who says (also today) *The British Prime Minister is a great man* would, if each knew that the two singular terms had the same reference, have said the same thing. But whatever decision is made about this question, the apparatus that I am about to provide will be capable of accounting for any implicatures that might depend on the presence of one rather than another of these singular terms in the sentence uttered. Such implicatures would merely be related to different maxims.

In some cases the conventional meaning of the words used will determine what is implicated, besides helping to determine what is said. If I say (smugly), *He is an Englishman; he is, therefore, brave*, I have certainly committed myself, by virtue of the meaning of my words, to its being the case that his being brave is a consequence of (follows from) his being an Englishman. But while I have said that he is an Englishman, and said that he is brave, I do not want to say that I have SAID (in the favored sense) that it follows from his being an Englishman that he is brave, though I have certainly indicated, and so implicated, that this is so. I do not want to say that my utterance of this sentence would be, STRICTLY SPEAKING, false should the consequence in question fail to hold. So SOME implicatures are conventional, unlike the one with which I introduced this discussion of implicature.

I wish to represent a certain subclass of nonconventional implicatures, which I shall call CONVERSATIONAL implicatures, as being essentially connected with certain general features of discourse; so my next step is to try to say what these features are.

The following may provide a first approximation to a general principle. Our talk exchanges do not normally consist of a succession of disconnected remarks, and would not be rational if they did. They are characteristically, to some degree at least, cooperative efforts; and each participant recognizes in them, to some extent, a common purpose or set of purposes, or at least a mutually accepted direction. This purpose or direction may be fixed from the start (e.g., by an initial proposal of a question for discussion), or it may evolve during the exchange; it may be fairly definite, or it may be so indefinite as to leave very considerable latitude to the participants (as in a casual conversation). But at each stage, SOME possible conversational moves would be excluded as conversationally unsuitable. We might then formulate a rough general principle which participants will be expected, other things being equal, to observe, namely: make your conversational contribution such as is required, at the stage at which it occurs, by the accepted purpose or direction of the talk exchange in which you are engaged. One might label this the Cooperative Principle [Grice later refers to this as the CP].

On the assumption that some such general principle as this is acceptable, one may perhaps distinguish four categories under one or another of which will fall certain more specific maxims and sub-maxims, the following of which will, in general, yield results in accordance with the Cooperative Principle. Echoing Kant, I call these categories Quantity, Quality, Relation, and Manner. The category of Quantity relates to the quantity of information to be provided, and under it fall the following maxims:

1   Make your contribution as informative as is required (for the current purposes of the exchange).
2   Do not make your contribution more informative than is required.

(The second maxim is disputable; it might be said that to be overinformative is not a transgression of the CP but merely a waste of time. However, it might be answered that such overinformativeness may be confusing in that it is liable to raise side issues; and there may also be an indirect effect, in that the hearers may be misled as a result of thinking that there is some particular POINT in the provision of the excess of information. However this may be, there is perhaps a different reason for doubt about the admission of this second maxim, namely, that its effect will be secured by a later maxim, which concerns relevance.)

Under the category of Quality falls a supermaxim – 'Try to make your contribution one that is true' – and two more specific maxims:

1   Do not say what you believe to be false.
2   Do not say that for which you lack adequate evidence.

Under the category of Relation I place a single maxim, namely, 'Be relevant.' Though the maxim itself is terse, its formulation conceals a number of problems that exercise me a good deal: questions about what different kinds and focuses of relevance there may be, how these shift in the course of a talk exchange, how to allow for the fact that subjects of conversation are legitimately changed, and so on. I find the treatment of such questions exceedingly difficult, and I hope to revert to them in a later work.

Finally, under the category of Manner, which I understand as relating not (like the previous categories) to what is said but, rather, to HOW what is said is to be said, I include the supermaxim – 'Be perspicuous' – and various maxims such as:

1   Avoid obscurity of expression.
2   Avoid ambiguity.
3   Be brief (avoid unnecessary prolixity).
4   Be orderly.

And one might need others.

It is obvious that the observance of some of these maxims is a matter of less urgency than is the observance of others; a man who has expressed himself with undue prolixity would, in general, be open to milder comment than would a man who has said something he believes to be false. Indeed, it might be felt that the importance of at least the first maxim of Quality is such that it should not be included in a scheme of the kind I am constructing; other maxims come into operation only on the assumption that this maxim of Quality is satisfied. While this may be correct, so far as the generation of implicatures is concerned it seems to play a role not totally different from the other maxims, and it will be convenient, for the present at least, to treat it as a member of the list of maxims.

There are, of course, all sorts of other maxims (aesthetic, social, or moral in character), such as 'Be polite', that are also normally observed by participants in talk exchanges, and these may also generate nonconventional implicatures. The conversational maxims, however, and the conversational implicatures connected with them, are specially connected (I hope) with the particular purposes that talk (and so, talk exchange) is adapted to serve and is primarily employed to serve. I have stated my maxims as if this purpose were a maximally effective exchange of information; this specification is, of course, too narrow, and the scheme needs to be generalized to allow for such general purposes as influencing or directing the actions of others.

As one of my avowed aims is to see talking as a special case or variety of purposive, indeed rational, behavior, it may be worth noting that the specific expectations or presumptions connected with at least some of the foregoing maxims have their analogues in the sphere of transactions that are not talk exchanges. I list briefly one such analog for each conversational category.

1 Quantity. If you are assisting me to mend a car, I expect your contribution to be neither more nor less than is required; if, for example, at a particular stage I need four screws, I expect you to hand me four, rather than two or six.

2 Quality. I expect your contributions to be genuine and not spurious. If I need sugar as an ingredient in the cake you are assisting me to make, I do not expect you to hand me salt; if I need a spoon, I do not expect a trick spoon made of rubber.

3 Relation. I expect a partner's contribution to be appropriate to immediate needs at each stage of the transaction; if I am mixing ingredients for a cake, I do not expect to be handed a good book, or even an oven cloth (though this might be an appropriate contribution at a later stage).

4 Manner. I expect a partner to make it clear what contribution he is making, and to execute his performance with reasonable dispatch.

These analogies are relevant to what I regard as a fundamental question about the CP and its attendant maxims, namely, what the basis is for the assumption which we seem to make, and on which (I hope) it will appear that a great range of implicatures depend, that talkers will in general (other things being equal and in the absence of indications to the contrary) proceed in the manner that these principles prescribe. A dull but, no doubt at a certain level, adequate answer is that it is just a well-recognized empirical fact that people DO behave in these ways; they have learned to do so in childhood and not lost the habit of doing so; and, indeed, it would involve a good deal of effort to make a radical departure from the habit. It is much easier, for example, to tell the truth than to invent lies.

I am, however, enough of a rationalist to want to find a basis that underlies these facts, undeniable though they may be; I would like to be able to think of the standard type of conversational practice not merely as something that all or most do IN FACT follow but as something that it is REASONABLE for us to follow, that we SHOULD NOT abandon. For a time, I was attracted by the idea that observance of the CP and the maxims, in a talk exchange, could be thought of as a quasi-contractual matter, with parallels outside the realm of discourse. If you pass by when I am struggling with my stranded car, I no doubt have some degree of expectation that you will offer help, but once you join me in tinkering under the hood, my expectations become stronger and take more specific forms (in the absence of indications that you are merely an incompetent meddler); and talk exchanges seemed to me to exhibit, characteristically, certain features that jointly distinguish cooperative transactions:

1   The participants have some common immediate aim, like getting a car mended; their ultimate aims may, of course, be independent and even in conflict – each may want to get the car mended in order to drive off, leaving the other stranded. In characteristic talk exchanges, there is a common aim even if, as in an over-the-wall chat, it is a second-order one, namely, that each party should, for the time being, identify himself with the transitory conversational interests of the other.
2   The contributions of the participants should be dovetailed, mutually dependent.
3   There is some sort of understanding (which may be explicit but which is often tacit) that, other things being equal, the transaction should continue in appropriate style unless both parties are agreeable that it should terminate. You do not just shove off or start doing something else.

But while some such quasi-contractual basis as this may apply to some cases, there are too many types of exchange, like quarrelling and letter writing, that it fails to fit comfortably. In any case, one feels that the talker who is irrelevant or obscure has primarily let down not his audience but himself. So I would like to be able to show that observance of the CP and maxims is reasonable (rational) along the following lines: that anyone who cares about goals that are central to conversation/communication (e.g. giving and receiving information, influencing and being influenced by others) must be expected to have an interest, given suitable circumstances, in participation in talk exchanges that will be profitable only on the assumption that they are conducted in general accordance with the CP and the maxims. Whether any such conclusion can be reached, I am uncertain; in any case, I am fairly sure that I cannot reach it until I am a good deal clearer about the nature of relevance and of the circumstances in which it is required.

It is now time to show the connection between the CP and maxims, on the one hand, and conversational implicature on the other.

A participant in a talk exchange may fail to fulfill a maxim in various ways, which include the following:

1   He may quietly and unostentatiously VIOLATE a maxim; if so, in some cases he will be liable to mislead.
2   He may OPT OUT from the operation both of the maxim and of the CP; he may say, indicate, or allow it to become plain that he is unwilling to cooperate in the way the maxim requires. He may say, for example, *I cannot say more; my lips are sealed.*

3   He may be faced by a CLASH: He may be unable, for example, to fulfill the first maxim of Quantity (Be as informative as is required) without violating the second maxim of Quality (Have adequate evidence for what you say).

4   He may FLOUT a maxim; that is, he may BLATANTLY fail to fulfill it. On the assumption that the speaker is able to fulfill the maxim and to do so without violating another maxim (because of a clash), is not opting out, and is not, in view of the blatancy of his performance, trying to mislead, the hearer is faced with a minor problem: How can his saying what he did say be reconciled with the supposition that he is observing the overall CP? This situation is one that characteristically gives rise to a conversational implicature; and when a conversational implicature is generated in this way, I shall say that a maxim is being EXPLOITED.

I am now in a position to characterize the notion of conversational implicature. A man who, by (in, when) saying (or making as if to say) that p has implicated that q, may be said to have conversationally implicated that q, PROVIDED THAT (1) he is to be presumed to be observing the conversational maxims, or at least the Cooperative Principle; (2) the supposition that he is aware that, or thinks that, q is required in order to make his saying or making as if to say p (or doing so in THOSE terms) consistent with this presumption; and (3) the speaker thinks (and would expect the hearer to think that the speaker thinks) that it is within the competence of the hearer to work out, or grasp intuitively, that the supposition mentioned in (2) IS required. Apply this to my initial example, to B's remark that C has not yet been to prison. In a suitable setting A might reason as follows: '(1) B has apparently violated the maxim "Be relevant" and so may be regarded as having flouted one of the maxims conjoining perspicuity, yet I have no reason to suppose that he is opting out from the operation of the CP; (2) given the circumstances, I can regard his irrelevance as only apparent if, and only if, I suppose him to think that C is potentially dishonest; (3) B knows that I am capable of working out step (2). So B implicates that C is potentially dishonest.'

The presence of a conversational implicature must be capable of being worked out; for even if it can in fact be intuitively grasped, unless the intuition is replaceable by an argument, the implicature (if present at all) will not count as a CONVERSATIONAL implicature; it will be a CONVENTIONAL implicature. To work out that a particular conversational implicature is present, the hearer will rely on the following data:

1   the conventional meaning of the words used, together with the identity of any references that may be involved;

2   the CP and its maxims;

3   the context, linguistic or otherwise, of the utterance;

4   other items of background knowledge; and

5   the fact (or supposed fact) that all relevant items falling under the previous headings are available to both participants and both participants know or assume this to be the case.

A general pattern for the working out of a conventional implicature might be given as follows: 'He has said that p; there is no reason to suppose that he is not observing the maxims, or at least the CP; he could not be doing this unless he thought that q;

he knows (and knows that I know that he knows) that I can see that the supposition that he thinks that *q* IS required; he has done nothing to stop me thinking that *q*; he intends me to think, or is at least willing to allow me to think, that *q*; and so he has implicated that *q*.'

I shall now offer a number of examples, which I shall divide into three groups.

Group A

Examples in which no maxim is violated, or at least in which it is not clear that any maxim is violated

A is standing by an obviously immobilized car and is approached by B; the following exchange takes place:

(1)   A: I am out of petrol.
    B: There is a garage round the corner.

(Gloss: B would be infringing the maxim 'Be relevant' unless he thinks, or thinks it possible, that the garage is open, and has petrol to sell; so he implicates that the garage is, or at least may be open, etc.)

In this example, unlike the case of the remark *He hasn't been to prison yet*, the unstated connection between B's remark and A's remark is so obvious that, even if one interprets the supermaxim of Manner, 'Be perspicious,' as applying not only to the expression of what is said but also to the connection of what is said with adjacent remarks, there seems to be no case for regarding that supermaxim as infringed in this example. The next example is perhaps a little less clear in this respect:

(2)   A: Smith doesn't seem to have a girlfriend these days.
    B: He has been paying a lot of visits to New York lately.

B implicates that Smith has, or may have, a girlfriend in New York. (A gloss is unnecessary in view of that given for the previous example.)

In both examples, the speaker implicates that which he must be assumed to believe in order to preserve the assumption that he is observing the maxim of Relation.

Group B

An example in which a maxim is violated, but its violation is to be explained by the supposition of a clash with another maxim

A is planning with B an itinerary for a holiday in France. Both know that A wants to see his friend C, if to do so would not involve too great a prolongation of his journey:

(3)   A: Where does C live?
    B: Somewhere in the south of France.

(Gloss: There is no reason to suppose that B is opting out; his answer is, as he well knows, less informative than is required to meet A's needs. This infringement of the first maxim of Quantity can be explained only by the supposition that B is aware that to be more informative would be to say something that infringed the maxim of Quality, 'Don't say what you lack adequate evidence for', so B implicates that he does not know in which town C lives.)

Group C

Examples that involve exploitation, that is, a procedure by which a maxim is flouted for the purpose of getting in a conversational implicature by means of something of the nature of a figure of speech

In these examples, though some maxim is violated at the level of what is said, the hearer is entitled to assume that that maxim, or at least the overall Cooperative Principle, is observed at the level of what is implicated.

A FLOUTING OF THE FIRST MAXIM OF QUANTITY

(4)   A is writing a testimonial about a pupil who is a candidate for a philosophy job, and his letter reads as follows: Dear Sir, Mr X's command of English is excellent, and his attendance at tutorials has been regular. Yours, etc.'

(Gloss: A cannot be opting out, since if he wished to be uncooperative, why write at all? He cannot be unable, through ignorance, to say more, since the man is his pupil; moreover, he knows that more information than this is wanted. He must, therefore, be wishing to impart information that he is reluctant to write down. This supposition is tenable only on the assumption that he thinks Mr X is no good at philosophy. This, then, is what he is implicating.)

Extreme examples of a flouting of the first maxim of Quantity are provided by utterances of patent tautologies like *Women are women* and *War is war*. I would wish to maintain that at the level of what is said, in my favored sense, such remarks are totally noninformative and so, at that level, cannot but infringe the first maxim of Quantity in any conversational context. They are, of course, informative at the level of what is implicated, and the hearer's identification of their informative content at this level is dependent on his ability to explain the speaker's selection of this PARTICULAR patent tautology.

. . .

EXAMPLES IN WHICH THE FIRST MAXIM OF QUALITY IS FLOUTED

(5)   *Irony*. X, with whom A has been on close terms until now, has betrayed a secret of A's to a business rival. A and his audience both know this. A says 'X is a fine friend.' (Gloss: It is perfectly obvious to A and his audience that what A has said or has made as if to say is something he does not believe, and the audience

knows that A knows that this is obvious to the audience. So, unless A's utterance is entirely pointless, A must be trying to get across some other proposition than the one he purports to be putting forward. This must be some obviously related proposition; the most obviously related proposition is the contradictory of the one he purports to be putting forward.)

(6)   *Metaphor*. Examples like *You are the cream in my coffee* characteristically involve categorical falsity, so the contradictory of what the speaker has made as if to say will, strictly speaking, be a truism; so it cannot be THAT that such a speaker is trying to get across. The most likely supposition is that the speaker is attributing to his audience some feature or features in respect of which the audience resembles (more or less fancifully) the mentioned substance.

It is possible to combine metaphor and irony by imposing on the hearer two stages of interpretation. I say *You are the cream in my coffee*, intending the hearer to reach first the metaphor interpretant 'You are my pride and joy' and then the irony interpretant 'You are my bane.'

(7)   *Meiosis*. Of a man known to have broken up all the furniture one says *He was a little intoxicated*.

(8)   *Hyperbole. Every nice girl loves a sailor.*

Examples in which the second maxim of Quality, 'Do not say that for which you lack adequate evidence', *is flouted* are perhaps not easy to find, but the following seems to be a specimen.

(9)   I say of X's wife, *She is probably deceiving him this evening*. In a suitable context, or with a suitable gesture or tone or voice, it may be clear that I have no adequate reason for supposing this to be the case. My partner, to preserve the assumption that the conversational game is still being played, assumes that I am getting at some related proposition for the acceptance of which I DO have a reasonable basis. The related proposition might well be that she is given to deceiving her husband, or possibly that she is the sort of person who would not stop short of such conduct.

Examples in which an implicature is achieved by real, as distinct from apparent, violation of the maxim of Relation are perhaps rare, but the following seems to be a good candidate.

(10)   At a genteel tea party, A says *Mrs X is an old bag*. There is a moment of appalled silence, and then B says *The weather has been quite delightful this summer, hasn't it?* B has blatantly refused to make what HE says relevant to A's preceding remark. He thereby indicates that A's remark should not be discussed and, perhaps more specifically, that A has committed a social gaffe.

· · ·

I have so far considered only cases of what I might call particularized conversational implicature – that is to say, cases in which an implicature is carried by saying that *p* on a particular occasion in virtue of special features of the context, cases in which there is no room for the idea that an implicature of this sort is

NORMALLY carried by saying that *p*. But there are cases of generalized conversational implicature. Sometimes one can say that the use of a certain form of words in an utterance would normally (in the ABSENCE of special circumstances) carry such-and-such an implicature or type of implicature. Noncontroversial examples are perhaps hard to find, since it is all too easy to treat a generalized conversational implicature as if it were a conventional implicature. I offer an example that I hope may be fairly noncontroversial.

(11) Anyone who uses a sentence of the form *X is meeting a woman this evening* would normally implicate that the person to be met was someone other than X's wife, mother, sister, or perhaps even close platonic friend. Similarly, if I were to say *X went into a house yesterday and found a tortoise inside the front door*, my hearer would normally be surprised if some time later I revealed that the house was X's own. I could produce similar linguistic phenomena involving the expressions *a garden, a car, a college*, and so on.

. . .

When someone, by using the form of expression *an X*, implicates that the X does not belong to or is not otherwise closely connected with some identifiable person, the implicature is present because the speaker has failed to be specific in a way in which he might have been expected to be specific, with the consequence that it is likely to be assumed that he is not in a position to be specific. This is a familiar implicature situation and is classifiable as a failure, for one reason or another, to fulfill the first maxim of Quantity. The only difficult question is why it should, in certain cases, be presumed, independently of information about particular contexts of utterance, that specification of the closeness or remoteness of the connection between a particular person or object and a further person who is mentioned or indicated by the utterance should be likely to be of interest. The answer must lie in the following region: transactions between a person and other persons or things closely connected with him are liable to be very different as regards their concomitants and results from the same sort of transactions involving only remotely connected persons or things; the concomitants and results, for instance, of my finding a hole in MY roof are likely to be very different from the concomitants and results of finding a hole in someone else's roof. Information, like money, is often given without the giver's knowing to just what use the recipient will want to put it. If someone to whom a transaction is mentioned gives it further consideration, he is likely to find himself wanting the answers to further questions that the speaker may not be able to identify in advance; if the appropriate specification will be likely to enable the hearer to answer a considerable variety of such questions for himself, then there is a presumption that the speaker should include it in his remark; if not, then there is no such presumption.

Finally, we can now show that, conversational implicature being what it is, it must possess certain features:

1   Since, to assume the presence of a conversational implicature, we have to assume that at least the Cooperative Principle is being observed, and since it is possible

to opt out of the observation of this principle, it follows that a generalized conversational implicature can be cancelled in a particular case. It may be explicitly cancelled, by the addition of a clause that states or implies that the speaker has opted out, or it may be contextually cancelled, if the form of utterance that usually carries it is used in a context that makes it clear that the speaker IS opting out.

2   Insofar as the calculation that a particular conversational implicature is present requires, besides contextual and background information, only a knowledge of what has been said (or of the conventional commitment of the utterance), and insofar as the manner of expression plays no role in the calculation, it will not be possible to find another way of saying the same thing, which simply lacks the implicature in question, except where some special feature of the substituted version is itself relevant to the determination of an implicature (in virtue of one of the maxims of Manner). If we call this feature NONDETACHABILITY, one may expect a generalized conversational implicature that is carried by a familiar, nonspecial locution to have a high degree of nondetachability.

3   To speak approximately, since the calculation of the presence of a conversational implicature presupposes an initial knowledge of the conventional force of the expression the utterance of which carries the implicature, a conversational implicatum will be a condition that is not included in the original specification of the expression's conventional force. Though it may not be impossible for what starts life, so to speak, as a conversational implicature to become conventionalized, to suppose that this is so in a given case would require special justification. So, initially at least, conversational implicata are not part of the meaning of the expressions to the employment of which they attach.

4   Since the truth of a conversational implicatum is not required by the truth of what is said (what is said may be true – what is implicated may be false), the implicature is not carried by what is said, but only by the saying of what is said, or by 'putting it that way.'

5   Since, to calculate a conversational implicature is to calculate what has to be supposed in order to preserve the supposition that the Cooperative Principle is being observed, and since there may be various possible specific explanations, a list of which may be open, the conversational implicatum in such cases will be disjunction of such specific explanations; and if the list of these is open, the implicatum will have just the kind of indeterminacy that many actual implicata do in fact seem to possess.

Chapter 4

M.M. Bakhtin

THE PROBLEM OF SPEECH GENRES

ALL THE DIVERSE AREAS of human activity involve the use of language. Quite understandably, the nature and forms of this use are just as diverse as are the areas of human activity. This, of course, in no way disaffirms the national unity of language. Language is realized in the form of individual concrete utterances (oral and written) by participants in the various areas of human activity. These utterances reflect the specific conditions and goals of each such area not only through their content (thematic) and linguistic style, that is, the selection of the lexical, phraseological, and grammatical resources of the language, but above all through their compositional structure. All three of these aspects – thematic content, style, and compositional structure – are inseparably linked to the *whole* of the utterance and are equally determined by the specific nature of the particular sphere of communication. Each separate utterance is individual, of course, but each sphere in which language is used develops its own *relatively stable types* of these utterances. These we may call *speech genres*.

The wealth and diversity of speech genres are boundless because the various possibilities of human activity are inexhaustible, and because each sphere of activity contains an entire repertoire of speech genres that differentiate and grow as the particular sphere develops and becomes more complex. Special emphasis should be placed on the extreme *heterogeneity* of speech genres (oral and written). In fact, the category of speech genres should include short rejoinders of daily dialogue (and these are extremely varied depending on the subject matter, situation, and participants), everyday narration, writing (in all its various forms), the brief standard military command, the elaborate and detailed order, the fairly variegated repertoire of business documents (for the most part standard), and the diverse world of commentary (in the broad sense of the word: social, political). And we must also

Source: M.M. Bakhtin, *Speech Genres and Other Late Essays*, translated by Vern W. McGee, edited by Caryl Emerson and Michael Holquist, Austin: University of Texas Press, 1986.

include here the diverse forms of scientific statements and all literary genres (from the proverb to the multivolume novel). It might seem that speech genres are so heterogeneous that they do not have and cannot have a single common level at which they can be studied. . . . One might think that such functional heterogeneity makes the common features of speech genres excessively abstract and empty. This probably explains why the general problem of speech genres has never really been raised. Literary genres have been studied more than anything else. But from antiquity to the present, they have been studied in terms of their specific literary and artistic features, in terms of the differences that distinguish one from the other (within the realm of literature), and not as specific types of utterances distinct from other types, but sharing with them a common *verbal* (language) nature. The general linguistic problem of the utterance and its types has hardly been considered at all. . . .

A clear idea of the nature of the utterance in general and of the peculiarities of the various types of utterances (primary and secondary), that is, of various speech genres, is necessary, we think, for research in any special area. To ignore the nature of the utterance or to fail to consider the peculiarities of generic subcategories of speech in any area of linguistic study leads to perfunctoriness and excessive abstractness, distorts the historicity of the research, and weakens the link between language and life. After all, language enters life through concrete utterances (which manifest language) and life enters language through concrete utterances as well. The utterance is an exceptionally important node of problems.

Any style is inseparably related to the utterance and to typical forms of utterances, that is, speech genres. Any utterance – oral or written, primary or secondary, and in any sphere of communication – is individual and therefore can reflect the individuality of the speaker (or writer); that is, it possesses individual style. But not all genres are equally conducive to reflecting the individuality of the speaker in the language of the utterance, that is, to an individual style. The most conducive genres are those of artistic literature: here the individual style enters directly into the very task of the utterance, and this is one of its main goals (but even within artistic literature various genres offer different possibilities for expressing individuality in language and various aspects of individuality). The least favorable conditions for reflecting individuality in language obtain in speech genres that require a standard form, for example, many kinds of business documents, military commands, verbal signals in industry, and so on. Here one can reflect only the most superficial, almost biological aspects of individuality (mainly in the oral manifestation of these standard types of utterances). In the vast majority of speech genres (except for literary-artistic ones), the individual style does not enter into the intent of the utterance, does not serve as its only goal, but is, as it were, an epiphenomenon of the utterance, one of its by-products. Various genres can reveal various layers and facets of the individual personality, and individual style can be found in various interrelations with the national language. The very problem of the national and the individual in language is basically the problem of the utterance (after all, only here, in the utterance, is the national language embodied in individual form). The very determination of style in general, and individual style in particular, requires deeper study of both the nature of the utterance and the diversity of speech genres.

. . .

It is especially harmful to separate style from genre when elaborating historical problems. Historical changes in language styles are inseparably linked to changes in speech genres. Literary language is a complex, dynamic system of linguistic styles. The proportions and interrelations of these styles in the system of literary language are constantly changing. Literary language, which also includes nonliterary styles, is an even more complex system, and it is organized on different bases. In order to puzzle out the complex historical dynamics of these systems and move from a simple (and, in the majority of cases, superficial) description of styles, which are always in evidence and alternating with one another, to a historical explanation of these changes, one must develop a special history of speech genres (and not only secondary, but also primary ones) that reflects more directly, clearly, and flexibly all the changes taking place in social life. Utterances and their types, that is, speech genres, are the drive belts from the history of society to the history of language. There is not a single new pheomenon (phonetic, lexical, or grammatical) that can enter the system of language without having traversed the long and complicated path of generic–stylistic testing and modification.

In each epoch, certain speech genres set the tone or the development of literary language. And these speech genres are not only secondary (literary, commentarial, and scientific), but also primary (certain types of oral dialogue – of the salon, of one's own circle, and other types as well, such as familiar, family – everyday, sociopolitical, philosophical, and so on). Any expansion of the literary language that results from drawing on various extraliterary strata of the national language inevitably entails some degree of penetration into all genres of written language (literary, scientific, commentarial, conversational, and so forth) to a greater or lesser degree, and entails new generic devices for the construction of the speech whole, its finalization, the accommodation of the listener or partner, and so forth. This leads to a more or less fundamental restructuring and renewal of speech genres.

. . .

Still current in linguistics are such *fictions* as the "listener" and "understander" (partners of the "speaker"), the "unified speech flow," and so on. These fictions produce a completely distorted idea of the complex and multifaceted process of active speech communication. Courses in general linguistics (even serious ones like Saussure's) frequently present graphic-schematic depictions of the two partners in speech communication – the speaker and the listener (who perceives the speech) – and provide diagrams of the active speech processes of the speaker and the corresponding passive processes of the listener's perception and understanding of the speech. One cannot say that these diagrams are false or that they do not correspond to certain aspects of reality. But when they are put forth as the actual whole of speech communication, they become a scientific fiction. The fact is that when the listener perceives and understands the meaning (the language meaning) of speech, he simultaneously takes an active, responsive attitude toward it. He either agrees or disagrees with it (completely or partially), augments it, applies it, prepares for its execution, and so on. And the listener adopts this responsive attitude for the entire duration of the process of listening and understanding, from the very beginning – sometimes literally from the speaker's first word. Any understanding of live speech, a live utterance, is inherently responsive, although the degree of this activity varies extremely. Any understanding is imbued with response and necessarily elicits it in one form or another: the listener becomes the speaker. . . .

Moreover, any speaker is himself a respondent to a greater or lesser degree. He is not, after all, the first speaker, the one who disturbs the eternal silence of the universe. And he presupposes not only the existence of the language system he is using, but also the existence of preceding utterances – his own and others' – with which his given utterance enters into one kind of relation or another (builds on them, polemicizes with them, or simply presumes that they are already known to the listener). Any utterance is a link in a very complexly organized chain of other utterances.

. . .

The boundaries of each concrete utterance as a unit of speech communication are determined by a *change of speaking subjects*, that is, a change of speakers. Any utterance – from a short (single-word) rejoinder in everyday dialogue to the large novel or scientific treatise – has, so to speak, an absolute beginning and an absolute end: its beginning is preceded by the utterances of others, and its end is followed by the responsive utterances of others (or, although it may be silent, others' active responsive understanding, or, finally, a responsive action based on this understanding). The speaker ends his utterance in order to relinquish the floor to the other or to make room for the other's active responsive understanding. The utterance is not a conventional unit, but a real unit, clearly delimited by the change of speaking subjects, which ends by relinquishing the floor to the other, as if with a silent *dixi*, perceived by the listeners (as a sign) that the speaker has finished.

This change of speaking subjects, which creates clear-cut boundaries of the utterance, varies in nature and acquires different forms in the heterogeneous spheres of human activity and life, depending on the functions of language and on the conditions and situations of communication. One observes this change of speaking subjects most simply and clearly in actual dialogue where the utterances of the interlocutors or partners in dialogue (which we shall call rejoinders) alternate. Because of its simplicity and clarity, dialogue is a classic form of speech communication. Each rejoinder, regardless of how brief and abrupt, has a specific quality of completion that expresses a particular position of the speaker, to which one may respond or may assume, with respect to it, a responsive position. But at the same time rejoinders are all linked to one another. And the sort of relations that exist among rejoinders of dialogue – relations between question and answer, assertion and objection, assertion and agreement, suggestion and acceptance, order and execution, and so forth – are impossible among units of language (words and sentences), either in the system of language (in the vertical cross section) or within the utterance (on the horizontal plane). These specific relations among rejoinders in a dialogue are only subcategories of specific relations among whole utterances in the process of speech communication. These relations are possible only among utterances of different speech subjects; they presuppose *other* (with respect to the speaker) participants in

speech communication. The relations among whole utterances cannot be treated grammatically since, we repeat, such relations are impossible among units of language,
and not only in the system of language, but within the utterance as well.

. . .

Complexly structured and specialized works of various scientific and artistic
genres, in spite of all the ways in which they differ from rejoinders in dialogue, are
by nature the same kind of units of speech communication. They, too, are clearly
demarcated by a change of speaking subjects, and these boundaries, while retaining
their *external* clarity, acquire here a special internal aspect because the speaking subject
– in this case, the *author* of the work – manifests his own individuality in his style,
his world-view, and in all aspects of the design of his work. This imprint of
individuality marking the work also creates special internal boundaries that distinguish
this work from other works connected with it in the overall processes of speech
communication in that particular cultural sphere: from the works of predecessors on
whom the author relies, from other works of the same school, from the works of
opposing schools with which the author is contending, and so on.

The work, like the rejoinder in dialogue, is oriented toward the response of the
other (others), toward his active responsive understanding, which can assume various
forms: educational influence on the readers, persuasion of them, critical responses,
influence on followers and successors, and so on. It can determine others' responsive
positions under the complex conditions of speech communication in a particular
cultural sphere. The work is a link in the chain of a speech communion. Like the
rejoinder in a dialogue, it is related to other work-utterances: both those to which
it responds and those that respond to it. At the same time, like the rejoinder in a
dialogue, it is separated from them by the absolute boundaries created by a change
of speaking subjects.

. . .

The speaker's speech will is manifested primarily in the *choice of a particular speech
genre*. This choice is determined by the specific nature of the given sphere
of speech communication, semantic (thematic) considerations, the concrete situation
of the speech communication, the personal composition of its participants, and so
on. And when the speaker's speech plan with all its individuality and subjectivity is
applied and adapted to a chosen genre, it is shaped and developed within a certain
generic form. Such genres exist above all in the great and multifarious sphere of
everyday oral communication, including the most familiar and the most intimate.

We speak only in definite speech genres, that is, all our utterances have definite
and relatively stable typical *forms of construction of the whole*. Our repertoire of
oral (and written) speech genres is rich. We use them confidently and skillfully *in
practice,* and it is quite possible for us not even to suspect their existence *in theory*.
Like Molière's Monsieur Jourdain who, when speaking in prose, had no idea that
was what he was doing; we speak in diverse genres without suspecting that they exist.
Even in the most free, the most unconstrained conversation, we cast our speech in
definite generic forms, sometimes rigid and trite ones, sometimes more flexible,

plastic, and creative ones (everyday communication also has creative genres at its disposal). We are given these speech genres in almost the same way that we are given our native language, which we master fluently long before we begin to study grammar. We know our native language – its lexical composition and grammatical structure – not from dictionaries and grammars but from concrete utterances that we hear and that we ourselves reproduce in live speech communication with people around us. We assimilate forms of language only in forms of utterances and in conjunction with these forms. The forms of language and the typical forms of utterances, that is, speech genres, enter our experience and our consciousness together, and in close connection with one another. To learn to speak means to learn to construct utterances (because we speak in utterances and not in individual sentences, and, of course, not in individual words). Speech genres organize our speech in almost the same way as grammatical (syntactical) forms do.

. . .

The generic forms in which we cast our speech, of course, differ essentially from language forms. The latter are stable and compulsory (normative) for the speaker, while generic forms are much more flexible, plastic, and free. Speech genres are very diverse in this respect. A large number of genres that are widespread in everyday life are so standard that the speaker's individual speech will is manifested only in its choice of a particular genre, and, perhaps, in its expressive intona-tion. Such, for example, are the various everyday genres of greetings, farewells, congratulations, all kinds of wishes, information about health, business, and so forth. These genres are so diverse because they differ depending on the situation, social position, and personal interrelations of the participants in the communication. These genres have high, strictly official, respectful forms as well as familiar ones. And there are forms with varying degrees of familiarity, as well as intimate forms (which differ from familiar ones). These genres also require a certain tone; their structure includes a certain expressive intonation. These genres, particularly the high and official ones, are compulsory and extremely stable. The speech will is usually limited here to a choice of a particular genre. And only slight nuances of expressive intonation (one can take a drier or more respectful tone, a colder or warmer one; one can introduce the intonation of joy, and so forth) can express the speaker's individuality (his emotional speech intent). But even here it is to re-accentuate genres. This is typical of speech communication: thus, for example, the generic form of greeting can move from the official sphere into the sphere of familiar communication, that is, it can be used with parodic-ironic re-accentuation. To a similar end, one can deliberately mix genres from various spheres.

In addition to these standard genres, of course, freer and more creative genres of oral speech communication have existed and still exist: genres of salon con-versations about everyday, social, aesthetic, and other subjects, genres of table conversation, intimate conversations among friends, intimate conversations within the family, and so on. (No list of oral speech genres yet exists, or even a principle on which such a list might be based.) The majority of these genres are subject to free creative reformulation (like artistic genres, and some, perhaps, to a greater degree).

But to use a genre freely and creatively is not the same as to create a genre from the beginning; genres must be fully mastered in order to be manipulated freely.

. . .

Any utterance is a link in the chain of speech communion. It is the active position of the speaker in one referentially semantic sphere or another. Therefore, each utterance is characterized primarily by a particular referentially semantic content. The choice of linguistic means and speech genre is determined primarily by the referentially semantic assignments (plan) of the speech subject (or author). This is the first aspect of the utterance that determines its compositional and stylistic features.

The second aspect of the utterance that determines its composition and style is the *expressive* aspect, that is, the speaker's subjective emotional evaluation of the referentially semantic content of his utterance. The expressive aspect has varying significance and varying degrees of force in various spheres of speech communication, but it exists everywhere. There can be no such thing as an absolutely neutral utterance. The speaker's evaluative attitude toward the subject of his speech (regardless of what his subject may be) also determines the choice of lexical, grammatical, and compositional means of the utterance. The individual style of the utterance is determined primarily by its expressive aspect. This is generally recognized in the area of stylistics. Certain investigators even reduce style directly to the emotionally evaluative aspect of speech.

. . .

When selecting words, we proceed from the planned whole of our utterance, and this whole that we have planned and created is always expressive. The utterance is what radiates its expression (rather, our expression) to the word we have selected, which is to say, invests the word with the expression of the whole. And we select the word because of its meaning, which is not in itself expressive but which can accommodate or not accommodate our expressive goals in combination with other words, that is, in combination with the whole of our utterance. The neutral meaning of the word applied to a particular actual reality under particular real conditions of speech communication creates a spark of expression. And, after all, this is precisely what takes place in the process of creating an utterance. . . .

A speech genre is not a form of language, but a typical form of utterance; as such the genre also includes a certain typical kind of expression that inheres in it. In the genre, the word acquires a particular typical expression. Genres correspond to typical situations of speech communication, typical themes, and, consequently, also to particular contacts between the *meanings* of words and actual concrete reality under certain typical circumstances. Hence also the possibility of typical expressions that seem to adhere to words. This typical expression (and the typical intonation that corresponds to it) does not have that force of compulsoriness that language forms have. . . . Speech genres in general submit fairly easily to re-accentuation, the sad can be made jocular and gay, but as a result something new is achieved (for example, the genre of comical epitaphs).

. . .

The words of a language belong to nobody, but still we hear those words only in particular individual utterances, we read them in particular individual works, and in such cases the words already have not only a typical, but also (depending on the genre) a more or less clearly reflected individual expression, which is determined by the unrepeatable individual context of the utterance.

Neutral dictionary meanings of the words of a language ensure their common features and guarantee that all speakers of a given language will understand one another, but the use of words in live speech communication is always individual and contextual in nature. Therefore, one can say that any word exists for the speaker in three aspects: as a neutral word of a language, belonging to nobody; as an *others'* word, which belongs to another person and is filled with echoes of the other's utterance; and, finally, as *my* word, for, since I am dealing with it in a particular situation, with a particular speech plan, it is already imbued with my expression. In both of the latter aspects, the word is expressive, but, we repeat, this expression does not inhere in the word itself. It originates at the point of contact between the word and actual reality, under the conditions of that real situation articulated by the individual utterance. In this case the word appears as an expression of some evaluative position of an individual person (authority, writer, scientist, father, mother, friend, teacher, and so forth), as an abbreviation of the utterance.

In each epoch, in each social circle, in each small world of family, friends, acquaintances, and comrades in which a human being grows and lives, there are always authoritative utterances that set the tone – artistic, scientific, and journalistic works on which one relies, to which one refers, which are cited, imitated, and followed. In each epoch, in all areas of life and activity, there are particular traditions that are expressed and retained in verbal vestments: in written works, in utterances, in sayings, and so forth. There are always some verbally expressed leading ideas of the "masters of thought" of a given epoch, some basic tasks, slogans, and so forth.

. . .

This is why the unique speech experience of each individual is shaped and developed in continuous and constant interaction with others' individual utterances. This experience can be characterized to some degree as the process of *assimilation* – more or less creative – of others' words (and not the words of a language). Our speech, that is, all our utterances (including creative works), is filled with others' words, varying degrees of otherness or varying degrees of "our-own-ness," varying degrees of awareness and detachment. These words of others carry with them their own expression, their own evaluative tone, which we assimilate, rework, and re-accentuate.

. . .

Utterances are not indifferent to one another, and are not self-sufficient; they are aware of and mutually reflect one another. These mutual reflections determine their character. Each utterance is filled with echoes and reverberations of other utterances to which it is related by the communality of the sphere of speech communication. Every utterance must be regarded primarily as a *response* to preceding utterances of the given sphere (we understand the word "response" here in the broadest sense). Each utterance refutes, affirms, supplements, and relies on the others, presupposes them to be known, and somehow takes them into account. After all, as regards a given question, in a given matter, and so forth, the utterance occupies a particular *definite* position in a given sphere of communication. It is impossible to determine its position without correlating it with other positions. Therefore, each utterance is filled with various kinds of responsive reactions to other utterances of the given sphere of speech communication. These reactions take various forms: others' utterances can be introduced directly into the utterance, or one may introduce words or sentences, which then act as representatives of the whole utterance. Both whole utterances and individual words can retain their alien expression, but they can also be re-accentuated (ironically, indignantly, reverently, and so forth). Others' utterances can be repeated with varying degrees of reinterpretation. They can be referred to as though the interlocutor were already well aware of them; they can be silently presupposed; or one's responsive reaction to them can be reflected only in the expression of one's own speech – in the selection of language means and intonations that are determined not by the topic of one's own speech but by the others' utterances concerning the same topic. . . . The utterance is filled with *dialogic overtones*, and they must be taken into account in order to understand fully the style of the utterance. After all, our thought itself – philosophical, scientific, and artistic – is born and shaped in the process of interaction and struggle with others' thought, and this cannot but be reflected in the forms that verbally express our thought as well.

· · ·

Any utterance, when it is studied in greater depth under the concrete conditions of speech communication, reveals to us many half-concealed or completely concealed words of others with varying degrees of foreignness. Therefore, the utterance appears to be furrowed with distant and barely audible echoes of changes of speech subjects and dialogic overtones, greatly weakened utterance boundaries that are completely permeable to the author's expression. The utterance proves to be a very complex and multiplanar phenomenon if considered not in isolation and with respect to its author (the speaker) only, but as a link in the chain of speech communication and with respect to other, related utterances (these relations are usually disclosed not on the verbal – compositional and stylistic – plane, but only on the referentially semantic plane).

· · ·

The topic of the speaker's speech, regardless of what this topic may be, does not become the object of speech for the first time in any given utterance; a given speaker is not the first to speak about it. The object, as it were, has already been articulated, disputed, elucidated, and evaluated in various ways. Various viewpoints, world-views, and trends cross, converge, and diverge in it. The speaker is not the biblical Adam, dealing only with virgin and still unnamed objects, giving them names for the first time. . . . The utterance is addressed not only to its own object, but also to others' speech about it. But still, even the slightest allusion to another's utterance gives the speech a dialogical turn that cannot be produced by any purely referential theme with its own object. The attitude toward another's word is in principle distinct from the attitude toward a referential object, but the former always accompanies the latter. We repeat, an utterance is a link in the chain of speech communication, and it cannot be broken off from the preceding links that determine it both from within and from without, giving rise within it to unmediated responsive reactions and dialogic reverberations. . . .

We have already said that the role of these others, for whom my thought becomes actual thought for the first time (and thus also for my own self as well) is not that of passive listeners, but of active participants in speech communication. From the very beginning, the speaker expects a response from them, an active responsive understanding. The entire utterance is constructed, as it were, in anticipation of encountering this response.

An essential (constitutive) marker of the utterance is its quality of being directed to someone, its *addressivity*. As distinct from the signifying units of a language – words and sentences – that are impersonal, belonging to nobody and addressed to nobody, the utterance has both an author (and, consequently, expression, which we have already discussed) and an addressee. This addressee can be an immediate participant-interlocutor in an everyday dialogue, a differentiated collective of specialists in some particular area of cultural communication, a more or less differentiated public, ethnic group, contemporaries, like-minded people, opponents and enemies, a subordinate, a superior, someone who is lower, higher, familiar, foreign, and so forth. And it can also be an indefinite, unconcretized *other* (with various kinds of monological utterances of an emotional type). All these varieties and conceptions of the addressee are determined by that area of human activity and everyday life to which the given utterance is related. Both the composition and, particularly, the style of the utterance depend on those to whom the utterance is addressed, how the speaker (or writer) senses and imagines his addressees, and the force of their effect on the utterance. Each speech genre in each area of speech communication has its own typical conception of the addressee, and this defines it as a genre.

. . .

Chapter 5

Norman Fairclough

TEXT RELATIONSHIPS

Texts and social agents

S OCIAL AGENTS ARE NOT 'FREE' AGENTS, they are socially constrained but their actions are not totally socially determined. Agents have their own 'causal powers' that are not reducible to the causal powers of social structures and practices (on this view of the relationship between structure and agency, see Archer 1995, 2000). Social agents texture texts, they set up relations between elements of texts. There are structural constraints on this process – for instance, the grammar of a language makes some combinations and orderings of grammatical forms possible but others (e.g., 'but book the' is not an English sentence); and if the social event is an interview, there are genre conventions for how the talk should be organized. But this still leaves social agents with a great deal of freedom in texturing texts.

Take the following extract as an example, where a manager is talking about the 'culture' of people in his native city of Liverpool:

> 'They are totally suspicious of any change. They are totally suspicious of anybody trying to help them. They immediately look for the rip-off. They have also been educated to believe that it is actually clever to get "one over on them". So they are all at it. And the demarcation lines that the unions have been allowed to impose in those areas, because of this, makes it totally inflexible to the point where it is destructive. I know it. I can see it.'
>
> 'And how does this relate to what is happening here?'
>
> 'Well, I was going to say, how do you change this sort of negative culture?'

Notice in particular the semantic relation which is set up between 'negative culture' and being 'totally suspicious' of change, 'looking for the rip-off', trying to 'get one over on them', 'demarcation lines', 'inflexible' and 'destructive'. We can see this as the texturing of a semantic relation of 'meronymy', i.e., a relation between the whole ('negative culture') and its parts. No dictionary would identify such a semantic relation between these expressions – the relation is textured by the manager. We can attribute this meaning-making to the manager as a social agent. And notice what the making of meaning involves here: putting existing expressions into a new relation of equivalence as co-instances of 'negative culture'. The meaning does not have a pre-existing presence in these words and expressions, it is an effect of the relations that are set up between them (Merleau-Ponty 1964).

Social events, social practices, social structures

Social structures are very abstract entities. One can think of a social structure (such as an economic structure, a social class or kinship system, or a language) as defining a potential, a set of possibilities. However, the relationship between what is structurally possible and what actually happens, between structures and events, is a very complex one. Events are not in any simple or direct way the effects of abstract social structures. Their relationship is mediated – there are intermediate organizational entities between structures and events. Let us call these 'social practices'. Examples would be practices of teaching and practices of management in educational institutions. Social practices can be thought of as ways of controlling the selection of certain structural possibilities and the exclusion of others, and the retention of these selections over time, in particular areas of social life. Social practices are networked together in particular and shifting ways – for instance, there has recently been a shift in the way in which practices of teaching and research are networked together with practices of management in institutions of higher education, a 'managerialization' (or more generally 'marketization', Fairclough 1993) of higher education.

Language (and more broadly 'semiosis', including for instance signification and communication through visual images) is an element of the social at all levels. Schematically:

Social structures: languages
Social practices: orders of discourse
Social events: texts

Languages can be regarded as among the abstract social structures to which I have just been referring. A language defines a certain potential, certain possibilities, and excludes others – certain ways of combining linguistic elements are possible, others are not (e.g., 'the book' is possible in English, 'book the' is not). But texts as elements of social events are not simply the effects of the potentials defined by languages. We need to recognize intermediate organizational entities of a specifically linguistic sort, the linguistic elements of networks of social practices. I shall call these *orders of discourse* (see Chouliaraki and Fairclough 1999; Fairclough 1992). An order of discourse is a network of social practices in its language aspect. The elements of orders of discourse are not things like nouns and sentences (elements of linguistic structures), but discourses, genres and styles (I shall differentiate them shortly). These elements select certain possibilities defined by languages and exclude others – they control linguistic variability for particular areas of social life. So orders of discourse can be seen as the social organization and control of linguistic variation.

There is a further point to make: as we move from abstract structures towards concrete events, it becomes increasingly difficult to separate language from other social elements. In the terminology of Althusser, language becomes increasingly 'overdetermined' by other social elements (Althusser and Balibar 1970). So at the level of abstract structures, we can talk more or less exclusively about language – more or less, because 'functional' theories of language see even the grammars of languages as socially shaped (Halliday 1978). The way I have defined orders of discourse makes it clear that at this intermediate level we are dealing with a much greater 'overdetermination' of language by other social elements – orders of discourse are the *social* organization and control of linguistic variation, and their elements (discourses, genres, styles) are correspondingly not purely linguistic categories but categories that cut across the division between language and 'non-language', the discoursal and the non-discoursal. When we come to texts as elements of social events, the 'overdetermination' of language by other social elements becomes massive: texts are not just effects of linguistic structures and orders of discourse, they are also effects of other social structures, and of social practices in all their aspects, so that it becomes difficult to separate out the factors shaping texts.

Social practices

Social practices can be seen as articulations of different types of social element that are associated with particular areas of social life – the social practice of classroom teaching in contemporary British education, for example. The important point about social practices from the perspective of this book is that they articulate discourse (hence language) together with other non-discoursal social elements. We might see any social practice as an articulation of these elements:

Action and interaction
Social relations
Persons (with beliefs, attitudes, histories, etc.)
The material world
Discourse

So, for instance, classroom teaching articulates together particular ways of using language (on the part of both teachers and learners) with the social relations of the classroom, the structuring and use of the classroom as a physical space, and so forth. The relationship between these different elements of social practices is dialectical, as Harvey argues (Fairclough 2001; Harvey 1996): this is a way of putting the apparently paradoxical fact that although the discourse element of a social practice is not the same as for example its social relations, each in a sense contains or internalizes the other – social relations *are* partly discoursal in nature, discourse *is* partly social relations. Social events are causally shaped by (networks of) social practices – social practices define particular ways of acting, and although actual events may more or less diverge from these definitions and expectations (because they cut across different social practices, and because of the causal powers of social agents), they are still partly shaped by them.

Discourse as an element of social practices: genres, discourses and styles

We can say that discourse figures in three main ways in social practice. It figures as:

Genres (ways of acting)
Discourses (ways of representing)
Styles (ways of being)

One way of acting and interacting is through speaking or writing, so discourse figures first as 'part of the action'. We can distinguish different genres as different ways of (inter)acting discoursally – interviewing is a genre, for example. Second, discourse figures in the representations that are always a part of social practices – representations of the material world, of other social practices, reflexive self-representations of the practice in question. Representation is clearly a discoursal matter, and we can distinguish different discourses, which may represent the same area of the world from different perspectives or positions. Notice that 'discourse' is being used here in two senses: abstractly, as an abstract noun, meaning language and other types of semiosis as elements of social life; more concretely, as a count noun, meaning particular ways of representing part of the world. An example of a discourse in the latter sense would be the political discourse of New Labour, as opposed to the political discourse of 'old' Labour, or the political discourse of 'Thatcherism' (Fairclough 2000). Third and finally, discourse figures alongside bodily behaviour in constituting particular ways of being, particular social or personal identities. I shall call the discoursal aspect of this a style. An example would be the style of a particular type of manager – his or her way of using language as a resource for self-identifying.

The concepts of 'discourse' and 'genre' in particular are used in a variety of disciplines and theories. The popularity of 'discourse' in social research owes a lot in particular to Foucault (1972). 'Genre' is used in cultural studies, media studies, film theory and so forth (see for instance Fiske 1987; Silverstone 1999). These concepts cut across disciplines and theories, and can operate as 'bridges' between them – as focuses for a dialogue between them through which perspectives in the one can be drawn upon in the development of the other.

Text as action, representation, identification

'Functional' approaches to language have emphasized the 'multi-functionality' of texts. Systemic Functional Linguistics, for instance, claims that texts simultaneously have 'ideational', 'interpersonal' and 'textual' functions. That is, texts simultaneously represent aspects of the world (the physical world, the social world, the mental world); enact social relations between participants in social events and the attitudes, desires and values of participants; and coherently and cohesively connect parts of texts together, and connect texts with their situational contexts (Halliday 1978, 1994). Or rather, people do these things in the process of meaning-making in social events, which includes texturing, making texts.

I shall also view texts as multi-functional in this sort of sense, though in a rather different way, in accordance with the distinction between genres, discourses and styles as the three main ways in which discourse figures as a part of social practice – ways of acting, ways of representing, ways of being. Or to put it differently: the relationship of the text to the event, to the wider physical and social world, and to the persons involved in the event. However, I prefer to talk about three major *types of meaning*, rather than functions:

Action
Representation
Identification

Representation corresponds to Halliday's 'ideational' function; Action is closest to his 'interpersonal' function, although it puts more emphasis on text as a way of (inter)acting in social events, and it can be seen as incorporating Relation (enacting social relations); Halliday does not differentiate a separate function to do with identification – most of what I include in Identification is in his 'interpersonal' function. I do not distinguish a separate 'textual' function, rather I incorporate it within Action.

We can see Action, Representation and Identification simultaneously through whole texts and in small parts of texts. Take for example the following sentence: 'The culture in successful businesses is different from in failing businesses.' What is represented here (Representation) is a relation between two entities – 'x is different from y'. The sentence is also (Action) an action, which implies a social relation: the manager is giving the interviewer information, telling him something, and that implies in broad terms a social relation between someone who knows and someone who doesn't – the social relations of this sort of interview are a specific variant of this, the relations between someone who has knowledge and opinions and someone who is eliciting them. Informing, advising, promising, warning and so forth are ways of acting. The sentence is also (Identification) an undertaking, a commitment, a judgement: in saying 'is different' rather than 'is perhaps different' or 'may be different', the manager is strongly committing himself. Focusing analysis of texts on the interplay of Action, Representation and Identification brings a social perspective into the heart and fine detail of the text.

There is, as I have indicated, a correspondence between Action and genres, Representation and discourses, Identification and styles. Genres, discourses and styles are respectively relatively stable and durable ways of acting, representing and identifying. They are identified as elements of orders of discourse at the level of social practices. When we analyse specific texts as part of specific events, we are doing two interconnected things: (a) looking at them in terms of the three aspects of meaning – Action, Representation and Identification – and how these are realized in the various features of texts (their vocabulary, their grammar, and so forth); (b) making a connection between the concrete social event and more abstract social practices by asking which genres, discourses, and styles are drawn upon here, and how are the different genres, discourses and styles articulated together in the text?

Dialectical relations

I have so far written as if the three aspects of meaning (and genres, discourses and styles) were quite separate from one another, but the relation between them is a rather more subtle and complex one – a dialectical relation. Foucault (1994: 318) makes distinctions that are very similar to the three aspects of meaning, and he also suggests the dialectical character of the relationship between them (although he does not use the category of *dialectics*):

> These practical systems stem from three broad areas: relations of control over things, relations of action upon others, relations with oneself. This does not mean that each of these three areas is completely foreign to the others. It is well known that control over things is mediated by relations with others; and relations with others in turn always entails relations with oneself, and vice versa. But we have three axes whose specificity and whose interconnections have to be analyzed: the axis of knowledge, the axis of power, the axis of ethics . . . How are we constituted as subjects of our own knowledge? How are we constituted as subjects who exercise or submit to power relations? How are we constituted as moral subjects of our own actions?

There are several points here. First, Foucault's various formulations point to complexity within each of the three aspects of meaning (which correspond to Foucault's three 'axes'): Representation is to do with knowledge but also thereby 'control over things'; Action is to do generally with relations with others, but also 'action on others', and power; Identification is to do with relations with oneself, ethics and the 'moral subject'. What these various formulations point to is the possibility of enriching our understanding of texts by connecting each of the three aspects of meaning with a variety of categories in social theories. Another example might be to see Identification as bringing what Bourdieu (Bourdieu and Wacquant 1992) calls the 'habitus' of the persons involved in the event into consideration in text analysis, i.e., their embodied dispositions to see and act in certain ways based upon socialization and experience, which is partly dispositions to talk and write in certain ways.

Second, although the three aspects of meaning need to be distinguished for analytical purposes and are in that sense different from one another, they are not *discrete,* not totally separate. I shall say, rather differently from Foucault, that they are dialectically related, i.e., there is a sense in which each 'internalizes' the others (Harvey 1996). This is suggested in the three questions at the end of the quotation: all three can be seen in terms of a relation involving the persons in the event ('subjects') – their relation to knowledge, their relation with others (power relations) and their relation with themselves (as 'moral subjects'). Or we can say for instance that particular Representations (discourses) may be enacted in particular ways of

Acting and Relating (genres), and inculcated in particular ways of Identifying (styles). Schematically, dialectics of discourse are as follows:

Discourses (representational meanings) enacted in genres (actional meanings)
Discourses (representational meanings) inculcated in styles (identificational meanings)
Actions and identities (including genres and styles) represented in discourses (representational meanings).

Mediation

The relationship between texts and social events is often more complex than I have indicated so far. Many texts are 'mediated' by the 'mass media', i.e., institutions that 'make use of copying technologies to disseminate communication' (Luhmann 2000). They involve media such as print, telephone, radio, television, the internet. In some cases – most obviously the telephone – people are co-present in time but distant in space, and the interaction is one-to-one. These are closest to ordinary conversation. Others are very different from ordinary conversation – for instance, a printed book is written by one or a small number of authors but read by indefinitely many people who may be widely dispersed in time and space. In this case, the text connects different social events – the writing of a book on the one hand, and the many and various social events that include reading (glancing at, referring to, etc.) the book – a train journey, a class in a school, a visit to a bookshop, and so forth.

Mediation, according to Silverstone (1999), involves the 'movement of meaning' – from one social practice to another, from one event to another, from one text to another. As this implies, mediation does not just involve individual texts or types of text, it is in many cases a complex process that involves what I shall call 'chains' or 'networks' of texts. Think, for example, of a story in a newspaper. Journalists write newspaper articles on the basis of a variety of sources – written documents, speeches, interviews and so forth – and the articles are read by those who buy the newspaper and may be responded to in a variety of other texts – conversations about the news, perhaps, if the story is a particularly significant one, further stories in other newspapers or on television and so on. The 'chain' or 'network' of texts in this case thus includes quite a number of different types of text. There are fairly regular and systematic relationships between some of them – for instance, journalists produce articles on the basis of sources in fairly regular and predictable ways, transforming the source materials according to quite well-established conventions (e.g., for turning an interview into a report).

Complex modern societies involve the networking together of different social practices across different domains or fields of social life (e.g. the economy, education, family life) and across different scales of social life (global, regional, national, local). Texts are a crucial part of these networking relations – the orders of discourse associated with networks of social practices specify particular chaining and networking relationships between types of text. The transformations of new capitalism can be seen as transformations in the networking of social practices, which include transformations in orders of discourse, and transformations in the chaining and networking of texts, and in 'genre chains' (see below). For instance, the process of 'globalization' includes the enhanced capacity for some people to act upon and shape the actions of others over considerable distances of space and time (Giddens 1991; Harvey 1990). This partly depends upon more complex processes of textual mediation of social events, and more complex chaining and networking relations between different types of text (facilitated through new communication technologies, notably the internet). And the capacity to influence or control processes of mediation is an important aspect of power in contemporary societies.

'Genre chains' are of particular significance: these are different genres that are regularly linked together, involving systematic transformations from genre to genre. Genre chains contribute to the possibility of actions that transcend differences in space and time, linking together social events in different social practices, different countries and different times, facilitating the enhanced capacity for 'action at a distance', which has been taken to be a defining feature of contemporary 'globalization', and therefore facilitating the exercise of power.

Genres and governance

Genres are important in sustaining the institutional structure of contemporary society – structural relations between (local) government, business, universities, the media, etc. We can think of such institutions as interlocking elements in the governance of society (Bjerke 2000), and of such genres as genres of governance. I am using 'governance' here in a very broad sense for any activity within an institution or organization directed at regulating or managing some other (network of) social practice(s). The increasing popularity of the term 'governance' is associated with a search for ways of managing social life (often referred to as 'networks', 'partnerships', etc.) that avoid both the chaotic effects of markets and the top-down hierarchies of states. Although, as Jessop points out, contemporary governance can be seen as combining all of these forms – markets, hierarchies, networks (Jessop 1998). We can contrast genres of governance with 'practical genres' – roughly, genres that figure in doing things rather than governing the way things are done.

The genres of governance are characterized by specific properties of recontextualization – the appropriation of elements of one social practice within another, placing the former within the context of the latter, and transforming it in particular ways in the process (Bernstein 1990; Chouliaraki and Fairclough 1999). 'Recontextualization' is a concept developed in the sociology of education (Bernstein 1990), which can be fruitfully operationalized, put to work, within discourse and text analysis.

Much action and interaction in modern societies is 'mediated', as I pointed out above. Mediated (inter)action is 'action at a distance', action involving participants who are distant from one another in space and/or time, which depends upon some communication technology (print, television, the internet etc.). The genres of governance are essentially mediated genres specialized for 'action at a distance'. What are usually referred to as 'the mass media' are, one might argue, a part of the apparatus of governance – a media genre such as television news recontextualizes and transforms other social practices, such as politics and government, and is in turn recontextualized in the texts and interactions of different practices, including, crucially, everyday life, where it contributes to the shaping of how we live, and the meanings we give to our lives (Silverstone 1999).

Genre mixing

The relationship between texts and genres is a potentially complex one: a text may not be 'in' a single genre, it may 'mix' or hybridize genres.

A genre within a chain characteristically enters both 'retrospective' and 'prospective' relations with the genres 'preceding' and 'following' it in the chain, which may progressively lead to hybridization of the genre through a sort of assimilation to these preceding and following genres. For example the incorporation of corporate advertising into a local authority genre can be seen as a form of prospective interdiscursivity – the local authority anticipating the practices of business within which it hopes its publicity will be taken up. Another widespread example is the 'conversationalization' of various genres such as radio talks or broadcast news – they take on certain features of the conversational language within the (anticipated) contexts in which they are listened to or watched (typically in the home).

A number of social researchers and theorists have drawn attention to ways in which social boundaries are blurred in contemporary social life, and to the forms of 'hybridity' or mixing of social practices that results. This is widely seen for instance as a feature of 'postmodernity', which writers such as Jameson (1991) and Harvey (1990) view as the cultural facet of what I am calling new capitalism. One area of social life where hybridity has received particularly intense attention is media – the texts of mass media can be seen as instantiating the blurring of boundaries of various sorts: fact and fiction, news and entertainment, drama and documentary, and so forth (McLuhan 1964; Silverstone 1999). The analysis of interdiscursive hybridity in texts provides a potentially valuable resource for enhancing research based upon these perspectives, offering a level of detailed analysis that is not achievable within other methods.

Relational approach to text analysis

I shall adopt a relational view of texts and a relational approach to text analysis. We are concerned with several 'levels' of analysis, and relations between these 'levels':

Social structures
Social practices
Social events
Actions and their social relations
Identification of persons
Representations of the world
Discourse (genres, discourses, styles)
Semantics
Grammar and vocabulary
Phonology/graphology

We can distinguish the 'external' relations of texts and the 'internal' relations of texts. Analysis of the 'external' relations of texts is analysis of their relations with other elements of social events and, more abstractly, social practices and social structures. Analysis of relations of texts to other elements of social events includes analysis of how they figure in Actions, Identifications, and Representations (the basis for differentiating the three major aspects of text meaning). There is another dimension to 'external' relations: relations between a text and other ('external') texts, how elements of other texts are 'intertextually' incorporated and, since these may be 'other people's' texts, how the voices of others are incorporated; how other texts are alluded to, assumed, dialogued with and so forth (see below).

Analysis of the 'internal relations' of texts includes analysis of:

Semantic relations: Meaning relations between words and longer expressions, between elements of clauses, between clauses and between sentences, and over larger stretches of text.

Grammatical relations: The relationship between 'morphemes' in words (e.g., 'sick' and 'ness' in 'sickness'), between words in phrases (e.g., between definite article ('the'), adjective ('old') and noun ('house') in 'the old house'), between phrases within clauses, and between clauses in sentences (e.g., clauses may be *paratactically* or *hypotactically* related – i.e., have equal grammatical status, or be in a superordinate/subordinate relationship).

Vocabulary (or 'lexical') relations: Relations of collocation, i.e., patterns of co-occurrence between items of vocabulary (words or expressions). For example, 'work' collocates with 'into' and 'back to' more than with 'out of' in the texts of Blair's New Labour Party in the UK, whereas in earlier Labour texts the pattern was reversed (Fairclough 2000).

Phonological relations: Relations in spoken language, including prosodic patterns of intonation and rhythm; graphological relations in written language – e.g., relations between different fonts or type sizes in a written text. I do not deal with phonological or graphological relations in this chapter.

Internal relations are both, in a classical terminology, 'relations in *praesentia*' and relations 'in *absentia*' – syntagmatic relations, and paradigmatic relations. The examples I have just given are examples of syntagmatic relations, relations between elements that are actually present in a text. Paradigmatic relations are relations of choice, and they draw attention to relations between what is actually present and what might have been present but is not – 'significant absences'. This applies on different levels – the text includes certain grammatical structures and a certain vocabulary and certain semantic relations and certain discourses or genres; it might have included others, which were available and possible but not selected.

The level of discourse is the level at which relations between genres, discourses and styles are analysed – 'interdiscursive' relations as I call them. The level of discourse is an intermediate level, a mediating level between the text *per se* and its social context (social events, social practices, social structures). Discourses, genres and styles are both elements of texts and social elements. In texts they are organized together in interdiscursive relations, relations in which different genres, discourses and styles may be 'mixed', articulated and textured together in particular ways. As social elements, they are articulated together in particular ways in orders of discourse – the language aspects of social practices in which language variation is socially controlled. They make the link between the text and other elements of the social, between the internal relations of the text and its external relations.

The relations between the discourse, semantic, and grammatical and vocabulary levels are relations of 'realization' (Halliday 1994). That is, interdiscursive relations between genres, discourses and styles are realized, or instantiated, as semantic relations, which are realized as ('formal') grammatical and vocabulary relations.

Intertextuality and assumptions

Both intertextuality and assumption can be seen in terms of claims on the part of the 'author' – the claim that what is reported was actually said, that what is assumed has indeed been said or written elsewhere, that one's interlocutors have indeed heard it or read it elsewhere. Such claims may or may not be substantiated. People may mistakenly, dishonestly or manipulatively make such implicit claims – assertions may for instance be manipulatively passed off as assumptions, statements may mistakenly or dishonestly be attributed to others.

Difference and dialogicality

An important contrast between intertextuality and assumption is that the former broadly opens up difference by bringing other 'voices' into a text, whereas the latter broadly reduces difference by assuming common ground. Or to put it differently, the former accentuates the dialogicality of a text, the dialogue between the voice of the author of a text and other voices, the latter diminishes it. The term 'voice' is in part similar to the way I use the term 'style' (meaning ways of being or identities in their linguistic and more broadly semiotic aspects), but it is useful in also allowing us to focus on the co-presence in texts of the 'voices' of particular individuals (Bakhtin 1981; Ivanic 1998; Wertsch 1991). People differ in all sorts of ways, and orientation to difference is fundamental to social interaction. Giddens suggested that 'the production of interaction has three fundamental elements: its constitution as "meaningful"; its constitution as a moral order; and its constitution as the operation of relations of power' (1993: 104). Orientation to difference is central to the account of these three elements that he went on to give. The production of interaction as meaningful entails active and continual 'negotiation' of differences of meaning; the 'norms' of interaction as a moral order are oriented to and interpreted differently by different social actors, and these differences are negotiated. Power in its most general sense of 'the transformative capacity of human action', the capacity to 'intervene in a series of events so as to alter their course', depends upon 'resources or facilities' that are differentially available to social actors; and power in the 'relational' sense of 'the capability to secure outcomes where the realization of these outcomes depends upon the agency of others' is also differentially available to different social actors.

But social events and interaction vary in the nature of their orientation to difference, as do texts as elements of social events. We can schematically differentiate five scenarios at a very general level:

(a)   an openness to, acceptance of, recognition of difference; an exploration of difference, as in 'dialogue' in the richest sense of the term;

(b)   an accentuation of difference, conflict, polemic, a struggle over meaning, norms, power;

(c)   an attempt to resolve or overcome difference;

(d)   a bracketing of difference, a focus on commonality, solidarity;

(e)   consensus, a normalization and acceptance of differences of power that brackets or suppresses differences of meaning and norms.

This is not a typology of actual social events and interactions; social events, and texts, may combine these scenarios in various ways.

Kress suggested a number of years ago that it is productive to see texts in terms of orientation to difference: 'difference is the motor that produces texts' (Kress 1985). However, Kress's view of difference is rather limited, focusing in particular on scenario (c) above, the resolution of differences. As Kress points out, difference is most immediately accessible in actual dialogue, text that is co-produced by two or more people, and the five scenarios above provide a basis of comparison between dialogues in terms of how difference is oriented to. But difference is no less central in 'monological' texts, including written texts – most obviously because all texts are addressed, have particular addressees and readers in view, and assume and anticipate differences between 'author' and addressees. On one level, orientation to difference can be understood as a matter of the dynamics of the interaction itself. But differences are not only or even mainly occasioned, local effects of specific encounters. This is clear from Kress's focus upon differences between people as differences between discourses. Discourses are durable entities that take us to the more abstract level of social practices, and we must clearly include the question of how longer-term orientations to difference at this level are instantiated in particular social events – and interactionally worked upon, for, as I have already stressed, events (and hence texts) are shaped by the agency of participants as well as social structures and social practices.

Orientation to difference brings into focus degrees and forms of dialogicality in texts. What I am referring to here is an aspect of Bakhktin's 'dialogical' theory of language: 'a word, discourse, language or culture undergoes "dialogization" when it becomes relativized, deprivileged, aware of competing definitions for the same things. Undialogized language is authoritative or absolute' (Holquist 1981: 427). Texts are inevitably and unavoidably dialogical in the sense that 'any utterance is a link in a very complexly organized chain of other utterances' with which it 'enters into one kind of relation or another' (Bakhtin 1986: 69). But as the Holquist quotation suggests, texts differ in their orientation to difference, i.e., in respect of 'dialogization'. Bakhtin points to such differences in noting that the relation of an utterance to others may be a matter of 'building on' them, 'polemicizing with' them, or simply 'presuming that they are already known to the listener' (1986: 69). And as Holquist suggests, one option is 'undialogized language', corresponding to scenario (e) above: excluding dialogicality and difference.

The public sphere

One might consider this way of dealing with difference in terms of the 'public sphere' (Arendt 1958; Calhoun 1992; Fairclough 1999; Habermas 1989). The public sphere is in Habermas's terms (1984) a zone of connection between social systems and the 'lifeworld', the domain of everyday living, in which people can deliberate on matters of social and political concern as citizens and, in principle, influence policy decisions. The contemporary status of the public sphere has attracted a great deal of debate, much of it about the 'crisis' of the public sphere, its problematic character in contemporary societies in which it tends to get 'squeezed out', especially by the mass media. One limitation of 'debates' from this perspective is that they don't go beyond confrontation and polemic. One might see effective public sphere debate or dialogue as reasonably including an element of polemic, but also incorporating elements of scenarios (a) and (c), and exploration of differences, and a move towards resolving them so as to reach agreement and form alliances. Without that element it is difficult to see how 'debates' can influence the formation of policy.

Hegemony, universal and particular

The concept of 'hegemony' is central to the version of Marxism associated with Antonio Gramsci (1971). In a Gramscian view, politics is seen as a struggle for hegemony, a particular way of conceptualizing power that, among other things, emphasizes how power depends upon achieving consent or at least acquiescence rather than just having the resources to use force, and the importance of ideology in sustaining relations of power. The concept of 'hegemony' has recently been approached in terms of a version of discourse theory in the 'post-Marxist' political theory of Ernesto Laclau (Laclau and Mouffe 1985). The hegemonic struggle between political forces can be seen as partly a contention over the claims of their particular visions and representations of the world to having a universal status (Butler et al 2000).

Intertextuality

We can begin by noting that for any particular text or type of text, there is a set of other texts and a set of voices that are potentially relevant and potentially incorporated into the text. It may not be possible to identify these sets with great precision, and they may be rather extensive and complex. But it is analytically useful to begin with some rough idea of them, for a significant initial question is: which texts and voices are included, which are excluded, and what significant absences are there?

Where other texts are intertextually incorporated in a text, they may or may not be attributed. For instance, an extract from Tony Blair's speech following the attack on the World Trade Center in September 2001 includes quite a lot of non-attributed intertextuality, and this is true of the speech as a whole. One example is:

> In the world of the internet, information technology and TV, there will be globalization. And in trade, the problem is not that there's too much of it; on the contrary there's too little of it. The issue is not how to stop globalization. The issue is how we use the power of the community to combine it with justice.

There is a repeated pattern here of denial followed by assertion – negative clause followed by positive clause. Denials imply the assertion 'elsewhere' of what is being denied – in this case, that someone has asserted that there is too much globalization in trade, and that the issue is how to stop globalization. In the context from which this extract comes, Blair has been referring to people who 'protest against globalization'. What he is implying is that these people do assert or have asserted these things, but he is not actually attributing these assertions to them. In fact, many who 'protest against globalization' are not claiming that there is 'too much' of it in trade or that it should be 'stopped', but rather that there is a need to redress imbalances of power in the way in which international trade in increasing.

When intertextuality is attributed, it may be specifically attributed to particular people, or non-specifically (vaguely) attributed. Elsewhere in the same speech, for instance, Blair says:

> Don't overreact, some say. We aren't. We haven't lashed out. No missiles on the first night just for effect.

> Don't kill innocent people. We are not the ones who waged war on the innocent. We seek the guilty.

> Look for a diplomatic solution. There is no diplomacy with Bin Laden or the Taliban regime.

> State an ultimatum and get their response. We stated the ultimatum, they haven't responded.

> Understand the causes of terror. Yes, we should try, but let there be no moral ambiguity about this: nothing could ever justify the events of September 11, and it is to turn justice on its head to pretend it could.

This is a simulated dialogue in which Blair does not so much represent a critical voice as dramatically enact a dialogue with such a voice, which appears as a series of injunctions. Yet he does attribute the words of his imaginary interlocutor, although vaguely, to 'some'. One can see this vagueness as giving Blair a licence to represent what critics of the war were saying in a way which a more specific attribution would make it easier to challenge. The final sentence is the significant one in this regard. It begins with a qualified acceptance of the injunction to 'understand the causes of terror' ('we should try'), but this is followed by an objection that rests upon the implication that those who call for an understanding of causes are thereby seeking to justify the events of September 11. Notice that, as with the previous example, there is a denial ('nothing could ever justify the events of September 11') which implies the assertion 'elsewhere' that 'terror' may be justified by its 'causes'. Of course, calling for a better understanding of why people resort to terrorism does not imply, and did not imply for critics of the policies of Bush and Blair at the time, that terrorism is justified so long as the causes are sufficiently compelling.

When the speech, writing or thought of another is reported, two different texts, two different voices are brought into dialogue, and potentially two different perspectives, objectives, interests and so forth (Volosinov 1973). There is always likely to be a tension between what is going on in the reporting text, including the work that the reporting of other texts is doing within that text, and what was going on in the reported text. I earlier suggested a broad contrast between intertextuality and assumption in terms of the openness of the former, but not the latter, to difference and dialogicality. The form of intertextuality I particularly had in mind is direct reporting, quoted speech or writing. But as soon as we get into the detail of how the speech and writing and thought of others can be reported, the diverse possible forms that it can take, it becomes clear that the picture is more complicated – that reporting, as a form of intertextuality, itself subsumes much of the range of orientations to difference which I summed up in the five scenarios above.

One important contrast in reporting is between reports that are relatively 'faithful' to what is reported, quoting it, claiming to reproduce what was actually said or written, and those which are not. Or, to put it differently, reports that keep a relatively strong and clear boundary between the speech, writing or thought that is reported and the text in which they are reported, and those that do not (Fairclough 1988; Volosinov 1973). This is the difference between 'direct' and 'indirect' reporting. We can differentiate four ways of reporting (see Leech and Short 1981 for a fuller account):

Direct reporting: Quotation, purportedly the actual words used, in quotation marks, with a reporting clause (e.g., She said: 'He'll be there by now.').

Indirect reporting: Summary, the content of what was said or written, not the actual words used, no quotation marks, with a reporting clause (e.g., She said he'd be there by then.). Shifts in the tense ('he'll' becomes 'he'd') and deixis ('now' becomes 'then') of direct reports.

Free indirect reporting: Intermediate between direct and indirect – it has some of the tense and deixis shifts typical of indirect speech, but without a reporting clause. It is mainly significant in literary language (e.g., Mary gazed out of the window. *He would be there by now.* She smiled to herself.).

Narrative report of speech act: Reports the sort of speech act without reporting its content (e.g. She made a prediction.).

One issue is 'framing': when the voice of another is incorporated into a text, there are always choices about how to 'frame' it, how to contextualize it, in terms of other parts of the text – about relations between report and authorial account.

Assumptions

Implicitness is a pervasive property of texts, and a property of considerable social importance. All forms of fellowship, community and solidarity depend upon meanings that are shared and can be taken as given, and no form of social communication or interaction is conceivable without some such 'common ground'. On the other hand, the capacity to exercise social power, domination and hegemony includes the capacity to shape to some significant degree the nature and content of this 'common ground', which makes implicitness and assumptions an important issue with respect to ideology.

We can distinguish three main types of assumptions:

Existential assumptions: Assumptions about what exists.
Propositional assumptions: Assumptions about what is or can be or will be the case.
Value assumptions: Assumptions about what is good or desirable.

Each of these may be marked or 'triggered' (Levinson 1983) by linguistic features of a text, although not all assumptions are 'triggered'. For example, existential assumptions are triggered by markers of definite reference such as definite articles and demonstratives (the, this, that, these, those). Factual assumptions are triggered by certain verbs ('factive verbs') – for instance 'I *realized* (*forgot, remembered*) that managers have to be flexible' assumes that managers have to be flexible. Value assumptions can also be triggered by certain verbs – for instance, 'help' (e.g., 'a good training programme can *help* develop flexibility') assumes that developing flexibility is desirable.

An extract from a European Union policy paper illustrates these types of assumption.

1   But it [globalization] is also a demanding process, and often a painful one.
2   Economic progress has always been accompanied by destruction of obsolete activities and creation of new ones.
3   The pace has become swifter and the game has taken on planetary dimensions.
4   It imposes deep and rapid adjustments on all countries – including European countries, where industrial civilization was born.
5   Social cohesion is threatened by a widespread sense of unease, inequality and polarization.
6   There is a risk of a disjunct between the hopes and aspirations of people and the demands of a global economy.
7   And yet social cohesion is not only a worthwhile social and political goal; it is also a source of efficiency and adaptability in a knowledge-based economy that increasingly depends on human quality and the ability to work as a team.
8   It is more than ever the duty of governments, trade-unions and employers to work together

- to describe the stakes and refute a number of mistakes;
- to stress that our countries should have high ambitions and they can be realized; and
- to implement the necessary reforms consistently and without delay.

9   Failure to move quickly and decisively will result in loss of resources, both human and capital, which will leave for more promising parts of the world if Europe provides less attractive opportunities.

Existential assumptions include the assumption that there are such things as globalization (pronominalized as 'it' in sentence 1) and as social cohesion (sentence 5); that there is a widespread sense of unease, inequality and polarization (sentence 5); that there is a global economy (sentence 6) and a knowledge-based economy (sentence 7). Propositional assumptions include the assumption that globalization is a process (in sentence 1 – what is asserted is the *sort* of process that it is, i.e., 'demanding'); that globalization is or constitutes economic progress (sentences 1 and 2); that people have hopes and aspirations and that the global economy makes demands (sentence 6); that social cohesion is a worthwhile social and political goal and that the knowledge-based economy does increasingly depend on human quality and the ability to work as a team (sentence 7); that reforms are necessary (sentence 8). The assumption that globalization constitutes economic progress is an example of the relationship between assumptions and coherence of meaning: we can talk about 'bridging assumptions', assumptions that are necessary to create a coherent link or 'bridge' between parts of a text, so that a text 'makes sense'. In this case, it is a bridging assumption that allows a coherent semantic connection to be made between sentences 1 and 2. There is also a propositional assumption associated with 'obsolete activities' in sentence 2: that (economic) activities can become obsolete.

Texts may include explicit evaluation ('That's wonderful/excellent!'), but most evaluation in texts is assumed. Value assumptions are triggered by 'threatened' in sentence 5 and by 'risk' in sentence 6. If X threatens (is a threat to) Y, there is an assumption that X is undesirable and Y is desirable; similarly if there is a risk that X, there is assumption that X is undesirable. In this case, social cohesion is assumed to be desirable, a widespread sense of unease, inequality and polarization to be undesirable; and a disjunct between hopes and demands to be undesirable. But value assumptions are not necessarily triggered. There is no need for a trigger such as 'threaten' for 'a sense of unease, inequality and polarization' to be implicitly undesirable, one can interpret it as such on the basis of one's knowledge and recognition of the value system which underlies the text. In sentence 7, it is clear that within the value system of the text social cohesion is being represented as desirable – as is anything that enhances 'efficiency and adaptability'. Notice that one can as a reader recognize the value system and therefore the assumed meaning without accepting or agreeing with it – critics of the new 'global economy' do not accept that efficiency and adaptability are unconditional goods, but they are still likely to be able to recognize that assumption. The corollary is that one's interpretation of texts in terms of values depends upon one's knowledge and recognition of such value systems.

Questions of implicitness and assumptions take us into territory which is conventionally seen as that of linguistic pragmatics (Blakemore 1992; Levinson 1983; Mey 1993; Verschueren 1999). Linguistic pragmatics is the study of 'language in relation to its users' (Mey 1993). It focuses on meaning, but the making of meaning in actual communication, as opposed to what is often seen as the concern of linguistic semantics with semantic relations that can be attributed to a language as such, in abstraction from actual communication. Linguistic pragmatics has produced valuable insights about assumptions (presuppositions, implicatures), speech acts and so forth that have been drawn upon in critical discourse analysis (e.g., Fairclough 1992), but it is also (at least in its Anglo-American as opposed to continental European versions) sometimes problematic in overstating social agency and tending to work with isolated (often invented) utterances (Fairclough 2001).

Ideologies and assumptions

Value systems and associated assumptions can be regarded as belonging to particular discourses – a neoliberal economic and political discourse in the case of the assumption that anything that enhances 'efficiency and adaptability' is desirable. Existential and propositional assumptions may also be discourse-specific – a particular discourse includes assumptions about what there is, what is the case, what is possible, what is necessary, what will be the case and so forth. In some instances, one might argue that such assumptions, and indeed the discourses they are associated with, are ideological. Assumed meanings are of particular ideological significance – one can argue that relations of power are best served by meanings that are widely taken as given. The ideological work of texts is connected to what I said earlier about hegemony and universalization. Seeking hegemony is a matter of seeking to universalize particular meanings in the service of achieving and maintaining dominance, and this is ideological work. So for instance texts can be seen as doing ideological work in assuming, taking as an unquestioned and unavoidable reality, the factuality of a global economy. In the European Union text, both the assumption that globalization is a reality and the assumption that globalization is economic progress might be seen as doing ideological work.

To make such claims, however, one needs to go beyond textual analysis. Let us take a very different example, an extract from a horoscope (*Lancaster Guardian*, 23 November 2001).

Virgo

Spiritual growth will be more important to you than outer ambition for a few weeks. Rather inward looking, you would like to feel more in touch with your soul. If you can push heavier chores at work to one side for a few weeks it will help. Though it may not be easy since you will be fizzing at points. Think about anger as blocked assertion and you can see why it is better to constantly put forward what you need and don't need. If you don't assert yourself in small ways, the resentment builds up, and then suddenly you let fly.

A number of propositional assumptions can be identified here. First, there is a dualist and religious assumption that the 'spirit' stands in contrast with the body, the inner self with the 'outer' self. Second, it is assumed that focusing on 'spiritual growth' means being 'inward looking' and 'feeling in touch with your soul', a bridging assumption that is necessary for a coherent semantic relation between the first two sentences. There is also an existential assumption that there are such things as 'souls' – or that people have souls. Third, there is an assumption that if one is 'fizzing', it is difficult to 'push heavier chores to one side'. Fourth, that thinking about things in certain ways allows one to understand things, that it's better to constantly put forward what you need and don't need, that you need some things and you don't need others. Fifth, that when resentment builds up, people are liable to suddenly let fly.

One might argue that the 'dualist' and religious assumption of a contrast between an inner, spiritual self and an outer self is ideological. This is the classic argument about religion as ideology, as the 'opiate of the masses' in Marx's famous phrase. But to claim that it is an ideological assumption, one would need a plausible argument that it is indeed effective, along with other related propositions and beliefs, in sustaining relations of power. This would need to be based upon a complex social scientific analysis of the relationship between religious beliefs and power relations, and of course such a claim would be controversial. The analysis would have to go beyond texts, although a textual analysis showing that such religious dualism is pervasively assumed, taken for granted, could be seen as a significant part of the analysis. Certainly one cannot simply look at a text, identify assumptions, and decide on textual evidence alone which of them are ideological.

Other types of assumptions

What I have been calling 'assumptions' are one of the types of implicitness generally distinguished in linguistic pragmatics – presuppositions. Verschueren (1999) differentiates four (I have changed his terminology somewhat):

Presuppositions (what I am calling 'assumptions')
Logical implications
Standard conversational implicatures
Non-standard conversational implicatures

Logical implications are implicit meanings that can be logically inferred from features of language – for example, 'I have been married for 20 years' implies that I am (still) married (because of the perfect aspect, 'have been'), or 'he is poor but honest' implies that poor people can be expected to be dishonest (because of the contrastive meaning of 'but'). Standard conversational implicatures are implicit meanings that can conventionally be inferred on the basis of our normal assumption that people are adhering to what Grice (1975) called conversational 'maxims'. The four maxims are:

Quantity: Give as much information, and no more information than is required in the context.

Quality: Try to speak the truth.
Relevance: Be relevant.
Manner: Be clear.

For example, if I ask 'Is there anything to see in Lancaster?', you can infer on the basis of the second of these maxims (the maxim of Quality) that I don't know much about Lancaster.

The most interesting type apart from presuppositions is the fourth, non-standard conversational implicatures. The basic contrast between presuppositions and such implicatures is that the former take as given what is assumed to be known or believed, whereas the latter are fundamentally about the strategic avoidance of explicitness. However, this contrast is made less simple by the possibility of strategically purporting to assume that something is known or believed when one has reason to believe it isn't – for instance, passing off something contentious as if it were uncontentious (e.g., saying 'I didn't realize that Fred was paid by the CIA' as a way of getting one's interlocutor to accept that he is paid by the CIA). While implicatures are inherently strategic, assumptions may be strategic.

This type of implicature arises from what Grice called the 'flouting' of a maxim – apparently breaking a maxim, but adhering to it on an implicit level of meaning. To take a classic example, if I write in a reference for an academic post only that the candidate is 'well-dressed and punctual', this appears to break the maxims of Quantity (it doesn't provide enough information) and Relevance (what information it does provide is not relevant). But if a person reading the reference assumes that I am being cooperative rather than perverse, s/he may inter that the candidate does not have the qualifications or qualities needed for the post, which is both informative enough (if curt) and relevant.

References

Althusser, L. and Balibar, E. (1970) *Reading Capital*, London: New Left Books.

Archer, M. (1995) *Realist Social Theory: The Morphogenetic Approach*, Cambridge: Cambridge University Press.

—— (2000) *Being Human: The Problem of Agency*, Cambridge: Cambridge University Press.

Arendt, H. (1958) *The Human Condition*, Chicago: University of Chicago Press.

Bakhtin, M. (1981) *The Dialogical Imagination*, Austin: University of Texas Press.

—— (1986) 'The problem of speech genres', in *Speech Genres and Other Late Essays*, Austin: University of Texas Press, 60–102.

Bernstein, B. (1990) *The Structuring of Pedagogic Discourse*, London: Routledge.

Bjerke, F. (2000) *Discursive Governance Structures*, Working Paper, Institute of Social Sciences and Business Economics, Roskilde University, Denmark.

Blakemore, D. (1992) *Understanding Utterances: An Introduction to Pragmatics*, Oxford: Blackwell.

Bourdieu, P. and Wacquant, L. (1992) *An Invitation to Reflexive Sociology*, Cambridge: Polity Press.

Butler, J., Laclau, E. and Žižek, S. (2000) *Contingency, Hegemony, Universality*, London: Verso.

Calhoun, C. (1992) *Habermas and the Public Sphere*, Cambridge, MA: MIT Press.

Chouliaraki, L. and Fairclough, N. (1999) *Discourse in Late Modernity*, Edinburgh: Edinburgh University Press.

Fairclough, N. (1988) 'Discourse representation in media discourse', *Sociolinguistics* 17: 125–39.

—— (1992) *Discourse and Social Change*, Cambridge: Polity Press.

—— (1993) 'Critical discourse analysis and the marketisation of public discourse: the universities', *Discourse and Society* 4: 133–68.

—— (1999) 'Democracy and the public sphere in critical research on discourse', in R. Wodak and C. Ludwig (eds) *Challenges in a Changing World: Issues in Critical Discourse Analysis*, Vienna: Passagen Verlag.

—— (2000) *New Labour, New Language?*, London: Routledge.

—— (2001) 'The dialectics of discourse', *Textus* 14: 231–42.

Fiske, J. (1987) *Television Culture*, London: Routledge.

Foucault, M. (1972) *The Archaeology of Knowledge*, New York: Pantheon.

—— (1994) 'What is enlightenment?', in P. Rabinow (ed.) *Michel Foucault: Essential Works vol 1 (Ethics)*, Harmondsworth: Penguin, 303–19.

Giddens, A. (1991) *Modernity and Self Identity*, Cambridge: Polity Press.

—— (1993) *New Rules of Sociological Method*, 2nd edition, Cambridge: Polity Press.

Gramsci, A. (1971) *Selections from the Prison Notebooks*, London: Lawrence & Wishart.

Grice, H.P. (1975) 'Logic and conversation', in P. Cole and J. Morgan (eds) *Syntax and Semantics 3: Speech Acts*, New York: Academic Press.

Habermas, J. (1984) *Theory of Communicative Action*, Vol. 1, London: Heinemann.

—— (1989) *The Structural Transformational of the Public Sphere*, Cambridge: Polity Press.

Halliday, M. (1978) 'The sociosemantic nature of discourse', in *Language as Social Semiotic*, London: Edward Arnold.

—— (1994) *An Introduction to Functional Grammar*, 2nd edition, London: Edward Arnold.

Harvey, D. (1990) *The Condition of Postmodernity*, Oxford: Blackwell.

—— (1996) *Justice, Nature and the Geography of Difference*, Oxford: Blackwell.

Holquist, M. (1981) *Dialogism: Bakhtin and his Works*, London: Routledge.

Ivanic, R. (1998) *Writing and Identity*, Amsterdam: John Benjamins.

Jameson, F. (1991) *Postmodernism, Or the Cultural Logic of Late Capitalism*, London: Verso.

Jessop, B. (1998) 'The rise of governance and the risks of failure: the case of economic development', *International Social Science Journal* 155: 29–45.

Kress, G. (1985) *Linguistic Processes in Sociocultural Practice*, Geelong, Victoria: Deakin University Press.

Laclau, E. and Mouffe, C. (1985) *Hegemony and Socialist Strategy*, London: Verso.

Leech, G.N. and Short, M. (1981) *Style in Fiction*, London: Longman.

Levinson, S. (1983) *Pragmatics*, Cambridge: Cambridge University Press.

Luhmann, N. (2000) *The Reality of the Mass Media*, Cambridge: Polity Press.

McLuhan, M. (1964) *Understanding Media*, New York: McGraw Hill.

Merleau-Ponty, M. (1964) *Signs*, Evanston, IL: Northwestern University Press.

Mey, J. (1993) *Pragmatics: An Introduction*, Oxford: Blackwell.

Silverstone, R. (1999) *Why Study the Media?* London: Sage.

Verschueren, J. (1999) *Understanding Pragmatics*, London: Arnold.

Volosinov, V.I. (1973) *Marxism and the Philosophy of Language*, Cambridge, MA: Harvard University Press.

Wertsch, J. (1991) *Voices of the Mind*, Hemel Hempstead: Harvester Wheatsheaf.

Chapter 6

Ron Scollon

MODES AND MODALITY

The multimodal shaping of reality in public discourse

Communicative modes: form and action

WE COMMUNICATE IN MANY different modes: we talk, write, gesture, pose, gaze, and dress ourselves in particular ways. And we make drawings, photos, films, or videos, or buildings and other artifacts. And we never do just one of these and only one of these at a time: we talk while we are gazing at the person we are speaking to or, perhaps, looking over their shoulder. In the morning before an important meeting we dress in a way that we feel will suit the tenor of the meeting and as we speak we sit or stand in particular ways and gesture in accompaniment of our speech.

Some of the modes we use are embodied modes – ways of communicating that are performed through our own bodies and are perceived by others who are together with us face-to-face as we communicate. Other modes transform actions of our body into more or less permanent records of those actions and these work at greater or lesser distance from our bodies.

In Figure 6.1 the signature of Thomas A. Readinger along with the rubber-stamped date, July 2, 2004, makes it legal to undertake the second sale of oil and

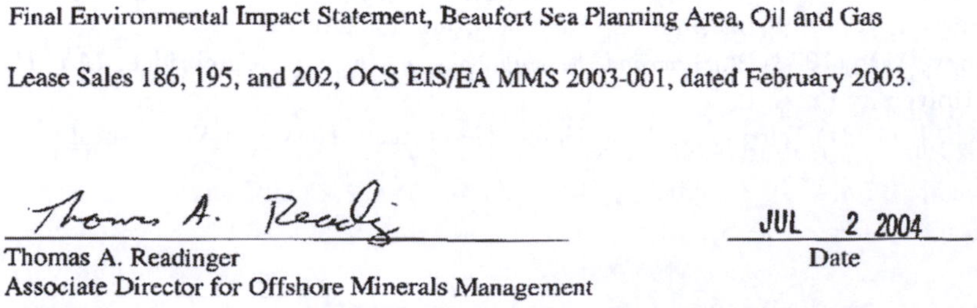

Final Environmental Impact Statement, Beaufort Sea Planning Area, Oil and Gas

Lease Sales 186, 195, and 202, OCS EIS/EA MMS 2003-001, dated February 2003.

Thomas A. Readinger
Associate Director for Offshore Minerals Management

JUL   2 2004
Date

Figure 6.1 Minerals Management Service, US Department of the Interior

gas leases in the Beaufort Sea (Sale 195). The 'Finding of No Significant Impacts' is the official document that enables the second sale (195) to go ahead. After the first sale (186) a call was issued for new information, an environmental assessment was prepared to evaluate any changes that might have occurred since the Environmental Impact Assessment; this was reviewed by the Minerals Management Service, and this finding was declared, signed, and dated. The signature tells us that it was the associate director himself who authorized this as a legally binding document. Perhaps he did not put the rubber-stamped date on himself and he quite certainly did not type the letter. But the signature tells us that this real-world, identifiable historical body took an action with his own hand for which he claims and accepts the responsibility within his official government authority. The signature inscription on this letter leaves a permanent trace in which we see the movements of the associate director's hand, but the typography of the letter that he has signed is so distant that we cannot tell whose body did the word processing and printing.

Whether communicative modes are embodied ones or distant, disembodied ones, to a great extent we make conventional judgments about truth and reality, reliability or official status or the binding nature of communications on the basis of the modes which are used to perform the action of communication. If the 'Finding of No Significant Impacts' appeared, for example, as in the photographically doctored image in Figure 6.2, with a different font and a printed date, we might assume that it was designed as a copy of some original with a signature which was being held elsewhere, but not that it was a copy of the signed document itself.

In pre-photocopying days this is, in fact, how legal copies of documents were made. They were typed 'exactly' and then an affidavit swearing the exactness of the copy was signed by the animator of the document, the typist. This was, in fact, one of my jobs in the army – to be a human 'photocopier'.

This is what occurs in notices that appear in the Federal Register, such as in Figure 6.3, which is the 'signature block' for the Final Notice of Sale. In this case the bolded name of the acting director and the italicized title under the name indicate by contrast with the other typefaces that these are facsimiles of what has been registered and archived elsewhere as the official, authorizing letter.

There is no very clear or widely agreed upon definition of the word 'mode' among researchers on communicative modes, whether in communication, psychology, or linguistics, but in most cases a distinction is made between mode and medium. A mode is a configuration of expressions that is conventionally recognized as being a symbolic system. A medium is the physical or material substance (paper, ink, pixels

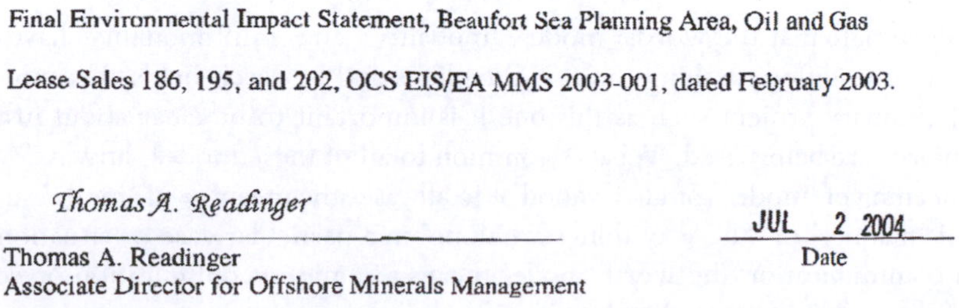

Final Environmental Impact Statement, Beaufort Sea Planning Area, Oil and Gas

Lease Sales 186, 195, and 202, OCS EIS/EA MMS 2003-001, dated February 2003.

Thomas A. Readinger   JUL   2 2004

Thomas A. Readinger   Date
Associate Director for Offshore Minerals Management

Figure 6.2 A photographically doctored version of Figure 6.1

Provisions, Sale 186" included in the
FNOS 186 package.

Dated: August 15, 2003.

Thomas A. Readinger,

Acting Director, Minerals Management Service.

[FR Doc. 03–21472 Filed 8–20–03; 8:45 am]

BILLING CODE 4310–MR–P

Figure 6.3 A Federal Register notice

on a screen, clothing, or even parts of the body such as the hands, arms, trunk, tongue, teeth, and larynx) in which a mode is formed. Generally we recognize the distinction, for example, between writing as the physical process of making marks (the medium) and writing as the semiotic process of making shapes within an alphabet (mode).

Of course these relate to the production/reception roles. The principal and the author of a document are concerned with the mode and the animator is concerned with the medium (typeface, paper choice, digital format of HTML or PDF). A signature is, then, an interesting case in which we take it as legally binding when the animator and the principal are the same person or social actor; that is, the person who takes ultimate responsibility must be the same person who animates the text 'Thomas A. Readinger' with his own handwriting.

Our concern in this chapter, then, is to discuss several ways in which communications may take on different statuses in relationship to the real world of social action through the mechanisms not only of lexicogrammar and discourse, but now also through the modes and media in which they are physically produced as objects in the world.

For public consultative discourse analysis we are mostly concerned with the modes and media of documentation and these are mostly print/text modes, although the use of images has increasingly entered into consideration through letterheads and through the use of color and images on websites. Even public testimony that is produced in the mode of speech is normally transformed into the mode of written text as part of making it a legitimate part of the public consultative process.

Truth and reality in public discourse: modality

It is unfortunate that the words 'mode', 'modality', and 'multimodality' have come to mean quite different things across disciplines and research fields, because in an interdisciplinary project such as this one it is important to be clear about just how these words are being used. What is common to all of these modes, however, is the basic meaning of 'mode' (or also 'mood'). In all cases the meaning of 'mode' suggests ideas of 'manner' or 'the way things are done' in a particular case or situation.

In communication the word 'mode' means a semiotic configuration or code in which a meaning is expressed such as writing, speech, gesture, posture, gaze, painting, architecture, interior design, or urban design, as we have noted above. That is, in communication the focus is on the manner of communicating. In linguistics the word 'mode' means the logical truth or reality status of a statement or sentence, as indicated by such means as modal verb auxiliaries like 'would,' 'could,' 'should.' For our purposes here it may help to use the term 'mode' as it is used in communication and the term 'modality' for the linguistic use of the term.

We can make this clearer by looking at several statements that were made in public hearings concerning the multiple oil and gas lease sales in the Beaufort Sea:

> Anchorage, 30 July 2002
> These comments that we get here at this public hearing and the other public hearings will be used by the Secretary of Interior in making her decision on the proposed sale, on each of these three proposed sales.

> Barrow, 1 August 2002
> I doubt if the Secretary of Interior or the Director of the Minerals Management Service would sign a contract between you and them. . .

> Nuiqsut, 24 July 2002
> The first sale is in 2003. The second sale is in 2005. The third sale is in 2007. These are proposed sales.

> Kaktovik, 26 July 2002
> What we mean by deferral is these are alternatives that are in the EIS that could be selected by the Secretary of Interior where leasing would not occur.
>
> We will, this fall, produce a – or I guess it's in February, will produce a Final Environmental Impact Statement, and then there will ultimately be a decision by the Secretary and the sale will occur a little more than a year from now.
>
> Let's say as a hypothetical, the Secretary decided to pick one of the alternatives. Let's just say hypothetically the Secretary decided to pick the Kaktovik green deferral and say I won't have leasing there.

Will the sale occur or won't it? Will these comments be used by the Secretary or won't they? Will the Secretary sign or won't she? Will the alternatives be selected or not? Will there be a sale in a year, in 2005, and in 2007? The verbs that tell us these things are modal verbs (or auxiliaries) like 'would,' 'could,' 'should,' 'might,' 'ought.' These verbs do not assert what we can observe to have happened; they present an imagined or alternate reality – usually one somewhere in the future, sometimes conditional on other events or occurrences.

'I will go to the store after a while,' conveys the idea that it is definite that I plan to go to the store. 'I would go to the store after a while,' conveys the more tentative notion that this action requires certain conditions to be met for it to happen – 'If you would do the dishes, I would go to the store.' 'I could go to the store after a while,' focuses on the speaker's ability to do the action. It is possible but no commitment is made. 'I should go to the store after a while,' suggests that the speaker thinks it would be right for that action to happen, but he or she remains doubtful that it will happen.

'Modality' is the word linguists use to talk about these varying states of projected reality or truth status. As we shall see below, these are far from being trivial grammatical matters of choice of words as we might have thought from our experiences of grammar in school; they are the material out of which political discourse and ideology are crafted.

Of course, it is not always the verb that tells us the truth or reality of what someone is saying, because we can also say, 'These are proposed,' or 'Let's say as a hypothetical,' but often the way we set up the truth or reality status of what we are saying is through the use of these verbs. This whole process of making the metacommunication about how we are to take a statement is called modality.

The central distinction in modality is between *realis* and *irrealis*. *Realis* is something that is 'real,' 'definite,' 'perceived by the person speaking' (or, of course, assumed to be perceived by the listener or a third person). *Irrealis* is 'imagined,' 'unreal,' 'indefinite,' 'unknown,' or 'unknowable'. And the modality might not just be located in the view or position of the speaker. It can be attributed to the hearer or even some other third person. 'I should go to the store this afternoon,' 'You ought to go to the store this afternoon,' 'He might go to the store this afternoon.'

Sometimes the modality distinction between *realis* 'real' and *irrealis* 'unreal' is not directly visible. If we have just the sentence, 'I need to buy a book,' we don't know precisely whether this is *realis* or *irrealis*. We can compare two fuller sentences:

I need to buy a book that I read about in a review yesterday (*realis*).

and

I need to buy a book because it's a long flight to Hong Kong (*irrealis*).

In the first case the speaker is talking about a concrete, specific book and so it is known (at least to her or him) exactly which book is being referred to, but in the second case it is just some book or any book, and so linguistically it is categorized as *irrealis*. In common conversations these are just the kinds of things that we respond to for clarifications, 'Does it matter what kind of book, or is there a particular book you are looking for?' In conversation we don't ask: is that a *realis* or an *irrealis* statement you are making? Wherever modality is placed interactionally, or whether it is marked in the verb or elsewhere in the lexicogrammatical system, we must successfully interpret the modality of communications in order to be able to respond or to act upon them appropriately.

Our sense of truth and reality lie at the very heart of our ability to undertake action in the world. And because public discourse on social policy is our major guide to sociopolitical actions in the future, modality, both lexicogrammatical modality and the modality that comes from multiple communicative modes, is central in public discourse.

Knowledge and agency in anticipatory discourse

Future national energy needs are not a fact (*realis*); they are a theory (*irrealis*). This is simply for the logical reason that the future is not known to us; it is a constructed world. It is constructed out of language, images, memories, stories, our artifacts, the objects we buy, treasure and discard, and the built and natural environment we move around in. Linguistically speaking, truth and reality are always from a point of view; the point of view of someone who makes a claim about reality or who attributes it to someone else. In the public hearing in Anchorage, Jim Sykes says:

> The oil is not needed.

This is a simple, declarative *realis* statement about the oil to be extracted from the Beaufort Sea. He did not say, 'The oil may not be needed,' 'The oil should not be needed,' 'The oil would not be needed.' He did not even say, 'The oil will not be needed.' He took a clear, declarative, *realis* stand in the present: it is not needed. This is a reality for Sykes, a truth that he is willing to directly assert and to stand behind.

The statement in the Environmental Assessment of July 2004 contrasts very strongly with the statement of Sykes:

> Oil from the adjacent Beaufort Sea shelf can help to reduce the Nation's need for oil imports.

The modal is 'can,' not 'will.' The verb phrase is 'help to reduce,' not 'reduce.' It is the 'need' that may be reduced, not necessarily the oil imports themselves. Hedged in this way, and cast in the *irrealis* modality with 'can,' the environmental assessment takes an anticipatory stance that is somewhat agnostic, that is, the environmental assessment is not ready to assert, at least within the scope of that statement, that the oil from the Beaufort Sea will either be needed or, more finely put, reduce the need for oil imports.

Work in the area of linguistics and discourse analysis that is sometimes discussed as anticipatory discourse focuses on such future-oriented statements (as well as other semiotic communications). There are many different stances that can be taken about the future which then shape the way we speak about actions yet to come. These can be plotted along two axes; one is a knowledge axis and the other is an agency axis, as diagrammed in Figure 6.4.

The range on the knowledge axis is from oracular to agnostic, from claims of certainty to the profession of ignorance. At the oracular end, at the top of the graph,

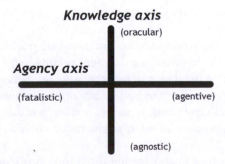

Figure 6.4 A two-dimensional model of future discourse

one takes the stance that what one is talking about is absolutely certain; although it has not yet happened one is certain that it will. Most of us, in talking about tomorrow's sunrise, are likely to take an oracular stance toward this event. We would be shocked if it did not happen. In the quotation above, Jim Sykes takes an oracular stance. There is no doubt left; he feels he *knows* with certainty that the oil is not needed.

Whether we are talking about the sunrise tomorrow or about the need for oil from the Beaufort Sea over the next decade or two, this oracular position is based on making many assumptions about the world that are so deeply buried in our historical bodies that we are not able to make ourselves aware of them, or we are strategically hiding those assumptions from others in a rhetorical move to be persuasive. Needless to say, much political discourse would be plotted at the top end of this knowledge axis, as political discourse frequently takes a stance of certainty toward future events and actions.

At the other end of this knowledge axis is the agnostic position. Here the person takes the position that he or she does not know at all what might happen. In Nuiqsut, Paul Stang comments on a question concerning environmental justice in two parts. The first part of the question is whether or not there would be adverse effects on a minority population (the people of Nuiqsut) and the second part is whether or not those would be highly adverse effects. He answers by saying that the Minerals Management Service recognizes that there would be some effects, but concerning the second issue of whether these would be highly adverse, he says:

> No one really knows until any development proceeds.

This statement would be plotted at the far bottom end of the knowledge axis, the agnostic end. Paul Stang does not claim any knowledge about this and goes so far as to suggest that nobody else could have that knowledge either. Of course such an agnostic position, like the extreme opposite oracular position, is based on many assumptions about the world, perhaps never articulated and, like the oracular position, it can be used for strategic purposes. It might indicate a bureaucratic dodge of responsibility or it might indicate a careful assessment of a scientifically supportable conclusion.

In responding to a question in Kaktovik concerning the distance from an oil spill at which negative effects could be measured, the same speaker, Paul Stang, comments:

> Our analysts look at those specific issues and they make their best judgment
> based on the data that they've got available.

Here he takes a much more mitigated and intermediate position, perhaps somewhat toward the middle of the knowledge axis: there is knowledge concerning effects; it is partial; analysts need to use their judgment to make predictions based on this partial knowledge. It is fair to say that the bulk of scientific discourse is positioned about where this statement is positioned. It asserts neither oracular knowledge about the future nor agnostic ignorance of what might occur. It is a 'best informed guess' position.

The modality involved in anticipating the future in discourse is not, however, governed solely by knowledge. The second dimension that is represented by the agency axis represents whether or not it is believed that social actors have the power to influence the outcomes of actions. Again, this varies quite a lot across discourses, persons, and situations. When we go into a restaurant we most likely take a relatively high agentive position – we will decide what we will order – but along with this we take a relatively low knowledge position – we do not know what is possible and so ask for the menu. When we are guests at a formal dinner we are likely to be considerably more fatalistic and assume that it will be a set meal with only the option of eating a prepared dish or leaving it untouched. Concerning the rising of the sun tomorrow, perhaps most humans would take a fatalistic position: whether we do anything or not, or even whether we know for certain that it will rise or not, the sun will do what it is going to do.

The people of Kaktovik prepared what they have called *In This Place: A Guide for Those Who Would Work in the Country of the Kaktovikmiut. An Unfinished and Ongoing Work of the People of Kaktovik, Alaska*, which is available on the Minerals Management Service website as document 1.12.3,b. As part of their general position statement they write:

> Outsiders constantly ask us if we are 'for' or 'against' oil development. These are outsider positions, commitments by outside interests, to be for or against whatever the industry does. Neither makes any sense to us, and we reject them both. How can anybody be for or against something that remains to be defined? Surely oil development is yet to be defined here, its impact on us yet unclear. Nobody else knows and neither do we. Instead, we choose a third path, our own, one that makes sense to us.
>
> This third path, the one we choose, is to be responsible, as we have always been, for the well being of our people and the well being of this country to which we are attached. We expect to control what is done here and how it is done. We also expect to be accountable for our decisions. This is our country, and we cannot allow anyone to come here who would damage it. We shall not permit the country to be harmed nor will we permit our use of it or responsibility for it to be questioned or restricted. Our position is that there will be no damages to our country nor to us but instead that we will control and gain from whatever activity we permit here. We propose in other documents our plans for maintaining that control.

The Kaktovik people set out their position on the knowledge axis in the first paragraph. It is agnostic. They do not know what the impact of these developments on them will be. But then, in the second paragraph, they turn to the agency axis. Here they express no doubt about their agency; they will control their country and what is done there. This position would be located at the far right end of the agency axis, but, because of the agnostic view of the future, in the lower right quadrant. It is a position of agnostic agency. 'We do not know but we assert our agency,' summarizes this position.

Perhaps it is obvious that political discourse makes ample use of the agency axis in strategizing positions. As Fairclough and other critical discourse analysts have observed, a rhetorical strategy within neoliberal discourse is to assert that globalization is absolutely inevitable; there is nothing anyone can do about it other than to position oneself in relationship to it. This neoliberal discourse achieves its power to persuade through adopting a fatalistic-oracular position, a position in the upper left hand quadrant in Figure 6.4. 'We know with certainty and there is nothing to be done about it,' summarizes this position. Thus there is a stark contrast between these two positions: globalization is inevitable and there is nothing you can do about it; the impacts of oil development cannot be known in advance but we will control those impacts.

The discursive means for talking about the future and for positioning ourselves as social actors in that future can be located anywhere on this graph. A strong upper left position (fatalistic-oracular) would be expressed as: 'We are certain X will happen, but there is nothing we can do about it.' A strong lower left position (fatalistic-agnostic) would be expressed as: 'We have no idea what will happen, and anyway there is nothing we can do about it.' A strong upper right position (agentive-oracular) would be expressed as: 'We are certain X will happen, and we will do Y about the consequences of that.' A strong lower right position (agentive-agnostic) would be expressed as: 'We have no idea what will happen, but we will be ready to act as soon as we find out.' A public consultative discourse analysis needs to examine where participants and documents position themselves when they make statements in anticipation of future actions.

The concern of this chapter follows from this: social actors who are located in different discourses as they speak and as they act may profoundly disagree with the actions and motives of others at this level of modality. Both individuals and discourses may take up positions of modality. While the public discourse may be carried out on a surface level of scientific (or bureaucratic or legal) discourse, underlying this discourse is a rock-solid ideological position about the nature of the world, the nature of our knowledge about the world, and the degree of human agency which is thought to be possible in having impacts on the world.

A public consultative discourse analysis may not be able to move social actors from their ideological positions concerning the basis of human actions, but it can and should make it clear how and where different positions are being taken up as part of the process of opening public discourse to a fuller examination of social actions.

Modality in science and politics: global warming

Linguistic modality can be used as a potent tool of political discourse. Scientific discourse is cautious in drawing conclusions from experimental data. Conclusions are built on an extended series of studies, each of which more closely refines our understanding of a phenomenon. Scientists insist on cross-checking findings through replication studies and through closely examining research results in review by peers before publication. At the same time, scientists are also very unlikely to make statements that are simply fatalistic or agnostic. Scientists would not be scientists if they took the position that there is nothing we can know and nothing we can do about our world. Science is a discourse within which participants are schooled and credentialed in an ideology of accumulated human knowledge as the basis for careful human action. In terms of modality, then, only when most of the ramifications of a theory have been filled out by experimental data do scientists feel comfortable making either very oracular or very agentive statements.

Our contemporary knowledge of global warming is based on a large body of scientific studies carried out throughout the world by scientists who themselves conduct their research within very different sociocultural or political environments. It is therefore striking when they come to the widespread agreement they have expressed concerning the imminent danger to life on the earth that global warming threatens. They have further expressed widespread agreement that a major cause of this global warming is under the control of human agency. In a few words, the scientific consensus is that, taken together, we are burning too much fossil fuel for the survival of life as we now know it. The position of scientists on global warming is, for science, surprisingly oracular and agentive. Rarely do scientists agree to such a great extent that we actually do know enough about the phenomenon to do something and also that there is something we can and should do.

There are political interests, however, which see the issue from a different ideological standpoint. That standpoint holds a considerably more agnostic and non-agentive position concerning global warming. The position taken is that we do not know much about what causes global warming or even if there is such a phenomenon at all. Further, that position asserts that even if there is some evidence of global warming, it is a purely natural phenomenon about which humans can do nothing. It is not surprising that this is the position taken by a substantial segment of the petroleum industry.

New York Times articles by Andrew C. Revkin in June 2005 tell the story of the whistleblower Rick S. Piltz, senior associate at the Climate Change Science Program Office of the US government and editor of *Our Changing Planet*, a regular government publication concerning global warming. According to the *New York Times*, as well as subsequent interviews with Piltz, scientific reports made by his agency were regularly edited by White House staffer Philip A. Cooney, chief of staff for the White House Council on Environmental Quality. Before joining the White House staff, Cooney was a leader in the petroleum industry's aggressive campaign to debunk the concept of global warming through greenhouse gases, gases that result in part from the burning of petroleum products.

An example cited by Revkin shows how Cooney edited Piltz's report *Our Changing Planet* over time with a steady remodalization that drew the statements into line with Cooney's, the White House's, and the petroleum industry's political ideology concerning global warming.

For example, the following paragraph first appeared in the draft text of October 2002 as follows:

> Warming will also cause reductions in mountain glaciers and advance the timing of the melt of mountain snow packs in polar regions. In turn runoff rates will change and flood potential will be altered in ways that are currently not well understood. There will be significant shifts in the seasonality of runoff that will have serious impacts on native populations that rely on fishing and hunting for their livelihood. These changes will

be further complicated by shifts in precipitation regimes and possible intensification and increased frequency of extreme hydrologic events.

In response to this draft the White House editor, Cooney, made suggestions to alter this draft, which are indicated below in bold type.

Warming **would** also cause reductions in mountain glaciers and advance the timing of the melt of mountain snow packs in polar regions. In turn runoff rates **would** change and flood potential **would** be altered in ways that are currently not well understood. There will be significant shifts in the seasonality of runoff that will have serious impacts on native populations that rely on fishing and hunting for their livelihood. These changes will be further complicated by shifts in precipitation regimes and possible intensification and increased frequency of extreme hydrologic events.

The *realis* 'will' was changed to the *irrealis* 'would.' The modal auxiliary 'would' is a conditional: 'If X occurs then Y would occur.' The changes suggested by Cooney leave hanging the 'if' question. Since there is no suggestion of this precondition, the change of *realis* to *irrealis* is a direct shift from a scientific statement of cause and effect – 'Global warming will cause X' – to a non-scientific *irrealis* – 'Global warming would cause X (under unspecified conditions).'

When the public review draft was made available in November of 2002, the lead sentence read:

Warming **could** also **lead to changes in the water cycle in polar regions. etc.**

The implied conditional of 'would' is reduced still further to the merely probabilistic 'could.' 'Cause reductions' is reduced to 'lead to changes.' Still further changes occurred throughout the paragraph.

Finally, when the report was published in July of 2003 the entire paragraph was simply deleted. Next to the paragraph had appeared Cooney's comment:

straying from research strategy into speculative findings/musings here.

'Warming will cause reductions,' becomes 'Warming would cause reductions.' This, then, becomes 'Warming could lead to changes.' That is ultimately followed by full deletion.

Here we can note two things: first, over successive stages this remodalization moves the scientific statement from certainty to a conditional reality, *realis* to *irrealis*. Then, once it is posed as an *irrealis* 'truth' – something that might be true under some unspecific conditions – it is further shifted to merely probable 'truth.' The political discourse can take over at this point by arguing that there is no basis for administration policy to be set on merely probable statements. More studies are needed, stronger scientific evidence is required, the political process of taking action is conveniently deferred. That is the first point.

The second point is important for a public consultative discourse analysis. The editor requiring these revisions in a scientific document is not doing so on the basis of any scientific knowledge or credentials by which he could make a scientific judgment about the *realis/irrealis* status of the scientific statements. His editing is based, rather, on political ideology. But, having said that, Cooney used a common feature of scientific discourse for political purposes. Cooney used the propensity of science to avoid strongly oracular or agentive statements as major political weapon against scientific discourse itself.

The problem in discourse is that the use of multiple modes in all communicative expressions gives rise to multiple positions on the truth and reality of what is being communicated. Multimodality as it is used in this chapter refers both to the fact that all communications occur simultaneously in multiple modes and to the fact that this multimodality produces multiple stances toward truth and reality. Scientists, logicians, and some linguists and lawyers deplore this; politicians, bureaucrats, marketers, and advertisers exploit it to the fullest advantage.

Modalities of discourse

Modality in communicative modes other than lexicogrammar is not conventionally fixed but varies depending on the discourses within which the modes are used. In this, modality in non-grammatical modes is not so much like the modal auxiliaries ('could,' 'should,' 'ought') as it is like the example of the two sentences given earlier in this chapter in which 'book' may either be a general, non-specific book ('some book,' 'any book') or a specific book ('the one I read a review of' or *War and Peace*) depending on how it is used within a sentence.

In scientific discourse, careful argumentation and careful statement of conclusions means that statements are cautious and hedged. Scientific discourse does not easily or frequently say 'We know that. . .' but rather 'Scientific studies indicate that. . .' Likewise, scientific discourse is primarily presented in the printed textual mode. This mode includes, of course, much use of charts, maps, graphs, and other images, but these decontextualized semiotic modes in scientific discourse are pared down to the highly abstract lines and symbols of an analytical presentation.

To give an illustration of this difference, Figure 6.5 is a photograph taken by the author from the mountain above his hometown of Haines, Alaska. Photos much like this one, shot from exactly this place, appear in full-color travel brochures that advertise vacationing and hiking in this town. As travel advertisements we see them as being 'natural' and 'true' photos of the place.

In this published version the same photo is reproduced in black and white to reduce printing costs that, of course, translate into cover price for the book. Already this change from the mode of color photography to the mode of black and white printing signals a shift in reality status from 'the real place' to 'an image used in academic argument.' It is no less true or false a photograph, but by the same measure that the photograph loses *realis* value as a travel image it gains *realis* status as textbook illustration.

At a much higher degree of abstraction is the image of Haines that one gets from a topographical map of 'the same' view. Here in Figure 6.6 are the same mountains,

Figure 6.5 Photograph of Haines, Alaska

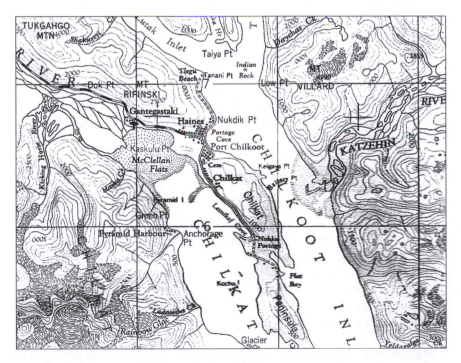

Figure 6.6 Topographical map of Haines, Alaska

the same town site, and the same ocean channel and river channel along the sides of the Chilkat Peninsula.

The scientific configuration of topographical cartography has translated the view of the mountain across the horizon into closed, irregular looping lines at fixed elevations. Land forms and sea are separated by outlines of the land forms and different shadings of gray. Further, the entire viewpoint is oriented so that north is squared to the top of the page, in contrast to the photograph, which takes the point of view of the hiker on the mountain who is looking south, down the Chilkat Peninsula. This, of course, is again very different from the perspective one would get from a bullet-pointed textual description you might find in a Chamber of Commerce fact sheet:

Haines and the Chilkat Peninsula
- Small, compact townsite (pop. 1811)
- High, relatively trackless mountains
- Glaciers
- Ocean
- Deep river valley

Like the difference between color and black and white modes, these differences among photographic, cartographic, and textual modes are not inherently tied to modality; that is, we cannot say independently of the discourse within which it is used that any one of these images is *realis* or any of them is *irrealis*. This can only be determined within a specific discourse and within its organizing purposes. The discourse of travel advertising generally works within the purpose of enticing the viewer to want to think in terms of the personal experience he or she will enjoy, and so full-color images taken on nice days have a *realis* status within this discourse and for this purpose. Within cartographic discourse the very different goal is to factor out all kinds of irrelevant detail so that the view can focus on land forms and elevations (among other things). Within that discourse and for that purpose, the topographical sheet of Haines in Figure 6.6 has *realis* status.

Modes, modality, and interdiscursivity

No mode of communication can automatically convert knowledge or information from another mode. Consequently, if there is a predominance of one or very few modes in a discourse or in a sequence of documents, it must be asked what modes are missing and what knowledge or information or even whole discourses this is obscuring. The public record of the multiple sale process for oil and gas leases is an extended series of documents that runs to thousands of pages. Among those thousands of pages relatively few modes beyond text and the corresponding scientific/ bureaucratic modes of graphs, charts, and tables are found. What's missing?

The public hearing that was held in Barrow on August 1, 2002, was held in the Iñupiat Heritage Center in Barrow. The Minerals Management Service has posted no photographs of the public hearings, although perhaps some are available in its archives. As far as the process of public consultation is concerned, only the written transcripts are considered relevant to the process. The photos in Figure 6.7 were

Figure 6.7 Photo-collage of the Iñupiaq Heritage Center

taken in the same room in the Iñupiat Heritage Center a year or so before the hearing, but these are not public hearings. We see a birthday party for a one-year-old boy, a college graduation ceremony, visiting Eskimo dancers at the State Library Conference, and a student art display.

In the documents and in the transcript of the Barrow hearing itself we have seen there is much blending of the discourses of science, energy development, and traditional knowledge as well as other interdiscursivities, but this interdiscursivity is presented largely in the form of print-text statements. In these photographs we also see some of these same blends. For example, the baby's grandfather is a whaler, an artist, and a teacher of carving. His grandmother is a mathematics teacher in the elementary school. His father is a counselor in the high school and a hunter.

While it is almost invisible to the eyes of people who do not live there, the most striking blend, perhaps, is lodged in the room itself and the building that encloses it. The Iñupiat Heritage Center was opened in 1999 after ten years of planning. It both houses permanent installations ranging from traditional whaling to global warming and is used constantly for activities from dances, conferences, and graduations to birthday parties, as shown in Figure 6.7. While the discourse of oil extraction is backgrounded in all of this – there are no exhibitions about the role of the oil industry in shaping traditional and contemporary life in Barrow or on the North Slope – both the North Slope Borough itself and this building are direct outcomes of the fossil fuel industry. The North Slope Borough arose in 1972 as part of a complex political response to Alaska statehood and to the development of the oil field at Prudhoe Bay. Its area of 88,000 square miles makes it the largest municipal government in the world – slightly smaller than the UK, larger than Austria and Hungary combined, about the same size as the Korean Peninsula or the US State of Minnesota – even though there are just 6,290 or so residents.

Now the majority of the residents live in homes of a style imported from the temperate zone of the south that have been adapted to Arctic conditions. Meeting the vision of Eben Hopson for the North Slope Borough that its residents have the same basic services and infrastructure as other Americans, the Iñupiat Heritage Center is a large, centrally heated building with large open spaces that, like the homes and other buildings of Barrow, is enabled both by the burning of fossil fuels (mostly natural gas) as its source of heat but also by the oil-fueled transportation system that has brought these materials to the Arctic Coast of Alaska by plane. As the website of the North Slope Borough notes, the borough is:

> home to resources like oil and gas, which have enabled our people, the Iñupiat, to enter the cash economy of the modern world with self-determination and an enduring respect for the survival skills taught to us by our ancestors.
>
> (www.north-slope.org/nsb/default.htm)

In a sense one could say that the discourse of oil extraction underwrites pretty much all of the infrastructure of the North Slope Borough and of Barrow, including the Iñupiat Heritage Center. This profound underwriting interdiscursivity of the discourse of oil and gas extraction with the support and sustenance of traditional whaling, as well as many other community discourses of schooling, and even religion, is visible wherever one might go in the community.

This interdiscursivity is captured in photos such as those in Figure 6.7. We can compare, then, two views of these interdiscursivities. The first is the view of these discourses and how they relate to each other that we might get by reading the documents of the Beaufort Sea Sales. The second is the view, really just a glimpse, that we get through a photographic collage of events in the community center in Barrow. This shift in modes makes it clear that whatever else might be said about the substance of the proposal to sell oil and gas leases in this particular way at this particular time, it is said against a background of not just dependence but active community support and ratification of the role of the petroleum industry in the development of the community, its political structure, and even its traditional whaling culture.

There is a large and rapidly growing research literature on multimodality covering face-to-face communication, visual images, objects, and the built environment. This example shows that while a linguistic basis for discourse analysis can be very fruitful, it should never be assumed to be showing us the whole picture. The documents of the Beaufort Sea Sale give us a particular view of the process of the sale that includes the texts of the public hearing. But the documents themselves present us with a distinctively text-based view of this process. Such a text-based modality is a view of reality that can be located in the discourses of science, law, and government. Presenting the multiple sale process as a matter of texts produces an eclipsing modality, a version of *realis* that claims that only text does or can present the reality of that sale. This *realis* eclipses all other views of the process that might be achieved by viewing the process through other modes, including images, face-to-face communication, song, or actional experience.

The ways in which a public consultative discourse analysis can make use of multimodal discourse analysis can be summarized with four points:

Modality is conveyed differently within the 'grammar' of each mode.

The modality of a particular mode is not fixed or inherent but varies with the discourse and the communicative purpose.

When communications occur across discourses, the modality (*realis*/*irrealis* status) of communication may become distorted either unwittingly or as a strategy to achieve political ascendancy.

The guiding analytical question is: what's missing? What is absent from the analysis because that knowledge or information is predominantly available in a different mode, and what might we see if it were presented in another way?

PART TWO

Methods and resources for analysing discourse

Editors' introduction
to Part Two

IN PREPARING THIS BOOK we at first resisted the suggestion of including a section on methods for the study of discourse. Discourse analysis, we wanted (and still want) to argue, is not simply a method. Its basic assumptions about the local and emergent construction of meaning and value would be obscured if we incorporated readings (and some do exist) that offered set rules and procedures for discourse analysts to follow. It is important to hold on to this objection. At the same time, studying language as discourse *does* mean adopting a certain perspective on the asking and answering of study questions, on treating language and other types of texts as 'data', on representing language and semiotic material, and on interacting with people treated as 'social actors'. The concept of discourse brings with it an agenda of theoretical issues that are related to how research is and can be done, and these are the themes we want to pick up in this part of the book.

First, we should make it clear that there are some senses of the term 'discourse' that are too abstract to lead to any detailed, direct, empirical procedures for doing discourse analysis. This is the point that James Paul Gee makes when he identifies discourses with a capital 'D', or 'big D Discourses' (Chapter 8), which he describes as abstract cultural models, or sense-making procedures that delineate social categories such as identities, group membership, acceptable modes of conduct, recognizable classes of objects and events. They closely resemble what Michel Foucault has called 'discourses' (Foucault 1966) or 'orders of discourse' (Foucault 1972). This very definition of discourse requires it to be an elusive and veiled phenomenon. It can be contrasted with Gee's 'social languages', or specific ways of using different styles or varieties of language (and, we might add, other modes of meaning-making), which is where (big D) Discourses *are* systematically linked to data – to specific texts, which are potential sites for empirical investigation. As we explained in the general Introduction, we give priority to this sort of discourse analysis in the *Reader*, where engaging in empirical linguistic/textual study leads to better understanding of the dynamics of social life. But this forces us to be as clear as possible about the principles according to which empirical investigation may proceed.

The chapter by Deborah Cameron, Elizabeth Frazer, Penelope Harvey, Ben Rampton and Kay Richardson (Chapter 7) is a wide-ranging and stimulating discussion not only of some practical aspects of linguistic research but also of its theoretical grounding. Cameron et al begin with clear outlines of three general orientations in social research: *positivism*, *relativism* and *realism*. Their arguments lead them to dismiss the positivist orientation absolutely. They say that 'the limits of positivism are severe and restrictive' (p. 136) for the study of language use, even though positivism is widely endorsed in many disciplines as the basis of 'good science', and indeed as the basis of *the* scientific approach. As Cameron and colleagues suggest, studying the local contextualization of meaning is incompatible with a formal, measurement-based, distributional, empiricist orientation to 'language behaviour'. Discourse theory itself rules out certain research methods.

Cameron and colleagues then consider relativist research approaches, and specifically the radical ethnomethodological arguments we met in Part One of the *Reader* about the interactional construction of social reality. Their line is that language research, like their own, which addresses various sorts of social inequality cannot avoid the 'reality' of social structures, structures that do have an existence outside of language and interaction. They are therefore committed to what one might call a 'mild', or 'less-than-radical' social relativism, and they take this forward into their discussion of relationships between researchers and the people they research – and this is the main thrust of their chapter. Cameron et al sketch out three idealized patterns of relationship – *ethical*, *advocacy* and *empowerment* relationships – arguing that the third is the morally and theoretically required option. It should be valuable to bear these ideal types in mind when reading the particular studies of discourse reported in later parts of the *Reader*. At that point, the empowerment stance, whereby people who feature as social actors in research designs are empowered through the research process itself, will probably appear to be not only idealized but unattainable in its full form. We might ask whether the phenomenon called 'academic research' is in fact able to encompass the ideal of 'researching on, for and with' researched populations, as part of a process of empowering them. Cameron and colleagues acknowledge this in their own discussion, but this does not prevent the chapter being a compelling discussion of the moral and sociopolitical framing of research, and of how discourse analysis should position itself as a research practice.

In Chapter 8, James Paul Gee introduces four 'tools of inquiry' or theoretical resources for engaging in discourse analysis: 'social languages', 'Discourses' (with a capital 'D'), 'Conversations' (with a capital 'C') and 'intertextuality'. We have alluded to some of these terms already. Intertextuality, as mentioned in relation to Bakhtin's work, may take the form of a quotation, pastiche or parody, i.e., making explicit or implicit reference to an earlier utterance or a 'pre-text'. Discourses, the central concept taken up by Gee in his chapter, can be characterized broadly as ways through which societies organize themselves. These are ways of being, doing and participating that allow us to enact specific socially relevant roles, and for others to recognize us in those roles. Social languages, different ways of speaking and writing – what Gee has also called 'small d discourses', language-in-use in particular social settings – combine with other ways of acting, beliefs, attitudes, values, tools, objects, times and places, etc., to form Discourses. In other words, Discourses are ways of combining and coordinating social languages with other cultural and material resources – bodies, actions, objects, etc. – in a kind of dance (Gee's metaphor) through which social actors express, or are expected to express, who they are. Finally, social languages and Discourses are sites and vehicles for specific social debates, long-standing and significant themes or ideas that are maintained over long stretches of times and in different public, institutional and private contexts. Gee calls them 'big C' Conversations, for example debates over abortion, smoking and related health risks, war and terrorism, privacy and security, and so on. There are clear echoes here of the critical and constructionist stances of Norman Fairclough (Chapter 5) and Ron Scollon (Chapter 6), and of Deborah Cameron and her colleagues' arguments about social realism.

These grand themes do, however, need to connect to 'on-the-ground' analysis of text. Discourse analysis needs to be a to-ing and fro-ing between more abstract/theoretical and more concrete/textual phenomena, an alternation between what are often called micro and macro levels of analysis. At the micro level we have texts and data which, first, need to be 'captured', held in some way to become available for analysis. For interactional data this will usually involve electronic audio recording or audio-visual recording. We have not included a chapter that reviews and advises on such techniques, but Duranti (1997) is a particularly helpful source. Further detail on methods in sociolinguistics, which overlap with those used in many studies of spoken discourse (e.g., interviewing procedures, sampling of spontaneous uses of language, issues of 'naturalness', and methods in observational research) can be found in Coupland and Jaworski (1997: Chapters 8–11).

In Chapter 9 Wolfram Bublitz discusses two important aspects for our understanding of how stretches of spoken or written discourse 'hang together' so that we recognize them as unified texts and can make sense of their cumulative meaning. *Coherence* is the familiar concept here, which we usually use to describe texts, arguments, conversations, etc., that 'make sense' and have no significantly incompatible meaningful elements. *Cohesion* is then a more technical concept, referring to how the more formal elements of a text, particularly its words and grammatical structures, are woven together in sequence. Bublitz follows Halliday and Hasan in describing five types of cohesive ties, or formal linkages within texts: reference; substitution; ellipsis; conjunction; lexical cohesion (or collocation). He explains that any text that is woven together using these devices is likely to be read or heard to be coherent. In fact, these cohesion devices urge us, as listeners or readers, to *find* coherence in the text. Our search for coherence, moreover, happens even in cases where there are no (or very few) cohesive devices, because (as established in Grice's Cooperative Principle and maxims – see Part One) we anticipate that texts will be coherent and that communicators will intend their communication to be coherent. Taking a more sociocultural view of discourse, Bublitz comments that coherence has recently come to be associated with sense-making procedures, taking into account this collaborative context of text production and the joint negotiation of meaning. Rather than an inherent property of texts, therefore, coherence is viewed as emerging in the process of interpretation or inference. As Bublitz writes, 'it is not texts that cohere but rather people who make texts cohere' (p. 162). And this is an imperfect process, where many personal, social and cultural considerations can intervene.

Chapter 10, by Jenny Thomas, introduces an influential concept of *activity types* first proposed by Steven Levinson (1979) following Wittgenstein's (1958) notion of *language games*. The main concern behind this chapter is how particular uses of language can be said to fall into types, categories, genres or styles. When we use any of these terms, we are recognizing that, for all its fluidity and 'online' constructed character, discourse in interaction does pattern into types, and types that are important for how we understand what discourse achieves. In the example that Thomas considers in her chapter, it is important for a university student and her research supervisor to know whether they are engaged in what we might call 'an academic supervision' or 'a friendly chat'. Thomas is able to show how the type of activity that these two individuals are engaged in is marked in the discourse of their exchanges.

Levinson defines an activity type as 'a fuzzy category whose focal members are goal-defined, socially constituted, bounded, events with *constraints* on participants, settings, and so on, but above all on the kinds of allowable contributions. Paradigm examples would be teaching, a job interview, a jural interrogation, a football game, a task in a workshop, a dinner party and so on' (Levinson 1979: 368). Activity types can be then seen as speech events or contexts in which specific speech acts are realized along the lines proposed in the Ethnography of Speaking (see our general Introduction to the *Reader*). However, both Levinson and Thomas emphasize a more inclusive and dynamic view of activity types that allows to account for stretches of culturally recognizable activities whether or not they are coextensive with speech or indeed whether or not any speech takes place at all. Generally, the notion of activity types bridges the ethnographic approaches (especially Hymes's model of communicative competence) and inferential approaches (especially the Gricean model of conversational inference, see Chapter 3) in emphasizing constraints on possible contributions as well as inferential schemata that aid understanding. In Levinson's terms, activity types 'play a central role in language usage . . . On the one hand they constrain what will count as an allowable contribution to each activity and on the other hand they help to determine how what one says will be "taken" – that is what kinds of inferences will be made from what is said' (Levinson 1979: 393).

The last chapter in this part of the *Reader* discusses another key term in the toolkit of any discourse analyst, and one that relates closely to activity type – *genre*. Many writers would see no significant differences between the concepts of activity type and genre, and it would be a useful exercise to compare the Chapter 10 and Chapter 11 accounts and examples. In Chapter 11 David Machin and Theo Van Leeuwen provide a particularly clear and helpful account of genre, first by contrasting 'discourse' – in the specific sense what a text is 'about' (cf. Gee's Discourses and Conversations) – and genre. In their definition genre refers to a type of text that has specific functions and is aimed at achieving particular communicative goals, e.g., persuasion, instruction, entertainment or maintaining relationships between people.

Thus, genres 'do something' for the producers of texts and their addressees; they allow communicators to take specific subject positions, such as 'expert', 'educator' or 'entertainer', and to position others, say as 'novice', 'pupil' or 'spectator'.

Genres are organized into stages or moves. In the most basic sense, all texts have a beginning, middle and end, but Machin and Van Leeuwen illustrate this underlying genre structure with reference to William Labov's well-known template of narrative components or stages: *abstract, orientation, complication, evaluation, resolution* and *coda* (see our general Introduction and Chapter 12). They also introduce two non-linear features of (written) genres – *information structure* and *modality* (see Scollon, Chapter 6). As noted by Hanks (1987), a speaker or writer may endeavour to adhere closely to conventional genre expectations, or s/he may deviate from them in a variety of ways. For example, stylistic features associated with different genres may be fused together, or framing devices and contextualization cues may be manipulated to create novel and emergent forms and meanings.

Machin and Van Leeuwen illustrate just some of these processes by developing an analysis of several articles relating to women's work in various national editions of *Cosmopolitan* magazine. Where 'women's work' can be taken as the dominant discourse of the articles, Machin and Van Leeuwen illustrate how manipulation of genre conventions across different editions, e.g., low naturalistic modality of images depicting 'women at work', positions women as glamorous but not fully in control of the work environment. Or again, the 'hot tips' problem–solution genre for dealing with 'women's work problems' offers lists of authoritative solutions in the form of unordered 'tips' of the sort we find in magazine articles on such lifestyle issues as 'gossip' or 'embarrassment'. The 'hot tips' problem–solution genre for dealing with work problems has the potential to gloss over a number of serious, structural problems in the job market, such as job cuts or inadequate provision of child care. This genre offers 'solutions' that sound authoritative but are also one-sided and monologic. By eschewing a more heteroglossic or dialogic style, the genre establishes a hegemonic view of women's work based on a set of implicit assumptions and adherence to a 'common ground' (cf. Fairclough, Chapter 5). To use Ron Scollon's terminology in Chapter 6, the problem–solution genre in the *Cosmopolitan* magazine *eclipses* alternative ideologies of gender and work. Thus, it is an essential task of discourse analysis to ask: what are we not seeing or hearing or otherwise perceiving in the documents under analysis?

References

Coupland, N. and Jaworski, A. (eds.) (1997) *Sociolinguistics: A Reader and Coursebook*, London: Macmillan.

Duranti, A. (1997) *Linguistic Anthropology*, Cambridge: Cambridge University Press.

Foucault, M. (1966) *The Order of Things: An Archaeology of Human Sciences,* New York: Random House.

—— (1972) *The Archaeology of Knowledge*, New York: Pantheon.

Hanks, W. (1987) 'Discourse genres in a theory of practice', *American Ethnologist* 14: 666–92.

Levinson, S.C. (1979) 'Activity types and language', *Linguistics* 17: 365–99.

Wittgenstein, L. (1958) *Philosophical Investigations*, Oxford: Blackwell.

Chapter 7

Deborah Cameron, Elizabeth Frazer, Penelope Harvey, Ben Rampton and Kay Richardson

ETHICS, ADVOCACY AND EMPOWERMENT

A S MANY COMMENTATORS HAVE pointed out – perhaps the fullest and most insistent statement can be found in the various works of Michel Foucault – social science is not and has never been a neutral enquiry into human behaviour and institutions. It is strongly implicated in the project of social control, whether by the state or by other agencies that ultimately serve the interests of a dominant group.

As a very obvious illustration, we may notice what an enormous proportion of all social research is conducted on populations of relatively powerless people. It is factory workers, criminals and juvenile delinquents as opposed to their bosses or victims who fill the pages of social science texts. Doubtless this is partly because members of powerful elites often refuse to submit to the probing of researchers – their time is valuable, their privacy jealously guarded. But it is also because a lot of social research is directly inspired by the need to understand and sometimes even to contain 'social problems' – the threats (such as crime or industrial disruption) that powerless groups are felt to pose to powerful ones.

Foucault observes, putting a new spin on the familiar saying 'knowledge is power', that the citizens of modern democracies are controlled less by naked violence or the economic power of the boss and the landlord than by the pronouncements of expert discourse, organised in what he calls 'regimes of truth' – sets of understandings which legitimate particular social attitudes and practices. Evidently, programmes of social scientific research on such subjects as 'criminality' or 'sexual deviance' or 'teenage motherhood' have contributed to 'regimes of truth'. In studying and presenting the 'facts' about these phenomena, they have both helped to construct particular people ('criminals', 'deviants', 'teenage mothers') as targets for social control and influenced the form the control itself will take.

Source: Deborah Cameron, Elizabeth Frazer, Penelope Harvey, M.B.H. Rampton and Kay Richardson, *Researching Language: Issues of Power and Method*, London: Routledge, 1992.

We could consider, for example, the medico-legal discourses interpreting but also, crucially, regulating the behaviour of women. Recently, some acts of aggression by women have been explained as a consequence of hormonal disturbance ('pre-menstrual syndrome'); conversely, some instances of women drinking while pregnant have been explained (and indeed punished) as acts of conscious negligence (since they may lead to problems for the newborn, most seriously 'foetal alcohol syndrome'). There are two things to note here. One is that although the categories 'pre-menstrual syndrome' and 'foetal alcohol syndrome' are presented as objective and value-free scientific discoveries, it is clear that these new pieces of knowledge function as forms of social control over women. The other is that although they may seem to contradict one another (since one makes women less responsible for damage they cause while the other makes them more responsible than in the past) they nevertheless complement each other at a higher level of analysis: they fit and reinforce the logic of that broader control discourse feminists call 'sexism'.

This interplay of power and knowledge (Foucaultians write 'power/knowledge') and the historical link between social science and social control pose obvious dilemmas for the radical social scientist. We have to recognise that we are inevitably part of a tradition of knowledge, one which we may criticise, certainly, but which we cannot entirely escape. Even the most iconoclastic scholar is always in dialogue with those who went before. Our own disciplines, anthropology, sociology and linguistics, have problematic histories. Scholars of language and society may be less powerful than lawyers and doctors, but we have certainly contributed to 'regimes of truth' and regulatory practices which are hard to defend.

. . .

It would be quite irresponsible to deny the real effects of research in our disciplines or to play down the contribution they have made to maintaining and legitimating unequal social arrangements. And in this light, our hopes of 'empowering' the subjects of linguistic research might start to look at best naïve. Perhaps it would be better to stop doing social science research altogether?

The questions of how 'empowering' social research can hope to be, and whether in the end certain kinds of research should be undertaken at all are certainly serious ones. . . . For us, though, the starting point was that we had done research in situations of inequality, and we felt a need to reappraise critically the ways we had gone about it, making explicit issues of method that were not necessarily foregrounded at the time.

Linguistic interaction is social interaction, and therefore the study of language use is fundamental to our understanding of how oppressive social relations are created and reproduced. If, as we believed, the politics of language is real politics, it is at least worth considering whether knowledge about it could be framed in a way that research subjects themselves would find relevant and useful.

Theoretical issues: the status of academic knowledge

Our early discussions of how research on language might empower its subjects raised general theoretical questions in two main areas: one was the status of academic knowledge itself and the other concerned the relation between researcher and researched in the making of knowledge. . . .

We will go on to distinguish a number of approaches or 'isms', which differ in their conceptions of reality, the object of knowledge, and therefore in their opinions about how it can be described and explained. Initially we will distinguish two broad categories among scientists and social scientists: those who subscribe to *positivism* and those who do not. Among the non-positivists we will further distinguish between *relativist* and *realist* approaches.

It must be acknowledged that positivism, relativism and realism are complex positions whose definition is contested rather than fixed. Our presentation of them will simplify the picture by describing a sort of 'ideal-typical' position rather than the nuances of any specific theorist's actual position. . . .

Positivism

Positivism entails a commitment to study of the frequency, distribution and patterning of observable phenomena, and the description, in law-like general terms, of the relationship between those phenomena. . . . Positivism is strongly averse to postulating the reality of entities, forces or mechanisms that human observers cannot see. Such things are myths, mere theoretical inventions which enable us to predict and explain observable events but cannot be seen as the stuff of reality itself. At the same time, positivism is strongly committed to the obviousness and unproblematic status of what we *can* observe: observations procured in a scientific manner have the status of value-free facts.

This distinction between fact and value is important. Though confident that there are methods which can provide a clear view of reality, positivism is very much aware of the potential for observation to be value laden, especially in the social as opposed to natural sciences. Indeed, for many it is a mark of 'pseudoscientific' theories like Marxism and psychoanalysis that their adherents will see what they want, or what the theory dictates they should; such theories are shot through with political bias. Nor can you set up a controlled experiment to test Marx's hypothesis that the class in society which owns the means of production will also have control of political and cultural institutions by virtue of their economic dominance. It might well be true that there are no known counterexamples to Marx's statement, but we still cannot say that the statement itself holds up. It would be difficult to set out to falsify this statement, as positivism requires, because so many variables are involved and there seems to be no way of isolating and manipulating the relevant one. Because it does not provide us with hypotheses that can be in principle falsified, Marxism for strict positivists is a pseudoscience rather than a science.

. . .

Challenges to positivism

Positivism is the 'hegemonic' position, the one scientists have generally been taught to regard not as a scientific method but as *the* scientific method. That is why we have grouped alternative positions as 'challenges to positivism': however different they may be from one another, they are obliged to define themselves first and foremost in opposition to positivism, the dominant 'common sense' of modern science. As this section makes clear, though, the two main challenges we identify – relativism and realism – are by no means 'the same thing'.

Relativism

Relativism does not recognise the observer's paradox (see p. 135) as a problem because relativism does not recognise the fact/value distinction. Reality for a relativist is not a fixed entity independent of our perceptions of it. Our perceptions in turn depend on (are relative to) the concepts and theories we are working with whenever we observe. We invariably have some preconceived notion of what is there to be seen, and it affects what we actually see. Thus someone training as a doctor, say, has to learn to see in a different way: the 'reality' she sees in a chest X-ray is different from what she saw before she did her training, and different again from what a traditional healer from a non-allopathic perspective would see. The history of ideas and the sociology of knowledge provide many examples of scientific theories having close links with the oral and cultural values of their time and place.

Dale Spender (1980) cites a good example of how language plays a part in linking scientific theories with social assumptions. Psychologists investigating people's visual perception discovered two ways of responding to a figure on a ground: abstracting it from its context (the ground) or relating it to its context. These responses were labelled 'field independence' and 'field dependence' respectively. They were also associated with the behaviour of male subjects ('field independence') and female subjects ('field dependence'). Spender's point is that it is not a coincidence that the male-associated strategy was given a label implying a more positive evaluation – 'independence' is conceived as both a positive and a male characteristic. The female tendency could have been called 'context awareness' and the male tendency 'context unawareness'. That this alternative did not occur to the scientist has nothing to do with the nature of his findings about visual perception, and everything to do with his social preconceptions (i.e. he took it for granted that the positive term must be accorded to what men do).

Relativism in the social sciences particularly addresses the role of language in shaping an actor's social reality, as opposed to merely reflecting or expressing some pre-existent, non-linguistic order. The 'Sapir-Whorf hypothesis of linguistic relativity' has inspired a great deal of discussion on the language dependence of social reality. As Sapir argued:

> The fact of the matter is that the 'real world' is to a large extent unconsciously built up on the language habits of the group. No two languages are ever sufficiently similar to be considered as representing the same social reality. The worlds in which different societies live are different worlds, not the same world with different labels attached.
>
> (Sapir 1949: 162)

Subsequently, many social theorists and philosophers in the phenomenological tradition have stressed that social order exists *only* as a product of human activity.

For some, this can even mean that there is no social reality, no facts, other than the actor's subjective experience.

Ethnomethodology [see Chapters 14–17] is a development of this tradition which illustrates both the strengths and the weaknesses of relativism. Ethnomethodology takes very seriously indeed the actor's subjective experience of a situation, to the point of denying any other reality. In particular, it is hostile to the Marxist notion of historical forces determining actors' lives, and to the structuralist postulation of social structures which coerce people into social roles and hierarchical relations. In this view, a social researcher is just like anyone else, an actor experiencing a situation: all research can really ever amount to is the reporting of one's experience. Clearly, this is an extreme anti-positivist position.

The problem here, though, is that in their zeal to emphasise the actor's own role in constructing a social world, ethnomethodologists have left us with a picture which implies that social actors could in principle construct the world exactly as they pleased. More precisely, they have given no account of why we cannot do this.

What makes this problematic? Very crudely, you might say it is a variant of not being able to see the wood for the trees. Indeed, since they deny the existence of higher-level social structures or social forces that the individual actor is unaware of, ethnomethodologists must be sceptical of the idea that the trees in any sense add up to a wood. For them there is no 'big picture' into which the study of some particular phenomenon like a tree must be fitted.

We can put the point a bit more technically. Ethnomethodology is one of those approaches that emphasise the 'micro' level of social organisation – a single interaction between two people, say – over the 'macro' level of institutions and classes, and so forth. In contrast to positivists, who conceive of explanation as stating general statistical regularities, ethnomethodologists give explanatory weight to the subject's account of herself. This means that if a woman says something like 'being a woman has made no difference to my life', the ethnomethodologist has no theoretical warrant for invoking the macro-category of gender. Here the ethnomethodologist is reacting against the Marxist idea of 'false consciousness', which implies that people are entirely deluded about the circumstances of their lives and that nothing a subject says should be taken at face value. Ethnomethodologists find this too deterministic (as well as condescending). For them, the way things are is the way subjects say they are.

For us, though we do not necessarily embrace the idea of false consciousness, this absolute faith in the subject's own account poses very serious problems. We do want to pay attention to actors' own understandings, but do we want to give them the last word in every case? We would prefer to say that whatever they say, people are not completely free to do what they want to do, be what they want to be. For we would want to claim that on the contrary, social actors are schooled and corrected, they come under pressure to take up certain roles and occupations, they are born into relations of class, race, gender, generation, they occupy specific cultural positions, negotiate particular value systems, conceptual frameworks and social institutions, have more or less wealth and opportunity . . . and so on, *ad infinitum*. As Berger and Luckmann say (1967), social reality may be a human product but it faces humans like a coercive force. It is a grave weakness of ethnomethodology, and more generally of relativism, that it offers no convincing account of that fact.

This critical view of relativism brings us closer to a 'realist' position, arguing that there is indeed a social reality for actors and researchers to study and understand.

Realism

Realism, like relativism, accepts the theory ladenness of observation but not the theory-dependent nature of reality itself. Realism posits a reality existing outside and independent of the observer, but also stresses that this reality may be impossible to observe or to describe definitively.

Realism parts company with positivism on the question of reality being only what we can observe. Neither the social order nor gravity can be observed, and therefore in positivist terms neither is 'real' (strictly speaking, only the observable effects of a gravitational field are real; the gravitational field for positivists is an artificial theoretical construct). Realism, as its name suggests, is committed to the notion that things like gravity *are* real, though at any time an observer might describe them incorrectly and so give a misleading or mistaken account of their real character. It follows, too, that for realism explanation is more than just stating regularities or predicting outcomes (the positivist model). When a realist describes the workings of gravity she believes she is giving an account of how the world works and not just stating what would be likely to happen if you conducted a particular operation in the world.

In the philosophical project of deciding what counts as 'real' – atoms and molecules, tables and chairs, rainbows, societies, classes and genders – there is still everything to play for. The area is full of ambiguities: for example, does the Sapir-Whorf hypothesis imply that reality itself is linguistically determined or that actors' experience of it, their 'mental reality', is? Commentators have expressed differing opinions on this. And does a 'mental reality' count as 'real'? These are hard questions, and philosophers have not resolved them.

What is hard to dispute, though, is the proposition that whatever the ultimate status of 'social reality', it is, partly at least, a *human* product. The continuing existence of such phenomena as social rules, behavioural rituals, institutions, e.g., marriage and government, is dependent on human action. Human action maintains these phenomena, and they are therefore susceptible to change and transformation by human beings.

The study of social reality

The challenges to positivism we have just considered have implications for the study of social reality. For if the experience of social actors is language and culture dependent, and if we grant that there are many languages and cultures, a number of problems for social science present themselves at once.

To begin with, and whether or not she believes it has an independent objective reality, the social researcher cannot take it for granted that she knows or recognises exactly what a social phenomenon or event is when she sees it. A woman turning over the earth in a flower bed with a spade might immediately be understood by an observer to be 'digging the garden'. In fact, though, the digger's own understandings and intentions would be an important part of the reality – she might not be gardening, but preparing to bury the budgie. Even if she were gardening, the observer who simply recorded this might miss some very important aspects of the scene: the gardener might be letting off steam after a row with her children, relaxing after a hard day at the office or worshipping the Goddess Earth by cultivating her. These meanings are properly a part of the reality being observed; the question 'what is going on here' cannot be answered without reference to the agent's own understanding of what she is doing.

If there are problems discovering exactly what is going on in one's own backyard, so to speak, if the objective and non-interactive observation assumed by positivism as the ideal is impossible or useless even so close to home, the problems for social scientists who study cultures and social groups not their own are even more acute. There are two main problems: the existence of differing and shifting conceptual frameworks, and the difficulty of translating from one to another. Can the researcher situate herself within the conceptual framework of the researched and thereby understand what is going on? And can she give an account of this 'otherness' for an audience of readers who can relate to her (original) conceptual framework but not the framework of her subjects? We might be alive to the dangers of ethnocentrism, but in the end, can anything be done about it?

Some influential philosophers have replied in the negative, arguing that there are no universally valid standards by which to judge the rightness or wrongness of belief systems; conceptual frameworks cannot validly be compared. This is a strongly relativist position. It has also been strongly opposed by those who argue that there is in fact a fundamental level of shared human experience and concepts. We are all sentient, rational beings who inhabit a world of solid objects: we must all have an understanding of the continued existence of objects in time and space, of cause and effect, and so on. Given such a 'bridgehead' between different human societies it is not so hard to see how we come to understand that someone else can have a different idea from ours of what causes rain, for instance. In other words, it is at least arguable that even radically unfamiliar conceptual frameworks can come to make sense to the observer.

But whether or not one holds an extreme relativist position, this debate highlights the problem that social reality is not just transparent to the observer. The social scientist must validate her understandings and interpretations with the community of researchers of which she is part (thus again raising the issue of theory-dependence in social scientific observation), but also and crucially she must validate her observations with the actors being observed. Asking what people are doing and why, as social scientists must, makes interaction with them inescapable.

You cannot validate a particular observation simply by repeating it. However many questionnaires you give out or interviews you conduct, it is impossible to be sure that all respondents who gave the 'same' answer meant the same thing by it, and that their responses are a direct representation of the truth. Furthermore, since persons are social actors the researcher cannot treat descriptions of their behaviour as chains of cause and effect, in the way one might describe the motion of billiard balls. To be sure, there are regularities to be discovered in the social world, but they are there because of people's habits, intentions, understandings and learning. Social scientists have to be concerned with what produces regularities as well as with the regularities themselves; and once again, this implies interaction with the researched.

. . .

The relations between researcher and researched: ethics, advocacy and empowerment

. . .

In this section we will distinguish three positions researchers may take up *vis-à-vis* their subjects: ethics, advocacy and empowerment. We will argue that ethics and advocacy are linked to positivist assumptions, while the more radical project of empowerment comes out of relativist and realist understandings.

Ethics

The potentially exploitative and damaging effects of being researched on have long been recognised by social scientists. We touched earlier on one important source of potential damage, the way social science is used within regimes of truth, or directly for social control. Even when you do not work for a government agency, and whatever your own political views, it is always necessary to think long and hard about the uses to which findings might be put, or the effects they might have contrary to the interests of subjects. If a researcher observes, for example, that the average attainment of some group of schoolchildren is less than might be anticipated, that can colour the expectations of teachers and contribute to the repetition of under-achievement by the same group in future. That might be very far from what the researcher intended, but an ethically aware social scientist will see the possible dangers and perhaps try to forestall them.

A second worry is that the researcher might exploit subjects during the research process. One controversy here concerns the acceptability of covert research, in which subjects cannot give full informed consent because the researcher is deliberately misleading them as to the nature and purpose of the research, or perhaps concealing the fact that research is going on at all. For instance, a great deal of research in social psychology relies on subjects thinking the experimenter is looking for one thing when she is really looking for something else. Some sociological studies have involved the researcher 'passing' as a community member; and some sociolinguists have used the technique of getting subjects to recount traumatic experiences because the surge of powerful emotions stops them from being self-conscious about their pronunciation, circumventing the observer's paradox. In cases like these one wonders how far the end justifies the means. Even when the deception is on the face of it innocuous, it raises ethical problems because it is a deception.

. . .

Apart from preventing the abuse of subjects, an ethical researcher will be advised to ensure that their privacy is protected (e.g. by the use of pseudonyms when the findings are published) and where appropriate to compensate them for inconvenience or discomfort (whether in cash, as commonly happens in psychology, or in gifts, as from anthropologists to a community, or in services rendered, as with many sociolinguistic studies).

In ethical research, then, there is a wholly proper concern to minimise damage and offset inconvenience to the researched, and to acknowledge their contribution (even where they are unpaid, they will probably be thanked in the researcher's book or article). But the underlying model is one of 'research *on*' social subjects. Human subjects deserve special ethical consideration, but they no more set the researcher's agenda than the bottle of sulphuric acid sets the chemist's agenda. This position follows, of course, from the positivist emphasis on distance to avoid interference or bias. However, it is also open to positivistically inclined researchers to go beyond this idea of ethics and make themselves more directly accountable to the researched. They may move, in other words, to an *advocacy* position.

Advocacy

What we are calling the 'advocacy position' is characerised by a commitment on the part of the researcher not just to do research *on* subjects but research *on and for* subjects. Such a commitment formalises what is actually a rather common development in field situations, where a researcher is asked to use her skills or her authority as an 'expert' to defend subjects' interests, getting involved in their campaigns for healthcare or education, cultural autonomy or political and land rights, and speaking on their behalf.

. . .

Labov (1982) suggests two principles. One is the principle of 'error correction': if we as researchers know that people hold erroneous views on something, we have a responsibility to attempt to correct those views. (This, incidentally, is a clear example of 'commitment' and 'objectivity' serving the exact same ends; Labov believes in or is committed to putting truth in place of error.) The second principle is that of 'the debt incurred'. When a community has enabled linguists to gain important knowledge, the linguist incurs a debt which must be repaid by using the said knowledge on the community's behalf when they need it. This is clearly an advocacy position.

Labov further stresses that the advocate serves the community, and that political direction is the community's responsibility. As an outsider, Labov accepts – and counsels others to accept – an auxiliary role. 'They [linguists] don't claim for themselves the right to speak for the community or make the decision on what forms of language should be used' (Labov 1982: 186).

. . . The important point we want to make is that while Labov's position is in some ways extremely radical, it is so *within a positivist framework*. That framework sets limits on Labov's advocacy, and without underestimating the usefulness and sincerity of what he says and what he has done, we have to add that in our view the limits of positivism are severe and restrictive.

Labov's positivism is clearly visible in his uneasy juxtaposition of 'objectivity' and 'commitment'. Obviously he is worried that a researcher's advocacy might undermine the validity of her findings (the 'bias' or 'pseudoscience' problem). He gets around the problem by claiming that [in the specific case of the Ann Arbor 'Black English' trial], the one reinforced or enhanced the other. It was the work of African

American linguists, many motivated at least partly by social and political considerations, that resolved the disagreements, anomalies, distortions and errors of previous work on 'Black English'. The field became better, more objective and more scientific as a result of these linguists' commitment.

This is a powerful and effective argument if one is inclined to place emphasis on notions of factual truth, error, bias, etc. – in other words, it is a positivistic argument. For a non-positivist it concedes too much – the absolute fact/value distinction for example, and the notion that there is one true account that we will ultimately be able to agree on. . . .

Empowerment

So far we have spoken of 'empowerment' and 'empowering research' as if the meaning of those expressions were self-evident. It will surprise no one if we now admit that they are not transparent or straightforward terms. As soon as we have dealt with the positivist objection that 'empowering research' is biased and invalid, we are likely to face more sophisticated questions from more radical quarters, in particular, 'what do you mean by power and what is empowerment?', followed swiftly by 'and how do you know who needs or wants to be "empowered"?' . . .

Our own position on power draws on both Foucaultian and non-Foucaultian understandings. We do treat power metaphorically as a property which some people in some contexts can have more of than others – that is, we cannot follow Foucault all the way in his rejection of the 'economic' metaphor. On the other hand we follow him in understanding it as a multiple relation (not something that has a single source, as in Marxism or Maoism); in emphasising its connection with knowledge and 'regimes of truth'; and in recognising the links between power and resistance.

Our decision to retain some notion of people or groups being more or less powerful exposes us to a further challenge, however. A sceptic might well ask how the would-be empowering researcher recognises who has more and who has less power: are we implying that the powerful and the powerless are recognisable to researchers as the poor and the wealthy are recognisable to economists? Obviously, if we were Marxists or Maoists who took economic ownership or gun-holding as straightforward indicators of power we could answer 'yes' to the sceptic's question. Since we find these views simplistic we are obliged to answer more thoughtfully. For if the 'real' centre of power is impossible to locate and we cannot identify who has power and who has not, how can we talk blithely about 'empowering research' as if it were easy to see where power lies and to alter its distribution?

We think this question lends weight to our argument that people's own definitions and experiences have to be considered. But consulting those involved, though it tells us something about how they perceive the question of power, does not automatically solve the problem: once again, we encounter the issue we discussed in relation to ethnomethodology, whether the actor's subjective account is the ultimate or only truth. Is, say, the happy slave's account of her experience the final account of it? To that we have to respond that the spectre of moral relativism is a frightening one. We would not want to be in a position where we could not assert, for instance, that slavery is wrong, or that extremes of wealth and poverty are unjust and undesirable.

The sceptic who thinks our notion of power simplistic, and challenges us to identify these 'powerless' people whom we propose to empower, has perhaps oversimplified the notion of empowerment. We must return here to the principle that power is not monolithic – the population does not divide neatly into two groups, the powerful and the powerless – from which it follows that 'empowering' cannot be a simple matter of transferring power from one group to the other, or giving people power when before they had none. Precisely because power operates across so many social divisions, any individual must have a complex and multiple identity: the person becomes an intricate mosaic of differing power potentials in different social relations. And we should not forget a further complication, that those who are dominated in particular social relations can and do develop powerful oppositional discourses of resistance – feminism, Black power, gay pride, for example – to which, again, people respond in complex ways. Importantly, though, the extent to which oppositional discourses and groupings are organised or alternative meanings generated varies: some groups are more cohesive and more effective in resistance than others. . . .

Empowering research

. . .

We have characterised 'ethical research' as *research on* and 'advocacy research' as *research on and for*. We understand 'empowering research' as *research on, for and with*. One of the things we take that additional 'with' to imply is the use of interactive or dialogic research methods, as opposed to the distancing or objectifying strategies positivists are constrained to use. It is the centrality of interaction 'with' the researched that enables research to be empowering in our sense; though we understand this as a necessary rather than a sufficient condition.

We should also point out that we do not think of empowerment as an absolute requirement on all research projects. There are instances where one would not wish to empower research subjects: though arguably there is political value in researching on powerful groups, such an enterprise might well be one instance where 'research on' would be the more appropriate model. But if we are going to raise the possibility of 'research on, for and with' as an appropriate goal in some contexts, we must also acknowledge that the standards and constraints of positivist 'research on' – objectivity, disinterestedness, non-interaction – will not be appropriate in those contexts. This raises the question: what alternative standards would be appropriate?

Whatever standards we propose at this stage can only be provisional: much more discussion is needed. . . .

The three main issues we will take up in this provisional way are (a) the use of interactive methods; (b) the importance of subjects' own agendas; and (c) the question of 'feedback' and sharing knowledge. On each of these points we will begin with a programmatic statement and then pose various questions in relation to it.

(a)   'Persons are not objects and should not be treated as objects.'
      The point of this statement is not one that needs to be laboured, since we believe most researchers would find it wholly uncontentious that persons are not

objects, and are entitled to respectful treatment. What is more contentious is how strictly we define 'treating persons as objects', and whether if we make the definition a strict one we can avoid objectification and still do good ('valid') research.

We have raised the question of whether 'ethical research' permits methods (e.g., concealment of the researcher's purpose) that might be regarded as objectifying. Indeed, we have asked whether non-interactive methods are by definition objectifying, and thus inappropriate for empowering research. If empowering research is research done 'with' subjects as well as 'on' them it must seek their active co-operation, which requires disclosure of the researcher's goals, assumptions and procedures.

On the question of whether this kind of openness undermines the quality or validity of the research, it will already be clear what we are suggesting. We have devoted a great deal of space in this chapter to the argument that interaction *enhances* our understanding of what we observe, while the claims made for non-interaction as a guarantee of objectivity and validity are philosophically naïve.

The question before us, then, is how we can make our research methods more open, interactive and dialogic. This is not a simple matter, particularly in situations of inequality.

(b) 'Subjects have their own agendas and research should try to address them.'
One of the ways in which researchers are powerful is that they set the agenda for any given project: what it will be about, what activities it will involve, and so on. But from our insistence that 'persons are not objects' it obviously follows that researched persons may have agendas of their own, things they would like the researcher to address. If we are researching 'with' them as well as 'on and for' them, do we have a responsibility to acknowledge their agendas and deal with them in addition to our own?

This might involve only fairly minor adjustments to research procedures: making it clear, for instance, that asking questions and introducing topics is not the sole prerogative of the researcher. While traditional handbooks for positivist research warn against addressing questions subjects might ask, interactive methods oblige the researcher not only to listen but also, if called upon, to respond. But making space for subjects' agendas might mean rather more than this. It might mean allowing the researched to select focus for joint work, or serving as a resource or facilitator for research they undertake themselves. . . .

Activities that are 'added on' in order to meet subjects' needs may turn out to generate new insights into the activities the researcher defined: in other words, 'our' agenda and 'theirs' may sometimes intertwine.

(c) 'If knowledge is worth having, it is worth sharing.'
This is perhaps the most complicated of the issues we are raising here. Is it, or should it be, part of the researcher's brief to 'empower' people in an educational sense, by giving them access to expert knowledge, including the knowledge a research project itself has generated?

First, let us backtrack: what is this 'expert knowledge'? For, to a very substantial degree, social researchers' knowledge is and must be constructed out of subjects' own knowledge; if this is made explicit (as arguably it should be) the effect might be to demystify 'expert knowledge' as a category. Such a blurring of the boundary between what 'we' know and what 'they' know, brought about by making explicit the processes whereby knowledge acquires its authority and prestige, might itself be empowering. But it does complicate the picture of 'sharing knowledge', suggesting that there are different sorts of knowledge to be shared and different ways of sharing.

. . .

Most research, even when it is precisely concerned with finding out what subjects think, does not provide opportunities for reinterpretation [allowing informants to gain new perspective on what they know or believe]. Indeed, for the positivist researcher such intervention would be anathema, since a cardinal rule is to leave your subjects' beliefs as far as possible undistributed. Needless to say, we are not greatly upset if our practice separates us from positivist researchers. But it might also seem to separate us from the many researchers who, sincerely and properly concerned about the imbalance of power between themselves and their subjects, follow the apparently very different practice of 'letting subjects speak for themselves'. There is a convention in some contemporary research of reproducing subjects' own words on the page unmediated by authorial comment, in order to give the subject a voice of her own and validate her opinions. This *non*-intervention might also be claimed as an empowering move.

In assessing these two strategies, intervention versus 'giving a voice', one might want to distinguish between what is empowering in the context of *representing* subjects (that is, in a text such as an article, a book or a film) and what is empowering in the context of *interacting* with them. In the former context we see that there may be value in non-intervention (though see Bhavnani (1988), who criticises some instances for perpetuating stereotypes and reproducing disinformation). But in the latter context we have our doubts whether subjects are most empowered by a principled refusal to intervene in their discourse. Discourse after all is a historical construct: whether or not intervention changes someone's opinions, it is arguable that they gain by knowing where those opinions have 'come from' and how they might be challenged or more powerfully formulated. Clearly, it is a principle we use when we teach: not only do we engage with students' views, we engage with them *critically*. The question we are raising, then, is whether there is some merit in extending that practice from the context of the classroom to the context of research.

Even if we decide to answer this question in the affirmative, other questions remain as to how knowledge can be shared, and what the effects might be. There is also the question of how to integrate educational or knowledge-sharing aims into the broader scope of a researched project. . . .

References

Berger, P. and Luckmann, T. (1967) *The Social Construction of Reality*, Harmondsworth: Penguin.

Bhavnani, K. (1988) 'Empowerment and social research: some comments', *Text* 81(2): 41–50.

Labov, W. (1982) 'Objectivity and commitment in linguistic science: the case of the Black English trial in Ann Arbor', *Language in Society* 11: 165–201.

Sapir, E. (1949) *Selected Writings in Language, Culture and Personality*, Mandelbaum, D. (ed.) Berkeley, CA: University of California Press.

Spender, D. (1980) *Man Made Language*, London: Routledge & Kegan Paul.

Chapter 8

James Paul Gee

TOOLS OF INQUIRY AND DISCOURSES

Tools

THE TOOLS OF INQUIRY I INTRODUCE in this chapter are primarily relevant to how people build identities and activities and recognize identities and activities that others are building around them. In summary, they are:

Social languages: People use different styles or varieties of language for different purposes. They use different varieties of language to enact and recognize different identities in different settings. I will call each such variety a 'social language.' For example, a student studying hornworms might say in everyday language, a variety of language often referred to as 'vernacular language,' something like 'Hornworms sure vary a lot in how big they get,' while the same student might use a more technical variety of language to say or write something like 'Hornworm growth exhibits a significant amount of variation.' The vernacular version is one social language and the technical version is another. Investigating how different social languages are used and mixed is one tool of inquiry for engaging in discourse analysis.

Discourses: People build identities and activities not just through language but by using language together with other 'stuff' that isn't language. If you want to get recognized as a street-gang member of a certain sort you have to speak in the 'right' way, but you have to act and dress in the 'right' way, as well. You also have to engage (or, at least, behave as if you are engaging) in characteristic ways of thinking, acting, interacting, valuing, feeling, and believing. You also have to use or be able to use various sorts of symbols (e.g., graffiti), tools (e.g., a weapon), and objects (e.g., street corners) in the 'right' places and at the 'right' times. You can't just 'talk the talk,' you have to 'walk the walk' as well. The same is true of doing/being a corporate lawyer, marine sergeant, radical feminist, or a regular at the local bar. One and the same person might talk, act, and interact in such a way as to get recognized as a 'street-gang member' in one context and, in another context, talk, act, and interact in quite different ways so as to get recognized as a 'gifted student.' And, indeed, these two identities, and their concomitant ways of talking, acting, and interacting, may well conflict with each other in some circumstances (in which different people expect different identities from the person), as well as in the person's own mind. I use the term 'Discourse,' with a capital 'D,' for ways of combining and integrating language, actions, interactions, ways of thinking, believing, valuing, and using various symbols, tools, and objects to enact a particular sort of socially recognizable identity. Thinking about the different Discourses a piece of language is part of is another tool for engaging in discourse analysis.

Intertextuality: When we speak or write, our words often allude to or relate to, in some fashion, other 'texts' or certain types of 'texts,' where by 'texts' I mean words that other people have said or written. For example, *Wired* magazine once printed a story with this title: 'The new face of the silicon age: tech jobs are fleeing to India faster than ever. You got a problem with that?' (February 2004). The sentence 'You got a problem with that?' reminds us of 'tough guy' talk we have heard in many movies or read in books. It intrigues us that such talk occurs written in a magazine devoted to technology. This sort of cross-reference to another text or type of text I will refer to as 'inter-textuality.' In instances of intertextuality, one spoken or written text alludes to, quotes, or otherwise relates to, another one.

Conversations: Sometimes when we talk or write, our words don't just allude or relate to someone else's words (as in the case of intertextuality), but to themes, debates, or motifs that have been the focus of much talk and writing in some social group with which we are familiar or in our society as a whole. These themes, debates, or motifs play a role in how language is interpreted. For example, how do you know that when I tell you 'Smoking is associated with health problems' that I mean to say that smoking leads to health problems and not that health problems lead people to smoke because, say, their health problems are making them nervous and they are smoking in order to calm down (the most probable meaning for a sentence like 'Writing a will is associated with health problems')? You know this because you are well aware of the long-running discussions in our society over the ill-effects of smoking. I refer to all the talk and writing that has gone on in a specific social group or in society at large around a major theme, debate, or motif as a 'Conversation' with a capital 'C,' using the term metaphorically, of course. Most of us today are aware of the societal Conversations going on around us about issues such as abortion, creationism, global warming, terrorism, and so on and so forth. To know about these Conversations is to know about the various sides one can take in debates about these issues and what sorts of people are usually on each side. As members of various social groups and of our society as a whole, we are privy to (know something about) a great many such Conversations. People interpret our language – and we interpret theirs – partly through such knowledge. Thinking about the different Conversations a piece of language impinges on or relates to is another tool for engaging in discourse analysis.

Discourses: *whos* and *whats*

Let's start by trying to get at the notion of a 'big D' Discourse. We begin with the question of *who* you are when you speak or write and *what* you are doing. When you speak or write anything, you use the resources of English to project yourself as a certain kind of person, a different kind in different circumstances. You also project yourself as engaged in a certain kind of activity, a different kind in different circumstances. If I have no idea who you are and what you are doing, then I cannot make sense of what you have said, written, or done.

You project a different identity at a formal dinner party than you do at the family dinner table. And, though these are both dinner, they are nonetheless different activities. The fact that people have differential access to different identities and activities, connected to different sorts of status and social goods, is a root source of inequality in society. Intervening in such matters can be a contribution to social justice. Since different identities and activities are enacted in and through language, the study of language is integrally connected to matters of equity and justice.

An oral or written 'utterance' has meaning, then, only if and when it communicates a *who* and a *what* (Wieder and Pratt 1990). What I mean by a 'who' is a *socially situated identity*, the 'kind of person' one is seeking to be and enact here-and-now. What I mean by a 'what' is a socially situated *activity* that the utterance helps to constitute.

Lots of interesting complications can set in when we think about identity enacted in and through language. *Whos* can be multiple and they need not always be people. The president's press secretary can issue an utterance that is, in fact, authored by a speech writer and authorized (and even claimed) by the president. In this case, the utterance communicates a sort of overlapping and compound *who*. The press secretary, even if she is directly quoting the speech writer, must inflect the remark with her own voice. In turn, the speech writer is both 'mimicking' the president's 'voice' and creating an identity for him.

This does not just apply to individuals. Institutions, through the 'anonymous' texts and products they circulate, can also author or issue 'utterances.' For example, the warning on an aspirin bottle actually communicates multiple *whos*. An utterance can be authored, authorized by, or issued by a group or a single individual.

Finally, we can point out that *whos* and *whats* are not really discrete and separable. You are *who* you are partly through *what* you are doing and *what* you are doing is partly recognized for what it is by *who* is doing it. So it is better, in fact, to say that utterances communicate an integrated, although often multiple or 'heteroglossic,' *who-doing-what*.

'Real Indians'

Although I have focused on language thus far, it is important to see that making visible and recognizable *who* we are and *what* we are doing always requires more than language. It requires, as well, that we act, think, value, and interact in ways that together with language render *who* we are and *what* we are doing recognizable to others (and ourselves). In fact, to be a particular *who* and to pull off a particular *what* requires that we act, value, interact, and use language *in sync with* or *in coordination with* other people and with various objects ('props') in appropriate locations and at appropriate times.

To see this wider notion of language as integrated with 'other stuff' (other people, objects, values, times and places), we will briefly consider Wieder and Pratt's (1990) fascinating work on how Native Americans recognize each other as 'really Indian' (their work is based on a variety of different groups, although no claim is made that it is true of all Native American groups). Wieder and Pratt point out that '[real Indians] refer to persons who are "really Indian" in just those words with regularity and standardization' (1990: 48). Wieder and Pratt's work will also make clear how the identities (the *whos*) we take on are flexibly negotiated in actual contexts of practice.

The term 'real Indian' is, of course, an 'insiders' term.' The fact that it is used by some Native Americans in enacting their own identity work does not license non-Native Americans to use the term. Thus, although it may clutter the text, I will below always place the term 'real Indian' in quotes to make clear that I am talking about the term and not claiming that I have the 'right' to actually use it of anyone. Finally, let me say that I am not discussing Native Americans here because I think they are 'esoteric.' In fact, I am using this example, because I think it is a clear and dramatic example of what we *all* do all the time, although in different ways.

The problem of 'recognition and being recognized' is very consequential and problematic for Native Americans. While, in order to be considered a 'real Indian,' one must be able to make some claims to kinship with others who are recognized as 'real Indians,' this by no means settles the matter. People with such (biological) ties can fail to get recognized as 'really Indian,' and people of mixed kinship can be so recognized.

A 'real Indian' is not something one can simply be. Rather, it something that one becomes or is *in the doing* of it, that is, in the performance. Although one must have certain kinship ties to get in the 'game,' beyond this entry criterion, there is no *being* (once and for all) a 'real Indian,' rather there is only *doing being-or-becoming-a-'real-Indian.'* If one does not continue to 'practice' being a 'real Indian,' one ceases to be one.

Finally, 'doing' being-or-becoming-a-'real-Indian' is not something that one can do all by oneself. It requires the participation of others. One cannot be a 'real Indian' unless one appropriately recognizes other 'real Indians' and gets recognized by others as a 'real Indian' in the practices of doing being-or-becoming-a-'real-Indian.' Being a 'real Indian' also requires appropriate accompanying objects (props), times, and places.

There are many ways one can do being-and-becoming-a-'real-Indian.' Some of these are (following Wieder and Pratt 1990): 'real Indians' prefer to avoid conversation with strangers, Native American or otherwise; they cannot be related to one another as 'mere acquaintances,' as some 'non-Indians' might put it. So, for 'real Indians,' any conversation they do have with a stranger who may turn out to be a 'real Indian' will, in the discovery of the other's 'Indianness,' establish substantial obligations between the conversational partners just through the mutual acknowledgment that they are 'Indians' and that they are now no longer strangers to one another.

In their search for the other's 'real Indianness' and in their display of their own 'Indianness,' 'real Indians' frequently engage in a distinctive form of verbal sparring. By correctly responding to and correctly engaging in this sparring, which 'real Indians' call 'razzing,' each participant further establishes cultural competency in the eyes of the other.

'Real Indians' manage face-to-face relations with others in such a way that they appear to be in agreement with them (or, at least, they do not overtly disagree); they are modest and 'fit in.' They show accord and harmony and are reserved about their own interests, skills, attainments, and positions. 'Real Indians' understand that they should not elevate themselves over other 'real Indians.' And they understand that the complex system of obligations they have to kin and other 'real Indians' takes priority over those contractual obligations and pursuit of self-interest that some 'non-Indians' prize so highly.

'Real Indians' must be competent in 'doing their part' in participating in conversations that begin with the participants exchanging greetings and other amenities and then lapsing into extended periods of silence. They must know that neither they nor the others have an obligation to speak – that silence on the part of all conversants is permissible.

When they are among 'Indians,' 'real Indians' must also be able to perform in the roles of 'student' and 'teacher' and be able to recognize the behaviors appropriate to these roles. These roles are brought into play exclusively when the appropriate occasion arises for transmitting cultural knowledge (i.e., things pertinent to being a 'real Indian'). Although many 'non-Indians' find it proper to ask questions of someone who is instructing them, 'Indians' regard questions in such a situation as being inattentive, rude, insolent, and so forth. The person who has taken the role of 'student' shows attentiveness by avoiding eye contact and by being silent. The teaching situation, then, as a witnessed monolog, lacks the dialogical features that characterize some Western instruction.

While the above sort of information gives us something of the flavor of what sorts of things one must do and say to get recognized as a 'real Indian,' such information can lead to a bad mistake. It can sound as if the above features are necessary and sufficient criteria for doing being-and-becoming-a-'real-Indian.' But this is not true.

These features are not a test that can be or ever is administered all at once, and once and for all, to determine who is or is not a 'real Indian.' Rather, the circumstances under which these features are employed by 'Indians' emerge over the course of a developing history among groups of people. They are employed always in the context of actual situations, and at different times in the life history of groups of people. The ways in which the judgment 'He (or she) is (or is not) a "real Indian"' is embedded within situations that motivate it make such judgments intrinsically provisional. Those now recognized can spoil their acceptance or have it spoiled and those not now accepted can have another chance, even when others are reluctant to extend it.

The same thing applies, in fact, in regard to many other social identities, not just being a 'real Indian.' There are no once and for all tests for who is a 'real' feminist, gang member, patriot, humanist, cutting-edge scientist, 'yuppie,' or 'regular' at the local bar. These matters are settled provisionally and continually, in practice, as part and parcel of shared histories and ongoing activities.

Different social identities (different *whos*) may seriously conflict with one another. For instance, Scollon and Scollon (1981) point out that, for the Native Americans they studied (Athabaskans in Canada and the US), writing essays, a practice common in school, can constitute a crisis in identity. To produce an essay requires the Athabaskan to produce a major self-display, which is appropriate to Athabaskans only when a person is in a position of dominance in relation to the audience (in the case of school, this is the teacher, not the student). Furthermore, in essayist prose, the audience and the author are 'fictionalized' (not really me and you, but decontextualized and rather generic 'types' of readers and writers) and the text is decontextualized from specific social networks and relationships. Where the relationship of the communicants is decontextualized and unknown, Athabaskans prefer silence.

The paradox of prose for Athabaskans, the Scollons point out, is that if it is communication between known author and audience it is contextualized and compatible with Athabaskan values, but not good essayist prose. To the extent that it becomes decontextualized and thus good essayist prose, it becomes uncharacteristic of what Athabaskans seek to communicate. What is required to do and be an Athabaskan is in large part mutually exclusive with what is required to do and be a writer of school-based essayist prose. This doesn't mean that Athabaskans cannot do both (remember, we are all multiple), it simply means that they may face very real conflicts in terms of values and identity. And, as the Scollons point out, many other groups of people have similar or related 'identity issues' with essayist literacy.

Discourses (with a big 'D')

So how does someone get recognized as a 'real Indian' (a *who*) engaged in verbal sparring of the sort 'real Indians' do (a *what*)? Such matters are consequential, as we said above. By correctly responding to and correctly engaging in this sparring, which 'Indians' call 'razzing,' participants establish their cultural competency to and for each other. This is a problem of 'recognition and being recognized.'

The problem of 'recognition and being recognized' is very consequential not only for Native Americans, but for all of us all the time. And, as we saw above, making visible and recognizable *who* we are and *what* we are doing always involves a great deal more than 'just language.' Think of how someone gets recognized as a 'good student,' a 'good cook,' a 'gang member,' a 'competent lawyer,' a 'real basketball fan,' or a 'real Catholic.' These all involve acting-interacting-thinking-valuing-talking (sometimes writing-reading) in the 'appropriate way' with the 'appropriate' props at the 'appropriate' times in the 'appropriate' places. For example, 'good cooks' cannot just talk a good game. They have to be able to use recipes, utensils, and ingredients in a sort of 'dance' of coordinating everything together. They also have to value certain things (e.g., presentation of food, combinations of tastes, pairings of food and wine, in certain ways).

How do we know a young child is becoming part of a literate Discourse (being-doing literacy of a certain sort)? We test that the child can turn a book right side up, knows what books are for, can interact with a parent appropriately while being read too, can engage in pretend book readings (i.e., 'talk like a book'), and values books enough not to tear them apart. We test all this before a child can actually decode print (it is all part of what we call 'emergent literacy,' by which we mean a child is emerging into a 'literate' sort of person). Such socially accepted associations among ways of using language, of thinking, valuing, acting, and interacting, in the 'right' places and at the 'right' times with the 'right' objects (associations that can be used to identify oneself as a member of a socially meaningful group or 'social network'), I will refer to as 'Discourses,' with a capital 'D.' I will reserve the word 'discourse,' with a little 'd,' to mean language-in-use or stretches of language (such as conversations or stories). 'Big D' Discourses are always language *plus* 'other stuff.'

There are innumerable Discourses in any modern, technological, urban-based society: for example, (enacting) being something as general as a type of African-American or Anglo-Australian or something as specific as a type of modern British young second-generation affluent Sikh woman. Being a type of middle-class American, factory worker, or executive, doctor or hospital patient, teacher, administrator, or student, student of physics or of literature, member of a club or street gang, regular at the local bar, or – as we have just seen – 'real Indian' are all Discourses. Discourses are about being different 'kinds of people.'

The key to Discourses is 'recognition.' If you put language, action, interaction, values, beliefs, symbols, objects, tools, and places together in such a way that others *recognize* you as a particular type of who (identity) engaged in a particular type of what (activity), here-and-now, then you have pulled off a Discourse (and thereby continued it through history, if only for a while longer). Whatever you have done must be similar enough to other performances to be recognizable. However, if it is different enough from what has gone before, but still recognizable, it can simultaneously change and transform Discourses. If it is not recognizable, then you're not 'in' the Discourse.

Discourses are always embedded in a medley of social institutions, and often involve various 'props' such as books and magazines of various sorts, laboratories, classrooms, buildings of various sorts, various technologies, and a myriad of other objects from sewing needles (for sewing circles) through birds (for bird watchers) to basketball courts and basketballs (for basketball players). Think of all the words, symbols, deeds, objects, clothes, and tools you need to coordinate in the right way at the right time and place to 'pull off' (or recognize someone as) being a cutting-edge particle physicist or a Los Angeles Latino street-gang member or a sensitive high-culture humanist (of old).

It is sometimes helpful to think about social and political issues as if it is not just us humans who are talking and interacting with each other, but, rather, the Discourses we represent and enact, and for which we are 'carriers.' The Discourses we enact existed before each of us came on the scene and most of them will exist long after we have left the scene. Discourses, through our words and deeds, have talked to each other through history, and, in doing so, form human history. Think, for instance, of the long-running and ever-changing historical interchange in the US and Canada between the Discourses of 'being an Indian' and 'being an Anglo' or of the different, but equally long-running, historical interchange in New Zealand between 'being a Maori' and 'being an Anglo' (or, for that matter, think of the long-running interchange between 'being a British Anglo' and 'being an American Anglo'). Think of the long-running and ever-changing interchange between creationists and biologists. Think of the long-running and ever-changing interchange in Los Angeles between African-American teenage gang members and the Los Angeles police (some of whom, for instance, are leading experts, even academically speaking, on the 'grammar' of gang graffiti, which varies significantly between African-American gangs and Latino gangs). Intriguingly, we humans are very often unaware of the history of these interchanges, and, thus, in a deep sense, not fully aware of what we mean when we act and talk.

When we discussed being a 'real Indian,' we argued that 'knowing how to be a "real Indian"' rests on one's being able to be in sync with other 'real Indians' and with objects (e.g., the material items of the culture) in the appropriate times and places. Recent studies of science suggest much the same thing is true for scientists. For example, these studies argue that the physics experimental physicists 'know' is, in large part, *not* in their heads. Rather, it is spread out (distributed), inscribed in (and often trapped in) scientific apparatus, symbolic systems, books, papers, and journals, institutions, habits of bodies, routines of practice, and other people. Each domain of practice, each scientific Discourse – for example, a specific area within physics or biology – *attunes* actions, expressions, objects, and people (the scientists themselves) so that they become 'workable' in *relation* to each other and in relation to tools, technologies, symbols, texts, and the objects they study in the world. They are 'in sync.'

Just as there are verbal and non-verbal ways to be a 'real Indian,' there are verbal and non-verbal ways to be a 'real experimental physicist.' Being an experimental physicist or being a 'real Indian' are ways with words, feelings, values, beliefs, emotions, people, actions, things, tools, and places that allow us to display and recognize characteristic *whos* doing characteristic *whats*. They are both, then, Discourses.

The scientist's 'knowhow' is the ability to *coordinate* and *be coordinated by* constellations of expressions, actions, objects, and people. In a sense, the scientist is *both* an actor (coordinating other people, and various things, tools, technologies, and symbol systems) and a *patient* (being coordinated by other people and various things, tools, technologies, and symbol systems). Scientists become *agent-patients* 'in sync with,' 'linked with,' 'in association with,' 'in coordination with' – however we want to put it – other 'actants' (adapting a term from Latour 2005), such as particular forms of language, other people, objects (e.g., scientific equipment, atoms, molecules, or birds), places (e.g., laboratories or fields), and non-verbal practices.

In the end, a Discourse is a 'dance' that exists in the abstract as a coordinated pattern of words, deeds, values, beliefs, symbols, tools, objects, times, and places, and in the here-and-now as a performance that is recognizable as just such a coordination. Like a dance, the performance here-and-now is never exactly the same. It all comes down, often, to what the 'masters of the dance' (the people who inhabit the Discourse) will allow to be recognized or will be forced to recognize as a possible instantiation of the dance.

Discourses are not 'units' with clear boundaries

Imagine I freeze a moment of thought, talk, action, or interaction for you, in the way that a projector can freeze a piece of film. To make sense of that moment, you have to recognize the identities and activities involved in it. Perhaps, for this frozen moment, you can't do so, so you move the film back and forward enough until you can make such a recognition judgment. 'Oh, now I see,' you say, 'It's a "real Indian" razzing another "real Indian,"' or 'It's a radical feminist berating a male for a crass patriarchal remark,' or 'It's a laboratory physicist orienting colleagues to a graph,' or 'It's a first-grader in Ms. X's class starting a sharing time story.' Perhaps, if you now move the film backwards and forwards a bit more, you will change your judgments a little, a lot, or not at all.

Perhaps you aren't sure. You and I even argue about the matter. You say that 'It's a skinhead sending intimating glances to a passing adult on the street,' and I say, 'No, it's just a wannabe trying to act tough.' You say, 'It's a modern classroom teacher leading a discussion,' and I say, 'No, it's a traditional teacher giving a hidden lecture in the guise of a series of known-answer questions to the students.'

This is what I call 'recognition work.' People engage in such work when they try to make visible to others (and to themselves, as well) who they are and what they are doing. People engage in such work when they try to recognize others for who they are and what they are doing. People engage in such work within interactions, moment by moment. They engage in such work when they reflect on their interactions later. They engage in such work, as well, when they try to understand human interaction as researchers, practitioners, theoreticians, or interventionists of various sorts. Sometimes such recognition work is conscious, sometimes it is not. Sometimes people have labels they can articulate for the *whos* and *whats* they recognize, sometimes they don't. Sometimes they fight over the labels, sometimes they don't. And the labels change over time.

Thanks to the fact that we humans engage in recognition work, Discourses exist in the world. For example, there is a way of being a kindergarten student in Ms. X's class with its associated activities and ways with words, deeds, and things. Ms. X, her students, her classroom, with its objects and artifacts, and characteristic activities, are all in the Discourse she and her students create. These same people and things, of course, can be in other Discourses as well. Recognition work and Discourses out in the world go hand-in-hand. Ms. X and her students engage in recognition work, for example when a certain sort of sharing time ('show and tell') story isn't recognized as 'acceptable' in this class and another type is. That recognition work creates a Discourse, that is, ways with words, actions, beliefs, emotions, values, interactions, people, objects, tools, and technologies that come to constitute 'being and doing a student in Ms. X's class.' In turn, this Discourse renders recognition work possible and meaningful. It's another 'chicken and egg' question, then: which comes first, recognition work or Discourses? Neither. They are reflexively related, such that each creates the other.

Discourses have no discrete boundaries because people are always, in history, creating new Discourses, changing old ones, and contesting and pushing the boundaries of Discourses. You, an African-American male, speak and act here-and-now in an attempt to get recognized as a 'new capitalist manager coaching a project team.' If you get recognized as such, then your performance is *in the Discourse* of new capitalist management. If you don't, it isn't. If your performance has been influenced, intentionally or not, by another one of your Discourses (say, your membership in the Discourse of doing and being a jazz fan or your membership in a certain version of African-American culture as a Discourse), and it gets recognized in the new capitalist management Discourse, then you just, at least for here-and-now, 'infected' one Discourse with another and widened what 'counts' in the new capitalist management Discourse. You pushed the boundaries. In another time and place they may get narrowed.

You can get several of your Discourses recognized all at once. You (thinking of one of my esteemed colleagues at a university where I previously worked) 'pull off' being here-and-now, in a class or meeting, for example, 'a British, twice-migrant, globally oriented, traditional and modern, fashionable, female, Sikh, American professor of cultural studies and feminist postmodern anthropology' by weaving strands of your multiple Discourses together. If this sort of thing gets enacted and recognized enough, by enough people, then it will become not multiple strands of multiple Discourses interwoven, but a single Discourse whose hybridity may ultimately be forgotten. The point is *not* how we 'count' Discourses; the point is the performance, negotiation, and recognition work that goes into creating, sustaining, and transforming them, and the role of language (always with other things) in this process.

Let me make several other brief, but important points about Discourses:

Discourses can split into two or more Discourses. For example medieval 'natural philosophy' eventually split into philosophy and physics and other sciences.

Two or more Discourses can meld together. For example, after the movie *Colors* came out some years ago, mixed Latino, African-American, and white gangs emerged. Prior to that, Latinos, African-American, and whites had quite separate ways of being and doing gangs, as they still do in the case of segregated gangs.

It can be problematic whether a Discourse today is or is not the same as one in the past. For example, modern medicine bears little similarity to medicine before the nineteenth century, but, perhaps, enough to draw some important parallels for some purposes though not for others.

New Discourses emerge and old ones die all the time. For example in Palmdale, California (a desert community outside Los Angeles), and I assume other places as well, an anti-racist skinhead Discourse is dying because people, including the police, tend to confuse its members with a quite separate, but similar looking racist neo-Nazi skinhead Discourse.

Discourses are always defined in relationship of complicity and contestation with other Discourses, and so they change when other Discourses in a society emerge or die. For example, the emergence of a 'new male' Discourse in the 1970s (ways of doing and being a 'new male') happened in response to various gender-based Discourses (e.g., various sorts of feminism) and class-based Discourses (the baby-boom middle class was too big for all young males to stay in it, so those who 'made it' needed to mark their difference from those who did not), and, in turn, changed the meaning and actions of these other Discourses.

Discourses need by no means be 'grand' or large scale. I used to eat regularly at a restaurant with a long bar. Among regulars there were two different Discourses at opposite ends of the bar, that is, ways of being and doing at each end of the bar. One involved young men and women and a lot of male-dominated sexual bantering; the other involved older people and lots of hard-luck stories. The restaurant assigned different bartenders to each end (always a young female at the young end) and many of the bartenders could fully articulate the Discourse at their end of the bar and their role in it.

Discourses can be hybrids of other Discourses. For example, the school yards of many urban middle and high school are places where teenagers of different ethnic groups come together and engage in what I have elsewhere called a 'borderland Discourse' of doing and being urban teenager peers when they cannot safely go into each other's neighborhoods and when they each have their own neighborhood peer-based Discourses. The borderland Discourse is quite manifestly a mixture of the various neighborhood peer Discourses, with some emergent properties of its own.

There are limitless Discourses and no way to count them, both because new ones, even quite non-grand ones, can always emerge and because boundaries are always contestable.

Discourses are out in the world and history as coordinations ('a dance') of people, places, times, actions, interactions, verbal and non-verbal expression, symbols, things, tools, and technologies that betoken certain identities and associated activities. Thus, they are material realities. But Discourses exist, also, as work we humans do to get ourselves and things recognized in certain ways and not others. They are also the 'maps' in our heads by which we understand society. Discourses, then, are social practices and mental entities, as well as material realities.

Discourses as 'kits'

If you are having trouble understanding the notion of 'big D' Discourses, maybe this will help. Think for a minute of all the stuff you would put into the 'Barbie doll' Discourse, restricting ourselves for the moment just to Barbie dolls and their accoutrements. How do you recognize something as in the 'Barbie doll' world or Discourse, even if it hasn't got the Barbie logo on it? Girl and boy (e.g., Ken) Barbie dolls look a certain way (e.g., their bodies have certain sorts of shapes and not others). They have characteristic sorts of clothes and accessories. They talk and act in certain ways in books, games, and television shows. They display certain sorts of values and attitudes. This configuration of words and things is the Barbie doll Discourse. You interpret everything Barbie within this frame. It is a sort of kit made of words, things, clothes, values, attitudes, and so forth, from which one could build Barbie doll meanings. Even if you want to demean the Barbie doll Discourse by making a parody Barbie doll (such as Australia's 'Feral Cheryl'), you have to recognize the Discourse in the first place.

Now imagine real people wanted to enact a Barbie Discourse. We know what they would have to look, act, interact, and talk like. We know what values and attitudes they would have to display. We know what sorts of objects, accessories, and places they would associate themselves with. They would draw these out of their now real-world Barbie kit. In fact, young people sometimes talk about someone, usually a girl, as being or trying to be a Barbie doll type of person.

The workings of society and history have given rise to innumerable kits with which we can live out our social lives as different and multiple kinds of people, different for different times and places – hopefully not as Barbie dolls but as men, women, workers, students, gamers, lovers, bird watchers, environmentalists, radicals, conservatives, feminists, African-Americans, scientists, bar members (lawyers or drinkers) of different types, and so on and so forth through an endless and changing list.

References

Latour, B. (2005) *Reassembling the Social: An Introduction to Actor-Network-Theory*, Oxford: Oxford University Press.

Scollon, R. and Scollon, S.W. (1981) *Narrative, Literacy and Face in Interethnic Communication*, Norwood, NJ: Ablex.

Wieder, D.L. and Pratt, S. (1990) 'On becoming a recognizable Indian among Indians,' in D. Carbaugh (ed.) *Cultural Communication and Intercultural Contact*, Hillsdale, NJ: Lawrence Erlbaum, 45–64.

Chapter 9

Wolfram Bublitz

COHESION AND COHERENCE

Introduction

LINGUISTS USE THE TWO notions of cohesion and coherence to refer to the (linguistically encoded or just assumed) connectedness of spoken as well as written discourse or text. Of course, connecting relations also hold among elements of structure within grammatical units such as word, phrase, clause or sentence. But these intra-sentential relations are different in kind because they are determined by phonological and grammatical rules and described, *inter alia*, as syntactic-semantic relations of valency, dependency, constituency, modification. Cohesion, operating inter-sententially, and coherence are key notions in text and discourse analysis, as well as in pragmatics because they also relate to the complex interrelationship between form, meaning and use of linguistic expressions in specific (social) contexts.

Native speakers have intuitions about which sequences of utterances do or do not constitute discourse or text. If, by way of an experiment, we deliberately distort a perfectly comprehensible and acceptable text by, for example, changing the order of its utterances or its linguistic, situational or sociocultural context, the effect will be one of confusion on the part of our hearers or readers. They may still understand each individual utterance but not the resulting string of utterances as a whole, i.e., as one unit with a definite function in its environment. In the eye of the language user who is trying to interpret them, they do not 'hang together' in a reasonable way. They do not display order and do not form a meaningful gestalt that fits both into the linguistic environment as well as the social situation, serves the accepted communicative goal and contributes to the topic at hand; in other words, they are not coherent. Accordingly, the defining characteristic of such instances of discourse

Wolfram Bublitz, 'Cohesion and Coherence' in Jan Zienkowski, Prof. Dr. Jan-Ola Östman and Prof. Dr. Jef Verschueren (eds.) *Discursive Pragmatics*, 2001, pp 37–49. With kind permission by John Benjamins Publishing Company, Amsterdam/Philadelphia. www.benjamins.com

or text is coherence, which itself rests on text-forming resources such as cohesion and general structural properties determined by register or genre.

Although both cohesion and coherence refer to meaning resting on relations of connectedness (between individual propositions and sets of propositions), which may or may not be linguistically encoded, they are descriptive categories that differ in kind. Cohesion refers to inter-sentential semantic relations that link current items with preceding or following ones by lexical and structural means. Cohesion is a kind of textual prosody. Since J.R. Firth, who perceived prosodic effects as phonological colouring, we use *prosody* to refer to the property of a feature to extend its domain, stretch over and affect not just one but several units. Analogously, textual prosody refers to cohesive colouring involving more than one element in discourse or text. As cohesion is anchored in its forms, we can argue that it is an invariant, user and context independent property of a piece of discourse or text. Coherence, on the other hand, is a cognitive category that depends on the language user's interpretation and is not an invariant property of discourse or text.

Although both cohesion and coherence have found their place as key terms in text and discourse analysis, they still mean different things to different people. Simplifying matters drastically, we can say that form and structure oriented linguists, who regard a text as a kind of long sentence, i.e., as a unit beyond the sentence, focus on cohesion as an essential feature of textuality. Function-oriented linguists, on the other hand, who equate text with any linguistic expression of any length that is used to perform a specific function, focus on coherence as the defining feature of textuality.

Focus on form: cohesion

The most influential account of cohesion was developed by Halliday and Hasan in their book *Cohesion in English*. Their concept of cohesion is 'a semantic one' because it refers 'to relations of meaning that exist within the text' (Halliday and Hasan 1976: 4) and 'enable one part of the text to function as the context for another' (Halliday and Hasan 1989: 489). Cohesion manifests itself in linguistic means that appear at the surface level of language. An example of such a cohesive means is *them* in 'Wash and core six cooking apples. Put them into a fireproof dish' (Halliday and Hasan 1976: 2), which 'presupposes for its interpretation something other than itself' (1976: 4), here the expression *six cooking apples* in the preceding sentence. 'Cohesion,' the authors argue, 'occurs where the *interpretation* of some element in the discourse is dependent on that of another. The one *presupposes* the other, in the sense that it cannot be effectively decoded except by recourse to it. When this happens, a relation of cohesion is set up' (1976: 4).

Halliday and Hasan focus on five kinds of cohesive ties between utterances: reference, substitution, ellipsis, conjunction and lexical cohesion. Reference is described as situational or exophoric, resting on means that refer to the situation at hand (as in *Would you like to join me for a cup of tea this afternoon?*), and as textual or endophoric reference, resting on anaphora or cataphora that refer to participant roles (personal reference as in *Doris likes him very much*), to (degrees of) proximity (demonstrative reference as in *Joe won't get tenure. This is what I can't understand*), or to (degrees of) similarity (comparative reference as in *He always eats meat balls with his fingers. I detest such manners*).

Substitution involves noun phrases (*My beer is warm. Please get me a chilled one*), verb phrases (*I have never talked in Jena before. But I did in Halle a couple of years ago*) and clauses (*I trust you know how to open a bottle of wine? I believe so*). Ellipsis is described as 'substitution by zero' (Halliday and Hasan 1976: 142) and likewise involves noun phrases, verb phrases and clauses.

There are four types of conjunction: additive (expressed by *and*, *or*, *furthermore*, etc.), adversative (*but*, *however*, etc.), causal (*so*, *therefore*, etc.), temporal (*then*, *next*, *finally*, etc.). Lexical cohesion, which rests on 'identity of reference' between two items, is realized by forms of reiteration such as word-for-word repetitions, synonyms, superordinates, general words, so-called collocations, i.e., members of the same lexical field (*euro*, *cent*; *mountain*, *climb*, *peak*) and items that, although they are not hyponyms or synonyms in the language system, are nonetheless used as such in discourse or text, acquiring their coreferential status only 'instantially' (1976: 289).

In the wake of Halliday and Hasan's proposal, much work has been devoted to re-classify and extend their inventory of cohesive means (see Martin 1992). Essentially, all means can be categorized into three types because cohesion stretches three ways: there is reference to what has been said, to what will be said and also to what could have been said instead. This three-way distinction corresponds to Roman Jakobson's well-known two modes of arrangement of verbal means, selection (paradigmatic choice, relatedness in the system) and combination (syntagmatic relatedness), to which, for a higher degree of delicacy, we can add the two vectors of retrospection and prospection (see Hasan 1984). The following overview categorizes cohesive means into classes according to their prospective or retrospective orientation.

Retrospective cohesive means are proforms (as anaphora), substitutions, synonyms, hyponyms, word-for-word repetitions, general words or labels and second pair parts of adjacency pairs. Except for the latter, they are based on similarity of form, structure, content and function and can therefore be labelled 'forms of repetition' (or 'parallelism'). The three essential properties of repetition are quality, quantity and distribution. Quality is best described as a scale that represents a continuum of fixity vs. looseness of form and indicates the degree of formal as well as semantic correspondence between the parallel items involved; there is a cline from total equivalence to paraphrastic substitution. Quantity refers to the length of the repeating item and is likewise best represented on a scale with a single word (or even phone) at one end and a string of utterances at the other. Distribution refers to the distance between the repeated and the repeating item, which can be anywhere between closely adjacent and considerably removed.

Prospective devices are used to create a slot (to be filled), thereby reducing the number of options and, generally, setting up expectations. They include proforms (as cataphora), text structuring discourse markers (*incidentally*, *actually*, see Lenk 1998) and gambits (*first of all*, *before I forget*, *and another thing*), and also general nouns or labels (Francis 1994) such as *aspect*, *dilemma*, *episode*, *pattern*, *problem*. Labels do not just refer to sections but categorize them; in the extract below there is both a prospective (*stuff*) and a retrospective (*things*) label:

> I always meant going down to the shops on Saturday to get fresh all the *stuff* to get meat and vegetables beefburgers sausages all these *things* the children eat for tea.
>
> (*London Lund Corpus* 4.3.90 ff)

To these two classes of cohesive means we can add forms of ordered arrangements that function both prospectively and retrospectively at the same time. They rest on principles such as information assessment and iconicity. The former has been described from a variety of different points of view, prominent among them the Prague School's principle of *functional sentence perspective*, according to which each sentence part is evaluated for its relative importance for the information carried by the sentence as a whole and thus for its communicative function within its contextual environment. Known or given information (i.e., theme or topic status) has a low degree of communicative dynamism (because it contributes little to informational progress) while new information (i.e., rheme or comment status) has a high degree of communicative dynamism. The assignment of theme and rheme to parts of an utterance has a clear cohesive function because it sets up links with preceding and following utterances (see Firbas 1992). The second principle of arrangement, iconicity, is easiest illustrated by Harvey Sacks' much-quoted example 'The baby cried. The mommy picked it up' (see Sacks, Chapter 14, this volume) where the temporal sequence of events is reflected in the linear sequence of the two adjacent utterances. Adjacency based on iconicity is thus another powerful means of creating cohesive linkage.

Cohesion as a condition for coherence

Cohesion should be kept strictly apart from coherence. It is neither a sufficient nor a necessary condition for coherence. Referring to van Dijk's example

> We will have guests for lunch. Calderón was a great Spanish writer
>
> (van Dijk 1972: 40)

Edmondson shows that, although the two utterances are not cohesively connected, they are nonetheless coherent in a context like:

> Do you know Calderón died exactly 100 years ago today? – Good heavens! I'd forgotten. The occasion shall not pass unnoticed. We will have guests for lunch. Calderón was a great Spanish writer. I shall invite Professor Wilson and Senor Castellano right away.
>
> (Edmondson 1981: 13)

Furthermore, in authentic discourse or text, we can encounter long stretches of utterances that, although they are not cohesively connected, are nonetheless accepted as coherent texts because they are, for example, parts of enumerations or cases of dissociated interior monologue.

However, while cohesion is not a necessary condition of coherence, studies have shown that discourse and text tend to be cohesive to a greater or lesser extent, depending on genre. Following a general principle of cooperation, speakers/writers are anxious to generate cohesion as a means of guiding their recipients' interpretation of coherence and thus, ultimately, of securing comprehension. Cohesive means are cues that 'signal' or indicate the preferred line of coherence interpretation. A lack of cohesive means may disturb the hearer's/reader's interpretation of coherence.

Easy and unimpeded interpretation of both discourse and text as coherent depends considerably on the presence of communicative and meta-communicative textual links.

Of course, the equation 'more cohesion = more coherence' is not valid *per se*. And yet, there are genres, among them everyday face-to-face conversation, in which the wealth and abundance of cohesive means is quite extraordinary, as in the extract below:

A   well I must admit I feel I mean Edward's mother and his great and his grandfather will come up on Christmas Day but I feel somehow the sheer fact of not having to have to have this really sort of it's for one thing it does nark me that it's so bloody expensive that he won't eat anything except the largest most splendid pieces of meat you know

B   how annoying

A   and it upsets me you know if he needed it I wouldn't mind

D   come to think of it he's also he's also an extremely greedy individual who

A   yeah so that if you buy enough [f]

D   he isn't satisfied with a normal portion

A   for cheese for for three days if he sees it's there he'll eat it you know

(*London Lund Corpus* 4.3)

Cohesive means come on all levels. In the extract above we find on the level of phonetics and prosody alliteration, assonance, rhythm (see Couper-Kuhlen 1983) and 'sound-rows' or '-sequences' as in *cheese – three-he-sees – eat* (Sacks 1992). On the lexico-syntactic level we notice articles, proforms, deictics, conjunctions, complementizers, labels (*somehow, do, anything, individual*) and members of a common script or semantic field (*mother, grandfather; eat, meat, greedy, portion; nark, upset, annoy*). And from a pragmatic and text-analytic viewpoint we recognize speech act pairs ('statement' – 'supportive statement' accompanied by supportive elements such as *yes, how annoying, yeah*), hedges, gambits, discourse markers, collocations and tags (*well, I mean, sort of, you know, come to think of it, I must admit, I feel somehow, the sheer fact, I wouldn't mind, for one thing*). There is an abundance of cohesive means to the point where they add up to a rather high degree of redundancy. Hearers, however, who have to process online, to interpret ongoing talk *in actu* (without the possibility to look ahead or the time to recall what was said before in any detail) depend on a certain degree of redundancy. Redundancy helps relieve their memory and gives them time to understand. In everyday face-to-face discourse, at least, securing comprehension as a principle ranks higher than avoiding redundancy. Occasionally, speakers may come up with too many cohesive cues that add up to a degree of redundancy that is no longer tolerable and can irritate or even annoy the hearer. Such cases of 'cohesive overkill' are triggered by the speakers misjudgement of the hearer's interpretive competence and range of knowledge.

While there is no *direct* correlation between (lack of) cohesion and (lack of) coherence, to claim that cohesion is not a sufficient condition for coherence is much more arguable especially if we accept that the speaker's/writer's primary motive for using cohesive means is to help secure coherence. And indeed, the examples which are given to prove that cohesion alone does not generate coherence, are not very convincing:

> The heads of the city's uniformed services polished their contingency plans for a strike. Queen Wilhelmina finalized her own plans for the evening. In a nearby Danish town, two fishmongers exchanged blows. Anders, by far the stronger, had a cousin in prison. Many criminals are in prison.
>
> (Samet and Schank 1984: 63)

The authors claim that the above extract is cohesive but not coherent because the utterances 'exhibit . . . connections but "make no sense at all"' (Samet and Schank 1984: 63). However, as we saw when we looked at Edmondson's reading of the non-cohesive sequence of utterances in the earlier example, judgements of coherence, or, for that matter, incoherence are not invariably triggered by the text at hand for any hearer or reader alike. If the text in Samet and Schank was authentic, i.e., an instance of naturally occurring data such as a narrative, its hearers or readers would easily succeed in reaching a plausible interpretation of coherence by resorting to the larger context, to the situation at hand, to the overall communicative goal, to their encyclopaedic knowledge and to other sources of supporting data. But even as a piece of constructed, context and situation free text, the Samet and Schank example allows for a coherent reading. To ask people whether or not an isolated sequence of utterances 'has coherence' is tantamount to asking whether or not they have enough imagination to come up with a context in which the sequence is indeed coherent. To reach coherence, they will then quite naturally rely on the cohesive means given in the text. Hence, cohesion is *normally* a sufficient condition for coherence because it serves as a powerful and suggestive guideline for the hearer's/reader's interpretation.

Focus on meaning: connectivity

It has been argued that text which is not cohesive can, nonetheless, be coherent provided the propositions underlying its utterances are semantically related to each other. In this view, coherence is a semantic notion resting on (a net of) semantic relations. The variety of semantic or connectivity relations that have been described in the literature so far can be categorized into a few core classes. Among them we find causality, reference, coordination (parallel, contrastive), elaboration (example, generalization, paraphrase), overlap and contiguity (temporal, spatial, aspectual, referential) (see Samet and Schank 1984) as well as so-called scripts, schemata or frames that refer to socially defined activities and events and help 'participants apply their knowledge of the world to the interpretation of what goes on in an encounter' (Gumperz 1982: 154). Viewing coherence as a semantic notion usually leads to the assumption that it is a feature of, or rather *in* the text. It is 'there', 'in' the text for people to 'find' it. Returning to the earlier example from van Dijk with its interpretation in Edmondson, we can now argue that its coherence rests on the semantic relations of causality and coordination, which do not only link the propositions of the two utterances but also two additional although latent – i.e., not realized – propositions; here is a possible paraphrase: *We will have guests for lunch – because – we want to celebrate – because – it is Calderón's birthday today – and because – Calderón was a great Spanish writer*. The connectivity is only partly reflected on the surface level of cohesion by the linear ordering of the two utterances. To make a clear distinction between connectivity and cohesion (with coherence resting on either or on both of these), is justified on theoretical grounds. In practical discourse analysis, however, the two concepts are not always easy to keep apart.

Semantic connectivity as a condition for coherence

From the fact that coherence is frequently based on semantic connectivity we may conclude that the latter is both a sufficient and a necessary condition for coherence. It has been argued, however, that this is too strong a claim. Basically, the argument is supported by five observations. First, adjacent utterances can be semantically related without being coherent. In the Samet and Schank extract there is connectivity (resting on the semantic relations of contiguity, time and coordination) but not coherence. Samet and Schank point out that 'our ability to render certain elements of a text understandable by using these [semantic] connections cannot itself make a text coherent to the point of making sense' (1984: 64). Second, semantic relations can involve utterances that are not adjacent as, for example, in enumerations where they are related to a superordinate topic but not to each other. Third, utterances can be semantically related in ways that are not clearly identifiable or that allow for alternative identification. Thus, in authentic discourse or text it may be difficult or even impossible to figure out exactly which semantic relation is involved, as in the Morris and Hirst example below:

> John bought a raincoat. He went shopping yesterday on Queen Street and it rained.
>
> (Morris and Hirst 1991: 25)

Each of several connectivity relations is a likely candidate for coherence: 'The coherence relation here could be elaboration (on the buying), or explanation (of when, how, or why), or cause (he bought the raincoat because it was raining out)' (Morris and Hirst 1991: 25). Fourth, two adjacent utterances can be semantically related (and thus possibly coherent) for one hearer/reader but not for another, as in this Vuchinich example:

> S   Well unless you're not a member, if yer a member of TM people
>   do, ah simply because it's such a fucking high price to get in there
>   (1.0 sec) it's like thirty five dollars
> C   it's like water polo (2.0 sec)
> S   Why, is it expensive
>
> (Vuchinich 1977: 246)

This exchange is part of an experiment. In order to test the reaction of his/her interlocutor the organizer C makes a deliberately incoherent contribution, i.e., one that is not semantically related to the preceding utterances. However, as is clear from his/her reaction, S does see a semantic relation (of comparison) between *it's like water polo* and the preceding text and understands it as coherent (although not straight away, he/she needs more processing time than usual). Fifth, two or more utterances can be connected by a semantic relation that, however, cannot be inferred from the linguistic or the non-linguistic context but only from previously acquired knowledge or from experience (as is often the case with allusions).

Of course, not one of these five lines of reasoning precludes connectivity from being at least a *major* condition for coherence. After all, connectivity rests on semantic relations of the kinds mentioned above rather than on transparence, adjacency or absoluteness.

Coherence: a general view

Coherence is a concept that in its complexity is still not fully understood and is a matter of continuing debate. Although it has doubtless found its place as a key term in text and discourse analysis, its usage continues to vary to the extent that to give a comprehensive overview of even the major views advocated goes well beyond the scope of a handbook article. While after the publication of Halliday and Hasan (1976) the notion of cohesion was widely welcomed and accepted as a well-defined and useful category, coherence was often regarded or even occasionally dismissed as a vague, fuzzy and 'rather mystical notion' (Sinclair 1991: 102) with little practical value for the text or discourse analyst. This view was held by parts of the linguistic community with, however, some notable exceptions, prominent among them hermeneutic, context- and interpretation-based dynamic concepts of coherence. Since the late 1980s, there has been renewed interest in the intriguing notion of coherence. The remarkable number of almost 500 titles listed in a recent bibliography (Bublitz 2010) bears witness to this development and to a rapidly changing scene in coherence research that is moving away from reducing coherence to a mere product of (formally represented) cohesion and/or (semantically established) connectivity.

In her overview, Hellman (1995) distinguishes, *inter alia*, between approaches that see coherence (a) 'as a formal property of texts' (1995: 191ff), (b) 'as a discourse processing concept' (1995: 194f), referring primarily to work by Sanders and Spooren (who, in a 1999 paper, juxtapose the linguists' view of coherence as a relational concept and the cognitivists' view of coherence as a realization of participant intentions manifest in each section of a discourse), (c) 'as a result of computing referential, causal or other relations', i.e., 'of a complex problem-solving process in which the reader infers relations among the ideas, events and states that are described in the text' (Hellman 1995: 195), and (d) 'as a result of computing', i.e., recognizing 'the intention(s) of a discourse producer' (1995: 196).

A hermeneutic, context- and interpretation-based view of coherence

Much recent work describes coherence as a mental notion that is interactively negotiated within a given sociocultural setting and less dependent on the language of discourse or text itself (see, for example, the readers by Gernsbacher and Givón 1995; Bublitz et al 1999). Such a hermeneutic approach describes coherence as a context-dependent, user-oriented and comprehension-based notion. This view, which dominates work by Fritz (1982), Brown and Yule (1983) and many others, is in accordance with a fairly long interpretive tradition in Europe (represented by Ludwig Wittgenstein, Alfred Schütz, Harold Garfinkel, Hans-Georg Gadamer, Anthony Giddens and others) and the USA. Within a sociological and ethnographic framework, Dell Hymes, John Gumperz and others (see the reader edited by Bauman and Sherzer 1974) argue for analysing language within its sociocultural settings. Speakers and hearers alike come to an understanding of the ongoing communicative interaction by linking linguistic and non-linguistic cues with their background knowledge. They thus continually and jointly negotiate meaning by constructing a shared context. From such a contextualizing, interpretive viewpoint, speakers/writers are said to intend, anticipate and (overtly and/or covertly) suggest coherence while hearers/readers ascribe coherence to utterances within their linguistic, situational and sociocultural context.

Because much recent research into coherence follows a context-, negotiation-, interpretation-dependent view of coherence, a snapshot account of it seems indicated. According to this view, coherence is not a discourse or text inherent property, i.e., it is not given in discourse or text independently of interpretation. Consequently, one cannot say 'a text has coherence' in the same way as one can say 'a text has a beginning or an end', or indeed, 'a text has cohesion' (the latter being a text inherent property). We can only say 'someone understands a text as coherent'. Of course, coherence is based on the language of the text in the same way as it is based on other information provided by the linguistic context, the sociocultural environment, the valid communicative principles and maxims, the interpreter's encyclopaedic knowledge, etc.

Since it is not texts that cohere but rather people who make texts cohere, we can say that for one and the same text there exist a speaker's/writer's, a hearer's/reader's and an analyst's coherence, which may or may not match. Typically, different interpretations of the coherence of a text depend on its linguistic complexity, the temporal, local and social setting, the interpreter's familiarity with genre and content as well as his/her knowledge of the speaker's/writer's background (motives, preferences, interests). Being dependent on interpretation means that speakers/writers can never produce coherence that is binding for hearers/readers. It is the latter who have to arrive at their own understanding of coherence. Normally speakers/writers are set to help create coherence by (more or less subtly) guiding their hearers/readers to a suggested line of understanding. Conversely, hearers/readers use these guiding signals as instructions to align their interpretations with what they take to be the speaker's/writer's intentions. Hearers/readers assemble and subsequently test a view of coherence that they assume comes closest to that of the speaker/writer. Hence, coherence is rarely static but frequently dynamic, i.e., a process rather than a state. It can be tentative and temporary because it is continually checked against any new information that may make adaption and updating necessary. Of course, eventually, coherence (especially of written texts) can lose some of its provisional and temporary character and acquire a higher degree of permanence.

Coherence is the outcome of the language user's gestalt creating power. People are driven by a strong desire to identify forms, relations, connections that they can maximize in order to turn fragments into whole gestalts, i.e., to 'see' coherence in strings of utterances. Coherence is also a cooperative achievement (in ongoing discourse more than in 'petrified' text) because it depends on both the speaker's/ writer's and the hearer's/reader's willingness to negotiate coherence. Mutual understanding not only rests on the participants sharing the same sociocultural background, the same range of knowledge and communicative assumptions, but also on their ability to figure out unshared experience, i.e., to adjust their own worldview to that of their interlocutors. Hearers/readers are constantly engaged in trying to re-create coherence as an equivalent of the speaker's/writer's coherence, but despite their efforts they can never succeed in coming up with an exact copy. Coherence is only approximate and a matter of degree and best described as a scalar notion. Any interpretation of coherence is restricted and, accordingly, partial to different degrees.

Coherence as a default assumption

As a rule, speakers/writers and hearers/readers alike operate on a standard or default assumption of coherence. This explains why despite the fact that ascribing coherence frequently involves making difficult and complex acts of inference, cases of disturbed coherence are not abundant, and why people try to understand coherence even though the data to go by may look sadly insufficient. As long as there is no evidence to the contrary, they proceed from the assumption that what they hear and read can be made coherent, even if this involves making extremely remote and unlikely connections. Speakers/writers likewise rely on the default principle and expect hearers/readers to assume that what they say or write is coherent. The default principle of coherence is accepted for two reasons. First, it relates to a more general strategy according to which it is normally assumed by the interactants that hearers/readers 'do as little processing as possible' (Brown and Yule 1983: 60), opting for the obvious and likely reading. Second, it follows from the general principle of cooperation (in the Gricean sense) and is therefore an essential normative basis of communication, which leads to rational behaviour as the only path to efficient communication (see also Linde's (1993: 16) observation that 'the process of creating coherence' is 'a social obligation').

Perspectives

This overview can only touch upon a limited number of methodological and theoretical approaches to the description of cohesion and coherence, on the one hand, and of ways and means of (re-)creating them, on the other. For some time now there have been several common tendencies, among them the tendency to describe a far larger inventory of cohesive means than originally proposed by Halliday and Hasan, the tendency to refrain from accepting only one canonic definition of coherence, and the tendency to observe a basic stock of fundamental theoretical and methodological assumptions. Much recent work demands such descriptive principles as the need to rely on authentic data, to proceed in an interdisciplinary way, to assume a cultural and 'common sense' basis for coherence (see Linde 1993: 192ff), to relate micro-linguistic to macro-linguistic (e.g. sociocultural) issues, and to focus on the powerful coherence-securing role of such (sometimes long neglected) means as gestures (see McNeill and Levy 1993), discourse topics, collocational orientation.

Discourse topic and the various procedures of handling it (introducing, changing, shifting, digressing from it) are prevalent and strong means of (re-)creating coherence (see Geluykens 1999). In many societies, speakers/writers are expected to stick to a topic. Taking up social space is only justified if an utterance is evidently a contribution to the topic at hand, i.e., an acceptable answer to 'the generic question . . . "why that now"' (Schegloff 1990: 55). The relationship between discourse topic and overarching communicative goals is one of the stubborn problems that future research has to address. Collocations based on shared polarity, following from the node's negative or positive semantic prosody, contribute to coherence because they are likely to recur in the local as well as global environment. The semantic orientation of the individual collocation is then not regarded as a single occurrence with no bearing on context but rather as indicating the overall tenor of the discourse, i.e., its general semantic orientation. On account of such predictive force, they are regularly instrumental in dispersing meaning in discourse (see Bublitz 1996).

Future research will also have to deal with unsolved problems such as how means of securing coherence (and ways of describing them) vary from spoken to written language, from genre to genre, from text type to text type (see, for example, Fritz 1999 on coherence in hypertext), from one society to another, from earlier to later stages of a language (the diachronic perspective), and from earlier to later stages of acquiring a language (both as a native speaker and a foreign language learner).

References

Bauman, R. and Sherzer, J. (eds.) (1974) *Explorations in the Ethnography of Speaking*, Cambridge: Cambridge University Press.

Brown, G. and Yule, G. (1983) *Discourse Analysis*, Cambridge: Cambridge University Press.

Bublitz, W. (1996) 'Semantic prosody and cohesive company', *Leuvense Bijdragen* 85: 1–32.

—— (2010) *A Bibliography of Coherence and Cohesion*, www.philhist.uni-augsburg.de/de/lehrstuehle/anglistik/sprachwissenschaft/Interne_Dateien/bibliographien/Bibliography_of_Coherence.pdf

Bublitz, W., Lenk, U. and Ventola, E. (eds.) (1999) *Coherence in Spoken and Written Discourse: How to Create it and How to Describe it*, Amsterdam: John Benjamins.

Couper-Kuhlen, E. (1983) 'Intonatorische Kohäsion', *Zeitschrift für Literaturwissenschaft und Linguistik* 49: 74–100.

Edmondson, W. (1981) *Spoken Discourse*, London: Longman.

Firbas, J. (1992) *Functional Sentence Perspective in Written and Spoken Communication*, Cambridge: Cambridge University Press.

Francis, G. (1994) 'Labelling discourse: an aspect of nominal-group lexical cohesion', in M. Coulthard (ed.) *Advances in Written Text Analysis*, London: Routledge, 83–101.

Fritz, G. (1982) *Kohärenz*, Württemberg: Narr.

—— (1999) 'Coherence in hypertext', in W. Bublitz, U. Lenk and E. Ventola (eds.) *Coherence in Spoken and Written Discourse: How to Create it and How to Describe it*, Amsterdam: John Benjamins, 221–32.

Geluykens, R. (1999). 'It takes two to cohere: the collaborative dimension of topical coherence in conversation', in W. Bublitz, U. Lenk and E. Ventola (eds.) *Coherence in Spoken and Written Discourse*: *How to Create it and How to Describe it*, Amsterdam: John Benjamins, 33–53.

Gernsbacher, M.A. and Givón, T. (eds.) (1995) *Coherence in Spontaneous Text*, Amsterdam: John Benjamins.

Gumperz, J.J. (1982) *Discourse Strategies*, Cambridge: Cambridge University Press.

Halliday, M.A.K. and Hasan, R. (1976) *Cohesion in English*, London: Longman.

—— (1989) *Language, Context, and Text*: *Aspects of Language in a Social-semiotic Perspective*, Oxford: Oxford University Press.

Hasan, R. (1984) 'Coherence and cohesive harmony', in J. Flood (ed.) *Understanding Reading Comprehension*, Newark, DE: International Reading Association, 181–219.

Hellman, C. (1995) 'The notion of coherence in discourse', in G. Rickheit and C. Habel (eds.) *Focus and Coherence in Discourse Processing*, Berlin: De Gruyter, 190–202.

Lenk, U. (1998) *Marking Discourse Coherence*, Württemberg: Narr.

Linde, C. (1993) *Life Stories: The Creation of Coherence*, Oxford: Oxford University Press.

Martin, J.R. (1992) *English Text: System and Structure*, Amsterdam: John Benjamins.

McNeill, D. and Levy, E.T. (1993) 'Cohesion and gesture', *Discourse Processes* 16: 363–86.

Morris, J. and Hirst, G. (1991) 'Lexical cohesion computed by thesaural relations as an indicator of the structure of text', *Computational Linguistics* 17: 21–48.

Sacks, H. (1992) *Lectures on Conversation*, Oxford: Blackwell.

Samet, J. and Schank, R. (1984) 'Coherence and connectivity', *Linguistics and Philosophy* 7: 57–82.

Sanders, T. and Spooren, W. (1999) 'Communicative intentions and coherence relations', in W. Bublitz, U. Lenk and E. Ventola (eds.) *Coherence in Spoken and Written Discourse*: *How to Create it and How to Describe it*, Amsterdam: John Benjamins, 235–50.

Schegloff, E. (1990) 'On the organization of sequences as a source of "coherence" in talk-in-interaction', in B. Dorval (ed.) *Conversational Organization and its Development*, New York: Ablex, 51–78

Sinclair, J. (1991) *Corpus, Concordance, Collocation*, Oxford: Oxford University Press.

van Dijk, T. (1972) *Some Aspects of Text Grammars*, Berlin: Mouton.

Vuchinich, S. (1977) 'Elements of cohesion between turns in ordinary conversation', *Semiotics* 20: 229–57.

Chapter 10

Jenny Thomas

ACTIVITY TYPES VERSUS SPEECH EVENTS

S OCIOLINGUISTICS AND PRAGMATICS are both centrally concerned with the effect of context on language: the sociolinguist is primarily interested in the *systematic* linguistic correlates of social and contextual variables. Within sociolinguistics, the most fully developed and best known framework for describing context is the one proposed by Hymes (1962) in his seminal article 'The ethnography of speaking'. With his SPEAKING mnemonic he offers a comprehensive checklist for the description of what he terms 'speech events'. These are summarized in the table below:

Table 10.1 The SPEAKING mnemonic

Situation	This can be a physical setting (e.g., classroom) or an abstract setting (e.g., a committee meeting, a graduation ceremony).
Participants	Speaker, hearer, audience, etc.
Ends	Some speech events have conventional outcomes (e.g., 'diagnosis,' 'verdict'). Can also include individual goals.
Act sequences	Message form, message content.
Key	Tone, manner or spirit of act (e.g., serious, ironic).
Instrumentalities	Channel or mode (is the language spoken, written, etc.?). Forms of speech (which dialect, accent or other variety does the speaker employ?).
Norms	Norms of interpretation. Norms of interaction.
Genre	Categories such as joke, lecture, advertisement.

This same framework is often used by pragmaticists for describing context, but it is not obvious that it is the most appropriate one. Hymes, it should be noted, was primarily interested in describing rather formal, often highly ritualized events, such as weddings, funerals, welcoming ceremonies (see Hymes 1962 or, for a clear and simple overview, Saville-Troike 1982). It is not necessarily the case that less formal, rigid or predictable events, such as 'a university admissions interview', 'a visit to the doctor's', 'a dressing down by the headmaster' are well-handled within this framework and casual conversations certainly are not.

Hymes's framework does an excellent job of revealing to us the taken-for-granted aspects of interactions, but the most interesting features can be obscured by a welter of (frequently incidental) detail. Moreover it does not enable us (nor was it so designed) to explain why it is that one person performs very differently from another in the 'same' linguistic situation (for example, why one student emerges from an interview having succeeded in gaining a university place, while another does not; why one person succeeds in talking his or her way into a private function, while another does not). Hymes's framework leaves no room for the individual's contribution, for showing how one speaker successfully exploits a situation to achieve his or her goals, while the other fails dismally.

So, although pragmaticists might want to use a framework such as Hymes's as a point of departure, we cannot leave it there. A possible way forward is suggested by Levinson's notion of *activity type*. Taking his approach and terminology from prototype theory, Levinson defines an activity type as:

> a fuzzy category whose focal members are goal-defined, socially constituted, bounded, events with *constraints* on participants, setting, and so on, but above all on the kinds of allowable contributions. Paradigm examples would be teaching, a job interview, a jural interrogation, a football game, a task in a workshop, a dinner party and so on.
>
> (Levinson 1979: 368)

It is surprising how few pragmaticists have adopted this, in my view, very promising framework. Hymes's framework for describing a speech event has many points in common with Levinson's activity type, but there is an important difference in emphasis (precisely reflecting the different approaches of the sociolinguist and the pragmaticist to the description of linguistic interaction). Put very simply, Hymes sees context as constraining the way the individual speaks; Levinson sees the individual's use of language as shaping the 'event'. The sociolinguist tries to show how features of context *systematically* constrain language use. The pragmaticist tries to show how speakers use language in order to change the situation they find themselves in. Now some events (and this is particularly true of the type of ritualistic events that most concerned Hymes) clearly give little or no room for manoeuvre; to give a very extreme example, the coronation of a British monarch gives virtually no opportunity for the individual participant to change anything – every word is scripted, every gesture rehearsed, each burst of 'spontaneous applause' elaborately choreographed.[1] At the other extreme, some situations can be completely transformed by a particular use of language – a particularly dramatic example of this is the way in which a single courageous heckler began the process that turned President Ceauşescu's rally for the

Communist Party faithful into a ferocious anti-government protest.[2] Less sensationally, tense situations can be defused by a particular speaker's contribution; a skilful speaker can use language in a multitude of ways in order to turn the tables on an opponent.

Clearly most situations lie between the totally pre-scripted and the totally unscripted and a good description of context could usefully take as its point of departure the sociolinguist's description of givens (in this and many other regards pragmatics can be seen to be parasitic upon sociolinguistics), but it would not stop there. The pragmaticist will go on to explore how individuals, given the situation in which they find themselves and the linguistic means at their disposal, use their linguistic resources to try to achieve their goals. So how do we describe an activity type? An activity type description could include a statement of:

The goals of the participants: Notice that we are talking about the goals of the individuals, rather than the goals of the event (as in Hymes's model). The goals of one participant may be different from those of another. For example, the goal of a trial is to come up with a fair verdict, but the goals of the prosecution lawyer (to get a verdict of 'guilty') are diametrically opposed to those of the defence lawyer and the defendant. An individual's goals may change during the course of the interaction.

Allowable contributions: Some interactions are characterized by social or legal constraints on what participants may say. For example, in courts of law the prosecution is not allowed to refer to a defendant's previous convictions; in the British House of Commons members may not use certain abusive terms; at academic conferences you are not supposed to make *ad hominem* comments. What is pragmatically interesting is the way in which people will work round these restrictions. Coulthard (1989), for example, relates how one prosecution lawyer was able to indicate that the defendant had previous convictions by referring to the circumstances in which the defendant had injured his foot (it had been broken during a burglary); Churchill (prohibited from calling an opponent a 'liar'), famously came up with the phrase 'guilty of a terminological inexactitude'.[3]

The degree to which Gricean maxims are adhered to or are suspended: The expectation of the way in which the maxims will be observed varies considerably from culture to culture and from activity type to activity type. In some activity types (e.g., in Parliament, in media interviews with politicians or in the law courts), there is a very low expectation that what is said (or implied) will be the whole truth; in other activity types (such as going to Confession) the expectation that the speaker will tell the whole truth without prevarication is extremely high (see Grice, Chapter 3, this volume). Some inferences can only be drawn in relation to the activity type. For example, the actor Nigel Hawthorne, talking about unsuccessful plays he had been in before he became famous,[4] said: 'Friends would come backstage and talk about the weather.' The irrelevance of the friends' comments can only be judged in relation to an activity type in which there was a powerful expectation that they would congratulate Hawthorne on the excellence of his performance.

The degree to which interpersonal maxims are adhered to or are suspended: As with the Gricean maxims, the expectation of the way in which interpersonal maxims (see Grice, Chapter 3, this volume) will be observed varies from culture to culture and from activity type to activity type. Thus, the modesty maxim is more highly valued in Japan than in Britain, but within Britain it would be more highly valued in some activity types than in others. For example, at an awards ceremony, the person receiving an award (an actor, say) would be expected to minimize his or her own achievements and give credit to the director, producer, fellow actors and so on; at a job interview, by contrast, the interviewee would try to maximize his or her achievements, while striving not to appear big-headed.

Turn-taking and topic control: To what degree can an individual exploit turn-taking norms in order to control an interaction, establish his or her own agenda, etc.?

The manipulation of pragmatic parameters: To what degree can an interactant use language in order to increase or decrease social distance (e.g., by the use of intimate or formal address terms), power, rights and obligations and size of imposition? To what extent (e.g., by the strategic use of different registers) can the individual increase or decrease the formality of the situation?

The two examples that follow are both taken from the same 'speech event' – a PhD supervision. Speaker A is a male academic, speaker B a female research student. They have known each other for several years and are good friends. The interaction took place in A's office and the two examples occurred within a few minutes of one another. The symbol / is used to indicate overlapping speech, italics are used to indicate an interpolation (generally a backchannel) by the other speaker:

Example 1

A   That's right. But then, there's a difference between that and what your um *[mm]* ultimate sort of social *[mm]* if you like purpose *[mm]* or objective *[mm mm]* is in the encounter *[mm]*. Okay? Now, would there be . . . would there be a further subdivision . . . I mean that's a question, would there be a further subdivision between, as it were tactical goal-sharing and long-term goal-sharing and would the tactical goal-sharing be equivalent to what you're calling 'observance of the conventions of the language game' or not? Because it did seem to me when I was reading this that I could see the difference you were drawing between linguistic cooperation and goal-sharing but I wondered whether there wasn't a further sub-division within goal-sharing between the tactical and the strategic?

B   Okay well/

A   and that the 'tactical' might be . . . might be in harmony with 'observance of the conventions of the language game' *[mm]* but might not, actually.

B   Well um er um what I was trying to get at here was why so many otherwise intelligent people have completely and utterly rejected Grice *[mm hmm]* and they have *[sure]* and it seems to me that why they've done it is because they do not see man as a fundamentally cooperative animal *[that's right]*. Now. . .

Example 2

A   Oh, 'e's back is 'e? From Columbia?

B   Mm and I snapped off his fl. . . you know how I fidget when I'm nervous and there was this 'orrible looking thing and I thought it was a a a spider on the end of a cobweb and I snapped it off and apparently he'd been nurturing it in his breast for about two years.

A   What was it?

B   I don't know. Some silly plant but he was obviously/

A   /our plants got nicked.

B   Really?

A   In the last week yeah we've had all our plants knocked off

B   What where from?

A   Here.

B   Really?

A   Must've been stolen from here and the Institute and the Literature Department.

B   How strange. Oh and a bird shat on my head and then/

A   /I thought that was good luck!

B   Yes. You wouldn't've if it had happened to you. And and I thought all that remains is for me drawers to fall down and my happiness is complete. Well the lecture went very well indeed and er there was him there was a man called somebody or other Charles or Charles somebody.

A   Charl. . . No. I don't know him.

B   And he said he's got a good friend in Finland and apparently she heard this lecture I gave over there. She's doing her bloody PhD on it.

A   Is she?

B   Yeah. On pragmatic failure.

A   Oh well, I mean, it's a. . .it's quite a likely phenomenon I would have thought.

B   Anyway

A   Anyway, it went all right?

The point I am concerned to make here is that a sociolinguistic (Hymesian) description of context would not explain the differences between the two examples. The physical setting (the supervisor's office), the participants, etc., all remain constant. An 'activity type' approach would show that what is different is the participants' use of language. From within their respective (socio)linguistic resources each speaker has drawn upon a range of pragmatic strategies to change the nature of the activity in which each is involved. At every level of linguistics, we can observe deliberate choices which, in example 2, have the effect of systematically reducing the social distance between A and B, emphasizing common ground and shared values.

Although both speakers clearly *can* pronounce /h/ and both do so all the time in example 1 (harmony, here, have), both 'drop their h's' and used stigmatized forms in example 2: '*e's back is* 'e and '*orrible looking thing*. At the level of syntax, we see that the grammatical structure of example 1 is more formal (e.g., use of *do not* instead of *don't*, compared with the informal *wouldn't've* in example 2) and more complex (compare the number of subordinate clauses that occur in A's first contribution in example 1 with the simple coordination that occurs in B's first contribution in example 2). The vocabulary in example 1 is formal and technical; example 2 has a plethora of informal, slang and taboo terms (*drawers, nicked, knocked off, shot, bloody*). Example 1 has a number of polite hedges to mitigate face-threat (*I wondered. . ., it did seem to me. . .*), metapragmatic comment (*I mean that's a question*) that are in contrast to the direct contradiction that occurs in example 2 (*You wouldn't've if it had happened to you*). The turn-taking and topic control in the two extracts are strikingly different: in example 1, A controls both; in example 2, the turns are very evenly distributed and both participants have their own topic (B wants to talk about the lecture she had just given at Aston University, A wants to talk about the theft) that each develops successfully, although in the end B's topic is jointly developed by both speakers.

In short, what we see in examples 1 and 2 is language that is not simply a reflection of the physical or social context, or of the role relationship between the two speakers, but language used in order to establish and then change the nature of the relationship between A and B and the nature of the activity type in which they are participating.

References

Coulthard, M. (1989) *Unpublished paper read at Linguistics Circle* (February 1989), Lancaster University, UK.

Hymes, D. (1962) 'The ethnography of speaking', in T. Gladwin and W.C. Sturtevant (eds) *Anthropology and Human Behavior*, Washington, DC: Anthropological Society of Washington, 13–53.

Levinson, S. C. (1979) 'Activity types and language', *Linguistics* 17(5/6): 365–99.

Saville-Troike, M. (1982) *The Ethnography of Communication: An Introduction*, Oxford: Basil Blackwell, 7–22.

Notes

1   Although in 1821 Queen Caroline, consort of George IV, had a good stab at disrupting the coronation of her estranged husband.

2   Bucharest, 22 December 1989.

3   *Hansard*, 22 February 1906, column 555.

4   *Desert Island Discs*, BBC Radio 4, 30 November 1986.

Chapter 11

David Machin and
Theo Van Leeuwen

GENRE ANALYSIS IN
MEDIA DISCOURSE

Introduction: a linguistic approach to genre

IN MANY ACADEMIC DISCIPLINES, for instance media and cultural studies or film studies, the term 'genre' tends to have a rather loose and flexible meaning. It can mean the subject matter of a film or other medium, such as 'science fiction' or 'horror', or the effect of the contents, such as 'thriller' or 'comedy'. Or it can refer to communication functions such as 'advertisements' or 'news', or to truth claims such as 'documentary' or 'reality television'. Here the use of the term is rather fluid and context-dependent. Linguists have developed more precise and systematic kinds of genre analysis, aimed at bringing out that genres are kinds of communicative acts that involve particular kinds of interaction and set up particular kinds of relationships between interactants. For example, a conversation is a different genre of communication than a lecture. A game is a different genre than a speech. Each sets up different relationships between the participants. Each fulfils specific communicative functions such as persuasion, entertainment, teaching, bonding, etc. And each involves a sequence of 'stages' or 'moves' that interactants immediately recognize as realizing such relationships and functions. Without this level of anticipation communication would be very difficult.

It is important to point at the differences between genre and discourse, as well as at their interaction. The same discourse can be realized through different genres of communication, and the same genre can realize different discourses. For example, a president might address his nation about the need to go to war for humanitarian reasons to defeat terrorists who threaten a local people. This presents a particular discourse of war in which war is about humanitarian intervention, rather than about territory, resources or proud nationalism. This same humanitarian discourse, however, can be realized through a number of different genres, for instance not only political speeches, but also computer video games where the gamer can play as a soldier defeating a terrorist enemy to help local civilians, or play where children play as soldiers with plastic guns battling an evil nameless enemy in the name of protecting the vulnerable locals.

Genres will also have different linguistic characteristics and draw on different modes of communication. For example, a genre intended to instruct a soldier about a particular military engagement will use language differently from a genre through which a politician seeks to explain this to the public. And, importantly, genres need not be linear and may include images and other communicative modes. A computer video game might not tell us about who 'we' are linguistically but communicate this visually through images of powerful-looking highly individualized soldiers. A toy soldier to be used in play would carry the same discourses on its packaging through images, fonts and colours.

Genres can be seen as containers for discourses in use. But it is important to note, as we show in this chapter, that they are not simply neutral communicative acts. As containers they can shape and control how the discourses are communicated and act upon the social world.

In sum, a linguistic approach to genre makes the following assumptions:

Genres are defined as habitual, conventional means for doing specific kinds of social work: instructing teachers, reassuring children, selling products, solving problems, and so on.

Genres are also and at the same time defined in terms of the social relations they encode, which can be equal or unequal in status, formal, casual or intimate, and so on.

Genres can be described as a series of stages, each fulfilling a particular communicative function. Together, and in their particular sequences, these stages do the communicative work that defines the genre as a whole.

In the rest of this chapter we will first clarify how genre and discourse are different and how they interact. In the second part we will draw on the work of a number of writers to demonstrate an approach to the systematic and detailed analysis of genres. In the third and final section we move on to show how genres, while appearing as neutral containers for discourse, are ideological, arguing that it is precisely their neutral appearance that allows them to carry out their ideological work so effectively. In this third section we look at a number of texts from the international versions of the women's lifestyle magazine *Cosmopolitan*. We show how genres in these texts carry important ideological content. While carrying out a research project on how transnational media corporations adapt their globally branded products for local markets, we found that while there was often an attempt to localize content to speak to certain specific cultural values, identities and scenarios, what remained constant was the generic structure of the 'hot tips' problem–solution genre. While this genre may represent the world in localized ways, the way it presents these discourses is global and the same the world over. This can be seen in Figure 11.1. Here a career issue is presented in the form of a simple 'problem–solution' genre. In the left column we place the text as it develops and on the right we label the communicative function of each 'stage'. As we move through the chapter we explain how these functions can be established.

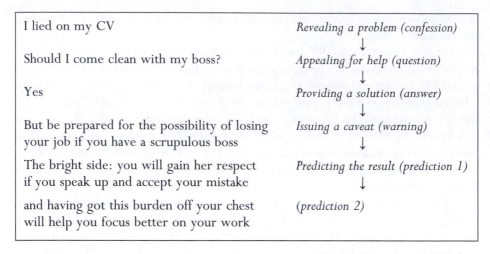

I lied on my CV	*Revealing a problem (confession)*
	↓
Should I come clean with my boss?	*Appealing for help (question)*
	↓
Yes	*Providing a solution (answer)*
	↓
But be prepared for the possibility of losing your job if you have a scrupulous boss	*Issuing a caveat (warning)*
	↓
The bright side: you will gain her respect if you speak up and accept your mistake	*Predicting the result (prediction 1)*
	↓
and having got this burden off your chest will help you focus better on your work	*(prediction 2)*

Figure 11.1 Advice column in *Cosmopolitan* magazine (Indian version, November 2001: 58)

We will argue that this genre, while seemingly offering a practical solution to a common problem, is ideological and constructs women's identities and agency as intertwined with the values of the neo-capitalist order. It presents the solutions to life's problems as consumer goods on a supermarket shelf, and neither presents the possibility of sustenance and support from fellow human beings, nor a recognition of the fact that these problems have political and social dimensions. There is only the individual. While much attention is given to the global dissemination of consumer brands of food and drink, clothing and movies, much less attention has been given to the way that the local can become a simple adornment used to gloss over the more basic architecture of the global. Genre analysis can reveal this and draw out the ideological dimensions of the *forms* of texts and the kinds of social and political relations these forms create between interactants.

Doing genre analysis

Since for linguists genre is a piece of interaction that fulfils specific communicative functions and creates specific kinds of relations between interactants, analysis of texts in terms of genre therefore involves:

Describing what people do to, for or with each other by means of texts and communicative events.

Describing how the way in which they do this helps set up or maintain specific relationships (formal or informal, equal or unequal, etc.).

One of the first linguists to attempt a systematic account of genre was Longacre (1974) who distinguished four basic types of genre: the *narrative* genre, which entertains; the *procedural* genre (the 'how-to-do-it' or 'how-it-is-done' text); the *expository* genre, which describes, explains and interprets the world; and the *hortatory* genre, which aims to 'influence conduct', to get people to feel or think or do in certain ways. He argued that these genres are universal, presenting examples from a number of societies (Longacre, 1971), correlating their functions (entertaining, instructing, explaining, persuading, etc.) to the linguistic features that typically manifests them. This is summarized in Table 11.1.

The table places the different genres chronologically as regards whether people and actions are linked in terms of chronology. So narratives clearly must be and deal with events that have already happened or are happening and are told in first or third person. But narratives are not necessarily prescriptive as they do not seek to provide any kind of guidance nor establish norms and rules. A narrative about the growing love between a woman and man seeks to entertain rather that persuade about a way of thinking or procedure. Procedural texts must also have chronology for the purposes of how to do something, such as how to make a cake, but no specific people are addressed. These texts can use imperatives ('first break two eggs in a bowl') or 'you' ('you first break two eggs in a bowl'). Procedural texts are projected into the future, in other words to a task not yet performed. They are clearly prescriptive as they seek to provide guidance to change behaviour to establish norms or rules of doing something.

Expository texts do not place events in chronological order but link general statements into a logical structure as in an explanation. Their structure is logical since reason must be given for why things are the way that is proposed such as why the ocean is influenced by gravity. These are not prescriptive in that they do not seek to change behaviour but rather to provide information. Hortatory texts are like procedural texts as they address the listener or reader directly and are prescriptive as their aim is influence and guide attitudes and behaviour. Their structure must also be logical as reasons must be given for the way. But unlike prescriptive texts they

Table 11.1 Longacre's discourse genres

	− prescriptive	*+ prescriptive*

+ chronological	*Narrative*
	First or third person
	Actor-oriented
	Accomplished time
	  (encoded as past or present)
	Chronological linkage
		Procedural
		Non-specific person
		Goal-oriented
		Projected time (encoded as
		  past, present or future)
		Chronological linkage

− chronological	*Expository*
	Any person (usually third)
	Subject matter oriented
	Time not focal
	Logical linkage
		Hortatory
		Second person
		Addressee oriented
		Commands, suggestions
		  (encoded as imperatives
		  or 'soft' commands)
		Logical linkage

do not have to be chronological. One of the skills of persuasive texts can be to link events in creative ways.

Longacre stresses that these genres should be seen as 'deep structures'. A procedural text, for instance, may have a narrative 'surface', for instance in a story of children baking a cake with their mother. On the surface it appears to be a narrative, but a closer look shows that all the stages of baking a cake are included, so that the text can serve as instruction just as well as a straightforwardly procedural text. Such a text will combine the entertainment function of the narrative with the instructional function of the procedural text. Anthropologists such as Lévi-Strauss (1978) have shown that traditional narratives often embed instruction. And while these stories may on the one hand entertain and on the other provide instructions, the evaluations and procedures may suit particular power interests in that society. Having the surface appearance of entertainment can gloss over the ideological nature and aims of the definition of how things should be done. It is common in today's media as well for instance in celebrity profiles in women's magazines, which often provide what is, from the point of narrative flow, an excess of detail on the beauty and health regimes that keep them young, slim and beautiful. Yet these texts at root naturalize procedures oriented towards notions of the body and appearance that are deeply ideological. As our analysis progresses, we will show that genres are not as homogeneous as Longacre described. Nevertheless his account was a significant step forward in thinking about genres as fulfilling specific communicative functions and as being able to be combined for ideological purposes.

Where Longacre provided an early account of the communicative functions of genres, William Labov (1972), in his work on the 'beginning-middle-end' structure of narrative, first divided narratives into the stages that develop the communicative function of the narrative as a whole, in other words, stages of the act of storytelling, rather than stages of the story told. His ideas have since been applied to non-narrative genres as well (e.g., Hasan 1978; Martin 1985, 1992; Swales 1990; Van Leeuwen 1987; Ventola 1987; Machin and Van Leeuwen 2007). Here we use a feature article, titled 'Her bridesmaids were killed on their way to the wedding', from *Cosmopolitan* magazine (USA version, November 2004: 92–5) to describe Labov's stages. We then show how this technique can be extended to other genres:

1 Abstract

The storyteller begins with a brief summary or indication of the topic of the story, to attract the listener's attention and interest:

> Her bridesmaids were killed on their way to the wedding
> What was to be the happiest day of Bree Mayer's life turned into the worst with one phone call. She shared her heartbreaking experience with *Cosmo*

2 Orientation

The storyteller then introduces the setting – who is involved, when and where – and the 'initial event', the event that kicks off the story. This provides orientation for the listener. Elements of orientation may also occur later in the story as new people, places and things are introduced.

> Joey and I met in 2000, when we were both freshmen at North Central University in Minnesota. We were in a gospel band on campus; he played the guitar and I sang. I was intrigued by Joey because he seemed kind of mysterious . . . One day, Joey invited me on a boat ride, but we ran out of gas in the middle of the lake. Since we didn't have any oars, we were stuck, so we started talking. By the time someone paddled out to rescue us I knew I wanted to spend a lot more time with this guy.

3 Complication

The story then moves into the events that make up its core.

> Joey and Bree decide to get married. Joey's three sisters will be brides-maids and are due to attend the pre-wedding 'bachelorette's party'. They are late to arrive. Then there is a phonecall and Bree learns that all three have died in a road accident.

4 Evaluation

Throughout the development of the story there are moments of evaluation. At such moments the storyteller reasserts the relevance, importance and interest of the story. In this story this is done mostly by indicating and reinforcing the narrator's *feelings* about the events.

> I was in total shock. . .
> I felt completely numb. . .

5 Resolution

The final event, the outcome of the story, provides the listener with meaning. Stories are told to convey ideas about life. They have an issue, a life problem, to resolve. In this case the issue in need of resolution is whether, such a short time after the tragedy, the wedding should or should not go ahead. The resolution is that it should.

> Marriage is a celebration of love, and 'love can heal'.

6 Coda

This stage, which is 'optional', has the storyteller signing off and making a bridge from the resolution to the 'here and now' of the telling of the story, and to its continuing relevance for the storyteller and/or the listeners. Here is the coda of the *Cosmopolitan* story.

> Now we try to take it one day at a time. Some are more difficult than others, but we're settling into the routine of any couple. We miss the

girls terribly. But we are helping each other deal with the loss and learning to balance grief with joy.

All these stages are realized by specific linguistic features, as indicated by the examples in Table 11.2.

The basic characteristics of this approach therefore are:

A genre is described as a series of 'stages', each of which has a specific function in moving the text or communicative event forwards towards the realization of its communicative aim. In the analysis each stage is given a functional label to bring out this function. We can see this in the advice column shown as Figure 11.1 earlier in the chapter such as 'revealing a problem' or 'appealing for help'.

Each stage consists of one or more of the same speech acts (e.g., 'question', 'answer', 'warning') as we saw in this example. In Figure 11.1, the first stage contains only 'confession' but other advice columns may contain more that may come in the form of a narrative.

The sequence of these stages as a whole realizes a particular strategy for achieving an overall communicative goal, in this case the solution of a problem.

Table 11.2 Speech acts and their realizations

Stages and their typical speech acts	Typical realizations	Examples
Abstract (speech acts of summarizing and attracting interest)	Action clauses summarizing the story; relational clauses with evaluative attribute	Her bridesmaids were killed on their way to the wedding. What was to be the happiest day of Bree Mayer's life turned into the worst.
Orientation (speech acts of description)	E.g., relational clauses describing people and places	He seemed mysterious. We were in a band.
Complication (speech acts of narration)	Action clauses	Alyssa then called the highway patrol. He looked at me and said: 'They're dead. They're all dead.'
Evaluation (speech acts of emotive expression)	E.g., first-person relational clauses with mental process attributes	I was in shock. I felt completely numb.
Coda (general observations of the impact of the narrated events)	E.g., clauses of habitualized action or relational clauses with mental process attribute	We are helping each other deal with the loss. Some [days] are more difficult than others.

Because each stage is homogeneous in terms of the communicative acts it contains, it will also be relatively homogeneous in terms of the linguistic features that characterize it. We can see this in Figure 11.1. In this case the 'revealing a problem' stage of the advice column has the typical features of a confession: first person, statements, past tense and verbs that are presented as a deviant action or state (lying on your CV).

Non-linear aspects of genre

The approach we have been drawing on so far has been designed for linear texts. However, many texts are partially or wholly non-linear. The magazine texts we analyse in this chapter for instance, include spatial and visual elements – particular kinds of images that have been placed in particular ways on the page in relation to the written text. It is therefore important to ask how these elements contribute to the communicative function of each stage and to the communicative function of the text as a whole.

Information structure

Kress and Van Leeuwen (1996) recognize three key principles of visual composition. First, information may be organized along a horizontal axis, with one element (e.g., a picture) on the left, and another (e.g., text) on the right. The left element is then presented as Given, that is, positioned as something already known to the reader or viewer, while the information on the right is presented as New, as something not yet known to the reader or viewer, and hence as something to which attention must be paid, and which is – at least in principle – negotiable or contestable in the larger communicative context.

Second, if information is organized vertically, with two different elements positioned one above the other, the information on top is presented as Ideal, that is, as the more abstract or generalized essence of the message, and the information below as Real, that is, as more down to earth and practical, and/or more detailed and specific information. Finally, information can be organized concentrically. In that case the Centre contains the information that is presented as the core, and the Margins contain information that is presented as in some sense subservient or complementary to the Centre, and deriving its identity and meaning from it. Combinations of the three principles are also possible.

Kress and Van Leeuwen (1996) also describe two other aspects of the spatial organization of information, the *salience* of the different elements, which can be realized by the size of the elements, or, for instance, by means of conspicuous colouring or tonal contrast, and the *framing* of the different elements, which signifies to which degree they are meant to be read as separate items or as 'belonging together', and which can be realized, for instance, by frame lines, or by the use of colour that can either make distinct elements cohere (e.g., through recurring colours) or contrast (e.g., through contrasting colours).

The kind of genre analysis described here is particularly useful for our purposes. As mentioned, a given genre can accommodate many different contents. The 'problem–solution' genre, for instance, can accommodate many different kinds of problem and many different kinds of solution. It is easily transferred from one context to another.

Modality

Our second methodological tool is modality analysis. The term 'modality' refers to semiotic resources for indicating as how true or as how real communication content is to be taken. In this chapter, as part of our analysis, we will deal primarily with the modality of images, the question of how images signify their status as factual or fictional, truth or fantasy, and so on. Kress and Van Leeuwen (1996) offer a list of eight visual qualities involved in judgements of visual modality. For our purposes here this involves whether the details of the objects and background depicted in the image are represented in full grained detail and focus or whether this detail has been reduced. We also ask how colour is represented. Do colour saturation, modulation and differentiation correspond to the realities of the photographed scene or are they either exaggerated or flattened and reduced? In the same way we ask whether the representation of light and shadow is realistic in its modality or either amplified or reduced.

For an initial example, consider again the advertising image. In many single-page magazine advertisements, the top part of the page shows the 'promise' of the product – how beautiful or glamorous or successful you will become if you buy the product, or how cool or soft or luxurious it will feel or taste or smell. The bottom part then provides factual detail and/or a picture of the product itself. In such advertisements the modality value of the two parts of the advertisement tend to differ. The top (Ideal) usually shows what you *might* be or *could* be (relatively low modality), the bottom (Real) what *is*, what you can *actually* buy right now in the shop if you want to (high modality). This is then expressed through subtle differences in the way certain means of visual expression are used. The top part may feature a photograph in a sepia-tinted black and white and the bottom part a photo of the product in full colour. The picture showing the 'promise of the product' may have soft focus, the photo in the bottom part may show the product in sharp detail. This illustrates how visual modality works. Increases or decreases in the degree to which certain means of visual expression are used (colour, sharpness, etc.) express increases or decreases in 'as how real' the image is meant to be taken.

Our reasons for using modality as a methodological tool in our study of *Cosmopolitan* are specific. We assume that *Cosmopolitan* communicates certain truths (e.g., those of the various experts on which it relies and the truths that go with certain forms of social, and especially sexual, behaviour) and that it seeks to extend these truths and these behaviours globally.

The problem–solution genre in the international versions of *Cosmopolitan* magazine

Case study 1: women's work in the Dutch version of *Cosmopolitan*

Every issue of every *Cosmopolitan* contains a section relating to work. Historically, the representation of the (largely corporate) workplace has been important in

Cosmopolitan, alongside sex, as signifying women having a place outside of the domestic environment, which itself indexes agency (men's magazines rarely represent men in work settings). We have chosen to look at representations of women at work in the different versions.

In the Dutch *Cosmopolitan* of November 2001, this section is titled 'Werk en reizen' ('Work and travel'). Only two of the five items in this section deal with work. A page titled 'Career' has five mixed items, among them the one shown in Figure 11.2 and a five-page feature has interviews with young Dutch women working in PR for, respectively, a fashion house, a theatre company, a zoo and a beauty products manufacturer. But work also appears in many other contexts. An article on gossip contains a section 'Gossip at work', and an article on dealing with anger uses many work-related examples – always set in unspecified office environments. Profiles of actresses and singers also deal with work-related issues, e.g. stress. The agony column includes a letter from a woman who cannot choose between her job (she is given a chance to work abroad) and her boyfriend, and the astrology column also contains a range of references to work ('Book a holiday for the 14th because there will many conflicts in the office that day'). Finally, although the vast majority of the 62 advertisements are for lingerie, perfumes, shampoo and other beauty products, there are five work-related advertisements, four of them for internet job-search sites. One of them ('A career in fashion looks good on you') in fact masquerades as a lingerie advertisement, with the copy in white lettering on a bluish photograph of a bra. The text in Figure 11.2 is from the 'Career' page.

The text in Figure 11.2 is analysed as follows in Table 11.3 (our translation).

Below, we discuss three key characteristics of this item:

THE PHOTOGRAPH HAS RELATIVELY LOW NATURALISTIC MODALITY AND DEPICTS 'WOMAN AT WORK' AS GLAMOROUS, BUT ALSO AS VULNERABLE AND NOT FULLY IN CONTROL

The picture, (left centre) shows an attractive model standing near a row of files. Although it illustrates a factual item, it has the sensory qualities of highly produced fashion and advertising photographs. There is an emphasis on the shimmering slinky, clingy fabrics of the model's dress and on her loose and lavish hair. The background is reduced, perhaps suggesting the photographer's studio rather than a real office location. The files in front of her only hint at a work setting. This is typical for *Cosmopolitan* work images (and for the work images in many advertisements and fashion shots): a few attributes – a computer, a pen, files, a plant – stand for work, in an abstracted, stylized way. Equally typical is the way the woman relates to – or rather, does not relate to – this attribute of work. Her position in relation to the files, and her way of touching them, do not clearly show her as actually searching for something. She is merely using the files as a support for her pose. And she is looking away, at something we cannot see, something left open for the viewer to fill in, or to supply from the context. Is she looking back, at the past, remembering that holiday? Frequently such wistful looks at something unseen are used of vulnerable people – refugees, victims of famines and other calamities, people who are no longer in control of their destinies. Here, then, we see a woman at work, glamorous, but also vulnerable, almost helpless, in a picture with a distinct air of unreality. In terms of

Figure 11.2 Careers section in *Cosmopolitan* magazine (Dutch version, November 2001)

Table 11.3 Genre analysis of text in Figure 11.2

Text	Genre analysis
Post-holiday stress?	**Problem**
There are jobs in which the jobs pile up while you're on holiday.	
It takes less than a day before stress makes you forget your beautiful trip.	**Elaboration of problem**
With these tips that won't happen:	**Goal**
If you need to keep something put it in a folder.	**Tip**
Before you go on holiday, reserve time to clean the 'rubbish' when you come back.	**Tip**
Make sure you have no appointments on your first morning back. This will give you a chance to look through the stuff that has piled up on your desk.	**Tip**
If there are any jobs waiting for you, put them on a to-do list.	**Tip**
And throw out anything you don't need any more.	**Tip?**
Want to read more? Look in the book 'Time Management for Dummies', by Jeffrey J. Mayer, ISBN 906789981 X	**Tip?**

the genre stages we can say that, on the one hand, it provides orientation. It is about a beautiful woman who is hesitant. It also provides an evaluation through implied mental processes. She appears to be uncertain. Such images are common to lifestyle magazines and advertising. While the text is in one sense expository and procedural these images do not illustrate nor provide evidence – the how-to-bake-a-cake would have diagrams or images to show how to do something or what something should look like, for example. Here the image plays a symbolic role.

THE TEXT HAS HIGH MODALITY AND USES A 'HOT TIPS' PROBLEM–SOLUTION GENRE

The text, on the other hand, is relatively straightforward. It fits Hodge and Kress's description of high modality (Hodge and Kress 1988: 121): 'emphatic, without qualifications . . . we know that we are being asked to believe that it is true.' It directly addresses the reader, first describing a familiar enough problem and then providing the solution in the form of a relatively unordered list of 'tips', which, as it happens, do not envisage the possibility that stress at work may derive from structural problems such as overwork due to staff cuts or fatigue from doing two jobs in order to meet living costs, and displace it to the level of minor organizational problems, suggesting that problems will go away when you get yourself organized.

Problem–solution genres pervade magazines like *Cosmopolitan*. Articles on subjects such as 'gossip', 'anger', 'embarrassing moments', etc., may be interrupted by tips, or contain tips in boxes, and profiles of stars may go quite deeply into the details of how such stars deal with stress, or keep themselves looking young and fit. A feature on the 'negative sides of autumn and winter' (*Cosmopolitan* magazine, Dutch version, November 2001: 5) starts with a problem and then offers the solution ('boost your resistance'), a solution worked out in sections on 'eating with more energy', vitamin pills, exercise and the 'power nap' and boxes on aromatherapy and an 'instant energy' lamp:

> You tire more easily, you have problems concentrating, you are irritable, you feel listless and you have difficulty sleeping. Sounds like diminished resistance. In this condition you're more likely to catch a cold or some other disease. Time to boost your resistance.

Again we find here that tiredness is not considered in relation to personal/ social/economic issues. For example the woman could be living off a low income with three young children, unable to afford proper childcare. Workloads could be heavy due to staff cutbacks to reduce operating costs. Yet issues are framed not in ways that point to required collective action or structural issues but are shared only in the sense that they have common solutions that can be applied to individual and isolated cases.

The issue also contains tips on how to calm down when overwhelmed with anger, how to keep your cool in the traffic, how to be hip without losing your own personality, and how to apply make-up and yet look 'natural'. The latter belongs to a slightly different category, however, as the 'tips', the direct 'what to do' instructions, are ordered sequentially, as in a recipe, while the tips in a 'hot tips' problem–solution text can appear in any order. In problem–solution advertisements, finally, there is only one solution, buy the product or obtain the service, even though there may, of course, be several problems – the more problems a product can solve, the better. There are therefore at least three problem–solution genres, a 'single-solution' genre, a 'hot tips' multiple-solution genre (an unordered list of 'instructions') and a 'procedure' multiple-solution genre (a time-ordered list of 'instructions').

THE PICTURE IS THE IDEAL AND THE TEXT THE REAL

The photograph and the text are spatially organized in terms of an Ideal–Real syntagm. The enticingly glamorous but also vulnerable and somewhat helpless *Cosmopolitan* woman is positioned as the idealized essence of the message, which not only emphasizes the problem (lack of control) over the solution (regaining a sense of control by getting organized), and links it to a particular kind of woman, but also creates contradictions between the fantasy of pleasurable glamour and the reality of the reader's life and work.

Cosmopolitan also includes texts that claim to be about real people doing real jobs. The images that accompany the profiles of women working in public relations in the Dutch version are higher in modality and less glamorous. For example, in an article about Linda Teeling, the picture shows her slightly from above and smiling at the camera, somewhat self-consciously, perhaps. The picture is clearly taken on location and the colours do not have the enhanced saturation and texture of those in Figure 11.2. High naturalistic, but lower sensory modality, therefore – the look of a snapshot, of a record of a real person in a real environment. But the image is still softened, we might argue, and it has the slightly blurred setting and sense of high-key lighting which is also characteristic of stock images such as that used in Figure 11.2.

Although starting like a narrative, the text for this article follows the genre of the testimonial (see Table 11.4). The first stage describes the 'conversion', the way in which Linda became involved with the Kuyichi brand. In the next stage Linda describes the brand identity, the Kuyichi message. Next she describes her own role in disseminating the message, her mission, and finally she gives an account of her identification with that role, first in a more specific way, and then again by means of

Table 11.4 Genre analysis of text in Linda Teeling article

Text	Genre analysis
I already worked here during the last few months of my studies. For my final project I did a communications plan for Kuyichi, and after I graduated I could start with them straightaway. Some parts from my plan are now actually implemented, but that's still a secret.	**'Conversion'**
What we have already done is send woollen socks with the invitation to the press to introduce the Fair Trade aspect in a humorous way. Kuyichi is a new fun brand with a story. Our jeans are made in accordance with Fair Trade practices: better working conditions, no child labour, that kind of thing. They cost the same as the competition but part of the profit goes to the people in Peru.	**Brand message**
As marketing- and PR-worker I have to promote the brand in the right way, through promotions and advertisements. I have to ensure that the brand radiates to others what we feel for it here.	**Mission**
At the moment I have only got one pair of Kuyichi jeans. I always wear them at work. Soon we'll be getting more stock in and I can choose whatever I want. They are special fun clothes which I would have chosen myself anyway. That's why I identify with the brand and that's just as well. It would be hard to promote something you didn't believe in.	**Identification with role (1)**
You have to relate to people to be able to do this work. I see the brand as a relationship: you put a lot of energy in it. Some things go well, some don't. You feel that immediately and you've got to keep working at it.	**Identification with role (2)**

an analogy in which she talks of her work as a personal relationship, in terms that are very compatible with the *Cosmopolitan* 'philosophy'. What is excluded here is as interesting as what is included: there are no managers telling Linda what to do, no other employees in fact, except through the use of 'we' and 'our' in the 'message' stage. Everything she does stems from her own initiative and her own total commitment to, and personal identification with, the brand. As far as the article is concerned, she has no boyfriend, no friends, no family, no hobbies – her work for the company is everything. The breakdown in Table 11.4 on p. 185 provides a genre analysis.

As mentioned before, the boundaries between stages are recognized by changes in the way language (or other modes) are used, and/or by framings, such as white space between blocks of text or framelines. In labelling the stages we first of all assume that every 'problem–solution' genre has at least a 'problem' and a 'solution'. The solution may be a single authoritative solution or a series of possible solutions, in which case terms such as 'recommendation' or 'tip' will be more appropriate. The text may be expanded in a number of ways, e.g., by elaborations or explanations or exemplifications of either the problem or the solution or the 'tips'. Overall, it is a matter of finding terms that adequately represent the communicative act realized by a given stage.

This testimonial has all the hallmarks of a religious testimonial: it tells a story of looking for the truth and finding it, and then testifies to this truth, and to the speaker's unstinting, personal and all-inclusive devotion to its dissemination.

As for the spatial organization of the page, this time it is horizontal. The picture is Given and the text New. We are therefore encouraged to think of the girl as someone 'already known', perhaps as someone just like us, the real Dutch readers of *Cosmopolitan*, who do not necessarily look like supermodels. The New is her devotion to a fashion brand and to the kind of total and quasi-religious devotion that many contemporary corporations require of their employees, and which, it is suggested here, combines fun, looking good, hard work and – important in a Dutch context – 'good works', charity.

Case study 2: women's work in the Indian version of *Cosmopolitan*

The 'Cosmo careers' section of the same month's Indian issue of *Cosmopolitan* is shown in Figure 11.3. It contains four items. The article '4 ways to win them over' aims to help managers to improve their communication skills. 'My brilliant career' is a short profile of the senior vice-president of a cable TV company. And then there are 'I lied on my CV. Should I come clean with my boss?' and a quote from the 'president of Indian Business and Professional Women': 'The successful women in technology I know don't believe in a glass ceiling.' Clearly, this magazine does not address the same kind of reader as the Dutch version. It assumes its readers are an elite of managers and bosses, while in European versions women's work almost always means office work, and the problem is not how to relate to your subordinates but how to relate to your boss.

In the index of the Indian *Cosmopolitan*, this 'Careers' page is listed under the heading 'Life and work'. The articles included in this section all apply the same ideas to work and life (love life, that is, for in the world of the 'fun, fearless female' there is only love and work). The article '9 ways to be a bad chick' gives tongue-in-cheek

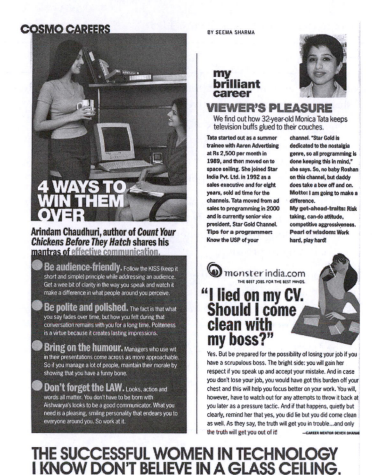

Figure 11.3 Careers section in *Cosmopolitan* magazine (Indian version, November 2001)

advice on love ('get down and dirty to snag your man') as well as work ('cuss out a pushy boss'). 'Great advice for 30 somethings' counsels the 30-something reader to 'stop job-hopping' and 'find someone who wants a commitment'. In 'Live your dream destiny' 'bad-vibe backlash' catches up with a woman who 'hooked up with her friend's guy' as well as with a woman who 'secretly went after a job her friend had applied for'. And 'How to change your life for the better' profiles four women who overcame obstacles and realized their dreams – of getting a steady boyfriend, recuperating from depression, slimming down and making a career in fashion. Some of the articles in the other sections also mix work life and intimate life in this way, e.g., 'Hit the big time', the 'Cosmo quiz' ('How independent are you?') and the profile of the 'fun, fearless female' of the month.

Comparing the Indian 'Cosmo careers' page (Figure 11.3) with its Dutch counterpart (Figure 11.2) shows a similar layout and a similar generic structure of the items included. Again, a 'hot tips' item is prominently featured.

Table 11.5 Genre analysis of text in Figure 11.3

4 ways to win them over	Goal
Arindham Chaudhuri, author of *Count Your Chickens Before They Hatch,* shares his mantras of effective communication.	Restatement of goal
<u>Be audience-friendly</u>. Follow the KISS (keep it short and simple) principle while addressing an audience. Get a wee bit of clarity in the way you speak and watch it make a difference in what people around you perceive.	Tip 1
<u>Be polite and polished.</u> The fact is that what you say fades over time, but how you felt during that conversation remains with you for a long time. Politeness is a virtue because it creates lasting impressions.	Tip 2
<u>Bring on the humour</u>. Managers who use wit in their presentations come across as more approachable. So if you manage a lot of people, maintain their morale by showing that you have a funny bone	Tip 3
<u>Don't forget the LAW</u>. Looks, action and words all matter. You don't have to be born with Aishwarya's looks to be a good communicator. What you need is a pleasing, smiling personality that endears you to everyone around you. So work at it.	Tip 4

An analysis of this item brings out further similarities:

THE PHOTOGRAPH HAS RELATIVELY LOW NATURALISTIC MODALITY AND SHOWS WOMEN AS GLAMOROUS, BUT NOT AS BEING IN CONTROL OF A SITUATION OR ACTIVITY

The picture shows two models in front of a desk. As in the Dutch version, the models are attractive, with lavish hair and radiant smiles, but not strikingly beautiful. The modality is both abstract and sensory. It is abstract, and hence slightly unreal from a naturalistic point of view, because of the reduced colour differentiation (an overall emphasis on blue) and the reduced background, with its use of just a few props (computer, files) to suggest an office setting. On the other hand, the picture is sensory, and reminiscent of advertising and fashion photography in its use of very vivid, sensual colour. *Cosmopolitan* photographer Michael Wray told us that the magazine prefers photos that 'look great', and are 'joyful', but also blend into the design of the page. People should forget them instantly and not even be directly drawn towards them, he said.

And why, when the item addresses women who 'manage a lot of people', do we see two women smiling blankly (and not particularly confidently) at each other over a cup of tea? Why are they not actually shown in their role as managers?

THE TEXT HAS HIGH MODALITY AND USES A 'HOT TIPS' PROBLEM–SOLUTION GENRE

As in the Dutch version, the text uses a 'hot tips' format and is relatively straightforward, lacking the air of unreality of the photograph. The format is graphically realized by having the underlined words from Table 11.5 in large blue font and the tips bullet-pointed in a box, and it is expanded by using 'maxims', pieces of expert wisdom such as 'the fact is that what you say fades over time', to lend authority to the directives. Typically the tips start with a directive (e.g., 'be audience friendly') and then link this to a maxim (see Table 11.6).

The same format is found elsewhere, e.g., in the above-mentioned '9 ways to be a bad chick'. The genre analysis for this text can be seen in Table 11.7 where mundane acts are fashioned in high modality through directives, maxims and expert wisdom. This text too carried a photograph of relatively low naturalistic modality showing a glamorous woman.

In longer versions, tips may be endorsed by expert opinions and/or illustrated with case stories. Such variations and expansions of the 'hot tips' genre form a key aspect of *Cosmopolitan* writing – even articles that at first sight seem to deal with an issue or to tell a story turn out to be a 'hot tips' format in disguise. Thus the magazine positions itself as expert and friend, drawing on case stories to give a sense of real women and common interests.

Table 11.6 Genre analysis of text in Figure 11.3 (extract)

Bring on the humour.	**Directive**
Managers who use wit in their presentations come across as more approachable.	**Maxim**
So if you manage a lot of people, maintain their morale by showing that you have a funny bone.	**Elaboration of directive**

Table 11.7 Genre analysis of '9 ways to be a bad chick'

Smoke a cigar.	**Directive**
Leave the ultrathins to the wuss.	**Directive**
Nothing's worse than a girl with a mean cigar tucked between her teeth.	**Maxim**
Wrap your scarlet pouters around a Habano and blow smoke rings as you discuss the stock market with your contemporaries.	**Elaboration of directive**

THE PICTURE IS THE IDEAL AND THE TEXT IS THE REAL

As in the Dutch version, fantasy and reality are ambiguously juxtaposed. The somewhat unreal picture, showing women as glamorous but not 'in control', is positioned as the idealized essence of the message, and the more straightforward text, seeking to help women to gain greater control over a specific aspect of their reality, is positioned as the Real.

'My brilliant career', taken from the same page as '4 ways to win them over', can be compared with the 'real woman' profile in the Dutch version. Here, too, the 'passport photo' image has higher modality, to indicate a real person. The lighting is realistic and what little can be seen of the background is highly articulated. *Cosmopolitan* photographers have spoken to us of the way make-up and hair have to be modified to give the sense of a real person (Romilly Lockyer) and of the need for higher colour modulation in photographs of this kind (Michael Wray). Table 11.8 provides a genre analysis.

Like the Dutch text, this text indicates total support for, and total dedication to, work and its values. But unlike Linda, Tata is a boss, and she is in it for herself. If she adheres to the 'mission' of the channel she works for, she does so in the first place to further her own career, and the Dutch emphasis on *believing* in that mission is lacking. Linda, the employee, is happy to 'serve'. She seeks job satisfaction ('it's like a relationship') rather than career advancement. Tata, the boss, on the other hand, aggressively seeks career advancement and success.

As for the genre, although it is in principle a story, a 'how to' element has been worked into both the title and the body of the article (the tip). In fact the whole

Table 11.8 Genre analysis of 'My brilliant career' from Figure 11.3

We find out how 32-year-old Monica Tata keeps television buffs glued to their couches.	**Problem (narrativized)**
Tata started out as a summer trainee with Aron Advertising at Rs 2,500 per month in 1989, and then moved on to space selling. She joined Star India Pvt. Ltd. in 1992 as a sales executive and for eight years, sold ad time for the channels.	**Tip (career history)**
Tata moved from ad sales to programming in 2000 and is currently senior vice president, Star Gold Channel.	**Tip**
Tips for a programmer: Know the USP of your Channel. 'Star Gold is dedicated to the nostalgia genre, so all programming is done keeping this in mind,' she says. So, no baby Roshan on this Channel, but daddy does take a bow off and on. Motto: I am going to make a difference.	**Directive (career attitudes)**
My get-ahead-traits: Risk taking, can-do attitude, Competitive aggressiveness.	**Directive (maxim)**
Pearl of wisdom: Work hard, play hard!	**Directive (maxim)**

story can be seen as a piece of advice, a model for how to succeed in the commercial world. The final part of the text has intertextual affinities with the Q&A genre in that the introductions to each 'career attitude' could be seen as questions (e.g., 'What is your motto?') and also with CVs, those documents in which we must narrativize ourselves in such a way that companies will 'buy'.

Conclusion

Genre analysis involves describing the stages or moves texts use to carry out specific communicative acts. Through this we can point to kinds of social relations that they build and the discourses they carry. Most importantly this allows us to point to the ideological work that they do. The texts we have analysed in this chapter combine genres to, in the first place, appear entertaining, fun and not so serious. They also provide exposition and procedure that suggest learning. But within these texts, the views of the world they present, the discourses they disseminate around the planet are neither neutral expositions nor simple and natural procedures. And just because they are presented as fun, often with playful language, this does not mean that they should be easily dismissed. These genres represent women as acting alone and selfishly in the world and strategically in a context devoid of issues that require collective actions and decisions. Such texts can deal with issues such as career advancement, even in times of layoffs, yet avoid political issues or responsibilities to fellow workers and the social consequences of large scale redundancies, reducing this rather to mundane tips about appearing to be enthusiastic and avoiding being seen with those most likely to be laid off. Tiredness and fatigue are related not to work overload and staff shortages but to petty matters of personal organization and aromatherapy. In each case we see images of young attractive women in pleasant settings symbolizing on the one hand the glamour of this world but also providing an element of evaluation. Tired women are not pictured in bleak work environments or holding three children along with their briefcase but looking thoughtful or determined.

We have also shown that while there can be different levels of localization by the magazines in order to meet local expectations of women's status and expecta- tions, this is little more than a gloss that is laid over the global architecture of the problem–solution format. Women around the world increasingly find what is wrong in their lives and the ways that these can be addressed cut off from sociopolitical reality and oriented to individualized selfish strategic action. Work becomes indistinguishably mixed in with the sphere of women's libidinal and personal lives and with fantasies of glamour, which at the same time perpetuate women's vulnera- bility and lack of control.

What genre analysis shows us is that it is not so much the immediate surface part of the story or text, but the deeper structure that can carry its core ideas about agency, roles and social organization. As global corporations enter new territories they may set their stories in different locations and populate them with different characters but the fundamental reasons for the behaviour of these characters, for what they want and how they seek to attain it, follows one and the same logic wherever these stories are told.

References

Hasan, R. (1978) 'Text in the systemic-functional model', in W.U. Dressler (ed.) *Current Trends in Textlinguistics*, Berlin: De Gruyter.

Hodge, R. and Kress, G. (1988) *Social Semiotics*, Cambridge: Polity

Kress, G. and Van Leeuwen, T. (1996) *Reading Images – The Grammar of Visual Design*, London: Routledge.

Labov, W. (1972) *Language in the Inner City*, Philadelphia: University of Philadelphia Press.

Lévi-Strauss, C. (1978) *Myth and Meaning*, London: Routledge & Kegan Paul.

Longacre, R.E. (ed.) (1971) *Philippine Discourse and Paragraph Studies in memory of Betty McLachli*, Canberra: Pacific Linguistics.

—— (1974) 'Narrative versus other discourse genre', in R. Brend (ed.) *Advances in Tagmemics*, Amsterdam: North Holland.

Machin, D. and Van Leeuwen, T. (2007) *Global Media Discourse*, London: Routledge.

Martin, J.R. (1985) *Factual Writing: Exploring and Challenging Social Reality*, Geelong: Deakin University Press.

—— (1992) *English Text: System and Structure*, Amsterdam/Philadelphia: John Benjamins.

Swales, J. (1990) *Genre Analysis: English in Academic and Research Settings*, Cambridge: Cambridge University Press.

Van Leeuwen, T. (1987) 'Generic strategies in press journalism', *Australian Review of Applied Linguistics* 10(2): 199–221.

Ventola, E.M. (1987) *The Structure of Social Interaction: A Systemic Approach to the Semiotics of Service Encounters*, London: Frances Pinter.

PART THREE

Sequence and structure

Editors' introduction
to Part Three

WE HAVE SEEN that sequence and structure are the focal concerns of conversation analysis (CA). Many other approaches to discourse emphasize how texts and (in the more material sense of the term) discourses are organized as patterned entities. To some extent this reflects the long-standing concerns of linguistics with matters of composition and structure (and see Bublitz's concern with cohesion and coherence in Chapter 9). But there are also some more important reasons for attending to discourse structure, some of which we have already encountered. If, as Bakhtin suggests, we need to see language-in-use as organized into various speech genres, and, more generally, if discourses (in Fairclough's definition) are organized as sets of ideological meanings and values, then discovering patterns in discourse is a primary objective. We could argue that patterns in discourse relate to structures or 'orders' of society and ideology. In CA terms, the sorts of structuring that interactants submit to conversationally, and that they reproduce in their talk, already form a core dimension of *social* structure. This is Emanuel Schegloff's (1991) argument, and it connects to what Giddens (1991) has called the process of 'structuration'. Therefore, as we have said before, there is a direct link between conversational production of the interaction order and production of the social order. Here we see one of the main ways in which discourse analysis is able to use micro-level (linguistic, textual, intertextual) commentary to help explain macro-level (societal, cultural, ideological) processes. (Papers collected in Coupland et al 2001 treat this question in more depth; it is briefly discussed by Cameron et al in Chapter 7 of the *Reader*.)

In Labov and Waletzky's (1967) structural analysis of the stories told by street-gang youngsters, summarized in William Labov's single-authored paper (Chapter 12), we are introduced to some core concepts for the analysis of *narrative* or storytelling. They have been used productively for analysing narratives in many other social settings. For example, Allan Bell's (1991) analysis of newspaper 'stories' builds directly on Labov's narrative categories. Labov's structural analysis is in itself very valuable, but it is worth emphasizing the title of Labov's text – the 'transformation of experience in narrative'. Labov shows how discourse structuring in the genre of narrative not only recounts but refashions experience. This is most apparent in the 'evaluation' component of narrative – the means by which a narrator explains the purpose and 'so what' of a story. Stories, for example among young street-gang members, function to establish social status for the narrator-protagonist, in both dimensions of context – the story context and the storytelling context. This is why we find features in narratives that Labov calls 'intensifiers'. These include non-verbal gestures, expressive pronunciation and repetition. Similarly, 'comparators' compare events that did occur with those that did not; 'correlatives' combine events into single accounts; 'explicatives' explain complications inherent in the narrative for listeners (these are sets of syntactic and pragmatic devices that Labov considers in the source article, although they are not included in the excerpted text). They are some of the means by which experience, in the telling of it, is transformed when it is animated and performed.

By way of contrast, we have included Derek Edwards's article (Chapter 13). Edwards suggests that to take Labov's schema and to impose it on any narrative has a limiting effect on the analysis. For Edwards, such a rigid schema is not capable of accounting for the rhetorical and interactional intricacy of narratives. First, the scene-setting 'orientation' may in fact provide relevant information about the recounted events. There is a high degree of idealization in categories such as 'complicating action' and 'evaluation'. Then, 'evaluation' may be a more pervasive feature running through entire narrative episodes rather than in a limited number of selected clauses. Also, with 'abstract' and 'orientation' being optional elements in Labov's model, most of the representational and categorial work is left to just one element: 'complicating action'. Edwards is pointing to the limitations of bringing any pre-formed category system to bear on narrative (or any other genre of) discourse, even though he would admit that Labov's template does capture a useful generalization about typical narrative structure.

Consistent with the tenets of CA and discursive psychology (a version of CA developed in the psychology literature), Edwards prefers to analyse narratives (as well as other forms of discourse) by examining their interactional and *emergent* structure. In order to make sense of the storyteller's unfolding account of the events and his/her own position-taking in relation to these events and other participants, Edwards focuses on the step-by-step rhetorical design. Where does a story begin? Which social categories are constructed and used? Are there competing stories or accounts? Which ones does the teller align with? The general CA question is: 'What's going on here?' – What is being accomplished in the ongoing business of talk? The sequencing of events in narrative is not the playing out of a universal narrative structure but something a speaker achieves when (re-)presenting events and legitimating some account of events that is relevant for the current activity. In narrative activity people take stances and authenticate versions of events, and versions of themselves as speakers.

Harvey Sacks's essay, Chapter 14, introduces the methodology of membership category analysis (MCA), which has its roots in CA and ethnomethodology. It is concerned with the sequential organization of talk, the way category descriptions are used in conversation especially with regard to their sequential relevance. Sacks illustrates his point with the following two-sentence mini-story: 'The baby cried. The mommy picked it up.' Through a rather elaborate analysis of this short example, Sacks demonstrates how the organization of social knowledge relies upon conventional categories and our understanding of how they interrelate in order to 'make sense'. He explains why, other things being equal, most people would understand the story as the 'mommy' picking up *her* 'baby', *in response to* the previous activity of the baby crying. The explanation lies partly in the iconic properties of talk. In this case these include the assumption that actions in two consecutive utterances, without any temporal markers, will be understood to be ordered in the same sequence as the utterances themselves – the 'picking up' is understood to come after the 'crying'. Sacks introduces the term 'membership categorization device' to refer to the meanings that people-categories achieve in talk. We understand that 'the mommy' picks up 'the baby' because we commonsensically associate the categories of 'baby' and 'mommy'. The relevant (but implied) membership categorization device is 'the family', forming a 'team' relationship between the categories mentioned. Additionally, the notion of 'category-bound activities' ties the activity of 'crying' to the category 'baby' – crying is what we commonsensically expect babies to do. It is in this way, Sacks argues, that people's capacity for practical sense-making is based on their capacity to recognize such categorizations and devices.

'Opening up closings' by Emanuel Schegloff and Harvey Sacks (Chapter 15) is one of the truly classic papers in CA. We can read it for its richly detailed insights into the structural patterns that speakers deploy when they close conversations. But it is probably more important to read it as an agenda-setting statement for the discipline of CA, and as an outline of its principles and methodological priorities. To this extent it follows on directly from the Sacks chapter and confirms many of its central points. Schegloff and Sacks are very explicit, early in the chapter, about the 'technical' nature of CA, and this term resurfaces at several points. They refer to CA as striving to be 'a naturalistic observational discipline' able to 'deal with the details of social action(s) rigorously, empirically and formally' (p. 239). We can make sense of these claims when we see the emphasis CA places on 'actual data' and when we consider the interpretive restrictions that Schegloff (1991) argues should apply in how analysts use contextual information. There is certainly a sort of 'formalism' in CA. Its transcribing conventions suggest a particular form of rigour in the representation of data. At the same time, terms such as 'formal' and 'empirical' run counter to the general priorities that linguists and philosophers have brought to the study of discourse – as evidenced in Part One of the *Reader*. For them, discourse deals in function as much as form. It reaches out to understandings of social context to build its analyses, rather than ruling some aspects of social context out-of-bounds. This is why there are enduring tensions between CA and discourse analysis, despite their many shared ambitions and insights (see Hutchby's chapter, Chapter 28). There is an irony in sociologists (in the name of CA) striving for naturalism and empiricism in their dealings with discourse, while linguists are very largely striving to shake off the formalism and empiricism of early versions of linguistics. (These issues are debated in more detail in Coupland and Jaworski 1997).

In Chapter 16 Geoffrey Raymond and Jack Sidnell offer a critical retrospective on CA. They draw together major influences on the discipline, e.g., from Harold Garfinkel, Gail Jefferson, Harvey Sacks (see Chapters 14 and 15), Emmanuel Schegloff (Chapter 15) and Erving Goffman (Chapter 19). They draw out many important generalizations from these early studies that have an enduring relevance for discourse analysis. One of these is the relationship between rule-governed social action and the emergence of meaning in interaction. Raymond and Sidnell explain that CA did not formalize rules of interactional conduct, but allowed us to understand the frameworks through which social conduct and talk-in-interaction becomes both intelligible (to social actors and to analysts), and possible. This is the 'methodology' that features in the label 'ethnomethodology' – a set of methods for understanding and enacting cultural practices (see our introduction to Part One).

Raymond and Sidnell then focus on three key analytic foci of CA: *turn-taking*, the *sequencing* of conversational actions and *repair*. It would be useful to cross-refer between this chapter's discussion and the accounts of sequence and structure that we have already encountered in this part of the *Reader*. But Chapter 16 makes it clear that CA has given us some very subtle and precise tools for analysing discourse structure, based around social actors' ability to anticipate the completion of turns-at-talk as discourse units, to select themselves or others as next speakers, to construct conversations on the basis of paired functional units (e.g., an offer followed by an acceptance, a greeting followed by a reciprocal greeting), to model the relevance (and indeed the coherence) of structural terms, and so on. 'Repair' refers to a particularly interesting conversational resource for 'making good' problems of sequence and coherence. Raymond and Sidnell explain that conversationalists have a general 'preference for self-correction' – they organize their talk to minimize or 'correct' the troubles that talk inevitably throws up. The fact that conversationalists know when and how to make good a troublesome bit of talk, either in retrospect or in prospect, stands as useful further evidence that the conversational systems are in place and being actively monitored by interactants.

In Deborah Schiffrin's work (Chapter 17) we see how CA's passion for analysing structure can usefully be developed into close analysis of individual discourse particles – in the case Schiffrin considers in Chapter 17, the particle *oh*. It is through discourse analysis that many of the linguistic features excluded from most traditional accounts of sentence structure and meaning come to prominence. As Schiffrin says, it is difficult to attribute much semantic or grammatical meaning to *oh*, yet it makes an important regular contribution to discourse structure – particularly through marking how listeners receive new and newly salient information from speakers, and how this changes their knowledge states. The initial motivation for a speaker to use the particle *oh* is therefore primarily a cognitive one. To put it another way, *oh* is the linguistic reflex of cognitive realignment. We may well be able to detect a speaker's (or our own) cognitive realignment to information without a discourse marker being present in the text. But the fact of marking these realignments, in all of the many sub-contexts

Schiffrin illustrates, does conversational work in the relational or interpersonal dimension too. *Oh* can mark that a speaker is occupying a 'listener' role, or perhaps the role of a 'supportive listener'. It can signal that a consensus of understanding has been achieved, at a particular moment in talk. Alternatively, it can signal disjunction and a listener's surprise at not sharing a point of view or a knowledge state.

So the general view of discourse functioning that Schiffrin's analysis gives us is the same multi-functional one we saw in many of the introductory chapters in Part One. Talk realizes and fulfils multiple communicative goals and functions simultaneously – ideational (or information-related), relational (or interpersonal) and identity-related. It performs these functions simultaneously and in a multilayered fashion. In Schiffrin's study of *oh* we can see how a tiny discourse particle helps to manage the informational/ ideational structure of talk, while also functioning at the level of negotiating social roles and relationships.

References

Bell, A. (1991) *The Language of News Media*, Oxford: Blackwell.

Coupland, N. and Jaworski, A. (1997) 'Relevance, accommodation and conversation: modelling the social dimension of communication', *Multilingua* 16: 233–58.

Coupland, N., Sarangi, S. and Candlin, C.N. (eds.) (2001) *Sociolinguistics and Social Theory*, London: Longman.

Giddens, A. (1991) *Modernity and Self-identity: Self and Identity in the Late Modern Age*, Cambridge: Polity Press.

Labov, W. and Waletzky, J. (1967) 'Narrative analysis: oral versions of personal experience', in J. Helm (ed.) *Essays on the Verbal and Visual Arts: Proceedings of the 1966 Annual Spring Meeting of the American Ethnological Society*, Seattle: University of Washington Press. 12–44. [Reprinted in *Journal of Narrative and Life History* 7/1–4, special issue: *Oral Versions of Personal Experience: Three Decades of Narrative Analysis*, M.G.W. Bamberg (ed.), 3–38.]

Schegloff, E. (1991) 'Reflections on talk and social structure', in D. Boden and D.H. Zimmerman (eds.) *Talk and Social Structure: Studies in Ethnomethodology and Conversation Analysis*, Cambridge: Polity Press, 44–70.

Chapter 12

William Labov

THE TRANSFORMATION OF
EXPERIENCE IN NARRATIVE

. . .

IN A PREVIOUS STUDY we have presented a general framework for the analysis of narrative which shows how verbal skills are used to evaluate experience (Labov and Waletzky 1967). In this chapter we examine the narratives we obtained in our study of south-central Harlem from pre-adolescents (9 to 13 years old), adolescents (14 to 19), and adults to see what linguistic techniques are used to evaluate experience within the black English [BE] vernacular culture . . .

It will be helpful for the reader to be acquainted with the general character and impact of narratives in black vernacular style. We will cite here in full three fight narratives from leaders of vernacular peer groups in south-central Harlem who are widely recognized for their verbal skills and refer to these throughout the discussion to illustrate the structural feature of narrative. The first is by Boot.[1]

Extract 1
(Something Calvin did that was really wild?)
　　　Yeah.
a　It was on a Sunday
b　and we didn't have nothin' to do after I – after we
　　came from church.
c　Then we ain't had nothin' to do.
d　So I say, "Calvin, let's go get our – out our dirty clothes on
　　and play in the dirt."
e　And so Calvin say, "Let's have a rock – a rock war."
f　And I say, "All right."

Source: William Labov, *Language in the Inner City: Studies in the Black English Vernacular*, Philadelphia, PA: University of Pennsylvania Press and Oxford: Blackwell, 1972.

g   So Calvin had a rock.
h   And we as – you know, here go a wall
i   and a far away here go a wall.
j   Calvin th'ew a rock.
k   I was lookin' and – uh –
l   And Calvin th'ew a rock.
m   It oh – it almost hit me
n   And so I looked down to get another rock;
o   Say "Ssh!"
p   An' it pass me.
q   I say, "Calvin, I'm bust your head for that!"
r   Calvin stuck his head out.
s   I th'ew the rock
t   An' the rock went up,
u   I mean – went up –
v   came down
w   an' say [slap!]
x   an' smacked him in the head
y   an' his head busted.

The second narrative is by Larry H., a core member of the Jets gang. This is one of three fight stories told by Larry which match in verbal skill his outstanding performance in argument, ritual insults, and other speech events of the black vernacular culture.

Extract 2

a   An' then, three weeks ago I had a fight with this
        other dude outside
b   He got mad
        'cause I wouldn't give him a cigarette.
c   Ain't that a bitch?
        (Oh yeah?)
d   Yeah, you know, I was sittin' on the corner an' shit,
        smokin' my cigarette, you know
e   I was high, an' shit.
f   He walked over to me,
g   "Can I have a cigarette?"
h   He was a little taller than me,
        but not that much.
i   I said, "I ain't got no more, man,"
j   'cause, you know, all I had was one left.
k   An' I ain't gon' give up my last cigarette unless I got some more.
l   So I said, "I don't have no more, man."
m   So he, you know, dug on the pack,
        'cause the pack was in my pocket.
n   So he said, "Eh man, I can't get a cigarette, man?
o   I mean – I mean we supposed to be brothers, an' shit,"

p   So I say, "Yeah, well, you know, man, all I got is one, you dig it?"

q   An' I won't give up my las' one to nobody.

r   So you know, the dude, he looks at me,

s   An' he – I 'on' know –
     he jus' thought he gon' rough that motherfucker up.

t   He said, "I can't get a cigarette."

u   I said, "Tha's what I said, my man."

v   You know, so he said, "What you supposed to be *bad*, an' shit?

w   What, you think you *bad* an' shit?"

x   So I said, "Look here, my man,

y   I don't think I'm bad, you understand?

z   But I mean, you know, if I had it,
     you could git it

aa   I like to see you with it, you dig it?

bb   But the sad part about it,

cc   You got to do without it.

dd   That's all, my man."

ee   So the dude, he 'on' to pushin' me, man.
     (Oh he pushed you?)

ff   An' why he do that?

gg   *Everytime somebody fuck with me,*
     why they do it?

hh   I put that cigarette down,

ii   An' boy, let me tell you,
     I beat the shit outa that motherfucker.

jj   I tried to *kill* 'im – over one cigarette"

kk   I tried to *kill* 'im. Square business!

ll   After I got through stompin' him in the face, man,

mm   You know, all of a sudden I went crazy!

nn   I jus' went crazy.

oo   An' I jus' wouldn't stop hittin the motherfucker.

pp   Dig it, I couldn't stop hittin' 'im, man,
     till the teacher pulled me off o' him.

qq   An' guess what? After all that I gave the dude the cigarette,
     after all that.

rr   Ain't that a bitch?
     (How come you gave 'im a cigarette?)

ss   I 'on' know.

tt   I jus' gave it to him.

uu   An' he smoked it, too!

Among the young adults we interviewed in our preliminary exploration of south-central Harlem, John L. struck us immediately as a gifted story teller; the following is one of many narratives that have been highly regarded by many listeners.

Extract 3
(What was the most important fight that you remember, one that sticks in your mind . . .)

a	Well, one (I think) was with a girl.
b	Like I was a kid, you know,
c	And she was the baddest girl, *the baddest girl in the neighborhood.*
d	If you didn't bring her candy to school, she would punch you in the mouth;
e	And you had to kiss her when she'd tell you.
f	This girl was only about 12 years old, man,
g	but she was a killer.
h	She didn't take no junk;
i	She whupped all her brothers.
j	And I came to school one day
k	and I didn't have no money.
l	My ma wouldn't give me no money.
m	And I played hookies one day,
n	(She) put something on me.[2]
o	I played hookies, man,
p	so I said, you know, I'm not gonna play hookies no more 'cause I don't wanna get a whupping
q	So I go to school
r	and this girl says, "Where's the candy?"
s	I said, "I don't have it."
t	She says, powww!
u	So I says to myself, "There's gonna be times my mother won't give me money because (we're) a poor family
v	And I can't take this all, you know, every time she don't give me any money."
w	So I say, "Well, I just gotta fight this girl.
x	She gonna hafta whup me.
y	I hope she don't whup me."
z	And I hit the girl: powwww!
aa	and I put something on it.
bb	I win the fight.
cc	That was one of the most important.

This discussion will first review briefly the general definition of narrative and its overall structure. . . . The main body of narratives cited are from our work in south-central Harlem, but references will be made to materials drawn from other urban and rural areas, from both white and black subjects.

Definition of narrative

We define narrative as one method of recapitulating past experience by matching a verbal sequence of clauses to the sequence of events which (it is inferred) actually occurred. For example, a pre-adolescent narrative:

> **Extract 4**
> a   This boy punched me
> b   and I punched him
> c   and the teacher came in
> d   and stopped the fight.

An adult narrative:

> **Extract 5**
> a   Well this person had a little too much to drink
> b   and he attacked me
> c   and the friend came in
> d   and she stopped it.

In each case we have four independent clauses which match the order of the inferred events. It is important to note that other means of recapitulating these experiences are available which do not follow the same sequence; syntactic embedding can be used:

> **Extract 6**
> a   A friend of mine came in just
>   in time to stop
>   this person who had a little too much to drink
>   from attacking me.

Or else the past perfect can be used to reverse the order:

> **Extract 7**
> a   The teacher stopped the fight.
> b   She had just come in.
> c   I had punched this boy.
> d   He had punched me.

Narrative, then, is only one way of recapitulating this past experience: the clauses are characteristically ordered in temporal sequence; if narrative clauses are reversed, the inferred temporal sequence of the original semantic interpretation is altered: *I punched this boy/and he punched me* instead of *This boy punched me/and I punched him*.

With this conception of narrative, we can define a *minimal narrative* as a sequence of two clauses which are *temporally ordered*: that is, a change in their order will result in a change in the temporal sequence of the original semantic interpretation. In alternative terminology, there is temporal juncture between the two clauses, and a minimal narrative is defined as one containing a single temporal juncture.

The skeleton of a narrative then consists of a series of temporally ordered clauses which we may call *narrative clauses*. A narrative such as 4 or 5 consists entirely of narrative clauses. Here is a minimal narrative which contains only two:

Extract 8
a   I know a boy named Harry.
b   Another boy threw a bottle at him right in the head
c   and he had to get seven stitches.

This narrative contains three clauses, but only two are narrative clauses. The first has no temporal juncture, and might be placed after *b* or after *c* without disturbing temporal order. It is equally true at the end and at the beginning that the narrator knows a boy named Harry. Clause *a* may be called a *free clause* since it is not confined by any temporal juncture. . . .

It is only independent clauses which can function as narrative clauses – and as we will see below, only particular kinds of independent clauses. In the representation of narratives in this section, we will list each clause on a separate line, but letter only the independent clauses. . . .

The overall structure of narrative

Some narratives, like 4, contain only narrative clauses; they are complete in the sense that they have a beginning, a middle, and an end. But there are other elements of narrative structure found in more fully developed types. Briefly, a fully-formed narrative may show the following:

Extract 9
1   Abstract.
2   Orientation.
3   Complicating action.
4   Evaluation.
5   Result or resolution.
6   Coda.

Of course there are complex chainings and embeddings of these elements, but here we are dealing with the simpler forms. Complicating action has been characterized above, and the result may be regarded for the moment as the termination of that series of events. We will consider briefly the nature and function of the abstract, orientation, coda, and evaluation.

The abstract

It is not uncommon for narrators to begin with one or two clauses summarizing the whole story.

Extract 10

(Were you ever in a situation where you thought you were in serious danger of being killed?)

    I talked a man out of – Old Doc Simon I talked him out of pulling the trigger.

When this story is heard, it can be seen that the abstract does encapsulate the point of the story. In 11 there is a sequence of two such abstracts.

Extract 11

(Were you ever in a situation where you were in serious danger of being killed?)

a   My brother put a knife in my head.
     (How'd that happen?)
b   Like kids, you get into a fight
c   and I twisted his arm up behind him.
d   This was just a few days after my father died . . .

Here the speaker gives one abstract and follows it with another after the interviewer's question. Then without further prompting, he begins the narrative proper. The narrative might just as well have begun with the free clause *d; b* and *c* in this sense are not absolutely required, since they cover the same ground as the narrative as a whole. Larry's narrative (see Extract 2) is the third of a series of three, and there is no question just before the narrative itself, but there is a well-formed abstract:

a   An' then, three weeks ago I had a fight with this other
     dude outside.
b   He got mad
     'cause I wouldn't give him a cigarette.
c   Ain't that a bitch?

Larry does not give the abstract in *place* of the story; he has no intention of stopping there, but goes on to give the full account.

    What then is the function of the abstract? It is not an advertisement or a warning: the narrator does not wait for the listener to say, "I've heard about that," or "Don't tell me that now." If the abstract covers the same ground as the story, what does it add? We will consider this problem further in discussing the evaluation section below.

Orientation

At the outset, it is necessary to identify in some way the time, place, persons, and their activity or the situation. This can be done in the course of the first several narrative clauses, but more commonly there is an orientation section composed of free clauses. In Boot's narrative (Extract 1), clause *a* sets the time (*Sunday*); clause *b* the persons (*we*), the situation (*nothin' to do*) and further specification of the time (*after we come from church*); the first narrative clause follows. In Larry's narrative

(Extract 2), some information is already available in the abstract (the time – *three weeks ago*; the place – *outside of school*); and the persons – *this other dude and Larry*). The orientation section then begins with a detailed picture of the situation – *Larry sittin' on the corner, high*.

Many of John L.'s narratives begin with an elaborate portrait of the main character – in this case, clauses *a–i* are all devoted to *the baddest girl in the neighborhood*, and the first narrative clause brings John L. and the girl face to face in the schoolyard.

The orientation section has some interesting syntactic properties; it is quite common to find a great many past progressive clauses in the orientation section – sketching the kind of thing that was going on before the first event of the narrative occurred or during the entire episode. But the most interesting thing about orientation is its *placement*. It is theoretically possible for all free orientation clauses to be placed at the beginning of the narrative, but in practice, we find much of this material is placed at strategic points later on, for reasons to be examined below.

The coda

There are also free clauses to be found at the ends of narratives; for example, John L.'s narrative ends:

cc. That was one of the most important

This clause forms the *coda*. It is one of the many options open to the narrator for signalling that the narrative is finished. We find many similar forms.

Extract 12
And that was that.

Extract 13
And that – that was it, you know.

Codas may also contain general observations or show the effects of the events of the narrator. At the end of one fight narrative, we have

Extract 14
I was given the rest of the day off.
And ever since then I haven't seen the guy
'cause I quit.
I quit, you know.
No more problems.

Some codas which strike us as particularly skillful are strangely disconnected from the main narrative. One New Jersey woman told a story about how, as a little girl, she thought she was drowning, until a man came along and stood her on her feet – the water was only four-feet deep.

Extract 15
And you know that man who picked me out of the water?
He's a detective in Union City
And I see him every now and again.

These codas (14, 15) have the property of bridging the gap between the moment of time at the end of the narrative proper and the present. They bring the narrator and the listener back to the point at which they entered the narrative. There are many ways of doing this: in 15, the other main actor is brought up to the present: in 14, the narrator. But there is a more general function of codas which subsumes both the examples of 14, 15 and the simpler forms of 12, 13. Codas close off the sequence of complicating actions and indicate that none of the events that followed were important to the narrative. A chain of actions may be thought of as successive answers to the question "Then what happened?"; "And then what happened?" After a coda such as *That was that*, the question "Then what happened?" is properly answered, "Nothing; I just told you what happened." It is even more obvious after the more complex codas of 14 and 15; the time reference of the discourse has been reshifted to the present, so that "what happened then?" can only be interpreted as a question about the present; the answer is "Nothing; here I am." Thus the "Disjunctive" codas of 14 and 15 forestall further questions about the narrative itself: the narrative events are pushed away and sealed off.[3]

Evaluation

Beginnings, middles, and ends of narratives have been analyzed in many accounts of folklore or narrative. But there is one important aspect of narrative which has not been discussed – perhaps the most important element in addition to the basic narrative clause. That is what we term the *evaluation* of the narrative: the means used by the narrator to indicate the point of the narrative, its *raison d'être*: why it was told, and what the narrator is getting at. There are many ways to tell the same story, to make very different points, or to make no point at all. Pointless stories are met (in English) with the withering rejoinder, "So what?" Every good narrator is continually warding off this question; when his narrative is over, it should be unthinkable for a bystander to say, "So what?" Instead, the appropriate remark would be, "He did?" or similar means of registering the reportable character of the events of the narrative.

The difference between evaluated and unevaluated narrative appears most clearly when we examine narrative of vicarious experience. In our first series of interviews with pre-adolescents in south-central Harlem, we asked for accounts of favorite television programs; the most popular at the time was "The Man from U.N.C.L.E."

Extract 16
a   This kid – Napoleon got shot
b   and he had to go on a mission,
c   And so this kid, he went with Solo.

d   So they went
e   And this guy – they went through the window,
f   and they caught him.
g   And then he beat up them other people.
h   And they went
i   and then he said
     that this old lady was his mother
j   and then he – and at the end he say
     that he was the guy's friend.

This is typical of many such narratives of vicarious experience that we collected. We begin in the middle of things without any orientation section; pronominal reference in many ways ambiguous and obscure throughout. But the meaningless and disorientated effect of 16 has deeper roots. None of the remarkable events that occur *is evaluated*. We may compare 16 with a narrative of personal experience told by Norris W., eleven years old:

Extract 17
a   When I was in fourth grade –
     no, it was in third grade –
b   This boy he stole my glove.
c   He took my glove
d   and said that his father found it downtown on the ground
     (And you fight him?)
e   I told him that it was impossible for him to find downtown
     'cause all those people were walking by
     and just the father was the only one that found it?
f   So he got all (mad).
g   Then I fought him.
h   I knocked him all out in the street.
i   So he say he give.
j   and I kept on hitting him.
k   Then he started crying
l   and ran home to his father.
m   And the father told him
n   that he ain't find no glove.

This narrative is diametrically opposed to 16 in its degree of evaluation. Every line and almost every element of the syntax contributes to the point, and that point is self-aggrandizement. Each element of the narrative is designed to make Norris look good and "this boy" look bad. Norris knew that this boy stole his glove – had the nerve to just walk off with it and then make up a big story to claim that it was his. Norris didn't lose his cool and started swinging; first he destroyed this boy's fabrication by logic, so that everyone could see how phony the kid was. Then this boy lost his head and got mad and started fighting. Norris beat him up, and was so outraged at the phony way he had acted that he didn't stop when the kid surrendered – he "went crazy" and kept on hitting him. Then this punk started crying, and ran home to his father like a baby. Then his father – his *very own father* told him that his story wasn't true.

Norris's story follows the characteristic two-part structure of fight narratives in the BE vernacular; each part shows a different side of his ideal character. In the account of the verbal exchange that led up to the fight, Norris is cool, logical, good with his mouth, and strong in insisting on his own right. In the second part, dealing with the action, he appears as the most dangerous kind of fighter, who "just goes crazy" and "doesn't know what he did." On the other hand, his opponent is shown as dishonest, clumsy in argument, unable to control his temper, a punk, a lame, and a coward. Though Norris does not display the same degree of verbal skill that Larry shows in Extract 2, there is an exact point-by-point match in the structure and evaluative features of the two narratives. No one listening to Norris's story within the framework of the vernacular value system will say "So what?" The narrative makes its point and effectively bars this question.

If we were to look for an evaluation section in 17 concentrating upon clause ordering as in Labov and Waletzky (1967), we would have to point to *d–e*, in which the action is suspended while elaborate arguments are developed. This is indeed the major point of the argument, as shown again in the dramatic coda *m–n*. But it would be a mistake to limit the evaluation of 17 to *d–e*, since evaluative devices are distributed throughout the narrative. We must therefore modify the scheme of Labov and Waletzky (1967) by indicating E as the focus of waves of evaluation that penetrate the narrative as in Figure 12.1.

A complete narrative begins with an orientation, proceeds to the complicating action, is suspended at the focus of evaluation before the resolution, concludes with the resolution, and returns the listener to the present time with the coda. The evaluation of the narrative forms a secondary structure which is concentrated in the evaluation section but may be found in various forms throughout the narrative. . . .

We can also look at narrative as a series of answers to underlying questions:

a   Abstract: what was this about?
b   Orientation: who, when, what, where?
c   Complicating action: then what happened?
d   Evaluation: so what?
e   Result: what finally happened?

Only *c*, the complicating action, is essential if we are to recognize a narrative, as pointed out above. The abstract, the orientation, the resolution, and the evaluation answer questions which relate to the function of effective narrative: the first three to clarify referential functions, the last to answer the functional question *d* – why the story was told in the first place. But the reference of the abstract is broader than the orientation and complicating action: it includes these and the evaluation so that the abstract not only states what the narrative is about, but why it was told. The coda is not given in answer to any of these five questions, and it is accordingly found less frequently than any other element of the narrative. The coda *puts off* a question – it signals that questions *c* and *d* are no longer relevant.

. . .

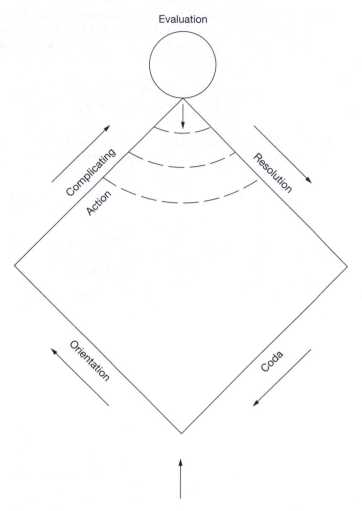

Figure 12.1 Narrative structure

Notes

1   Remarks in parentheses are by the interviewer. The initial questions asked by the interviewer are also given to help clarify the evaluative focus of the narrative.

2   To *put something on someone* means to 'hit him hard'. See also aa, *I put something on it* 'I hit hard'.

3   The coda can thus be seen as one means of solving the problem of indicating the end of a "turn" at speaking. As Harvey Sacks has pointed out, a sentence is an optimal unit for the utterance, in that the listener's syntactic competence is employed in a double sense – to let him know when the sentence is complete and also when it is his turn to talk. Narratives require other means for the narrator to signal the fact that he is beginning a long series of sentences which will form one "turn" and to mark the end of that sequence. Many of the devices we have been discussing here are best understood in terms of how the speaker and the listener let each other know whose turn it is to talk. Traditional folk tales and fairy tales have fixed formulas which do this at the beginning

and the end, but these are not available for personal narratives. It can also be said that a good coda provides more than a mechanical solution for the sequencing problem: it leaves the listener with a feeling of satisfaction and completeness that matters have been rounded off and accounted for.

Reference

Labov, W. and Waletzky, J. (1967) 'Narrative analysis,' in *Essays on the Verbal and Visual Arts*, Helm, J. (ed.), Seattle, WA: University of Washington Press, 12–44.

Chapter 13

Derek Edwards

NARRATIVE ANALYSIS

. . .

THERE ARE THREE KINDS of objects at which any analysis of narratives might be aimed: (1) the nature of the *events* narrated; (2) people's perception or *understanding* of events; and (3) the *discourse* of such understandings and events. We can think of these as three crudely separated kinds of analysis.

Type 1: pictures of events
Type 2: pictures of mind
Type 3: discursive actions

Of course, these are ways of approaching any discourse, not just narrative.

Type 1 corresponds to the basic aims of ethnography and oral histories, in which stories and descriptions are collected as a route (however compromised) to the things that are their topic – to matters and events beyond the talk. It is also part of common-sense practices, in ordinary talk, texts, courtrooms, classrooms, and scientific publications, that discourse about events is produced as, and taken to be, a way of telling and finding out about those events, with due caution for lies and errors. Type 2 takes one step back from events themselves, and takes a psychological interest in the speaker. It treats people's discourse as how they 'see' things (again, through a glass however darkly), whether as representatives of groups or cultures, or as individuals. This corresponds to much of cognitive and narrative psychology and cognitive anthropology.

Type 3 focuses on discourse itself, as a performative domain of social action. Both the nature of events (type 1), and the nature of people's perspectives on events

Source: Derek Edwards, *Discourse and Cognition*, London: Sage, 1997.

(type 2), are considered to be *at stake* here (worked up, managed, topicalized, implied, and so on), rather than simply available, in the discourse. Type 3 is broadly characteristic of discursive psychology, and of conversation analysis, rhetorical analysis, sociology of scientific knowledge (SSK), and some varieties of narratology. Type 3 essentially reverses the order of the three. Discourse is, analytically, what we have got, what we start with. Whereas we might assume, common-sensically, that events come first, followed by (distorted) understandings of them, followed by (distorted) verbal expressions of those understandings, type 3 inverts that, and treats both understandings and events themselves as participants' concerns – the stuff the talk works up and deals with.

With these three types in mind we may turn to some ways of defining and analysing narrative, starting with Jerome Bruner's.

> Narrative requires . . . four crucial grammatical constituents if it is to be effectively carried out. It requires, first, a means for emphasizing human '*agentivity*' – action directed toward goals controlled by agents. It requires, secondly, that a sequential order be established and maintained – that events and states be '*linearized*' in a standard way. Narrative, thirdly, also requires a sensitivity to what is canonical and what violates canonicality in human interaction. Finally, narrative requires something approximating a narrator's *perspective*: it cannot, in the jargon of narratology, be 'voiceless'.
>
> (Bruner 1990: 77, emphasis added)

Bruner's broad definition is a useful place to start, in that it is specifically oriented to narrative *psychology*, and because it includes elements of various other descriptive schemes and definitions, such as Kenneth Burke's (1945). Burke suggested a scheme which he called 'dramatism', which deals with matters such as motives, persuasion, stories, and so on, by defining five elements that make up a well-formed story: 'What was done (act), when or where it was done (scene), who did it (agent), how he [*sic*] did it (agency), and why (purpose)' (1945: xv). Bruner (1990) glosses these five elements as: Action, Scene, Actor, Instrument, and Goal. Into these elements is then inserted Trouble, in the form of some kind of imbalance or conflict between the five elements, and this is what gives rise to the subsequent actions, events, and resolutions that make up a coherent, bounded narrative.

A related set of criteria is provided by Kenneth Gergen (1994: 189–90). Well-formed narratives have (1) a valued endpoint, goal, or 'point'; (2) an ordering of events, not necessarily told in the order in which they occur (flashbacks, insertions, etc., are possible); (3) stable identities for the main characters, which may develop; (4) causal links and explained outcomes; (5) demarcation signs – in conversations especially, marking where stories start and end. Gergen's list is clearly similar to Bruner's and to Burke's, and there are others which also draw on general narratology, but none of them are identical. Why not? Are the differences minor and terminological, or are they matters that the authors might insist on? How might the differences be resolved, or, alternatively, by what criteria should we prefer one definition to another? It is not simply a matter of pointing to actual instances of stories and showing that one definition fits better than another, because each definition specifies, somewhat circularly, what would count as a good ('well-formed') example.

Definitions of this kind can be understood as analysts' efforts at nailing down common-sense categories: efforts at defining what a story or narrative is, as distinct from, say, a sermon, lecture, scientific explanation, or any other discourse category. The participants themselves display sensitivity to what *that* story should contain, and one imagines that Bruner's, Burke's, and Gergen's lists accord with those kinds of participants' sensibilities, although that would be a matter for research rather than stipulation.

. . .

The more detailed definitions of narrative become, then the more specific they are to particular genres (for example, Propp 1928/1968) or events, and the less generally applicable they are as analytic schemes. On the other hand, the looser their definition, the more they dissolve into the tropes, concerns, and devices of discourse in general. The problem of too broad a definition, of seeing virtually all discourse as narrative, is that it starts to lose explanatory power. As Kenneth Gergen suggests, definitions of narrative can only be definitions of specific cultural forms: 'rather than seek a definitive account [of narrative structure] . . . there is a virtual infinity of possible story forms, but due to the exigencies of social co-ordination, certain modalities are favored over others in various historical periods' (1994: 195).

Narratology deals with the internal structures of narratives, with distinctions between narratives of different kinds, and also with distinctions between narratives and other kinds of discourse. Hayden White (1973) takes from literary theory four basic categories, *tragedy*, *comedy*, *romance*, and *satire*, and suggests that these are appropriate labels for a wide range of literary, historical, and everyday narratives. The four categories have been taken up and applied in a variety of psychologically oriented treatments of personal narratives, including Gergen and Gergen (1988), Murray (1989), and Schafer (1976). Kevin Murray provides a concise summary, which I condense a little further here:

> . . . 'comedy' involves the victory of youth and desire over age and death . . . 'Romance' concerns the restoration of the honoured past through a series of events that involve a struggle . . . between a hero and forces of evil . . . In 'tragedy' the individual fails to conquer evil and is excluded from the social unit. The nobility of this failure is contrasted with the satire of 'irony', which deals in the discovery that comedy, romance, and tragedy are mere schemes of mortals to control experience: individuals are not so pure, nor is the social order so healthy.
>
> (1989: 181–2)

It is easy to see how these categories might be applied to actual instances. But even literary works, let alone ordinary talk, have to be *fitted* to the four types, giving rise to various sub-types, overlaps, and mixtures. The problem for narrative analysis is that of *idealization* – the adoption of an analytic category scheme in advance of examining specific instances, perhaps even a scheme whose original domain of application was different (in this case, literary genres), and seeing how something such as stories collected in interviews can be fitted to them.

In order to illustrate the problems of applying category schemes, let us briefly consider a particularly influential one that is widely used in narrative analysis: that of William Labov (1972; Labov and Waletzky 1967; see Chapter 12). Labov's categories of the structure and functions of oral narratives are shown in Extract 13.1, which is an example provided by Catherine Kohler Riessman (1993: 59) in a book on the methodology of narrative analysis. Riessman presents the example positively, as one to which Labov's categories can be usefully applied (Riessman uses the scheme in her own research), rather than as one of the 'many narratives [that] do not lend themselves to Labov's framework' (1993: 59).

Labov's categories are signalled by the letter codes assigned to each numbered line. The codes, as glossed by Riessman, are as follows: 'to provide an Abstract for what follows (A), Orient the listener (O), carry the Complicating Action (CA), Evaluate its meaning (E), and Resolve the action (R)' (1993: 59; note that Labov's scheme also specifies an optional sixth item, a 'Coda' that brings us back to the present). Extract 13.1 is taken from a husband's talk about incidents leading up to a divorce. . . .

Extract 13.1 (Applying Labov's categories)

30	and (.) finally, ah, it's, this is actually a crucial incident	A
31	because I <u>finally</u> got up and (.)	CA
32	and (.) went into the other room	CA
33	(.) she was in the laundry room with the door closed and	O
34	(.) knocked on the door and said	CA
35	'When are you going to be done with this?'	CA
36	'cause we, we were going to talk.	O
37	And she kind of held up her hand like this and went 'no'.	CA
38	And I got absolutely bullshit	E
39	I put my <u>fist</u> through the door ((*Interviewer*: uh-huh))	R
40	which is not the kind of stuff that I, that I do, you know	E
41	I'm <u>not</u> a real physically violent person at <u>all</u>.	E

(Riessman 1993: 59, untimed pauses)

Some of the problems of *applying* Labov's categories *as an analytic scheme*, and by extension other related pre-defined analytic codes and categories, can be seen in this example. The thing to do is to try assigning alternative categories, and see how plausible, or strained, that becomes. Of course, this leaves aside the appropriateness of having subdivided the talk into precisely those twelve discrete 'clauses' (the twelve lines) in the first place. Line 30 is coded as an 'Abstract', although 'a crucial incident' might reasonably be judged an Evaluation rather than a summary of events. Less obviously, try considering line 31 as an Evaluation. The expression 'because I finally got up', including the emphasis on 'finally', surely reinforces the notion of a 'crucial incident' having just taken place, together with a sense of the narrator's judgment (evaluation) of that incident – enough to 'finally' make him get up. Again, it is not clear why 'And I got absolutely bullshit' (line 38) is not a next occurrence or Complicating Action (CA) rather than an Evaluation (E), unless all emotion descriptions are automatically considered Evaluations. Part of the problem here is that the single category 'Complicating Action' (CA) seems to contain the bulk of what one might common-sensically assume is the basic storyline, the sequence of events, which means that, as an analytic scheme for stories, much of the content must remain largely unanalysed.

The category 'Orientation', in Labov's scheme, supposedly informs the listener of the circumstances of the action, a kind of contextual scene-setting – time, place, situation, participants. But surely this under-specifies what is going on in lines 33 and 36. The narrative sense of 'she was in the laundry room with the door closed' is not merely circumstantial; she was not doing the laundry. Rather, it helps define the nature of the wife's actions at that juncture, making a secretive and illicit phone call (she was 'talking to her lover on the phone', Riessman 1993: 59), just as 'we were going to talk' establishes, in contrast to that, the less objectionable activity she was (according to him) supposed to be doing at that time with her husband. . . . What matters with these utterances is not that we categorize them under Orientation, or Complicating Action, or Evaluation, or whatever, and then deal with those categories, but, rather, that we grasp what they are doing, as specific, precisely worded, occasioned formulations.

Without labouring the point, similar kinds of reassignments and complications are possible for the rest of the narrative in Extract 13.1. 'Evaluation' is likely to be a pervasively relevant concern in story-telling, rather than something exclusively coded in a specific item or slot, while the inclusion of an Abstract and Orientation are in any case considered optional in oral narratives (Labov 1972), again leaving 'Complicating Action' with a very heavy and rather uninformative analytic burden. 'Orientation' includes the kinds of story details that can occur anywhere in a narrative, and perform significant business (see Drew 1978, and Schegloff, 1972, on 'formulating place'). In other words, when we come to dealing with specific story details, we are immediately dealing with the contingencies of discourse per se, of descriptions, reports, accounts, and so on, rather than something specific about narrative. It is by collecting stories through interviews, taking them out of the inter-actional (and rhetorical) contexts of their production, and formulating check-list categories of their structural components that we obtain a rather idealized notion of how they work.

The identification of general story schemas across a wide range of stories is clearly an important analytic goal. But despite being derived from and for empirical analysis, Labov's categories are idealized as well as empirical. That is, they define the kinds of things a story *ought* to contain, theoretically, in order to count as a story. They become less useful when used as a set of pre-coded analytic slots into which we should try to place an actual story's contents. The temptation for analysts using the scheme is to start with the categories and see how the things people say can be fitted into them, and, having coded everything as one category or another, to call that the analysis, and then compare it to other findings. In that role, as a coding scheme, these kinds of structural categories impose rather than reveal, obscuring the particularity of specific details, and how that particularity is crucial for the occasioned, action-performative workings of discourse (cf. discussions in Langellier 1989: 248; Linde 1993: 66).

Competing stories

. . . Stories may be rhetorically designed to manage their own credibility, and to counter alternatives. . . . The point I want to emphasize here, which both Bruner and (more emphatically) Gergen also appreciate, is the rhetorical, interaction-oriented nature not only of those kinds of formulations, but of narratives generally.

A basic issue in telling a story of events in your life is where to begin: 'Where one chooses to begin and end a narrative can profoundly alter its shape and meaning' (Riessman 1993: 18). Where to start a story is a major, and rhetorically potent, way of managing causality and accountability. It is an issue not only for personal narratives, but for accounts of all kinds, including histories of nation states, and stories of immigration and ethnicity: who actually belongs where? Starting when? Whose country *is* it? From Britain to Bosnia to New Zealand (Wetherell and Potter 1992), and the so-called 'Indian' natives of North America (Cronon 1992), alternative narratives compete in terms of precisely when and where they start.

Then there is what to include: which words/categories to use? To whom, for whom, for what, and at what juncture is the story told? What alternatives are being countered or aligned with? What current interactional business is being managed? It is not just a matter of possessing a narrative mind, whose mental operations turn events into best-sense personal stories. Telling stories is discursive action doing discursive business. This certainly emerges when studying research interviews, but those essentially work *against* interactional considerations, because they tend to substitute, for the ordinary occasions on which stories might be told, got-up occasions for set-piece performances-for-interview. It is better to collect samples of natural talk, where possible, if we want to see how talk performs interactional work other than informing researchers who are interested in narratives, in family relations, in violence, or social attitudes, or whatever.

As an example of 'where to start', consider Extract 13.2, which occurs near the beginning of Jeff's and Mary's first session with their relationship counsellor. Jeff, it may be noted (for brevity's sake), places his wife's recent affair with another man as the origin of their current marital difficulties. But it is Mary who takes the first opportunity to outline their troubles.

Extract 13.2

```
1   Counsellor:  (. . .) P'haps (.) uh in in in your words
2                or (.) either of your words you better (0.8)
3                st↑art from the beginning as to why:, you
4                went to Relate in the first place, (0.6)
5                and then the difference between the ⌈:n and now.
6   Jeff:                                           ⌊ Shall I
7                (        ) start now or (      )?=
```

```
 8    Mary:      =Uh? (.)
 9    Jeff:      °'n you jus (.) keep on going.°
10               (.)
11    Mary:      Yeh. (.) U:m (3.0) well. What happened,
12               Jeff started doing some exa:ms (.) which (.)
13               la:sted abou:t (0.2) four years.= And before that,
14               (0.8) >this is when we were living in the
15               hospital,< (.) we was always doing some exa:ms,
16               (1.0) since we've me:t, (0.5) at some point, (.)
17               which has lasted some time.
18               (0.8)
19               Anyway Jeff was doing u:m (.) a degree:, (.) that
20               (0.3) la:sted must've bee:n about (0.5) we were
21               just coming to the e:nd. (0.7) Just last summer.
22               (1.0)
23               A:nd during that time I felt that, (0.8) u:m (1.0)
24               he didn't pay any attention to me: that (0.4) um
25               (0.2) ↑alth↑ough we had a s- we still had a fairly
26               good relationship, .hh I didn't feel there was
27               anything wro:ng, .h but (.) at the time, (.)
28               I ↑didn't really think anything too much abou:t
29               (0.2) these pr↑oblems. (0.6) but (.) it must have
30               all like come to a head. (0.8) Then I felt like
31               he was neglecting me:, he didn't wanna know,
32               I was working too har:d, .hh u:m, (0.8) and then
33               I had the two children I felt I was being left on
34               my ow:n, (0.8) uhh (.) an' the:n (.) I started
35               going round with my friends quite a bit, (1.6)
36               u:m, (0.4) ↑just to get out of the house.
37               (0.4)
38               For some rel↑ief.
39               (1.0)
40               And then: I met °somebody e:lse,° (0.8) an:d u:m
41               (1.4) had (0.6) an affair, (.) uh (.) and then I
```

Rather than starting with her recent affair, Mary starts several years back (lines 12–17) with events that (according to her) led up to it, and therefore somewhat account for it. According to Mary, Jeff's continual and long-term exam preparations led to her feeling neglected (lines 30–1), even though she herself was 'working too har:d' (line 32) and had the children to look after. Mary's own hard work stands as a counter to any suggestion (which Jeff actually develops later) that he was doing all the work for the family while she went off and indulged herself. The affair itself is offered by Mary as an understandable event-in-sequence, a sequence culpably implicating Jeff, and an unlooked-for consequence of her going out with friends, '↑just to get out of the house. (0.4) For some rel↑ief' (lines 34–8).

The rhetorical design of Mary's story (which continues beyond the extract provided) is clear, even without a full interactional analysis of her various accounts, and of Jeff's, which I shall not provide here. In starting her story with events prior to the affair, and in formulating those events in specific ways, Mary manages to provide an accountable basis for her actions, while at the same time attending to likely (and no doubt familiar, and in any case forthcoming) counter-versions from Jeff. Any notion of an irresponsible *neglect* of her family (a notion which Jeff later develops) is countered, ahead of its production in counselling, by an account of *his prior* neglect of her. Any notion that their problems are those of a *happy marriage* spoiled by a wife's sexual adventures (another of Jeff's themes) are countered by the prior problems she outlines. And, should Jeff try to claim that everything was *basically* fine between them prior to the affair (which he does), Mary attends to that ('we still had a fairly good relationship, .hh I didn't feel there was anything wro:ng', lines 25–7), while recounting the underlying, partly unnoticed (and therefore uncomplained-of, should he point that out) pattern of neglect. There is an interaction-oriented exquisiteness in the detail and subtlety of these kinds of stories (and more that I have not picked out here) that is easily missed on a first reading, and missable altogether where stories of this kind are collected and analysed structurally, and in isolation, or as reflections of events or cognitions.

Narrative truth and authenticity

In the social and human sciences, in anthropological, ethnographic, psychological, and other research domains, narrative analysis is generally a matter of collecting interviews about particular kinds of life experiences (for example Linde 1993, recorded interviews on choice of profession), and fitting them to various analytical categories and schemas.

> The purpose is to see how respondents in interviews impose order on the flow of experience to make sense of events and actions in their lives. The methodological approach examines the informant's story and analyses how it is put together, the linguistic and cultural resources it draws on, and how it persuades a listener of authenticity.
>
> (Riessman 1993: 2)

These notions of 'persuasion' and 'authenticity' reflect a recurrent theme in narrative theory, which is the interpersonal functions of story-telling. Despite that theme, interactional orientations tend to be underplayed *in actual analyses* of narratives, by virtue of the focus on structural story schemas, data from interviews and written literature, and in the location of narrative studies within the theoretical domains of self, identity, and personal growth.

As Riessman (1993) notes, in the 'life story method' (for example, Bruner 1990; Josselson and Lieblich 1993; Murray 1989; Plummer 1995) the usual thing is to mix analysis and data, and blur the distinction. Rather than focusing analysis on transcribed materials and their interactional settings, the analyst uses quotations from informants' talk as illustrations of analysts' summaries, gists, generalizations, and glosses. This glosses-and-quotes treatment of discourse materials is reminiscent of essays on works of literature, though sometimes transcripts are also used (Linde 1993; Young 1987). Generally, the analyst's 'authorial voice and interpretative commentary knit the disparate elements together and determine how readers are to understand [the informant's] experience. . . . Illustrative quotes from the interview provide evidence for the investigator's interpretation of the plot twists' (Riessman 1993: 30).

One advantage of interviewing-for-narratives is that it allows participants to develop long turns and tell things 'in their own way', in contrast to the more question–answer kinds of format used in other interview research, where personal narratives and 'anecdotal' replies may even be systematically prevented from developing. More structured research methods (questionnaires, experiments, structured interviews, etc.) may treat personal stories as some kind of noise or nuisance, to be discouraged by the use of standard questions, fixed topics, a fixed range of possible responses, and/or analytic methods that break up and lose whatever conversational or narrative flow might still have been captured on audiotape. Nevertheless, narrative interviewing is still interviewing, and 'in their own way' tends to be treated as definitive of how respondents 'see' things, rather than an instance of interaction-oriented talk.

'Authenticity' in life story interview studies is generally taken not as a participants' concerted accomplishment, something discursively constructed, but, rather, as some kind of built-in feature bequeathed by the methodology of collecting personal stories (in contrast to more impersonal methodologies). *Non*-authenticity in such settings may be treated as a kind of forgivable *aberration*, behind which may nevertheless lie a deeper, and recoverable, psychological truth: 'When talking about their lives, people lie sometimes, forget a lot, exaggerate, become confused, and get things wrong. Yet they *are* revealing truths. These truths don't reveal the past "as it actually was", aspiring to a standard of objectivity. They give us instead the truths of our experiences' (Personal Narratives Group 1989: 261, original emphasis).

This is a 'type 2' treatment of discourse, approaching it as a kind of window on participants' perspectives. Again, it is essential to separate the notion I am promoting here of discourse's action-orientation from any notion that this is a cynical and mistrusting way to deal with people. It is neither to trust nor to mistrust, but to analyse. It is to treat *all* talk as performative, as action-oriented, as doing something, such that issues of sincerity, truth, honest confession, lies, errors, confabulations, and so on, are matters that talk itself must manage, and *does* manage, in analysable ways. The management of authenticity, as a participants' concern or accomplishment, is explored in a wide variety of discourse studies. These include Edwards and Potter (1992), Lynch and Bogen (1996), and Wooffitt (1992) on factual authenticity and the credibility of reports; Widdicombe (1993) and Widdicombe and Wooffitt (1995) on persons as authentic members, holders of, or spokespersons for a particular social identity; and Whalen and Zimmerman (1990) on how those two things (personal identity and the authenticity of reports) may be managed simultaneously.

For example, Sue Widdicombe and Robin Wooffitt (1995) are concerned with the discourse of social identity. In their materials, 'authenticity' is at stake with regard to membership (and therefore speakers' rights to talk *as* members) of a youth sub-culture whose appearance, tastes, and other preferences might be taken as signs of mere conformity to a standard group image. Respondents deal with that issue by telling fragments of life stories that build authentic membership in terms of self-expression or personal choice. Like Mary does with regard to Jeff (Extract 13.2 above) . . . one way they do it is to place decisive details *further back* in the 'taleworld' of events than the rhetorical alternative would require. In Extract 13.3, 'MR1' is a 'goth' talking to an interviewer, 'I'. The important notion here, in the context of analysing personal narratives, is how the notion of a 'true self' is discursively managed, rather than being something that is simply available in this kind of talk, lying behind and generating it.

Extract 13.3

```
1    MR1:    yeah 'cos I started wearing make up, and I
2            didn't even know about other people wearing it
3            1 st- I star- I just started wearing it and
4            putting on these black clothes and things like
5            that an' then ⌈ I went
6    I:                    ⌊ ahha
7    MR1     I went into town one week because like I was
8            considered really freaky by everybody
9            because .hh all these people who lived on this
10           estate hadn't ever seen anybody like me before (.)
11           I went into town one evening an' walked by this
12           pub an' saw loads of people with hair, spiked up
13           an' things like that an' er a lot more way out than
14           me even though I was considered the biggest freak
15           of the area- they were a lot more way out than me-
                     (from Widdicombe and Wooffitt 1995: 148)
```

Widdicombe and Wooffitt focus on how, in snatches of 'autobiography', respondent 'MR1' manages his authenticity, both as an independent agent, and also as a member of a sub-cultural group. His narrated change of appearance, in the way it is described as personal and spontaneous, and in its sequential placing prior to his knowledge of other people looking similar (lines 1–4), follows a pattern of narrative accountability found across a range of other interviews. MR1's story rhetorically counters any 'negative inferences regarding the reasons for that change . . . that speakers were copying or influenced by others, or conforming to a particular image' (1995: 149). The narrative in lines 7 to 15 (which runs on after line 15) is produced as a specific episode within a larger pattern of events, in which the speaker had already started, spontaneously, to adopt the persona that would eventually make him identifiable as a member of a group.

Widdicombe and Wooffitt's analysis brings out the way in which autobiographical stories are intrinsically, and in detail, interaction-oriented and rhetorical. Personal stories attend to motive and accountability, to alternative readings, alternative identities. Bruner suggests that young children learn to narrate events within the context of family relations, disputes, and the negotiation of identities, where 'narrative becomes an instrument for telling not only what happened but also why it justified the action recounted . . . narrating becomes not only an expository act but a rhetorical one' (1990: 86–7). This should not be thought of as something restricted to people with especially delicate identities to manage. It is an issue also even for the most literary and interactionally marooned of written autobiographies (Freeman 1993), although the interaction-oriented nature of autobiographical discourse emerges most clearly in spoken interaction, and through applying the kinds of discursive and conversation analytic methods used by Widdicombe and Wooffitt.

References

Bruner, J.S. (1990) *Acts of Meaning*, Cambridge, MA: Harvard University Press.

Burke, K. (1945) *A Grammar of Motives*, New York: Prentice Hall.

Cronon, W. (1992) 'A place for stories: nature, history, and narrative', *Journal of American History* 78(4): 1347–76.

Drew, P. (1978) 'Accusations: the occasioned use of members' knowledge of "religious geography" in describing events', *Sociology* 12: 1–22.

Edwards, D. and Potter, J. (1992) *Discursive Psychology*, London: Sage.

Freeman, M. (1993) *Rewriting the Self: History, Memory, Narrative*, London: Routledge.

Gergen, K.J. (1994) *Realities and Relationships*, Cambridge, MA: Harvard University Press.

—— and Gergen, M.M. (1988) 'Narrative and self as relationship', in L. Berkowitz (ed.) *Advances in Experimental Social Psychology*, New York: Academic Press.

Josselson, R. and Lieblich, A. (eds) (1993) *The Narrative Study of Lives*, volume 1, London: Sage.

Labov, W. (1972) *Language of the Inner City*, Philadelphia, PA: Philadelphia University Press.

—— and Waletzky, J. (1967) 'Narrative analysis: oral versions of personal experience', in J. Helm (ed.) *Essays on the Verbal and Visual Arts*, Seattle, WA: University of Washington Press.

Langellier, K.M. (1989) 'Personal narratives: perspectives on theory and research', *Text and Performance Quarterly* 9(4): 243–76.

Linde, C. (1993) *Life Stories: The Creation of Coherence*, Oxford: Oxford University Press.

Lynch, M. and Bogen, D. (1996) *The Spectacle of History: Speech, Text, and Memory at the Iran–Contra Hearings*, Durham, NC: Duke University Press.

Murray, K.D. (1989) 'The construction of identity in the narratives of romance and comedy', in J. Shotter and K.J. Gergen (eds) *Texts of Identity*, London: Sage.

Personal Narratives Group (eds) (1989) *Interpreting Women's Lives: Feminist Theory and Personal Narratives*, Indianapolis, IN: Indiana University Press.

Plummer, K. (1995) 'Life story research', in J.A. Smith, R. Harré and L. Van Langenhove (eds) *Rethinking Methods in Psychology*, London: Sage.

Propp, V.J. (1928/1968) *Morphology of the Folktale*, Austin, TX: University of Texas Press.

Riessman, C.K. (1993) *Narrative Analysis*, London: Sage.

Schafer, R. (1976) *A New Language for Psychoanalysis*, New Haven, CT: Yale University Press.

Schegloff, E.A. (1972) 'Notes on a conversational practice: formulating place', in D. Sudnow (ed.) *Studies in Social Interaction*, Glencoe, IL: Free Press.

Wetherell, M. and Potter, J. (1992) *Mapping the Language of Racism: Discourse and the Legitimation of Exploitation*, Hemel Hempstead: Harvester Wheatsheaf.

Whalen, M.R. and Zimmerman, D.H. (1990) 'Describing trouble: practical epistemology in citizen calls to the police', *Language and Society* 19: 465–92.

White, H. (1973) *Metahistory: The Historical Imagination in Nineteenth Century Europe*, Baltimore, MD: Johns Hopkins University Press.

Widdicombe, S. (1993) 'Autobiography and change: rhetoric and authenticity of "gothic" style', in E. Burman and I. Parker (eds) *Discourse Analytic Research: Repertoires and Readings of Texts in Action*, Hemel Hempstead: Harvester Wheatsheaf.

—— and Wooffitt, R. (1995) *The Language of Youth Subcultures: Social Identity in Action*, Hemel Hempstead: Harvester Wheatsheaf.

Wooffitt, R.C. (1992) *Telling Tales of the Unexpected: The Organization of Factual Discourse*, Hemel Hempstead: Harvester Wheatsheaf.

Young, K.G. (1987) *Taleworlds and Storyrealms: The Phenomenology of Narrative*, Dordrecht: Martinus Nijhoff.

Chapter 14

Harvey Sacks

ON THE ANALYZABILITY OF STORIES BY CHILDREN

Problems in recognizing possible descriptions

THE INITIAL DATA are the first two sentences from a "story" offered by a two-year-and-nine-month-old girl to the author of the book *Children Tell Stories*. They are: "The baby cried. The mommy picked it up." I shall first make several observations about these sentences. Before doing so, however, let me note: if these observations strike you as a ranker sort of subjectivism, then I ask you to read on just far enough to see whether it is or is not the case that the observations are both relevant and defensible. When I hear "The baby cried. The mommy picked it up," one thing I hear is that the "mommy" who picks the "baby" up is the mommy of that baby. That is a first observation. (You will, of course, notice that the second sentence does not contain a genitive. It does not read, "Its mommy picked it up," or variants thereof.) Now it is not only that *I* hear that the mommy is the mommy of that baby, but I feel rather confident that at least many of the natives among you hear that also. That is a second observation. One of my tasks is going to be to construct an apparatus that will provide for the foregoing facts to have occurred; an apparatus, i.e., which will show how it is that we come to hear the fragment as we do.

Some more: I take it we hear two sentences. Call the first S_1 and the second S_2; the first reports an occurrence O_1 and the second reports an occurrence O_2. Now, I take it we hear that as S_2 follows S_1, so O_2 follows O_1. That is a third observation. And also, we hear that O_2 occurs because of O_1: i.e., the explanation for O_2 occurring is that O_1 did. That is a fourth observation. I want the apparatus to show how we come to hear those facts also.

If I asked you to explain the group of observations that I have made, observations that you could have made just as well—and let me note, they are *not* proposed as sociological findings, but rather do they pose some of the problems that social science shall have to resolve—you might well say something like the following: we hear that it is the mommy of the baby who picks the baby up because she's the one who ought to pick it up, and (you might eventually add) if she's the one who ought to pick it up, and it was picked up by somebody who could be her, then it was her, or was probably her.

You might go on: while it is quite clear that not any two consecutive sentences, not even any consecutive sentences that report occurrences, are heard, and properly heard, as reporting that the occurrences have occurred in the order which the sentences have, if the occurrences ought to occur in that order, and if there is no information to the contrary (such as a phrase at the beginning of the second, like "before that, however"), then the order of the sentences indicates the order of the occurrences. And these two sentences do present the order of the occurrences they report in the proper order for such occurrences. If the baby cried, it ought to have started crying before the mother picked it up, and not after. Hearing it that way, the second sentence is explained by the first; hearing them as consecutive or with the second preceding the first, some further explanation is needed, and none being present, we may suppose that it is not needed.

Now let me make a fifth observation: all of the foregoing can be done by many or perhaps any of us without knowing what baby or what mommy it is that might be being talked of.

With this fifth observation it may now be noticed that what we've essentially been saying so far is that the pair of sentences seems to satisfy what a member might require of some pair of sentences for them to be recognizable as "a possible description." They "sound like a description," and some form of words can, apparently, sound like a description. To recognize that some form of words is a possible description does not require that one must first inspect the circumstances it may be characterizing.

That "possible descriptions" are recognizable as such is quite an important fact, for members, and for social scientists. The reader ought to be able to think out some of its import for members, e.g., the economies it affords them. It is the latter clause, "and for social scientists," that I now wish to attend to.

Were it not so both that members have an activity they do, "describing," and that at least some cases of that activity produce, for them, forms of words recognizable as at least possible descriptions without having to do an inspection of the circumstances they might characterize, then it might well be that social science would necessarily be the last of the sciences to be made do-able. For, unless social scientists could study such things as these "recognizable descriptions," we might only be able to investigate such activities of members as in one or another way turned on "their knowledge of the world" when social scientists could employ some established, presumptively correct scientific characterizations of the phenomena members were presumably dealing with and knowing about.

If, however, members have a phenomenon, "possible descriptions" that are recognizable per se, then one need not in the instance know how it is that babies and mommies do behave to examine the composition of such possible descriptions as members produce and recognize. Sociology and anthropology need not await developments in botany or genetics or analyses of the light spectra to gain a secure position from which members' knowledge, and the activities for which it is relevant, might be investigated.

What one ought to seek to build is an apparatus that will provide for how it is that any activities, which members do in such a way as to be recognizable as such to members, are done, and done recognizably. Such an apparatus will, of course, have to generate and provide for the recognizability of more than just possible descriptions, and in later discussions we shall be engaged in providing for such activities as "inviting," "warning," and so forth, as the data we consider will permit and require.

My reason for having gone through the observations I have so far made was to give you some sense, right off, of the fine power of a culture. It does not, so to speak, merely fill brains in roughly the same way, it fills them so that they are alike in fine detail. The sentences we are considering are after all rather minor, and yet all of you, or many of you, hear just what I said you heard, and many of us are quite unacquainted with each other. I am, then, dealing with something real and something finely powerful.

Membership categorization devices

We may begin to work at the construction of the apparatus. I'm going to introduce several of the terms we need. The first term is *membership categorization device* (or just *categorization device*). By this term I shall intend any collection of membership categories, containing at least a category, which may be applied to some population containing at least a member, so as to provide, by the use of some rules of application, for the pairing of at least a population member and a categorization device member. A device is then a collection plus rules of application.

An instance of a categorization device is the one called "sex": Its collection is the two categories (male, female). It is important to observe that a collection consists of categories that "go together." For now that may merely be seen as a constraint of the following sort: I could say that some set of categories was a collection, and be wrong. I shall present some rules of application very shortly.

Before doing that, however, let me observe that "baby" and "mommy" can be seen to be categories from one collection: the collection whose device is called "family" and that consists of such categories as ("baby," "mommy," "daddy,". . .) where by ". . ." we mean that there are others, but not any others, e.g., "shortstop."

Let me introduce a few rules of application. It may be observed that if a member uses a single category from any membership categorization device, then they can be recognized to be doing *adequate reference* to a person. We may put the observation in a negative form: it is not necessary that some multiple of categories from categorization devices be employed for recognition that a person is being referred to, to be made; a single category will do. (I do not mean by this that more cannot be used, only that for reference to persons to be recognized more need not be used.) With that observation we can formulate a "reference satisfactoriness" rule, which we call "the economy rule." It holds: a single category from any membership categorization device can be referentially adequate.

A second rule I call "the consistency rule." It holds: if some population of persons is being categorized, and if a category from some device's collection has been used to categorize a first member of the population, then that category or other categories of the same collection *may* be used to categorize further members of the population.

The former rule was a "reference satisfactoriness" rule; this latter one is a "relevance" rule.

The economy rule having provided for the adequate reference of "baby," the consistency rule tells us that if the first person has been categorized as "baby," then further persons may be referred to by other categories of a collection of which they are a member, and thus that such other categories as "mommy" and "daddy" are relevant given the use of "baby."

While in its currently weak form and alone, the consistency rule may exclude no category of any device, even in this weak form (the "may" form—I shall eventually introduce a "must" form), a corollary of it will prove to be useful. The corollary is a "hearer's maxim." It holds: if two or more categories are used to categorize two or more members of some population, and those categories can be heard as categories from the same collection, then hear them that way. Let us call the foregoing "the consistency rule corollary." It has the following sort of usefulness. Various membership categorization-device categories can be said to be ambiguous. That is, the same categorial word is a term occurring in several distinct devices, and can in each have quite a different reference; they may or may not be combinably usable in regard to a single person. So, for example, "baby" occurs in the device "family" and also in the device "stage of life" whose categories are such as "baby," "child,". . . "adult." A hearer who can use the consistency rule corollary will regularly not even notice that there might be an ambiguity in the use of some category among a group which it can be used to hear as produced via the consistency rule.

It is, of course, clear that the two categories "baby" are sometimes combinably referential and sometimes not. A woman may refer to someone as "my baby" with no suggestion that she is using the category that occurs in the "stage of life" device; her baby may be a full-fledged adult. In the case at hand that problem does not occur, and we shall be able to provide the bases for it not occurring, i.e., the bases for the legitimacy of hearing the single term "baby" as referring to a person located by reference both to the device "family" and to the device "stage of life."

With this, let us modify the observation on the consistency rule as follows: the consistency rule tells us that if a first person has been categorized as "baby," the further persons may be referred to by categories from either the device "family" or from the device "stage of life." However, if a hearer has a second category that can be heard as consistent with one locus of a first, then the first is to be heard as *at least* consistent with the second.

Given the foregoing, we may proceed to show how the combined reference of "baby" is heard for our two sentences, and also how "the mommy" is heard as "the mommy of the baby." We shall deal with the latter task first, and we assume from now on that the consistency rule corollary has yielded at least that "baby" and "mommy" are heard as from the device "family." We assume that without prejudice to the further fact that "baby" is also heard as "baby" from the device "stage of life."

The device "family" is one of a series which you may think of by a prototypical name "team." One central property of such devices is that they are what I am going to call "duplicatively organized." I mean by the use of that term to point out the following: when such a device is used on a population, what is done is to take its categories, treat the set of categories as defining a unit, and place members of the population into cases of the unit. If a population is so treated and is then counted, one counts not numbers of daddies, numbers of mommies, and numbers of babies but numbers of families—numbers of "whole families," numbers of "families without fathers," etc. A population so treated is partitioned into cases of the unit, cases for which what properly holds is that the various persons partitioned into any case are "coincumbents" of that case.

There are hearer's maxims that correspond to these ways of dealing with populations categorized by way of duplicatively organized devices. One that is relevant to our current task holds: if some population has been categorized by use of categories from some device whose collection has the "duplicative organization" property, and a member is presented with a categorized population that *can be heard* as "coincumbents" of a case of that device's unit, then hear it that way. (I will consider the italicized phrase shortly.) Now let it be noticed that this rule is of far more general scope than we may seem to need. In focusing on a property such as duplicative organization it permits a determination of an expectation (of social scientists) as to how some categorized population will be heard independently of a determination of how it is heard. It is then formal and predictive, as well, of course, as quite general.

Now, by the phrase "can be heard" we mean to rule out predictions of the following sort. Some duplicatively organized devices have proper numbers of incumbents for certain categories of any unit (at any given time a nation-state may have but one president, a family but one father, a baseball team but one shortstop on the field, etc.). If more incumbents of a category are proposed as present in the population than a unit's case can properly take, then the "can be heard" constraint is not satisfied, and a prediction would not be made.

Category-bound activities

The foregoing analysis shows us then how it is that we come to hear, given the fact that the device "family" is duplicatively organized, and the "can be heard" constraint being satisfied, "the mommy" to be "the mommy of the baby." It does, of course, much more than that. It permits us to predict, and to understand how we can predict, that a statement such as "The first baseman looked around. The third baseman scratched himself." will be heard as saying "the first baseman of the team on which the third baseman is also a player" and its converse.

Or, putting the claim more precisely, it shows us how, in part—"in part" because for the materials at hand—it happens that there are other means for providing that the same hearing be made, means which can operate in combination with the foregoing, otherwise sufficient ones, to further assure the hearings we have observed. That will be done in the next section. Let us now undertake our second task, to show how "the baby" is heard in its combined form, i.e., as the category with that name from both the "stage of life" device and from the "family" device.

Let me introduce a term that I am going to call *category-bound activities*. While I shall not now give an intendedly careful definition of the term, I shall indicate what I mean to notice with it and then in a while offer a procedure for determining that some of its proposed cases are indeed cases of it. By the term I intend to notice that many activities are taken by members to be done by some particular or several particular categories of members where the categories are categories from membership categorization devices.

Let me notice then, as is obvious to you, that "cry" is bound to "baby," i.e., to the category "baby," which is a member of the collection from the "stage of life" device. Again, the fact that members know that this is so only serves, for the social scientist, to pose some problem. What we want is to construct some means by reference to which a class, which proposedly contains at least the activity-category "cry" and presumably others, may have the inclusion of its candidate-members assessed. We will not be claiming that the procedure is definitive as to exclusion of a candidate-member, but we will claim that it is definitive as to inclusion of a candidate-member.

It may be observed that the members of the "stage of life" collection are "positioned" ("baby" . . . "adolescent" . . . "adult" . . .), an observation that, for now, we shall leave unexamined. I want to describe a procedure for praising or degrading members, the operation of which consists of the use of the fact that some activities are category-bound. If there are such procedures, they will provide one strong sense of the notion "category-bound activities" and also will provide, for any given candidate activity, a means for warrantably deciding that it is a member of the class of category-bound activities.

For some positioned-category devices it can be said as between any two categories of such a device that A is either higher or lower than B, and if A is higher than B, and B is higher than C, then A is higher than C.

We have some activity which is a candidate-member of the class "category-bound activities" and which is proposedly bound to some category C. Then, a member of either A or B who does that activity may be seen to be degrading himself, and may be said to be "acting like a C." Alternatively, if some candidate activity is proposedly bound to A, a member of C who does it is subject to being said to be acting like an A, where that assertion constitutes "praising."

If, using the "stage of life" categories, we subject "crying" to such a test, we do find that its candidacy as a member of the class "category-bound activities" is warrantable. In the case of "crying" the results are even stronger. For, it appears, if a "baby" is subject to some circumstances that would for such a one warrant crying, and he does not, then his not crying is observable, and may be used to propose that "he is acting like a big boy," where that assertion is taken to be "praise."

The foregoing procedure can, obviously enough, be used for other devices and other candidate activities. Other procedures may also be used; for example, one way to decide that an activity is category-bound is to see whether—the fact of membership being unknown—it can be "hinted at" by naming the activity as something one does.

The following data are from a telephone call between a staff member (S) and a caller (C) to an emergency psychiatric clinic. Note the juxtaposition of "hair stylist" in turn 4 with suspected homosexuality in the last turn.

S   So, you can't watch television. Is there anything you can stay interested in?
C   No, not really.
S   What interests did you have before?
C   I was a hair stylist at one time. I did some fashions now and then. Things like that.

S   Then why aren't you working?

C   Because I don't want to, I guess. Maybe that's why.

S   But do you find that you just can't get yourself going?

C   No. Well, as far as the job goes?

S   Yes.

C   Well, I'll tell you. I'm afraid. I'm afraid to go out and look for a job. That's what I'm afraid of. But more, I think I'm afraid of myself because I don't know. I'm just terribly mixed up.

S   You haven't had any trouble with anyone close to you?

C   Close to me. Well, I've been married three times and I'm—close, you mean, as far as arguments or something like that?

S   Yes.

C   No, nobody real close. I'm just a very lonely person. I guess I'm very—

S   There's nobody who loves you.

C   Well, I feel that somebody must someplace, but I don't know where or who.

S   Have you been having some sexual problems?

C   All my life.

S   Uh huh. Yeah.

C   Naturally. You probably suspect—as far as the hair stylist and— either go one way or the other. There is a straight or homosexual, something like that. I'm telling you, my whole life is just completely mixed up and turned over and it's just smashed and I'm not kidding.

Having constructed a procedure that can warrant the candidacy of some activity as a member of the class "category-bound activities," and which warrants the membership of "cry" and provides for its being bound to "baby," i.e., the category "baby" that is a member of the "stage of life" collection, we move on to see how it is that "the baby" in our sentence is heard in the combined reference we have proposed.

We need, first, another "hearer's maxim." If a category-bound activity is asserted to have been done by a member of some category where, if that category is ambiguous (i.e., is a member of at least two different devices) but where, at least for one of those devices, the asserted activity is category-bound to the given category, then hear that *at least* the category from the device to which it is bound is being asserted to hold.

The foregoing maxim will then provide for hearing "The baby cried." as referring to at least "baby" from the "stage of life" device. The results obtained from the use of the consistency rule corollary, being independent of that, are combinable with it. The consistency rule corollary gave us at least that "the baby" was the category from the device "family." The combination gives us both.

If our analysis seems altogether too complicated for the rather simple facts we have been examining, then we invite the reader to consider that our machinery has intendedly been "overbuilt." That is to say it may turn out that the elaborateness of our analysis, or its apparent elaborateness, will disappear when one begins to consider the amount of work that the very same machinery can perform.

In the next section I will attempt to show that the two sentences we have been discussing—"The baby cried. The mommy picked it up."—constitute a possible description.

Identifying possible descriptions

I shall focus next on the fact that an activity can be category-bound and then on the import of there being a norm that provides for some second activity, given the occurrence of a first, considering both of these with regard to the "correctness," for members, of "possible description."

Let me for the moment leave aside our two sentences and consider some observations on how it is that I see, and take it you see, describable occurrences. Suppose you are standing somewhere, and you see a person you don't know. The person cries. Now, if I can, I will see that what has happened is that a baby cried. And I take it that you will, if you can, see that too. That's a first pair of observations. Suppose again you are standing somewhere and you see two people you don't know. Suppose further that one cries, and the other picks up the one who is crying. Now, if I can, I will see that what has happened is that a baby cried and its mother picked it up. And I take it that you will, if you can, see that too. That's a second pair of observations.

Consider the first pair of observations. The modifying phrases, to deal with them first, refer simply to the possibility that the category "baby" might be obviously inapplicable to the crier. By reference to the "stage of life" collection the crier may be seen to be an adult. And that being so, the "if. . .can" constraint wouldn't be satisfied. But there are certainly other possible characterizations of the crying person. For example, without respect to the fact that it is a baby, it could be either "male" or "female," and nonetheless I would not, and I take it you would not, seeing the scene, see that "a male cried" if we could see that "a baby cried."

The pair of observations suggest the following "viewer's maxim": if a member sees a category-bound activity being done, then, if one can see it being done by a member of a category to which the activity is bound, then see it that way. The viewer's maxim is another relevance rule in that it proposes that for an observer of a category-bound activity the category to which the activity is bound has a special relevance for formulating an identification of its doer.

Consider the second pair of observations. As members you, of course, know that there is a norm that might be written as: "A mother ought to try to soothe her crying baby." I, and you, not only know that there is such a norm but, as you may recall, we used it in doing our hearing of "The baby cried. The mommy picked it up." In addition to the fact of duplicative organization, the norm was relevant in bringing us to hear that it was the mommy of the baby who did the picking up. While we would have heard that it was the mommy of the baby for other pairs of activities in which the two were involved (but not any pair), the fact that the pair were relatable via a norm that assigns the mother of the baby that duty may have operated in combination with the duplicative organization to assure our hearing that it was she who did it.

Leaving aside the hearing of the sentence, we are led to construct another viewer's maxim: if one sees a pair of actions that can be related via the operation of a norm that provides for the second given the first, where the doers can be seen as members of the categories the norm provides as proper for that pair of actions, then: (a) see that the doers are such members; and (b) see the second as done in conformity with the norm.

This second viewer's maxim suggests an observation about norms. In the sociological and anthropological literature, the focus on norms is on the conditions under which and the extent to which they govern, or can be seen by social scientists to govern, the relevant actions of those members whose actions they ought to control. While such matters are, of course, important, our viewer's maxim suggests other importances of norms, for members.

Viewers use norms to provide some of the orderliness, and proper orderliness, of the activities they observe. Via some norm two activities may be made observable as a sequentially ordered pair. That is, viewers use norms to explain both the occurrence of some activity given the occurrence of another and also its sequential position with regard to the other, e.g., that it follows the other, or precedes it. That is a first importance. Second, viewers use norms to provide the relevant membership categories in terms of which they formulate identifications of the doers of those activities for which the norms are appropriate.

Now let me observe, viewers may use norms in each of the preceding ways, and feel confident in their usage without engaging in such an investigation as would serve to warrant the correctness of their usages. This last observation is worth some further thought.

We may, at least initially, put the matter thus: for viewers, the usability of the viewer's maxims serves to warrant the correctness of their observations. And that is then to say, the usability of the viewer's maxims provides for the recognizability of the correctness of the observations done via those maxims. And that is then to say, "correct observations" or, at least, "possible correct observations" are "recognizable." (Members feel no need in warranting their observation, in recognizing its correctness to do such a thing as to ask the woman whether she is the mother of the baby, or to ask her whether she picked it up because it was crying; i.e., they feel no such need so long as the viewer's maxims are usable.)

In short: "correctness" is recognizable, and there are some exceedingly nice ties between recognizably correct description and recognizably correct observations. One such tie that is relevant to the tasks we have undertaken is a string of sentences that may be heard, via the hearer's maxims, as having been produced by use of the viewer's maxims, will be heard as a "recognizably correct possible description."

Sequential ordering

The rest of this chapter will be devoted to two tasks. I shall try to develop some further rewards of the analysis so far assembled, some consequences it throws off; and to show also how it is that the two sentences—"The baby cried. The mommy picked it up."—can warrantably be said to be from "a story." I start with the latter task.

It ought to be apparent that the fact that the children whose talk is reported in *Children Tell Stories* were asked to tell a story is not definitive of their having done so. It is at least possible that the younger ones among them are not capable of building stories, of building talk that is recognizable as a "story," or, at least, as a "possible story."

It happens to be correct, for Western literature, that if some piece of talk is a possible description it is also, and thereby, a possible story or story part. It appears, therefore, that having established that the two sentences are a possible description, I have also, and thereby, established that they are possibly (at least part of) a story. To stop now would, however, involve ignoring some story-relevant aspects of the given sentences which are both interesting and subjectable to analysis. So, I go on.

Certain characteristics are quite distinctive to stories. For example, there are characteristic endings ("And they lived happily ever after") and characteristic beginnings ("Once upon a time"). I shall consider whether the possible story, a fragment of which we have been investigating, can be said (and I mean here, as throughout, "warrantably said") to close with what is recognizable as "an ending" and to start with what is recognizable as "a beginning."

In suggesting a difference between "starts" and proper "beginnings," and between "closes" and proper "endings," I am introducing a distinction that has some importance. The distinction, which is by no means original, may be developed by considering some very simple observations.

1. A piece of talk that regularly is used to do some activity—as "Hello" is used to do "greeting"—may not invariably be so used, but may do other activities as well—as "Hello" is used to check out whether another with whom one is talking on the phone is still there or has been cut off—where it is in part its occurrence in "the middle" and not "the start" of a conversation that serves to discriminate the use being made of it.

2. Certain activities not only have regular places in some sequence where they do get done but may, if their means of being done is not found there, be said, by members, to not have occurred, to be absent. For example, the absence of a greeting may be noticed, as the following conversation, from field observation, indicates. The scene involved two adult women, one the mother of two children, ages six and ten. The kids enter and the following ensues:

    WOMAN: Hi.
    BOY: Hi.
    WOMAN: Hi, Annie.
    MOTHER: Annie, don't you hear someone say hello to you?
    WOMAN: Oh, that's okay, she smiled hello.
    MOTHER: You know you're supposed to greet someone, don't you?
    ANNIE: [Hangs head] Hello.

3. Certain activities can only be done at certain places in a sequence. For example, a third strike can only be thrown by a pitcher after he has two strikes on a batter.

Observations such as these lead to a distinction between a "slot" and the "items" that fill it, and to proposing that certain activities are accomplished by a combination of some item and some slot.

The notion of slot serves for the social scientist to mark a class of relevance rules. Thus, if it can be said that for some assertable sequence there is a position in which one or more activities properly occur, or occur if they are to get done, then: The observability of either the occurrence or the nonoccurrence of those activities may be claimed by reference to having looked to the position and determined whether what occurs in it is a way of doing the activity.

An instance of the class of relevance rules might run: To see whether a conversation included "greetings," look to the first utterance of either party and see whether there occurs in it any item which passes as a greeting; items such as ("hello," "hi," "hi there,". . .). The fact that the list contains the ellipsis might be deeply troublesome were it not the case that while we are unable to list all the members of the class "greeting items," we can say that the class is bounded, and that there are some utterables that are not members of it, perhaps, for example, the sentence now being completed. If that and only that occurred in a first utterance, we might feel assured in saying that a greeting did not occur.

Consider just one way that this class of relevance rules is important. Roughly, it permits the social scientist to nontrivially assert that something is absent. Nontrivial talk of an absence requires that some means be available for showing both the relevance of occurrence of the activity that is proposedly absent and the location where it should be looked for to see that it did not occur. Lacking these, an indefinite set of other activities might equally well be asserted to be absent given some occurrence, and the assertion in question not being discriminable from the (other) members of that indefinite set, it is trivialized.

It does seem that for stories it is correct to say that they can have beginnings, and we can then inspect the items that occur at their start to see whether they can be seen to make a beginning. Given further that stories can have endings, we can inspect the items that occur at their close to see whether they can be seen to make an ending.

While my main interest will be with the story's start as a possible proper beginning, let me briefly consider its close: "She went to sleep." With this the speaker would seem to be not merely closing but closing making a proper ending. It so seems by virtue of the fact that such a sentence reports an occurrence, or can be heard as reporting an occurrence, which is a proper ending to something for which endings are relevant and standardized, that very regularly used unit of orientation, the day. A day being recognized as ending for some person when they go to sleep, so a story may be recognized as closing with an ending if at its close there is a report of the protagonist's having gone to sleep. This particular sort of ending is, of course, not at all particular to stories constructed by young children; it, and other endings like it, from "the last sleep" of death unto the shutting down of the world, are regular components of far more sophisticated ventures in Western literature.

Let me turn then to the start, to consider whether it can be said to be a beginning. I shall attempt to show that starting to talk to adults is for small children a rather special matter. I shall do that by focusing on a most characteristic way that small children, of around the age of the teller of the given story, characteristically open their talk to adults, i.e., the use of such items as "You know what?" I shall offer an analysis of that mode of starting off, which will characterize the problems such a start can be seen to operate as a methodical solution to.

The promised analysis will warrant my assertion that starting to talk is, for small children, a special matter. That having been established, I shall turn to see whether the particular start we have for this story may be seen as another type of solution to the same problem that I will have shown to be relevant.

If I can then show that another solution is employed in our problematic utterance (the sentence "The baby cried"), I will have shown that the story starts with something that is properly a beginning, and that therefore, both start and close are "proper" beginning and end. Such, in any event, are my intentions.

I begin, roughly and only as an assumption (although naively, the matter is obvious), by asserting that kids have restricted rights to talk. That being the case, by assumption, I want to see whether the ways that they go about starting to talk, with adults, can be most adequately seen to be solutions to the problem that focuses on needing to have a good start if one is going to get further than that. Starts that have that character can then be called beginnings.

Now, kids around the age of three go through a period when some of them have an almost universal way of beginning any piece of talk they make to adults. They use things like: "You know what, daddy?" or "You know something, mommy?"

I will introduce a few rules of conversational sequencing. I do that without presenting data now, but the facts are so obvious that you can check them out easily for yourself; you know the rules anyway. The sequencing rules are for two-party conversation; and, since two-party conversation is a special phenomenon, what I say is not intended as applying for three- or more party conversation.

One basic rule of two-party conversation concerns a pair of objects, questions and answers. It runs: if one party asks a question, when the question is complete, the other party properly speaks, and properly offers an answer to the question and says no more than that. The rule will need considerable explication, but for now, it will do as it stands.

A second rule, and it's quite a fundamental one, because by reference to it the infinite, in principle, character of a conversation can be seen as: a person who has asked a question can talk again, has, as we may put it, "a reserved right to talk again," after the one to whom he has addressed the question speaks. *And*, in using the reserved right he can ask a question. I call this rule the "chaining rule," and in combination with the first rule it provides for the occurrence of an indefinitely long conversation of the form Q-A-Q-A-Q-A-. . .

Now, the characteristic opener that we are considering is a question (e.g., "You know what?"). Having begun in that way, a user who did not have restricted rights to talk would be in a position of generating an indefinite set of further questions as each question was replied to, or as the other otherwise spoke on the completion of some question.

But the question we begin with is a rather curious one in that it is one of those fairly but not exceptionally rare questions that have as their answer another question, in this case the proper and recurrent answer is "What?". The use of initial questions of this sort has a variety of consequences. First, if a question that has another question as its proper answer is used and is properly replied to, i.e., is replied to with the proper question, then the chaining rule is turned around, i.e., it is the initial answerer and not the initial questioner who now has the reserved right to speak again after the other speaks. The initial questioner has by his question either not assumed that he can use the chaining rule or has chosen not to. (Note that we are not saying that he has not chosen to invoke the chaining rule but rather that he has instead given the choice of invoking it to the initial answerer. There are two different possibilities involved.)

Second, the initial questioner does not only not make his second speech by virtue of the chaining rule but he makes it by virtue of the first sequencing rule, i.e., by reference to the fact that a person who has been asked a question properly speaks and properly replies to it. His second speech is then not merely not made as a matter of either the chaining rule or his choice by some other means of making a second speech but it is something he makes by obligation, given the fact that he has been asked a question and is therefore obliged to answer.

Third, the question he is obliged to answer is, however, "an open one" in the sense that what it is that an answer would be is something that its asker does not know, and further is one that its answerer by the prior sequence should know. What an answer is then to the second question is whatever it is the kid takes to be an answer, and he is thereby provided with the opportunity to say whatever it is he wanted to say in the first place, not now, however, on his own say-so but as a matter of obligation.

In that case then—and the foregoing being a method whereby the production of the question "You know what?" may be explicated—we may take it that kids take it that they have restricted rights which consist of a right to begin, to make a first statement and not much more. Thereafter they proceed only if requested to. And if that is their situation as they see it, they surely have evolved a nice solution to it.

With the foregoing we can say then that a focus on the way kids begin to talk is appropriate, and we can see whether the beginnings of stories, if they are not made of the culturally standardized beginnings (such as "Once upon a time"), might be seen to be beginnings by virtue of the special situation which kids have vis-à-vis beginning to talk.

We may arrive at the status of "The baby cried" as a proper beginning, in particular as a start that is a beginning by virtue of being a proper opener for one who has restricted rights to talk, by proceeding in the following way. Let us consider another solution to the problem of starting talk under restricted rights. I'll begin by introducing a word, "ticket." I can show you what I mean to point to with the word by a hypothetical example. Suppose two adults are copresent and lack rights to talk to each other, they have never been introduced or whatever. For any such two persons there are conditions under which one can begin to talk to the other. And that those conditions are the conditions used to in fact begin talk is something that can be shown via a first piece of talk. Where that is done we will say that talk is begun with a ticket. That is, the item used to begin talk is an item that, rights not otherwise existing, serves to warrant one having begun to talk. For example, one turns to the other and says, "Your pants are on fire." It is not just any opening, but an opening that tells why it is that one has breached the correct silence, which warrants one having spoken. Tickets then are items specially usable as first items in talk by one who has restricted rights to talk to another. And the most prototypical class of tickets are "announcements of trouble relevant to the other."

Now it is clear enough that the occurrence of a baby crying is the occurrence of a piece of trouble relevant to some person, e.g., the mother of the baby. One who hears it gains a right to talk, i.e., to announce the fact that it has occurred, and can most efficiently speak via a ticket, i.e., "The baby cried." That being so, we can see then that the opener "The baby cried" is a proper beginning, i.e., it is something which can serve as a beginning for someone whose rights to talk are in the first instance restricted.

With the foregoing we have established that the story we have been examining has both a proper beginning and a proper end, and is thus not only a story by virtue of being a possible description but also by virtue of its employing, as parts, items that occur in positions that permit one to see that the user may know that stories have such positions, and that there are certain items that when used in them are satisfactory incumbents.

Chapter 15

Emanuel A. Schegloff and Harvey Sacks

OPENING UP CLOSINGS

OUR AIM IN THIS PAPER is to report in a preliminary fashion on analyses we have been developing of closings of conversation. Although it may be apparent to intuition that the unit 'a single conversation' does not simply end, but is brought to a close, our initial task is to develop a technical basis for a closing problem. This we try to derive from a consideration of some features of the most basic sequential organization of conversation we know of – the organization of speaker turns. . . .

This project is part of a program of work undertaken several years ago [this paper was first delivered to the American Sociological Association in 1969] to explore the possibility of achieving a naturalistic observational discipline that could deal with the details of social action(s) rigorously, empirically, and formally. For a variety of reasons that need not be spelled out here, our attention has focused on conversational materials; suffice it to say that this is not because of a special interest in language, or any theoretical primacy we accord conversation. Nonetheless, the character of our materials as conversational has attracted our attention to the study of conversation as an activity in its own right, and thereby to the ways in which any actions accomplished in conversation require reference to the properties and organization of conversation for their understanding and analysis, both by participants and by professional investigators. This last phrase requires emphasis and explication.

We have proceeded under the assumption (an assumption borne out by our research) that insofar as the materials we worked with exhibited orderliness, they did so not only for us, indeed not in the first place for us, but for the coparticipants who had produced them. If the materials (records of natural conversations) were orderly, they were so because they had been methodically produced by members of the society for one another, and it was a feature of the conversations that we treated as data that they were produced so as to allow the display by the

Source: Emanuel A. Schegloff and Harvey Sacks, 'Opening up closings', *Semiotica*, 1973, 8: 289–327.

coparticipants to each other of their orderliness, and to allow the participants to display to each other their analysis, appreciation, and use of that orderliness. Accordingly, our analysis has sought to explicate the ways in which the materials are produced by members in orderly ways that exhibit their orderliness, have their orderliness appreciated and used, and have that appreciation displayed and treated as the basis for subsequent action.

In the ensuing discussion, therefore, it should be clearly understood that the 'closing problem' we are discussing is proposed as a problem for conversationalists; we are not interested in it as a problem for analysts except insofar as, and in the ways, it is a problem for participants. (By 'problem' we do not intend puzzle, in the sense that participants need to ponder the matter of how to close a conversation. We mean that closings are to be seen as achievements, as solutions to certain problems of conversational organization.) . . .

The materials with which we have worked are audiotapes and transcripts of naturally occurring interactions (i.e., ones not produced by research intervention such as experiment or interview) with differing numbers of participants and different combinations or participant attributes. There is a danger attending this way of characterizing our materials, namely, that we be heard as proposing the assured relevance of numbers, attributes of participants, etc., to the way the data are produced, interpreted, or analyzed by investigators or by the participants themselves. Such a view carries considerable plausibility, but for precisely that reason it should be treated with extreme caution, and be introduced only where warrant can be offered for the relevance of such characterizations of the data from the data themselves.

. . .

It seems useful to begin by formulating the problem of closing technically in terms of the more fundamental order of organization, that of turns. Two basic features of conversation are proposed to be: (1) at least, and no more than, one party speaks at a time in a single conversation; and (2) speaker change recurs. The achievement of these features singly, and especially the achievement of their co-occurrence, is accomplished by co-conversationalists through the use of a 'machinery' for ordering speaker turns sequentially in conversation. The turn-taking machinery includes as one component a set of procedures for organizing the selection of 'next speakers', and, as another, a set of procedures for locating the occasions on which transition to a next speaker may or should occur. The turn-taking machinery operates utterance by utterance. That is to say . . . it is within any current utterance that possible next speaker selection is accomplished, and upon possible completion of any current utterance that such selection takes effect and transition to a next speaker becomes relevant. We shall speak of this as the 'transition relevance' of possible utterance completion. . . . Whereas these basic features . . . deal with a conversation's ongoing orderliness, they make no provision for the closing of conversation. A machinery that includes the transition relevance of possible utterance completion recurrently for any utterance in the conversation generates an indefinitely extendable string of turns to talk. Then, an initial problem concerning closings may be formulated: HOW TO ORGANIZE THE SIMULTANEOUS

ARRIVAL OF THE CO-CONVERSATIONALISTS AT A POINT WHERE ONE SPEAKER'S COMPLETION WILL NOT OCCASION ANOTHER SPEAKER'S TALK, AND THAT WILL NOT BE HEARD AS SOME SPEAKER'S SILENCE. The last qualification is necessary to differentiate closings from other places in conversation where one speaker's completion is not followed by a possible next speaker's talk, but where, given the continuing relevance of the basic features and the turn-taking machinery, what is heard is not termination but attributable silence, a pause in the last speaker's utterance, etc. It should suggest why simply to stop talking is not a solution to the closing problem: any first prospective speaker to do so would be hearable as 'being silent' in terms of the turn-taking machinery, rather than as having suspended its relevance. . . .

How is the transition relevance of possible utterance completion lifted? A proximate solution involves the use of a 'terminal exchange' composed of conventional parts, e.g., an exchange of 'good-byes'. . . . We note first that the terminal exchange is a case of a class of utterance sequences which we have been studying for some years, namely, the utterance pair, or, as we shall refer to it, the adjacency pair. . . . Briefly, adjacency pairs consist of sequences which properly have the following features: (1) two utterance length, (2) adjacent positioning of component utterances, (3) different speakers producing each utterance. The component utterances of such sequences have an achieved relatedness beyond that which may otherwise obtain between adjacent utterances. That relatedness is partially the product of the operation of a typology in the speakers' production of the sequences. The typology operates in two ways: it partitions utterance types into 'first pair parts' (i.e., first parts of pairs) and second pair parts; and it affiliates a first pair part and a second pair part to form a 'pair type'. 'Question-answer', 'greeting-greeting', 'offer-acceptance/refusal' are instances of pair types. . . . Adjacency pair sequences, then, exhibit the further features (4) relative ordering of parts (i.e. first pair parts precede second pair parts) and (5) discriminative relations (i.e., the pair type of which a first pair part is a member is relevant to the selection among second pair parts). . . .

In the case of that type of organization which we are calling 'overall structural organization', it may be noted that at least initial sequences (e.g., greeting exchanges), and ending sequences (i.e., terminal exchanges) employ adjacency pair formats. It is the recurrent, institutionalized use of adjacency pairs for such types of organization problems that suggests that these problems have, in part, a common character, and that adjacency pair organization . . . is specially fitted to the solution of problems of that character. . .

But it may be wondered, why are two utterances required for either opening or closing? . . . What two utterances produced by different speakers can do that one utterance cannot do is: by an adjacently positioned second, a speaker can show that he understood what a prior aimed at, and that he is willing to go along with that. Also, by virtue of the occurrence of an adjacently produced second, the doer of a first can see that what he intended was indeed understood, and that it was or was not accepted. . . .

We are then proposing: If WHERE transition relevance is to be lifted is a systematic problem, an adjacency pair solution can work because: by providing that transition relevance is to be lifted after the second pair part's occurrence, the occurrence of the second pair part can then reveal an appreciation of, and agreement to, the intention of closing NOW which a first part of a terminal exchange reveals its speaker to propose. Given the institutionalization of that solution, a range of ways of assuring that it be employed have been developed, which make a drastic difference between one party saying "good-bye" and not leaving a slot for the other to reply, and one party saying "good-bye" and leaving a slot for the other to reply. The former becomes a distinct sort of activity, expressing anger, brusqueness, and the like, and available to such a use by contrast with the latter. It is this consequentiality of alternatives that is the hallmark of an institutionalized solution. . . .

In referring to the components of terminal exchanges, we have so far employed "good-bye" as an exclusive instance. But, it plainly is not exclusively used. Such other components as "ok", "see you", "thank you", "you're welcome", and the like are also used. Since the latter items are used in other ways as well, the mere fact of their use does not mark them as unequivocal parts of terminal exchanges. . . .

The adjacency pair is one kind of 'local', i.e., utterance, organization. It does NOT appear that FIRST parts of terminal exchanges are placed by reference to that order of organization. While they, of course, occur after some utterance, they are not placed by reference to a location that might be formulated as 'next' after some 'last' utterance or class of utterances. Rather, their placement seems to be organized by reference to a properly initiated closing SECTION.

The [relevant] aspect of overall conversational organization concerns the organization of topic talk. . . . If we may refer to what gets talked about in a conversation as 'mentionables', then we can note that there are considerations relevant for conversationalists in ordering and distributing their talk about mentionables in a single conversation. There is, for example, a position in a single conversation for 'first topic'. We intend to mark by this term not the simple serial fact that some topic gets talked about temporally prior to others, for some temporally prior topics such as, for example, ones prefaced by "First, I just want to say . . .", or topics that are minor developments by the receiver of the conversational opening of "how are you" inquiries, are not heard or treated as 'first topic' is to accord it to a certain special status in the conversation. Thus, for example, to make a topic 'first topic' may provide for its analyzability (by coparticipants) as 'the reason for' the conversation, that being, furthermore, a preservable and reportable feature of the conversation. In addition, making a topic 'first topic' may accord it a special importance on the part of its initiator . . . .

These features of 'first topics' may pose a problem for conversationalists who may not wish to have special importance accorded some 'mentionable', and who may not want it preserved as 'the reason for the conversation'. It is by reference to such problems affiliated with the use of first topic position that we may appreciate such exchanges at the beginnings of conversations in which news IS later reported, as:

    A: What's up.
    B: Not much. What's up with you?
    A: Nothing.

Conversationalists, then, can have mentionables they do not want to put in first topic position, and there are ways of talking past first topic position without putting them in.

A further feature of the organization of topic talk seems to involve 'fitting' as a preferred procedure. That is, it appears that a preferred way of getting mentionables mentioned is to employ the resources of the local organization of utterances in the course of the conversation. That involves holding off the mention of a mentionable until it can 'occur naturally', that is, until it can be fitted to another conversationalist's prior utterance. . . .

There is, however, no guarantee that the course of the conversation will provide the occasion for any particular mentionable to 'come up naturally'.

This being the case, it would appear that an important virtue for a closing structure designed for this kind of topical structure would involve the provision for placement of hitherto unmentioned mentionables. The terminal exchange by itself makes no such provision. By exploiting the close organization resource of adjacency pairs, it provides for an immediate (i.e., next turn) closing of the conversation. That this close-ordering technique for terminating not exclude the possibility of inserting unmentioned mentionables can be achieved by placement restrictions on the first part of terminal exchanges, for example, by requiring 'advance note' or some form of foreshadowing.

. . .

The first proper way of initiating a closing section that we will discuss is one kind of (what we will call) 'pre-closing'. The kind of pre-closing we have in mind takes one of the following forms, "We-ell . . .", "O.K . . .", "So-oo", etc. (with downward intonation contours), these forms constituting the entire utterance. These pre-closings should properly be called 'POSSIBLE pre-closing', because providing the relevance of the initiation of a closing section is only one of the uses they have. One feature of their operation is that they occupy the floor for a speaker's turn without using it to produce either a topically coherent utterance or the initiation of a new topic. With them a speaker takes a turn whose business seems to be to 'pass,' i.e., to indicate that he has not now anything more or new to say, and also to give a 'free' turn to the next, who, because such an utterance can be treated as having broken with any prior topic, can without violating topical coherence take the occasion to introduce a new topic. . . . When this opportunity is exploited . . . then the local organization otherwise operative in conversation, including the fitting of topical talk, allows the same possibilities which obtain in any topical talk. The opening . . . may thus result in much more ensuing talk than the initial mentionable that is inserted. . . . The extendability of conversation to great lengths past a possible pre-closing is not a sign of the latter's defects with respect to initiating closings, but of its virtues in providing opportunities for further topic talk that is fitted to the topical structure of conversation.

. . . The other possibility is that co-conversationalists decline an opportunity to insert unmentioned mentionables. In that circumstance, the pre-closing may be answered with an acknowledgement, a return 'pass' yielding a sequence such as:

A: O.K.
B: O.K.

thereby setting up the relevance of further collaborating on a closing section. When the possible pre-closing is responded to in this manner, it may constitute the first part of the closing section.

. . .

Clearly, utterances such as "*O.K.*", "*We-ell*", etc. (where those forms are the whole of the utterance), occur in conversation in capacities other than that of 'pre-closing'. It is only on some occasions of use that these utterances are treated as pre-closings. . . .

[They] operate as possible pre-closings when placed at the analyzable (once again, TO PARTICIPANTS) end of a topic.

. . . Not all topics have an analyzable end. One procedure whereby talk moves off a topic might be called 'topic shading', in that it involves no specific attention to ending a topic at all, but rather the fitting of differently focused but related talk to some last utterance in a topic's development. But co-conversationalists may specifically attend to accomplishing a topic boundary, and there are various mechanisms for doing so; these may yield 'analyzable ends,' their analyzability to participants being displayed in the effective collaboration required to achieve them.

For example, there is a technique for 'closing down a topic' that seems to be a formal technique for a class of topic types, in the sense that for topics that are of the types that are members of the class, the technique operates without regard to what the particular topic is. . . . We have in mind such exchanges as:

A: Okay?
B: Alright

Such an exchange can serve, if completed, to accomplish a collaboration on the shutting down of a topic, and may thus mark the next slot in the conversational sequence as one in which, if an utterance of the form "We-ell", "*O.K.*", etc. should occur, it may be heard as a possible pre-closing.

Another 'topic-bounding' technique involves one party's offering of a proverbial or aphoristic formulation of conventional wisdom which can be heard as the 'moral' or 'lesson' of the topic being thereby possibly closed. Such formulations are 'agreeable with'. When such a formulation is offered by one party and agreed to by another, a topic may be seen (by them) to have been brought to a close. Again, an immediately following "We-ell" or "*O.K.*" may be analyzed by its placement as doing the alternative tasks a possible pre-closing can do.

(1) *Dorrinne:*   Uh-you know, it's just like bringin the- blood up.
    Theresa: Yeah well, THINGS UH ALWAYS WORK OUT FOR THE //
                 BEST
    Dorrinne: Oh certainly. Alright //Tess.

Theresa:	Oh huh,
Theresa:	Okay,
Dorrinne:	G'bye.
Theresa:	Goodnight,

(2) *Johnson:*   . . . and uh, uh we're gonna see if we can't uh tie in our
      plans a little better.
Baldwin: Okay // fine.
Johnson: ALRIGHT?
Baldwin: RIGHT.
Johnson: Okay boy,
Baldwin: Okay
Johnson: Bye // bye
Baldwin: G'night

. . .

What the preceding discussion suggests is that a closing section is initiated, i.e., turns out to have begun, when none of the parties to a conversation care or choose to continue it. Now that is a WARRANT for closing the conversation, and we may now be in a position to appreciate that the issue of placement, for the initiation of closing sections as for terminal exchanges, is the issue of warranting the placement of such items as will initiate the closing at some 'here and now' in the conversation. The kind of possible pre-closing we have been discussing – "O.K.", "We-ell", etc. – is a way of establishing one kind of warrant for undertaking to close a conversation. Its effectiveness can be seen in the feature noted above, that if the floor offering is declined, if the "O.K." is answered by another, then together these two utterances can constitute not a possible, but an actual first exchange of the closing section. The pre-closing ceases to be 'pre-' if accepted, for the acceptance establishes the warrant for undertaking a closing of the conversation at some 'here'.

We may now examine other kinds of pre-closings and the kinds of warrants they may invoke for initiating the beginning of a closing section. The floor-offering-exchange device [above] is one that can be initiated by any party to a conversation. In contrast to this, there are some . . . devices whose use is restricted to particular parties. We can offer some observations about telephone contacts, where the formulation of the parties can be specified in terms of the specific conversation, i.e., caller – called. What we find is that there are, so to speak, 'caller's techniques' and 'called's techniques' for inviting the initiation of closing sections. . . .

One feature that many of them have in common [is] that they employ as their warrant for initiating the closing the interests of the other party. It is in the specification of those interests that the techniques become assigned to one or another party. Thus, the following invitation to a closing is caller-specific and makes reference to the interests of the other.

A discussion about a possible luncheon has been proceeding:

A: Uhm livers 'n an gizzards 'n stuff like that makes it real yummy. Makes
it too rich for *me* but: makes it yummy.
A: *Well* I'll letchu go. I don't wanna tie up your phone.

And, on the other hand, there are such called-specific techniques, also making reference to the other's interests, as

A: This is costing you a lot of money.

There are, of course, devices usable by either party which do not make reference to the other's interests, most familiarly, "I gotta go".

. . .

The 'routine' questions employed at the beginnings of conversations, e.g., "what are you doing?", "where are you going?", "how are you feeling?", etc., can elicit those kinds of materials that will have a use at the ending of the conversation in warranting its closing, e.g., "Well, I'll let you get back to your books", "why don't you lie down and take a nap?", etc. By contrast with our earlier discussion of such possible pre-closings as "O.K." or "We-ell", which may be said to accomplish or embody a warrant for closing, these may be said to announce it. That they do so may be related to the possible places in which they may be used.

. . .

It is the import of some of the preceding discussion that there are slots in conversation 'ripe' for the initiation of closing, such that utterances inserted there may be inspected for their closing relevance. To cite an example, "why don't you lie down and take a nap" properly placed will be heard as an initiation of a closing section, not as a question to be answered with a "Because . . ." (although, of course, a coparticipant can seek to decline the closing offering by treating it as a question). To cite actual data:

B has called to invite C, but has been told C is going out to dinner:

B: Yeah. Well get on your clothes and get out and collect some of that
free food and we'll make it some other time Judy then.
C: Okay then Jack
B: Bye bye
C: Bye bye

While B's initial utterance in this excerpt might be grammatically characterized as an imperative or a command, and C's "Okay" as a submission or accession to it, in no sense but a technical syntactic one would those be anything but whimsical characterizations. While B's utterance has certain imperative aspects in its language form, those are not ones that count; his utterance is a closing initiation; and

C's utterance agrees not to a command to get dressed (nor would she be inconsistent if she failed to get dressed after the conversation), but to an invitation to close the conversation. The point is that no analysis – grammatical, semantic, pragmatic, etc. – of these utterances taken singly and out of sequence, will yield their import in use, will show what coparticipants might make of them and do about them. That B's utterance here accomplishes a form of closing initiation, and C's accepts the closing form and not what seems to be proposed in it, turns on the placement of these utterances in the conversation. Investigations which fail to attend to such considerations are bound to be misled. [Schegloff and Sacks go on to discuss 'pre-topic closing offerings', utterances like "Did I wake you up?", which offer listeners a means of moving into a closing section.]

. . .

Once properly initiated, a closing section may contain nothing but a terminal exchange and accomplish a proper closing thereby. Thus, a proper closing can be accomplished by:

> A: *O*.K.
> B: O.K.
> A: Bye Bye
> B: Bye

Closing sections may, however, include much more. There is a collection of possible component parts for closing sections which we cannot describe in the space available here. Among others, closings may include 'making arrangements', with varieties such as giving directions, arranging later meetings, invitations, and the like; reinvocation of certain sorts of materials talked of earlier in the conversation, in particular, reinvocations of earlier-made arrangements (e.g., "See you Wednesday") and reinvocations of the reason for initiating the conversation (e.g., "Well, I just wanted to find out how Bob was"), not to repeat here the earlier discussion of materials from earlier parts of the conversation to do possible pre-closings; and components that seem to give a 'signature' of sorts to the type of conversation, using the closing section as a place where recognition of the type of conversation can be displayed (e.g., "Thank you"). Collections of these and other components can be combined to yield extended closing sections, of which the following is but a modest example:

> B: Well that's why I *said* "I'm not gonna say anything, I'm not making
>   *any comments //* about anybody"
> C: Hmh
> C: Ehyeah
> B: Yeah
> C: Yeah
> B: *Alrighty.* Well *I'll* give you a call before we decide to come down.
>   O.K.?
> C: O.K.

B: *Al*righty
C: O.K.
B: We'll see you then
C: O.K.
B: *Bye* bye
C: Bye

However extensive the collection of components that are introduced, the two crucial components (FOR THE ACHIEVEMENT OF PROPER CLOSING; other components may be important for other reasons, but not for closing *per se*) are the terminal exchange which achieves the collaborative termination of the transition rule, and the proper initiation of the closing section which warrants the undertaking of the routine whose termination in the terminal exchange properly closes the conversation.

. . .

To capture the phenomenon of closings, one cannot treat it as the natural history of some particular conversation; one cannot treat it as a routine to be run through, inevitable in its course once initiated. Rather, it must be viewed, as much conversation as a whole, as a set of prospective possibilities opening up at various points in the conversation's course; there are possibilities throughout a closing, including the moments after a 'final' good-bye, for reopening the conversation. Getting to a termination, therefore, involves work at various points in the course of the conversation and of the closing section; it requires accomplishing. For the analyst, it requires a description of the prospects and possibilities available at the various points, how they work, what the resources are, etc., from which the participants produce what turns out to be the finally accomplished closing.

. . .

Symbols used in transcriptions

/	—	indicates upward intonation
//	—	indicates point at which following line interrupts
(n.0)	—	indicates pause of n.0 seconds
( )	—	indicates something said but not transcribable
(word)	—	indicates probable, but not certain, transcription
but	—	indicates accent
emPLOYee	—	indicates heavy accent
DO	—	indicates very heavy accent
: : : :	—	indicates stretching of sound immediately preceding, in proportion to number of colons inserted
becau-	—	indicates broken word

Chapter 16

Geoffrey Raymond and Jack Sidnell

CONVERSATION ANALYSIS

CONVERSATION ANALYSIS (CA) emerged through the collaboration of Harvey Sacks, Emanuel Schegloff, and Gail Jefferson in the late 1960s and early 1970s. Today it is one of the most well-established approaches to the study of social interaction across various disciplinary boundaries and is taught in universities throughout North America, Europe, and Asia. In what follows we present a brief sketch of CA beginning with the intellectual context within which it developed and proceeding to detail some of its methodologies and principal findings.

Introduction

Sacks and Schegloff were students of Erving Goffman, who was perhaps the first and certainly the most eloquent defender of the view that social interaction constituted a *sui generis* domain of social organization with properties not reducible to individual psychology or broader social processes (Goffman 1964, 1967). As Goffman observed, the social institution of interaction is of special interest to the human and social sciences because it is a main point of production for culture, social institutions, and other aspects of social life (Goffman 1983). At the same time Sacks and Schegloff were influenced by the highly original studies of Harold Garfinkel and the approach he developed known as ethnomethodology (Garfinkel 1974). Using a novel, and brilliant, set of experiments in which confederates sought to breach the norms and expectations of research subjects, Garfinkel exposed the underlying practices of reasoning that members of a society use in accomplishing everyday activities (Garfinkel 1967). For instance, Garfinkel instructed his students to act as if they were lodgers upon returning to their family homes. In doing so the students brought to light an immense range of unspoken assumptions that inform the production and interpretation of social actions—and social relations—in everyday life. For example, in the everyday life of families children are permitted to help themselves to food; by asking permission to eat, however, the students enacted the more formal relation of "guest" (or lodger). Although such conduct could be characterized as "polite," because it failed to draw on the relevant background knowledge used by family members they were typically confounded by it. Parents reacted to what they saw as bizarre behavior with confusion, annoyance, and frustration and, in some cases, concern for their children's mental health. A major part of Garfinkel's investigations was taken up with the question of how persons produce and make joint sense of action—including actions produced in and through talk—and the relevance of shared social norms and background knowledge to these achievements. These two approaches converged in their inversion of the common sense approaches to social action that dominated social theory at the time, as captured in Goffman's (1967) suggestion that the proper study of social interaction consisted not of "men and their moments; rather, moments and their men" (see also Schegloff 2010: 41, who paraphrases this as "not persons and their moments, but the organization of those moments"). The complementary perspectives of Goffman and Garfinkel provided inspiration for a new approach to the study of ordinary social interaction, but both drew on forms of data and methods (field notes drawn from direct observation and breaching experiments, respectively) that ultimately proved limiting. Sacks, Schegloff, and Jefferson's major innovations were enabled by their use of recorded interactions, and the development of the methods by which these recordings could be systematically studied.

Sacks, Schegloff, and Jefferson began their study of social interaction by examining audio recordings of telephone calls as well as co-present interaction and found there a locus of intricate order. Early studies showed that any given interaction could be broken down into parts and that these parts themselves consisted of orderly sequences. Moreover, in their studies, Sacks, Schegloff, and Jefferson (Jefferson 1973, 1974; Sacks 1974, 1995; Schegloff 1968; Sacks et al 1974; Schegloff and Sacks 1973) showed that this order is not the product of statistical regularities or of categorical imperatives but rather of a persistent and pervasive orientation by the participants to a set of norms or rules. In keeping with Garfinkel's findings regarding patterns of social action, the norms or rules that organize social interaction do not determine conduct but rather provide a framework through which it is made intelligible to the very people who produce it. Participants in interaction, that is, can be seen by others as following a rule, deviating from it, attempting but failing to follow it or simply violating it flat out—these various alternatives generating further informative inferences about what that participant intends by behaving in that way. The orderliness of interaction then is brought off by participants in interaction in each and every one of its local instantiations through the application of regular practices used in producing and recognizing social action. In the most basic sense, it is through the use of these practices that participants manage and track such routine matters as what (range of) action(s) is relevant next, just when it should be produced and by whom. Because participants cannot avoid having to manage this very basic— and inexorably local—form of social order, however, the linked actions that comprise encounters—specifically types of action they select, the methods used to design them (including their timing and placement relative to other actions) and the understandings these convey—produce a constantly updated, intersubjectively grounded definition of the situation. Thus, in contrast to traditional approaches that view matters of context as outside of interaction and impinging on it (what Goodwin and Heritage 1990: 286

call the "bucket theory of context"), CA shows that participants seamlessly interweave matters of social context—including who the parties are for one another and whatever social relations or identities may be relevant for them, and a range of other social, cultural, and institutional matters—in and through the linked actions that comprise the interaction itself.

The basic norms or rules that enable participants to accomplish this constitute a largely universal and generic underlying infrastructure of interaction. This infrastructure is organized into partially independent or semi-autonomous domains—or systems of practices—that emerge out of participants' efforts to manage a range of inescapable organizational contingencies that arise in encounters with others (Schegloff 2006). These organizational contingencies include how parties distribute opportunities to produce action (e.g., via talking), how adjacent actions are formed up as part of an overarching course of action, how troubles in speaking, hearing, and understanding are managed, how reference is made to persons, places, and objects, how stories are launched, composed, and responded to, how the overall organization of encounters is managed, and so on. Due to space limitations we can only sketch some basic features of three such domains—turn-taking, action sequencing, and repair—using these to illustrate the general approach we've outlined.

Turn-taking

First there is an organization of turn-taking that provides for the orderly distribution of opportunities to participate in talk-in-interaction. Sacks, Schegloff, and Jefferson (1974) described a system having two components: (1) a *turn constructional* component that defines the units out of which a possible turn can be constructed and by extension allows participants in interaction to independently anticipate the possible/probable extent and shape of any actual unit and thus to project its (possible) completion; (2) a *turn allocation* component that specifies an organized set of practices by which transition from a current speaker to a next speaker is managed at the possible completion of these units. Together these two components and the rules that organize their relation provide for the detailed orderliness of turn-taking in interaction (e.g., that one party speaks at a time, that these contributions are sequentially related, where simultaneous talk emerges it is brief, and so on). It can be seen, for instance, that overwhelmingly, self-selecting next speakers target possible unit completion points as places at which to start their own talk. In the following case a bracket marks the onset of overlapping talk. It can be observed in the example below that Parky twice attempts to begin his turn "That changed it" before it is eventually produced at line 06. Notice the split-second timing evidenced here with Parky attempting to come in at just those points where the old man has reached *possible* (although obviously not actual) completion of his current turn.

(1) Parky

```
01 Tourist:    Has the park cha:nged much,
02 Parky:      Oh:: ye:s,
03             (1.0)
```

04 Old man: Th'*Fun*fair changed it'n [ahful lot [didn'it.
05 Parky: [Th-   [That-
06 Parky: That changed it,

(Sacks et al 1974)

Clearly, in order to come in at just these points, Parky must have anticipated where the old man would reach the possible completion of each of the units used to construct his current turn (or 'turn constructional units' in Sacks et al 1974): "The funfair changed it" + "an awful lot" + "didn't it." Because participants—the current speaker and potential next speakers—orient to the possible completion of such units as places where transition to a next speaker is relevant, the system localizes the operation of turn allocation components. According to Sacks et al (1974), a current speaker is entitled (and obligated) to produce one such unit. At the first possible completion of a current turn constructional unit, transition to a next speaker becomes relevant in a way that it is not prior to reaching that point. There is a great deal of evidence to show that participants themselves orient to this relevance. This includes potential next speakers attempting to come in at just such points (as illustrated here), as well as current speaker "rushing-through" a point of possible completion (or otherwise suppressing its transition relevance) and thereby attempting to foreclose the possibility of another starting their own turn (see Sidnell 2010: ch. 3).

Thus far we have mainly emphasized how participants use the turn-construction component to organize their conduct by reference to "possible completion points." We now briefly consider the methods speakers use to effect transition to a next speaker—that is, the "turn allocation" component of the system described by Sacks et al (1974; and elaborated in Lerner 2003). In line 1, the tourist poses a question about the park, thereby selecting as next speaker a party with more extensive knowledge of it (to answer her). As Parky's response in line 2 illustrates, when a current speaker selects a next, transition to that party is relevant at the current unit's first possible completion. If the current speaker does not select a next, as in Parky's response (in line 2), any other party can *self*-select at the turn's possible completion with first starter gaining rights to the turn should more than one self-select (thereby, encouraging early starts in multi-party conversation). In this case the old man, another person with knowledge of the park, self-selects (in line 4) to elaborate Parky's answer before selecting him as next (using the tag question, "didn't it?"). The two methods used to distribute these turns—current selects next and next self-selects—are the most common practices for effecting transition to a next speaker. However, if the first is not used and the second does not occur the current speaker *can* continue, with the same set of ordered alternatives—(a) current selects next, (b) next self-selects, and (c) current continues, respectively—relevant at the next possible completion, and recursively until transfer to a next speaker is effected (see Sacks et al 1974). Across any conversation, then, participants' use of these components (for composing and allocating turns at talk) has profound consequences for what can be done (or even reliably contemplated) within it: their use locally distributes (at each next possible completion) opportunities for action to *current* and *next speakers*, while the content and composition of *current turns* shapes what can be relevantly produced in *next ones*. For example, it is by virtue of these operations that one can miss an opportunity to say something (once a next turn has been taken), or fail to realize (until it is too late) just what one should (or could) have said (see Schegloff and Sacks 1973: 297 on "close ordering", also Chapter 15 in this volume).

An important and widely underappreciated point is that this turn-taking system operates indiscriminately of whatever action is being pursued in and through the talk it organizes—i.e., whether persons are requesting, inviting, questioning, answering, agreeing, disagreeing, complaining, excusing, insulting, or whatever else, they do so in turns-at-talk constructed and distributed through an orientation to the turn-taking system. There is a single turn-taking system for ordinary talk in interaction not separate ones for arguing, complaining, complimenting, requesting, and so on. In this respect, the turn-taking system for conversation has a range of features that inhere across the various contexts in which it is used. At the same time, however, by virtue of the way opportunities to speak are locally distributed (on a turn-by-turn basis), participants' use of the turn-taking system will be sensitive to the specific projects they pursue, their identities or relations to one another, and even the types of encounters (and their boundaries) the use of this system partly organizes. It is in these senses that the system for turn-taking described by Sacks et al (1974) can be understood as a "context-free" form of social organization that is exploited in context sensitive ways.

Action sequencing

Despite the pervasive import of this organization for talk-in-interaction, speakers do not initiate social encounters with others simply to take turns speaking. Rather, participants use the opportunity (or responsibility) to speak to pursue (or participate in) courses of action with others. Thus a second key domain of organization in interaction concerns the ways in which sequences of action are composed using turns at talk. One can readily observe that a great many—although not all—courses of action in talk-in-interaction are produced through pairs of action, such as greetings and their return, request and granting (or rejection), invitation and acceptance (or refusal), complaint and excuse (or denial), and so on. The actions that compose what Schegloff (1968) called "adjacency pairs" are linked together by a relation of conditional relevance whereby (to paraphrase Schegloff 1968), given a first action (or "first pair part" such as a request, invitation, or complaint), a second (or "second pair part," such as a granting, acceptance, or excuse) is made expectable. Upon the occurrence of a second it can be seen to be a second item to the first (rather than an independent turn) and upon its nonoccurrence it can be seen to be absent (where an infinite number of other things did not occur but were not absent in the same way).

In this respect conditional relevance describes a relation between a first and second action that has both a prospective and a retrospective dimension. The prospective dimension allows participants to identify who is responsible for doing what next by virtue of the way in which a first action makes the doing of a responsive action relevant and noticeably absent if not produced. The retrospective dimension allows the first speaker to see if and how she was understood—e.g., production of a turn recognizable as an excuse in response will reveal to the first speaker that she was heard to be complaining or accusing, whether that was what she set out to do or not. Thus the production of actions within sequences constitutes an "architecture of intersubjectivity" by which understandings are publically displayed and ratified *en passant* in the course of whatever business the talk is occupied with (Sacks et al 1974; Heritage 1984). When used in conjunction with a practice for selecting a next speaker (see Sacks et al 1974; Lerner 2003), practices of action sequencing (i.e., producing an initiating action that makes a responsive one relevant next, producing responsive actions, etc.) provide one of the basic means humans have for making things happen in the world (see Schegloff 2007b).

Because the term "conditional relevance" names a very basic—and in many ways obvious—relationship between actions, it may not be immediately apparent how it can constitute a fine-grained interpretive framework for organizing social action, or how it can be used to coordinate longer stretches of talk. One can begin to appreciate both features by considering how the realization of many sequence types is shaped by the organization of "preference/dispreference." For many types of sequences the production of a first action makes relevant a choice between *alternative* next actions (e.g., as we noted above, invitations make *acceptance* or *refusal* relevant next, etc.). These alternative actions are *not* equivalent, however: one response promotes, or affiliates with, the course of action set in motion by the first, while the other disappoints (or blocks) it. These are respectively "preferred" and "dispreferred" responses (or better, preferred and dispreferred actions). It is important to note that these terms *do not* refer to the psychological states of the speakers who produced them; rather, they refer to the ways in which the practices used to produce these alternatives, and the organization of action sequencing more generally, are constitutive of a structural bias that makes some actions or outcomes (i.e., preferred ones) more likely than others. The simplest form this structural bias takes can be found in the differences between the alternative response forms themselves.

Typically, preferred responses are produced immediately and without qualification. So, for example, in the following case, which comes from a telephone conversation between two work colleagues (both are nurses), in accepting the invitation "Why don't you come and see me sometimes?", the recipient says, "I'd like to."

(2) SBL:1:1:10:r, p.7

```
01 Ros:     You know I have[a hou:se a big gahd'n=
02 Bea:                    [ˇYe:s.
03 Ros: -> hh ^Why ^dont'ohu come'n ^^see[me ˇso:me[t i : m e s.ˇ]
04 Bea: ->                               [ hh      [I would Li]:ke
05      -> ˇto:.
```

By contrast speakers usually design their dispreferred responses to include some or all of the following features: dispreferred responses may be (a) delayed by silence or other conduct; (b) prefaced by appreciations or other items; (c) mitigated or qualified; and (d) explained or accounted for. For example, in response to an invitation to "come over for coffee," taken from the same call as the previous example, the speaker declines by saying "(a) hehh (b) Well that's awfully sweet of you (c) I don't think I can make it this morning (d) I'm running an ad in the paper and I have to stay near the phone" (Heritage 1984).

(3) SBL:1:1:10:r, p.8–9

```
01 Ros:   And uh the: if you'd care tuh come ovuh, en Vis^it uh
02        little while this morn^ing I'll give you [cup a'^coffee.
03 Bea:                                           [khhh
04 Bea:   Uhhh-huh hh W'l thet's awf'lly sweet of yuh I ^don't
05        think I c'n make it this morning, hheeuhh uh:m (0.3)
06        'tch I'm running en a:d in the paper 'nd an:d uh hh I
07        haftih stay near the pho::ne,
```

The differences between these two responses suggest that speakers treat accepting an invitation as the preferred response—that is, as the default response form—while they treat declining an invitation as a dispreferred response, as the alternative to accepting, and as specifically accountable. We can further note that the account—or explanation—treats the dispreferred action it, in part, delivers as a product of the speaker's inability (as opposed to her unwillingness) to participate in the gathering, thereby limiting the degree to which the rejection can be taken as a comment on the participants' relationship.

These two cases exemplify a more general pattern in action sequencing: preferred actions (including responses) are simple and short, while dispreferred actions, or speakers' orientations to them, are associated with complexity and the expansion of basic units used to organize conduct. In the case we just examined, it was a *turn* that came to be expanded (by virtue of the number of distinct elements used to construct it); however (orientations to) dispreferred responses can also be reflected in the various ways *sequences of actions* can come to be expanded as well. To ground this point it will be useful to describe some basic features of sequence organization first.

Any sequence of actions can, itself, be expanded by turns at talk that are produced by reference to it—either before it (and so anticipating the sequence it thereby projects), or in its midst (and so delaying the response a sequence initiating action makes relevant), or after it (and so after a response, as part of an effort to deal with it, or any other as yet unresolved matters). In this way, a maximally simple ordering of utterances into adjacency pair sequences can nevertheless result in complex stretches of talk composed of multiple contributions by each party. The basic course of action pursued in a sequence—whether an invitation, request, offer, or other action—is called the "base" sequence, and other forms of sequence expansion are named by reference to the way they are positioned relative to it. Thus, speakers producing an initiating action can use "pre-sequences" (which are positioned *before* the base pair) to establish whether responding speakers will (likely) produce preferred responses to the base sequence they project, or otherwise establish a favorable basis for the action sequences they project. Following the production of an initiating action, responding speakers can use "insert sequences" (so named because they are positioned *between* a first and a second pair part) to deal with problems associated with an initiating action, clarify matters relating to the responding action it makes relevant, or (in other ways) foreshadow a dispreferred response. And following a second pair part, the first speaker has a further opportunity to manage the outcome of the sequence via talk in the next turn. Such "post-expansion" can take the form of a single turn (that registers the import or outcome of the sequence, especially preferred responses), or a post-expansion sequence that indicates some problem with the response (especially a dispreferred response), or deals with any other as yet unresolved matters associated with the course of action (e.g., as in lines 6–7 in example 3). For discussion and exemplification of these issues see Schegloff (2007b) and Sidnell (2010). The distribution of these practices, and the uses to which they are put suggest a close connection between sequence expansion and the organization of preference/ dispreference. Thus, as this overview suggests, sequences of action that come to be expanded reflect an orientation to—or an effort to deal with the implications of— dispreferred actions, while minimal or simple sequences of action are associated with preferred responses. Across virtually every facet of sequence organization, the practices that comprise it promote agreement and other preferred actions, while limiting the occasions for, and consequences of, disagreement and other dispreferred actions (e.g., Heritage 1984; Sacks 1987). Thus, the very methods that humans use to coordinate action in interaction have a built-in bias toward action completion quite apart from what the individual contributors to any specific course of action may want, wish, or believe is in their personal interest.

Repair

The third and final domain of organization to be described here is the system of repair. Troubles of speaking, hearing, and understanding are endemic to all forms of human interaction. The organized set of practices of repair constitute part of a natural, interactive system by which such troubles may be addressed at or near their point of production (or manifestation), thereby enabling their potential resolution more or less immediately lest they undermine the possibility of intersubjectively organized social action. The practices that make up the domain of repair are described in terms of the *personnel* who raise and deal with the trouble (self = speaker of trouble source, other = any other participant), the *positions* relative to the trouble source from which repair is initiated or indicated (same-turn, transition space between turns, next turn, third turn, third position, and fourth position), and the *components* through which it is carried out (initiation vs. repair proper, etc.) Consider for instance the following case excerpted from a talk show in which Ellen DeGeneres is interviewing Rashida Jones. The fragment begins with DeGeneres raising the topic of Jones' new television show, *Parks and Recreation*, with comedian Amy Poehler. DeGeneres initiates the topic by inviting Jones to tell the audience about the show. She then gives the title before concluding the turn with "an' you an' Amy Poehler how-how great is that," using an interrogative form that makes Jones' contribution relevant next. As we shall see, just what type of action Jones should (or does) produce in that turn emerges as a source of trouble.

(4) Rashida Jones on Ellen 04, 2009

```
01 El:          Al:right tell people about this hilarious
02              show. It's Parks and Recreation an' you
03      A ->    an' Amy Poehler how- How great is that. =
04 Ra:  B ->    = It's pretty great =
```

```
05 El:            = mm mh[m.
06 Ra:                    [It's- uhm- it- I just mean it- ek-
07                 experientially for me it's pr(h)etty
08                 [gr(h)ea(h)t(h)   [heh heh ha (      )
09 El:    C –>    [yeah.            [no. an' but I mean it's
10        C –>    a- I ah- know what you mea[nt. But I: say
11 Ra:                                      [hih huh ha hah ha
12                 [huh huh .hh hah
13 El:    C –>    [it's really great. The two of you. =
14 Ra:             nyeah.
15 El:             yeah. [an' it's about,
16 Ra:                   [(it is)
```

The final part of DeGeneres' turn (in lines 1–3) can be heard to make very different sorts of actions relevant next: Her use of interrogative syntax ("How great . . .") may treat as "in question" just how great "that" (the show?, working with Poehler?) is as a means of inviting Jones to respond with an answer. At the same time, this construction "How X is that?" is a familiar, idiomatic expression that, by virtue of the presupposition it carries, conveys "it's X" or, in this case, "it's great." On this hearing, DeGeneres' turn amounts to a positive evaluation of "that," which, given Jones' connection to the assessable, implies a compliment that Jones can accept (e.g., with "thank you") or agree with (e.g., "I really enjoy it").

While Jones' initial response (line 4) appears to be unproblematic for DeGeneres (as evidenced by the continuer in line 5, which passes on the opportunity to indicate trouble) what Jones adds in lines 6–8 attracts a different uptake. DeGeneres' turns (in lines 9–10, and 13, the C arrows) initiates repair, first by rejecting the understanding conveyed in Jones' turn (with "No"), and (after clarifying just what was being rejected) adding "But I: say it's really great. The two of you". In this way, DeGeneres conveys that she offered "How great is that" as an assertion (or more specifically an assessment) rather than a question. We call this repair in third *position*. The term "position" is used to capture the sequential location of the initiation of repair relative to the action it targets as a source of trouble. A first position (or sequence initiating) utterance ("How great is that") has been produced and the response to it, in second position, "it's pretty great. . ." reveals a problematic understanding of it. This problem in understanding is repaired in third position (the next action in the sequence following the response). Because this trouble is flagged, and managed (when she clarifies that she was asserting or assessing instead of asking), by the speaker of the first position utterance (the trouble source, "how great is that"), this is an instance of "self-initiated" repair (as are all "third position" repairs).

Given DeGeneres' initial acceptance of Jones' utterance (with a continuer in line 5), we might ask what about the talk she went on to produce revealed a form of trouble not apparent in the first part? First we can simply note that Jones evidently struggles in producing the utterance (in line 6) that follows her initial response. Before bringing her utterance to its first possible completion (at "great" in line 8) she restarts this portion of it three times ("Its-," "It-," and "I mean. . .") and encounters still more trouble in later parts ("I just mean it-" and "ek-"). In these cases, Jones treats aspects of her own in-progress turn as having been problematic in different ways. Because these efforts to initiate repair are launched before she reaches the first possible completion of her utterance and target an aspect of the turn *she* is currently producing (e.g., the "It" she begins with), these are instances of same turn, self-initiated repair. This is, by far, the most common form of repair in conversation, partly reflecting what Schegloff et al (1977) described as the "preference for self-correction." As with preference organization in action sequencing, the term is not used to describe the psychological desires of the participants; rather it refers to the way in which the organization of conversation makes some outcomes more likely than others. In the case of repair, opportunities for dealing with problems in speaking, hearing, and understanding are distributed through turns at talk: speakers have the first and second structurally provided opportunities for dealing with troubles associated with the turns they are producing (i.e., before their first possible completion, and in the transition space just after those turns are brought to a possible completion). By virtue of this, many forms of trouble are dealt with before any other speaker has a chance to talk.

Our account of Jones' turn documents that producing this utterance entailed a struggle of sorts. What made it so? If we examine the utterance Jones finally completes ("I just mean . . . experientially for me it's pretty great") we can note that it is devoted to revising (or reframing) the initial response she had just completed ("It's pretty great"). She does this by using the beginning of her utterance, "I just mean," to frame the turn as part of an effort to repair a potential problem of understanding, and completing her turn with a repetition of her prior turn ("it's pretty great"), locating it as the target of the repair. The talk she produces between these elements— "experientially for me"—adjusts or specifies both *what* she is describing as "pretty great" (the *experience,* rather than the show) and for *whom* this is so (i.e., herself). In this respect, both revisions target ways in which her prior turn could have amounted to a form of self-praise. In this case, the location of the repair initiation (following a continuer) and the scope of the repair itself (the prior turn) suggest that this is a different species of self-repair than the ones we just examined. Because the speaker initiates repair *after* both her own prior turn has been brought to a possible completion (which, as we noted above, is the *first* turn in which the trouble could have been dealt with), and her recipient has composed a brief second turn that acknowledges it ("mmhmm" in line 5), this is an instance of "third *turn* repair."

This analysis, then, also helps us to appreciate how a response initially treated as unproblematic by DeGeneres came to be viewed differently by her, and how the third position repair she launched by virtue of this was consequential for the sequence as a whole. As we noted in the prior paragraph, Jones uses third turn repair to adjust the action import of her initial response, producing an assessment that praises the experience of working with Poehler (most likely on the grounds that her initial simple assessment is potentially hearable as a form of self-praise). In so doing, however, Jones evidently invokes an experience that is uniquely her own (working with Poehler on *this* show) thereby limiting the degree to which DeGeneres (or the overhearing audience) can respond meaningfully to it. While this in itself may not pose insurmountable problems for DeGeneres, the adjustment Jones makes (in praising that experience) undercuts the degree to which DeGeneres' own prior turn (in line 4) was recognized as a compliment of her *in particular*. Thus, it is these two issues that DeGeneres addresses in her third-position repair: "But I say it's great" emphasizes that DeGeneres' initial turn was proposed as a compliment, while "The two of you" clarifies that Jones, in particular, was one of her intended recipients.

Finally for this excerpt, consider "it's really great. The two of you" at line 13. The resulting construction (specifically the addition of "the two of you") illustrates self-initiated "transition space repair." The addition of "the two of you" treats the initial reference with "it" as problematic, replacing it presumably in an effort to prevent any further misunderstanding of what exactly is being assessed. Because DeGeneres produced the initial reference, this is an instance of self-initiated repair, and because it is produced in a place where a turn has been brought to a possible completion (and so where another speaker could start, effecting a transition to next speaker), it is produced in the transition space.

The preceding excerpt contained examples of same turn, transition space, third turn, third position repair, all of which are forms of *self*-initiated repair. While it is similarly possible for *others* to initiate repair from more than one position, most cases of *other*-initiated repair occur in just one position: in the turn following the trouble source (Schegloff 2000). For example, in the following, taken from a call between two young women, directly following the opening of the call, Bee indicates trouble parsing an aspect of Ava's query (lines 7–8), briefly delaying her response to establish that she has heard Ava correctly.

(5) TG 1

```
04 Bee:     hHowuh you:?
05 Ava:     Oka:::y?hh =
06 Bee:     = Good. = Yihs[ou:nd  ] hh
07 Ava:                  [<I wan]'dih know if yih got a–uh:m
08          wutchimicawllit. A:: pah(hh)khing place °th's mornin'. hh
09 Bee: –> A pa:rking place,
10 Ava:     Mm hm,
11          (0.4)
12 Bee:     Whe:re.
13 Ava:     t! Oh: just anypla(h)ce? I wz jus' kidding yuh.
14 Bee:     Nno? =
```

In line 9 Bee initiates repair, indicating trouble with "parking place" by repeating it. We can note, then, that in doing so Bee indicates that what should relevantly come next—an answer to Ava's query—cannot be produced until the parties deal with this trouble. We can further note that unlike the previous cases (in which the same speaker initiates and manages the repair) in cases of other initiated repair, the "other" speaker leaves it to *self*—the speaker of the trouble source—to actually effect the repair itself. This appears to hold even in a number of cases in which the other "knows" the repair or correction—and so could provide it on his or her own (see Schegloff et al 1977: 377–8). Finally, this case illustrates the connection between the various domains that we've treated as partially independent or semi-autonomous in our account so far. Evidently next turn repair can be one basis for initiating an "insert sequence," thereby expanding the in-progress adjacency pair sequence. And though such instances of next turn repair usually target what are simply (or only) problems in hearing or understanding, they can also be used to foreshadow dispreferred responses, as in this case. More generally, the privileging of repair relative to any other activity in conversation, the distribution of opportunities for repair across any series of sequentially arrayed turns—beginning with the trouble source turn and extending to the fourth sequential position following it—and the allocation of resources (and responsibility) to *self* and *other(s)* for detecting and resolving troubles in speaking, hearing, and understanding, point to the centrality of this organization in sustaining the very possibility of a shared social world that transcends any single individual's experience or understanding of it.

Conclusion

As these cases illustrate, an important initial step in developing a rigorous account of interaction involved determining the different systems or domains out of which talk-in-interaction is composed. Understanding these basic domains, and how the participants' use of them contributes to any episode of interaction, provides analysts with powerful tools for developing analyses because they allow us to ground them in the methods by which participants composed their encounter in the first place. Although obviously interrelated in multiple ways these domains have their own distinctive properties and operate to some extent independently of one another— so, for instance, it may have been noted that the turn-taking system underlies all the practices of repair just described but does so indiscriminately of whether it is repair or something else that is being done. And both turn-taking and repair are informed by, and underwrite, the parties' conduct of courses of action—what they do with, to, and for one another in sequences of actions. These partially independent domains of organization, in turn, provide an infrastructure for a range of other basic constituents of human sociality and social life, including story telling (Jefferson 1978; Sacks 1978, 1986), how persons refer to one another (Schegloff 1996), the use of person categories as a basis for action and inference (Schegloff 2007a; Whitehead 2009; Whitehead and Lerner 2009), how persons manage the social distribution of knowledge, and rights to knowledge (or "epistemics," see Heritage and Raymond 2005; Raymond and Heritage 2006; Heritage 2012), and so on. Moreover, understanding these basic enabling organizations has opened up research into the myriad social institutions conducted in, and through, social interaction—such as classrooms, legal courts, emergency telecommunications, news interviews, doctor-patient interactions, and so on (e.g., see Drew and Heritage 1992 and Clayman and Heritage 2010 for introductions).

In the foregoing we have introduced by way of illustration some of the practices, and the systems of practices of which they are a part, that participants use to coordinate and conduct action in interaction with others. In doing so, we have both related some of the basic findings of Conversation Analysis, and exemplified aspects of its basic approach. As Schegloff noted in a recent account of the field:

> CA is most centrally focused on (a) the elements of conduct (principal among them actions); (b) the practices by which those elements are constituted, shaped, and deployed; and (c) the organization of those

practices that underwrite the forms and trajectories of human interaction, and the ways in which it shapes human experience.

(Schegloff 2010: 41)

But what about all of the other aspects of social life that such a view may appear to leave out? What about such features of conduct as the language participants use in speaking (including its features and organization), as well as other embodied resources—gaze, gesture, posture, the use of the material surround in which the encounter takes place? Of course these are key to analyses of conduct in interaction: they supply the basic resources parties use in organizing their encounters with others. Similarly, one might ask: what about the diverse relationships between participants that may inform their conduct in interaction, the differing contexts in which their interactions may be conducted, and the various institutional arrangements that provide occasions for those categories, identities, relationships, contexts, and other social-structural arrangements to be worked out? Where these are demonstrably relevant and consequential for the participants' doings, efforts to understand their import must be part of any serious analysis precisely because they matter to, and for, the parties themselves. But conversation analytic studies of interaction are

> addressed not to these forms, resources, and environments per se, but to the contribution they make to—their realization as and incorporation into—the elements of conduct, the practices by which those elements are deployed, and the organizations of those practices that are the constitutive components of human interaction; *it is the action that gives these resources their organizational relevance.*
>
> (Schegloff 2010: 41, emphasis added)

Indeed, it is this focus, and resulting ordering of priorities, that contributes most directly to the field's remarkable success producing a truly innovative and strongly cumulative body of findings. Thus, while we have described *people* (and speakers) as *using* practices in an effort to render our analyses readable, it is also the case that the ordering of these analytic elements can be reversed so that accounts emphasize, instead, the ways in which those *practices, and organizations*, unavoidably *shape the conduct of persons* in their temporally bounded encounters with others. People come and go, the relations and other outcomes that emerge in their interactions with others are variable and ephemeral, but the practices they use to organize those encounters— and the systematic organizational contingencies to which those practices are adapted—endure. Thus it is by uncovering and explicating these practices, systems and contingencies, that CA fulfills Goffman's profound suggestion that the study of interaction consists in ". . .not persons and their moments, but the organization of those moments" (Schegloff 2010: 41).

References

Clayman, S. and Heritage, J. (2010) *Talk in Action: Interaction Identities and Institutions*, Oxford: Wiley-Blackwell.

Drew, P. and Heritage, J. (1992) *Talk at Work: Interaction in Institutional Settings*, Cambridge: Cambridge University Press.

Garfinkel, H. (1967) *Studies in Ethnomethodology*, Englewood Cliffs, NJ: Prentice-Hall.

—— (1974) "On the origins of the term 'ethnomethodology,'" in R. Turner (ed.) *Ethnomethodology: Selected Readings*, Harmondsworth: Penguin, 15–18.

Goffman, E. (1964) "The neglected situation," *American Anthropologist* 66(6, pt.2): 133–6.

—— (1967) *Interaction Ritual: Essays in Face-to-Face Behavior*. Garden City, NY: Doubleday.

—— (1983) "The interaction order: American Sociological Association, 1982 Presidential Address," *American Sociological Review* 48(1): 1–17.

Goodwin, C. and Heritage, J. (1990) "Conversation analysis," *Annual Review of Anthropology* 19: 283–307.

Heritage, J. (1984) *Garfinkel and Ethnomethodology*, Cambridge: Polity Press.

—— (2012) "Epistemics in action: action formation and territories of knowledge," *Research on Language and Social Interaction* 45(1): 1–29.

Heritage, J. and Raymond, G. (2005) "The terms of agreement: indexing epistemic authority and subordination in assessment sequences," *Social Psychology Quarterly* 68: 15–38.

Jefferson, G. (1973) "A case of precision timing in ordinary conversation: overlapped tag-positioned address terms in closing sequences," *Semiotica* 9: 47–96.

—— (1974) "Error correction as an interactional resource," *Language in Society* 3(2): 181–99.

—— (1978) "Sequential aspects of storytelling in conversation," in J. Schenkein (ed.) *Studies in the Organization of Conversational Interaction*, New York: Academic Press, 219–48.

Lerner, G.H. (2003) "Selecting next speaker: the context-sensitive operation of a context-free organization," *Language in Society* 32: 177–201.

Raymond, G. and Heritage, J. (2006) "The epistemics of social relations: owning grandchildren," *Language in Society* 35: 677–70.

Sacks, H. (1974) "An analysis of the course of a joke's telling in conversation," in R. Bauman and J. Sherzer (eds.) *Explorations in the Ethnography of Speaking*, Cambridge: Cambridge University Press, 337–53.

—— (1978) "Some technical considerations of a dirty joke," in J. Schenkein (ed.) *Studies in the Organization of Conversational Interaction*, New York: Academic Press, 249–70.

—— (1986) "Some considerations of a story told in ordinary conversations," *Poetics* 15(2): 127–38.

—— (1987) "On the preferences for agreement and contiguity in sequences in conversation," in G. Button and J.R.E. Lee (eds.) *Talk and Social Organisation*, Clevedon: Multilingual Matters, 54–69.

—— (1995) *Lectures on Conversation*, Oxford: Blackwell.

Sacks, H., Schegloff, E.A., and Jefferson, G. (1974) "A simplest systematics for the organization of turn-taking for conversation," *Language* 50(4): 696–735.

Schegloff, E.A. (1968) "Sequencing in conversational openings," *American Anthropologist* 70(6): 1075–95.

—— (1996) "Some practices for referring to persons in talk-in-interaction: a partial sketch of a systematics," in B. Fox (ed.) *Studies in Anaphora*, Amsterdam: John Benjamins, 437–85.

—— (2000) "When 'others' initiate repair," *Applied Linguistics* 21(2): 205–43.

—— (2006) "Interaction: the infrastructure for social institutions, the natural ecological niche for language, and the arena in which culture is enacted," in N.J. Enfield and S.C. Levinson (eds.), *Roots of Human Sociality: Culture, Cognition, and Interaction*, Oxford: Berg, 70–96.

—— (2007a) "A tutorial on membership categorization," *Journal of Pragmatics* 39: 462–82.

—— (2007b) *Sequence Organization in Interaction: A Primer in Conversation Analysis*, Cambridge: Cambridge University Press.

—— (2010) "Commentary on Stivers and Rossano: 'Mobilizing Response,'" *Research on Language and Social Interaction* 43(1): 38–48.

Schegloff, E.A. and Sacks, H. (1973) "Opening up closings," *Semiotica* 8: 289–327.

Schegloff, E.A., Jefferson, G. and Sacks, H. (1977) "The preference for self-correction in the organization of repair in conversation," *Language* 53(2): 361–82.

Sidnell, J. (2010) *Conversation Analysis: An Introduction*, Oxford: Wiley/Blackwell.

Whitehead, K. (2009). "'Categorizing the categorizer': the management of racial common sense in interaction," *Social Psychology Quarterly* 72, 4: 325–42.

Whitehead, K. and Lerner, G. (2009) "When are persons 'white'?: on some practical asymmetries of racial reference in talk-in-interaction," *Discourse in Society* 20(5): 613–41.

Chapter 17

Deborah Schiffrin

OH AS A MARKER OF INFORMATION MANAGEMENT

UNDERSTANDING DISCOURSE MARKERS requires separating the contribution made by the marker itself from the contribution made by characteristics of the discourse slot in which the marker occurs. We must pose the following questions. Does an item used as a marker have semantic meaning and/or grammatical status which contributes to its discourse function? And how does such meaning interact with a sequential context of the marker to influence production and interpretation?

I examine [a] discourse marker in this chapter – *oh* – whose uses are not clearly based on semantic meaning or grammatical status. . . . *Oh* is traditionally viewed as an exclamation or interjection. When used alone, without the syntactic support of a sentence, *oh* is said to indicate emotional states, e.g. surprise, fear, or pain (*Oxford English Dictionary* 1971, Fries 1952). (1) and (2) illustrate *oh* as exclamation:

> (1) *Jack:*   Was that a serious picture?
>   *Freda:* **Oh**:! Gosh yes!
> (2) *Jack:*   Like I'd say, 'What d'y'mean you don't like classical music?'
>   *Freda:* '**Oh**! I can't stand it! It's draggy.'

Oh can also initiate utterances, either followed by a brief pause:

> (3) *Freda:* **Oh**, well they came when they were a year.

or with no pause preceding the rest of the tone unit:

> (4) *Jack:*   Does he like opera? **Oh** maybe he's too young.

Source: Deborah Schiffrin, *Discourse Markers*, Cambridge: Cambridge University Press, 1988.

We will see, regardless of its syntactic status or intonational contour, that *oh* occurs as speakers shift their orientation to information. (A very similar view of *oh* is Heritage (1984: 299), who views *oh* as a particle 'used to propose that its producer has undergone some kind of change in his or her locally current state of knowledge, information, orientation or awareness'.) We will see that speakers shift orientation during a conversation not only as they respond affectively to what is said (e.g., as they exclaim with surprise as in 1 and 2), but as they replace one information unit with another, as they recognize old information which has become conversationally relevant, and as they receive new information to integrate into an already present knowledge base. All of these are **information management tasks** in which *oh* has a role: *oh* pulls from the flow of information in discourse a temporary focus of attention which is the target of self and/or other management.

. . .

Oh in repairs

Repair is a speech activity during which speakers locate and replace a prior information unit. Because they focus on prior information, repairs achieve information transitions anaphorically – forcing speakers to adjust their orientation to what has been said before they respond to it in upcoming talk.

Almost anything that anyone says is a candidate for repair either by the speaker him/herself or by a listener. Once an utterance actually is subjected to repair, however, the method by which it is repaired is more restricted than its initial selection: although both repair initiation and completion can be performed by a listener (other-initiation, other-completion), speakers are more likely to participate in their own repairs either by initiating (self-initiation) or completing (self-completion) the repair. (Schegloff, Jefferson, and Sacks 1977 speak of this tendency as the preference for self-repair.)

Oh in repair initiation

Oh prefaces self-initiated and other-initiated repairs. Example 5 shows *oh* at self-initiated repairs. In (5), Freda is answering a question about whether she believes in extra-sensory perception (ESP) by describing her husband Jack's abilities to predict future political events.

> (5) I mean . . . he can almost foresee: . . . eh : : for instance with Nixon
> . . . . . . He said . . . now he's not in a medical field my husband.
> He said coagulating his blood, . . . uh thinning his – Nixon's blood
> . . . will not be good for him, if he should be operated on. **Oh** maybe
> it's just knowledge. I don't know if that's ESP or not in that c– in
> this case.

Freda recategorizes a particular description from an instance of ESP to an instance of knowledge: this self-repair is initiated with *oh*. Another self-repair from *coagulating* to *thinning* is marked with *uh*. Two other self-repairs, the addition of background information following *he said*, and replacement of *that c–* by *this case*, are not marked.

. . .

Not all self-initiated repairs are actual replacements of one unit of information with another: in some, speakers search for information to fill a temporary gap in recall. In (6), for example, Jack interrupts a story to provide background information about his age at the time of the reported experience – which he cannot then remember precisely. *Oh* fills the slot between his self-interruption and his first attempt at specifying his age.

> (6) There was a whole bunch of oth– I was about– **oh**: younger than
>   Robert. I was about uh . . . maybe Joe's age. Sixteen.

Note that *uh* seems to serve the same general function as *oh* in this example: both are place-holders for Jack as he searches for information. But *oh* initiates the repair (it is preceded by a self-interruption), whereas *uh* continues the repair.

Example (7) illustrates other-initiated repairs. (Differentiating other-initiated repairs from disagreements often requires interpretation of speaker intent, especially when the same phrases are used, e.g., *what do you mean X?*. Because it is not always possible (from either an analyst's or participant's viewpoint) to know whether it is one's information output that is being corrected (repair), or one's knowledge of information that is being assessed (disagreement), I am including any replacement by one speaker of what another has said as other-repair. Note that this ambiguity may be one reason why other-repairs are marked forms of repair.) In (7), I am explaining what I mean by 'ethnic group'.

> (7) *Debby:*   By ethnic group I meant nationality. Okay like um Irish
>   or:– I guess there aren't⎡too many Irish Jews but   ⎤=
>   *Jack:*   ⎣I see! Yeh yeh. **Oh** yes =⎦
>   *Debby:*   = Italian:
>   *Jack:*   = there is!

Jack's *I see* acknowledges my description of ethnic group. His *Oh yes there is!* is an other-initiated repair to my assertion about Irish Jews.

. . .

Oh in repair completion

Repairs are completed when the repairable is replaced by a new item; additional completion can be provided through confirmation of the replacement. When the replacement is issued by the same speaker who had issued the repairable, we can speak of self completion; when the repairable is replaced by another speaker, of other completion. *Oh* prefaces both self and other-completions. . . . Example (7) showed combinations of other-initiated and other-completed repairs. . . .

Oh also occurs when one party completes a repair initiated by the other – when other-initiated repairs are self-completed, and when self-initiated repairs are other-completed. In 8, for example, Zelda and Henry are answering my questions about who they visit.

> (8) *Henry:*   Ah: who can ⎡answer that,⎤ the kids. We have nobody =
> *Zelda:*   ⎣Our kids. ⎦
> *Henry:*   = else.   **Oh** yeh we– my sister =
> *Zelda:*   Yeh, you have a sister.
> *Henry:*   = we see in the summertime a lot.

Henry forgets to mention his sister: thus, Zelda other-initiates a repair to this effect. Henry then self-completes the repair by replacing his earlier answer with one which includes his sister as someone whom he visits.

. . .

In sum, that self and other participate in both initiation and completion of repair shows a speaker/hearer division of responsibility for information management. Self-initiation and completion of repair show speakers' sensitivity to their own **production** of discourse: by locating and replacing an item from an outgoing utterance, speakers display their productive efforts. Other-initiation and completion of repair show hearers' sensitivity to their **reception** of discourse: by locating and replacing an item from an incoming utterance, hearers display their pursual of understanding and their effort to interpret what is being said as it is being received. Thus, jointly managed repairs are evidence of a participation framework in which both producer and recipient of talk replace information units and publicly redistribute knowledge about them.

[We omit a detailed section where Schiffrin considers *oh* in repairs achieved through clarification sequences.]

Oh in question/answer/acknowledgement sequences

Another speech activity which explicitly manages and distributes information is the three-part sequence of question, answer, and acknowledgement. Question/answer pairs complete a proposition, which may then be verbally acknowledged by the questioner – the individual who first opened the proposition for completion. The conditions under which *oh* prefaces questions, answers, and acknowledgements are sensitive to the different information management tasks accomplished in these turns.

Question/answer pairs

Question/answer pairs are adjacency pairs, i.e., sequentially constrained pairs in which the occurrence of a first-pair-part creates a slot for the occurrence of a second-pair-part (a conditional relevance), such that the non-occurrence of that second-pair-part is heard as officially absent [see Chapter 15]. One reason why questions constrain the next conversational slot is semantic: WH-questions are incomplete propositions; yes–no questions are propositions whose polarity is unspecified (e.g., Carlson 1983). Completion of the proposition is up to the recipient of the question, who either fills in the WH-information or fixes the polarity. This semantic completion allows a speaker/hearer reorientation toward an information unit, i.e., redistribution of knowledge about a proposition.

OH WITH QUESTIONS

Question/answer pairs are rarely couplets which are totally disconnected from their containing discourse. In fact, some questions are quite explicitly connected to immediately prior utterances: for example, requests for clarification are often formulated as syntactic questions. Other questions are used to request elaboration of what has just been said. Example (9) shows that like requests for clarification, requests for elaboration may also be prefaced by *oh*.

> (9) *Val:*   Is it safe?
> *Freda:*   Uh: we found a safe way! But it's the long way!
> *Val:*   **Oh** it's a special way?

   Elaboration requests are similar to clarification requests because they, too, focus on prior information. There are two differences, however. First, clarification requests indicate a reception problem which will be resolved through upcoming clarification; elaboration requests acknowledge receipt of information which has been sufficiently interpreted to allow the receiver to prompt its further development. Second, compliance with a clarification request is the amendment of **old** information; compliance with an elaboration request is provision of **new** information.

   Despite these differences, both clarification and elaboration requests can be prefaced by *oh* because both display speakers' receipt of information (partial or complete) at the same time that they solicit further information. The only other questions prefaced by *oh* are those which are suddenly remembered by a speaker as previously intended. Prior to (10), for example, I had been checking my interview schedule, when I saw a question that I had not yet asked.

> (10) *Debby:*   **Oh** listen, I forgot to ask you what your father did when you were growing up.

Like requests for clarification and elaboration, the suddenly remembered question in (10) displays the questioner's receipt of information – although here, the just-received information may not be presented by an interlocutor, but may be recalled by the speaker him/herself. In short, questions through which speakers only solicit information are not prefaced by *oh*; it is only questions which are evoked by the reception of information which may be prefaced by *oh*.

OH WITH ANSWERS

Answers to questions are prefaced with *oh* when a question forces an answerer to reorientate him/herself to information – that is, when the question makes clear that information presumed to be shared is not so, or that a similar orientation toward information was wrongly assumed. At the same time, answers with *oh* make explicit to the questioner the violation of a prior expectation about information.

Such reorientations may be caused by a mismatch between the information that the questioner assumed to be shared: the questioner may have assumed too much or too little to be shared, or the questioner may have made a wrong assumption. Consider (11). I have told Irene that I am a student at a local university.

> (11) *Irene:*   How can I get an appointment t'go down there t'bring my son on a tour?
>
> *Debby:*   **Oh** I didn't even know they gave tours! I'm not the one t'ask about it.

Irene's son is interested in attending the university, and she assumes that I would know (as a student) that the university gives tours to prospective students. But since I had no knowledge of the tours, Irene's question had assumed more shared information than was warranted: my *oh* shows both my receipt of this new information and alerts Irene to her misguided expectation as to what information we had shared.

. . .

Oh with acknowledgement of answers

Question/answer pairs are often followed by the questioner's response to the informational content of the answer which had been elicited. Such responses may vary from evaluations of the answer (endorsements, challenges) to re-solicitations of the answer (as accomplished through requests for clarification). (That certain registers, such as teacher talk, use a three-part question/answer/evaluation format is well known. See e.g., Mehan 1979.) Another possible response is acknowledgement of the answer, i.e., the questioner's display of receipt of the answer.

Consider, however, that exactly **what** is acknowledged varies depending upon whether the questioner finds that the answer to his/her question contains anticipated information. . . .

In (12), for example, Irene's answer does not conform to the expectations encoded through my question:

> (12) *Debby:* So what, you have *three* kids?
>
> *Irene:* I have *four*. ⎡Three boys⎤ and a girl.
>
> *Debby:*   ⎣*Four* kids.⎦   **Oh** I didn't know that.

Note that I am not distinguishing old from new information: both anticipated and unanticipated answers provide **new** information. But new information which has been anticipated creates less of a reorientation than does new information which has not been anticipated. . . .

Oh and the status of information

Thus far we have focused on speech activities whose goal is the management of information and whose exchange structure helps accomplish that goal. We have seen that *oh* marks different tasks involved in this management: the production and reception of information, the replacement and redistribution of information, the receipt of solicited, but unanticipated, information. *Oh* is more likely to be used when locally provided information does not correspond to a speaker's prior expectations: in repairs, questions, answers, and acknowledgements, *oh* marks a shift in speaker's orientation to information.

Use of *oh* is hardly confined to speech activities whose exchange structure is focused on information management. In this section, I examine *oh* first, as a marker of recognition of familiar information – more specifically, old information which has become newly relevant – and second, as a marker of new information receipt.

Oh as recognition display

Recognition of familiar information is often conversationally triggered. In the following examples, one speaker prompts another into recall, which is then explicitly marked not only with *oh*, but with confirmation of the correctness of the prompt, and/or provision of information testifying to the speaker's prior knowledge.

In (13), I prompt Zelda and Henry through use of *do you know X?*

> (13) *Debby:*   No this–d'you–d'you know um: I was talkin' to the
>   Kramers, down, 4500.
>   *Zelda:*   **Oh** yeh, Freda?
>   *Debby:*   ⎡ Yeh. ⎤
>   *Henry:*   ⎣ **Oh** ⎦ yeh. Jack?

Both Zelda and Henry mark their recognition with *oh* and with elaboration of the topic which I have evoked (the Kramers' first names). . . . Recognition of familiar information may also result from the speaker's own cognitive search for a particular piece of known information. In (14), for example, Zelda and Henry are telling me about their favorite restuarants; Henry has just said that they have been eating out more than ever.

> (14) *Zelda:*   And uh– **Oh**! We– when we go to the kids, we always eat
>   out.
>   We eat at the F1– Blue Fountain.

It sounds as if Zelda is about to add another restaurant to her list of favorites (because of her initial *and*). But she switches to a reason for the frequency with which they have been dining out (*when we go to the kids, we always eat out*), and then mentions another restaurant (*Blue Fountain*). The reason seems to be a sudden recall, and it is the reason that is marked by *oh*.

. . .

Oh as information receipt

Oh also marks a speaker's receipt of new information. In (15), for example, Zelda doesn't know prior to Irene's telling her that Irene's husband Ken had been fixing their back door. Note how Irene prompts Zelda's realization by introducing the news discourse topic with *y'know*. . . .

(15) *Irene:*   You know who was bangin' out there for twenty minutes.
              Ken.   He didn't know where I was. =
    Zelda: **Oh**
    Irene: [= He was fixin' the back] door.
    Zelda: [**Oh** I didn't hear him!]

Speakers also introduce new discourse topics by tying them to information they assume their hearers will find familiar. Henry and Zelda know that my parents own a house near their summer home. In (16), they are trying to find a location with which I am familiar in order to locate their summer home for me.

(16) *Debby:* Where are you? Which— [which street?]
     Henry: [We're on] Arkansas.
           Right from— across from the bank.
    Zelda: D'y'know where the Montclair is? And the Sea View?
           D'you ever ride down the:– [uh]   The =
    Debby: [The] motels? There?
    Zelda: = motels. On the boardwalk. [D'you go bike riding?]
    Henry: [Do you know where Abe's]
          is?   Right across the =
    Debby: Yeh I know where Abe's is.
    Henry: = street.
    Debby: **Oh** it's that way.

When I finally do acknowledge a familiar location (*where Abe's is*), Henry locates his home in relation to that place. I then acknowledge receipt of this new piece of information.

. . .

Oh and shifts in subjective orientation

Speaker orientation to information is not just a matter of recognition and receipt of the informational content of ongoing discourse. Orientation also involves the **evaluation** of information: speakers respond affectively and subjectively to what is said, what they are thinking of, and what happens around them. Just as speakers display shifts in objective orientation, so too, do they display shifts in subjective orientation. And not surprisingly, *oh* can be used when speakers display shifts in expressive orientation.

One such subjective orientation is **intensity**: a speaker is so committed to the truth of a proposition that future estimates of his or her character hinge on that truth (Labov 1984). In (17), for example, I have unintentionally provoked a disagreement between Freda and Jack about something for which they both display strong feelings: girls' high schools. Note Freda's repetition, meta-talk, and contrastive stress on *do* – all expressions of intensity commonly used in argument (Schiffrin 1982: Chapter 8).

> (17a) *Debby:* Well I think there's a lot of competition between girls.
> In an *all* girls school. More than well– more
> academically ⎡anyway.⎤
> *Freda:* ⎣**Oh**⎦ yes. **Oh** yes. They're better
> students I *do* believe that.

Later in the argument, Freda responds to Jack's accusation that the girls' high school which she and I both attended is no longer academically respected. Her defense intensifies when Jack adds to his accusation the demise of the local boys' high school.

> (17b) *Jack:* In fact it had lost its popularity, didn't it.
> Girls' High. ⎡   ⎤ And Central High.
> *Freda:* ⎣ No. ⎦   **Oh** no.

She later solicits endorsement of her position from me. Note her use of *oh yes* upon receipt of my endorsement, and, as preface to her response to Jack's question – a response which intensifies her position about the academic quality of Girls' High still further.

> (17c) *Freda:* You went there more recently
> than ⎡I. ⎤
> *Debby:* ⎣Yeh.⎦ ⎡Um . . . it's–⎤
> *Jack:* ⎣Doesn't   ⎦
> hold the: . . like it *used* to.
> *Debby:* It still has a reputation. ⎡   ⎤ In some ways.
> *Freda:* ⎣**Oh** yes.⎦
> *Jack:* But, like it did?
> *Freda:* **Oh** yes. Girls' High is still rated. Y'know Girls' High is
> rated higher than Central. I just read recently that Girls'
> High is *still* rated the highest.

Thus, in (17), *oh* accompanies Freda's increasingly intensive orientation toward her position. The cumulative interactional effect of these progressive shifts in Freda's own commitment in her position is increased distance from Jack's position.

. . .

Why *oh*?

We have seen that *oh* marks different tasks of information management in discourse. These productive and receptive tasks, however, are hardly dependent on *oh*: speakers are certainly able to replace, recognize, receive, and re-evaluate information without verbalization through *oh*. Why, then, does *oh* occur?

Since the overall role of *oh* is in information state transitions, let us begin with this component of talk. One of the basic goals of talk is the exchange of information. This goal can be realized because speakers and hearers redistribute knowledge about entities, events, states, situations, and so on – whatever real world knowledge is being represented through talk. Furthermore, because discourse involves the **exchange** of information, knowledge and meta-knowledge are constantly in flux, as are degrees of certainty about, and salience of, information. Another way of saying this is that information states are constantly evolving over the course of a conversation: what speakers and hearers can reasonably expect one another to know, what they can expect about the other's knowledge of what they know, how certain they can expect one another to be about that knowledge, and how salient they can expect the other to find that knowledge are all constantly changing. In short, information states are dynamic processes which change as each one of their contributing factors changes.

Oh has a role in information state transitions because *oh* marks a focus of speaker's attention which then also becomes a candidate for hearer's attention. This creation of a joint focus of attention not only allows transitions in information state, but it marks information as more salient with a possible increase in speaker/hearer certainty as to shared knowledge and meta-knowledge. So it is by verbally marking a cognitive task, and opening an individual processing task to a hearer, that *oh* initiates an information state transition.

But suggesting that *oh* has a pragmatic effect – the creation of a joint focus – does not really answer the question of **why** *oh* has this pragmatic effect. To try to answer this question, let us consider in more detail how *oh* is situated in social interaction.

First, *oh* makes evident a very general and pervasive property of participation frameworks: the division of conversational labor between speaker and hearer. Back-channel *oh*, for example, ratifies the current participation structure of the conversation: speaker remains speaker, and hearer remains hearer. Thus, *oh* as back-channel not only marks information receipt, and marks an individual as an occupant of a specific participation status (active recipient), but it also ratifies the current division of turn-taking responsibilities in the exchange structure.

Second, *oh* displays individuals in specific participation statuses and frameworks. Because *oh* displays one's own ongoing management of information, its user is temporarily displayed as an individual active in the role of utterance reception. Recall that *oh* is used not only as a back-channel response, but to incorporate requested clarifications and unanticipated answers into talk. These uses display a hearer as an active recipient of information who acknowledges and integrates information as it is provided. This functional capacity is complementary to the speaker's capacity as animator (Goffman 1981: 144): both display individuals as occupants of mechanically defined nodes in a system of information transmission.

Oh displays still another aspect of participation frameworks: speaker/hearer alignment toward each other. We have seen that individuals evaluate each other's orientations: what one defines as an appropriate level of commitment to a proposition, another may define as inappropriate. Different speaker/hearer alignments can be characterized in part by whether individuals share subjective orientations toward a proposition. For example, we might characterize an argument as an alignment in which Speaker A is committed to the truth of a proposition to which B is not similarly committed, and Speaker B is committed to the truth of another proposition to which A is not similarly committed. When *oh* marks a speaker's realization of the other's unshared commitment, then, it may serve as a signal of a potentially argumentative stance. Thus, it is because *oh* makes accessible speaker/hearer assumptions about each others' subjective orientations toward information, that it can display speaker/hearer alignments toward each other.

And, finally, consider that conversation requires a delicate balance between the satisfaction of one's own needs and the satisfaction of others' needs. Included is not only an individual cognitive need – individuals need time (no matter how short) to transform the content that they have in mind into talk – but a reciprocal social need: individuals need to receive appreciation for self and show deference to others (Goffman 1967; Chapter 19; Lakoff 1973; Tannen 1984). *Oh* may help service individuals' cognitive needs by providing time to focus on informational tasks – while still displaying one's interactional presence in deference to the satisfaction of social needs.

In sum, although *oh* is a marker of information management tasks which are essentially cognitive, the fact that it verbalizes speakers' handling of those tasks has interactional consequences. Thus, use of *oh* may very well be cognitively motivated. But once an expression makes cognitive work accessible to another during the course of a conversation, it is open for pragmatic interpretation and effect – and such interpretations may become conventionally associated with the markers of that work. Intended interactional effects and meanings may thus account for the use of *oh* as readily as the initial cognitive motivation. Such conventionalized effects may further explain why speakers verbally mark information management tasks with *oh*.

References

Carlson, L. (1983) *Dialogue Games*, Dordrecht: Reidel.
Fries, C. (1952) *The Structure of English*, London: Longman.
Goffman, E. (1967) 'The nature of deference and demeanor', in *Interaction Ritual*, New York: Anchor Books, 49–95.

—— (1981) 'Footing', in *Forms of talk*, Philadelphia, PA: University of Pennsylvania Press, 124–57. (Originally published 1979 in *Semiotica* 25: 1–29.)

Heritage, J. (1984) 'A change-of-state token and aspects of its sequential placement', in Atkinson, J.M. and Heritage, J. (eds) *Structures of Social Action: Studies in Conversation Analysis*, Cambridge: Cambridge University Press, 299–345.

Labov, W. (1984) 'Intensity', in Schiffrin, D. (ed.) *Meaning, Form and Use in Context: Linguistic Applications,* Georgetown University Round Table on Languages and Linguistics 1984, Washington, DC: Georgetown University Press, 43–70.

Lakoff, R. (1973) 'The logic of politeness, or minding your p's and q's', *Papers from the 9th Regional Meeting, Chicago Linguistic Society,* Chicago, IL: Linguistics Department, University of Chicago, 292–305.

Mehan, H. (1979) *Learning Lessons: Social Organization in the Classroom*, Cambridge, MA: Harvard University Press.

Oxford English Dictionary (1971), Oxford: Oxford University Press.

Schegloff, E., Jefferson, G., and Sacks, H. (1977) 'The preference for self-correction in the organization of repair in conversation', *Language* 53: 361–82.

Schiffrin, D. (1982) 'Discourse markers: semantic resources for the construction of conversation', Ph.D. dissertation, University of Pennsylvania.

Tannen, D. (1984) *Conversational Style: Analyzing Talk Among Friends*, Norwood, NJ: Ablex.

PART FOUR

Negotiating social relationships

Editors' introduction
to Part Four

THE OPENING CHAPTER in this part of the *Reader* is a classic text by the anthropologist Bronislaw Malinowski, first published in 1923. The original date of publication is important for two reasons. First, it indicates Malinowski's pioneering theoretical work, establishing the basic theme of this part of the book – how language achieves closeness and intimacy between people, what he referred to as 'phatic communion'. Second, it explains the rather dated rhetoric of the paper, which, like most other writings of Malinowski's, is based on his research in the Pacific. Certainly, references by a white, middle-class anthropologist to 'savage tribes' or to 'the primitive mind . . . among savages or our own uneducated classes' are by today's standards the voice of colonial power and of ethnic and class prejudice. But regardless of these historical limitations, Malinowski's placing of language (and more specifically *talk*) at the centre of social relations is highly significant. Phatic communion, 'a type of speech in which ties of union are created by a mere exchange of words' (p. 285), is a prototypical manifestation of sociability through discourse.

One of the important aspects of phatic communion that drew analysts' interest was its ritualistic character. It was mainly John Laver's (1974, 1981) work that first refined the ideas put forward by Malinowski, and Laver pointed out that phatic communion is ritualized usage in at least two senses. First, phatic communion, like much of everyday conversation (Cheepen 1988), is highly predictable. Like other ritualistic behaviour, phatic communion proceeds according to well-established patterns or scripts. Anyone who has been to more than one drinks party can attest that 'all' conversations we had there were 'exactly the same'. But there is a good reason for this apparent repetitiveness of phatic communion, and that brings us to the second understanding of its ritualistic aspect. In line with a cultural anthropological approach to communication (e.g., Leach 1976), the term 'ritual' refers to the wide range of activities that people engage in during transitional or *liminal* (Turner 1969) moments in social time and space. These are ceremonies such as baptisms, weddings, funerals, initiation rites and birthdays, especially birthdays marking 'significant' ages, e.g., 18, 21, and all the 'round-number' birthdays at decade boundaries. In other words, all our *rites of passage*, big or small, tend to be marked by rituals. Verbal and non-verbal ritualistic activities help social actors in these situations to overcome the unusually significant face-threat associated with the uncertainty of the situation (moving from one state to another) and often being in the centre of attention. We might argue that having a script to follow makes such occasions (e.g., weddings) bearable and manageable by giving all the participants clear and predefined roles to play and things to say.

However, social rituals are enacted more often than this. Meeting new people, starting and closing conversations, or just having a chat while taking time off work in an office are, according to Laver, all marginal phases of interaction that resemble other rites of passage. They place social actors in liminal spaces. Phatic communion, then, offers us mini-scripts to pass through these moments in a non-threatening and socially acceptable way. Malinowski's original definition of phatic communion, and Laver's elaboration of it, centre on its use to deflect the potentially hostile effects of silence in situations where talk is conventionally anticipated. This, again, requires a brief comment. On the one hand, such an approach relegates phatic communion to the realm of trivial and unimportant talk. It may make the participants in a speech event comfortable, but in itself the talk is seemingly dismissed as a 'filler' for silence: we might call it 'small talk', 'gossip' or 'chit-chat'. Justine Coupland (2000, see also Coupland et al 1992) re-examines this relative negativity in academic and everyday metalanguage about phatic communion. She shows that 'phaticity' is an important and intricate discursive practice, co-constructed by all participants in delicate negotiations of face and social distance. Besides, silence need not always be a signal of interpersonal unease or 'problematic talk' (Jaworski 2000).

This discussion of the sociable nature of talk and treating everyday encounters as mini-performances or mini-rituals was developed with great insight by the American sociologist Erving Goffman, whose chapter 'On face-work' is reproduced as Chapter 19. We have already mentioned Goffman in our general Introduction, and his influence on discourse-analytic research on sociability (and social interaction generally) is so great that we would have wanted to devote far more space to his writing. Goffman takes us further towards a local perspective on communication. His analyses were grounded in his own informal observation of North American social and interactional styles of interaction. The subtitle of the book from which we have excerpted Chapter 19 is 'Essays on face-to-face behavior' (first published in 1967), and we have selected a famous essay dealing with the ritualized nature of talk, and with the intriguing and much-analysed concepts of 'face' and 'face-work'. The technical concept of face should be understood in the way we use it in the everyday expression 'saving face'. It refers to our public image or persona. It has become a major theme in discourse studies, most notably developed in Brown and Levinson's research on 'politeness' (see Chapter 20). Goffman uses the concept of face to analyse how a person's standing and integrity are 'managed' in everyday interaction, how people are attentive to their own and others' faces, and how they deal with moments that threaten esteem and credibility.

The metaphor that dominates Goffman's analyses is that of the theatre, and when he uses the terms 'actor' (often in preference to 'speaker' or 'listener') and 'performance' (often instead of 'talk' or 'behaviour') he is deliberately invoking the theatrical senses of these terms. The idea of 'poise' (self-control), but also the concept of face itself, both suggest stage-masks that people carefully select and wear to conjure up specific images and effects. Goffman strips away the levels of control and self-management that produce conventionalized social behaviour in public. He helps us recognize these traits and practices – in ourselves and others – but perhaps he also leaves us feeling rather like voyeurs, sneaking a look behind the surface level (or the 'front stage') of social and interactional processes. Goffman picks up what is most ordinary in social interaction and, brilliantly, identifies the goals, strategies and conceits that are interwoven into everyday face-to-face communication.

Not surprisingly, very many aspects of Goffman's work have left a deep imprint on the methods and assumptions of discourse analysis. We can list some of them:

- the view of language in use as social action, and, as we have just mentioned, seeing people as social 'actors';
- the assumption that discourse does not merely happen but is achieved, as part of strategic performances;
- the role of discourse in the construction and management of individuals and 'selfhood';
- the need to study how individuals' language and actions are co-ordinated with other people's language and actions, so that social interaction is a delicately collaborative achievement;
- the need to see discourse as, in many regards, pre-structured, predictable and ritualistic;
- the importance of the orderliness of talk (e.g., 'the little ceremonies of greeting and farewell', p. 297), which is explicable in terms of speakers' concerns for protecting and extending their relationships (see Schegloff and Sacks, Chapter 15);
- the need to build a sociological 'map' of social norms and customs through analysis of local patterns of talk ('the traffic rules of social interaction', p. 289).

Goffman's writings are clearly contributions to sociological analysis. His writing is peppered with phrases such as 'in our society' and comments on potentially different practices and norms for interaction in different cultural groups. Most obviously he is a sociologist mapping out the sociology of human relationships. Goffman does not give us examples of specific utterances, and his analyses are therefore largely built around general categories of utterance (e.g., 'employing courtesies', 'making a belittling demand' or 'providing explanations') or of non-verbal behaviour ('avoidance' or 'leave-taking'). But these categories, the building blocks of Goffman's interactional analysis which he sometimes calls 'moves', are of course speech-act types of the sort Austin (Chapter 2) and Grice (Chapter 3) were discussing in slightly more formal terms. They are functional and pragmatic units of the sort that Watzlawick et al

(1967) saw as the architecture of relational communication. Despite their widely differing origins, we again see a confluence of ideas and interests in these foundational texts — in studying the discursive basis of everyday communication.

A combination of Goffman's work on face and interaction and Grice's perspective on conversational cooperativity left Penelope Brown and Stephen Levinson two main legacies in formulating their politeness theory (Chapter 20). Grice (Chapter 3) in fact mentions politeness as a specific dimension of talk where it is possible to formulate general conversational maxims, and this is largely what Brown and Levinson have done. They built a model of the normal expectations communicators make about how to 'save face'. The extract we reproduce here comes from their original work (first published as an extended paper in 1978, and later reprinted in book form in 1987), and it gives an outline of the theory. Due to limited space we cannot reproduce their elaborate taxonomy of politeness strategies, which Brown and Levinson illustrate in their original text with numerous examples, mainly from English, Tamil and Tzeltal. But we have provided a short Appendix, summarizing these strategies (pp. 310–11).

As we have said, politeness theory has Goffman's notion of face at its heart. Face, for Brown and Levinson, has two aspects: a want to be liked and appreciated by others, *positive face*; and a want to be left free of imposition, *negative face*. Both positive and negative faces can be damaged or threatened in contact with others, when a *face-threatening act* (FTA) of some sort is performed. Thus, individuals adopt various politeness strategies to mitigate or avoid the face-threat associated with such speech acts as criticisms and accusations (which are usually threatening to positive face), or requests and orders (usually threatening to negative face). Mitigation strategies in discourse then take the form of either *indirectness* (in the sense of violating Grice's Cooperative Principle), or they can be *direct with a mitigating comment* before an FTA is performed. A rather crass example of this second case is when a criticism is preceded by a compliment. A less crass instance is when we criticize someone by saying 'I'm sorry to say this but . . .'. Another instance is when an accusation is accompanied by the speaker giving an account or a justification, as in 'Everybody knows you shouldn't act like that'.

Politeness theory has become an enormously influential paradigm in discourse analysis. It has spawned a large body of literature on politeness strategies and face in different contexts and in different social and cultural groups. It has offered a comprehensive system for describing and explaining the communicative behaviour of individuals across a wide range of speech events (e.g., Holmes 1995; Sifianou 1999; Mills 2003; Watts 2003; Culpeper 2011;Leech 2014).

Chapter 21, by Deborah Tannen and Cynthia Wallat, is concerned with a different aspect of interpersonal communication: discourse *framing*. Drawing on linguistic, sociological and cognitive work, Tannen and Wallat start with a helpful summary of related concepts such as 'frame', 'footing' and 'knowledge schema'. They apply these terms to an analysis of a paediatric consultation, in which the doctor shifts *register* (style of speaking), signalling how the speech event is restructured from moment to moment. Reminiscent of the data in Thomas's chapter (Chapter 10), we see how style shifts mark changes in the type of activity that the speaker is engaged in (a medical examination of the child, where the doctor gives explanations to the mother, gives explanations to students, and records a diagnosis), and changes in the 'participation framework' (speaking to the child, or mother, or student). This chapter shows also how frames are established interactively, as part of a negotiative process and through conversational work. The doctor alternates between the interactive frames of 'examination' and 'consultation' on the one hand, and 'social encounter' on the other. In this way she shows sensitivity to the mother, for whom unmitigated, matter-of-fact talk about her child's impairment could be emotionally difficult to cope with. Thus, to ease the mother's emotional burden, the doctor 'blunts the effect of the information she imparts by using circumlocutions and repetitions; pausing and hesitating; and minimizing the significant danger of the arteriovenous malformation by using the word "only" ("only danger"), by using the conditional tense ("that would be the danger"), and by stressing what sounds positive', and that the symptoms are 'not going to get worse' (p. 322). These framing devices, not unlike Gumperz's contextualization cues (see our general Introduction) perform the dual role of signalling what kind of frame is being established in interaction at the moment of speaking, and forming part of the message communicated within this frame too.

References

Cheepen, C. (1988) *The Predictability of Everyday Conversation*, London: Pinter.

Coupland, J. (2000) 'Introduction', in J. Coupland (ed.) *Small Talk*, London: Longman, 1–25.

Coupland, J., Coupland, N. and Robinson, J.D. (1992) '"How are you?": negotiating phatic communion', *Language in Society* 21: 207–30

Culpeper, J. (2011) *Impoliteness: Using Language to Cause Offence*, Cambridge: Cambridge University Press.

Holmes, J. (1995) *Women, Men and Politeness*. Harlow: Longman.

Jaworski, A. (2000) 'Silence and small talk', in. J. Coupland (ed.) *Small Talk*, London: Longman, 110–32.

Laver, J. (1974) 'Communicative functions of phatic communion', in A. Kendon, R.M. Harris and M. Ritchie Key (eds.) *Organization of Behavior in Face-to-Face Interaction*, The Hague: Mouton, 215–38.

—— (1981) 'Linguistic routines and politeness in greeting and parting', in F. Coulmas (ed.) *Conversational Routine: Explorations in Standardized Communication Situations and Prepatterned Speech*, The Hague: Mouton, 289–304.

Leach, E.R. (1976) *Culture and Communication: The Logic by which Symbols are Connected. An Introduction to the Use of Structuralist Analysis in Social Anthropology*, Cambridge: Cambridge University Press.

Leech, G. (2014) *Politeness*, New York: Oxford University Press.

Mills, S. (2003) *Gender and Politeness*, Cambridge: Cambridge University Press.

Sifianou, M. (1999) *Politeness Phenomena in England and Greece: A Cross-cultural Perspective*, Oxford: Oxford University Press.

Turner, V. (1969). *The Ritual Process: Structure and Anti-structure*, Chicago: Aldine.

Watzlawick, P., Beavin-Bavelas, J. and Jackson, D. (1967) *The Pragmatics of Human Communication*, New York: Norton.

Watts, R.J. (2003) *Politeness*, Cambridge: Cambridge University Press.

Chapter 18

Bronislaw Malinowski

ON PHATIC COMMUNION

. . .

THE CASE OF LANGUAGE used in free, aimless, social intercourse requires special consideration. When a number of people sit together at a village fire, after all the daily tasks are over, or when they chat, resting from work, or when they accompany some mere manual work by gossip quite unconnected with what they are doing – it is clear that here we have to do with another mode of using language, with another type of speech function. Language here is not dependent upon what happens at that moment, it seems to be even deprived of any context of situation. The meaning of any utterance cannot be connected with the speaker's or hearer's behaviour, with the purpose of what they are doing.

A mere phrase of politeness, in use as much among savage tribes as in a European drawing-room, fulfils a function to which the meaning of its words is almost completely irrelevant. Inquiries about health, comments on weather, affirmations of some supremely obvious state of things – all such are exchanged, not in order to inform, not in this case to connect people in action, certainly not in order to express any thought. It would be even incorrect, I think, to say that such words serve the purpose of establishing a common sentiment, for this is usually absent from such current phrases of intercourse; and where it purports to exist, as in expressions of sympathy, it is avowedly spurious on one side. What is the *raison d'être*, therefore, of such phrases as 'How do you do?' 'Ah, here you are,' 'Where do you come from?' 'Nice day to-day' – all of which serve in one society or another as formulae of greeting or approach?

I think that, in discussing the function of speech in mere sociabilities we come to one of the bedrock aspects of man's nature in society. There is in all human beings

Source: Bronislaw Malinowski, 'The problem of meaning in primitive languages' in C.K. Ogden and I.A. Richards (eds) *The Meaning of Meaning*, London: Routledge & Kegan Paul, 1946 [1923], 296–336.

the well-known tendency to congregate, to be together, to enjoy each other's company. Many instincts and innate trends, such as fear or pugnacity, all the types of social sentiments such as ambition, vanity, passion for power and wealth, are dependent upon and associated with the fundamental tendency which makes the mere presence of others a necessity for man.

Now speech is the intimate correlate of this tendency, for, to a natural man, another man's silence is not a reassuring factor, but, on the contrary, something alarming and dangerous. The stranger who cannot speak the language is to all savage tribesmen a natural enemy. To the primitive mind, whether among savages or our own uneducated classes, taciturnity means not only unfriendliness but directly a bad character. This no doubt varies greatly with the national character but remains true as a general rule. The breaking of silence, the communion of words is the first act to establish links of fellowship, which is consummated only by the breaking of bread and the communion of food. The modern English expression, 'Nice day to-day' or the Melanesian phrase, 'Whence comest thou?' are needed to get over the strange and unpleasant tension which men feel when facing each other in silence.

After the first formula, there comes a flow of language, purposeless expressions of preference or aversion, accounts of irrelevant happenings, comments on what is perfectly obvious. Such gossip, as found in primitive societies, differs only a little from our own. Always the same emphasis of affirmation and consent, mixed perhaps with an incidental disagreement which creates the bonds of antipathy. Or personal accounts of the speaker's views and life history, to which the hearer listens under some restraint and with slightly veiled impatience, waiting till his own turn arrives to speak. For in this use of speech the bonds created between hearer and speaker are not quite symmetrical, the man linguistically active receiving the greater share of social pleasure and self-enhancement. But though the hearing given to such utterances is as a rule not as intense as the speaker's own share, it is quite essential for his pleasure, and the reciprocity is established by the change of roles.

There can be no doubt that we have here a new type of linguistic use – *phatic communion* I am tempted to call it, actuated by the demon of terminological invention – a type of speech in which ties of union are created by a mere exchange of words. Let us look at it from the special point of view with which we are here concerned; let us ask what light it throws on the function or nature of language. Are words in phatic communion used primarily to convey meaning, the meaning which is symbolically theirs? Certainly not! They fulfil a social function and that is their principal aim, but they are neither the result of intellectual reflection, nor do they necessarily arouse reflection in the listener. Once again we may say that language does not function here as a means of transmission of thought.

But can we regard it as a mode of action? And in what relation does it stand to our crucial conception of context of situation? It is obvious that the outer situation does not enter directly into the technique of speaking. But what can be considered as *situation* when a number of people aimlessly gossip together? It consists in just this atmosphere of sociability and in the fact of the personal communion of these people. But this is in fact achieved by speech, and the situation in all such cases is created by the exchange of words, by the specific feelings which form convivial gregariousness, by the give and take of utterances which make up ordinary gossip. The whole situation consists in what happens linguistically. Each utterance is an act serving the direct aim of binding hearer to speaker by a tie of some social sentiment or other. Once more language appears to us in this function not as an instrument of reflection but as a mode of action.

I should like to add at once that though the examples discussed were taken from savage life, we could find among ourselves exact parallels to every type of linguistic use so far discussed. The binding tissue of words which unites the crew of a ship in bad weather, the verbal concomitants of a company of soldiers in action, the technical language running parallel to some practical work or sporting pursuit – all these resemble essentially the primitive uses of speech by man in action and our discussion could have been equally well conducted on a modern example. I have chosen the above from a savage community, because I wanted to emphasize that such and no other is the nature of *primitive* speech.

Again in pure sociabilities and gossip we use language exactly as savages do and our talk becomes the 'phatic communion' analysed above, which serves to establish bonds of personal union between people brought together by the mere need of companionship and does not serve any purpose of communicating ideas. . . . Indeed there need not or perhaps even there must not be anything to communicate. As long as there are words to exchange, phatic communion brings savage and civilized alike into the pleasant atmosphere of polite, social intercourse.

It is only in certain very special uses among a civilized community and only in its highest uses that language is employed to frame and express thoughts. In poetic and literary production, language is made to embody human feelings and passions, to render in a subtle and convincing manner certain inner states and processes of mind. In works of science and philosophy, highly developed types of speech are used to control ideas and to make them common property of civilized mankind.

Even in this function, however, it is not correct to regard language as a mere residuum of reflective thought. And the conception of speech as serving to translate the inner processes of the speaker to the hearer is one-sided and gives us, even with regard to the most highly developed and specialized uses of speech, only a partial and certainly not the most relevant view.

To restate the main position arrived at in this section we can say that language in its primitive function and original form has an essentially pragmatic character; that it is a mode of behaviour, an indispensable element of concerted human action. And negatively: that to regard it as a means for the embodiment or expression of thought is to take a one-sided view of one of its most derivate and specialized functions.

. . .

Chapter 19

Erving Goffman

ON FACE-WORK: AN ANALYSIS OF RITUAL ELEMENTS IN SOCIAL INTERACTION

EVERY PERSON LIVES IN A WORLD of social encounters, involving him either in face-to-face or mediated contact with other participants. In each of these contacts, he tends to act out what is sometimes called a *line* – that is, a pattern of verbal and nonverbal acts by which he expresses his view of the situation and through this his evaluation of the participants, especially himself. Regardless of whether a person intends to take a line, he will find that he has done so in effect. The other participants will assume that he has more or less willfully taken a stand, so that if he is to deal with their response to him he must take into consideration the impression they have possibly formed of him.

The term *face* may be defined as the positive social value a person effectively claims for himself by the line others assume he has taken during a particular contact. Face is an image of self delineated in terms of approved social attributes – albeit an image that others may share, as when a person makes a good showing for his profession or religion by making a good showing for himself.

A person tends to experience an immediate emotional response to the face which a contact with others allows him; he cathects his face; his "feelings" become attached to it. If the encounter sustains an image of him that he has long taken for granted, he probably will have few feelings about the matter. If events establish a face for him that is better than he might have expected, he is likely to "feel good"; if his ordinary expectations are not fulfilled, one expects that he will "feel bad" or "feel hurt." In general, a person's attachment to a particular face, coupled with the ease with which disconfirming information can be conveyed by himself and others, provides one reason why he finds that participation in any contact with others is a commitment. A person will also have feelings about the face sustained for the other participants, and while these feelings may differ in quantity and direction from those he has for his own face,

Source: Erving Goffman, *Interaction Ritual: Essays on Face-to-Face Behavior*, Garden City, NY: Anchor/ Doubleday, 1967.

they constitute an involvement in the face of others that is as immediate and spontaneous as the involvement he has in his own face. One's own face and the face of others are constructs of the same order; it is the rules of the group and the definition of the situation which determine how much feeling one is to have for face and how this feeling is to be distributed among the faces involved.

A person may be said to *have*, or *be in*, or *maintain* face when the line he effectively takes presents an image of him that is internally consistent, that is supported by judgements and evidence conveyed by other participants, and that is confirmed by evidence conveyed through impersonal agencies in the situation. At such times the person's face clearly is something that is not lodged in or on his body, but rather something that is diffusely located in the flow of events in the encounter and becomes manifest only when these events are read and interpreted for the appraisals expressed in them.

. . .

A person may be said to *be in wrong face* when information is brought forth in some way about his social worth which cannot be integrated, even with effort, into the line that is being sustained for him. A person may be said to *be out of face* when he participates in a contact with others without having ready a line of the kind participants in such situations are expected to take. The intent of many pranks is to lead a person into showing a wrong face or no face, but there will also be serious occasions, of course, when he will find himself expressively out of touch with the situation.

When a person senses that he is in face, he typically responds with feelings of confidence and assurance. Firm in the line he is taking, he feels that he can hold his head up and openly present himself to others. He feels some security and some relief – as he also can when the others feel he is in wrong face but successfully hide these feelings from him.

. . .

Following common usage, I shall employ the term *poise* to refer to the capacity to suppress and conceal any tendency to become shamefaced during encounters with others.

In our Anglo-American society, as in some others, the phrase "to lose face" seems to mean to be in wrong face, to be out of face, or to be shamefaced. The phrase "to save one's face" appears to refer to the process by which the person sustains an impression for others that he has not lost face. Following Chinese usage, one can say that "to give face" is to arrange for another to take a better line than he might otherwise have been able to take, the other thereby gets face given him, this being one way in which he can gain face.

As an aspect of the social code of any social circle, one may expect to find an understanding as to how far a person should go to save his face. Once he takes on a self-image expressed through face he will be expected to live up to it. In different ways in different societies he will be required to show self-respect, abjuring certain actions because they are above or beneath him, while forcing himself to perform

others even though they cost him dearly. By entering a situation in which he is given a face to maintain, a person takes on the responsibility of standing guard over the flow of events as they pass before him. He must ensure that a particular *expressive order* is sustained – an order that regulates the flow of events, large or small, so that anything that appears to be expressed by them will be consistent with his face.
. . .

Just as the member of any group is expected to have self-respect, so also he is expected to sustain a standard of considerateness; he is expected to go to certain lengths to save the feelings and the face of others present, and he is expected to do this willingly and spontaneously because of emotional identification with the others and with their feelings. In consequence, he is disinclined to witness the defacement of others. The person who can witness another's humiliation and unfeelingly retain a cool countenance himself is said in our society to be "heartless," just as he who can unfeelingly participate in his own defacement is thought to be "shameless."

The combined effect of the rule of self-respect and the rule of considerateness is that the person tends to conduct himself during an encounter so as to maintain both his own face and the face of the other participants. This means that the line taken by each participant is usually allowed to prevail, and each participant is allowed to carry off the role he appears to have chosen for himself. A state where everyone temporarily accepts everyone else's line is established. This kind of mutual acceptance seems to be a basic structural feature of interaction, especially the interaction of face-to-face talk. It is typically a "working" acceptance, not a "real" one, since it tends to be based not on agreement of candidly expressed heart-felt evaluations, but upon a willingness to give temporary lip service to judgements with which the participants do not really agree.

The mutual acceptance of lines has an important conservative effect upon encounters. Once the person initially presents a line, he and the others tend to build their later responses upon it, and in a sense become stuck with it. Should the person radically alter his line, or should it become discredited, then confusion results, for the participants will have prepared and committed themselves for actions that are now unsuitable.

Ordinarily, maintenance of face is a condition of interaction, not its objective. Usual objectives, such as gaining face for oneself, giving free expression to one's true beliefs, introducing depreciating information about the others, or solving problems and performing tasks, are typically pursued in such a way as to be consistent with the maintenance of face. To study face-saving is to study the traffic rules of social interaction; one learns about the code the person adheres to in his movement across the paths and designs of others, but not where he is going, or why he wants to get there. One does not even learn why he *is* ready to follow the code, for a large number of different motives can equally lead him to do so. He may want to save his own face because of his emotional attachment to the image of self which it expresses, because of his pride or honor, because of the power his presumed status allows him to exert over the other participants, and so on. He may want to save the others' face because of his emotional attachment to an image of them, or because he feels that his coparticipants have a moral right to this protection, or because he wants to avoid the hostility that may be directed toward him if they lose their face. He may feel that an assumption has been made that he is the sort of person who shows compassion and sympathy toward others, so that to retain his own face, he may feel obliged to be considerate of the line taken by the other participants.

By *face-work* I mean to designate the actions taken by a person to make whatever he is doing consistent with face. Face-work serves to counteract "incidents" – that is, events whose effective symbolic implications threaten face. Thus poise is one important type of face-work, for through poise the person controls his embarrassment and hence the embarrassment that he and others might have over his embarrassment. Whether or not the full consequences of face-saving actions are known to the person who employs them, they often become habitual and standardized practices; they are like traditional plays in a game or traditional steps in a dance. Each person, subculture, and society seems to have its own characteristic repertoire of face-saving practices. It is to this repertoire that people partly refer when they ask what a person or culture is "really" like. And yet the particular set of practices stressed by particular persons or groups seems to be drawn from a single logically coherent framework of possible practices. It is as if face, by its very nature, can be saved only in a certain number of ways, and as if each social grouping must make its selections from this single matrix of possibilities.

The members of every social circle may be expected to have some knowledge of face-work and some experience in its use. In our society, this kind of capacity is sometimes called tact, *savoir-faire*, diplomacy, or social skill. Variation in social skill pertains more to the efficacy of face-work than to the frequency of its application, for almost all acts involving others are modified, prescriptively or proscriptively, by considerations of face.

If a person is to employ his repertoire of face-saving practices, obviously he must first become aware of the interpretations that others may have placed upon his acts and the interpretations that he ought perhaps to place upon theirs. In other words, he must exercise perceptiveness. . . .

I have already said that the person will have two points of view – a defensive orientation toward saving his own face and a protective orientation toward saving the others' face. Some practices will be primarily defensive and others primarily protective, although in general one may expect these two perspectives to be taken at the same time. In trying to save the face of others, the person must choose a tack that will not lead to loss of his own; in trying to save his own face, he must consider the loss of face that his action may entail for others.

. . .

The basic kinds of face-work

The avoidance process

The surest way for a person to prevent threats to his face is to avoid contacts in which these threats are likely to occur. In all societies one can observe this in the avoidance relationship and in the tendency for certain delicate transactions to be conducted by go-betweens. Similarly, in many societies, members know the value of voluntarily making a gracious withdrawal before an anticipated threat to face has had a chance to occur.

Once the person does chance an encounter, other kinds of avoidance practices come into play. As defensive measures, he keeps off topics and away from activities that would lead to the expression of information that is inconsistent with the line he is maintaining. At opportune moments he will change the topic of conversation or the direction of activity. He will often present initially a front of diffidence and composure, suppressing any show of feeling until he has found out what kind of line the others will be ready to support for him. Any claims regarding self may be made with belittling modesty, with strong qualifications, or with a note of unseriousness; by hedging in these ways he will have prepared a self for himself that will not be discredited by exposure, personal failure, or the unanticipated acts of others. And if he does not hedge his claims about self, he will at least attempt to be realistic about them, knowing that otherwise events may discredit him and make him lose face.

Certain protective maneuvers are as common as these defensive ones. The person shows respect and politeness, making sure to extend to others any ceremonial treatment that might be their due. He employs discretion; he leaves unstated facts that might implicitly or explicitly contradict and embarrass the positive claims made by others. He employs circumlocutions and deception, phrasing his replies with careful ambiguity so that the others' face is preserved even if their welfare is not. He employs courtesies, making slight modifications of his demands on or appraisals of the others so that they will be able to define the situation as one in which their self-respect is not threatened. In making a belittling demand upon the others, or in imputing uncomplimentary attributes to them, he may employ a joking manner, allowing them to take the line that they are good sports, able to relax from their ordinary standards of pride and honor. And before engaging in a potentially offensive act, he may provide explanations as to why the others ought not to be affronted by it. For example, if he knows that it will be necessary to withdraw from the encounter before it has terminated, he may tell the others in advance that it is necessary for him to leave, so that they will have faces that are prepared for it. But neutralizing the potentially offensive act need not be done verbally; he may wait for a propitious moment or natural break – for example, in conversation, a momentary lull when no one speaker can be affronted – and then leave, in this way using the context instead of his words as a guarantee of inoffensiveness.

When a person fails to prevent an incident, he can still attempt to maintain the fiction that no threat to face has occurred. The most blatant example of this is found where the person acts as if an event that contains a threatening expression has not occurred at all. He may apply this studied nonobservance to his own acts – as when he does not by outward sign admit that his stomach is rumbling – or to the acts of others, as when he does not "see" that another has stumbled. Social life in mental hospitals owes much to this process; patients employ it in regard to their own peculiarities, and visitors employ it, often with tenuous desperation, in regard to patients. In general, tactful blindness of this kind is applied only to events that, if perceived at all, could be perceived and interpreted only as threats to face.

A more important, less spectacular kind of tactful overlooking is practiced when a person openly acknowledges an incident as an event that has occurred, but not as an event that contains a threatening expression. If he is not the one who is responsible for the incident, then his blindness will have to be supported by his forbearance; if he is the doer of the threatening deed, then his blindness will have to be supported by his willingness to seek a way of dealing with the matter, which leaves him dangerously dependent upon the cooperative forbearance of the others.

Another kind of avoidance occurs when a person loses control of his expressions during an encounter. At such times he may try not so much to overlook the incident as to hide or conceal his activity in some way, thus making it possible for the others to avoid some of the difficulties created by a participant who has not maintained face. Correspondingly, when a person is caught out of face because he had not expected to be thrust into interaction, or because strong feelings have disrupted his expressive mask, the others may protectively turn away from him or his activity for a moment, to give him time to assemble himself.

The corrective process

When the participants in an undertaking or encounter fail to prevent the occurrence of an event that is expressively incompatible with the judgements of social worth that are being maintained, and when the event is of the kind that is difficult to overlook, then the participants are likely to give it accredited status as an incident – to ratify it as a threat that deserves direct official attention – and to proceed to try to correct for its effects. At this point one or more participants find themselves in an established state of ritual disequilibrium or disgrace, and an attempt must be made to re-establish a satisfactory ritual state for them. I use the term *ritual* because I am dealing with acts through whose symbolic component the actor shows how worthy he is of respect or how worthy he feels others are of it. The imagery of equilibrium is apt here because the length and intensity of the corrective effort is nicely adapted to the persistence and intensity of the threat. One's face, then, is a sacred thing, and the expressive order required to sustain it is therefore a ritual one.

The sequence of acts set in motion by an acknowledged threat to face, and terminating in the re-establishment of ritual equilibrium, I shall call an *interchange*. Defining a message or move as everything conveyed by an actor during a turn at taking action, one can say that an interchange will involve two or more moves and two or more participants. Obvious examples in our society may be found in the sequence of "Excuse me" and "Certainly," and in the exchange of presents or visits. The interchange seems to be a basic concrete unit of social activity and provides one natural empirical way to study interaction of all kinds. Face-saving practices can be usefully classified according to their position in the natural sequence of moves that comprise this unit. Aside from the event which introduces the need for a corrective interchange, four classic moves seem to be involved.

There is, first, the *challenge*, by which participants take on the responsibility of calling attention to the misconduct; by implication they suggest that the threatened claims are to stand firm and that the threatening event itself will have to be brought back into line.

The second move consists of the *offering*, whereby a participant, typically the offender, is given a chance to correct for the offense and re-establish the expressive order. Some classic ways of making this move are available. On the one hand, an attempt can be made to show that what admittedly appeared to be a threatening expression is really a meaningless event, or an unintentional act, or a joke not meant to be taken seriously, or an unavoidable, "understandable" product of extenuating circumstances. On the other hand, the meaning of the event may be granted and effort concentrated on the creator of it. Information may be provided to show that the creator was under the influence of something and not himself, or that he was under the command of somebody else and not acting for himself. When a person claims that an act was meant in jest, he may go on and claim that the self that seemed to lie behind the act was also projected as a joke. When a person suddenly finds that he has demonstrably failed in capacities that the others assumed him to have and to claim for himself — such as the capacity to spell, to perform minor tasks, to talk without malapropisms, and so on — he may quickly add, in a serious or unserious way, that he claims these incapacities as part of his self. The meaning of the threatening incident thus stands, but it can now be incorporated smoothly into the flow of expressive events.

. . .

After the challenge and the offering have been made, the third move can occur: the persons to whom the offering is made can *accept* it as a satisfactory means of re-establishing the expressive order and the faces supported by this order. Only then can the offender cease the major part of his ritual offering.

In the terminal move of the interchange, the forgiven person conveys a sign of *gratitude* to those who have given him the indulgence of forgiveness.

The phases of the corrective process — challenge, offering, acceptance, and thanks — provide a model for interpersonal ritual behavior, but a model that may be departed from in significant ways. For example, the offended parties may give the offender a chance to initiate the offering on his own before a challenge is made and before they ratify the offense as an incident. This is a common courtesy, extended on the assumption that the recipient will introduce a self-challenge. Further, when the offended persons accept the corrective offering, the offender may suspect that this has been grudgingly done from tact, and so he may volunteer additional corrective offerings, not allowing the matter to rest until he has received a second or third acceptance of his repeated apology. Or the offended persons may tactfully take over the role of the offender and volunteer excuses for him that will, perforce, be acceptable to the offended persons.

An important departure from the standard corrective cycle occurs when a challenged offender patently refuses to heed the warning and continues with his offending behavior, instead of setting the activity to rights. This move shifts the play back to the challengers. If they countenance the refusal to meet their demands, then it will be plain that their challenge was a bluff and that the bluff has been called. This is an untenable position; a face for themselves cannot be derived from it, and they are left to bluster. To avoid this fate, some classic moves are open to them. For instance, they can resort to tactless, violent retaliation, destroying either themselves or the person who had refused to heed their warning. Or they can withdraw from the undertaking in a visible huff – righteously indignant, outraged, but confident of ultimate vindication. Both tacks provide a way of denying the offender his status as an interactant, and hence denying the reality of the offensive judgement he has made. Both strategies are ways of salvaging face, but for all concerned the costs are usually high. It is partly to forestall such scenes that an offender is usually quick to offer apologies; he does not want the affronted persons to trap themselves into the obligation to resort to desperate measures.

It is plain that emotions play a part in these cycles of response, as when anguish is expressed because of what one has done to another's face, or anger because of what has been done to one's own. I want to stress that these emotions function as moves, and fit so precisely into the logic of the ritual game that it would seem difficult to understand them without it. In fact, spontaneously expressed feelings are likely to fit into the formal pattern of the ritual interchange more elegantly than consciously designed ones.

Making points – the aggressive use of face-work

Every face-saving practice which is allowed to neutralize a particular threat opens up the possibility that the threat will be willfully introduced for what can be safely gained by it. If a person knows that his modesty will be answered by others' praise of him, he can fish for compliments. If his own appraisal of self will be checked against incidental events, then he can arrange for favorable incidental events to appear. If others are prepared to overlook an affront to them and act forbearantly, or to accept apologies, then he can rely on this as a basis for safely offending them. He can attempt by sudden withdrawal to force the others into a ritually unsatisfactory state, leaving them to flounder in an interchange that cannot readily be completed. Finally, at some expense to himself, he can arrange for the others to hurt his feelings, thus forcing them to feel guilt, remorse, and sustained ritual disequilibrium.

When a person treats face-work not as something he need be prepared to perform, but rather as something that others can be counted on to perform or to accept, then an encounter or an undertaking becomes less a scene of mutual considerateness than an arena in which a contest or match is held. The purpose of the game is to preserve everyone's line from an inexcusable contradiction, while scoring as many points as possible against one's adversaries and making as many gains as possible for oneself. An audience to the struggle is almost a necessity. The general method is for the person to introduce favorable facts about himself and unfavorable facts about the others in such a way that the only reply the others will be able to think up will be one that terminates the interchange in a grumble, a meager excuse, a face-saving I-can-take-a-joke laugh, or an empty stereotyped comeback of the "Oh yeah?" or "That's what you think" variety. The losers in such cases will have to cut their losses, tacitly grant the loss of a point, and attempt to do better in the next interchange. Points made by allusion to social class status are sometimes called snubs; those made by allusions to moral respectability are sometimes called digs; in either case one deals with a capacity at what is sometimes called "bitchiness."

. . .

Cooperation in face-work

When a face has been threatened, face-work must be done, but whether this is initiated and primarily carried through by the person whose face is threatened, or by the offender, or by a mere witness, is often of secondary importance. Lack of effort on the part of one person induces compensative effort from others; a contribution by one person relieves the others of the task. In fact, there are many minor incidents in which the offender and the offended simultaneously attempt to initiate an apology. Resolution of the situation to everyone's apparent satisfaction is the first requirement; correct apportionment of blame is typically a secondary consideration. Hence terms such as tact and *savoir-faire* fail to distinguish whether it is the person's own face that his diplomacy saves or the face of the others. Similarly, terms such as *gaffe* and *faux pas* fail to specify whether it is the actor's own face he has threatened or the face of other participants. . . . Tact in regard to face-work often relies for its operation on a tacit agreement to do business through the language of hint – the language of innuendo, ambiguities, well-placed pauses, carefully worded jokes, and so on. The rule regarding this official kind of communication is that the sender ought not to act as if he had officially conveyed the message he has hinted at, while the recipients have the right and the obligation to act as if they have not officially received the message contained in the hint. Hinted communication, then, is deniable communication; it need not be faced up to. It provides a means by which the person can be warned that his current line or the current situation is leading to loss of face, without this warning itself becoming an incident.

Another form of tacit cooperation, and one that seems to be much used in many societies, is reciprocal self-denial. Often the person does not have a clear idea of what would be a just or acceptable apportionment of judgements during the occasions, and so he voluntarily deprives or depreciates himself while indulging and complimenting the others, in both cases carrying the judgements safely past what is likely to be just. The favorable judgements about himself he allows to come from the others; the unfavorable judgements of himself are his own contributions. This "after you, Alphonse" technique works, of course, because in depriving himself he can reliably anticipate that the others will compliment or indulge him. Whatever allocation of favors is eventually established, all participants are first given a chance to show that they are not bound or constrained by their own desires and expectations, that they have a properly modest view of themselves, and that they can be counted upon to support the ritual code. Negative bargaining, through which each participant tries to make the terms of the trade more favorable to the other side, is another instance; as a form of exchange perhaps it is more widespread than the economist's kind.

A person's performance of face-work, extended by his tacit agreement to help others perform theirs, represents his willingness to abide by the ground rules of social interaction. Here is the hallmark of his socialization as an interactant. If he and the others were not socialized in this way, interaction in most societies and most situations would be a much more hazardous thing for feelings and faces. The person would find it impractical to be orientated to symbolically conveyed appraisals of social worth, or to be possessed of feelings – that is, it would be impractical for him to be a ritually delicate object. And as I shall suggest, if the person were not a ritually delicate object, occasions of talk could not be organized in the way they usually are. It is no wonder that trouble is caused by a person who cannot be relied upon to play the face-saving game.

The ritual roles of the self

So far I have implicitly been using a double definition of self: the self as an image pieced together from the expressive implications of the full flow of events in an undertaking; and the self as a kind of player in a ritual game who copes honorably or dishonorably, diplomatically or undiplomatically, with the judgemental contingencies of the situation. . . .

Once the two roles of the self have been separated, one can look to the ritual code implicit in face-work to learn how the two roles are related. When a person is responsible for introducing a threat to another's face, he apparently has a right, within limits, to wriggle out of the difficulty by means of self-abasement. When performed voluntarily these indignities do not seem to profane his own image. It is as if he had the right of insulation and could castigate himself qua actor without injuring himself qua object of ultimate worth. By token of the same insulation he can belittle himself and modestly underplay his positive qualities, with the understanding that no one will take his statements as a fair representation of his sacred self. On the other hand, if he is forced against his will to treat himself in these ways, his face, his pride, and his honor will be seriously threatened. Thus, in terms of the ritual code, the person seems to have a special license to accept mistreatment at his own hands that he does not have the right to accept from others. Perhaps this is a safe arrangement because he is not likely to carry this license too far, whereas the others, were they given this privilege, might be more likely to abuse it.

Further, within limits the person has a right to forgive other participants for affronts to his sacred image. He can forbearantly overlook minor slurs upon his face, and in regard to somewhat greater injuries he is the one person who is in a position to accept apologies on behalf of his sacred self. This is a relatively safe prerogative for the person to have in regard to himself, for it is one that is exercised in the interests of the others or of the undertaking. Interestingly enough, when the person commits a *gaffe* against himself, it is not he who has the license to forgive the event; only the others have that prerogative, and it is a safe prerogative for them to have because they can exercise it only in his interests or in the interests of the undertaking. One finds, then, a system of checks and balances by which each participant tends to be given the right to handle only those matters which he will have little motivation for mishandling. In short, the rights and obligations of an interactant are designed to prevent him from abusing his role as an object of sacred value.

. . .

Face and social relationships

When a person begins a mediated or immediate encounter, he already stands in some kind of social relationship to the others concerned, and expects to stand in a given relationship to them after the particular encounter ends. This, of course, is one of the ways in which social contacts are geared into the wider society. Much of the activity occurring during an encounter can be understood as an effort on everyone's part to get through the occasion and all the unanticipated and unintentional events that can cast participants in an undesirable light, without disrupting the relationships of the participants. And if relationships are in the process of change, the object will be to bring the encounter to a satisfactory close without altering the expected course of development. This perspective nicely accounts, for example, for the little ceremonies of greeting and farewell which occur when people begin a conversational encounter or depart from one. Greetings provide a way of showing that a relationship is still what it was at the termination of the previous coparticipation, and, typically, that this relationship involves sufficient suppression of hostility for the participants temporarily to drop their guards and talk. Farewells sum up the effect of the encounter upon the relationship and show what the participants may expect of one another when they next meet. The enthusiasm of greetings compensates for the weakening of the relationship caused by the absence just terminated, while the enthusiasm of farewells compensates the relationship for the harm that is about to be done to it by separation. Greetings, of course, serve to clarify and fix the roles that the participants will take during the occasion of talk and to commit participants to these roles, while farewells provide a way of unambiguously terminating the encounter. Greetings and farewells may also be used to state, and apologize for, extenuating circumstances – in the case of greetings for circumstances that have kept the participants from interacting until now, and in the case of farewells for circumstances that prevent the participants from continuing their display of solidarity. These apologies allow the impression to be maintained that the participants are more warmly related socially than may be the case. This positive stress, in turn, assures that they will act more ready to enter into contacts than they perhaps really feel inclined to do, thus guaranteeing that diffuse channels for potential communication will be kept open in the society.

It seems to be a characteristic obligation of many social relationships that each of the members guarantees to support a given face for the other members in given situations. To prevent disruption of these relationships, it is therefore necessary for each member to avoid destroying the others' face. . . . Furthermore, in many relationships, the members come to share a face, so that in the presence of third parties an improper act on the part of one member becomes a source of acute embarrassment to the other members. A social relationship, then, can be seen as a way in which the person is more than ordinarily forced to trust his self-image and face to the tact and good conduct of others.

The nature of the ritual order

. . .

Throughout this paper it has been implied that underneath their differences in culture, people everywhere are the same. If persons have a universal human nature, they themselves are not to be looked to for an explanation of it. One must look rather to the fact that societies everywhere, if they are to be societies, must mobilize their members as self-regulating participants in social encounters. One way of mobilizing the individual for this purpose is through ritual; he is taught to be perceptive, to have feelings attached to self and a self expressed through face, to have pride, honor, and dignity, to have considerateness, to have tact and a certain amount of poise. These are some of the elements of behavior which must be built into the person if practical use is to be made of him as an interactant, and it is these elements that are referred to in part when one speaks of universal human nature.

Universal human nature is not a very human thing. By acquiring it, the person becomes a kind of construct, built up not from inner psychic propensities but from moral rules that are impressed upon him from without. These rules, when followed, determine the evaluation he will make of himself and of his fellow-participants in the encounter, the distribution of his feelings, and the kinds of practices he will employ to maintain a specified and obligatory kind of ritual equilibrium. The general capacity to be bound by moral rules may well belong to the individual, but the particular set of rules which transforms him into a human being derives from requirements established in the ritual organization of social encounters. And if a particular person or group or society seems to have a unique character all its own, it is because its standard set of human-nature elements is pitched and combined in a particular way. Instead of much pride, there may be little. Instead of abiding by the rules, there may be much effort to break them safely. But if an encounter or undertaking is to be sustained as a viable system of interaction organized on ritual principles, then these variations must be held within certain bounds and nicely counterbalanced by corresponding modifications in some of the other rules and understandings. Similarly, the human nature of a particular set of persons may be specially designed for the special kind of undertakings in which they participate, but still each of these persons must have within him something of the balance of characteristics required of a usable participant in any ritually organized system of social activity.

Chapter 20

Penelope Brown and
Stephen C. Levinson

POLITENESS: SOME UNIVERSALS
IN LANGUAGE USAGE

Assumptions: properties of interactants

W E MAKE THE FOLLOWING assumptions: that all competent adult members of a society have (and know each other to have):

1   'Face', the public self-image that every member wants to claim for himself, consisting in two related aspects:
    (a) negative face: the basic claim to territories, personal preserves, rights to non-distraction – i.e., to freedom of action and freedom from imposition
    (b) positive face: the positive consistent self-image or 'personality' (crucially including the desire that this self-image be appreciated and approved of) claimed by interactants.
2   Certain rational capacities, in particular consistent modes of reasoning from ends to the means that will achieve those ends.

Face

Our notion of 'face' is derived from that of Goffman (1967; [see Chapter 19]) and from the English folk term, which ties face up with notions of being embarrassed or humiliated, or 'losing face'. Thus face is something that is emotionally invested, and that can be lost, maintained, or enhanced, and must be constantly attended to in interaction. In general, people cooperate (and assume each other's cooperation) in maintaining face in interaction, such cooperation being based on the mutual vulnerability of face. That is, normally everyone's face depends on everyone else's being maintained, and since people can be expected to defend their faces if

Source: Penelope Brown and Stephen C. Levinson, *Politeness: Some Universals in Language Usage*, Cambridge: Cambridge University Press, 1987.

threatened, and in defending their own to threaten others' faces, it is in general in every participant's best interest to maintain each other's face, that is to act in ways that assure the other participants that the agent is heedful of the assumptions concerning face given under (1) above. . . .

Furthermore, while the content of face will differ in different cultures (what the exact limits are to personal territories, and what the publicly relevant content of personality consists in), we are assuming that the mutual knowledge of members' public self-image or face, and the social necessity to orient oneself to it in interaction, are universal.

Face as wants

. . . We treat the aspects of face as basic wants, which every member knows every other member desires, and which in general it is in the interests of every member to partially satisfy. In other words, we take in Weberian terms the more strongly rational *zweckrational* model of individual action, because the *wertrational* model (which would treat face respect as an unquestionable value or norm) fails to account for the fact that face respect is not an unequivocal right. In particular, a mere bow to face acts like a diplomatic declaration of good intentions; it is not in general required that an actor fully satisfy another's face wants. Second, face can be, and routinely is, ignored, not just in cases of social breakdown (affrontery) but also in cases of urgent cooperation, or in the interests of efficiency.

Therefore, the components of face given above may be restated as follows. We define:

> **negative face**: the want of every 'competent adult member' that his actions be unimpeded by others;
> **positive face**: the want of every member that his wants be desirable to at least some others.

Negative face, with its derivative politeness of non-imposition, is familiar as the formal politeness that the notion 'politeness' immediately conjures up. But positive face, and its derivative forms of positive politeness, are less obvious. The reduction of a person's public self-image or personality to a want that one's wants be desirable to at least some others can be justified in this way. The most salient aspect of a person's personality in interaction is what that personality requires of other interactants – in particular, it includes the desire to be ratified, understood, approved of, liked or admired. The next step is to represent this desire as the want to have one's goals thought of as desirable. In the special sense of 'wanting' that we develop, we can then arrive at positive face as here defined. To give this some intuitive flesh, consider an example. Mrs B is a fervent gardener. Much of her time and effort are expended on her roses. She is proud of her roses, and she likes others to admire them. She is gratified when visitors say 'What lovely roses; I wish ours looked like that! How do you do it?', implying that they want just what she has wanted and achieved.

. . .

Rationality

We here define 'rationality' as the application of a specific mode of reasoning . . . which guarantees inferences from ends or goals to means that will satisfy those ends. Just as standard logics have a consequence relation that will take us from one proposition to another while preserving truth, a system of practical reasoning must allow one to pass from ends to means and further means while preserving the 'satisfactoriness' of those means. . . .

Intrinsic FTAs [face-threatening acts]

Given these assumptions of the universality of face and rationality, it is intuitively the case that certain kinds of acts intrinsically threaten face, namely those acts that by their nature run contrary to the face wants of the addressee and/or of the speaker. By 'act' we have in mind what is intended to be done by a verbal or non-verbal communication, just as one or more 'speech acts' can be assigned to an utterance.

First distinction: kinds of face threatened

We may make a first distinction between acts that threaten negative face and those that threaten positive face.

Those acts that primarily threaten the addressee's (H's) negative-face want, by indicating (potentially) that the speaker (S) does not intend to avoid impeding H's freedom of action, include:

1   Those acts that predicate some future act A of H, and in so doing put some pressure on H to do (or refrain from doing) the act A:
   (a) orders and requests (S indicates that he wants H to do, or refrain from doing, some act A)
   (b) suggestions, advice (S indicates that he thinks H ought to (perhaps) do some act A)
   (c) remindings (S indicates that H should remember to do some A)
   (d) threats, warnings, dares (S indicates that he – or someone, or something – will instigate sanctions against H unless he does A)
2   Those acts that predicate some positive future act of S toward H, and in so doing put some pressure on H to accept or reject them, and possibly to incur a debt:
   (a) offers (S indicates that he wants H to commit himself to whether or not he wants S to do some act for H, with H thereby incurring a possible debt)
   (b) promises (S commits himself to a future act for H's benefit)
3   Those acts that predicate some desire of S toward H or H's goods, giving H reason to think that he may have to take action to protect the object of S's desire, or give it to S:

(a) compliments, expressions of envy or admiration (S indicates that he likes or would like something of H's)
(b) expression of strong (negative) emotions toward H – e.g., hatred, anger, lust (S indicates possible motivation for harming H or H's goods)

Those acts that threaten the positive-face want, by indicating (potentially) that the speaker does not care about the addressee's feelings, wants, etc. – that in some important respect he doesn't want H's wants – include:

1   Those that show that S has a negative evaluation of some aspect of H's positive face:
   (a) expressions of disapproval, criticism, contempt or ridicule, complaints and reprimands, accusations, insults (S indicates that he doesn't like / want one or more of H's wants, acts, personal characteristics, goods, beliefs or values)
   (b) contradictions or disagreements, challenges (S indicates that he thinks H is wrong or misguided or unreasonable about some issue, such wrongness being associated with disapproval)
2   Those that show that S doesn't care about (or is indifferent to) H's positive face:
   (a) expressions of violent (out-of-control) emotions (S gives H possible reason to fear him or be embarrassed by him)
   (b) irreverence, mention of taboo topics, including those that are inappropriate in the context (S indicates that he doesn't value H's values and doesn't fear H's fears)
   (c) bringing of bad news about H, or good news (boasting) about S (S indicates that he is willing to cause distress to H, and/or doesn't care about H's feelings)
   (d) raising of dangerously emotional or divisive topics, e.g., politics, race, religion, women's liberation (S raises the possibility or likelihood of face-threatening acts (such as the above) occurring; i.e., S creates a dangerous-to-face atmosphere)
   (e) blatant non-cooperation in an activity – e.g., disruptively interrupting H's talk, making non-sequiturs or showing non-attention (S indicates that he doesn't care about H's negative- or positive-face wants)
   (f) use of address terms and other status-marked identifications in initial encounters (S may misidentify H in an offensive or embarrassing way, intentionally or accidentally)

Note that there is an overlap in this classification of FTAs, because some FTAs intrinsically threaten both negative and positive face (e.g., complaints, interruptions, threats, strong expressions of emotion, requests for personal information).

Second distinction: threats to H's face versus threats to S's

Second, we may distinguish between acts that primarily threaten *H's* face (as in the above list) and those that threaten primarily *S's* face. To the extent that S and H are cooperating to maintain face, the latter FTAs also potentially threaten H's face. FTAs that are threatening to S include:

1   Those that offend S's negative face:
    (a)   expressing thanks (S accepts a debt, humbles his own face)
    (b)   acceptance of H's thanks or H's apology (S may feel constrained to minimize H's debt or transgression, as in 'It was nothing, don't mention it.')
    (c)   excuses (S indicates that he thinks he had good reason to do, or fail to do, an act which H has just criticized; this may constitute in turn a criticism of H, or at least cause a confrontation between H's view of things and S's view)
    (d)   acceptance of offers (S is constrained to accept a debt, and to encroach upon H's negative face)
    (e)   responses to H's *faux pas* (if S visibly notices a prior *faux pas*, he may c ause embarrassment to H; if he pretends not to, he may be discomfited himself)
    (f)   unwilling promises and offers (S commits himself to some future action although he doesn't want to; therefore, if his unwillingness shows, he may also offend H's positive face)
2   Those that directly damage S's positive face:
    (a)   apologies (S indicates that he regrets doing a prior FTA, thereby damaging his own face to some degree – especially if the apology is at the same time a confession with H learning about the transgression through it, and the FTA thus conveys bad news)
    (b)   acceptance of a compliment (S may feel constrained to denigrate the object of H's prior compliment, thus damaging his own face; or he may feel constrained to compliment H in turn)
    (c)   breakdown of physical control over body, bodily leakage, stumbling or falling down, etc.
    (d)   self-humiliation, shuffling or cowering, acting stupid, self-contradicting
    (e)   confessions, admissions of guilt or responsibility – e.g., for having done or not done an act, or for ignorance of something that S is expected to know
    (f)   emotion leakage, non-control of laughter or tears

These two ways of classifying FTAs (by whether S's face or H's face is mainly threatened, or by whether it is mainly positive face or negative face that is at stake) give rise to a four-way grid which offers the possibility of cross-classifying at least some of the above FTAs. However, such a cross-classification has a complex relation to the ways in which FTAs are handled.

Strategies for doing FTAs

In the context of the mutual vulnerability of face, any rational agent will seek to avoid these face-threatening acts, or will employ certain strategies to minimize the threat. In other words, he will take into consideration the relative weightings of (at least)

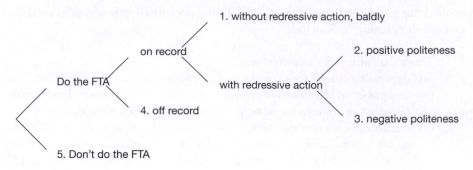

Figure 20.1 Possible strategies for doing FTAs

three wants: (a) the want to communicate the content of the FTA *x*, (b) the want to be efficient or urgent, and (c) the want to maintain H's face to any degree. Unless (b) is greater than (c), S will want to minimize the threat of his FTA.

The possible sets of strategies may be schematized exhaustively as in Figure 20.1. In this schema, we have in mind the following definitions.

An actor goes **on record** in doing an act A if it is clear to participants what communicative intention led the actor to do A (i.e., there is just one unambiguously attributable intention with which witnesses would concur). For instance, if I say 'I (hereby) promise to come tomorrow' and if participants would concur that, in saying that, I did unambiguously express the intention of committing myself to that future act, then in our terminology I went 'on record' as promising to do so.

In contrast, if an actor goes **off record** in doing A, then there is more than one unambiguously attributable intention so that the actor cannot be held to have committed himself to one particular intent. So, for instance, if I say 'Damn, I'm out of cash, I forgot to go to the bank today', I may be intending to get you to lend me some cash, but I cannot be held to have committed myself to that intent (as you would discover were you to challenge me with 'This is the seventeenth time you've asked me to lend you money'). Linguistic realizations of off-record strategies include metaphor and irony, rhetorical questions, understatement, tautologies, all kinds of hints as to what a speaker wants or means to communicate, without doing so directly, so that the meaning is to some degree negotiable.

Doing an act **baldly**, **without redress**, involves doing it in the most direct, clear, unambiguous and concise way possible (for example, for a request, saying 'Do X!'). This we shall identify roughly with following the specifications of Grice's maxims of cooperation [Chapter 3]. Normally, an FTA will be done in this way only if the speaker does not fear retribution from the addressee, for example in circumstances where (a) S and H both tacitly agree that the relevance of face demands may be suspended in the interests of urgency or efficiency; (b) where the danger to H's face is *very* small, as in offers, requests, suggestions that are clearly in H's interest and do not require great sacrifices of S (e.g., 'Come in' or 'Do sit down'); and (c) where S is vastly superior in power H, or can enlist audience support to destroy H's face without losing his own.

By **redressive action** we mean action that 'gives face' to the addressee, that is, that attempts to counteract the potential face damage of the FTA by doing it in such a way, or with such modifications or additions, that indicate clearly that no such face threat is intended or desired, and that S in general recognizes H's face wants and himself wants them to be achieved. Such redressive action takes one of two forms, depending on which aspect of face (negative or positive) is being stressed.

Positive politeness is orientated toward the positive face of H, the positive self-image that he claims for himself. Positive politeness is approach-based; it 'anoints' the face of the addressee by indicating that in some respects, S wants H's wants (e.g., by treating him as a member of an in-group, a friend, a person whose wants and personality traits are known and liked). The potential face threat of an act is minimized in this case by the assurance that in general S wants at least some of H's wants; for example, that S considers H to be in important respects, 'the same' as he, with in-group rights and duties and expectations of reciprocity, or by the implication that S likes H so that the FTA doesn't mean a negative evaluation in general of H's face.

Negative politeness, on the other hand, is orientated mainly toward partially satisfying (redressing) H's negative face, his basic want to maintain claims of territory and self-determination. Negative politeness, thus, is essentially avoidance based, and realizations of negative-politeness strategies consist in assurances that the speaker recognizes and respects the addressee's negative-face wants and will not (or will only minimally) interfere with the addressee's freedom of action. Hence negative politeness is characterized by self-effacement, formality and restraint, with attention to very restricted aspects of H's self-image, centring on his want to be unimpeded. Face-threatening acts are redressed with apologies for interfering or transgressing, with linguistic and non-linguistic deference, with hedges on the illocutionary force of the act, with impersonalizing mechanisms (such as passives) that distance S and H from the act, and with other softening mechanisms that give the addressee an 'out', a face-saving line of escape, permitting him to feel that his response is not coerced.

There is a natural tension in negative politeness, however, between (a) the desire to go on record as a prerequisite to being seen to pay face, and (b) the desire to go off record to avoid imposing. A compromise is reached in **conventionalized indirectness**, for whatever the indirect mechanism used to do an FTA, once fully conventionalized as a way of doing that FTA it is no longer off record. Thus many indirect requests, for example, are fully conventionalized in English so that they are on record (e.g., 'Can you pass the salt?' would be read as a request by all participants; there is no longer a viable alternative interpretation of the utterance except in very special circumstances). And between any two (or more) individuals, any utterance may become conventionalized and therefore on record, as is the case with passwords and codes.

A purely conventional 'out' works as redressive action in negative politeness because it pays a token bow to the negative-face wants of the addressee. That is, the fact that the speaker bothers to phrase his FTA in a conventionally indirect way shows that he is aware of and honours the negative-face wants of H.

Factors influencing the choice of strategies

. . . In this section we argue that any rational agent will tend to choose the same genus of strategy under the same conditions – that is, make the same moves as any other would make under the circumstances. This is by virtue of the fact that the particular strategies intrinsically afford certain payoffs or advantages, and the relevant circumstances are those in which one of these payoffs would be more advantageous than any other.

We consider these in turn – first the intrinsic payoffs and then the relevant circumstances – and then relate the two.

The payoffs: *a priori* considerations

Here we present a fairly complete list of the payoffs associated with each of the strategies, derived on *a priori* grounds.

By going *on record*, a speaker can potentially get any of the following advantages: he can enlist public pressure against the addressee or in support of himself; he can get credit for honesty, for indicating that he trusts the addressee; he can get credit for outspokenness, avoiding the danger of being seen to be a manipulator; he can avoid the danger of being misunderstood; and he can have the opportunity to pay back in face whatever he potentially takes away by the FTA.

By going *off record*, on the other hand, a speaker can profit in the following ways: he can get credit for being tactful, non-coercive; he can run less risk of his act entering the 'gossip biography' that others keep of him; and he can avoid responsibility for the potentially face-damaging interpretation. Furthermore, he can give (non-overtly) the addressee an opportunity to be seen to care for S (and thus he can test H's feelings towards him). In this latter case, if H chooses to pick up and respond to the potentially threatening interpretation of the act, he can give a 'gift' to the original speaker. Thus, if I say 'It's hot in here' and you say 'Oh, I'll open the window then!', you may get credit for being generous and cooperative, and I avoid the potential threat of ordering you around.

For going on record with *positive politeness*, a speaker can minimize the face-threatening aspects of an act by assuring the addressee that S considers himself to be 'of the same kind', that he likes him and wants his wants. Thus a criticism, with the assertion of mutual friendship, may lose much of its sting – indeed, in the assumption of a friendly context it often becomes a game and possibly even a compliment (as between opposite-sexed teenagers). Another possible payoff is that S can avoid or minimize the debt implications of FTAs such as requests and offers, either by referring (indirectly) to the reciprocity and on-going relationship between the addressee and himself (as in the reference to a pseudo prior agreement with *then* in 'How about a cookie, then') or by including the addressee and himself equally as participants in or as benefitors from the request or offer (for example, with an inclusive 'we', as in 'Let's get on with dinner' [to] the husband glued to the TV).

For going on record with *negative politeness*, a speaker can benefit in the following ways: he can pay respect, deference, to the addressee in return for the FTA, and can thereby avoid incurring (or can thereby lessen) a future debt; he can maintain social distance, and avoid the threat (or the potential face loss) of advancing familiarity towards the addressee; he can give a real 'out' to the addressee (for example, with a request or an offer, by making it clear that he doesn't really expect H to say 'Yes' unless he wants to, thereby minimizing the mutual face loss incurred if H has to say 'No'); and he can give conventional 'outs' to the addressee as opposed to real 'outs', that is, pretend to offer an escape route without really doing so, thereby indicating that he has the other person's face wants in mind.

Finally, the payoff for the fifth strategic choice, 'Don't do the FTA', is simply that S avoids offending H at all with this particular FTA. Of course S also fails to achieve his desired communication, and as there are naturally no interesting linguistic reflexes of this last-ditch strategy, we will ignore it in our discussion henceforth.

For our purpose, these payoffs may be simplified to the following summary: On-record payoffs:

(a)   clarity, perspicuousness
(b)   demonstrable non-manipulativeness

Bald-on-record (non-redressed) payoff:

efficiency (S can claim that other things are more important than face, or that the act is not an FTA at all)

Plus-redress payoff: S has the opportunity to give face

(a)   positive politeness – to satisfy H's positive face, in some respect
(b)   negative politeness – to satisfy H's negative face, to some degree

Off-record payoffs:

(a)   S can satisfy negative face to a degree greater than that afforded by the negative-politeness strategy
(b)   S can avoid the inescapable accountability, the responsibility for his action, that on-record strategies entail.

. . .

The circumstances: sociological variables

In this section we argue that the assessment of the seriousness of an FTA (that is, the calculations that members actually seem to make) involves the following factors in many and perhaps all cultures:

1   The 'social distance' (D) of S and H (a symmetric relation).
2   The relative 'power' (P) of S and H (an asymmetric relation).
3   The absolute ranking (R) of impositions in the particular culture.

An immediate clarification is in order. We are interested in D, P, and R only to the extent that the actors think it is mutual knowledge between them that these variables have some particular values. Thus these are not intended as *sociologists'* ratings of *actual* power, distance, etc., but only as *actors'* assumptions of such ratings, assumed to be mutually assumed, at least within certain limits.

Our argument here has an empirical basis, and we make the argument in as strong a form as our ethnographic data will allow.

COMPUTING THE WEIGHTINESS OF AN FTA

For each FTA, the seriousness or weightiness of a particular FTA *x* is compounded of both risk to S's face and risk to H's face, in a proportion relative to the nature of the FTA. Thus apologies and confessions are essentially threats to S's face (as we have seen), and advice and orders are basically threats to H's face, while requests and offers are likely to threaten the face of both participants. However, the way in which the seriousness of a particular FTA is weighed seems to be neutral as to whether it is S's or H's face that is threatened, or in what proportion. So let us say that the weightiness of an FTA is calculated thus:

$$W_x = D(S,H) + P(H,S) + R_x$$

where W_x is the numerical value that measures the weightiness of the FTA *x*, $D(S,H)$ is the value that measures the social distance between S and H, $P(H,S)$ is a measure of the power that H has over S, and R_x is a value that measures the degree to which the FTA *x* is rated an imposition in that culture. We assume that each of these values can be measured on a scale of 1 to *n*, where *n* is some small number. Our formula assumes that the function that assigns a value to W_x on the basis of the three social parameters does so on a simple summative basis. Such an assumption seems to work surprisingly well, but we allow that in fact some more complex composition of values may be involved. In any case, the function must capture the fact that all three dimensions P, D, and R contribute to the seriousness of an FTA, and thus to a determination of the level of politeness with which, other things being equal, an FTA will be communicated.

First, we must clarify our intent. By D and P we intend very general pan-cultural social dimensions which nevertheless probably have 'emic' correlates. We are not here interested in what factors are compounded to estimate these complex parameters; such factors are certainly culture-specific. For instance, $P(H,S)$ may be assessed as being great because H is eloquent and influential, or is a prince, a witch, a thug, or a priest; $D(S,H)$ as great because H speaks another dialect or language, or lives in the next valley, or is not a kinsman. More specifically, we can describe these factors as follows.

D is a symmetric social dimension of similarity/difference within which S and H stand for the purposes of this act. In many cases (but not all), it is based on an assessment of the frequency of interaction and the kinds of material or non-material goods (including face) exchanged between S and H (or parties representing S or H, or for whom S and H are representatives). An important part of the assessment of D will usually be measures of social distance based on stable social attributes.

The reflex of social closeness is, generally, the reciprocal giving and receiving of positive face.

P is an asymmetric social dimension of relative power, roughly in Weber's sense. That is, P(H,S) is the degree to which H can impose his own plans and his own self-evaluation (face) at the expense of S's plans and self-evaluation. In general there are two sources of P, either of which may be authorized or unauthorized – material control (over economic distribution and physical force) and metaphysical control (over the actions of others, by virtue of metaphysical forces subscribed to by those others). In most cases an individual's power is drawn from both these sources, or is thought to overlap them. The reflex of a great P differential is perhaps archetypally 'deference', as discussed below.

R is a culturally and situationally defined ranking of impositions by the degree to which they are considered to interfere with an agent's wants of self-determination or of approval (his negative- and positive-face wants). In general there are probably two such scales or ranks that are emically identifiable for negative-face FTAs: a ranking of impositions in proportion to the expenditure (a) of services (including the provision of time) and (b) of goods (including non-material goods like information, as well as the expression of regard and other face payments). These intra-culturally defined costings of impositions on an individual's preserve are in general constant only in their rank order from one situation to another. However, even the rank order is subject to a set of operations that shuffles the impositions according to whether actors have specific rights or obligations to perform the act, whether they have specific reasons (ritual or physical) for not performing them, and whether actors are known to actually *enjoy* being imposed upon in some way.

So an outline of the rankings of negative-face impositions for a particular domain of FTAs in a particular culture involves a complex description like the following:

1 (a) rank order of impositions requiring services
   (b) rank order of impositions requiring goods

2 Functions on (1):
   (a) the lessening of certain impositions on a given actor determined by the obligation (legally, morally, by virtue of employment, etc.) to do the act A; and also by the enjoyment that the actor gets out of performing the required act
   (b) the increasing of certain impositions determined by reasons why the actor *shouldn't* do them, and reasons why the actor *couldn't* (easily) do them

For FTAs against positive face, the ranking involves an assessment of the amount of 'pain' given to H's face, based on the discrepancy between H's own desired self-image and that presented (blatantly or tacitly) in the FTA. There will be cultural rankings of aspects of positive face (for example, 'success', 'niceness', 'beauty', 'generosity'), which can be re-ranked in particular circumstances, just as can negative-face rankings. And there are personal (idiosyncratic) functions on these rankings; some people object to certain kinds of FTAs more than others. A person who is skilled at assessing such rankings, and the circumstances in which they vary, is considered to be graced with 'tact', 'charm', or 'poise'.

We associate with each of these variables D, P, and R, a value from 1 to *n* assigned by an actor in particular circumstances. No special substantial claim is intended; the valuation simply represents the way in which (for instance) as S's power over H increases, the weightiness of the FTA diminishes. One interesting side effect of this numerical representation is that it can describe these intuitive facts: the threshold value of risk which triggers the choice of another strategy is a constant, independent of the way in which the value is composed and assessed. Thus one goes off record where an imposition is small but relative S–H distance and H's power are great, and also where H is an intimate equal of S's but the imposition is very great.

. . .

Editors' appendix: list of politeness strategies

Positive politeness strategies:

Notice, attend to H (his/her interests, wants, needs, goods)
Exaggerate (interest, approval, sympathy with H)
Intensify interest to H
Use in-group identity markers
Seek agreement
Avoid disagreement
Presuppose/raise/assert common ground
Joke
Assert or presuppose S's knowledge of and concern for H's wants
Offer, promise
Be optimistic
Include both S and H in the activity
Give (or ask for) reasons
Assume or assert reciprocity
Give gifts to H (goods, sympathy, understanding, cooperation)

Negative politeness strategies:

Be direct/conventionally indirect
Question, hedge
Be pessimistic
Minimize the size of imposition on H
Give deference
Apologize
Impersonalize S and H: avoid pronouns 'I' and 'you'
State the FTA as a general rule
Nominalize
Go on record as incurring a debt, or as not indebting H

Off-record strategies:

Those violating Grice's conversational maxims, see Chapter 3.

VIOLATE MAXIM OF RELEVANCE

Give hints/clues
Give association clues
Presuppose

VIOLATE MAXIM OF QUALITY

Understate
Overstate
Use tautologies
Use contradictions
Be ironic
Use metaphors
Use rhetorical questions

VIOLATE MAXIM OF MANNER

Be ambiguous
Be vague
Over-generalize
Displace H
Be incomplete, use ellipsis

Reference

Goffman, E. (1967) *Interaction Ritual*, New York: Anchor Books. [See also Chapter 19 of this *Reader*.]

Chapter 21

Deborah Tannen and Cynthia Wallat

INTERACTIVE FRAMES AND KNOWLEDGE SCHEMAS IN INTERACTION: EXAMPLES FROM A MEDICAL EXAMINATION/ INTERVIEW[1]

Introduction

GOFFMAN (1981a) INTRODUCED the term "footing" as "another way of talking about a change in our frame for events," "a change in the alignment we take up to ourselves and the others present as expressed in the way we manage the production or reception of an utterance" (p. 128). He describes the ability to shift footing within an interaction as "the capacity of a dexterous speaker to jump back and forth, keeping different circles in play" (p. 156). Goffman asserts that "linguistics provides us with the cues and markers through which such footings become manifest, helping us to find our way to a structural basis for analyzing them" (p. 157). Using linguistic "cues and markers" as a "structural basis for analyzing" talk in a pediatric interaction, we show that a mismatch of knowledge schemas can trigger frame switches which constitute a significant burden on the pediatrician when she conducts her examination of a child in the mother's presence. Combining the perspectives of a social psychologist (Wallat) and a linguist (Tannen), we thus examine the specifics of talk in interaction in a particular setting to provide a basis for understanding talk in terms of shifting frames.

Like many of our colleagues, we make use of video-tape to analyze interaction which is evanescent in nature. In his description of the theoretical and methodological complexity of making informed use of filmed records in social psychological research, Kendon (1979) cautions that micro-analytic analysis must be based on a theoretical perspective involving "context analysis." He sees context analysis as a conceptual framework which presumes that participants are not isolated senders and receivers of messages. When people are in each other's presence, all their verbal and nonverbal behaviors are potential sources of communication, and their

Source: Deborah Tannen and Cynthia Wallat, 'Interactive frames and knowledge schemas in interaction: examples from a medical examination/interview', *Social Psychology Quarterly*, 50(2): 205–16, 1987.

actions and meanings can be understood only in relation to the immediate context, including what preceded and may follow it. Thus, interaction can be understood only in context: a specific context. We have chosen the pediatric setting as an exemplary context of interaction. Understanding how communication works in this context provides a model which can be applied in other contexts as well.

In examining talk in a pediatric setting, we are interested in the duality of what emerges in interaction: the stability of what occurs as a consequence of the social context, and the variability of particular interactions which results from the emergent nature of discourse. On one hand, meanings emerge which are not given in advance; on the other, meanings which are shaped by the doctor's or patient's prior assumptions (as we will argue, their knowledge schemas) may be resistant to change by the interlocutor's talk.

As Cicourel (1975) cautioned over a decade ago, when social scientists create a database for addressing the issues involved in integrating structure and process in the study of participants in medical settings, their textual material should "reflect the complexities of the different modalities and emergent contextual knowledge inherent in social interaction" (p. 34). One important way that Cicourel, and after him Richard Frankel (1989), sought to observe such complexities has been to compare discourse produced in spoken and written modalities. We have adopted this practice and have also developed a method of analyzing video-tapes of participants in more than one setting.

. . .

Frames and schemas

The term "frame," and related terms such as "script," "schema," "prototype," "speech activity," "template" and "module," have been variously used in linguistics, artificial intelligence, anthropology and psychology. Tannen (1979) reviews this literature and suggests that all these concepts reflect the notion of structures of expectation. Yet that early treatment of a variety of concepts of frames and schemas in the disciplines of linguistics, cognitive psychology and artificial intelligence said little about the type of frames that Goffman (1974) so exhaustively analyzed, as he himself observed (Goffman 1981b). The present paper broadens the discussion of frames to encompass and integrate the anthropological/sociological sense of the term.

The various uses of "frame" and related terms fall into two categories. One is interactive "frames of interpretation" which characterize the work of anthropologists and sociologists. We refer to these "frames," following Bateson (1972), who introduced the term, as well as most of those who have built on his work, including scholars in the fields of anthropology (Frake 1977), sociology (Goffman 1974) and linguistic anthropology (Gumperz 1982; Hymes 1974). The other category is knowledge structures, which we refer to as "schemas," but which have been variously labeled in work in artificial intelligence (Minsky 1975; Schank and Abelson 1977), cognitive psychology (Rumelhart 1975), and linguistic semantics (Chafe 1977; Fillmore 1976; 1976).

Interactive frames

The interactive notion of frame refers to a definition of what is going on in interaction, without which no utterance (or movement or gesture) could be interpreted. To use Bateson's classic example, a monkey needs to know whether a bite from another monkey is intended within the frame of play or the frame of fighting. People are continually confronted with the same interpretative task. In order to comprehend any utterance, a listener (and a speaker) must know within which frame it is intended: for example, is this joking? Is it fighting? Something intended as a joke but interpreted as an insult (it could of course be both) can trigger a fight.

Goffman (1974) sketched the theoretical foundations of frame analysis in the work of William James, Alfred Schutz and Harold Garfinkel to investigate the socially constructed nature of reality. Building on their work, as well as that of linguistic philosophers John Austin and Ludwig Wittgenstein, Goffman developed a complex system of terms and concepts to illustrate how people use multiple frameworks to make sense of events even as they construct those events. Exploring in more detail the linguistic basis of such frameworks, Goffman (1981a) introduced the term "footing" to describe how, at the same time that participants frame events, they negotiate the interpersonal relationships, or "alignments," that constitute those events.

The interactive notion of frame, then, refers to a sense of what activity is being engaged in, how speakers mean what they say. As Ortega y Gasset (1959: 3), a student of Heidegger, puts it, "Before understanding any concrete statement, it is necessary to perceive clearly 'what it is all about' in this statement and 'what game is being played.'"[2] Since this sense is gleaned from the way participants behave in interaction, frames emerge in and are constituted by verbal and nonverbal interaction.

Knowledge schemas

We use the term "knowledge schema" to refer to participants' expectations about people, objects, events and settings in the world, as distinguished from alignments being negotiated in a particular interaction. Linguistic semanticists have been interested in this phenomenon, as they have observed that even the literal meaning of an utterance can be understood only by reference to a pattern of prior knowledge. This is fundamental to the writing of Heidegger (for example, 1962: 199), as in his often quoted argument (p. 196) that the word "hammer" can have no meaning to someone who has never seen a hammer used. To borrow an example from Fillmore (1976), the difference between the phrases "on land" and "on the ground" can be understood only by reference to an expected sequence of actions associated with travel on water and in the air, respectively. Moreover, the only way anyone can understand any discourse is by filling in unstated information which is known from prior experience in the world. This became clear to researchers in artificial intelligence as soon as they tried to get computers to understand even the simplest discourse – hence, for example, the need for Schank and Abelson's (1977) restaurant script to account for the use of the definite article "the" in a minimal discourse such as, "John went into a restaurant; he asked the waitress for a menu."

Researchers in the area of medical sociology and anthropology such as Kleinman (1980) and Mishler (1984) have observed the problem of doctors' and patients' divergent knowledge schemas, although they may not have used this terminology. Cicourel (1983), for example, describes the effects of differing "structures of belief" in a gynecological case. The contribution of our analysis is to show the distinction and interaction between knowledge schemas and interactive frames.

At an earlier stage of this study, we referred to an interactive notion of frame as "dynamic" and the knowledge structure notion of schema as "static," but we now realize that all types of structures of expectations are dynamic, as Bartlett (1932), whose work underlies much of present-day schema theory, pointed out, and as others (for example, Frake 1977) have emphasized. That is, expectations about objects, people, settings, ways to interact, and anything else in the world are continually checked against experience and revised.

The interaction of frames and schemas

We demonstrate here a particular relationship between interactive frames and knowledge schemas by which a mismatch in schemas triggers a shifting of frames. Before proceeding to demonstrate this by reference to detailed analysis of pediatric interaction, we will illustrate briefly with reference to an example of a trivial, fleeting and mundane interchange that was part of a telephone conversation.

One author (Tannen) was talking to a friend on the telephone, when he suddenly yelled, "YOU STOP THAT!" She knew from the way he uttered this command that it was addressed to a dog and not her. She remarked on the fact that when he addressed the dog, he spoke in something approximating a southern accent. The friend explained that this was because the dog had learned to respond to commands in that accent, and, to give another example, he illustrated the way he plays with the dog: "I say, 'GO GIT THAT BALL!'" Hearing this, the dog began running about the room looking for something to fetch. The dog recognized the frame "play" in the tone of the command; he could not, however, understand the words that identified an outer frame, "*referring* to playing with the dog," and mistook the reference for a literal invitation to play.

This example illustrates, as well, that people (and dogs) identify frames in interaction by association with linguistic and paralinguistic cues – the way words are uttered – in addition to what they say. That is, the way the speaker uttered "You stop that!" was associated with the frame "disciplining a pet" rather than "chatting with a friend." Tannen drew on her familiarity with the use of linguistic cues to signal frames when she identified her friend's interjection "You stop that!" as addressed to a dog, not her. But she also drew on the knowledge that her friend was taking care of someone's dog. This was part of her knowledge schema about her friend. Had her schema included the information that he had a small child and was allergic to dogs, she might have interpreted the same linguistic cues as signaling the related frame, "disciplining a misbehaving child." Furthermore, her expectations about how any speaker might express orders or emotions, i.e. frame such expressions, were brought to bear in this instance in conjunction with her expectations about how this particular friend is likely to speak to her, to a dog and to a child; that is, a schema for this friend's personal style. Thus frames and schemas interacted in her comprehension of the specific utterance.

The remainder of this paper illustrates frames and schemas in a video-taped interaction in a medical setting: the examination of a child by a pediatrician in the presence of the mother. It demonstrates that an understanding of interactive frames accounts for conflicting demands on the pediatrician. In addition to communicative demands arising from multiple interactive frames, much of the talk in the pediatric encounter can be understood as resulting from differing knowledge schemas of the mother and the pediatrician. This will be illustrated with reference to their schemas for health and cerebral palsy. Finally, it is the mismatch in knowledge structure schemas that prompts the mother to ask questions which require the doctor to switch frames.

Background of the study

The video-tapes on which our analysis is based were obtained from the Child Development Center of the Georgetown University Medical School, following our presentation of a proposal to the Center's Interdisciplinary Research Committee. The video-tapes had been made as raw material for a demonstration tape giving an overview of the Center's services, and therefore documented all the encounters involving a single family and Center staff, which took place over three weeks.

The primary goal of the Center is to provide interdisciplinary training to future professionals in serving developmentally disabled children and their families. Staff members work in interdisciplinary teams which include an audiologist, speech pathologist, pediatrician, social worker, nutritionist, dentist, nurses and an occupational, an educational and a physical therapist. Each professional meets with the child and, in some cases, other family members; then all meet to pool the results of their evaluations, which are presented to the parents in a group meeting.

The parents of Jody, the 8-year-old cerebral palsied child in this study, were referred to the Center by the parents of another child. Their chief concern was Jody's public school placement in a class for mentally retarded children. Their objective, which was met, was to have a Center representative meet with the supervisor of special education in their district and have Jody placed in a class for the orthopedically rather than mentally handicapped.

In addition to the spastic cerebral palsy (paralysis resulting from damage to the brain before or during birth), Jody was diagnosed as having a seizure disorder; a potentially lethal arteriovenous malformation in her brain (this was subsequently, and happily, rediagnosed as a less dangerous malformation involving veins only, rather than both arteries and veins); facial hemangiomas (red spots composed of blood-filled capillaries); and slight scoliosis (curvature of the spine).

We began our analysis by focusing on the pediatrician's examination/interview, which took place with the mother present. As part of our analysis, we met, separately, with the doctor and the mother, first talking with them and then reviewing segments of the tape. The mother expressed the opinion that this doctor "was great," in explicit contrast with others who "cut you off and make you feel stupid" and deliver devastating information (for example, "she'd be a vegetable") in an offhand manner.

Interactive frames in the pediatric examination

The goal of this paper is to show that examining Jody in her mother's presence constituted a significant burden on the pediatrician, which can be attributed to a conflict in framing resulting from mismatched schemas. To demonstrate this inter-action between frames and schemas, we will first show what framing is and how it works, beginning with the crucial linguistic component of register.

Linguistic registers

A key element in framing is the use of identifiable linguistic registers. Register, as Ferguson (1985) defines it, is simply "variation conditioned by use": conventionalized lexical, syntactic and prosodic choices deemed appropriate for the setting and audience. . . .

In addressing the child, the pediatrician uses "motherese": a teasing register characterized by exaggerated shifts in pitch, marked prosody (long pauses followed by bursts of vocalization), and drawn out vowel sounds, accompanied by smiling. For example, while examining Jody's ears with an ophthalmoscope (ear light), the pediatrician pretends to be looking for various creatures, and Jody responds with delighted laughter:

> Doctor: Let me look in your ear. Do you have a monkey in your ear?
> Child: [laughing] No::::.
> Doctor: No:::? . . . Let's see. . . . I . . see . . . . . . a birdie!
> Child: [laughing] No:::.
> Doctor: [smiling] No.

In stark contrast to this intonationally exaggerated register, the pediatrician uses a markedly flat intonation to give a running account of the findings of her examination, addressed to no present party, but designed for the benefit of pediatric residents who might later view the video-tape in the teaching facility. We call this "reporting register." For example, looking in Jody's throat, the doctor says, with only slight stumbling:

> Doctor: Her canals are are fine, they're open, um her tympanic mem-
> brane was thin, and light,

Finally, in addressing the mother, the pediatrician uses conventional conversational register, as for example:

> Doctor: As you know, the important thing is that she does have difficulty
> with the use of her muscles.

Register shifting

Throughout the examination the doctor moves among these registers. Some-times she shifts from one to another in very short spaces of time, as in the following example in which she moves smoothly from teasing the child while examining her throat, to reporting her findings, to explaining to the mother what she is looking for and how this relates to the mother's expressed concern with the child's breathing at night.

[Teasing register]

Doctor: Let's see. Can you open up like this, Jody. Look.
          [Doctor opens her own mouth]
Child: Aaaaaaaaaaaaah.
Doctor: ⌜Good. That's good.
Child: ⌞Aaaaaaaaaaah

[Reporting register]

Doctor: /Seeing/ for the palate, she ⌜has a high arched palate →
Child: ⌞Aaaaaaaaaaaaaaaaaaaaaaaaaah
Doctor: but there's no cleft,
          [maneuvers to grasp child's jaw]

[Conversational register]

> . . . what we'd want to look for is to see how she . . . moves her palate. . . . Which may be some of the difficulty with breathing that we're talking about.

The pediatrician's shifts from one register to another are sometimes abrupt (for example, when she turns to the child and begins teasing) and sometimes gradual (for example, her reporting register in "high arched palate" begins to fade into conversational register with "but there's no cleft," and come to rest firmly in conversational register with "what we'd want to look for . . ."). In the following example, she shifts from entertaining Jody to reporting findings and back to managing Jody in a teasing tone:

[Teasing register]

Doctor: That's my light.
Child: /This goes up there./
Doctor: It goes up there. That's right.

[Reporting register]

> Now while we're examining her head we're feeling for lymph nodes in her neck . . . or for any masses . . . okay . . . also you palpate the midline for thyroid, for goiter . . . if there's any.

[Teasing register]

> Now let us look in your mouth. Okay? With my light. Can you
> open up real big? . . . Oh, bigger. . . . Oh bigger. . . . Bigger.

Frame shifting

Although register shifting is one way of accomplishing frame shifts, it is not the only way. Frames are more complex than register. Whereas each audience is associated with an identifiable register, the pediatrician shifts footings with each audience. In other words, she not only talks differently to the mother, the child and the future video audience, but she also deals with each of these audiences in different ways, depending upon the frame in which she is operating.

The three most important frames in this interaction are the social encounter, examination of the child and a related outer frame of its video-taping, and consultation with the mother. Each of the three frames entails addressing each of the three audiences in different ways. For example, the social encounter requires that the doctor entertain the child, establish rapport with the mother and ignore the video camera and crew. The examination frame requires that she ignore the mother, make sure the video crew is ready and then ignore them, examine the child, and explain what she is doing for the future video audience of pediatric residents. The consultation frame requires that she talk to the mother and ignore the crew and the child – or, rather, keep the child "on hold," to use Goffman's term, while she answers the mother's questions. These frames are balanced nonverbally as well as verbally. Thus the pediatrician keeps one arm outstretched to rest her hand on the child while she turns away to talk to the mother, palpably keeping the child "on hold."

Juggling frames

Often these frames must be served simultaneously, such as when the pediatrician entertains the child and examines her at the same time, as seen in the example where she looks in her ear and teases Jody that she is looking for a monkey. The pediatrician's reporting register reveals what she was actually looking at (Jody's ear canals and tympanic membrane). But balancing frames is an extra cognitive burden, as seen when the doctor accidentally mixes the vocabulary of her diagnostic report into her teasing while examining Jody's stomach:

[Teasing register]

Doctor: Okay. All right. Now let me /?/ let me see what I
         can find in there. Is there peanut butter and jelly?
         Wait a minute.⌐
Child: ⌊No⌐
Doctor: ⌊No peanut butter and jelly in there?
Child: No.

[Conversational register]

Doctor: Bend your legs up a little bit. . . . That's right.

[Teasing register]

```
                Okay? Okay. Any peanut butter and jelly in here?⌐
Child:                                                          └ No⌐
Doctor:                                                              └No.
                No. There's nothing in there. Is your spleen palpable over
                there?⌐
Child:                └No.
```

The pediatrician says the last line, "Is your spleen palpable over there?" in the same teasing register she was using for peanut butter and jelly, and Jody responds with the same delighted giggling "No" with which she responded to the teasing questions about peanut butter and jelly. The power of the paralinguistic cues with which the doctor signals the frame "teasing" is greater than that of the words spoken, which in this case leak out of the examination frame into the teasing register.

In other words, for the pediatrician, each interactive frame, that is, each identifiable activity that she is engaged in within the interaction, entails her establishing a distinct footing with respect to the other participants.

The interactive production of frames

Our analysis focuses on the pediatrician's speech because our goal is to show that the mismatch of schemas triggers the frame switches which make this interaction burdensome for her. Similar analyses could be performed for any participant in any interaction. Furthermore, all participants in any interaction collaborate in the negotiation of all frames operative within that interaction. Thus, the mother and child collaborate in the negotiation of frames which are seen in the pediatrician's speech and behavior.

For example, consider the examination frame as evidence in the pediatrician's running report of her procedures and findings for the benefit of the video audience. Although the mother interrupts with questions at many points in the examination, she does not do so when the pediatrician is reporting her findings in what we have called reporting register.[3] Her silence contributes to the maintenance of this frame. Furthermore, on the three of seventeen occasions of reporting register when the mother does offer a contribution, she does so in keeping with the physician's style: Her utterances have a comparable clipped style.

The homonymy of behaviors

Activities which appear the same on the surface can have very different meanings and consequences for the participants if they are understood as associated with different frames. For example, the pediatrician examines various parts of the child's body in accordance with what she describes at the start as a "standard pediatric evaluation." At times she asks the mother for information relevant to the child's condition, still adhering to the sequence of foci of attention prescribed by the pediatric evaluation. At one point, the mother asks about a skin condition behind the child's right ear, causing the doctor to examine that part of Jody's body. What on the surface appears to be the same activity – examining the child – is really very different. In the first case the doctor is adhering to a preset sequence of procedures in the examination, and in the second she is interrupting that sequence to focus on something else, following which she will have to recover her place in the standard sequence.

Conflicting frames

Each frame entails ways of behaving that potentially conflict with the demands of other frames. For example, consulting with the mother entails not only interrupting the examination sequence but also taking extra time to answer her questions, and this means that the child will get more restless and more difficult to manage as the examination proceeds. Reporting findings to the video audience may upset the mother, necessitating more explanation in the consultation frame. Perhaps that is the reason the pediatrician frequently explains to the mother what she is doing and finding and why.

Another example will illustrate that the demands associated with the consultation frame can conflict with those of the examination frame, and that these frames and associated demands are seen in linguistic evidence, in this case by contrasting the pediatrician's discourse to the mother in the examination setting with her report to the staff of the Child Development Center about the same problem. Having recently learned that Jody has an arteriovenous malformation in her brain, the mother asks the doctor during the examination how dangerous this condition is. The doctor responds in a way that balances the demands of several frames:

Mother: I often worry about the danger involved too. →
Doctor: ˪Yes.
            Cause she's well I mean like right now, . . . uh . . . in
            her present condition. →
Doctor: ˪mhm
Mother: I've often wondered about how dangerous they they are
            to her right now.
Doctor: We:ll . . . um . . . the only danger would be from
            bleeding. . . . Fróm them. If there was any rupture, or
            anything like that. Which CAN happen. . . . um . . .
            that would be the danger.
Mother: ˪mhm
Doctor: . . . Fór that. But they're . . . . . . mm . . . nót going
            to be something that will get worse as time goes on.
Mother: Oh I see.
Doctor: But they're just thére. Okay?

The mother's question invoked the consultation frame, requiring the doctor to give the mother the information based on her medical knowledge, plus take into account the effect on the mother of the information that the child's life is in danger. However, the considerable time that would normally be required for such a task is limited because of the conflicting demands of the examination frame: the child is "on hold" for the exam to proceed. (Notice that it is admirable sensitivity of this doctor that makes her aware of the needs of both frames. According to this mother, many doctors have informed her in matter-of-fact tones of potentially devastating information about her child's condition, without showing any sign of awareness that such information will have emotional impact on the parent. In our terms, such doctors acknowledge only one frame – examination – in order to avoid the demands of conflicting frames – consultation and social encounter. Observing the burden on this pediatrician, who successfully balances the demands of multiple frames, makes it easy to understand why others might avoid this.)

The pediatrician blunts the effect of the information she imparts by using circumlocutions and repetitions; pausing and hesitating; and minimizing the significant danger of the arteriovenous malformation by using the word "only" ("only danger"), by using the conditional tense ("that would be the danger"), and by stressing what sounds positive, that they're not going to get worse. She further creates a reassuring effect by smiling, nodding and using a soothing tone of voice. In reviewing the video-tape with us several years after the taping, the pediatrician was surprised to see that she had expressed the prognosis in this way, and furthermore that the mother seemed to be reassured by what was in fact distressing information. The reason she did so, we suggest, is that she was responding to the immediate and conflicting demands of the two frames she was operating in: consulting with the mother in the context of the examination.

Evidence that this doctor indeed felt great concern for the seriousness of the child's condition is seen in her report to the staff regarding the same issue:

> Doctor: . . . uh: I'm not sure how much counseling has been dóne, . . . wíth these parents, . . . around . . . the issue . . . of the a-v malformation. Mother asked me questions, . . . about the operability, inoperability of it, . . . u:m . . . which I was not able to answer. She was told it was inoperable, and I had to say well yes some of them are and some of them aren't. . . . And I think that this is a . . . a . . . an important point. Because I don't know whether . . . the possibility of sudden death, intra-cranial hemorrhage, if any of this has ever been discússed with these parents.

Here the pediatrician speaks faster, with fluency and without hesitation or circum-locution. Her tone of voice conveys a sense of urgency and grave concern. Whereas the construction used with the mother, "only danger," seemed to minimize the danger, the listing construction used with the staff ("sudden death, intracranial hemorrhage"), which actually refers to a single possible event, gives the impression that even more dangers are present than those listed.

Thus the demands on the pediatrician associated with consultation with the mother; those associated with examining the child and reporting her findings to the video audience; and those associated with managing the interaction as a social encounter are potentially in conflict and result in competing demands on the doctor's cognitive and social capacities.

Knowledge schemas in the pediatric interaction

Just as ways of talking (that is, of expressing and establishing footing) at any point in interaction reflect the operation of multiple frames, similarly, what individuals choose to say in an interaction grows out of multiple knowledge schemas regarding the issues under discussion, the participants, the setting, and so on. We have seen that conflicts can arise when participants are orientated toward different interactive frames, or have different expectations associated with frames. Topics that the mother introduces in the consultation frame sometimes interfere with the doctor's conducting the examination, and time the doctor spends examining Jody in areas in which she has had no problems does not help the mother in terms of what prompted her to take Jody to the Child Development Center: a concern that she was regressing rather than improving in skills. Similarly, when participants have different schemas, the result can be confusion and talking at cross-purposes, and, frequently, the triggering of switches in interactive frames. We will demonstrate this with examples from the pediatrician's and mother's discussions of a number of issues related to the child's health and her cerebral palsy.

Mismatched schemas

Before examining Jody, the pediatrician conducts a medical interview in which she fills out a form by asking the mother a series of questions about Jody's health history and current health condition. After receiving negative answers to a series of questions concerning such potential conditions as bowel problems, bronchitis, pneumonia and ear infections, the pediatrician summarizes her perception of the information the mother has just given her. However, the mother does not concur with this paraphrase:

> Doctor: Okay. And so her general overall health has been good.
> Mother: . . . . . . [sighs] Not really. . . . uh: . . . back . . . uh . . .
>   after she had her last seizure, . . . uh . . . uh . . . it was
>   pretty cold during this . . . that time . . . a:nd uh . . . it
>   seemed that she just didn't have much energy,⌐
> Doctor: ⌐mm
> Mother: . . . and she uh . . . her uh . . . . . . motor abilities at the
>   time didn't seem . . . very good. . . . She kept bumping into
>   walls, . . . and falling, and . . . uh

The mother's schema for health is a comprehensive one, including the child's total physical well-being. The child's motor abilities have not been good; therefore her health has not been good. In contrast, the pediatrician does not consider motor abilities to be included in a schema of health. Moreover, the pediatrician has a schema for cerebral palsy (cp): she knows what a child with cp can be expected to do or not do, i.e. what is "normal" for a child with cp. In contrast, as emerged in discussion during a staff meeting, the mother has little experience with other cp children, so she can only compare Jody's condition and development to those of non-cp children.

Throughout our tapes of interaction between Jody's mother and the pediatrician, questions are asked and much talk is generated because of unreconciled differences between the mother's and doctor's knowledge schemas regarding health and cerebral palsy, resulting from the doctor's experience and training and the mother's differing experience and personal involvement.

Mismatches based on the cp schema account for numerous interruptions of the examination frame by the mother invoking the consultation frame. For example, as briefly mentioned earlier, the mother interrupts the doctor's examination to ask about a skin eruption behind the child's ear. The mother goes on to ask whether there is a connection between the cerebral palsy and the skin condition because both afflict Jody's right side. The doctor explains that there is no connection. The mother's schema for cp does not include the knowledge that it would not cause drying and breaking of skin. Rather, for her, the skin condition and the cp become linked in a "right-sided weakness" schema.

Similar knowledge schema mismatches account for extensive demands on the pediatrician to switch from the examination to the consultation frame. When Jody sleeps, her breathing sounds noisy, as if she were gasping for air. The mother is very concerned that the child might not be getting enough oxygen. When the doctor finishes examining the child's throat and moves on to examine her ears, the mother takes the opportunity to interrupt and state her concern. The doctor halts the examination, turns to the mother and switches to the consultation frame, explaining that the muscle weakness entailed in cp also affects the muscles used in breathing; therefore Jody's breathing sounds "coarse" or "floppy." However, this does not mean that she is having trouble breathing.

> Doctor: Jody? . . . I want to look in your ears. . . . Jody?
> Mother: This problem that she hás, . . . is not . . . interfering
> with her breathing, is it?
> Child: /Hello/ [spoken into ophthalmoscope]
> Doctor: No.
> Mother: It just appears that way?
> Doctor: Yes. It's very . . . it's . . . really . . . it's like flóppy you
> know that that's why it sounds the way it is.
> Mother: She worries me at night.
> Doctor: Yes
> Mother: Because uh . . . when she's asleep I keep checking on hér
> so she doesn't⌐
> Doctor: ⌐ As you know the important⌐
> Mother: ⌐ I keep
> thinking she's not breathing properly.
> [spoken while chuckling]
> Doctor: As you know, the impórtant thing is that she dóes have
> difficulty with the use of her muscles.⌐
> Mother: ⌐ mhm

> Doctor: So she has difficulty with the use of muscles, . . . as far
> as the muscles of her chest, that are used with breathing.
> Y'know as well as the drooling, the muscles with swallowing,
> and all that ⌈ so all her muscles
> Mother:　　　　　　　⌊ Is there some exercise
> /to strengthen or help that/.

The mother's schemas for health and cerebral palsy do not give her the expectation that the child's breathing should sound noisy. Rather, for her, noisy breathing is "wheezing," which fits into a schema for ill health: noisy breathing is associated with difficulty breathing. In fact, the parents, in the initial medical interview at the Child Development Center, characterize Jody as having difficulty breathing, and this is entered into the written record of the interview.

These schemas are not easily altered. The pediatrician's assurance that Jody is not having trouble breathing goes on for some time, yet the mother brings it up again when the doctor is listening to Jody's chest through a stethoscope. Again the doctor shifts from the examination frame to the consultation frame to reassure her at length that the child is not having trouble breathing, that these sounds are "normal" for a child with cerebral palsy.

> Doctor: Now I want you to listen, Jody. We're going to listen to you
> breathe. Can you? Look at me. Can you go like this? [inhales]
> Good. Oh you know how to do all this. You've been to a lot
> of doctors. [Jody inhales] Good. Good. Once . . . good. Okay.
> Once more. Oh you have a lot of extra noise on this side.
> Go ahead. Do it once more. ⌈ Once more.
> Mother:　　　　　　　　　　　⌊ That's the particular noise she
> makes when she sleeps. [chuckle]
> Doctor: Once more. Yeah I hear all that. One more. One more.
> [laughs] Once more. Okay. That's good. She has very coarse
> breath sounds um . . . and you can hear a lot of the noises
> you hear when she breathes you can hear when you listen.
> But there's nothing that's ⌉
> Mother:　　　　　　　　　　⌊That's the kind of noise I hear
> when she's sleeping at night.
> Doctor:　　　　　　　　⌊Yes,⌋
> Yes. There's nothing really as far as a pneumonia is concerned
> or as far as any um anything here. There's no wheezing um
> which would suggest a tightness or a constriction of the thing.
> There's no wheezing at all. What it is is mainly very coarse
> due to the . . . the wide open kind of flopping.

Nonetheless, during the session in which the staff report their findings to the parents, when the pediatrician makes her report, the mother again voices her concern that the child is having trouble breathing and refers to the sound of Jody's breathing as "wheezing." At this point the doctor adamantly reasserts that there is no wheezing. What for the mother is a general descriptive term for the sound of noisy breathing is for the doctor a technical term denoting a condition by which the throat passages are constricted.

An understanding of the mother's schemas accounts for the resilience of her concern about the child's breathing, despite the doctor's repeated and lengthy reassurances. Our point here is that the mismatch in schemas – that is, the mother's association of noisy breathing with difficulty breathing and the doctor's dissociation of these two conditions and her emphasis on the medical definition of "wheezing" (irrelevant to the mother) – creates a mismatch in expectations about what counts as adequate reassurance. This mismatch causes the mother to ask questions which require the doctor to shift frames from examination to consultation.

Summary and conclusion

We have used the term "frame" to refer to the anthropological/sociological notion of a frame, as developed by Bateson and Goffman, and as Gumperz (1982) uses the term "speech activity." It refers to participants' sense of what is being done, and reflects Goffman's notion of footing: the alignment participants take up to themselves and others in the situation. We use the term "schema" to refer to patterns of knowledge such as those discussed in cognitive psychology and artificial intelligence. These are patterns of expectations and assumptions about the world, its inhabitants and objects.

We have shown how frames and schemas together account for interaction in a pediatric interview/examination, and how linguistic cues, or ways of talking, evidence and signal the shifting frames and schemas. An understanding of frames accounts for the exceedingly complex, indeed burdensome nature of the pediatrician's task in examining a child in the mother's presence. An understanding of schemas accounts for many of the doctor's lengthy explanations, as well as the mother's apparent discomfort and hedging when her schemas lead her to contradict those of the doctor. Moreover, and most significantly, it is the mismatch of schemas that frequently occasions the mother's recurrent questions which, in their turn, require the doctor to interrupt the examination frame and switch to a consultation frame.

The usefulness of such an analysis for those concerned with medical interaction is significant. On a global level, this approach begins to answer the call by physicians (for example, Brody 1980 and Lipp 1980) for deeper understanding of the use of language in order to improve services in their profession. On a local level, the pediatrician, on hearing our analysis, was pleased to see a theoretical basis for what she had instinctively sensed. Indeed, she had developed the method in her private practice of having parents observe examinations, paper in hand, from behind a one-way mirror, rather than examining children in the parents' presence.

The significance of the study, however, goes beyond the disciplinary limits of medical settings. There is every reason to believe that frames and schemas operate in similar ways in all face-to-face interaction, although the particular frames and schemas will necessarily differ in different settings. We may also expect, and must further investigate, individual and social differences both in frames and schemas and in the linguistic as well as nonverbal cues and markers by which they are identified and created.

Transcription conventions

[	Brackets linking two lines show overlap: Two voices heard at once
]	Reversed-flap brackets shows latching⌐ ⌐No pause between lines
/ /	/words/ in slashes reflect uncertain transcription
/?/	indicates inaudible words
?	indicates rising intonation, not grammatical question
.	indicates falling intonation, not grammatical sentence
:	following vowels indicates elongation of sound
..	Two dots indicate brief pause, less than half second
...	Three dots indicate pause of at least half second; more dots indicate longer pauses
→	Arrow at left highlights key line in example Arrow at right means talk continues without interruption→ on succeeding lines of text
′	Accent mark indicates primary stress
CAPS	indicate emphatic stress

Notes

1   This chapter . . . is a final synthesis of a long-term project analyzing video-tapes made at Georgetown University's Child Development Center. We are grateful to the Center administrators and staff who gave us permission to use the tapes, and to the pediatrician, the mother, and the parent coordinator for permission to use the tapes and for taking the time to view and discuss them with us. We thank Dell Hymes for his observations on how our work blends social psychological and sociolinguistic concerns. Tannen is grateful to Lambros Comitas and the Department of Philosophy and the Social Sciences of Teachers College Columbia University for providing affiliation during her sabbatical leave which made possible the revision of the manuscript. We thank Douglas Maynard for incisive editorial suggestions. . . .

2   Thanks to A.L. Becker for the reference to Ortega y Gasset. For a discussion on framing based on numerous examples from everyday life, see chapter 5, "Framing and Reframing," in Tannen (1986).

3   The notion of "reporting register" accounts for a similar phenomenon described by Cicourel (1975) in an analysis of a medical interview.

References

Bartlett, F.C. (1932) *Remembering*, Cambridge: Cambridge University Press.

Bateson, G. (1972) *Steps to an Ecology of Mind*, New York: Ballantine.

Brody, D.S. (1980) 'Feedback from patients as a means of teaching non-technological aspects of medical care', *Journal of Medical Education* 55: 34–41.

Chafe, W. (1977) 'Creativity in verbalization and its implications for the nature of stored knowledge', in Freedle, R. (ed.) *Discourse Production and Comprehension*, Norwood, NJ: Ablex, 41–55.

Cicourel, A.V. (1975) 'Discourse and text: cognitive and linguistic processes in studies of social structure', *Versus* 12: 33–84.

—— (1983) 'Language and the structure of belief in medical communication', in Fisher, S. and Dundas Todd, A. (eds) *The Social Organization of Doctor–Patient Communication*, Washington, DC: Center for Applied Linguistics, 221–39.

Ferguson, C.A. (1985) Editor's introduction. Special language registers, Special issue of *Discourse Processes* 8: 391–4.

Fillmore, C.J. (1976) 'The need for a frame semantics within linguistics', *Statistical Methods in Linguistics*, 5–29, Stockholm: Skriptor.

Frake, C.O. (1977) 'Plying frames can be dangerous: some reflections on methodology in cognitive anthropology', *The Quarterly Newsletter of the Institute for Comparative Human Cognition* 1: 1–7.

Frankel, R.M. (1989) '"I was wondering – could Raid affect the brain permanently d'y'know?": Some observations on the intersection of speaking and writing in calls to a poison control center', *Western Journal of Speech Communication* 53: 195–226.

Goffman, E. (1974) *Frame Analysis*, New York: Harper & Row.

—— (1981a) *Forms of Talk*, Philadelphia, PA: University of Pennsylvania Press.

—— (1981b) 'Reply to review of frame analysis by Norma Denzin', *Contemporary Sociology* 10: 60–8.

Gumperz, J.J. (1982) *Discourse Strategies*, Cambridge: Cambridge University Press.

Heidegger, M. (1962) *Being and Time*, New York: Harper & Row.

Hymes, D. (1974) 'Ways of speaking', in Bauman, R. and Sherzer, J. (eds) *Explorations in the Ethnography of Speaking*, Cambridge: Cambridge University Press, 433–510.

Kendon, A. (1979) 'Some theoretical and methodological aspects of the use of film in the study of social interaction', in Ginsburg, G.P. (ed.) *Emerging Strategies in Social Psychological Research*, New York: Wiley, 67–94.

Kleinman, A. (1980) *Patients and Healers in the Context of Culture: An Exploration of the Borderland Between Anthropology, Medicine and Psychiatry*, Berkeley, CA: University of California Press.

Lipp, M.R. (1980) *The Bitter Pill: Doctors, Patients and Failed Expectations*, New York: Harper & Row.

Minsky, M. (1975) 'A framework for representing knowledge', in Winston, P.H. (ed.) *The Psychology of Computer Vision*, New York: McGraw Hill, 211–77.

Mishler, E. (1984) *The Discourse of Medicine: Dialectics of Medical Interviews*, Norwood, NJ: Ablex.

Ortega y Gasset, J. (1959) 'The difficulty of reading', *Diogenes* 28: 1–17.

Rumelhart, D.E. (1975) 'Notes on a schema for stories', in Bobrow, D.G. and Collins, A. (eds) *Representation and Understanding*, New York: Academic Press, 211–36.

Schank, R.C. and Abelson, R.P. (1977) *Scripts, Plans, Goals, and Understanding: An Inquiry into Human Knowledge Structures*, Hillsdale, NJ: Erlbaum.

Tannen, D. (1979) 'What's in a frame? Surface evidence for underlying expectations', in Freedle, R. (ed.) *New Directions in Discourse Processing*, Norwood, NJ: Ablex.

—— (1986) *That's Not What I Meant!: How Conversational Style Makes or Breaks your Relations with Others*, New York: William Morrow.

Identity and subjectivity

PART THREE

Identity and
subjectivity

Editors' introduction
to Part Five

AS WE SAW IN DISCUSSING Harvey Sacks' idea of membership categorization devices (Introduction to Part Three), the discursive world is populated by familiar categories of people. We tend to accept many people-categories as natural ones, even though, from a different point of view, we are endorsing distinctions and identities that people may well not feel they actually inhabit. Social identity, and the process of social identification, has become a key theme in discourse analysis where the ambition is often to scrutinize the use of identity categories and to challenge the 'natural' assumptions that follow.

The fact that we need to look closely at the local contextualization of identity in itself establishes the need for a discourse analysis perspective. Many other sorts of research – such as simple, quantitative surveys of media content – can give us overviews of how often and in what general ways social and ethnic groups are represented in mass media. Results from such research are important, but they need to be complemented by closer, text-based analysis. What often emerges from close analysis is that identity is rarely a fixed and immutable attribute that people are comfortable to display on all occasions. Rather, identity is a subtle and multilayered phenomenon, to the extent that, individually, we are usually reticent to accept (or, to use a more consumerist metaphor, to 'buy into') identity categories with reference to ourselves. We often experience identity as complex, and the term 'identity hybridity' has come into common usage in academic research. It refers to a sense of people being not fully contained by singular social categories of race, gender, age, place, and so on. It stands in opposition to what are often called 'essentialist' readings of identity – reducing identity simplistically to lists of who and what people 'essentially' are.

A good deal of sociological writing on selfhood echoes these sentiments. Not only should we recognize a multiplicity of personal and social identities, but we have to see identities being worked through discursive processes. For example, Anthony Giddens refers to 'the reflexive project of the self' (1990, 1991). He conceptualizes identity as a process, not as a state, and as a series of choices one continually makes about one's self and one's lifestyle rather than a set of personal attributes, and as emerging from one's relationships with others. Although Giddens does not offer an empirically oriented programme for the analysis of how these processes are actually mediated in discourse, he puts discourse at the centre of his theory of selfhood by adopting a discursive metaphor of identities construed as 'biographical narratives':

> The reflexive project of the self, which consists in the sustaining of coherent, yet continuously revised, biographical narratives, takes place in the context of multiple choice as filtered through abstract systems. In modern social life, the notion of lifestyle takes on a particular significance. The more tradition loses its hold, and the more daily life is reconstituted in terms of the dialectical interplay of the local and the global, the more individuals are forced to negotiate lifestyle choices among a diversity of options.
>
> (Giddens 1991: 5)

However, as Giddens points out, the new conditions of life that have contributed to this 'dynamization' of selfhood have generated restlessness and anxiety. Traditional systems of belief based on faith have given way to secularization and the emergence of a multitude of competing ideologies (of which religious faith is only one). The versions of self that people can choose for themselves come from an increasing pool of options that are often unfamiliar to them, bringing new risks and conflicting interests. Consumerist discourse and the discourse of lifestyle choice, propagated by advertising for example (see also the example of *Cosmopolitan* magazine in Chapter 11), stands in conflict with the discourse/lifestyle of prudence that dominates discussions of welfare system reforms. Giddens refers to these problems as 'tribulations of the self', and discusses them in terms of four pairs of oppositions: unification versus fragmentation, powerlessness versus appropriation, authority versus uncertainty, personalized versus commodified experience.

These dilemmas are ongoing in contemporary life and can only be resolved temporarily by engaging a particular type of ideology, relationship or activity, through which an individual can show his or her stance or allegiance towards a particular way of living. The sites for such position-taking are to be found in interaction between the self and the contexts in which the person operates, whether we think of other human agents, mediated communication or more abstract notions such as ideologies. In all these processes, discourse constitutes not only identities, but also social relations and categories, and other aspects of people's social lives (cf. Shotter 1993). The social constructionist approach to identity (e.g., Gergen 1985; Potter and Wetherell 1987; Potter 1996) is echoed quite explicitly in all the other chapters in this part of the *Reader*.

Deborah Cameron's chapter (Chapter 22) focuses on the discursive construction of heterosexual male identity in an informal conversation among five American college students. Rather like Giddens's 'reflexive project of the self', Cameron views gender identity as social performances (cf. Austin, Chapter 2, and our discussion of Goffman in the Introduction to Part Four). She draws on Judith Butler's ideas about gender as 'the repeated stylization of the body' (p. 339), which has a conventionalizing but not essentializing effect on how people enact and read masculinity or femininity – or preferably, masculinities and femininities in the plural. Thus, gender roles are not given, static attributes but recursive, dynamic patterns of *being* and *doing*.

Two resources that people have available to them to construct gender identities are, of course, *discourses of gender* and *gendered speech*. Cameron examines how the students in her study enact their male, heterosexual identity by engaging in a disparaging exchange of opinions about other men as 'gays'. In this specific instance and frame of talk, references to 'gayness' are largely a ritualistic, boundary-marking activity, as the classification of people as 'gay' in their conversation has little to do with the known sexuality of the objects of their gossip. However, displaying hostility to gay men is a way for these students to establish their preferred version of masculinity in this particular context of an all-male peer group. In other contexts, for example at a party with their girlfriends present, the heterosexual masculine identity of the same men could be enacted in totally different, possibly non-verbal ways.

Another interesting aspect of Cameron's chapter is the role of stereotypes and expectations in attributing meaning to the communicative strategies used by males and females. The five men engage in acts of asserting their solidarity and in-groupness through a stereotypically female verbal activity: gossip. However, their competent gossip is precisely used to allow them to dissociate themselves from the stereotypically non-masculine concerns (e.g., the supposed preoccupation of females and gays with their bodies). Besides, the men display certain conversational features (joint discourse production through interruptions and overlapping talk), which in female talk is associated with conversational cooperativity. In male talk, it seems more like competitiveness. Cameron shows how both these interpretations (cooperativity and competitiveness) may suit her data, and she warns against 'gender stereotyping that causes us to miss or minimize the status-seeking element in women friends' talk, and the connection-making dimension in men's' (p. 347).

We could also argue that by adopting a particular social language (Gee, Chapter 8) – gossip that 'others' gay people – the young men in Cameron's chapter style themselves as heterosexual males. *Style* and *stylization* are among key terms in current sociolinguistics and discourse analysis, especially in the way these terms relate to the discursive conditions of late-modern life (which is Anthony Giddens's term) and the globalized service-based industry (e.g. Heller 2011). The term 'style' typically refers to how an individual speaker uses language differently in different social circumstances – 'the range of variation within the speech of an individual speaker' (Bell 2009: 265). The older term 'register' is used with the same meaning (see Johnstone, Chapter 24). Traditionally, style shifts have been thought to occur in accordance with varying degrees of situational formality/informality (Joos 1961) or the degree of attention paid to speech by the speaker (Labov 1972). In these approaches, style has been treated as a correlate of rather simple and stable types of situations, and speakers' demographic characteristics. However, in more 'dynamic' approaches, style is not so much a stable attribute of a particular type of speaker or situation, but a reflexively managed resource for performing 'acts of identity' (Le Page and Tabouret-Keller 1985). It is in this tradition that Nikolas Coupland (2007) argues for style to be treated as a resource for strategic positioning of self and others in discourse. Style allows us to enact particular social personas, a form of self-identification with and self-differentiation from particular groups or group-orientations.

A related though narrower concept is *stylization*, i.e. a knowing display of language style(s) deemed in a particular situation to be non-normative, unpredictable, or an 'as if' construction (Rampton 1995; Coupland 2001). Stylization has its origins in the work of Mikhail Bakhtin on multiple voicing (Bakhtin 1981, 1986; Chapter 4) and in performative language use (Austin, Chapter 2; Bauman and Briggs 1990; Butler 1990). According to Bakhtin, language is always dialogic, which presupposes a rich mixing and multiplicity of voices, or the condition of 'heteroglossia', in all texts. Thus, identities are not autonomous and separate but involved and intercorporeal, produced as a series of stylizations by appropriating, reworking and subverting different voices. We can talk of identities being actively 'styled' (see Bell 2009) and of people 'crossing' (Rampton 1995) from one identity format into another. In her study of call centre employees, Deborah Cameron (2000) finds telephone workers modifying their speech, not because they are making choices about their own linguistic performance (*self*-styling in the traditional sense), but because they are given a script and a way of delivering this script by others. Their talk can be said to be stylized because they are involved in 'giving a performance, the "script" for which has been written by someone else' (Cameron 2000: 327). In this context, being scripted into stylized performance is a form of what Cameron calls 'verbal hygiene' (Cameron 1995), the imposition of a style complete with its commodification as a work-related skill or a lifestyle choice (cf. Thurlow and Jaworski 2006).

We chose to include Don Zimmerman's account of identity (Chapter 23) here because it shows how considerations of identity can be accommodated within CA frameworks. As we saw elsewhere (in the Introduction to Part Three), CA has tended to be rather silent about the social contexts in which it analyses conversational data. At least, CA is wary, on principle, of allowing conventional understandings of context to impinge on its own analyses. For example, CA researchers would argue that the fact that a speaker is a woman, or an older person, or a student, whatever, should not be presumed to be relevant to how talk proceeds. It would be necessary to *demonstrate* that this or that membership category is in fact relevant, presumably by showing that participants orient to it directly. This stance has always been controversial among non-CA discourse analysts, who would say that *not* to attend to identity categories is closing one's eyes, analytically speaking, to contextual considerations that *might well* be relevant, even though we don't have direct evidence that this is so. This is the controversy that Zimmerman sets out to resolve.

The key point Zimmerman makes is that we need to recognize what he calls *discourse identities*, and to distinguish them from *situated identities*. In the first data extract that Zimmerman considers, it emerges that the 'prank' caller to an emergency police telephone service has the situated identity of 'prank caller', which is out of tune with the police representative's situated identity of being an emergency call receiver, and out of tune with the identity that the situation tends to project onto callers to the emergency line. The discourse identities of the caller, as someone who embarks on 'an emergency call' in this context, discursively invites a response from the representative, and so on, turns out to be incompatible with the situated identity that we would expect to be in place (i.e., as someone in need of police help). Zimmerman goes on to add a third type of identity, *transportable identities,* which 'travel with individuals across situations' (p. 354), but which may remain latent or unactivated in discourse. Transportable identities include those linked to visible social category identifiers, such as maleness, youth, ethnicity, and so on, which may or may not become consequential in a given interaction. On the other hand, Zimmerman shows that situated identities (perhaps particularly in institutionalized interactions) and discourse identities are inevitably brought into play relative to each other. Once a situated identity (such as being a *bona fide* caller to an emergency service) is confirmed, it will shape the emergent structure of discourse. For example, once an emergency call handler has heard the salient initial details of the emergency situation, it becomes her or his turn to lead the conversation and solicit further details that will dictate the nature of the emergency response. Zimmerman's approach is particularly helpful in bridging a former gap between CA and other discourse analysts' concerns with context and genre, but staying within the disciplined remit of CA.

Identity and language come together in many ways. One of the strongest associations is to be found under the heading of *indexicality* (or indexical relations), when particular features of speech or a consolidated speech-style are taken to index social belonging. The concepts of accent and dialect are based in indexical relations between ways of speaking and regional community or social class memberships, and this makes it possible to talk of 'Cardiff dialect' (in Wales in the UK) or 'Pittsburgh English' (in the USA). Sociolinguists have been interested in speech style as an index of social belonging for many decades, although social change is complicating the circumstances under which we experience this sort of sociolinguistic identity. It may well be true that, overall, the range and diversity of indexical diversity indexed through speech is declining, but, as arguably a more significant change, it is also becoming less feasible for people to feel that their accents and dialects adequately define them. What does 'localness' mean nowadays, and how do people mark and orient to their own local circumstances?

Barbara Johnstone picks up these questions directly (in Chapter 24) in relation to Pittsburgh and the dialect phenomenon of 'Pittsburguese' (ways of speaking believed to be local to Pittsburgh). Johnstone finds that the idea of Pittsburguese is well-established in the city, and that many people literally 'buy into' Pittsburguese by purchasing and displaying products that celebrate it – bumper stickers, coffee mugs, etc., and, not least, the T-shirts that are Johnstone's main interest in the chapter. T-shirts can be thought of as mobile bits of 'linguistic landscaping', personalized resources to get commodified discourses and representations of Pittsburguese into circulation, and to imply links between discourse and local identification. One stimulating idea in Johnstone's analyses of the T-shirt data is that Pittsburguese has entered a new phase of indexical representation whereby the dialect as such has lost its intimate association with working-class Pittsburgh life and with the idea of being 'incorrect' local speech. It seems to have become a resource for people to express pride and nostalgia, but for people who may *not* claim to belong to the indexed social categories. Pittsburguese is 'enregistered' as a local way of speaking, and indeed as a local identity, but it circulates as a commodity whose social meaning is probably ephemeral and framed as ironic or playful.

In the final chapter in Part Five, Gerlinde Mautner extends the theme of 'discourses made public' in her analyses of public signage. Her main question is the fundamental question of discourse analysis: how, and by virtue of what, do texts carry the meanings attributed to them, and for whom? These questions are highly pertinent here, because Mautner is concerned with establishing how public signs gain and assert their legal authority over us as individuals and groups. As in Johnstone's T-shirt data, the texts in question are multi-modal, combining linguistic resources with visual (spatial, typographical, iconographic, material, etc.) resources. Since she is dealing with the political and legal contexts of public discourses, Mautner takes a self-consciously 'critical' line in her analyses, helping us to reassess what the 'C' in CDA implies (see our general Introduction and chapters in Part Six).

Mautner's chapter also develops an original account of the importance of social context, referring not only to the physical emplacement of signs and notices but to how they colour the physical spaces we inhabit as being 'more local, private and informal' or 'more global and more public'. Principally at issue is how signs explicitly or implicitly reference their own legal authority over us, for example as prescriptions or proscriptions backed by the force of specific laws and institutions. The fundamental issue is, therefore, not so much 'how signs work as texts', but 'why they work as discourse' (p. 396). The answer to this question takes us into issues we have already considered to some extent — the authority of convention and of institutionalized assumptions; the power of cultural ideologies; the constitutive and performative functions of discourse.

As we have argued in this Introduction, the emergence and re-emergence of the self is a process that is a function of a number of situational, social, cultural and historical factors. The role of discourse, in its various multi-modal guises, and its meaning-making capacity is paramount. Thus, the ways we speak (as males, females, doctors, patients, call centre operators, callers to the emergency services, and so on), the ways we speak to and about ourselves and others (the 'gays' in Cameron's data, Pittsburghers in Johnstone's data), the ways we are addressed (by the public signs in Mautner's data), turn individuals into *subjective* and *discursively constructed* selves. Even though we mistakenly treat our descriptive categories as 'natural' (cf. our general Introduction), and our descriptions of self and other may indeed be meant 'objectively', various private and institutional discourses are constitutive of us and others as *social* subjects. In other words, these discourses fabricate our subjectivities (Foucault 1972; see also Potter 1996; Mills 1997).

Deborah Cameron gives one compelling example of how our gendered social subjectivities are fabricated discursively from the day we are born:

> Recently a woman who had just had a baby told me that in the hospital nursery, each newborn's crib bore a label announcing its sex. The label said either "I'm a boy" or "It's a girl". Obviously none of the infants

was yet capable of speech. But on the day they were born, the culture hailed them differently: boys were hailed as active 'speaking subjects', unproblematically 'I'; girls were not. This is the order which, as they grow older, these children will be forced to enter.

(Cameron 1992: 161–2)

Subjectivity is the site of our consciousness, but far from being a fully independent entity, it is bound up by the structures and discourses of institutional and interpersonal order, power and ideology.

References

Bakhtin, M.M. (1981) *The Dialogic Imagination: Four Essays*, edited by M. Holquist, translated by Vern W. McGee, Austin: University of Texas Press.

—— (1986) *Speech Genres and Other Late Essays*, translated by Vern W. McGee, Austin: University of Texas Press.

Bauman, R. and Briggs, C. (1990) 'Poetics and performance as critical perspectives on language and social life', *Annual Review of Anthropology* 19: 59–88.

Bell, A. (2009) 'Language style as audience design', in N. Coupland and A. Jaworski (eds.) *The New Sociolinguistics Reader*, Basingstoke: Macmillan, 265–75.

Butler, J. (1990) *Gender Trouble: Feminism and the Subversion of Identity*, New York: Routledge.

Cameron, D. (1992) *Feminism and Linguistic Theory*, 2nd edition, London: Macmillan.

—— (1995) *Verbal Hygiene*, London: Routledge.

—— (2000) 'Styling the worker: gender and the commodification of language in the globalized service economy', *Journal of Sociolinguistics* 4(3): 323–47.

Coupland, N. (2001) 'Dialect stylisation in radio talk', *Language in Society* 30: 345–75.

—— (2007) *Style: Language Variation and Identity*, Cambridge: Cambridge University Press.

Foucault, M. (1972) *The Archaeology of Knowledge*, translated by S. Smith, London: Tavistock.

Gergen, K.J. (1985) 'Social constructionist inquiry: context and implications', in K.J. Gergen and K.E. Davis (eds.) *The Social Construction of the Person*, New York: Springer-Verlag.

Giddens, A. (1990) *The Consequences of Modernity*, Cambridge: Polity.

—— (1991) *Modernity and Self-Identity: Self and Society in the Late Modern Age*, Cambridge: Polity.

Heller, M. (2011) *Paths to Postnationalisms: A Critical Ethnography of Language and Identity*, New York: Oxford University Press.

Joos, M. (1961) *The Five Clocks*, New York: Harcourt Brace.

Labov, W. (1972) *Sociolinguistic Patterns*, Philadelphia: Pennsylvania University Press.

Le Page, R.B. and Tabouret-Keller, A. (1985) *Acts of Identity: Creole-based Approaches to Language and Ethnicity*, Cambridge: Cambridge University Press.

Mills, S. (1997) *Discourse*, London: Routledge.

Potter, J. (1996) *Representing Reality: Discourse, Rhetoric and Social Construction*, London: Sage.

Potter, J. and Wetherell, M. (1987) *Discourse and Social Psychology: Beyond Attitudes and Behaviour*, London: Sage.

Rampton, B. (1995) *Crossing: Language and Ethnicity among Adolescents*, London: Longman.

Shotter, J. (1993) 'Becoming someone', in N. Coupland and J.F. Nussbaum (eds.) *Discourse and Lifespan Identity*, Newbury Park, CA: Sage, 5–27.

Thurlow, C. and Jaworski, A. (2006) 'The alchemy of the upwardly mobile: symbolic capital and the stylization of elites in frequent-flyer programs', *Discourse and Society* 17: 131–67.

Chapter 22

Deborah Cameron

PERFORMING GENDER IDENTITY: YOUNG MEN'S TALK AND THE CONSTRUCTION OF HETEROSEXUAL MASCULINITY

Introduction

IN 1990, A 21-YEAR-OLD STUDENT in a language and gender class I was teaching at a college in the southern USA tape-recorded a sequence of casual conversation among five men; himself and four friends. This young man, whom I will call 'Danny',[1] had decided to investigate whether the informal talk of male friends would bear out generalizations about 'men's talk' that are often encountered in discussions of gender differences in conversational style – for example that it is competitive, hierarchically organized, centres on 'impersonal' topics and the exchange of information, and foregrounds speech genres such as joking, trading insults and sports statistics.

Danny reported that the stereotype of all-male interaction was borne out by the data he recorded. He gave his paper the title 'Wine, women, and sports'. Yet although I could agree that the data did contain the stereotypical features he reported, the more I looked at it, the more I saw other things in it too. Danny's analysis was not inaccurate, his conclusions were not unwarranted, but his description of the data was (in both senses) *partial*: it was shaped by expectations that caused some things to leap out of the record as 'significant', while other things went unremarked.

I am interested in the possibility that Danny's selective reading of his data was not just the understandable error of an inexperienced analyst. Analysis is never done without preconceptions, we can never be absolutely non-selective in our observations, and where the object of observation and analysis has to do with gender it is extraordinarily difficult to subdue certain expectations.

Source: Deborah Cameron, 'Performing gender identity: young men's talk and the construction of heterosexual identity', in Sally Johnson and Ulrike Hanna Meinhof (eds) *Language and Masculinity*, Oxford: Blackwell, 1997, 47–64.

One might speculate, for example, on why the vignettes of 'typical' masculine and feminine behaviour presented in popular books like Deborah Tannen's *You Just Don't Understand* (1990) are so often apprehended as immediately *recognizable*.[2] Is it because we have actually witnessed these scenarios occurring in real life, or is it because we can so readily supply the cultural script that makes them meaningful and 'typical'? One argument for the latter possibility is that if you *reverse* the genders in Tannen's anecdotes, it is still possible to supply a script which makes sense of the alleged gender difference. For example, Tannen remarks on men's reluctance to ask for directions while driving, and attributes it to men's greater concern for status (asking for help suggests helplessness). But if, as an experiment, you tell people it is women rather than men who are more reluctant to ask for directions, they will have no difficulty coming up with a different and equally plausible explanation – for instance that the reluctance reflects a typically feminine desire to avoid imposing on others, or perhaps a well-founded fear of stopping to talk to strangers.[3]

What this suggests is that the behaviour of men and women, whatever its substance may happen to be in any specific instance, is invariably read through a more general discourse on gender difference itself. That discourse is subsequently invoked to *explain* the pattern of gender differentiation in people's behaviour; whereas it might be more enlightening to say the discourse *constructs* the differentiation, makes it visible *as* differentiation.

I want to propose that conversationalists themselves often do the same thing I have just suggested analysts do. Analysts construct stories about other people's behaviour, with a view to making it exemplify certain patterns of gender difference; conversationalists construct stories about themselves and others, with a view to performing certain kinds of gender identity.

Identity and performativity

In 1990, the philosopher Judith Butler published an influential book called *Gender Trouble: Feminism and the Subversion of Identity*. Butler's essay is a postmodernist reconceptualization of gender, and it makes use of a concept familiar to linguists and discourse analysts from speech-act theory: *performativity*. For Butler, gender is *performative* – in her suggestive phrase 'constituting the identity it is purported to be'. Just as J.L. Austin [Chapter 2] maintained that illocutions like 'I promise' do not describe a pre-existing state of affairs but actually bring one into being, so Butler claims that 'feminine' and 'masculine' are not what we are, nor traits we *have*, but effects we produce by way of particular things we *do*: 'Gender is the repeated stylization of the body, a set of repeated acts within a rigid regulatory frame which congeal over time to produce the appearance of substance, of a "natural" kind of being' (p. 33).

This extends the traditional feminist account whereby gender is socially con-structed rather than 'natural', famously expressed in Simone de Beauvoir's dictum that 'one is not born, but rather becomes a woman'. Butler is saying that 'becoming a woman' (or a man) is not something you accomplish once and for all at an early stage of life. Gender has constantly to be reaffirmed and publicly displayed by repeatedly performing particular acts in accordance with the cultural norms (themselves historically and socially constructed, and consequently variable) which define 'masculinity' and 'femininity'.

This 'performative' model sheds an interesting light on the phenomenon of gendered *speech*. Speech too is a 'repeated stylization of the body'; the 'masculine' and 'feminine' styles of talking identified by researchers might be thought of as the 'congealed' result of repeated acts by social actors who are striving to constitute themselves as 'proper' men and women. Whereas sociolinguistics traditionally assume that people talk the way they do because of who they (already) are, the postmodernist approach suggests that people are who they are because of (among other things) the way they talk. This shifts the focus away from a simple cataloguing of differences between men and women to a subtler and more complex inquiry into how people use linguistic resources to produce gender differentiation. It also obliges us to attend to the 'rigid regulatory frame' within which people must make their choices – the norms that define what kinds of language are possible, intelligible and appropriate resources for performing masculinity or femininity.

A further advantage of this approach is that it acknowledges the instability and variability of gender identities, and therefore of the behaviour in which those identities are performed. While Judith Butler rightly insists that gender is regulated and policed by rather rigid social norms, she does not reduce men and women to automata, programmed by their early socialization to repeat forever the appropriate gendered behaviour, but treats them as conscious agents who may – albeit often at some social cost – engage in acts of transgression, subversion and resistance. As active producers rather than passive reproducers of gendered behaviour, men and women may use their awareness of the gendered meanings that attach to particular ways of speaking and acting to produce a variety of effects. This is important, because few, if any, analysts of data on men's and women's speech would maintain that the differences are as clear-cut and invariant as one might gather from such oft-cited dichotomies as 'competitive/cooperative' and 'report talk/rapport talk'. People *do* perform gender differently in different contexts, and do sometimes behave in ways we would normally associate with the 'other' gender. The conversation to which we now turn is a notable case in point.

The conversation: wine, women, sports . . . and other men

The five men who took part in the conversation, and to whom I will give the pseudonyms Al, Bryan, Carl, Danny and Ed, were demographically a homogeneous group: white, middle-class American suburbanites aged 21, who attended the same university and belonged to the same social network on campus. This particular conversation occurred in the context of one of their commonest shared leisure activities: watching sports at home on television.

Throughout the period covered by the tape-recording there is a basketball game on screen, and participants regularly make reference to what is going on in the game. Sometimes these references are just brief interpolated comments, which do not disrupt the flow of ongoing talk on some other topic; sometimes they lead to extended discussion. At all times, however, it is a legitimate conversational move to comment on the basketball game. The student who collected the data drew attention to the status of sport as a resource for talk available to North American men of all classes and racial/ethnic groups, to strangers as well as friends, suggesting that 'sports talk' is a typically 'masculine' conversational genre in the US, something all culturally competent males know how to do.

But 'sports talk' is by no means the only kind of talk being done. The men also recount the events of their day – what classes they had and how these went; they discuss mundane details of their domestic arrangements, such as who is going to pick up groceries; there is a debate about the merits of a certain kind of wine; there are a couple of longer narratives, notably one about an incident when two men sharing a room each invited a girlfriend back without their room-mate's knowledge – and discovered this at the most embarrassing moment possible. Danny's title 'Wine, women, and sports' is accurate insofar as all these subjects are discussed at some length.

When one examines the data, however, it becomes clear there is one very significant omission in Danny's title. Apart from basketball, the single most prominent theme in the recorded conversation, as measured by the amount of time devoted to it, is 'gossip': discussion of several persons not present but known to the participants, with a strong focus on critically examining these individuals' appearance, dress, social behaviour and sexual mores. Like the conversationalists themselves, the individuals under discussion are all men. Unlike the conversationalists, however, the individuals under discussion are identified as 'gay'.

The topic of 'gays' is raised by Ed, only a few seconds into the tape-recorded conversation:

> ED: Mugsy Bogues (.) my name is Lloyd Gompers I am a homosexual (.) you know what the (.) I saw the new Remnant I should have grabbed you know the title? Like the head thing?

'Mugsy Bogues' (the name of a basketball player) is an acknowledgement of the previous turn, which concerned the on-screen game. Ed's next comment appears off-topic, but he immediately supplies a rationale for it, explaining that he 'saw the new Remnant' – *The Remnant* being a deliberately provocative right-wing campus newspaper whose main story that week had been an attack on the 'Gay Ball', a dance sponsored by the college's Gay Society.

The next few turns are devoted to establishing a shared view of the Gay Ball and of homosexuality generally. Three of the men, Al, Bryan and Ed, are actively involved in this exchange. A typical sequence is the following:

> AL: gays=
> ED: =gays w[hy? that's what it should read [gays why?
> BRYAN: [gays]   [I know]

What is being established as 'shared' here is a view of gays as alien (that is, the group defines itself as heterosexual and puzzled by homosexuality ('gays, why?'), and also to some extent comical. Danny comments at one point, 'it's hilarious', and Ed caps the sequence discussing the Gay Ball with the witticism:

> ED: the question is who wears the boutonnière and who wears the
>   corsage, flip for it? or do they both just wear flowers coz they're
>   fruits

It is at this point that Danny introduces the theme that will dominate the conversation for some time: gossip about individual men who are said to be gay. Referring to the only other man in his language and gender class, Danny begins

> DANNY: My boy Ronnie was uh speaking up on the male perspective
>   today (.) way too much

The section following this contribution is structured around a series of references to other 'gay' individuals known to the participants as classmates. Bryan mentions 'the most effeminate guy I've ever met' and 'that really gay guy in our Age of Revolution class'. Ed remarks that 'you have never seen more homos than we have in our class. Homos, dykes, homos, dykes, everybody is a homo or a dyke'. He then focuses on a 'fat, queer, goofy guy . . . [who's] as gay as night' [sic], and on a 'blond hair, snide little queer weird shit', who is further described as a 'butt pirate'. Some of these references, but not all, initiate an extended discussion of the individual concerned. The content of these discussions will bear closer examination.

'The antithesis of man'

One of the things I initially found most puzzling about the whole 'gays' sequence was that the group's criteria for categorizing people as gay appeared to have little to do with those people's known or suspected sexual preferences or practices. The terms 'butt pirate' and 'butt cutter' were used, but surprisingly seldom; it was unclear to me that the individuals referred to really were homosexual, and in one case where I actually knew the subject of discussion, I seriously doubted it.

Most puzzling is an exchange between Bryan and Ed about the class where 'everybody is a homo or a dyke', in which they complain that 'four homos' are continually 'hitting on' [making sexual overtures to] one of the women, described as 'the ugliest-ass bitch in the history of the world'. One might have thought that a defining feature of a 'homo' would be his lack of interest in 'hitting on' women. Yet no one seems aware of any contradiction in this exchange.

I think this is because the deviance indicated for this group by the term 'gay' is not so much *sexual* deviance as *gender* deviance. Being 'gay' means failing to measure up to the group's standards of masculinity or femininity. This is why it makes sense to call someone '*really* gay': unlike same- versus other-sex preference, conformity to gender norms can be a matter of degree. It is also why hitting on an 'ugly-ass bitch' can be classed as 'homosexual' behaviour – proper masculinity requires that the object of public sexual interest be not just female, but minimally attractive.

Applied by the group to men, 'gay' refers in particular to insufficiently masculine appearance, clothing and speech. To illustrate this I will reproduce a longer sequence of conversation about the 'really gay guy in our Age of Revolution class', which ends with Ed declaring: 'he's the antithesis of man'.

BRYAN: uh you know that really gay guy in our Age of Revolution
         class who sits in front of us? he wore shorts again, by
         the way, it's like 42 degrees out he wore shorts again
         [laughter] [Ed: That guy] it's like a speedo, he wears a
         speedo to class (.) he's got incredibly skinny legs [Ed:
         it's worse] you know=
ED: =you know
         like those shorts women volleyball players wear? it's like those (.)
         it's l[ike
BRYAN: [you know what's even more ridicu[lous? When
ED: [French cut spandex]
BRYAN: you wear those shorts and like a parka on . . .
(5 lines omitted)
BRYAN: he's either got some condition that he's got to like have
         his legs exposed at all times or else he's got really good
         legs=
ED: =he's probably he'[s like
CARL: [he really likes
BRYAN: =he
ED: =he's like at home combing his leg hairs=
CARL: his legs =
BRYAN: he doesn't have any leg hair though=   [yes and oh
ED: =he real[ly likes
ED: his legs =
AL: =very long very white and very skinny
BRYAN: those ridiculous Reeboks that are always (indeciph)
         and goofy white socks always striped=   [tube socks
ED: =that's [right
ED: he's the antithesis of man

In order to demonstrate that certain individuals are 'the antithesis of man', the group
engages in a kind of conversation that might well strike us as the antithesis of 'men's
talk'. It is unlike the 'wine, women, and sports' stereotype of men's talk – indeed,
rather closer to the stereotype of 'women's talk' – in various ways, some obvious,
and some less so.

     The obvious ways in which this sequence resembles conventional notions of
'women's talk' concern its purpose and subject-matter. This is talk about people,
not things, and 'rapport talk' rather than 'report talk' – the main point is clearly not
to exchange information. It is 'gossip', and serves one of the most common purposes
of gossip, namely affirming the solidarity of an in-group by constructing absent others
as an out-group, whose behaviour is minutely examined and found wanting.

     The specific subjects on which the talk dwells are conventionally 'feminine' ones:
clothing and bodily appearance. The men are caught up in a contradiction: their
criticism of the 'gays' centres on their unmanly interest in displaying their bodies,
and the inappropriate garments they choose for this purpose (bathing costumes worn
to class, shorts worn in cold weather with parkas which render the effect ludicrous,
clothing which resembles the outfits of 'women volleyball players'). The implication

is that real men just pull on their jeans and leave it at that. But in order to pursue this line of criticism, the conversationalists themselves must show an acute awareness of such 'unmanly' concerns as styles and materials. ('French cut spandex', 'tube socks'), what kind of clothes go together, and which men have 'good legs'. They are impelled, paradoxically, to talk about men's bodies as a way of demonstrating their own total lack of sexual interest in those bodies.

The less obvious ways in which this conversation departs from stereotypical notions of 'men's talk' concern its *formal* features. Analyses of men's and women's speech style are commonly organized around a series of global oppositions, e.g. men's talk is 'competitive', whereas women's is 'cooperative'; men talk to gain 'status', whereas women talk to forge 'intimacy' and 'connection'; men do 'report talk' and women 'rapport talk'. Analysts working with these oppositions typically identify certain formal or organizational features of talk as markers of 'competition' and 'cooperation' etc. The analyst then examines which kinds of features predominate in a set of conversational data, and how they are being used.

In the following discussion, I too will make use of the conventional oppositions as tools for describing data, but I will be trying to build up an argument that their use is problematic. The problem is not merely that the men in my data fail to fit their gender stereotype perfectly. More importantly, I think it is often the stereotype itself that underpins analytic judgements that a certain form is cooperative rather than competitive, or that people are seeking status rather than connection in their talk. As I observed about Deborah Tannen's vignettes, many instances of behaviour will support either interpretation, or both; we use the speaker's gender, and our beliefs about what sort of behaviour makes sense for members of that gender, to rule some interpretations in and others out.

Cooperation

Various scholars, notably Jennifer Coates (1989), have remarked on the 'cooperative' nature of informal talk among female friends, drawing attention to a number of linguistic features which are prominent in data on all-female groups. Some of these, like hedging and the use of epistemic modals, are signs of attention to others' face, aimed at minimizing conflict and securing agreement. Others, such as latching of turns, simultaneous speech where this is not interpreted by participants as a violation of turn-taking rights, and the repetition or recycling of lexical items and phrases across turns, are signals that a conversation is a 'joint production': that participants are building on one another's contributions so that ideas are felt to be group property rather than the property of a single speaker.

On these criteria, the conversation here must be judged as highly cooperative. For example, in the extract reproduced above, a strikingly large number of turns (around half) begin with 'you know' and/or contain the marker 'like' ('you know like those shorts women volleyball players wear?'). The functions of these items (especially 'like') in younger Americans' English are complex and multiple, and may include the cooperative, mitigating/face-protecting functions that Coates and Janet Holmes (1984) associate with hedging. Even where they are not clearly hedges, however, in this interaction they function in ways that relate to the building of group involvement and consensus. They often seem to mark information as 'given' within the group's discourse (that is, 'you know', 'like', 'X' presupposes that the addressee is indeed familiar with X); 'you know' has the kind of hearer-orientated affective function (taking others into account or inviting their agreement) which Holmes attributes to certain tag-questions; while 'like' in addition seems to function for these speakers as a marker of high involvement. It appears most frequently at moments when the interactants are, by other criteria such as intonation, pitch, loudness, speech rate, incidence of simultaneous speech, and of 'strong' or taboo language, noticeably excited, such as the following:

> ED: he's I mean he **like** a real artsy fartsy fag he's **like** (indeciph)
>   he's so gay he's got this **like** really high voice and wire rim
>   glasses and he sits next to the ugliest-ass bitch in the history
>   of the world
> ED: [and
> BRYAN: [and they're all hitting on her too, **like** four
> ED: [I know it's **like** four homos hitting on her
> BRYAN: guys [hitting on her

It is also noticeable throughout the long extract reproduced earlier how much latching and simultaneous speech there is, as compared to other forms of turn transition involving either short or long pauses and gaps, or interruptions which silence the interruptee. Latching – turn transition without pause or overlap – is often taken as a mark of cooperation because in order to latch a turn so precisely onto the preceding turn, the speaker has to attend closely to others' contributions.

The last part of the reproduced extract, discussing the 'really gay' guy's legs, is an excellent example of jointly produced discourse, as the speakers cooperate to build a detailed picture of the legs and what is worn on them, a picture which overall could not be attributed to any single speaker. This sequence contains many instances of latching, repetition of one speaker's words by another speaker (Ed recycles Carl's whole turn, 'he really likes his legs', with added emphasis), and it also contains something that is relatively rare in the conversation as a whole, repeated tokens of hearer support like 'yes' and 'that's right'.[4]

There are, then, points of resemblance worth remarking on between these men's talk and similar talk among women as reported by previous studies. The question does arise, however, whether this male conversation has the other important hallmark of women's gossip, namely an egalitarian or non-hierarchical organization of the floor.

Competition

In purely quantitative terms, this conversation cannot be said to be egalitarian. The extracts reproduced so far are representative of the whole insofar as they show Ed and Bryan as the dominant speakers, while Al and Carl contribute fewer and shorter turns (Danny is variable; there are sequences where he contributes very little, but when he talks he often contributes turns as long as Ed's and Bryan's, and he also initiates topics). Evidence thus exists to support an argument that there is a hierarchy in this conversation, and there is competition, particularly between the two dominant speakers, Bryan and Ed (and to a lesser extent Ed and Danny). Let us pursue this by looking more closely at Ed's behaviour.

Ed introduces the topic of homosexuality, and initially attempts to keep 'ownership' of it. He cuts off Danny's first remark on the subject with a reference to *The Remnant*: 'what was the article? cause you know they bashed them they were like'. At this point Danny interrupts: it is clearly an interruption because in this context the preferred interpretation of 'like' is quotative – Ed is about to repeat what the gay-bashing article in *The Remnant* said. In addition to interrupting so that Ed falls silent, Danny contradicts Ed, saying 'they didn't actually (.) cut into them big'. A little later on during the discussion of the Gay Ball, Ed makes use of a common competitive strategy, the joke or witty remark which 'caps' other contributions (the 'flowers and fruits' joke quoted above). This, however, elicits no laughter, no matching jokes and indeed no take-up of any kind. It is followed by a pause and a change of direction if not of subject, as Danny begins the gossip that will dominate talk for several minutes.

This immediately elicits a matching contribution from Bryan. As he and Danny talk, Ed makes two unsuccessful attempts to regain the floor. One, where he utters the prefatory remark 'I'm gonna be very honest', is simply ignored. His second strategy is to ask (about the person Bryan and Danny are discussing) 'what's this guy's last name?'. First Bryan asks him to repeat the question, then Danny replies 'I don't know what the hell it is'.

A similar pattern is seen in the long extract reproduced above, where Ed makes two attempts to interrupt Bryan's first turn ('That guy' and 'it's worse'), neither of which succeeds. He gets the floor eventually by using the 'you know, like' strategy. And from that point, Ed does orient more to the norms of joint production; he overlaps others to produce simultaneous speech but does not interrupt; he produces more latched turns, recyclings and support tokens.

So far I have been arguing that even if the speakers, or some of them, compete, they are basically engaged in a collaborative and solidary enterprise (reinforcing the bonds within the group by denigrating people outside it), an activity in which all speakers participate, even if some are more active than others. Therefore I have drawn attention to the presence of 'cooperative' features, and have argued that more extreme forms of hierarchical and competitive behaviour are not rewarded by the group. I could, indeed, have argued that by the end, Ed and Bryan are not so much 'competing' – after all, their contributions are not antagonistic to one another but tend to reinforce one another – as engaging in a version of the 'joint production of discourse'.

Yet the data might also support a different analysis in which Ed and Bryan are simply *using* the collaborative enterprise of putting down gay men as an occasion to engage in verbal duelling where points are scored – against fellow group members rather than against the absent gay men – by dominating the floor and coming up with more and more extravagant put-downs. In this alternative analysis, Ed does not so much modify his behaviour as 'lose' his duel with Bryan. 'Joint production' or 'verbal duelling' – how do we decide?

Deconstructing oppositions

One response to the problem of competing interpretations raised above might be that the opposition I have been working with – 'competitive' versus 'cooperative' behaviour – is inherently problematic, particularly if one is taken to exclude the other. Conversation can and usually does contain both cooperative and competitive elements: one could argue (along with Grice [Chapter 3]) that talk must by definition involve a certain minimum of cooperation, and also that there will usually be some degree of competition among speakers, if not for the floor itself then for the attention or the approval of others.

The global competitive/cooperative opposition also encourages the lumping together under one heading or the other of things that could in principle be distinguished. 'Cooperation' might refer to agreement on the aims of talk, respect for other speakers' rights or support for their contributions; but there is not always perfect co-occurrence among these aspects, and the presence of any one of them need not rule out a 'competitive' element. Participants in a conversation or other speech event may compete with each other and at the same time be pursuing a shared project or common agenda (as in ritual insult sessions); they may be in severe disagreement but punctiliously observant of one another's speaking rights (as in a formal debate, say); they may be overtly supportive, and at the same time covertly hoping to score points for their supportiveness.

This last point is strangely overlooked in some discussions of women's talk. Women who pay solicitous attention to one another's face are often said to be seeking connection or good social relations *rather than* status; yet one could surely argue that attending to others' face and attending to one's own are not mutually exclusive here. The 'egalitarian' norms of female friendship groups are, like all norms, to some degree coercive: the rewards and punishments precisely concern one's status within the group (among women, however, this status is called 'popularity' rather than 'dominance'). A woman may gain status by displaying the correct degree of concern for others, and lose status by displaying too little concern for others and too much for herself. Arguably, it is gender-stereotyping that causes us to miss or minimize the status-seeking element in women friends' talk, and the connection-making dimension of men's.

How to do gender with language

I hope it will be clear by now that my intention in analysing male gossip is not to suggest that the young men involved have adopted a 'feminine' conversational style. On the contrary, the main theoretical point I want to make concerns the folly of making any such claim. To characterize the conversation I have been considering as 'feminine' on the basis that it bears a significant resemblance to conversations among women friends would be to miss the most important point about it, that it is not only *about* masculinity, it is a sustained performance *of* masculinity. What is important in gendering talk is the 'performative gender work' the talk is doing; its role in constituting people as gendered subjects.

To put matters in these terms is not to deny that there may be an empirically observable association between a certain genre or style of speech and speakers of a particular gender. In practice this is undeniable. But we do need to ask: in virtue of what does the association hold? Can we give an account that will not be vitiated by cases where it does *not* hold? For it seems to me that conversations like the one I have analysed leave, say, Deborah Tannen's contention that men do not do 'women's talk', because they simply *do not know how*, looking lame and unconvincing. If men rarely engage in a certain kind of talk, an explanation is called for; but if they do engage in it even very occasionally, an explanation in terms of pure ignorance will not do.

I suggest the following explanation. Men and women do not live on different planets, but are members of cultures in which a large amount of discourse about gender is constantly circulating. They do not only learn, and then mechanically reproduce, ways of speaking 'appropriate' to their own sex; they learn a much broader set of gendered meanings that attach in rather complex ways to different ways of speaking, and they produce their own behaviour in the light of those meanings.

This behaviour will vary. Even the individual who is most unambiguously committed to traditional notions of gender has a range of possible gender identities to draw on. Performing masculinity or femininity 'appropriately' cannot mean giving exactly the same performance regardless of the circumstances. It may involve different strategies in mixed and single-sex company, in private and in public settings, in the various social positions (parent, lover, professional, friend) that someone might regularly occupy in the course of everyday life.

Since gender is a relational term, and the minimal requirement for 'being a man' is 'not being a woman', we may find that in many circumstances, men are under pressure to constitute themselves as masculine linguistically by avoiding forms of talk whose primary association is with women/femininity. But this is not invariant, which begs the question: under what circumstances does the contrast with women lose its salience as a constraint on men's behaviour? When can men do so-called 'feminine' talk without threatening their constitution as men? Are there cases when it might actually be to their advantage to do this?

When and why do men gossip?

Many researchers have reported that both sexes engage in gossip, since its social functions (like affirming group solidarity and serving as an unofficial conduit for information) are of universal relevance, but its cultural meaning (for us) is undeniably 'feminine'. Therefore we might expect to find most men avoiding it, or disguising it as something else, especially in mixed settings where they are concerned to mark their difference from women. In the conversation discussed above, however, there are no women for the men to differentiate themselves from; whereas *there is* the perceived danger that so often accompanies western male homosociality: homosexuality. Under these circumstances perhaps it becomes acceptable to transgress one gender norm ('men don't gossip, gossip is for girls') in order to affirm what in this context is a more important norm ('men in all-male groups must unambiguously display their heterosexual orientation').

In these speakers' understanding of gender, gay men, like women, provide a contrast group against whom masculinity can be defined. This principle of contrast seems to set limits on the permissibility of gossip for these young men. Although they discuss other men besides the 'gays' – professional basketball players – they could not be said to gossip about them. They talk about the players' skills and their records, not their appearance, personal lives or sexual activities. Since the men admire the basketball players, identifying *with* them rather than *against* them, such talk would border dangerously on what for them is obviously taboo: desire for other men.

Ironically, it seems likely that the despised gay men are the *only* men about whom these male friends can legitimately talk among themselves in such intimate terms without compromising the heterosexual masculinity they are so anxious to display – though in a different context, say with their girlfriends, they might be able to discuss the basketball players differently. The presence of a woman, especially a heterosexual partner, displaces the dread spectre of homosexuality, and makes other kinds of talk possible; though by the same token her presence might make certain kinds of talk that take place among men *im*possible. What counts as acceptable talk for men is a complex matter in which all kinds of contextual variables play a part.

In this context – a private conversation among male friends – it could be argued that to gossip, either about your sexual exploits with women or about the repulsiveness of gay men (these speakers do both), is not just one way, but the most appropriate way to display heterosexual masculinity. In another context (in public, or with a larger and less close-knit group of men), the same objective might well be pursued through explicitly agonistic strategies, such as yelling abuse at women or gays in the street, or exchanging sexist and homophobic jokes. *Both* strategies could be said to do performative gender work: in terms of what they do for the speakers involved, one is not more 'masculine' than the other, they simply belong to different settings in which heterosexual masculinity may (or must) be put on display.

Conclusion

I hope that my discussion of the conversation I have analysed makes the point that it is unhelpful for linguists to continue to use models of gendered speech which imply that masculinity and femininity are monolithic constructs, automatically giving rise to predictable (and utterly different) patterns of verbal interaction. At the same time, I hope it might make us think twice about the sort of analysis that implicitly seeks the meaning (and sometimes the *value*) of an interaction among men or women primarily in the style, rather than the substance, of what is said. For although, as I noted earlier in relation to Judith Butler's work, it is possible for men and women to performatively subvert or resist the prevailing codes of gender, there can surely be no convincing argument that this is what Danny and his friends are doing. Their conversation is animated by entirely traditional anxieties about being seen at all times as red-blooded heterosexual males: not women and not queers. Their skill as performers does not alter the fact that what they perform is the same old gendered script.

Transcription conventions

=	latching
[	turn onset overlaps previous turn
[ ]	turn is completely contained within another speaker's turn
?	rising intonation on utterance
(.)	short pause
(indeciph)	indecipherable speech
italics	emphatic stress on italicized item

Notes

1   Because the student concerned is one of the speakers in the conversation I analyse, and the nature of the conversation makes it desirable to conceal participants' identities (indeed, this was one of the conditions on which the data were collected and subsequently passed on to me), I will not give his real name here, but I want to acknowledge his generosity in making his recording and transcript available to me, and to thank him for a number of insights I gained by discussing the data with him as well as by reading his paper. I am also grateful to the other young men who participated. All their names, and the names of other people they mention, have been changed, and all pseudonyms used are (I hope) entirely fictitious.

2   I base this assessment of reader response on my own research with readers of Tannen's book (see Cameron 1995: Chapter 5), on non-scholarly reviews of the book, and on reader studies of popular self-help generally (e.g., Lichterman 1992; Simonds 1992).

3   I am indebted to Penelope Eckert for describing this 'thought experiment', which she has used in her own teaching (though the specific details of the example are not an exact rendition of Eckert's observations).

4   It is a rather consistent research finding that men use such minimal responses significantly less often than women, and in this respect the present data conform to expectations – there are very few minimal responses of any kind. I would argue, however, that active listenership, involvement and support are not *absent* in the talk of this group; they are marked by other means such as high levels of latching/simultaneous speech, lexical recycling and the use of *like*.

References

Butler, J. (1990) *Gender Trouble: Feminism and the Subversion of Identity*, New York: Routledge.
Cameron, D. (1995) *Verbal Hygiene*, London: Routledge.
Coates, J. (1989) 'Gossip revisited: language in all-female groups', in Coates, J. and Cameron, D. (eds) *Women in their Speech Communities*, Harlow: Longman, 94–121.

Chapter 23

Don H. Zimmerman

IDENTITY, CONTEXT AND INTERACTION

THE CONCEPT OF 'IDENTITY', particularly in relation to discourse, can be variously specified, for example, as an independent variable accounting for participants' use of particular linguistic or discourse devices; as a means of referring to and making inferences about self and other; as a constructed display of group membership; as a rhetorical device; and so on. In this chapter, I propose to treat identity as an element of context for talk-in-interaction. Indeed, any of the previously listed applications of the concept would depend in some way on identity as a contextual element of a given discourse. I note here that I use the term 'discourse' in this chapter as shorthand for referring to talk-in-interaction, the domain of concerted social activity pursued through the use of linguistic, sequential and gestural resources. In this usage, it is primarily a behavioural rather than symbolic domain, less a 'text' to be interpreted than a texture of orderly, repetitive and reproducible activities to be described and analysed. Shortly, I will elaborate on the notion of identity-as-context and distinguish between different types of identity. First, however, I briefly consider the link between interaction and the social order.

Erving Goffman (1983) proposed that there is a domain of face-to-face interaction – what he termed the interaction order – that is only loosely coupled with what is generally taken to be the 'macro' social order. This proposal suggests that the organization of social interaction can be looked at as a phenomenon in its own right, and although conversation analysis antedates Goffman's valedictory formulation, it nevertheless abundantly confirms that suggestion. However, I want here to go a step further and propose that although social interaction has a detailed organization that is largely independent of social structure, the 'loose coupling' that Goffman refers to, it nevertheless is tightly articulated with the environing social world. I propose further that participants' orientations to this or that identity – their own and others'

Source: Don H. Zimmerman, 'Identity, context and interaction', in Charles Antaki and Sue Widdicombe (eds) *Identities in Talk*, London: Sage, 1998, 87–106.

– is a crucial link between interaction on concrete occasions and encompassing social orders (see Wilson 1991). Indeed, in so far as a social order presupposes recurrent patterns of action, its fundamental substrate is the organization of interaction – a view of which Goffman was wary (1983: 8–9). However, to view the interaction order as furnishing the building blocks for a social world beyond the instant situation is not to say that the 'larger' social order is 'nothing but' interaction; rather, that the interaction order provides the mechanisms that enable not only interaction between social actors, but also larger formations that arise from such activities (see Schegloff 1991, 1996: 54).

The main focus of this chapter is how oriented-to identities provide both the *proximal* context (the turn-by-turn orientation to developing sequences of action at the interactional level) and the *distal* context for social activities (the oriented-to 'extra-situational' agendas and concerns accomplished *through* such endogenously developing sequences of interaction). Discourse identities bring into play relevant components of conversational machinery, while situated identities deliver pertinent agendas, skills and relevant knowledge, allowing participants to accomplish various projects in an orderly and reproducible way. Activities in a given setting achieve their distinctive shape through an *articulation* of discourse and situated identities for each participant and an *alignment* of these identities across participants, linking the proximal and distal contexts of action. Thus, in the most general sense, the notion of identity-as-context refers to the way in which the articulation/alignment of discourse and situated identities furnishes for the participants a continuously evolving framework within which their actions, vocal or otherwise, assume a particular meaning, import and interactional consequentiality (see Goodwin 1996: 374–6).

The linking of proximate and distal contexts of action through the alignment of discourse and situated identities is a fundamental interactional issue. This can be seen most clearly when troubles of articulation or alignment occur. Consider the following [call] to an emergency number in the Midwestern United States:

(1) (MCE 20–10/196)

```
 1   CT: Mid-City police an fire
 2       ((background noise and music on the line))
 3   C: (YA:H) Thiz iz thuh () ((voice is very
 4       slurred))
 5       (1.5) ((loud background noise))
 6   CT: Hello:?
 7       (0.4)
 8   C: YEA:H?
 9   → CT: Wadidja want'?
10       (0.5)
11   C: Yea:h we-we wan' forn'ca:y (h) heh
12       (0.6) ((background voices, noise))
13   → CT: 'Bout wha:t?
14       (5.3)
15       ((noise, voice: 'hey gimme dat. . .'))
16   C: Hay =l've = uh ri:ddle for ya:
```

```
17    (0.3)
18    CT: HU:H?
19    C: I have uh ri:ddle for ya
20    (0.3)
21  → CT: I don't have ti:me f'r riddles = do-ya wanna
22    squa:d'rno:t =
23    C: = NO: jes' uh simple que:stion,
24    (0.4) ((loud music)) Wha' fucks an leaks
25    like uh ti:ger,
26    (0.2)
27    CT: HU:H?
28    C: What fucks an leaks like uh ti:ger,
29    Huh? ((background noise))
30    CT: Good bye
31    C: Why:?
32    ((disconnect))
```

Below, I will discuss in more detail the organization of calls to emergency numbers, and particularly how this organization aligns caller and the answerer. For present purposes, the call may be glossed as follows (see Zimmerman 1990). To begin, the caller seeks explicitly to take the discourse identity (see below) of a story teller or a riddler (line 16, 'hay =I've = uh ri:ddle for ya'). When the call-taker refuses to be a recipient for the riddle and asks (lines 21–2) if he needs police services (thereby explicitly proposing the capacity in which he should be calling), he appears momentarily to shift identities, countering that he wants 'an answer to a simple question', which, of course, turns out to be the riddle (lines 23–5).

Each party proposes a different footing for the call, that is, a different alignment of situated identities within which the sense and relevance of the exchange is to be understood and responded to. While the call-taker speaks 'seriously', that is, in her identity as call-taker, the caller aligns himself not as a 'serious' complainant, but as its alternative, a non-serious identity, 'prank' caller.

Thus, to the extent that this sequence is in fact a 'prank' being played on the complaint-taker, this is an instance of an attempt to alter the routine framing of citizen calls to the police (Whalen and Zimmerman 1990; Zimmerman 1984, 1992a, 1992b). It is important to observe in this regard the almost heroic character of the call-taker's attempt to manage the call on a routine footing. For example, in lines 9 and 13 she seeks to elicit some indication that the call is a request for service. When the caller then offers to tell her a riddle, the dispatcher rebukes him with 'I don't have ti:me for riddles', but mounts yet another attempt to allow the caller to disclose a possible emergency with her query ('do = ya = wanna squa:d'rno:t?') in line 21. When it becomes clear to her that the caller proposes a different footing for the encounter (line 28), she initiates a closing of the call (line 30).

Note that the problems of this call stem from the misalignment of situated identities across the participants. Moreover, this call shows that alignment is an interactional issue, that is, it is something that cannot be secured unilaterally. Neither party was successful in inducing the other to align with their proposed identity sets and this impasse ultimately leads to the termination of the call. This suggests that when alignment is achieved, it must entail interactional ratification by the parties involved, and also that the interaction will be troubled to the extent that alignment is problematic (see the discussion of the Dallas Fire Department call, below).

The riddle call is useful in that it permits us to see how crucial the alignment of discourse and situated identities is for the conduct of an emergency call. I want to turn now to a brief examination of the nature of discourse and situated identities, and of a third type, transportable identities.

Discourse, situational and transportable identities

Discourse, situational and transportable identities have different home territories. Discourse identities are integral to the moment-by-moment organization of the interaction. Participants assume discourse identities as they engage in the various sequentially organized activities: current speaker, listener, story teller, story recipient, questioner, answerer, repair initiator and so on (see below). In initiating an action, one party assumes a particular identity and projects a reciprocal identity for co-participant(s). As suggested in the discussion of the riddle call just above, such projections are subject to ratification (the recipient assuming the projected identity) or revision (in the case where, for example, a recipient of a question locates some aspect of that action as a trouble source, becoming a repair initiator instead of the answerer).

Situated identities come into play within the precincts of particular types of situation. Indeed, such situations are effectively brought into being and sustained by participants engaging in activities and respecting agendas that display an orientation to, and an alignment of, particular identity sets, for example, in the case of emergency telephone calls, citizen-complainant and call-taker. In turn, the pursuit of such agendas rests on the underlying alignment of discourse identities.

Finally, transportable identities travel with individuals across situations and are potentially relevant in and for any situation and in and for any spate of interaction. They are latent identities that 'tag along' with individuals as they move through their daily routines in the following sense: they are identities that are usually visible, that is, assignable or claimable on the basis of physical or culturally based insignia which furnish the intersubjective basis for categorization. Here, it is important to distinguish between the registering of *visible* indicators of identity and *oriented-to* identity which pertains to the capacity in which an individual should *act* in a particular situation. Thus, a participant may be *aware* of the fact that a co-interactant is classifiable as a young person or a male without orienting to those identities as being relevant to the instant interaction.

The distinction between *apprehension* of the transportable identity of the other, and the *orientation to* incumbency in that category as the basis of action, is critical for empirical investigation. Parties to an interaction may recognize at some level that they and their co-interactants can be classified in particular ways. Moreover, such classificatory information could be used to refer to or characterize individuals as a means of *accounting for* the course of some interactional episode. This does not entail that such identity assignments provided the *operative* context for the interaction, although such tacit identity work may affect how participants subsequently describe or evaluate the interaction. Thus, for example, a given interaction may, behaviourally, be gender neutral while participants' perceptions or professional accounts of it may invoke gender-relevant meanings and inferences (see Garcia 1998). That such perceptions occur, or that gender-based accounts are offered, are, of course, significant phenomena in their own right, and can have important consequences (see Ridgeway 1997).

In the analyses of emergency calls reported below, however, there is little evidence that participants treat transportable identities such as gender as relevant to their interaction. To be sure, reference to such matters as the age, sex and race of third parties do occur in emergency calls, but this is for the purpose of locating and apprehending those persons. For reasons of space, I will confine my attention in this chapter to oriented-to discourse and situated identities. This is not, I emphasize, to suggest that the latter identities are unimportant, for it is clear that they are a way of encoding some of the major structural features of a society in a fashion that is capable of bearing directly on concrete social activities. I turn next to a closer examination of discourse and situated identities.

Discourse identities

First, notice that the parties to an interaction do different things over the course of talk. They ask questions, tell stories, issue and defend against complaints, do repairs on problems of hearing and understanding, offer and respond to assessments of persons and events – this list is far from exhaustive. Moreover, who is doing what varies over the interaction, and the procession of discourse identities is interactionally contingent rather than determined, that is, one party's initiation of a discourse activity does not preclude a shift to another activity by another party. The mundane activity of talking with one another is coincident with assuming and leaving discourse identities.

Discourse identities furnish the focus for the type of discourse activity projected and recognized by participants, what they are *doing* interactionally in a particular spate of talk. For example, for all types of spoken discourse, the pervasive identities are that of *speaker/hearer*. It matters for participants who has the floor to speak, and who is assigned the tasks associated with listening. For specific types of discourse such as telephone calls, the relevant identities are *caller/answerer*. It matters who placed the call and who received it. For specific segments or sequences within a discourse, *story teller/recipient*, *inviter/invitee* or *questioner/answerer* and so on become important. In so far as an activity is enabled and advanced through discourse, participants recognizably act in the capacity of one or another discourse identity. For example, in locating topics for discussion, a participant may ask a question directed at some aspect of another's situated identity, thereby inviting a recipient to pursue a particular line of talk, and an invitation a recipient can accept or decline (see Maynard and Zimmerman 1984).

I argue that discourse identities emerge as a feature of the sequential organization of talk-in-interaction, orienting participants to the type of activity underway and their respective roles within it. Indeed, the alignment of discourse identities figures in the maintenance of sequential ordering and the 'architecture of intersubjectivity' it sustains (Heritage 1984: 254–60). The initiation of a given sequence projects (but does not assure) a restricted range of next actions and selects particular parties, either individuals or larger units (see Lerner 1992, 1993) as the animator of those actions.

Consider the following call to a Midwestern emergency dispatch centre:

(2a) (MCE 30–20.18)

```
1    CT: Mid-City emergency
2  → C: 'hhh Yeah um I'd like tu:h report something weird
3    that happened abou:t (0.1) um five minutes ago?
```

Notice that the caller/citizen-complainant (C) initiates what at first looks to be the first component of the standard report format: *I'd like to*, *report categorization of problem*, for example, an accident/robbery/loud party, etc. Routinely, call-takers respond to this format by initiating a series of questions, which I have called the 'interrogative series' as in the following:

(3) (MCE 23–14.22)

```
1    CT: 'hh Mid-City emergency.
2    C: 'h Yes urn (.) I would like to: (.) u:h 'port uh,
3    .'hhh uh break in.
4  → CT: To your home?
5    C: Yes. (.) Well: (.) we're babysitting.
6    CT: Okay what's the address there? =
7    C: = It's forty one forty four (.) [eighteenth avenue. =
8    CT: [uh huh,
9  → CT: Is this a one family dwelling or a duplex.
10   (0.5)
11   C: It's u:h h =
12 → CT: = Is it a house or a dupl[ex.
13   C: [It's like 'hhh yeah a
14   duplex. We're-[ih-upstairs.
15   CT: [Up'r down.
16 → CT: And what's thuh last name there?
```

However, in the case of the previous extract (2a), the 'report' is transformed into a characterization of an as yet unspecified event, 'something weird'. This can be considered an instance of what Goodwin (1996: 384) calls a 'prospective indexical', namely, an expression which orients recipient to the 'yet to be discovered' sense of the event (in this case, its status as a 'policeable' matter). Examining an extended version of this transcript (2b) we see that the characterization of the problem is followed by try-marked temporal and locational information. The call-taker's 'yeah?' (line 4) displays a readiness to receive an explication of the 'weird' event (see Goodwin 1984: 226). The caller then continues, completing the locational information and launching into a narrative account of how they came to encounter the 'weird' happening:

(2b) (MCE: 30–20.18)

```
 1    C: 'hhh Yeah um I'd like tu:h report something weird
 2       that happened abou:t (0.1) um five minutes ago?
 3       In front of our apartment building?
 4    → CT: Yeah?
 5    C: On eight fourteen eleventh avenue southeast,
 6    → CT: Mmhm,
 7    C: 'hh We were just (.) um (.) sittin' in the room and
 8       we heard this cra:nking you know like someone was
 9       pulling something behind their ca:r an' we
10       looked out the window 'hhh an' there was this (0.1)
11       light blue: (.) smashed up u:m (0.1) station wagon
12       and 'hh a:nd (.) thuh guy made a U-turn = we live
13       on a dead end 'hh and (.) thuh whole front end of
14       thuh-thuh car was smashed up 'hhh and (.) he jumped
15       out of the car and I remember he-he tried to push
16       the hood down on something and then he jus' (.)
17       started running an' he took off,
18    → CT: Mmhm.
19    C: A:nd we think that maybe 'e could've (.) you know
20       stolen the car and abandoned it or something.
21    → CT: What kinda car is it?
22    C: 'h It's a blue station wagon 'hh hh We just (.) have
23       seen it from the window.
24    CT: We'll get somebody over there. . .
```

The caller, by moving from report format (which projects the call-taker as report-recipient and usually leads, as indicated above, to the initiation of a series of questions) to a narrative format, projects the call-taker as, in effect, story recipient. The call-taker exhibits her orientation to a multiple turn unit in progress by issuing continuers. When the narrative is apparently brought to a close in lines 19–20, the call-taker initiates questioning at that point. A report or request format thus initiates one type of discourse structure (interrogation) early on in the call (recall extract 3) whereas a narrative or story format initiates another (extracts 2a and 2b), namely an extended turn by the caller supported by continuers from the call-taker. Interrogation, if it occurs, comes after the completion of the narrative.

Conversational sequences and their discourse identities thus provide the resources for the pursuit of an array of activity types, for example, question-answer sequences as a species of adjacency-pair organization provide the means to pursue activities as courtroom examinations (Atkinson and Drew 1979; Drew 1992), police interrogations (Watson 1990), television news interviews (Heritage and Greatbatch 1991), and many types of service calls, including emergency telephone calls (Drew and Heritage 1992: 43–5; Zimmerman 1992a, 1992b).

Situated identities

By virtue of their ubiquity as an element of the general organization of talk-in-interaction, discourse identities do not by themselves account for the variation in the nature of these activities, for example, the difference between courtroom interrogation and a television news interview (both of which involve questioning and answering). Discourse identities can shift turn by turn. In the immediately preceding example, the situated identities of citizen-complainant and call-taker remain constant, while the discourse identities shift, or rather become layered, as the caller assumes the task of narrator and the call-taker the narrative recipient. The shifting of identities repositions the parties to address particular tasks as they arise, in this case, the characterization of an event that the caller could not, or would not code in the report format. When the narrative is concluded, the call-taker becomes interrogator, the caller the interogatee, as further information of a particular sort is elicited. This play of discourse identities is tied to the situated identities of the parties, which in turn link these local activities to standing social arrangements and institutions through the socially distributed knowledge participants have about them. For Wilson, the term 'social structure' is a covering concept for orientation to such extra-situational formations:

> . . . social structure consists of matters that are described and oriented
> to by members of society on relevant occasions as essential resources
> for conducting their affairs and, at the same time, reproduced as external
> and constraining social facts through that same social interaction.
>
> (Wilson 1991: 27)

In these terms, oriented-to situated identities circumscribe and make available those extra-situational resources participants need to accomplish a particular activity by articulating with the discourse identities embedded in the sequential organization that enables the accomplishment of these activities. They are the portal through which the setting of the talk and its institutional surround (Wilson's 'social structure') enters and helps to shape the interaction, which in turn actualizes the occasion and its institutional provenance.

A perspicuous example of how situated identities function in talk-in-interaction can be found in Heritage and Sefi's (1992) study of health visitors in Britain. Health visitors are nurses who, by law, must call on mothers who have recently given birth. Heritage and Sefi observe (1992: 365–6) that these interactions were mutually regarded as a service encounter (see Jefferson and Lee 1992): the mothers oriented to health visitors as 'baby experts' and hence knowledgeable judges of mothers' competence as caregivers, and the nurses usually comported themselves as such. This is shown, in extract 4, by a mother's (M) uptake of an observation by a health visitor (HV):

(4)   (from Heritage and Sefi 1992 [4A 1:1])

1   HV: He's enjoying that [isn't he.
2   F: [°Yes he certainly is = °

3   M: = He's not hungry 'cuz (h)he's ju(h)st (h)had
4   'iz bo:ttle 'hhh

Heritage and Sefi point out that health visitor's observation is regarded by the mother as offered in her professional capacity and hence as an implicit negative assessment of her (the mother's) care of the infant. The mother's response exhibits both her orientation to the situated identity of the health visitor, which comprises, among other things, expertise in matters of infant care, and her orientation to her own identity as a mother who, in that capacity, may feel accountable with regard to any noticing offered by the health visitor concerning the state of her infant. As Heritage and Sefi observe, the father (F) and mother have a different take on the upshot of the assessment: the father apparently does not view the query as professionally motivated (i.e., at just this juncture, produced by reference to the health visitor identity) whereas the mother does, shaping the defensive stance of her answer.

In what follows, I will use materials from several studies of emergency telephone calls that my collaborators and I (separately or together) have done, drawing them together in a fashion that focuses more closely on the problem of identity-as-context.

Identity and interaction in emergency calls

Drew and Heritage (1992: 43–4) in their introduction to a collection of studies of talk in institutional settings observe that in contrast to ordinary conversation, which, apart from opening and closings, is not constrained by some overarching organization or 'standard pattern', institutional interactions follow a 'task-related standard shape', whether this be prescribed or the product of 'locally managed routines'. The 'locally managed routines' characteristic of service calls can be characterized as follows:

Pre-beginning/summons

Opening/identification /acknowledgement

REQUEST [caller's first turn]

INTERROGATIVE SERIES [contingencies of response]

RESPONSE [promise or provision of service]

Closing

Figure 23.1 The organization of service calls (modified from Zimmerman 1992b: 419)

For present purposes, I will consider identity-as-context with respect to the pre-beginning, opening identification/acknowledgement, the caller's first turn, and interrogative series 'phases' of the call.

Pre-beginnings and openings

Conversation on the telephone is, of course, conversation, and is organized in much the same way as face-to-face encounters. However, parties to telephone talk cannot see one another, and special steps have to be taken to achieve the mutual recognition accomplished in other circumstances by a glance (Schiffrin 1977; see also Schegloff 1979: 71).

The accomplishment of identification and, thereby, an alignment of identities, provides for reciprocal understanding of just what sectors of one's self and one's social knowledge are now relevant to the upcoming interaction. To fully appreciate this fact it is necessary to consider what occurs just before the opening in such calls.

A call to an emergency service like 911 in the USA begins prior to the opening identification sequence. There is, in short, a 'pre-beginning'. Generally, it consists of the activity of dialling a telephone number, which summons another to interact (Schegloff 1968). For most casual telephone calls, the answerer does not and cannot know who, in particular, is calling and for what reasons, although prearranged calls can overcome these constraints.[1] The caller has selected a recipient, although, similar to the answerer's circumstances, the caller cannot be certain who will answer (the number dialled may be incorrect, or answered by some party other than the one sought).

In the case of dialling the number of a service port like the police, the situation is modified in several respects. First, the caller is selecting an organization (and a service) rather than a particular individual, although individuals known as agents of the organization may be sought. Second, the answerer can presume that callers who have correctly selected the number are members of a class of callers who have appropriate business to transact. The organization of identity alignment in emergency calls can be summarized as follows:

- In answering the telephone summons, the answerer from the outset treats incoming calls to that number as selected by callers in terms of the purposes which that number exists to serve. Incoming calls to emergency numbers are thus treated as *virtual emergencies* (Whalen and Zimmerman 1990; Zimmerman 1992b); the *placing* of the call itself assuming the status of a *request* for service.
- By providing a self-identification appropriate to that number, the answerer announces to the caller the character of the service port reached.
- The caller, upon hearing the answerer's self-identification, ordinarily acknowledges having reached the intended service port, completing the opening identification sequence.

In terms of identity, then, what transpires in the pre-beginning is a *pre-alignment* (caller/called and citizen-complainant/call-taker) subject to ratification in the opening/identification sequence. In a routine opening sequence where the caller has dialled 911, the call-taker answers with a categorical self-identification and an offer of assistance.

The sequences themselves, including those that figure in the emergency telephone calls, are indifferent to the particular situated identities of the parties who animate them. Yet, as Wilson (1991: 37–8) argues, they can be articulated with particular discourse identities such that, for example, call-takers ask the questions, and callers return the floor when they complete their answer, allowing for a series of question-and-answer pairs (see below). Speaking of the distribution of events found across emergency calls, Wilson goes on to observe that:

In effect, routine use of the mechanisms of interaction passes an antecedent distribution [citizen requests for service] through to a final distribution [call-takers ask questions]. In this sense, then, one can account for the distribution of subsequent events as a product of sequential mechanisms, but only if the distribution of antecedent events is already given. . . . [T]he initial distribution of requests, such that these are made by citizen complainants rather than complaint takers, arises from the institutional context that the participants establish as relevant. Thus, ultimately, distributional phenomena in interaction may reflect elements of institutional context.

(Wilson 1991: 37–8)

This distributional regularity is achieved by virtue of the way in which participants *enter* the sequential space within which the interactionally organized pursuit of the institution's work is sustained, namely, through a set of sequences initiated by the pre-beginning. The 'institutional context' Wilson refers to is first provided by the designation of a seven-digit or three-digit telephone number as an emergency number, and second, embodied in the call-taker who is positioned in her identity by the alignment in the opening sequence to perform the interactional work necessary for the institution's purposes.

The point I wish to stress here is that the opening of the call, and in particular, the first component or components of the first turn of the answerer and caller are regularly devoted to establishing a mutually oriented-to set of identities implicative for the shape of what is to follow – the *footing* (Goffman 1981: 128), as it were, of the encounter. Moreover, the sequence of events – dialling 911 (or other emergency number), answering the summons with a categorical self-identification, acknowledging having reached the intended number – projects a particular line of activity and, to use Wilson's phrase, a 'continuity of relevancies' (1991: 25). This not to say that this initial establishment of the relevance of the institutional context automatically 'covers' all else that follows. As Wilson (1991: 25–6) notes, to establish a presumption is one thing, to fulfil it, and fulfil it recognizably, is another. The notion of continuity suggests that relevance does not have to be *established anew* at each turn, but it does have to be *extended*, and failure to extend or reconfirm by producing some behaviour under- standable in a different context is a method of renegotiating what is going on in the situation – recall here the discussion of the riddle call (extract 1) above. The issue of the 'continuity of relevance' underscores the irreducibly interactional character of the alignment.

I want to turn now to the more routine features of call-processing to explore how identity-as-context functions to undergird the practical activity of seeking and receiving emergency services.

Caller's first turn

The caller's first turn ordinarily consists of an acknowledgement token (which completes the ratification of pre-alignment identities) followed by one or more possible utterances. Such utterances function as some version of the 'reason for the call'. The format by which callers engage emergency dispatch services reflects their analysis of both 'who' they are addressing (recipient design), the nature of the problem, and their own relationship to it, that is, their 'stance' (Whalen and Zimmerman 1990). That is, the format of the caller's first turn projects a further identity alignment of caller and the answerer. These formats include *reports*, *narratives* and *requests*:

> (5) (MCE 21–16a/21) Report format
>
> 1   CT: Mid-City emergency.
> 2   C: hh u:h Yeah I wanna report a: (.) real bad accident h hh

> (6) (MCE 20–15/207) Narrative format
>
> 1   CT: Mid-City police an' fire
> 2   C: Hi um (.) I'm uh (.) I work at thuh University
> 3   Hospital and I was riding my bike home
> 4   tanight from (.) *work-*
> 5   CT: Mm
> 6   C: 'bout (.) ten minutes ago, 'hh as I was riding
> 7   past Mercy Hospital (.) which is uh few blocks
> 8   from there 'hh () urn () I *think* uh couple vans
> 9   full uh kids pulled up (.) an started um (.)
> 10   they went down thuh trail an(h)d are *beating* up
> 11   people down there I'm not sure (.) but it
> 12   sounded like (something) 'hh

> (7) (MCE 21–24a/4) Request format
>
> 1   C: I need the paramedics please?

The report format ('I want to report . . .') is typically an account of a 'codeable' problem delivered to an 'authority' by a citizen. A codeable problem is one that can be named or characterized in a word or two. Its codeability is reflected in the fact that little, if any, elaboration is requested; rather, the call-taker will proceed to determine location and ancillary features of the reported problem, for example, whether personal injuries were sustained. Narratives are chronologically organized descriptions or accounts, often extended, leading up to a discursive characterization of a possible trouble, as was seen in extract 2a and 2b discussed above, in which what began as a report was transformed into a narrative. Finally, the request format is a request for service delivered to a service provider. It can be the sole component of the caller's first turn after the acknowledgement token, or be followed with a statement of a codeable problem.

Callers also employ a proprietary format which can deploy one or both of the following components: a categorical self-identification ('This is . . .') and a proprietorial we ('We have a . . .):

> (8) (MCE 7–3.56) Categorical self-identification
>
> 1   CT: Mid-City emergency.
> 2   (.)

3   C: tch 'hh u:h This is u:h () Knights of Columbus
4   Hall at uh: twenty twenty ni:ne West Broadway
5   North? =
6   CT: = Mmhm, ((*keyboard sounds*))
7   C: U:h we had some u:h women's purses u:h stolen,

(9) (MCE 21–13.10) Proprietorial format

1   CT: Mid-City emergency.
2   C: 'hh tch Hi: we got u:h (.) this is security at thuh
3   bus depot, Greyhound bus depot? =
4   CT: = Yes ma'am =
5   → C: = An' we got a guy down here that's uh:
6   (0.6) ((*background noise*))
7   C: over intoxicated, hhh 'hh He just-he's passed out.

In employing a report format, the caller assumes a particular stance, as a gloss, a 'citizen' reporting an incident to an 'authority' for whom the information is a warrant for taking action of some sort. Indeed, engaging in such an activity displays the caller's orientation to the call-taker as a representative of the organization.

Narrative accounts deal with problems that are less readily codeable, which is to say that they are less clear-cut and seem to require some explanation of how the caller came to know of them and why they might think them worthy of report to authorities. This format allows callers to present their noticing of ambiguous events in a way that portrays them as ordinary, disinterested, reasonable witnesses (see Bergmann 1987).

Requests, while they intimate that some type of policeable trouble or medical emergency is involved, do not specify the exact nature of the problem, projecting a particular response without providing its warrant. A report establishes the substantive reason for a call, although it does not clarify the caller's identity beyond that of 'citizen' (e.g., whether the citizen-caller is a victim or a witness).

Proprietorial formats establish a communication from 'my organization' to 'your organization', that is, as a report of a 'responsible party'. Proprietorial formats also report particular types of repetitive incident (often dealing with problems occurring within the realm of the caller's occupational responsibilities).

Whatever the format, the call-taker will usually have further work to do in processing the call. The work involved in identity alignment, and the role that identities play in shaping the character of reported troubles and the trajectory of the call can be found in situations like the following which present ambiguous features to call-takers. Consider the following:

(10) (MCE 21–27/39)

1   CT: Mid-City emergency
2   C: Yes sir uh go' uh couple gu:ys over here ma:n
3   they thin' they bunch uh wi:se ((*background*
4   *noise*)) =

5   CT: = Are they in yur house? or is this uh busness?
6   C: They're over here ah Quick Stop (.) They (fuckin)
7   come over here an pulled up at thuh Quick Stop
8   slammin' their doors intuh my truck.
9   CT: Quick Stop? =
10   C: = Yeah.
11 → CT: Okay Uh-were you uh customer at that store?
12   C: Yeah.
13   CT: What thee address there or thee uhm:. . .

The call-taker's question 'in yur house? or is this uh business' (line 5) is not simply locational in its import. She is asking for the setting of the problem and hence, on the basis of the inferential tie between setting and identity, 'in what capacity' the caller is reporting. His answer adds further ambiguity for, although he selects 'business' as opposed to 'home' (line 6), he does not clarify his relationship to the business establishment. This much is evident when the call-taker asks if he is a customer (versus an employee) at the store in question (line 11). There are several issues implicated here. The police-relevant nature of the trouble is shaped by its location, and by who reports it. A disturbance of some sort on a public street is a different event from a disturbance occurring on private property, and the person reporting the problem may stand in a different relationship to it depending on the nature of his or her tie to the territory in question. 'Citizens', for example, may report disturbances occurring in public places, while 'proprietors' may report disturbances occurring in stores or other places of business (and may be heard as more reliable sources of information since they are accountable for managing such events as part of their occupational responsibilities). The categories of place, identity and problem are thus linked in consequential ways for the handling of emergency calls.

As I hope to show in the following section, the identities thus far displayed and aligned in the opening of the call (and as subsequently developed within it) will continue to play an important role in the intelligibility and practicability of the work of emergency dispatching.

The interrogative series

As noted earlier, the core organization of the emergency call, like many service calls in general, is a single adjacency repair (request/response) with an insertion sequence – what I have called the 'interrogative series' (see Figure 23.1). An insertion sequence, a series of one or more question-answer pairs, serves to clarify or determine matters necessary to provide a response to the initial 'pair part', in this case, the request for service. Sequentially, reports (including narratives) and requests are oriented to by citizen-complainant and call-taker as initiating the first adjacency pair, that is, each of these forms achieves functional status as a request for service (see Wilson 1991). The embedding of a series of adjacency pairs within an adjacency pair requires participants to sustain the relevance of each embedded pair to the ultimate provision of a response to the initial pair part, in this case, the 'request for service' (however formatted).

The interrogative series is the sequential space in which the call-taker addresses the *contingencies of response*, that is, he or she determines that there is a legitimate need for police, fire or paramedic services, and assembles the information necessary to dispatch the response effectively. Such information includes the location to which the responding unit or units are to be sent (which can involve fairly extensive questioning) as well as relevant features of the problem itself, for example, the nature of medical problems (for which 'pre-arrival instruction' in first aid may be indicated), whether or not a reported auto accident involves injuries, and details pertinent to any reported crime (whether it is in progress or just completed, suspect descriptions, direction and mode of flight, the presence of weapons, etc.). These questions stem from, and exhibit the special occupational competence and responsibility of the call-taker; indeed, their form and manner of execution constitute the call-taker's activity as call-taker. The caller's recognition of this, implied in the alignment of identities and the receptiveness such alignment establishes, provides for the routine character of most emergency calls.

It is instructive to consider instances where alignment is problematic or not maintained. In one instance, a woman called Central County 911 and made a terse report of some activity at the corner of her street and then hung up. The enraged CT called the woman back and chastised her for breaking off the contact after an initial, if inadequate, report of possible trouble:

(11) (Central County (VIDEO TAPE) (*CT1 has redialled a caller who has hung up prematurely; transcript displays only* CT's *side of the conversation*))

1   CT1: HELLO! CAN YOU HEAR ME?
2   ((*CT2 looks towards CT1*))
3   CT2: I can.
4   CT1: This is 911 emergency (1.0) W-I you don't report
5   something an' just hang up

Note here that CT1's identity as call-taker – a position that carries with it the responsibility to determine the need for police or other forms of assistance as well as a location to which they can be sent – provides a warrant for insisting on cooperation from callers.

We can begin to see how identity works in this fashion by first considering the constraints call-takers' situated identity places on their mode of responding to callers. The first such constraint is the requirement that a problem of an appropriate sort exists. Expressed need for service is insufficient, as is clear in the following call from an Ambassador Hotel operator to the Los Angeles Police Department on the occasion of the shooting of Robert Kennedy in the hotel kitchen:

(12) (RFK)

1   CT: Police Department.
2   (.)
3   C: Yes This is the Ambassador Hotel Em
4   CT: Ambassador Hotel?

```
5    ((echo: Hotel))
6    C: Do you hear me?
7    (.)
8    CT: Yeah I hear you.
9    C: Uh they have an emergency = They want thuh
10   police to thuh kitchen right away.
11   CT: What kind of an emergency?
12   C: I don't know honey They hung up I don't know
13   [what's happening
14   CT: [Well find out. (.) We don't send out without =
15   C: = I beg your pardon?
16   (.)
17   CT: We have to know what we're sending on,
```

The delay in responding to this incident may have embarrassed the police department, but it is evident that C, a hotel operator, was not in a position to provide the required information. Pressing her to obtain the information, the call-taker explicitly formulates the critical issue: 'We have to know what we're sending on.' The mere assertion that an event is an emergency is, other things being equal, not enough.

In the case of the assassination of Robert Kennedy, the caller was initially unable to provide a characterization of the problem satisfactory to the call-taker. The difficulties that plagued a call to the Dallas Fire Department (Whalen et al 1988) was largely due to a *misalignment* of caller and call-taker (a 'nurse-dispatcher' in this case). As a consequence, the dispatch of an ambulance was delayed, and the afflicted party was dead upon its arrival. The encounter begins when the Dallas Fire Department operator (who screens and routes calls according to their need for fire or medical response) answers a call:

(13) (Dallas FD/B1)

```
1    O: Fire department
2    (0.8)
3    C: Yes, I'd like tuh have an ambulance at forty one thirty
4    nine Haverford please
5    (0.5)
6    O: What's thuh problem sir?
7    C: I: don't know, 'n if I knew I wouldn't be ca:lling you all
```

The caller begins with a request for service which is followed by a routine query by O concerning the nature of the problem (line 6). The caller responds by averring that he does not know the nature of the problem, and indeed, should not be expected to know (line 7). After an attempt by O to clarify the caller's inability to address the problem query (not shown in extract 13), he is transferred to the nurse-dispatcher who initiates a series of questions concerning the destination to which the paramedics are to be sent and the caller's telephone number. She then asks the caller about the problem. However, C responds with an utterance nearly identical to that of line 7 in extract 13. The nurse-dispatcher interrupts and attempts to align the caller as the answerer in the question-answer sequence she has initiated. This time, the caller responds with a characterization of the problem (someone having difficulty breathing) that could count as a 'priority symptom', one requiring an immediate response of the mobile life support ambulance dispatched by the Fire Department.

For reasons that I won't go into here (see Whalen et al 1988: 351–2), the call from that point on rapidly dissolves into a dispute focusing on the caller's 'refusal' to let the nurse-dispatcher speak with the caller's stepmother who is experiencing the breathing difficulties. The identity alignment of caller and nurse-dispatcher has become significantly (and as it turned out, disastrously) altered, the two parties realigning as *disputants*. In their capacity as disputants, what each says to the other is in the service of the pursuit of an argument rather than the orderly elicitation and provision of information satisfying the contingencies of response for dispatching a paramedic ambulance. The nurse-dispatcher treats the caller as uncooperative, refusing to answer questions and comply with requests, while the caller treats the nurse-dispatcher as incompetently impeding the satisfaction of his request.

As noted above, queries as to the nature of the problem for which help is sought are routine, and are routinely answered. Against that background, the caller's denial of knowledge about the problem and indeed, the legitimacy of the question itself requires explanation. Whalen et al (1988: 346) suggest that the caller, for whatever reason, misunderstood the contingencies of the service offered by the Fire Department, treating it as relatively unconditional like, for example, the request for the delivery of a pizza for which only an address and an order are necessary. I am entertaining a conjecture not reported in the 1988 paper, namely, that on the assumption of unconditional service, when the caller was confronted with a request for a statement of the 'problem', he understood it within the device *lay versus professional* (see Sacks 1972a, 1972b), that is, in terms of the distribution of competency on such matters in the population. Classifying himself in this situation as a *layperson* to the Fire Department's *professional*, he rejected the question as beyond his scope but within that of Fire Department personnel. That is, within such an understanding, the specifically medical reasons for requesting an ambulance are not relevant, it being the responsibility of Fire Department paramedics to deal with such matters. Hence, the hearing of the problem queries as requests for *diagnosis* rather than for a descriptive statement of the observable features of the medical emergency. Of course, virtually any caller would call in the capacity of a layperson vis-à-vis any call-taker, but an insufficient understanding of the nature of the professional constraints on the latter (in the case of Dallas, call screening in terms of a medical protocol) can also lead to insufficient understanding of what matters fall within a layperson's capacity (being able to describe the publicly observable features of the problem). And, as we saw, when realignment momentarily occurred, the caller was able to produce such a description.

The Dallas call rather dramatically underlines the importance of appropriate identity alignment for the routine (and successful) processing of emergency calls – as well as for the necessity of call-taker and dispatchers to *recognize* and deal effectively with misalignments when they occur (see Whalen 1990 for other circumstances that can affect the nature of the alignment between caller and call-taker).

Concluding comments

In the preceding discussion, I tried to show how discourse and situated identities provide both the proximal and distal contexts for a range of activities within the domain of emergency telephone calls. Discourse identities implicate a sequential machinery by which participants manage their interaction. On this view, conversational organization is the fundamental resource for engaging in social (i.e., intersubjectively coordinated) action, the platform on which activities of various sorts are built. The substantive shape of these activities, the agendas they embody and the goals that they pursue, emerge from the situated identities of participants. Coorientation to particular, articulated discourse and situated identities joins a given sector of distributed social knowledge (both tacit and explicit) and interactional know-how to produce repetitive, reproducible, recognizable activities. This emphasis on participants' orientations to features of the interactional situation (such as discourse and situated identities) does not presuppose that they possess 'theories' of discourse or of society, but rather that they can manage their local affairs in systematic ways that have consequences, intended and unintended, some of which are beyond their reach or notice. To echo a theme from early on in this chapter, while the interaction order is loosely coupled to social structure, it is tightly articulated with it. Indeed, the coordination of activities within the interaction order provides the fundamental sociality which makes socially structured actions of diverse sorts possible.

The empirical case in point, which I used to illustrate these ideas, is the emergency telephone call. What recommends this sort of call as a focus of investigation is that it is at once close kin to 'ordinary', non-institutional telephone interactions while at the same time bearing the imprint of a particular institutional arrangement. That is, it displays the generalized shape of a service call (a sequence organization that can be found in many transactions with businesses of various sorts). Such calls allow us repeatedly to encounter the contingent achievement of this form of activity while displaying in relatively accessible ways the workings of discourse (i.e., interactional) and situated (i.e., institutional) identities, and in particular how these identities are articulated and aligned. I have tried to show in this chapter how such articulation and alignment operate to generate the routine features of emergency calls, and I have also attempted to point out how failure of articulation and alignment produces trouble for this type of activity. More important, it should be clear from the discussion that the articulation of discourse and situated identities is a *contingent* matter: the alignment of identities is an achievement, and the shape of the interaction that results is a local crafting out of the resources of talk-in-interaction and materials of human social agendas.

References

Atkinson, J.M. and Drew, P. (1979) *Order in Court: The Organization of Verbal Interaction in Judicial Settings*, London: Macmillan.
Bergmann, J.R. (1987) *Klatsch: Zur Socialform der disketen Indiskretion*, Berlin: de Gruyter.
Drew, P. (1992) 'Contested evidence in courtroom cross-examination: the case of a trial for rape', in P. Drew and J. Heritage (eds.) *Talk at Work: Interaction in Institutional Settings*, Cambridge: Cambridge University Press.

Drew, P. and Heritage, J. (1992) *Talk at Work: Interaction in Institutional Settings*, Cambridge: Cambridge University Press.

Garcia, A. (1998) 'The relevance of interactional and institutional contexts for the study of gender difference: a demonstrative case study', *Symbolic Interaction* 21: 35–58.

Goffman, E. (1981) *Forms of Talk*, Philadelphia: University of Pennsylvania Press.

—— (1983) 'The interaction order', *American Sociological Review* 48: 1–17.

Goodwin, C. (1984) 'Notes on story structure and the organization of participation', in J.M. Atkinson and J. Heritage (eds.) *Structures of Social Action: Studies in Conversation Analysis*, Cambridge: Cambridge University Press.

—— (1996) 'Transparent vision', in E. Ochs, E.A. Schegloff and S.A. Thompson (eds.) *Interaction and Grammar*, Cambridge: Cambridge University Press.

Heritage, J. (1984) *Garfinkel and Ethnomethodology*, Oxford: Polity Press.

Heritage, J. and Greatbatch, D. (1991) 'On the institutional character of institutional talk: the case of news interviews', in D. Boden and D.H. Zimmerman (eds.) *Talk and Social Structure: Studies in Ethnomethodology and Conversation Analysis*, Oxford: Polity Press.

Heritage, J. and Sefi, S. (1992) 'Dilemmas of advice: aspects of the delivery and reception of advice in interactions between health visitors and first-time mothers', in P. Drew and J.C. Heritage (eds.) *Talk at Work: Interaction in Institutional Settings*, Cambridge: Cambridge University Press.

Jefferson, G. and Lee, J.R.L. (1992) 'The rejection of advice: managing the problematic convergence of a "troubles teller" and a "service encounter"', in P. Drew and J. Heritage (eds.) *Talk at Work: Interaction in Institutional Settings*, Cambridge: Cambridge University Press.

Lerner, G. (1992) 'Assisted story telling: deploying shared knowledge as a practical matter', *Qualitative Sociology* 15: 247–71.

—— (1993) 'Collectivities in action: establishing the relevance of cojoined participation in conversation', *Text* 13: 213–45.

Maynard, D.W. and Zimmerman, D.H. (1984) 'Topical talk, ritual, and the social organization of relationships', *Social Psychology Quarterly* 47: 301–16.

Ridgeway, C.L. (1997) 'Interaction and the conservation of gender inequality: considering employment', *American Sociological Review* 62: 218–35.

Sacks, H. (1972a) 'Notes on police assessment of moral character', in D. Sudnow (ed.) *Studies in Social Interaction*, New York: Free Press.

—— (1972b) 'An initial investigation of the usability of conversational data for doing sociology', in D. Sudnow (ed.) *Studies in Social Interaction*, New York: Free Press.

Schegloff, E.A. (1968) 'Sequencing in conversational openings', *American Anthropologist* 70: 1075–95.

—— (1979) 'Identification and recognition in telephone openings', in G. Psathas (ed.) *Everyday Language: Studies in Ethnomethodology*, New York: Irvington Press.

—— (1991) 'Reflections on talk and social structure', in D. Boden and D.H. Zimmerman (eds.) *Talk and Social Structure: Studies in Ethnomethodology and Conversation Analysis*, Oxford: Polity Press.

—— (1996) 'Turn organization: one intersection of grammar and interaction', in E. Ochs, E.A. Schegloff and S.A. Thompson (eds.) *Interaction and Grammar*, Cambridge: Cambridge University Press.

Schiffrin, D. (1977) 'Opening encounters', *American Sociological Review* 44: 679–91.

Watson, D.R. (1990) 'Some features of the elicitation of confessions in murder interrogations', in G. Psathas (ed.) *Interactional Competence*, Lanham, MD: University Press of America.

Whalen, J., Zimmerman, D.H. and Whalen, M.R. (1988) 'When words fail: a single case analysis', *Social Problems* 35: 335–62.

Whalen, M.R. (1990) 'Ordinary talk in extraordinary situations: the social organization of interrogation in calls for help', unpublished PhD dissertation, University of California, Santa Barbara.

Whalen, M.R. and Zimmerman, D.H. (1990) 'Describing trouble: epistemology in citizen calls to the police', *Language in Society* 19: 465–92.

Wilson, I. (1987) *The After Death Experience*, London: Sidgwick & Jackson.

Zimmerman, D.H. (1984) 'Talk and its occasion: the case of calling the police', in D. Schiffrin (ed.) *Meaning, Form, and Use in Context: Linguistic Applications*, Washington, DC: Georgetown University Roundtable on Language and Linguistics.

—— (1990) 'Prendre position [Accomplishing footing]', in *Le parler frais d'Erving Goffman*, Paris: Les Editions de Minuit.

—— (1992a) 'Achieving context: openings in emergency calls', in G. Watson and R.M. Seiler (eds.) *Text in Context: Contributions to Ethnomethodology*, Newbury Park, CA: Sage.

—— (1992b) 'The interactional organization of calls for emergency assistance', in P. Drew and J. Heritage (eds.) *Talk at Work: Interaction in Institutional Settings*, Cambridge: Cambridge University Press.

Note

I want to thank Thomas P. Wilson, Angela Garcia and Gene Lerner for their helpful comments on earlier drafts of this chapter.

1   Obviously, Zimmerman's analysis predates mobile and smartphone technology which, in most cases, makes it possible for the answerer to know the identity of the caller before answering the call – *eds*.

Chapter 24

Barbara Johnstone

PITTSBURGHESE SHIRTS: COMMODIFICATION AND THE ENREGISTERMENT OF AN URBAN DIALECT

IN THE COURSE OF sociolinguistic interviews in the Pittsburgh area, I and my fellow fieldworkers asked our interviewees what they knew about "Pittsburghese," the local name for what is thought to be a distinctive Pittsburgh dialect. Their answers were sometimes supported by material artifacts bearing representations of "Pittsburghese." When I asked for examples of local peculiarities of speech, one interviewee produced a coffee mug decorated with "Pittsburghese" words. Another interviewee, when asked if he had ever heard of the dialect, opened a bag he had brought along and dramatically produced a white T-shirt with letters and images in black and gold. The front of the shirt depicted the city's skyline with words like *pop*, *redd up*, *keller*, *hans*, and *sammich* superimposed on it. On the back was a dictionary-like list of words and phrases with definitions and sample sentences. "This," he told us, holding up the shirt, "is Pittsburghese." In another interview, Jenn R., a speaker of the local dialect in Pittsburgh, responded:[1]

> Oh yes. I mean, there's that store over on the Southside, in Station Square that has the Pittsburghese shirts. In fact, I remember when my friend Karen moved out of state, with—her husband's job took them out of state and to many other states, I remember sending her a couple Pittsburghese shirts for them.

As in the interview with Jenn R., "Pittsburghese shirts" were often among the first things mentioned when people talked to us about local speech in Pittsburgh. These shirts, for sale at sidewalk markets, in souvenir shops, and online, often look like the one we were shown by the man described above. Figure 24.1 shows the front and back of a typical Pittsburghese shirt.

Source: Barbara Johnstone, 'Pittsburghese shirts: commodification and the enregisterment of an urban dialect', *American Speech* (2009) 84, 2: 157–175.

PITTSBURGHESE
DEFINITIONS

aht: *adv.* opposite of in
babushka: *n.* a headscarf used for a bad hair day
blitzburgh: *n.* a drinking town with a football problem
chipped ham: *n.* thinly sliced ham sold only in the Burg
chitchat: *v.* idle conversation
dahntahn: *n.* opposite of uptahn
gumban: *n.* rubber band
hans: *n.* a part of the body used to hold a cold Iron
iron: *n.* the beer of champions
jaggers: *n.* thorns
jagoff: *adj.* anyone who pisses off a Pittsburger
Jeetjet? No, J'ew?: Did you eat yet? No, did you?
jumbo: *n.* bologna
jynt iggle: *n.* a popular supermarket
keller: *n.* black and gold to name a few
nebby: *adj.* nosey to a fault
pensivania: *n.* The state where friends and memories last a lifetime
picksburgh: *n.* the greatest city in pensivania
pop: *n.* a carbonated beverage, soda
redd up: *v.* to straighten or clean up an area
sammitch: *n.* chipped ham or jumbo between two pieces of Town Talk bread
N'alfberry: *n.* end of town opposite of Wes'liberty
slippey: *adj.* slippery
spicket: *n.* a tap on a barrel of Iron
stillers: *n.* four time super bowl champs with unfinished business
stillmill: *n.* factory where steel is produced
telepole: *n.* telephone pole
the burg: *n.* a helluva cool place
the mon: *n.* the Monongahela River
the point: *n.* the meeting place of Pittsburgh's Three Rivers
yuns: *n.* 'yous' to the east and 'yall' to the south

Figure 24.1 Front and back of a Pittsburghese shirt

The shirts are almost always either white, black, or a yellow-orange color thought of locally as "gold," with printing in white, black, and/or gold. The front typically depicts the cityscape and includes the word "Pittsburghese" (sometimes "Pixburghese") together with a scattering of words spelled phonetically to represent local pronunciation (*dahntahn* "downtown," *worsh* "wash," *jynt iggle* "Giant Eagle" supermarkets), vocabulary (*gumban* "rubber band," *redd up* "tidy up," *slippy* or *slippey* "slippery"), and sometimes syntax (*needs washed* "needs to be washed"). On the back there is typically a dictionary-like alphabetical list. Newer designs are often simpler, involving a single black word or phrase on the front of a white shirt: *YNZ* (*yinz* "you, pl."), *I'm surrounded by jagoffs!* "jerks, irritating people."[2]

As is suggested by the fact that all but a handful of more than 100 interviewees had heard of "Pittsburghese" and could talk about it, there is a very high level of dialect awareness in Pittsburgh. This is true even among people who do not themselves have strong local accents, including outsiders who live in the area and many local African Americans.[3] Unelicited, naturally occurring evidence of dialect awareness is provided by the ubiquity and variety of items representing "Pittsburghese" that are for sale in the city: coffee mugs, shot glasses, beer steins, refrigerator magnets, postcards, talking dolls, bumper stickers, dog clothing, shirts, and hats. The most prevalent—in that it is among the oldest and most widely available and in that it displays the most variety and reflects changes fastest—is the Pittsburghese shirt.

In this article I argue that Pittsburghese shirts are not simply evidence of dialect awareness, however. Rather, I claim, these T-shirts, seen for themselves and in the context of their production, distribution, and consumption, are part of a process leading to the creation and focusing of the idea that there is a Pittsburgh dialect in the first place. To make this argument, I invoke the concept of "enregisterment" (Agha 2003, 2007), the processes by which particular linguistic forms become linked with "social" meaning. In Pittsburgh a set of locally hearable forms have become linked with an imagined (in Anderson's 1991 sense) "dialect" called "Pittsburghese." To understand why this has happened at the time and in the way it has and why T-shirts have become part of the process, I draw on the literature from critical discourse analysis, anthropological linguistics, and cultural anthropology about globalization and commodification and on eight years of ethnographic participant-observation, more than 100 sociolinguistic interviews, and several collections of texts and other artifacts (including T-shirts collected between 1997 and 2008) that represent local speech in Pittsburgh. I show that a set of material, ideological, and historical facts have come together to make Pittsburgh speech into a commodity that can add value to items like T-shirts. Finally, I suggest that Pittsburghese shirts contribute to dialect enregisterment in at least four ways: they put local speech on display; they imbue local speech with value; they standardize local speech; and they link local speech with particular social meanings.

Enregisterment

Although linguistic variation is audible to someone listening for it, a dialect is not. What linguists and laypeople alike encounter in lived experience are particular speakers, writers, or signers, saying particular things in particular ways. The variation between one speaker and another, or between the same person's speech in one situation as opposed to another, is often unnoticeable to a particular hearer. In order to become noticeable, a particular variant must be linked with an ideological scheme that can be used to evaluate it in contrast to another variant. For example, if, according to the ideological scheme that comes into play, women are expected to act differently than men, particular features may come to sound gendered (Ochs 1992). Alternatively, the scheme to which a hearer orients may be one that links variation with class, carefulness, correctness, place, or any other framework in terms of which people position one another socially, each associated with a set of stereotypical personas.

Ideas about how linguistic variants are associated with identities may be quite idiosyncratic. (A particular way of saying a particular word may remind you of your grandfather.) However, some of these linkages can come to be shared via "metapragmatic" practices (Silverstein 1993) by which people indicate to one another what particular forms mean. (Someone may point out that your grandfather sounded like a Philadelphian, upon which you are able to transform the idiosyncratic linkage of a form with an individual's personal identity to a more widely shared linkage of the form with a regional dialect.) Form-meaning links can be suggested directly, in explicit talk about talk ("People who say 'dahntahn' sound ignorant"), or indirectly, by associating forms with social stereotypes in other ways. Once it comes to be interpreted and evaluated with reference to an ideological scheme, a linguistic form has been "enregistered." A form that is enregistered is one that is linked with a way of speaking or "register" associated with a personal or social identity.

The same feature can be enregistered in multiple ways. For example, in the history of English, alveolar (ing) (the pronunciation of the morpheme -ing as [n]) has been associated with both upper-class and lower-class speech. In Pittsburgh, the same features that are in some situations, by some people, associated with uneducated, sloppy, or working-class speech can, in other situations and sometimes by other people, be associated with the city's identity, with local pride and authenticity. Over time, the indexical linkages between linguistic forms and social meanings can evolve so that one ideological scheme used to link forms and meanings can be replaced by another. By virtue of a variety of discursive and metadiscursive activities, a set of features associated with an accent can come to be represented collectively in the public imagination as a stable register (in the case in question in this chapter, the sort of place-linked register that is typically called a "dialect") and maintained across time via practices that reiterate and reinforce the evaluation of the register and its link to the social identity associated with a particular type of persona (the authentic Pittsburgher, in this case).

Commodification

Although the term "commodification" is used in a variety of ways, sometimes to refer to any reification of a social process, a narrower and more literal conceptualization captures the process represented by Pittsburghese shirts. Borrowing Fairclough's (1992: 207) definition, I conceptualize commodification as "the process whereby social domains and institutions, whose concern is not producing commodities in the narrower economic sense of goods for sale, come nevertheless to be organized and conceptualized in terms of commodity production, distribution, and consumption." A linguistic variety or a set of varieties is commodified when it is available for purchase and people will pay for it. For example, Hall (1995) explores the commodification of an intimate register of talk by telephone sex workers who are paid for intimacy. Cameron (2000) discusses the commodification not only of speech styles but of particular scripted utterances in new-economy jobs such as telephone marketing, consumer service, and opinion polling, where highly standardized speech has economic value and people are paid to produce it. Gaudio (2003) explores how conversation is commodified by a coffeehouse chain, and Bucholtz (1999, 2008) shows how linguistic styles can involve ways of talking associated with material goods. English has become a valuable commodity worldwide, and other languages more locally (Tan and Rubdy 2008). Heller (2003) shows how French-English bilingualism, once associated with Francophone Canadian identity but stigmatized on the economic market, has come to be a valuable commodity in the call-center sector, as call centers locate where bilinguals can be hired.

What people are buying when they buy a Pittsburghese shirt is not only an item of clothing but also the words and images on it. A men's plain white Hanes T-shirt is available for retail purchase for as little as $2.19 but will sell for $5 or $8 with Pittsburghese printed on it. What has happened, locally and in popular culture at large, to enable Pittsburgh speech to add value to a shirt in this way? Appadurai's (1986) description of the "commodity situation" is a useful heuristic for exploring the conditions and processes that have led to the viability of Pittsburghese shirts.

According to Appadurai, the "commodity situation in the social life of any 'thing' [can] be defined as the situation in which its exchangeability (past, present, or future) for some other thing is its socially relevant feature." In order to enter into a commodity situation, a "thing" (in our case, the imagined dialect people call "Pittsburghese") must, historically, be in a "commodity phase," it must be a potential "commodity candidate," and it must be in a viable "commodity context" (Appadurai 1986: 13–15). In other words, to understand how and why Pittsburghese has become a commodity bought and sold in the form of T-shirts, we need to answer these questions:

Commodity phase: When and how did local speech in Pittsburgh acquire the potential for commodification? What set of ideas about local speech had to be in place before people could begin to think of it as having economic value in this way? Answering these questions requires taking a historical perspective on the indexical meanings of Pittsburgh linguistic forms.

Commodity candidacy: What makes something like local speech a potential commodity? What is the larger cultural framework in which it makes sense to people to buy and sell Pittsburghese? Answering these questions requires thinking about more widely circulating ideas about place, identity, and authenticity that shape how vernacular practices like regional speech are evaluated.

Commodity context: In what ideological and material contexts can local speech be a viable commodity? Answering this question requires taking a close look at the economics of T-shirt sales and the ideas about T-shirts as a medium of communication that encourage people to produce and purchase Pittsburghese shirts.

In what follows, I discuss each of these issues in turn. Since each of these sections could itself be an article, these discussions are necessarily brief. Rather than touching on every element of the context that makes Pittsburghese shirts possible, I focus on a few key elements in each category.

Commodity phase

When is Pittsburgh speech in a commodity phase? In other words, when does local speech become a potential commodity? To answer this question, I turn again to the process by which speech features can become enregistered in multiple ways that change over time. One way of thinking about this process is in terms of "orders of indexicality" (Silverstein 2003). According to Silverstein, linguistic features that are correlated with demographic facts about people (adapting Silverstein's more abstract terminology to an actual historical context, I call these first-order indexicals) can come to do social work, as people enregister these features in terms of some set of ideas about the people who use them. A group of features that have been enregistered in terms of an ideological schema that divides languages into neatly bounded sets of varieties, some of which can be mapped onto places, can come to be thought of as a "dialect." This is the ideological schema that typically shapes dialectologists' (and to some extent sociolinguists') experience with variation. But what may start out sounding like a dialect to linguists may not start out sounding that way to local laypeople, and even once they come to hear a particular set of local features as a regional dialect, the indexical meaning of using the dialect can vary and change.

   In Pittsburgh, local forms were at first only correlated with demographic facts about their users. Because there was no metapragmatic activity calling attention to the first-order correlation, the forms had no indexical meaning. Only when alternative forms began to be heard did some Pittsburgh forms become hearable, by contrast with the alternatives. It should be noted that the set of forms that have become hearable in Pittsburgh includes many forms also heard outside of Pittsburgh and does not include some forms that are heard in Pittsburgh. With the exception of the monophthongization of /aw/, usually represented on T-shirts as <ah> in words like "dahntahn," all occur elsewhere in western and central Pennsylvania, along the Ohio River valley, or in Appalachia. Of interest in this article is not which elements of "Pittsburghese" a linguist would associate with Pittsburgh as opposed to other places, but why and how a particular set of features comes to be associated with Pittsburgh in the popular imagination. In other words, the set of forms associated with "Pittsburghese" in the local imagination is not the same as the set of forms a linguist, operating with a different set of assumptions about language, class, and place, would identify with Pittsburgh speech.

Once they became hearable, features of local-sounding speech were first linked ideologically with working-class identity, incorrectness, and/or lack of education.[4] These are the "second-order" indexical meanings of the dialect. Gradually, however, the set of features enregistered as "Pittsburghese" and the indexical meaning of using them have started to shift, so that now many people hear a slightly different subset of features of local speech as expressing local identity and some can use it to project localness. These are "third-order" indexical links. Table 24.1 sketches this process.

Pittsburgh speech entered a commodity phase only when local forms were socially meaningful at the third-order level, that is, when they were no longer linked exclusively with class or correctness but also (or, for some people, instead) with local identity. It is at this stage that a Pittsburgh word or phrase can come to evoke local pride or nostalgia, even among people who do not identify themselves as working class or as speakers of a nonstandard variety. While the earlier (and, for some people, still exclusively) more stigmatized meanings of local forms still resonate, so that a Pittsburghese shirt may still call to mind working-class pride and disregard for correctness, this link is now indirect, mediated by the association of local forms with authentic localness.

As we have shown in more detail elsewhere (Johnstone et al 2006), moves from first- to second-order and from second- to third-order indexicality of local speech forms have been enabled by social and geographical mobility. When Pittsburgh women began to get jobs as secretaries and receptionists, they came into contact with other social classes and their ways of talking and had to learn to vary their speech in order to sound more correct and careful, or, alternatively, to sound more like their peers. When Pittsburghers began to travel, in the military and on vacation, and came into contact with people from other places who sounded different and noticed that the Pittsburghers sounded different to them, they began to connect local speech with place and identity. Mobility has thus been perhaps the crucial factor in putting Pittsburgh speech into a commodity phase.

Commodity candidacy

One of the many intersecting sets of ideas that make local speech a potential commodity is the ideology about language, place, and tradition that underlies what Bendix (1988) calls "folklorism." This is the idea, which originates in nineteenth-

Table 24.1 Indexical change in Pittsburgh

Silverstein (2003)	In Pittsburgh
"*n*-th-order indexical": A feature whose use can be correlated with a sociodemographic identity (e.g., region or class) or a semantic function (e.g., number-marking).	**First-order indexicality:** The frequency of regional variants in a person's speech can be correlated with whether he/she is from southwestern Penn. (especially from Pittsburgh), working-class, and/or male.
"*n*+1-th-order indexical": An *n*-th order indexical feature that has been assigned "an ethno-metapragmatically driven native interpretation" (Silverstein 2003: 212), i.e., a meaning in terms of one or more native ideologies (the idea that certain people speak more correctly than others, for example).	**Second-order indexicality:** Regional features become available for social work; speakers start to notice and attribute meaning to regional variants and shift styles in their own speech. The meaning of these forms is shaped, for many, by ideologies about class and correctness.
"(n+l)+l-th-order indexical": An indexical phenomenon at order *n*+1 can come to have another, (n+l)+l-th-order, indexical meaning when a subset of its features come to be perceived as meaningful according to another ideological schema.	**Third-order indexicality:** People who notice the existence of second-order stylistic variation in Pittsburghers' speech link the regional variants they are most likely to hear with Pittsburgh identity, drawing on the idea that places and dialects are essentially linked.

century Romanticism and continues to circulate today, that old, vernacular practices and artifacts are the most authentic. According to the ideology of folklorism, "authentic" folk ways are untainted, desirable in a way that newer practices are not, even if newer ways are more practical. Ideas like these lead people to want to preserve old things and old ways of doing things even if—or even to show that—they do not do things that way themselves. In Pittsburgh, being able to cite the older form of a local word can be a useful way of claiming expertise about local speech (Johnstone 2007).

According to the ideology of folklorism, cultural authenticity is also linked with connectedness to place. This is because older social practices last longer in isolated places, where it is less likely that new practices will be imported. People and practices that have never moved, or that have generations of rootedness in a particular geographic area, are, according to this set of ideas, better and more authentic than others. When this ideological scheme is in play, Appalachian folk-songs collected in remote valleys trump contemporary or even classical forms, Texas roper boots and broad-brimmed hats trump contemporary clothing, "Downeaster" accents from Maine trump more regional or national varieties. In Pittsburgh, the display of local speech is sometimes part and parcel of the display of other elements of local cultural heritage, like steelworkers' hard hats, plaques and signs commemorating local people and historical moments, buildings where memorable events occurred, and the like. The Pittsburgh historical museum has at times had a small informational poster about Pittsburgh speech on display, and a film and a museum exhibit on the theme of "Pittsburgh A to Z" both featured the pronoun *yinz* ("you, pl."; a form of *you ones*) to fill the slot for Y. Knowing what local linguistic forms mean is sometimes explicitly linked with Pittsburgh authenticity, as in the T-shirt in Figure 24.2.

Commodity context

When the right historical and ideological factors are in place, economic and technical factors must also line up in such a way as to make Pittsburghese shirts viable as a commodity. First, it must make sense in the context of local resources and practices to sell and buy T-shirts with words and images printed on them. People must know by whom and why such shirts can be worn, and the shirts must seem affordable. As Miller (2002) points out in a study of T-shirts produced by fans of the rock band Phish, there is a tradition in the US and elsewhere of playful T-shirts, often featuring borrowed and recontextualized images. Such shirts are purchased and worn because of their "badging" function (Symes 1987; Kelly 2003). People who see Pittsburghese shirts for sale tend, in other words, to know how to consume them, both in the sense of how to interpret them and in the sense of who might wear them and in what contexts.

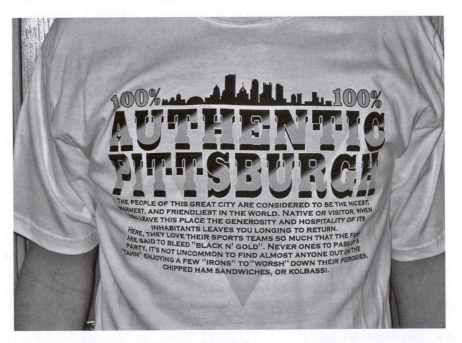

Figure 24.2 "100% Authentic Pittsburgh" T-shirt. The final sentence reads "It's not uncommon to find almost anyone out on the 'tahn' enjoying a few 'irons' to 'worsh' down their pierogies, chipped ham sandwiches, or kolbassi."

Second, elements of the shirts' design must be available. The designers of Pittsburghese shirts draw heavily for the shirts' content on Internet lists of Pittsburghese words, such as those found at www.pittsburghese.com. The shirt in Figure 24.3 borrows a well-known phrase, "I'm surrounded by idiots," and reworks it with a local word, *jagoff.*

Ideas for the shirts' visual design are also borrowed and reused. Black and gold, the colors of the city's sports teams and the city shield and flag, are almost compulsory for any item alluding to local identity. Images of the downtown cityscape have been featured on Pittsburghese shirts since they were first produced. Other elements of visual design are also borrowed. During the 1990s, automobile bumper-stickers that identify vacation spots in a design borrowed from European country-identification stickers became common in the Pittsburgh area and elsewhere in the United States. For example, OBX, in black on white and enclosed in a black-bordered oval, means the Outer Banks, while HHI means Hilton Head Island—both popular beach destinations for Pittsburghers. The T-shirt in Figure 24.4 borrows this design and reworks it with a designation based not on a place-name abbreviation but on the word *yinz,* which is thought to be an exclusively Pittsburghese form.

Third, producing and selling Pittsburghese shirts must be economically feasible. The availability of wholesale T-shirts and sweatshirts at low cost, together with inexpensive reproduction technology that is available locally, makes the shirts relatively disposable, so people are willing to purchase them without much forethought. According to the website of Berda CompuGraphix (www.berda.com), a T-shirt wholesaler and printer located near Pittsburgh, a white, 100% cotton, heavyweight or 50/50% cotton/poly blend T-shirt, including one-color printing in one location, wholesales for $3.29 per shirt if 500 shirts are purchased. Selling such a shirt for as little as $5 represents a 50% markup. Gold shirts with black printing

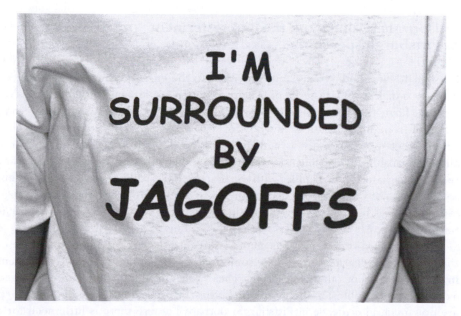

Figure 24.3 "I'm surrounded by Jagoffs" T-shirt

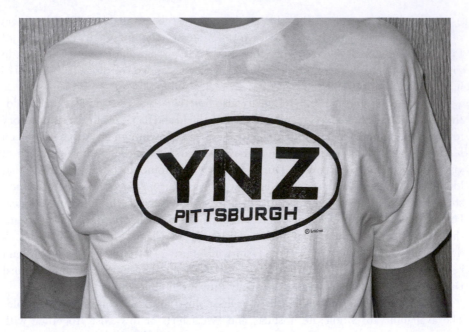

Figure 24.4 "YNZ Pittsburgh" shirt

are $5.29 per shirt for 500 shirts; these often sell for $8, which again represents a 50% markup. Dealers' overhead costs are low, since the shirts can be produced nearby and are often sold on the street. In sum, it makes economic sense both to sell Pittsburghese shirts and to buy them.

Pittsburghese shirts and the enregisterment of Pittsburgh speech

Pittsburgh shirts both require and contribute to the enregisterment of local speech forms as a dialect. Enregisterment is a precondition for Pittsburghese shirts for two reasons. First, the shirts appeal to people who are able to hear Pittsburgh speech as different from other varieties and who link Pittsburgh speech not with working-class or incorrect speech as much as with authentic local identity. Second, they require already-available lists of linguistic forms identified with "Pittsburghese," and they require purchasers to be familiar with the practice of respelling words to make them sound local. As I have argued above, these conditions are met only when a set of local forms has been enregistered, and in particular only when their indexicality is third order.

But the third-order enregisterment of Pittsburgh speech is also an outcome of the production, distribution, and consumption of Pittsburghese shirts. This happens in several ways. For one thing, Pittsburghese shirts put local speech on display, on sidewalk display tables, in shops, and on bodies. (People actually wearing the shirts are not much in evidence in Pittsburgh, perhaps because there is little need for a person in Pittsburgh to "badge" the fact that he or she is a Pittsburgher. Pittsburghers living elsewhere and tourists who visit the city would have a greater use for the identity-badging afforded by the shirts.) Second, Pittsburghese shirts link local speech with social and economic value. T-shirts were once men's underwear, and many people who buy or wear them think they are appropriate only for casual-dress situations. Pittsburghese shirts are also relatively inexpensive. This both mirrors and suggests the idea that Pittsburgh speech has limited value but may be appropriate in some contexts.

Third, Pittsburghese shirts help standardize Pittsburghese, the imagined dialect. This is by virtue of their intertextuality with one another and with representations of Pittsburgh speech in other media, such as online lists and McCool's (1982) well-known folk dictionary. A comparison of one T-shirt from the late 1990s with the McCool dictionary makes this clear. Of the 32 words on the shirt, 26 were also in the folk dictionary, and 20 of these were spelled the same way on the shirt as in the book. When asked, during fieldwork, where they get their ideas, T-shirt vendors sometimes refer to "lists on the internet." This degree of intertextuality is made possible in large part by the fact that Pittsburghese shirts are bought and sold in a grassroots, often literally person-on-the-street market that is not quite legitimate, if not quite illegitimate. Trademarking is rare, and designers and vendors are unlikely to sue one another for copying their ideas, word lists, or designs.[5]

Finally, Pittsburghese shirts, and the economic practices in which they participate, lend specific meanings to local speech. They link dialect and place by juxtaposing local words on images of the city, sometimes directly, as when local words are enclosed in speech balloons emanating from downtown windows (see Figure 24.5; see also Figure 24.1 above).

Figure 24.5 Linking speech and place on the front of a T-shirt

As noted, their colors—the city's colors and those of the city's professional football, baseball, and hockey teams—also link the speech forms represented on the shirts with the city of Pittsburgh. The words that are included and the way words are defined on the backs of many of the shirts serves also to link the forms with local practices. Of the 31 items listed on the back of the shirt depicted in Figure 24.1 above, 13 (arguably more if one includes more indirect allusions to the city) are forms that are explicitly linked with the Pittsburgh area, by virtue either of how they are defined or of their inclusion at all:

> **blitzburgh: n.** a drinking town with a football problem
> **chipped ham: n.** thinly sliced ham sold only in the Burg
> **hans: n.** a part of the body used to hold a cold Iron [Iron City is a Pittsburgh beer]
> **jagoff: n.** anyone who pisses off a Pittsburger [*sic*, Pittsburgher]
> **jynt iggle: n.** a popular supermarket [Giant Eagle]
> **keller: n.** black and gold to name a few
> **picksburgh: n.** the greatest city in pensivania [Pennsylvania]
> **sammich: n.** chipped ham or jumbo between two pieces of Town Talk bread [a local bakery]
> **spicket: n.** a tap on a barrel of Iron
> **stillers: n.** four time super bowl champs with unfinished business [Steelers, Pittsburgh's professional football team]
> **the burgh: n.** a helluva cool place
> **the mon: n.** the Monogahela [*sic*, Monongahela] River
> **the point: n.** the meeting place of Pittsburgh's Three Rivers

The venues where Pittsburghese shirts are sold and the people who sell them reinforce the idea that local speech is casual and fun, linked with working-class mores, and in some cases even a bit shady. They are sold at airport newsstands and gift shops where tourists congregate and, probably more than anywhere else, in the wholesale market area called the Strip, now also a destination for "ethnic" foods sold in rundown but charming old buildings, a café where Italian can still be heard, and a number of more upscale kitchen-supply and home decorating stores. Pittsburghers of Italian heritage go to the Strip to shop for Italian breads, cheeses, and pastry, seafood for the traditional seven-fishes Christmas Eve dinner, and grapes for wine-making. There are also Greek, Arab, Asian, and Mexican shops. On the sidewalk, ready-made food, flowers, and a variety of other items such as cheap clothing and jewelry are sold from folding tables. On any Saturday, at least three T-shirt vendors open up or set up shop, one in an old, windowless storefront, one at a permanent wooden booth, and at least one at a folding table. Their location is thus associated experientially with traditional food ways and with an informal, leisurely way of shopping, for fun, in a somewhat grubby but comfortable environment. The Strip experience attracts tourists, reminds Pittsburghers of their heritage, and encourages impulse buying, which makes it an ideal site for the sale of Pittsburghese shirts.

The merchandise with which Pittsburghese shirts are juxtaposed on tables and hanging displays also reinforces its connection with local vernacular practices. Especially prominent are sports T-shirts, particularly ones celebrating the Pittsburgh

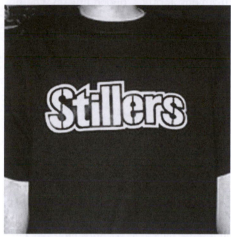

Figure 24.6 Pittsburgh Steelers/
Pittsburghese shirts (rings and
footballs on pedestals refer to the
Steelers' Superbowl championships)

Steelers. Some shirts combine Pittsburghese and sports imagery. Figure 24.6 shows
three such shirts.

The first two refer to the team's fifth national championship victory in ways that
include Pittsburghese forms (*n'at*, *yinz*); the third spells the team's name in a way
that purports to represent how it is locally pronounced. In addition, Pittsburghese
shirts are sometimes sold alongside shirts that disparage Cleveland, Pittsburgh's
traditional sports rival.

Discussion

The production and circulation of Pittsburghese shirts is one of the many ways in
which many Pittsburghers, ex-Pittsburghers, and visitors come to share ideas about
what Pittsburgh speech consists of and what it means. It is also evidence that this
process has been going on for some time. Appadurai's heuristic provides a useful way
of exploring the details about what makes Pittsburghese shirts viable. It would no

doubt also be useful for exploring the circumstances under which other media for Pittsburghese have been produced, circulated, and consumed, although the details would be slightly different for coffee mugs or postcards than for T-shirts. As I hope to have shown, exploring the process of commodification of dialect also requires exploring the process of enregisterment of dialect. Dialect enregisterment is both a precondition for and an outcome of dialect commodification.

Exploring this process in detail is worthwhile not only because it is important for understanding the history of "Pittsburghese" and its impact on how Pittsburghers talk, but also because it is important for understanding the object of dialectologists' and sociolinguists' study in general. As we see here, dialects do not exist in the world. Both we and the people we study create dialects as we use a variety of media and genres to exchange ideas about how people talk. These metapragmatic practices serve to link particular speech features with indexical meanings, by evoking ideological schemes in order to attribute certain social characteristics to people who use certain forms. Linguists' evolving ideas about language, place, and identity have led to a number of ways of demarcating dialect areas from one another, depending on whether the focus is on sounds (Labov et al 2006) or words (Carver 1987; Kretzschmar 2005). Laypeople's evolving ideas about language, place, and identity lead them to demarcate dialects from one another in different ways, ways that are often less systematic and seem less "objective." But the process is the same. We need, then, to be a more reflexive than we have been about where our own ideas about dialects come from and how they function.

References

Agha, A. (2003) "The social life of cultural value," *Language and Communication* 23: 231–73.
—— (2007) *Language and Social Relations*, New York: Cambridge University Press.
Anderson, B. (1991) *Imagined Communities: Reflections on the Origin and Spread of Nationalism*, revised and extended edition, London: Verso.
Appadurai, A. (1986) "Commodities and the politics of value," in A. Appadurai (ed.) *The Social Life of Things: Commodities in Cultural Perspective*, Cambridge: Cambridge University Press, 3–63.
Bendix, R. (1988) "Folklorism: the challenge of a concept," *International Folklore Review* 6: 5–15.
Bucholtz, M. (1999) "Purchasing power: the gender and class imaginary on the shopping channel," in M. Bucholtz, A.C. Liang, and L.A. Sutton (eds.) *Reinventing Identities: The Gendered Self in Discourse*, New York: Oxford University Press, 348–68.
—— (2008) "Shop talk: branding, consumption and gender in American middle-class youth interaction," in B.S. McElhinny (ed.) *Words, Worlds, and Material Girls: Language, Gender, Globalization*, Berlin: Mouton de Gruyter, 371–403.
Cameron, D. (2000) "Styling the worker: gender and the commodification of language in the globalized service economy," *Journal of Sociolinguistics* 4: 323–47.
Carver, C.M. (1987) *American Regional Dialects: A Word Geography*, Ann Arbor: University of Michigan Press.
Eberhardt, M. (2008) "The low-back merger in the Steel City: African American English in Pittsburgh," *American Speech* 83: 284–311.
Fairclough, N. (1992) *Discourse and Social Change*, Cambridge: Polity.
Gaudio, R.P. (2003) "Coffeetalk: Starbucks™ and the commercialization of casual conversation," *Language in Society* 32: 659–91.

Hall, K. (1995) "Lip service on the fantasy lines," in K. Hall and M. Bucholtz (eds.) *Gender Articulated: Language and the Socially Constructed Self*, New York: Routledge, 183–216.

Heller, M. (2003) "Globalization, the new economy, and the commodification of language and identity," *Journal of Sociolinguistics* 7: 473–92.

Johnstone, B. (2007) "Linking identity and dialect through stancetaking," in R. Englebretson (ed.) *Stancetaking in Discourse: Subjectivity, Evaluation, Interaction*, Amsterdam: Benjamins, 49–68.

Johnstone, B., Andrus, J., and Danielson, A.E. (2006) "Mobility, indexicality, and the enregisterment of 'Pittsburghese,'" *Journal of English Linguistics* 34: 77–104.

Kelly, M. (2003) "Projecting an image and expressing identity: T-shirts in Hawaii," *Fashion Theory* 7: 191–212.

Kretzschmar, W.A., Jr. (2005) *Linguistic Atlas Projects*, http://us.english.uga.edu.

Labov, W., Ash, S., and Boberg, C. (2006) *Atlas of North American English: Phonetics, Phonology and Sound Change*, Berlin: Mouton de Gruyter.

McCool, S. (1982) *Sam McCool's New Pittsburghese: How to Speak Like a Pittsburgher*, Pittsburgh, PA: Hayford.

Miller, S.J. (2002) "Phish Phan pholklore: identity and community through commodities in the Phish parking lot scene," *Midwestern Folklore* 28: 42–60.

Ochs, E. (1992) "Indexing gender," in A. Duranti and C. Goodwin (eds.) *Rethinking Context: Language as an Interactive Phenomenon*, New York: Cambridge University Press, 335–58.

Silverstein, M. (1993) "Metapragmatic discourse and metapragmatic function," in J.A. Lucy (ed.) *Reflexive Language: Reported Speech and Metapragmatics*, Cambridge: Cambridge University Press, 33–58.

—— (2003) "Indexical order and the dialectics of sociolinguistic life," *Language and Communication* 23: 193–229.

Symes, C. (1987) "Keeping abreast with the times: towards an iconography of T-shirts," *Studies in Popular Culture* 12: 87–100.

Tan, P.K.W. and Rubdy, R. (eds.) (2008) *Language as Commodity: Global Structures, Local Marketplaces*, London: Continuum.

Notes

1   I have edited this transcript to make it as readable as possible, since hesitations, back channeling, and the like are not germane to my analysis.

2   *Jagoff* derives from *jag* "to poke, tease, annoy." *Jag* in this sense occurs in other local words and phrases such as *jaggerbush* "briar bush" and *jag around* "fool around." It has recently become associated with the unrelated vulgarity *jack off* and is accordingly used less frequently than it once was.

3   Sociolinguists have typically not expected African Americans to share local whites' speech features or participate in local whites' patterns of language change. Thus, interactions between African Americans' and whites' speech and ideas about speech have largely escaped scholarly notice. Eberhardt (2008) shows, however, that Pittsburgh African Americans do in fact share one phonological feature (the merger of the low back vowels /ɑ/ and /ɔ/) with white Pittsburghers and not with African Americans elsewhere, and my research shows that Pittsburgh African Americans use a number of lexical items common to local whites but not to African Americans in other cities.

4   I do not mean to suggest that all urban dialects are initially enregistered as working-class, simply that this is what happened in Pittsburgh.

5   In this, Pittsburghese shirts are very different from the sports-team shirts they are usually sold with. Unlicensed uses of logos and other design elements of sports T-shirts can result in legal action by the national sports federations.

Chapter 25

Gerlinde Mautner

SIGNS OF THE TIMES

A discourse perspective on public signage, urban space and the law

Introduction: why study signs?

IN URBAN ENVIRONMENTS, we are constantly exposed to a variety of directions, warnings and prohibitions, and most of them appear on signs. Walking as little as a few hundred metres along any street in a modern city will easily prove this point. You will be admonished, for example, not to *loiter* outside an office block's back entrance (Figure 25.1) and not to assume you were in truly public space just because you had been given access to it (Figure 25.2); you will be warned that you are being filmed by surveillance cameras (Figure 25.3), and that if you want to hand out leaflets outside a supermarket – whether for commercial or political purposes – you will have to get the management's permission first (Figure 25.4). Even the simplest everyday activity, it seems, comes with instructions (Figure 25.5), and the most commonsensically obvious world knowledge is pointed out (Figure 25.6[1]). Although all these examples, and others to be discussed later in the paper, come from Britain, readers from other national backgrounds will readily recognize the general phenomenon.

While signs' ubiquity is in itself striking, it is far from the only thing that makes them interesting. To the discourse analyst, they are worthwhile objects of study for various other reasons.

1. As texts, they are unusual in that their meaning and performative potential are partly derived from exophoric reference to their immediate physical environment, a phenomenon which Scollon and Wong Scollon (2003) refer to as 'emplacement'. For the emplaced sign, the space surrounding it is not merely a contextual factor affecting the interpretation of what the sign *says*; it also has a direct bearing on what the sign *does*. In other words, signs exemplify a particular relationship between language and space.

Figure 25.1 Bloomsbury, London

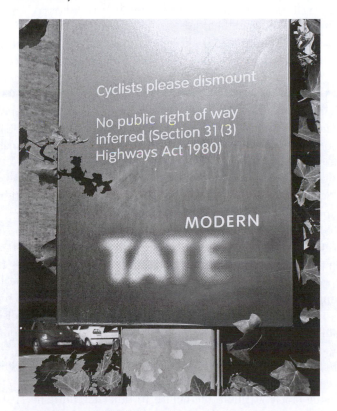

Figure 25.2 Near the Tate Modern, London

Figure 25.3 Clapham Junction Railway Station, South London

Figure 25.4 Outside Morrisons supermarket, Cardiff Bay, Cardiff, UK

Figure 25.5 Railway Station, Bath, UK

Figure 25.6 Cardiff Bay, Cardiff, UK

2.   The type of directive sign studied here also illustrates how intertextuality – that is, cross-referencing between a sign and other texts – can be crucial in order to ensure that the sign can actually do the 'work' it is meant to do. As we shall see, signs often derive their authority from the law (and statutes may be mentioned explicitly on the sign itself); in turn, for some legal provisions to take effect, signs actually have to be where the law says they should be. In these cases, the intertextual links do more than just help readers interpret the sign; they are a necessary condition for the sign to have its desired legal effect.

3.   Signs are richly multimodal, often combining text, symbols and pictures. In addition, some of their performative quality is derived from the material on which the signs are printed and the fixings used. That is, we are more likely to act as signs urge us to if they *look* legitimate.

4.   Signs make a significant contribution to 'linguistic landscapes', the study of which is an exciting, burgeoning new field (Shohamy and Gorter 2009; Jaworski and Thurlow 2010). To date, linguistic landscape research has looked at signage primarily through the lens of multilingualism, investigating how signs both reflect and constitute the complex linguistic environments of modern cities. Also, the emphasis has been mostly on commercial signs, such as those on shop fronts. Concentrating on directive signs, and taking legal issues into account, as the present chapter does, might thus take us in a useful new direction.

5.   Signs are implicated in socio-legal and socio-spatial issues such as the demarcation between public and private space, social exclusion, the social construction of risk and, crucially, the question of who has the power to control access to space. Studying signs is therefore also a good entry point to a range of social questions which are familiar territory for discourse analysis in general, and for critical discourse analysis (CDA) in particular.

Thus, apart from any intrinsic analytical interest that signage may generate, it can serve well as a test case for both broadening and deepening our understanding of how discourse works. Of course, signs are not 'mainstream' texts of the two-dimensional, paper-based variety that most discourse analysts study. Yet, arguably, it is precisely because signs are unusual kinds of texts that they can help to throw light on discursive phenomena that are of interest over and above their relevance for the study of signs.

The above list provides the road map for the present chapter. The next section outlines what I mean by approaching signage from a discourse perspective. After that, I consider textual issues (relating to points one to three) and then social issues (points four and five). Finally, the chapter will conclude with some thoughts on open questions and wider implications for discourse analysis.

Adopting a discourse perspective

In the context of studying signage, what does it mean to adopt a discourse perspective, and specifically one inspired by CDA? On the basis of the many programmatic statements that now exist about CDA (e.g., van Dijk 1993; Wodak and Meyer 2009), such an approach to signage will:

- start with an observation grounded in social life – the recognition that signs 'do' things to people and have tangible effects on communities; in other words, that signage, as discourse, not only reflects social reality but contributes to shaping it;
- examine the spatial, socio-political, economic and legal context as a core element of the analysis rather than a peripheral one;
- challenge the notion that the social structures reflected in and shaped by signs are 'natural' and inevitable, instead treating them as contingent and amenable to change;
- use authentic data collected *in situ*, that is, in signs' original environments;
- give potentially equal weight to all linguistic levels – lexis, syntax and text – as well as to non-verbal means of expression.

For any one study, it may be neither possible nor advisable to try and cover all of the above ground. Yet, combined in creative ways to suit the data at hand, these principles ensure that signs are not treated purely as a surface phenomenon, but are seen as indexing social structures and processes. It is these deeper layers of social organization that the discourse analyst driven by a 'critical impetus' (Wodak and Meyer 2009: 6) aims to penetrate. In the process, linguistic landscapes, and the familiar signs in them, are defamiliarized and denaturalized, to borrow terms from critical sociology (Bauman and May 2001: 10) and critical management studies (Alvesson and Willmott 1992: 13). Apparently mundane signs such as *Private Property* (Figure 25.1) are so widespread in today's cityscapes that they seem to blend into their environments, so that their legal and socio-political underpinnings can easily go unnoticed. However, when scrutinized through a critical lens, such signs emerge as key instruments for regulating public space and thus effectively constructing it (Lefebvre 1991). And how *that* is done is never 'natural' but always a question of social convention and power mediated through institutions. One of these institutions is the law. It establishes and enforces the rights associated with private property (such as the right to exclusive use), while also specifying property owners' liability. The law also defines and penalizes deviant behaviour (such as drinking alcohol in certain public places). The law thus forms the institutional backdrop for the directives that appear on signs.

Textual issues[2]

Signs probably rank among the texts read most frequently by the largest number of people. Yet, as texts go, what you see on signs is rather unusual, and this is not just because they contain relatively few words (if any). The aim of the present section is to explore the other peculiarities of signage – emplacement, intertextuality and materiality.

Emplacement

Directive signs mean what they mean and get people to do certain things because they reach outside the text and into the specific environment in which they are located.

Remove them from this environment and they cease to be performative, at least in the way that was originally intended. This is because, to use a concept from speech act theory (Austin 1962), a key felicity condition for the directive speech act is no longer present once the sign is removed from its original environment. The sign *Water can be dangerous* is literally and figuratively 'out of place' if, say, propped up against a wall in a built-up area without any body of water close by. Similarly, a sign saying *Naturist Beach* (Figure 25.7) depends on the presence of a beach for its readers to be informed that, in the area so designated, specific social rules apply.

This particular quality of signs is indeed distinctive and not a quality of texts in general. For the sake of comparison, take a newspaper article. *Where* you read it – in which country, city, or room of the house – may not be completely irrelevant for how you do so, but the location will not materially affect its meaning. By contrast, the *implied grammatical* object of the phrase *Do not touch* written on a sign is inevitably the *physical* object to which the sign refers by virtue of spatial proximity. Significantly changing the position of the sign means changing that referent.

This inevitable effect of emplacement on meaning and performativity does not necessarily imply that a sign's sphere of applicability is unambiguously demarcated. Sometimes it is (See Figure 25.9: *The land lying between this notice and the brass studs . . .*), and sometimes it isn't (Figures 25.7 and 25.8). In the latter case, the resulting fuzziness can lead to confusion, conflict and even legal disputes (as will be readily testified by anyone who has had their car clamped, paid a hefty release fee – and then wondered whether their car really was parked *inside* the area designated as a clamping zone).

The legal implications of emplacement go even further. In some cases, laws do not apply at all unless the signs are displayed as stipulated in the relevant statute. For example, fining an unauthorized person for entering a port's 'restricted area', or forcibly removing them from it, is lawful only if 'at the material time, notices stating that the area concerned was a restricted area were posted so as to be readily seen and read by persons entering the restricted area' (*Ship and Port Facility (Security) Regulations 2004*, 11(2)). Thus, the sign is not just socially but legally performative: without it, the legal norm stated in the statute is not applicable – a consideration that leads us straight to the issue of intertextuality.

Intertextuality

The Ship and Port Facility example has shown the importance of intertextual connections between signage and legislation. In this particular case, the connection works both ways. Not only does the statute mention the necessary signs, but the signs displayed *in situ*, in turn, mention the law. The relevant sign, attached to a wire fence around Cardiff Harbour, reads:

> Restricted Area. Entry into this area without authorisation is a breach of security and will render you liable to prosecution under the Ship and Port Facility (Security) Regulations 2004.

References to the law can be explicit, and either precise (see Figures 25.2 and 25.9, for example, referring to *Section 31(3) Highways Act 1980*) or vague (as in Figure 25.3,

Figure 25.7 Brighton, UK

Figure 25.8 Southwark, London

Figure 25.9 Near Victoria Station, London

Figure 25.10 Islington, London

announcing CCTV surveillance and saying that *Evidence can be used in a court of law*). Alternatively, legal authority may be merely implied and inferred. For example, it can nowadays be taken as common knowledge in many countries that *No smoking* signs have legal backing; they will be interpreted accordingly, even when they do not quote any anti-smoking legislation (although some do, as in signs saying *Smoke-free in accordance with the Health Act 2006*, for example). Whether people actually comply is, of course, a different matter, but there can be no question that even non-compliers will have understood the directive speech act and will be aware of their non-compliance.

Another way in which legal authority can be implied rather than stated is through the verbal and/or visual presence of the institutional author of the sign, such as a city council. Social agents legitimated to issue directives may be named or represented visually through their logos (e.g., Figures 25.6 and 25.7). In the Tate Modern example (Figure 25.2), legal authority is signalled both explicitly and implicitly – on the one hand, through reference to the Highways Act, and on the other, through the logo, the gallery's corporate design, and the professional presentation of the sign as a whole. It thus shows neatly how intertextuality can interact with another dimension of meaning-making on signs, namely their visual and material quality.

Materiality

We have noted that a directive sign's performative potential depends on where the sign is (*emplacement*) and how it indexes legal authority through implicit and/or explicit references to the law (*intertextuality*). It seems intuitively obvious, however, that another factor plays a part in our assessment of signs: quite simply, whether they *look* official enough to be taken seriously. Use of the corporate design associated with an authorized social agent is one type of indicator; another is the material quality of the sign. A sign saying *Any bicycles chained to these railings will be removed* has different performative potential depending on whether it is an A4-sized handwritten note on flimsy paper taped to a fence, or a large, professionally printed sign with a metal back and firmly screwed to the railings in question (see Figure 25.10).

This strong link between the material presentation of a text and its assessment as authoritative may not be unique to signage. There are other text types, too, that we are more likely to accept as authentic if the material they are printed on conforms to legal requirements and our expectations – parking tickets, for example, or passports and banknotes. Still, the relevance of materiality is a feature of signs special enough to be worth noting, particularly in comparison to types of text that are not legally performative, such as novels. Whether you read *Oliver Twist* in hardback, paperback or e-book form may affect your subjective reading experience, but does not fundamentally affect its content.

Of course, it is possible to fake authority by making signs look official. This happened in Vienna recently when, in response to road closures, signs marking an 'alternative cycle route' appeared. Although to all intents and purposes the signs looked fully authorized, news reports[3] claimed that they had not in fact been put up by either the Vienna Transport Authority or the City Council. Instead they were attributed to an unnamed 'guerrilla' group of cycling activists. Surprisingly, the signs were not removed and were allowed to serve their purpose for the whole duration of the road closures – an example of successful grassroots activism played out through the medium of the sign.

Interestingly, there are echoes here of what Rose-Redwood (2008) calls 'performative resistance'. By this, he means the 'subversion' of a performative act by the purposeful, collective non-compliance of those it addresses, even though all felicity conditions have apparently been met. (Rose-Redwood's example shows how the official codification of street names may be resisted by citizens through 'myriad counter-performances', Rose-Redwood 2008: 890–1.) It would seem that this concept can usefully be extended to cover situations like the cycling route example. Here, the resistance consists in appropriating the semiotic resources that are known to index socio-legal authority, in order to claim power over space.

Faking authority on signs has its limits, however. While it is true that a convincing appearance of authenticity can be sufficient to influence people's behaviour, such semblance alone will not produce the desired legal effect. If I marked my favourite parking space in the public street outside my house with a sign saying *No Parking*, this sign might well deter some people from using it. But those parking in the space despite the sign would not be trespassing: if I tried to sue them, there would be no case to answer. It therefore seems useful to regard signs' performativity as two-dimensional, one dimension being social, the other legal (Mautner 2012).

Socio-legal issues

In the previous section, we were concerned mainly with how signs work as texts. Here, we are going to look at why they work as discourse, and how signage discourse is implicated in various socio-legal structures and processes.

Space, power and exclusion

My earlier observations about emplacement and intertextuality helped us to identify the felicity conditions for directive signs to be performative in social and legal terms. Now it is time to dig deeper and ask how those conditions, in turn, depend on underlying social conventions. When we argue, for example, that a sign saying *Private Property* is socially and legally performative because it has been put up by someone legitimated to do so, we have in a sense only told half the story. The other half, which the critical gaze should also be keen to explore, is the status of property as an instrument for exercising control over space and, crucially, over people's behaviour in that space. In all its stark and apparently innocuous simplicity, the *Private Property* sign speaks to us of power and exclusion. This is widely recognized, one should add, among lawyers too; it does not in fact require a particularly radical take on things to view property in this way. As one mainstream treatise on land law explains:

> 'Property' is simply the word used to describe particular concentra-
> tions of power over things and resources, and every claim of 'property'
> comprises the assertion of some *quantum* (or amount) of socially

permissible power as exercisable in respect of some socially valued resource.

(Gray and Gray 2011: 34, emphasis in original)

Seen in this way, property emerges as what Searle calls an 'institutional fact', that is, a fact 'by human agreement or acceptance' (Searle 2010: 10). The sign *Private Property* is accepted because the underlying institutional fact is. As Rousseau famously remarked:

> The first man who, after enclosing a piece of ground, took it into his head to say, 'This is mine,' *and found people simple enough to believe him*, was the true founder of civil society.
>
> (Rousseau 2012 [1755]: Second Part, first paragraph, emphasis added)

The recognition that the link between texts and the institutional facts underpinning them is not only relevant but also a necessary and legitimate part of linguistic inquiry lies at the very heart of a discourse-based approach to signage and indeed to any other text or genre.

Furthermore, the exercise of control over space, which often crystallizes in directive signs, has implications beyond questions of access. Quite often it amounts to controlling certain types of behaviour and then, by extension, certain kinds of people. Land use and land users are implicitly conflated. That is, while signs ostensibly talk about the former, often they really mean the latter. The *Private Property* sign discussed above is a case in point. Apart from *No Smoking*, it also states *No Loitering* (Figure 25.1). Arguably, that directive is less about loitering, as such, than about the people typically considered to be doing the loitering – youngsters 'hanging about', drug addicts, the homeless. The dictionary definition of *loiter*, 'to stand or wait somewhere especially with no obvious reason',[4] does not do justice to the word's associative and social meaning. However, the latter does emerge indirectly from the example sentences that the dictionaries provide: 'unemployed young men loiter at the entrance of the factory' in the *Collins Cobuild Advanced English Dictionary*, 'Teenagers were loitering in the street outside' in the *Oxford Advanced Learner's Dictionary*, 'Five or six teenagers were loitering in front of the newsagent's' in the *Longman Dictionary of Contemporary English,* and 'There's a group of kids loitering outside the shop' in the *Macmillan Dictionary*. By contrast, an expensively dressed middle-aged person is much less likely to be considered 'loitering' when they 'stand or wait with no obvious reason' on freely accessible private land (such as the area outside an office block which is shown in Figure 25.1); they are clearly not the kind of person to whom the directive on the sign is primarily addressed.

The implicit conflation of land *use* and land *users* also exists in the domain of public and administrative law. In the UK, for example, alcohol consumption in public can be regulated by so-called Designated Public Place Orders (DPPOs), which 'enable local authorities to designate places where restrictions on public drinking apply', in cases where 'alcohol-related disorder or nuisance' has occurred (Home Office, n.d. [2008]). The Home Office guidelines on the matter emphasize that 'these powers are not intended to disrupt peaceful activities, for example *families having a picnic in a park or on the beach with a glass of wine'* (emphasis added). However reasonable this may sound, the overtones of class-specific behaviour are unmissable. As Valverde (2005: 37) reminds us, 'legal tools designed to govern things, uses, and activities usually end up governing certain groups of persons'.

The Home Office guidelines on DPPOs, incidentally, also include a fairly detailed section on the design and wording of the relevant signs. The model sign shown in one of the appendices to the document not only establishes an explicit and precise intertextual link with the legislation governing DPPOs, but also specifies the maximum fine that non-compliance can entail.[5]

Public versus private space

As we noted earlier, signs play a key role in outwardly defining space, distinguishing private from public space and specifying what behaviours are acceptable where. Yet there is more to this than meets the eye. Public space may be an intuitively straightforward concept, but it becomes fiendishly complex and elusive as soon as one looks at it more closely – so much so, in fact, that the concept itself has been called into doubt (Kohn 2004: 11–12) and alternative typologies of space proposed (Carmona 2010: 169).

On the one hand, some areas that appear public in social terms are actually private in law, an obvious example being shopping malls. Many of these are deliberately designed not to look like standard department stores, but to have streets, plazas, indoor vegetation and other features that mimic public space. Some malls are even made to have a 'villagey' feel to them[6] – encouraging people to shop, eat and drink, and discouraging them from simply doing nothing (Minton 2009: 53). Rather oddly, the right to do nothing, and in particular, not to consume anything, appears to have become a privilege increasingly difficult to exercise in public.

On the other hand, areas that are public in legal terms may in practice be used very selectively, with their architectural, infrastructural, aesthetic and commercial qualities effectively inviting some people in and deterring others. Many gentrified neighbourhoods, with expensive retail outlets and sleek cafés, fall into that category.[7] Since they are defined primarily as spaces of consumption, the presence of the non-consuming public is covertly discouraged (Turner 2002: 543). As a result, 'this new public realm', Minton pointedly observes, 'is not really public at all' (Minton 2009: 52).

The public-private divide is also important from a civil rights perspective, namely where free speech is at stake. For example, the space outside a supermarket may look and feel public – it is outdoors and there are no physical barriers such as gates, to name just two of the typical clues to 'publicness' – but it is private land nonetheless. As the sign next to the supermarket's entrance (Figure 25.4) makes clear, access is restricted (*entry is only permitted to shoppers*), and free speech cannot be exercised (*Strictly no leaflets*). This is because the area in question has not been *dedicated as a public right of way*. A similar wording appears in Figure 25.2 (*no public right of way inferred*) and Figure 25.9 (*has not been dedicated and is not intended to become dedicated for public use as a highway*). The importance of right of way lies not only in facilitating transport and enabling recreational use, but also 'in underpinning vital liberties of movement, expression, association and assembly' (Gray and Gray 2011: 547). With these liberties curtailed, privatized space invariably becomes depoliticized space.

To complicate matters even further, it is becoming increasingly clear that the neat dichotomy 'public versus private' no longer captures contemporary socio-legal realities. Instead, hybrid regimes have emerged, with the public and private sectors frequently collaborating in the ownership and management of public space. Accordingly, concepts such as *pseudo-private* space have sprung up, that is, 'spaces that are formally owned by the state, by the public, but that are subject to control and regulation by private interests' (Mitchell and Staeheli 2006: 153). For 'private' read commercial and in particular retailing, because the overriding goal, in many British cities at least, is now to manage and police public space in a way that makes it conducive to shopping.[8]

The relevance of these developments for signage is twofold. On the one hand, changes in the definition of what constitutes publicness often have a visible corollary in signs intended to regulate behaviour – forbidding loitering, begging and busking, for example. On the other, the presence of signs can be stipulated by law. In the previous section, where the demarcation of private property was the main issue, we saw from the Port Facility example how the relevant warning sign becomes instrumental in defining and punishing trespass. In the present section, where our focus is on public space, a pertinent example would be the signs which, according to the Data Protection Act 1988, must accompany CCTV surveillance (see Figure 25.3). As the Code of Practice published by the Information Commissioner's Office explains:

> You must let people know that they are in an area where CCTV surveillance is being carried out. The most effective way of doing this is by using prominently placed signs at the entrance to the CCTV zone and reinforcing this with further signs inside the area.
>
> (Information Commissioner's Office 2008: 15)

The key phrase in this passage is *you must let people know* – a simple but forceful reminder of one of the cornerstones of the Rule of Law, namely the principle that norms have to be promulgated (i.e., made known) to those subject to them (Fuller 1969 quoted in Kramer 2007: 104). Thus, while the large number of *CCTV* signs in British cities indicates how widespread surveillance is, the signs themselves bear testimony to the elaborate legal framework within which surveillance is carried out. An important feature of that framework is accountability; as the Information Commissioner's Guidelines point out, the signs must contain details of who operates the CCTV system in question.[9] None of this will assuage concerns about CCTV infringing civil liberties, of course. However, what is significant for those studying public signage is that, in this context, signs have an officially defined role in both legal discourse and legal practice.

Liability and the risk society

Finally, let us return briefly to the signs warning us of dangers and advising caution in the face of 'threats' such as stairs, escalators and hot tap water. Again, these signs must be seen against both their social and legal backgrounds. From a wider social perspective, warning signs are textual symptoms of the 'risk society' (Beck 1992), which attempts to control all life's vicissitudes (or, failing that, at least aims to create the illusion that such control is possible). From a legal perspective, on the other hand, the reason why property owners put up such signs is that they wish to protect themselves – pre-emptively but not necessarily successfully – against liability lawsuits that might be brought were someone to be injured on their property. Thus, in areas with very fragmented ownership structures, the frequently observed proliferation of signs warning against the same danger can be explained by each owner wanting to be on the safe side, as it were, on their patch.

In litigious risk societies, therefore, the number of warning signs is less a function of the actual level of exposure to danger than of the way in which the society concerned deals with danger: how much responsibility the individual is entrusted with; what risks are considered acceptable; which duties of care on the part of owners are enshrined in the legal system; and how liability is regulated. Again, following Searle's distinction between different types of fact (Searle 1969: 50–3; 2010: 10) one could argue that while danger is a 'brute fact', risk is an 'institutional fact'. It is the latter that is reflected and reproduced by warning signs, not the former. This is why environments such as the mixed-use waterfronts typical of coastal cities can be replete with warning signs, as in Britain, or almost entirely devoid of them, as in some Scandinavian countries. The level of danger, in objective terms, may be the same everywhere, but the socio-legal construction of risk is not.

Conclusion and outlook

Contemporary linguistic landscapes are full of signs. Those that are directive perform a range of socio-legal functions, such as separating public from private space, defining deviant behaviour, and constraining civil rights while also explaining the legal basis for the constraint. Signs reflect socio-legal developments and contribute to reinforcing them. Current trends include the shrinking of public space, particularly for disadvantaged groups, and the concomitant emergence of 'pseudo-public' space dedicated predominantly to commercial uses – in particular to shopping. Furthermore, in the UK, concerns about property owners' liability have led to a proliferation of warning signs, reflecting broader social attitudes towards risk.

Recognizing the mutual influence between language and the social is at the core of the discourse perspective applied here, and it forms the backdrop against which the present chapter has outlined the most important characteristics of signs as texts. Three factors have emerged as distinctive: the close tie between a sign's meaning and its immediate environment (*emplacement*), the mutual dependence between signs and legal statutes (*intertextuality*) and the influence of the material quality of the sign on its perceived legal authority (*materiality*).

Inevitably, the approach to signs presented here has blind spots that need to be acknowledged and identified as possible themes for future research. For example, multimodality could and should be discussed in greater detail than was attempted here, in order to explore in greater depth the way in which verbal and visual elements interact, and how colour and typefaces are exploited as meaning-making resources.

Another obvious gap in the present chapter is the lack of ethnographic fieldwork exploring how citizens process directive signs: whether they read them at all and if so, where, when and how; what they make of the references to the law; whether they comply with the directives; and, how they justify non-compliance. Furthermore, the study of signs would also benefit from research into discourses *about* space, in policy documents and the media for example, so that a more rounded picture of the discursive construction of space can be built. And finally, systematic comparisons between directive signage in different places and different countries could shed more light on the influence of linguistic, cultural, historical and political factors, and so provide useful guidance for policymakers and urban space designers.

Whatever the precise purpose and research perspective applied, the study of signage highlights the interrelationships between discourse and space. It would probably be excessive to follow the example of the social sciences (Goodchild and Janelle 2010) and hail a 'spatial turn' for discourse analysis. Nevertheless, space deserves more attention in critical discourse studies than hitherto, and indications that research in this area is gaining momentum (see Gu 2012, for example) should be welcomed. For adding a spatial perspective to our discourse-analytic canon certainly promises valuable new insights, particularly where space is bound up in complex webs of relationships with society and the law.

References

Alvesson, M. and Willmott, H. (1992) 'Critical theory and management studies: an introduction', in M. Alvesson and H. Willmott (eds.) *Critical Management Studies*, London: Sage, 1–20.

Austin, J.L. (1962) *How to Do Things with Words*, Cambridge, MA: Harvard University Press.

Backhaus, P. (2007) *Linguistic Landscapes: A Comparative Study of Urban Multilingualism in Tokyo*, Clevedon: Multilingual Matters.

Bauman, Z. and May, T. (2001) *Thinking Sociologically*, 2nd edition, Oxford: Blackwell.

Beck, U. (1992) *The Risk Society: Towards a New Modernity*, London: Sage.

Carmona, M. (2010) 'Contemporary public space. Part two: classification', *Journal of Urban Design* 15(2): 157–73.

Coupland, N. (2012) 'Bilingualism on display: the framing of Welsh and English in Welsh public spaces', *Language in Society* 41(1): 1–27.

Edelman, L. and Gorter, D. (2010) 'Linguistic landscapes and the market', in H. Kelly-Holmes and G. Mautner (eds.) *Language and the Market*, Basingstoke: Palgrave, 96–108.

Fuller, L. (1969) *The Morality of Law*, New Haven, CT: Yale University Press.

Goodchild, M.F. and Janelle, D.G. (2010) 'Toward critical spatial thinking in the social sciences and humanities', *GeoJournal* 75: 3–13.

Gray, K.J. and Gray, S.F. (2011) *Land Law*, 7th edition, Oxford: Oxford University Press.

Gu, Y. (2012) 'Discourse geography', in J.P. Gee and M. Handford (eds.) *The Routledge Handbook of Discourse Analysis*, London and New York: Routledge, 541–57.

Home Office (n.d.) [2008] *Guidance on Designated Public Place Orders (DPPOs): For Local Authorities in England and Wales*, available at http://webarchive.nationalarchives.gov.uk/ 20100413151441/http://crimereduction.homeoffice.gov.uk/alcoholorders/alcoholor ders016.htm, accessed 18 August 2012.

Information Commissioner's Office (2008) *CCTV Code of Practice*, available at www.ico.gov. uk/for_the_public/topic_specific_guides/cctv.aspx, accessed 20 August 2012.

Jaworski, A. and Thurlow, C. (eds.) (2010) *Semiotic Landscapes: Language, Image, Space*, London and New York: Continuum.

Kohn, M. (2004) *Brave New Neighbourhoods: The Privatization of Public Space*, Oxford: Rowan and Littlefield.

Kramer, M.H. (2007) *Objectivity and the Rule of Law*, Cambridge: Cambridge University Press.

Lefebvre, H. (1991) *The Production of Space*, Oxford: Wiley-Blackwell.

Marquardt, N. and Füller, H. (2012) 'Spillover of the private city: BIDs as a pivot of social control in downtown Los Angeles', *European Urban and Regional Studies* 19(2): 153–66.

Mautner, G. (2012) 'Language, space and the law: a study of directive signs', *International Journal of Speech, Language and the Law* 19(2): 189–217.

Minton, A. (2009) *Ground Control: Fear and Happiness in the Twenty-First-Century City*, London: Penguin Books.

Mitchell, D. and Staeheli, L.A. (2006) 'Clean and safe? Property redevelopment, public space, and homelessness in downtown San Diego', in S. Low and N. Smith (eds.) *The Politics of Public Space*, New York and London: Routledge, 143–75.

Rose-Redwood, R. (2008) '"Sixth Avenue is now a memory": regimes of spatial inscription and the performative limits of the official city-text', *Political Geography* 27: 875–94.

Rousseau, J.-J. (2012 [1755]) *A Discourse upon the Origin and the Foundation of the Inequality Among Mankind*, Kindle edition, retrieved from amazon.de on 18 August 2012.

Scollon, R. and Wong Scollon, S. (2003) *Discourses in Place: Language in the Material World*, New York and London: Routledge.

Searle, J.R. (1969) *Speech Acts: An Essay in the Philosophy of Language*, Cambridge: Cambridge University Press.

——— (2010) *Making the Social World: The Structure of Human Civilization*, Oxford: Oxford University Press.

Shohamy, E. and Gorter, D. (eds.) (2009) *Linguistic Landscape: Expanding the Scenery*, New York and London: Routledge.

Turner, R.S. (2002) 'The politics of design and development in the postmodern downtown', *Journal of Urban Affairs* 24(5): 533–48.

Valverde, M. (2005) 'Taking "land use" seriously: toward an ontology of municipal law', *Law, Text, Culture* 9: 33–59.

van Dijk, T.A. (1993) 'Principles of critical discourse analysis', *Discourse and Society* 4(2): 249–83.

Wodak, R. and Meyer, M. (2009) 'Critical Discourse Analysis: history, agenda, theory and methodology', in R. Wodak and M. Meyer (eds.) *Methods of Critical Discourse Analysis*, 2nd edition, London: Sage, 1–33.

Notes

1   On this particular sign, located on the waterfront in Cardiff Bay, the obvious is pointed out in both English and Welsh following the country's language policy. For linguistic landscape research with a focus on multilingualism see, for example, Backhaus (2007), Edelman and Gorter (2010), and Coupland (2012).

2   The structure chosen for the rest of the chapter is not without its pitfalls, and a few words of clarification are in order. Separating the textual and social dimensions should not be taken as suggesting that the boundaries between them are neat and tidy. In fact, they are anything but. Any actual instance of a sign displayed in context will have several layers of meaning-making that all work together at the same time. If they are dealt with separately, this is purely for heuristic and practical reasons and not because they *are* separate.

3   http://wien.orf.at/news/stories/2541242, accessed 18 August 2012.
4   *Oxford Advanced Learner's Dictionary*, iPad edition.
5   The text of the model sign, in Annex A of the Home Office Guidance document reads as follows:

> This area has been designated under the Local Authorities (Alcohol Consumption in Designated Public Places) Regulations 2007. If you continue to drink alcohol in this area designated under section 13 of the Criminal Justice and Police Act 2001 when asked not to do so by a police officer or any other person designated to carry out this task under sections 41 and 42 of the Police Reform Act 2002, or fail to surrender any alcohol to a police officer in this area, you may be arrested and would be liable on conviction to a maximum fine of £500.

6   It is rather ironic that in the Westfield shopping centre in Shepherd's Bush, London, the area with the most exclusive luxury shops is called *The Village* (http://uk.westfield.com/thevillagelondon, accessed 20 August 2012).
7   Cardiff Bay, which I briefly mentioned earlier, is a case in point. Mermaid Quay, the shops and restaurants area at the heart of the Bay, is not secluded by physical barriers to entry, nor by off-putting signage. However, it is a decidedly middle-class recreational area used by everyone, it seems, except the residents of the immediately adjacent council estate in Bute Street, who are predominantly working class and members of so-called 'visible minorities'.
8   In this context, witness also the aptly named Business Improvement Districts (BIDs), which are private organizations that manage public space, providing infrastructure and security services. Safety, or the illusion of it, is promoted by blanket CCTV surveillance, and policing is done mainly by private security firms, not the police. On the controversial nature of BIDs see Marquardt and Füller (2012).
9   'Signs should . . . contain details of the organisation operating the system, the purpose for using CCTV and who to contact about the scheme (where these things are not obvious to those being monitored)' (Information Commissioner's Office 2008: 15).

Power, ideology and control

Editors' introduction
to Part Six

CHAPTERS IN PART FOUR dealt expressly with issues of intimacy, involvement, detachment and other manifestations of interpersonal distance. In Part Five the focus was mainly on identity work in discourse and the subjectivities of 'selfness' (self-identity) and 'groupness' (group-identity). Ever since the work of Roger Brown and his associates (Brown and Ford 1964; Brown and Gilman 1972) on pronouns and other forms of address, *power* and its relational counterpart *solidarity* have remained firmly at the centre of discourse analytic and sociolinguistic research into interpersonal and intergroup relations. Particular aspects of language in relation to social power and social solidarity have arisen in many chapters so far. But in this final part of the *Reader* we need to focus in closely on *power*, which is in many ways the primary concern of discourse analysis, particularly in its critical (CDA) version.

A related concept, which the seven chapters in this part of the book explore, is *ideology*, which refers to belief systems and cultural values underlying different power relations. (See our comments about discourse and ideology, and discussion of the work of Michel Foucault and Michel Pêcheux in the general Introduction.) Once again, the concept of ideology has already been inescapably present in the volume. Following the work of Michael Billig (e.g., 1990) in rhetoric and Van Dijk (e.g., 1998) in discourse analysis itself, it is demonstrably the case that ideology is intimately related to situated practices of day-to-day interaction. In fact Van Dijk argues that it is through discourse and other semiotic practices that ideologies are formulated, reproduced and reinforced. Accomplishing ideology is an important end in political discourse (including 'Political' discourse, where the 'P' might refer to formal, institutionalized political systems), because a discourse's acceptance by an audience, especially mass media audiences, ensures the establishment of group rapport and compliance. As Fowler (1985: 66) puts it, through the emergence of a 'community of ideology', a shared system of beliefs about reality comes into being and creates group identity.

We understand the term *ideology* as the set of social representations, both specific and more abstract, shared by members of a group and used by them to accomplish everyday social practices, including communication (e.g., Fowler et al 1979; Fowler 1985; Billig et al 1988; Van Dijk 1998). These representations are organized into systems that are deployed by social classes and other groups 'in order to make sense of, figure out and render intelligible the way society works' (Hall 1996: 26). Billig et al (1988) make a distinction between 'lived' and 'intellectual' ideology. Our definition, above, aligns with the idea of lived ideology. Intellectual ideology refers to an overall, coherent system of thought that is realized in textual form: political programmes or manifestos, philosophical doctrines or religious codifications. This distinction is useful because it reflects the workings of ideology on two levels: people's coherent, formal, explicit systems of belief (their intellectual ideologies) and the architecture of their everyday practices. This includes their objectives in self- and other-presentation, their expressions of opinions that represent and satisfy their own and their groups' preferred views of reality, constructed to suit local goals of interaction (see Jaworski and Galasiński, 2000). One of the ideologically relevant discourse structures pointed to by Van Dijk (1998: 209) is interactional control, where ideologies get legitimized (see Jaworski and Galasiński 1998). Who starts an interactional exchange, who ends it, who initiates new topics, who interrupts whom and which address forms are used in the course of interaction, may all be indicative of a person's power, and as such, these interactional designs are ideologically charged, or to use Van Dijk's (1998: 209) term, they have an 'ideological dimension'.

As we explained in the general Introduction (and see also Fairclough 1989), CDA's social constructionist view of language prevents it from treating language as a mirror of social relations. Thus, CDA examines the structure of spoken and written texts in search of politically and ideologically salient features, which index particular power relations and may be constitutive of them, often without being evident to participants. Some of the key linguistic/discursive features discussed by critical linguists include: nominalization, passivization and sequencing. They are used for ideological control as 'masking devices' (Ng and Bradac 1993), as they allow speakers or writers to withhold the identity of the actors and causality of events. For example, nominalization, as in '*Failure* to display this notice will result in *prosecution*', and passivization, as in 'John *was murdered*' (Fowler 1985: 71), remove the visible agents of verbal action and, consequently, deflect responsibility (compare: 'The fugitive was shot by police marksmen'). Exploitation of sequencing, as in: 'Fords I find particularly reliable' (Fowler 1985: 72), is a rhetorical device serving the purpose of manipulating the addressee's attention (by bringing forward the nominal 'Fords' into a marked position in the utterance). The seemingly semantically equivalent sentences, 'Employers always quarrel with unions' and 'Unions always quarrel with employers' (Ng and Bradac 1993: 156), apportion different degrees of responsibility and agency in 'quarrelling' – who 'quarrels' the most, who is responsible for conflict.

Another area of discourse analysis in which power, dominance and control have been major agenda-setting issues is one we have discussed briefly already – language and gender. Women have been shown to be linguistically dominated by men, whose assertive and aggressive communication strategies are not 'mere cultural differences' between the sexes but manifestations of male dominance over females (Henley and Kramarae 1991). However, as Tannen (1993) argues, different discourse strategies do not uniformly create dominance or powerlessness. One has to look at their meaning in relation to context, the conversational styles of the participants and the interaction between different speakers' styles and strategies. Only then might it be possible to interpret silence, interruption or indirectness as expressions of power, powerlessness, assertion, aggressiveness or cooperation (see also Machin and Van Leeuwen, Chapter 11; Cameron, Chapter 22).

The first chapter of this part of the *Reader* (Chapter 26) is a seminal source on discourse and power by a major social theorist, Pierre Bourdieu. As we pointed out in the general Introduction, Bourdieu's interest in discourse is not so much in empirical examination of particular sequences of interactional data, but, as in the case of Giddens (see the Introduction to Part Five), in discourse as an abstract vehicle for social and political processes. Language in Bourdieu's (1986, 1991, 1993) theory of social practice is related to his notion of *habitus*, the group norms or dispositions that people have internalized, whose task is to regulate and generate their actions (practices), perceptions and representations of individuals, and to mediate the social structures that they inhabit. Two important and interrelated aspects of habitus are that it reflects the social structures in which it was acquired and also reproduces these structures. Thus, a person who was brought up in a working-class background will, from this point of view, manifest a set of discursive dispositions that are different from those acquired by a person from a middle-class background. These differences will in turn reproduce the class divisions between individuals and their groups.

For Bourdieu, language is a locus of struggle for power and authority in that some types of language (speech styles, accents, dialects, codes, and so on) are presupposed to be 'correct', 'distinguished' or 'legitimate' in opposition to those which are 'incorrect' or 'vulgar'. Those who use (in speaking or writing) linguistic varieties ranked as acceptable exert a degree of control over those with a dominated linguistic habitus (Bourdieu 1991: 60). The field of linguistic production, however, can be manipulated in that the symbolic capital claimed by the authority of 'legitimate' language may be reclaimed in the process of negotiation 'by a metadiscourse concerning the conditions of use of discourse' (p. 417):

> The habitus . . . provides individuals with a sense of how to act and respond
> in the course of their daily lives. It 'orients' their actions and inclinations
> without strictly determining them. It gives them a 'feel for the game',
> a sense of what is appropriate in the circumstances and what is not, a
> 'practical sense'.
>
> (Thompson 1991: 13)

We have been unable to include any of Michel Foucault's original writing in the *Reader*, but it would be useful to follow up on Bourdieu's text by reading Foucault. Foucault's model of power is 'productive' (Mills 1997). For Foucault, power is dispersed throughout all social relations as a force that prevents some actions and enables others. However, power is not confined to large-scale, macro processes of politics and society. It is a *potential* present in all everyday exchanges and social encounters. In Foucault's system, one of the significant influences of power is in constituting different versions of individuals' subjectivity (see the Introduction to Part Five). For example, in *The History of Sexuality* (Foucault 1978, 1985, 1986) it transpires that in the Victorian era children's sexuality was not 'simply' suppressed. Rather, children faced a hegemonic discourse of 'acceptable' sexuality constructed for them. Another important aspect of Foucault's (1997) view of power is that it is explicitly linked to *knowledge*. Sarah Mills illustrates this as follows, in an example that fits well alongside the one used by Deborah Cameron, at the end of our Introduction to Part Five:

> [W]hat is studied in schools and universities is the result of struggles over whose version of events is sanctioned. Knowledge is often the product of the subjugation of objects, or perhaps it can be seen as the process through which subjects are constituted as subjugated; for example, when consulting a university library catalogue, if you search under the term 'women', you will find a vast selection of books and articles discussing the oppression of women, the psychology of women, the physical ailments that women suffer from, and so on. If you search under the term 'men' you will not find the same wealth of information.
>
> (Mills 1997: 21)

Teun Van Dijk (Chapter 27) discusses an example of the sinister and twisted working of discursive processes involved in the legitimizing of racist ideology, for example in face-to-face conversation, in a job interview or in a newspaper article. Van Dijk identifies a pattern in discourse whereby the speaker/writer overtly *denies* that there is an underlying racist ideology. It takes a fine-grained textual analysis of discourse for Van Dijk to demonstrate how socially unacceptable positions are overtly denied, but covertly present, in speakers' or writers' accounts of race and ethnic relations. The original article, too long for us to reproduce here in its entirety, offers a taxonomy of *denials of racism*:

> act-denial ('I did not do/ say that at all');
> control-denial ('I did not do/ say that on purpose', 'It was an accident')
> intention-denial ('I did not mean that', 'You got me wrong');
> goal-denial ('I did not do/ say that, in order to. . .').
>
> (Van Dijk 1992: 92)

Why do people put so much effort into disguising their racism? Racism is an ideology that officially, in public discourse in a liberal democracy, does not find social approval. Therefore, denying racism (despite one's beliefs or one's 'lived' ideology) is an important aspect of positive self-presentation, whether one is a private individual, journalist or Member of Parliament. (One part of the original article, not reproduced here, examines denials of racism in parliamentary debates.) On the other hand, maintaining racist ideology is an expression and reinforcement of white, middle-class power over ethnic 'others' and minorities.

Ian Hutchby (Chapter 28), in his analysis of locally produced patterns of power and resistance in argumentative talk of British phone-in radio programmes, takes up Foucault's point about the potential for all talk to embed power relationships. His methodology is conversation analytic (see Part Three). But like Foucault, he defines power not as a set of attributes characterizing any one person, but 'as a set of potentials which, while always present, can be variably exercised, resisted, shifted around and struggled over by social agents' (p. 449). Phone-ins are one sub-genre of media talk that have spawned their own normative structure, for example around who gets to decide what the agenda for talk is. Callers are positioned to make the first formulation of what might be a relevant topic for discussion. But Hutchby shows that the second position – allocated to the show's host – carries the power to challenge the first formulation of what the agenda is, and also to do this without the need for a detailed rationale or account. Although power in this instance isn't a particularly loaded social relation, Hutchby's analysis shows how institutions (such as radio broadcasting) generate power structures that we have to conform to.

Hugh Mehan's chapter, 'Oracular reasoning in a psychiatric exam' (Chapter 29), is a poignant and powerful demonstration of the power/knowledge interface in discourse. In his study, a panel of psychiatrists and a patient diagnosed as schizophrenic put forward their arguments to each other in order for the panel to decide whether the patient can be released from the mental hospital – a kind of negative gatekeeping exercise. As Mehan demonstrates, both sides come to the examination totally unprepared to accept the opposite (and conflicting) views of the other party. The patient claims he is ready to be released from the hospital, and the panel sees him as totally unfit to be released. Both sides engage in argument trying to sanction their own versions of reality. But in the end, it is the party that can command greater power, through institutional authority, i.e., the panel, whose version of 'the truth' about the patient comes to dominate. As Mehan (p. 462) aptly puts it:

> All people define situations as real; but when powerful people define situations as real, then they are real *for everybody involved* in their consequences.

In Chapter 30 Paul Baker and Tony McEnery return us to the social context of ethnic and in-group/out-group relations in their study of how 'foreign doctors' are represented in the British press. The discourse process they are concerned with could be referred to as 'othering', a stereotype-driven process of demeaning and subordinating people that one deems to be not only unlike oneself but inferior and undesirable (Coupland 2000). On the other hand, as the authors point out, their study deals with discursive targets who are highly qualified professional doctors, a group we might expect to be much less subject to prejudice and discrimination. Yet the study provides plenty of evidence of textual othering. The research methods that Baker and McEnery use are very distinctive in the field of discourse analysis (cf. our

Introduction to Part Two), illustrating the value of detailed quantitative analyses of large bodies of text data – over half a million words of news stories were examined as primary data in this case – as opposed to the close, qualitative analysis of particular extracts of talk or written text. The 'corpus linguistics' approach (see McEnery and Hardie 2011) allows the researchers to find statistical trends of different sorts in their data. They can provide empirically grounded, evidenced accounts of the frequency with which 'foreign doctors' are referred to in the British press, whether such mentions are becoming more or less frequent, and what linguistic (lexical) features tend to feature in those accounts. The method allows for a very precisely definable interpretation of what is meant by discursive construction – which lexical items co-occur in the representations of 'foreign doctors' constructed by journalists.

Some emerging patterns of collocation (co-presence of words) are highly suggestive of ideological skewing, from a CDA perspective, for example the relatively high frequency with which 'foreign doctors' are associated with incompetence, with frequent use of adjectives such as 'bungling' and 'incompetent'. Baker and McEnery are also able to follow through and compare particular aspects of their findings (such as the phrase 'at the hands of' in the primary corpus) with much larger corpora, mapping out tendencies in how particular English phrases carry particular ideological values. The statistical method of course has limitations as well as benefits, and Baker and McEnery provide a balanced view of this in their Conclusion.

For his title, Crispin Thurlow (Chapter 31) borrows Foucault's perspective on ideological 'disciplining' (Foucault 1977), and applies it to public and media 'moral panic' about innovations in digital discourse, particularly by young people. Using search techniques similar to those used in the previous chapter, Thurlow locates a corpus of English-language newspaper articles, but this time dealing with young people, language and new technology. Like Baker and McEnery, Thurlow is interested in dominant patterns of mass-mediated representation, but takes an interpretive approach rather than a statistical one. He organizes key parts of his critical interpretations around a well-known three-part schema for doing ideology-critique, based on the concepts of *erasure, iconization* and (*fractal*) *recursivity* (Irvine and Gal 2000). Erasure refers to the ideological process of suppressing alternative viewpoints (and details of what is *absent* from a discourse can't be adduced if we are quantifying what is *present*). In relation to erasure, Thurlow shows, for example, that the enormous complexity and range of 'new media' genres and practices is radically simplified in newspaper reports, constructing a demonized category of 'meaningless communication'. Iconization is the process of 'lifting' certain qualities or attributes to higher, more iconic levels of representation. Particular local characteristics of digital communication tend to be represented as general attributes of young people, pejoratively constructed, for example, as 'garrulous youngsters', or even using the label 'yoof' (which stylizes a supposed feature of young people's pronunciation, with the fronting of the 'th' consonant). Recursivity is the related process of extrapolating from a local instance to increasingly wider levels of generality. Thurlow's data include copious instances where economy and innovation in, for example, texting are given wildly exaggerated personal and cultural significance, such as eroding awareness of grammar or encouraging shallowness of thought! These 'hygienist' orientations to language and discourse (Cameron 1995) are not entirely new, but digital communication practices have clearly provided a new rallying point for conservative and repressive ideological forces.

We chose to put Jan Blommaert's chapter last in the *Reader* (Chapter 32) because it invites us to consider some of the taken-for-granted attributes of discourse analysis, and to reflect on discourse analysis in the context of social change. Our editorial material in the *Reader* has repeatedly emphasized the importance of social context in shaping the meaning and functioning of discourse, but context also shapes the functioning of discourse analysis. Blommaert picks up the theme of globalization as an ongoing social change, and he asks how linguists and discourse analysts are, or are not, responding to the globalizing world in which we all function. He reminds us of some of the key premises of discourse analysis, and particularly of the importance of relating linguistic 'order' to social order and social structure. (Recall Goffman on *the interaction order* in Chapter 19, and in our discussion of this in the Introductions to Parts Four and Five; also Foucault's notion of *orders of discourse*, and related discussion earlier in this Introduction). Blommaert then throws in the concepts of *the indexical order* and *orders of indexicality,* which amount to the idea that the social meanings we attach to linguistic features or styles are themselves socially structured, and often normatively so.

Blommaert's main point about globalization is that, as the contemporary world becomes more and more interconnected, complex and mobile, we need to recognize that linguistic and discursive resources have *different* values in different places, and that they are policed from different bases of authority. Ways of communicating, and indeed ways of being (social identities), are repositioned as they 'travel' (more or less literally) from one environment to another. There are competing power bases, or 'centres', in a 'polycentric' world. Globalization tends to erase some sources of authority (e.g., national governments, in at least some respects) and tends to empower and privilege others (e.g., multinational corporations). It has its egalitarian dimensions, but is certainly no panacea; globalization facilitates new forms of inequality, as well as opening up some new avenues for self-determination (Coupland 2010). Our practices as discourse analysts need to keep pace with these changes, and to reflect (as Blommaert says) new 'discourses-in-globalization' and the ideological matrices in which they function.

References

Billig, M. (1990) 'Stacking the cards of ideology: the history of the Sun Royal Album', *Discourse and Society* 1: 17–37.

Billig, M., Condor, S., Edwards, D., Gane, M., Middleton, D. and Radley, A.R. (1988) *Ideological Dilemmas*, London: Sage.

Bourdieu, P. (1986) *Distinction: A Social Critique of the Judgement of Taste*, London: Routledge.

—— (1991) *Language and Symbolic Power*, Cambridge: Polity Press.

—— (1993) *The Field of Cultural Production: Essays on Art and Literature*, Cambridge: Polity Press.

Brown, R. and Ford, M. (1964) 'Address in American English', in D. Hymes (ed.) *Language in Culture and Society*, New York: Harper and Row, 234–44.

Brown, R. and Gilman, A. (1972) 'The pronouns of power and solidarity', in P.P. Giglioli (ed.) *Language and Social Context*, Harmondsworth: Penguin, 256–82 [first published in: T.A. Sebeok (ed.) (1960) *Style in Language*, Cambridge, MA: MIT Press, 253–77].

Cameron, D. (1995) *Verbal Hygiene*, London: Routledge.

Coupland, N. (2000) '"Other" representation', in J. Verschueren, J.-O. Östman, J. Blommaert and C. Bulcaen (eds.) *Handbook of Pragmatics, 1999 Installment*, Amsterdam: John Benjamins, 1–24.

Coupland, N. (ed.) (2010) *Handbook of Language and Globalization*, Malden, MA and Oxford: Wiley-Blackwell.

Fairclough, N. (1989) *Language and Power*, London: Longman.

Foucault, M. (1977) *Discipline and Punish: The Birth of the Prison*, New York: Pantheon.

—— (1978, 1985, 1986) *The History of Sexuality* (three volumes), New York: Random House.

—— (1997) *Power/Knowledge*, Hemel Hempstead: Harvester.

Fowler, R. (1985) 'Power', in T. Van Dijk (ed.) *Handbook of Discourse Analysis*, vol. 4, London: Academic Press, 61–82.

Fowler, R., Hodge, R., Kress, G.R. and Trew, T. (1979) *Language and Control*, London: Routledge and Kegan Paul.

Hall, S. (1996) 'The problem of ideology: Marxism without guarantees', in D. Morley and K.H. Chen (eds.) *Stuart Hall: Critical Dialogues in Cultural Studies*, London: Routledge, 25–46.

Henley, N. and Kramarae, C. (1991) 'Miscommunication, gender, and power', in N. Coupland, J.M. Wiemann and H. Giles (eds.) *'Miscommunication' and Problematic Talk*, Newbury Park, CA: Sage, 18–43.

Irvine, J. and Gal, S. (2000) 'Language ideology and linguistic differentiation', in P.V. Kroskity (ed.) *Regimes of Language: Ideologies, Polities, and Identities*, Santa Fe, NM: School of American Research Press, 35–84.

Jaworski, A. and Galasiński, D. (1998) 'The last Romantic hero: Lech Walesa's image-building in TV presidential debates', *TEXT* 18: 525–44.

—— (2000) 'Vocative address forms and ideological legitimisation in political debates', *Discourse Studies* 2: 65–83.

McEnery, A. and Hardie, A. (2011) *Corpus Linguistics: Methods, Theory and Practice*, Cambridge: Cambridge University Press.

Mills, S. (1997) *Discourse*, London: Routledge.

Ng, S.H. and Bradac, J.J. (1993) *Power in Language: Verbal Communication and Social Influence*, Newbury Park, CA: Sage.

Tannen, D. (1993) 'The relativity of linguistic strategies: rethinking power and solidarity in gender and dominance', in D. Tannen (ed.) *Gender and Conversational Interaction*, New York: Oxford University Press, 165–88.

Thompson, J.B. (1991) 'Editor's introduction', in P. Bourdieu, *Language and Symbolic Power*, Cambridge: Polity Press. 1–31.

Van Dijk, T. A. (1992) 'Discourse and the denial of racism', *Discourse and Society* 3: 87–118.

—— (1998) *Ideology*, London: Sage.

Chapter 26

Pierre Bourdieu

LANGUAGE AND SYMBOLIC POWER

. . .

LINGUISTIC EXCHANGE – a relation of communication between a sender and a receiver, based on enciphering and deciphering, and therefore on the implementation of a code or a generative competence – is also an economic exchange which is established within a particular symbolic relation of power between a producer, endowed with a certain linguistic capital, and a consumer (or a market), and which is capable of procuring a certain material or symbolic profit. In other words, utterances are not only (save in exceptional circumstances) signs to be understood and deciphered; they are also *signs of wealth*, intended to be evaluated and appreciated, and *signs of authority*, intended to be believed and obeyed. Quite apart from the literary (and especially poetic) uses of language, it is rare in everyday life for language to function as a pure instrument of communication. The pursuit of maximum informative efficiency is only exceptionally the exclusive goal of linguistic production and the distinctly instrumental use of language which it implies generally clashes with the often unconscious pursuit of symbolic profit. For in addition to the information expressly declared, linguistic practice inevitably communicates information about the (differential) manner of communicating, i.e., about the *expressive style*, which, being perceived and appreciated with reference to the universe of theoretically or practically competing styles, takes on a social value and a symbolic efficacy.

Source: Pierre Bourdieu, *Language and Symbolic Power*, translated by Gino Raymond and Matthew Adamson. Edited by John B. Thompson. Cambridge: Polity Press in association with Blackwell, 1991.

Capital, market and price

Utterances receive their value (and their sense) only in their relation to a market, characterized by a particular law of price formation. The value of the utterance depends on the relation of power that is concretely established between the speakers' linguistic competences, understood both as their capacity for production and as their capacity for appropriation and appreciation; it depends, in other words, on the capacity of the various agents involved in the exchange to impose the criteria of appreciation most favourable to their own products. This capacity is not determined in linguistic terms alone. It is certain that the relation between linguistic competences – which, as socially classified productive capacities, characterize socially classified linguistic units of production and, as capacities of appropriation and appreciation, define markets that are themselves socially classified – helps to determine the law of price formation that obtains in a particular exchange. But the linguistic relation of power is not completely determined by the prevailing linguistic forces alone: by virtue of the languages spoken, the speakers who use them and the groups defined by possession of the corresponding competence, the whole social structure is present in each interaction (and thereby in the discourse uttered). That is what is ignored by the interactionist perspective, which treats interaction as a closed world, forgetting that what happens between two persons – between an employer and an employee or, in a colonial situation, between a French speaker and an Arabic speaker or, in the post-colonial situation, between two members of the formerly colonized nation, one Arabic-speaking, one French-speaking – derives its particular form from the objective relation between the corresponding languages or usages, that is, between the groups who speak those languages.

The concern to return to the things themselves and to get a firmer grip on 'reality', a concern which often inspires the projects of 'micro-sociology', can lead one purely and simply to miss a 'reality' that does not yield to immediate intuition because it lies in structures transcending the interaction which they inform. There is no better example of this than that provided by *strategies of condescension*. Thus a French-language newspaper published in Béarn (a province of south-west France) wrote of the mayor of Pau who, in the course of a ceremony in honour of a Béarnais poet, had addressed the assembled company in Béarnais: 'The audience was greatly moved by this thoughtful gesture' [*La République des Pyrénées*, 9 September 1974]. In order for an audience of people whose mother tongue is Béarnais to perceive as a 'thoughtful gesture' the fact that a Béarnais mayor should speak to them in Béarnais, they must tacitly recognize the unwritten law which prescribes French as the only acceptable language for formal speeches in formal situations. The strategy of condescension consists in deriving *profit* from the objective relation of power between the languages that confront one another in practice (even and especially when French is absent) in the very act of symbolically negating that relation, namely, the hierarchy of the languages and of those who speak them. Such a strategy is possible whenever the objective disparity between the persons present (that is, between their social properties) is sufficiently known and recognized by everyone (particularly those involved in the interaction, as agents or spectators) so that the symbolic negation of the hierarchy (by using the 'common touch', for instance) enables the speaker to combine the profits linked to the undiminished hierarchy with those derived from the distinctly symbolic negation of the hierarchy – not the least of which is the strengthening of the hierarchy implied by the recognition accorded to the way of using the hierarchical relation. In reality, the Béarnais mayor can create this condescension effect only because, as mayor of a large town, attesting to his urbanity, he also possesses all the titles (he is a qualified professor) which guarantee his rightful participation in the 'superiority' of the 'superior' language (no one, and especially not a provincial journalist, would think of praising the mayor's French in the same way as his Béarnais, since he is a qualified, licensed speaker who speaks 'good quality' French by definition, *ex officio*). What is praised as 'good quality Béarnais', coming from the mouth of the legitimate speaker of the legitimate language, would be totally devoid of value – and furthermore would be sociologically impossible in a formal situation – coming from the mouth of a peasant, such as the man who, in order to explain why he did not dream of becoming mayor of his village even though he had obtained the biggest share of the vote, said (in French) that he 'didn't know how to speak' (meaning French), implying a definition of linguistic competence that is entirely sociological. One can see in passing that strategies for the subversion of objective hierarchies in the sphere of language, as in the sphere of culture, are *also* likely to be strategies of condescension, reserved for those who are sufficiently confident of their position in the objective hierarchies to be able to deny them without appearing to be ignorant or incapable of satisfying their demands. If Béarnais (or, elsewhere, Creole) is one day spoken on formal occasions, this will be by virtue of its takeover by speakers of the dominant language, who have enough claims to linguistic legitimacy (at least in the eyes of their interlocutors) to avoid being suspected of resorting to the stigmatized language *faute de mieux*.

The relations of power that obtain in the linguistic market, and whose variations determine the variations in the price that the same discourse may receive on different markets, are manifested and realized in the fact that certain agents are incapable of applying to the linguistic products offered, either by themselves or others, the criteria that are most favourable to their own products. This effect of the imposition of legitimacy is greater – and the laws of the market are more favourable to the products offered by the holders of the greatest linguistic competence – when the use of the legitimate language is more imperative, that is, when the situation is more formal (and when it is more favourable, therefore, to those who are more or less formally delegated to speak), and when consumers grant more complete recognition to the legitimate language and legitimate competence (but a recognition which is relatively independent of their knowledge of that language). In other words, the more formal the market is, the more practically congruent with the norms of the legitimate language, the more it is dominated by the dominant, i.e., by the holders of the legitimate competence, authorized to speak with authority.

. . .

It is true that the definition of the symbolic relation of power which is constitutive of the market can be the subject of *negotiation* and that the market can be manipulated, within certain limits, by a metadiscourse concerning the conditions of use of discourse. This includes, for example, the expressions which are used to introduce or excuse speech which is too free or shocking ('with your permission', 'if I may say so', 'if you'll pardon the expression', 'with all due respect', etc.) or those which reinforce, through explicit articulation, the candour enjoyed on a particular market ('off the record', 'strictly between ourselves', etc.). But it goes without saying that the capacity to manipulate is greater the more capital one possesses, as is shown by the strategies of condescension. It is also true that the unification of the market is never so complete as to prevent dominated individuals from finding, in the space provided by private life, among friends, markets where the laws of price formation which apply to more formal markets are suspended. In these private exchanges between homogeneous partners, the 'illegitimate' linguistic products are judged according to criteria which, since they are adjusted to their principles of production, free them from the necessarily comparative logic of distinction and of value. Despite this, the formal law, which is thus provisionally suspended rather than truly transgressed, remains valid, and it re-imposes itself on dominated individuals once they leave the unregulated areas where they can be outspoken (and where they can spend all their lives), as is shown by the fact that it governs the production of their spokespersons as soon as they are placed in a formal situation.

. . .

The anticipation of profits

Since a discourse can only exist, in the form in which it exists, so long as it is not simply grammatically correct but also, and above all, socially acceptable, i.e., heard, believed, and therefore effective within a given state of relations of production and circulation, it follows that the scientific analysis of discourse must take into account the laws of price formation which characterize the market concerned or, in other words, the laws defining the social conditions of acceptability (which include the specifically linguistic laws of grammaticality). In reality, the conditions of reception envisaged are part of the conditions of production, and anticipation of the sanctions of the market helps to determine the production of the discourse. This anticipation, which bears no resemblance to a conscious calculation, is an aspect of the linguistic habitus which, being the product of a prolonged and primordial relation to the laws of a certain market, tends to function as a practical sense of the acceptability and the probable value of one's own linguistic productions and those of others on different markets. It is this sense of acceptability, and not some form of rational calculation oriented towards the maximization of symbolic profits, which, by encouraging one to take account of the probable value of discourse during the process of production, determines corrections and all forms of self-censorship – the concessions one makes to a social world by accepting to make oneself acceptable in it.

Since linguistic signs are also goods destined to be given a price by powers capable of providing credit (varying according to the laws of the market on which they are placed), linguistic production is inevitably affected by the anticipation of market sanctions: all verbal expressions – whether words exchanged between friends, the bureaucratic discourse of an authorized spokesperson or the academic discourse of a scientific paper – are marked by their conditions of reception and owe some of their properties (even at a grammatical level) to the fact that, on the basis of a practical anticipation of the laws of the market concerned, their authors, most often unwittingly, and without expressly seeking to do so, try to maximize the symbolic profit they can obtain – from practices which are, inseparably, oriented towards communication and exposed to evaluation. This means that the market fixes the price for a linguistic product, the nature, and therefore the objective value, of which the practical anticipation of this price helped to determine; and it means that the practical relation to the market (ease, timidity, tension, embarrassment, silence, etc.), which helps to establish the market sanction, thus provides an apparent justification for the sanction by which it is partly produced.

In the case of symbolic production, the constraint exercised by the market via the anticipation of possible profit naturally takes the form of an anticipated *censorship*, of a self-censorship which determines not only the manner of saying, that is, the choice of language – 'code switching' in situations of bilingualism – or the 'level' of language, but also what it will be possible or not possible to say.

. . .

What our social sense detects in a form which is a kind of symbolic expression of all the sociologically pertinent features of the market situation is precisely that which oriented the production of the discourse, namely, the entire set of characteristics of the social relation obtaining between the interlocutors and the expressive capacities which the speaker was able to invest in the process of euphemization. The interdependence between linguistic forms and the structure of the social relation within and for which it is produced can be seen clearly, in French, in the oscillations between the forms of address, *vous* and *tu*, which sometimes occur when the objective structure of the relation between two speakers (e.g., disparity in age or social status) conflicts with the length and continuity of their acquaintance, and therefore with the intimacy and familiarity of their interaction. It then seems as if they are feeling their way towards a readjustment of the mode of expression and of the social relation through spontaneous or calculated slips of the tongue and progressive lapses, which often culminate in a sort of linguistic contract designed to establish the new expressive order on an official basis: 'Let's use *tu*.' But the subordination of the form of discourse to the form of the social relationship in which it is used is most strikingly apparent in situations of *stylistic collision*, when the speaker is confronted with a socially heterogeneous audience or simply with two interlocutors socially and culturally so far apart that the sociologically exclusive modes of expression called for, which are normally produced through more or less conscious adjustment in separate social spaces, cannot be produced simultaneously.

What guides linguistic production is not the degree of tension of the market or, more precisely, its degree of formality, defined in the abstract, for any speaker, but rather the relation between a degree of 'average' objective tension and a linguistic habitus itself characterized by a particular degree of sensitivity to the tension of the market; or, in other words, it is the anticipation of profits, which can scarcely be called a subjective anticipation since it is the product of the encounter between an objective circumstance, that is, the average probability of success, and an incorporated objectivity, that is, the disposition towards a more or less rigorous evaluation of that probability. The practical anticipation of the potential rewards or penalties is a practical quasi-corporeal sense of the reality of the objective relation between a certain linguistic and social competence and a certain market, through which this relation is accomplished. It can range from the certainty of a positive sanction, which is the basis of *certitudo sui*, of *self-assurance*, to the certainty of a negative sanction, which induces surrender and silence, through all the intermediate forms of insecurity and timidity.

The linguistic habitus and bodily hexis

The definition of acceptability is found not in the situation but in the relationship between a market and a habitus, which itself is the product of the whole history of its relations with markets. The habitus is, indeed, linked to the market no less through its conditions of acquisition than through its conditions of use. We have not learned to speak simply by hearing a certain kind of speech spoken but also by speaking, thus by offering a determinate form of speech on a determinate market. This occurs through exchanges within a family occupying a particular position in the social space and thus presenting the child's imitative propensity with models and sanctions that diverge more or less from legitimate usage. And we have learned the value that the products offered on this primary market, together with the authority which it provides, receive on other markets (like that of the school). The system of successive reinforcements or refutations has thus constituted in each one of us a certain sense of the social value of linguistic usages and of the relation between the different usages and the different markets, which organizes all subsequent perceptions of linguistic products, tending to endow it with considerable stability. (We know, in general terms, that the effects that a new experience can have on the habitus depend on the relation of practical 'compatibility' between this experience and the experiences that have already been assimilated by the habitus, in the form of schemes of production and evaluation, and that, in the process of selective re-interpretation which results from this dialectic, the informative efficacy of all new experiences tends to diminish continuously.) This linguistic 'sense of place' governs the degree of constraint which a given field will bring to bear on the production of discourse, imposing silence or a hyper-controlled language on some people while allowing others the liberties of a language that is securely established. This means that competence, which is acquired in a social context and through practice, is inseparable from the practical mastery of a usage of language and the practical mastery of situations in which this usage of language is *socially acceptable*. The sense of the value of one's own linguistic products is a fundamental dimension of the sense of knowing the place which one occupies in the social space. One's original relation with different markets and the experience of the sanctions applied to one's own productions, together with the experience of the price attributed to one's own body, are doubtless some of the mediations which help to constitute that *sense of one's own social worth* which governs the practical relation to different markets (shyness, confidence, etc.) and, more generally, one's whole physical posture in the social world.

While every speaker is both a producer and a consumer of his own linguistic productions, not all speakers, as we have seen, are able to apply to their own products the schemes according to which they were produced. The unhappy relation which the petits bourgeois have to their own productions (and especially with regard to their pronunciation, which, as Labov shows, they judge with particular severity); their especially keen sensitivity to the tension of the market and, by the same token, to linguistic correction in themselves and in others, which pushes them to hyper-correction; their insecurity, which reaches a state of paroxysm on formal occasions, creating 'incorrectness' through hyper-correction or the embarrassingly rash utterances prompted by an artificial confidence – are all things that result from a divorce between the schemes of production and the schemes of evaluation. Divided against themselves, so to speak, the petits bourgeois are those who are both the most 'conscious' of the objective truth of their products (the one defined in the academic hypothesis of the perfectly unified market) and the most determined to reject it, deny it, and contradict it by their efforts. As is very evident in this case, what expresses itself through the linguistic habitus is the whole class habitus of which it is one dimension, which means in fact, the position that is occupied, synchronically and diachronically, in the social structure.

As we have seen, hyper-correction is inscribed in the logic of pretension which leads the petits bourgeois to attempt to appropriate prematurely, at the cost of constant tension, the properties of those who are dominant. The particular intensity of the insecurity and anxiety felt by women of the petite bourgeoisie with regard to language (and equally with regard to cosmetics or personal appearance) can be understood in the framework of the same logic: destined, by the division of labour between the sexes, to seek social mobility through their capacity for symbolic production and consumption, they are even more inclined to invest in the acquisition of legitimate competences. The linguistic practices of the petite bourgeoisie could not fail to strike those who, like Labov, observed them on the particularly tense markets created by linguistic investigation. Situated at the maximum point of subjective tension through their particular sensitivity to objective tension (which is the effect of an especially marked disparity between recognition and cognition), the petits bourgeois are distinct from members of the lower classes who, lacking the means to exercise the liberties of plain speaking, which they reserve for private usage, have no choice but to opt for the broken forms of a borrowed and clumsy language or to escape into abstention and silence. But the petits bourgeois are no less distinct from the members of the dominant class, whose linguistic habitus (especially if they were born in that class) is the *realization of the norm* and who can express all the self-confidence that is associated with a situation where the principles of evaluation and the principles of production coincide perfectly.

In this case, as, at the other extreme, in the case of popular outspokenness on the popular market, the demands of the market and the dispositions of the habitus are perfectly attuned; the law of the market does not need to be imposed by means of constraint or external censorship since it is accomplished through the relation to the market which is its incorporated form. When the objective structures which it confronts coincide with those which have produced it, the habitus antici-pates the objective demands of the field. Such is the basis of the most frequent and best concealed form of censorship, the kind which is applied by placing, in positions which imply the right to speak, those agents who are endowed with expressive dispositions that are 'censored' in advance, since they coincide with the exigencies inscribed in those positions. As the principle underlying all the distinctive features of the dominant mode of expression, *relaxation in tension* is the expression of a relation to the market which can only be acquired through prolonged and precocious familiarity with markets that are characterized, even under ordinary circumstances, by a high level of control and by that constantly sustained attention to forms and formalities which defines the 'stylization of life'.

. . .

It is no coincidence that bourgeois distinction invests the same intention in its relation to language as it invests in its relation to the body. The sense of acceptability which orients linguistic practices is inscribed in the most deep-rooted of bodily dispositions: it is the whole body which responds by its posture, but also by its inner reactions or, more specifically, the articulatory ones, to the tension of the market. Language is a body technique, and specifically linguistic, especially phonetic, competence is a dimension of bodily hexis in which one's whole relation to the social world, and one's whole socially informed relation to the world, are expressed. There is every reason to think that, through the mediation of what Pierre Guiraud calls 'articulatory style', the bodily hexis characteristic of a social class determines the system of phonological features which characterizes a class pronunciation. The most frequent articulatory position is an element in an *overall way of using the mouth* (in talking but also in eating, drinking, laughing, etc.) and therefore a component of the bodily hexis, which implies a *systematic informing* of the whole phonological aspect of speech. This 'articulatory style', a life-style 'made flesh', like the whole bodily hexis, welds phonological features – which are often studied in isolation, each one (the phoneme 'r', for example) being compared with its equivalent in other class pronunciations – into an indivisible totality which must be treated as such.

Thus, in the case of the lower classes, articulatory style is quite clearly part of a relation to the body that is dominated by the refusal of 'airs and graces' (i.e., the refusal of stylization and the imposition of form) and by the valorization of virility – one aspect of a more general disposition to appreciate what is 'natural'. Labov is no doubt right when he ascribes the resistance of male speakers in New York to the imposition of the legitimate language to the fact that they associate the idea of virility with their way of speaking or, more precisely, their way of using the mouth and throat when speaking. In France, it is surely no accident that popular usage condenses the opposition between the bourgeois relation and the popular relation to language in the sexually over-determined opposition between two words for the mouth: *la bouche*, which is more closed, pinched, i.e., tense and censored, and therefore feminine, and *la gueule*, unashamedly wide open, as in 'split' (*fendue, se fendre la gueule*, 'split oneself laughing'), i.e., relaxed and free, and therefore masculine. Bourgeois dispositions, as they are envisaged in the popular mind, and in their most caricatured, petit-bourgeois form, convey in their physical postures of tension and exertion (*bouche fine, pincée, lèvres pincées, serrées, du bout des lèvres, bouche en cul-de-poule* – to be fastidious, supercilious, 'tight-lipped') the bodily indices of quite general dispositions towards the world and other people (and particularly, in the case of the mouth, towards food), such as haughtiness and disdain (*faire la fine bouche, la petite bouche* – to be fussy about food, difficult to please), and the conspicuous distance from the things of the body and those who are unable to mark that distance. *La gueule*, by contrast, is associated with the manly dispositions which, according to the popular ideal, are rooted in the calm certainty of strength which rules out censorships – prudence and deviousness as well as 'airs and graces' – and which make it possible to be 'natural' (*la gueule* is on the side of nature), to be 'open' and 'outspoken' (*jouer franc-jeu, avoir son franc-parler*) or simply to sulk (*faire la gueule*). It designates a capacity for verbal violence, identified with the sheer strength of the voice (*fort en gueule, coup de gueule, grande gueule, engueuler, s'engueuler, gueuler, aller gueuler* – 'loud-mouthed', a 'dressing-down', 'bawl', 'have a slanging match', 'mouth-off'). It also designates a capacity for the physical violence to which it alludes, especially in insults (*casser la gueule, mon poing sur la gueule, ferme ta gueule* – 'smash your face in', 'a punch in the mouth', 'shut your face'), which, through the *gueule*, regarded both as the 'seat' of personal identity (*bonne gueule, sale gueule* – 'nice guy', 'ugly mug') and as its main means of expression (consider the meaning of *ouvrir sa gueule*, or *l'ouvrir*, as opposed to *la fermer, la boucler, taire sa gueule, s'écraser* – 'say one's piece', as opposed to 'shut it', 'belt up', 'shut your mouth', 'pipe down'), aims at the very essence of the interlocutor's social identity and self-image. Applying the same 'intention' to the site of food intake and the site of speech output, the popular vision, which has a clear grasp of the unity of habitus and bodily hexis, also associates *la gueule* with the frank acceptance (*s'en foutre plein la gueule, se rincer la gueule* – stuffing oneself with food and drink) and frank manifestation (*se fendre la gueule*) of elementary pleasure.

On the one hand, domesticated language, censorship made natural, which proscribes 'gross' remarks, 'coarse' jokes and 'thick' accents, goes hand in hand with the domestication of the body which excludes all excessive manifestations of appetites or feelings (exclamations as much as tears or sweeping gestures), and which subjects the body to all kinds of discipline and censorship aimed at denaturalizing it. On the other hand, the 'relaxation of articulatory tension', which leads, as Bernard Laks has pointed out, to the dropping of the final 'r' and 'l' (and which is probably not so much an effect of *laisser-aller* as the expression of a refusal to 'overdo it' to conform too strictly on the points most strictly demanded by the dominant code, even if the effort is made in other areas), is associated with rejection of the censorship which propriety imposes, particularly on the tabooed body, and with the outspokenness whose daring is less innocent than it seems since, in reducing humanity to its common nature – belly, bum, bollocks, grub, guts and shit – it tends to turn the social world upside down, arse over head. Popular festivity as described by Bakhtin and especially revolutionary crisis highlight, through the verbal explosion which they facilitate, the pressure and repression which the everyday order imposes, particularly on the dominated class, through the seemingly insignificant constraints and controls of politeness which, by means of the stylistic variations in ways of talking (the formulae of politeness) or of bodily deportment in relation to the degree of objective tension of the market, exacts recognition of the hierarchical differences between the classes, the sexes and the generations.

It is not surprising that, from the standpoint of the dominated classes, the adoption of the dominant style is seen as a denial of social and sexual identity, a repudiation of the virile values which constitute class membership. That is why women can identify with the dominant culture without cutting themselves off from their class as radically as men. 'Opening one's big mouth' (*ouvrir sa grande gueule*) means refusing to submit, refusing to 'shut it' (*la fermer*) and to manifest the signs of docility that are the precondition of mobility. To adopt the dominant style, especially a feature as marked as the legitimate pronunciation, is in a sense doubly to negate one's virility because the very fact of acquiring it requires docility, a disposition imposed on women by the traditional sexual division of labour (and the traditional division of sexual labour), and because this docility leads one towards dispositions that are themselves perceived as effeminate.

In drawing attention to the articulatory features which, like the degree of 'aperture', sonority or rhythm, best express, in their own logic, the deep-rooted dispositions of the habitus and, more precisely, of the bodily hexis, spontaneous sociolinguistics demonstrates that a differential phonology should never fail to select and interpret the articulatory features characteristic of a class or class fraction in relation not only to the other systems with reference to which they take on their distinctive value, and therefore their social value, but also in relation to the synthetic unity of the bodily hexis from which they spring, and by virtue of which they represent the ethical or aesthetic expression of the necessity inscribed in a social condition.

> The linguist, who has developed an abnormally acute perception (particularly at the phonological level), may notice differences where ordinary speakers hear none. Moreover, because he has to concentrate on discrete criteria (such as the dropping of the final 'r' or 'l') for the purposes of statistical measurement, he is inclined towards an analytical perception very different in its logic from the ordinary perception which underlies the classificatory judgements and the delimitation of homogeneous groups in everyday life. Not only are linguistic features never clearly separated from the speaker's whole set of social properties (bodily hexis, physiognomy, cosmetics, clothing), but phonological (or lexical, or any other) features are never clearly separated from other levels of language; and the judgement which classifies a speech form as 'popular' or a person as 'vulgar' is based, like all practical predication, on sets of indices which never impinge on consciousness in that form, even if those which are designated by stereotypes (such as the 'peasant' 'r' or the southern *ceusse*) have greater weight.

The close correspondence between the uses of the body, of language and no doubt also of time is due to the fact that it is essentially through bodily and linguistic disciplines and censorships, which often imply a temporal rule, that groups inculcate the virtues which are the transfigured form of their necessity, and to the fact that the 'choices' constitutive of a relationship with the economic and social world are incorporated in the form of durable frames that are partly beyond the grasp of consciousness and will.

Chapter 27

Teun A. Van Dijk

DISCOURSE AND THE
DENIAL OF RACISM

. . .

Discourse and racism

ONE OF THE CRUCIAL PROPERTIES of contemporary racism is its denial, typically illustrated in such well-known disclaimers as 'I have nothing against blacks, but . . .'. This article examines the discursive strategies, as well as the cognitive and social functions, of such and other forms of denial in different genres of text and talk about ethnic or racial affairs.

. . .

The guiding idea behind this research is that ethnic and racial prejudices are prominently acquired and shared within the white dominant group through everyday conversation and institutional text and talk. Such discourse serves to express, convey, legitimate or indeed to conceal or deny such negative ethnic attitudes. Therefore, a systematic and subtle discourse analytical approach should be able to reconstruct such social cognitions about other groups.

It is further assumed in this research programme that talk and text about minorities, immigrants, refugees or, more generally, about people of colour or Third World peoples and nations, also have broader societal, political and cultural functions. Besides positive self-presentation and negative other-presentation, such discourse signals group membership, white in-group allegiances and, more generally, the various conditions for the reproduction of the white group and their dominance in virtually all social, political and cultural domains.

Source: Teun A. Van Dijk, 'Discourse and the denial of racism', *Discourse & Society*, 1992, 3(1): 87–118.

. . .

Political, media, academic, corporate and other elites play an important role in the reproduction of racism. They are the ones who control or have access to many types of public discourse, have the largest stake in maintaining white group dominance, and are usually also most proficient in persuasively formulating their ethnic opinions. Although there is of course a continuous interplay between elite and popular forms of racism, analysis of many forms of discourse suggests that the elites in many respects 'preformulate' the kind of ethnic beliefs of which, sometimes more blatant, versions may then get popular currency. Indeed, many of the more 'subtle', 'modern', 'everyday' or 'new' forms of cultural racism, or ethnicism, studied below, are taken from elite discourse. This hypothesis is not inconsistent with the possibility that (smaller, oppositional) elite groups also play a prominent role in the pre-formulation of anti-racist ideologies.

. . .

The denial of racism

The denial of racism is one of the moves that is part of the latter strategy of positive in-group presentation. General norms and values, if not the law, prohibit (blatant) forms of ethnic prejudice and discrimination, and many if not most white group members are both aware of such social constraints and, up to a point, even share and acknowledge them (Billig 1988). Therefore, even the most blatantly racist discourse in our data routinely features denials or at least mitigations of racism. Interestingly, we have found that precisely the more racist discourse tends to have disclaimers and other denials. This suggests that language users who say negative things about minorities are well aware of the fact that they may be understood as breaking the social norm of tolerance or acceptance.

Denials of racism, and similar forms of positive self-presentation, have both an *individual* and a *social* dimension. Not only do most white speakers individually resent being perceived as racists, [but] also, and even more importantly, such strategies may at the same time aim at defending the in-group as a whole: 'We are not racists', 'We are not a racist society'.

Whereas the first, individual, form of denial is characteristic of informal every-day conversations, the second is typical for public discourse, for instance in politics, the media, education, corporations and other organizations. Since public discourse potentially reaches a large audience, it is this latter, social form of denial that is most influential and, therefore, also most damaging: it is the social discourse of denial that persuasively helps construct the dominant white consensus. Few white group members would have reason or interest, to doubt let alone to oppose such a claim.

. . .

Conversation

Everyday conversation is at the heart of social life. Whether in informal situations, with family members or friends, or on the job with colleagues or clients or within a multitude of institutions, informal talk constitutes a crucial mode of social interaction. At the same time, conversations are a major conduit of social 'information-processing', and provide the context for the expression and persuasive conveyance of shared knowledge and beliefs.

In ethnically mixed societies, minority groups and ethnic relations are a major topic of everyday conversation. Whether through direct personal experience, or indirectly through the mass media, white people in Europe and North America learn about minorities or immigrants, formulate their own opinions and thus informally reproduce – and occasionally challenge – the dominant consensus on ethnic affairs through informal everyday talk.

Our extensive discourse analytical research into the nature of such everyday talk about ethnic affairs, based on some 170 interviews conducted in the Netherlands and California, shows that such informal talk has a number of rather consistent properties:

1   Topics are selected from a rather small range of subjects, and focus on sociocultural differences, deviance and competition. Most topics explicitly or implicitly deal with interpersonal, social, cultural or economic 'threats' of the dominant white group, society or culture.

2   Storytelling is not, as would be usual, focused on entertaining, but takes place within an argumentative framework. Stories serve as the strong, while personally experienced, premises of a generally negative conclusion, such as 'We are not used to that here', 'They should learn the language' or 'The government should do something about that'.

3   Style, rhetoric and conversational interaction generally denote critical distance, if not negative attitudes towards minorities or immigration. However, current norms of tolerance control expressions of evaluations in such a way that discourse with strangers (such as interviewers) is generally rather mitigated. Strong verbal aggression tends to be avoided.

4   Overall, speakers follow a double strategy of positive self-presentation and negative other-presentation.

It is within this latter strategy also that disclaimers, such as 'I have nothing against Arabs, *but* . . .' have their specific functions. Such a denial may be called 'apparent', because the denial is not supported by evidence that the speaker does not have anything against 'them'. On the contrary, the denial often serves as the face-keeping move introducing a generally negative assertion, following the invariable *but*, sometimes stressed, as in the following example from a Dutch woman:

(1)   uhh . . . how they are and that is mostly just fine, people have their own religion have their own way of life, and I have abso*lutely* nothing against that, *but*, it *is* a fact that if their way of life begins to differ from mine to an *extent* that. . . .

Talking about the main topic of cultural difference, the denial here focuses on relative tolerance for such cultural differences, which, however, is clearly constrained. The differences should not be too great. So, on the one hand, the woman follows the norm of tolerance, but on the other hand, she feels justified to reject others when they 'go too far'. In other words, the denial here presupposes a form of limited social acceptance.

Speakers who are more aware of discrimination and racism, as is the case in California, are even more explicit about the possible inferences of their talk:

(2)   It sounds prejudiced, but I think if students only use English. . . .

The use of English, a prominent topic for 'ethnic' conversations in the USA, may be required for many practical reasons, but the speaker realizes that whatever the good arguments he or she may have, it may be heard as a form of prejudice against immigrants. Of course the use of 'It sounds' implies that the speaker does not think he is really prejudiced.

One major form of denial in everyday conversation is the denial of discrimination. Indeed, as also happens in the right-wing media (see below), we also find reversal in this case: we are the real victims of immigration and minorities. Here are some of the ways people in Amsterdam formulate their denials:

(3)   Yes, they have exploited them, that's what they say at least, you know, but well, I don't believe that either. . . .
(4)   Big cars, they are better off than we are. If anybody is being discriminated against, our children are. That's what I make of it.
(5)   And the only thing that came from her mouth was I am being discriminated against and the Dutch all have good housing, well it is a big lie, it is not true.
(6)   And they say that they are being dismi discri discriminated against. That is not true.
(7)   Listen, they always say that foreigners are being discriminated against here. No, *we* are being discriminated against. It is exactly the reverse.

In all these situations, the speakers talk about what they see as threats or lies by immigrants: a murder in (3), cheating on welfare in (4), a radio programme where a black woman says she is discriminated against in (5), and neighbourhood services in (6) and (7). In conversations such reversals may typically be heard in working-class neighbourhoods where crime is attributed to minorities, or where alleged favouritism (e.g., in housing) is resented. Poor whites thus feel that they are victims of inadequate social and urban policies, but instead of blaming the authorities or the politicians, they tend to blame the newcomers who, in their eyes, are so closely related to the changing, i.e., deteriorating, life in the inner city. And if *they* are defined as those who are responsible, such a role is inconsistent with the claim that *they* are discriminated against (Phizacklea and Miles 1979).

Note that this consensus is not universal. Negative behaviour may be observed, but without generalization and with relevant comparisons to Dutch youths:

(8)   And that was also, well I am sorry, but they were foreigners, they were apparently Moroccans who did that. But God, all young people are aggressive, whether it is Turkish youth, or Dutch youth, or Surinamese youth, is aggressive. Particularly because of discrimination uhh that we have here . . .

Here discrimination is not reversed, and the young immigrants are represented as victims of discrimination, which is used to explain and hence to excuse some of their 'aggressiveness'. Such talk, however, is rather exceptional.

The press

Many of the 'ethnic events' people talk about in everyday life are not known from personal experiences, but from the media. At least until recently, in many parts of Western Europe and even in some regions of North America, most white people had few face-to-face dealings with members of minority groups. Arguments in everyday talk, thus, may be about crime or cultural differences they read about in the press, and such reports are taken as 'proof' of the negative attitudes the speakers have about minorities.

Our analyses of thousands of reports in the press in Britain and the Netherlands (Van Dijk 1991), largely confirm the common-sense interpretations of the readers: a topical analysis shows that crime, cultural differences, violence ('riots'), social welfare and problematic immigration are among the major recurrent topics of ethnic affairs reporting. In other words, there are marked parallels between topics of talk and media topics.

Overall, with some changes over the last decade, the dominant picture of minorities and immigrants is that of *problems* (Hartmann and Husband 1974). Thus the conservative and right-wing press tends to focus on the problems minorities and immigrants are seen to create (in housing, schooling, unemployment, crime, etc.), whereas the more liberal press (also) focuses on the problems minorities have (poverty, discrimination), but which *we* (white liberals) do something about. On the other hand, many topics that are routine in the coverage of white people, groups or institutions tend to be ignored, such as their contribution to the economy, political organization, culture and in general all topics that characterize the everyday lives of minorities, and their own, active contributions to the society as a whole. Thus, in many respects, except when involved in conflicts or problems, minorities tend to be 'denied' by the press (Boskin 1980).

Practices of newsgathering as well as patterns of quotation also show that minorities and their institutions have literally little to say in the press. First of all, especially in Europe, there are virtually no minority journalists, so that the perspective, inside knowledge and experience, prevailing attitudes and necessary sources of journalists tend to be all white, as are also the government agencies, police and other institutions that are the main sources of news in the press (Van Dijk 1988a; 1988b). Even on ethnic events, minority spokespersons are less quoted, less credibly quoted, and if they are quoted their opinions are often 'balanced' by the more 'neutral' comments of white spokespersons. Especially on delicate topics, such as discrimination, prejudice and racism, minority representatives or experts are very seldom heard in a credible, authoritative way. If at all, such quotes are often presented as unwarranted or even ridiculous accusations.

It is at this point where the overall strategy of denial has one of its discursive manifestations in press reports. Of course, as may be expected, there is a difference between liberal, conservative and right-wing newspapers in this respect. Note, however, that there are virtually no explicitly anti-racist newspapers in Europe and North America. The official norm, even on the right, is that 'we are all against racism', and the overall message is, therefore, that serious accusations of racism are a figment of the imagination.

Liberal newspapers, however, do pay attention to stories of explicit discrimination, e.g., in employment (though *rarely* in their own newsrooms or news reports), whereas right-wing extremism is usually dealt with in critical terms, although such coverage may focus on violent or otherwise newsworthy incidents rather than on racist attitudes *per se*. By such means ethnic or racial inequality is redefined as marginal, that is, as individualized or outside the consensus. Thus, the Dutch liberal press extensively reports cases (accusations) of discrimination, and the same is true in the USA. In the right-wing press, discrimination is also covered, but from a different perspective. Here, it is usually covered as a preposterous accusation, preferably against 'ordinary' people, or embedded in explanations or excuses (the act was provoked).

Whereas discrimination gets rather wide attention in the press, racism does not. Indeed, discrimination is seldom qualified as a manifestation of racism. One of the reasons is that racism is still often understood as an ideology of white supremacy, or as the kind of practices of the extreme right. Since the large majority of the press does not identify with the extreme right, any qualification of everyday discriminatory practices as 'racism' is resolutely rejected.

For large sections of the press, only anti-racists see such everyday racism as racism, which results in the marginalization of anti-racists as a radical, 'loony' group. For much of the press, at least in Britain, the real enemies, therefore, are the anti-racists: they are intolerant, anti-British, busybodies, who see racism everywhere, even in 'innocent' children's books, and even in the press.

It is not surprising, therefore, that reports on general aspects of racism in one's own society or group tend to be rare, even in the liberal press. Anti-racist writers, researchers or action groups have less access to the media, and their activities or opinions tend to be more or less harshly scorned, if not ridiculed. For the right-wing press, moreover, they are the real source of the 'problems' attributed to a multicultural society, because they not only attack venerable institutions (such as the police, government or business), but also provide a competing but fully incompatible definition of the ethnic situation. It is this symbolic competition for the definition of the situation and the intellectual struggle over the definition of society's morals, that pitches the right-wing press against left-wing, anti-racist intellectuals, teachers, writers and action groups.

Let us examine in more detail how exactly the press engages in this denial of racism. Most of our examples are taken from the British press, but it would not be difficult to find similar examples in the Dutch, German and French press. Because of its long history of slavery and segregation, the notion of white racism is more broadly accepted in the USA, even when today's prevailing ideology is that, now minorities have equal rights, racism is largely a thing of the past.

Racism and the press

The denial of racism in and by the press is of course most vehement when the press itself is the target of accusations. Reflecting similar reactions by other editors of Dutch newspapers to our own research on racism in the press, the editor-in-chief of a major elite weekly, *Intermediair*, catering especially for social scientists and the business community, writes the following in a letter:

> (9)   In particular, what you state about the coverage of minorities remains unproven and an unacceptable caricature of reality. Your thesis 'that the tendency of most reports is that ethnic minorities cause problems for us' is in my opinion not only not proven, but simply incorrect.
>
> (Translated from the Dutch)

This reaction was inspired by a brief summary of mostly international research on the representation of minorities in the press. The editor's denial is not based on (other) research, but simply stated as a 'fact'.

. . .

Other editors take an even more furious stand, and challenge the very academic credentials of the researcher and the university, as is the case by the editor of the major conservative popular daily in the Netherlands, *De Telegraaf*, well known for its biased reporting on minorities, immigrants and refugees:

> (10)   Your so-called scientific research does not in any sense prove your slanderous insinuations regarding the contents of our newspaper, is completely irrelevant and raises doubt about the prevailing norms of scientific research and social prudence at the University of Amsterdam.
>
> (Translated from the Dutch)

We see that whatever 'proof' may be brought in one's painstaking analyses of news reports, the reaction is one of flat denial and counter-attack by discrediting the researcher. Examples like these may be multiplied at random. No newspaper, including (or especially) the more liberal ones, will accept even a moderate charge of being biased, while allegations of racism are rejected violently. Recall that these newspapers, especially in Europe, generally employ no, or only one or two token, minority journalists.

With such an editorial attitude towards racism, there is a general reluctance to identify racist events as such in society at large. Let us examine the principal modes of such denials in the press. Examples are taken from the British press coverage of ethnic affairs in 1985 (for analysis of other properties of these examples, see Van Dijk 1991). Brief summaries of the context of each fragment of news discourse are given between parentheses.

Positive self-presentation

The semantic basis of denial is 'truth' as the writer sees it. The denial of racism in the press, therefore, presupposes that the journalist or columnist believes that his or her own group or country is essentially 'tolerant' towards minorities or immigrants. Positive self-presentation, thus, is an important move in journalistic discourse, and should be seen as the argumentative denial of the accusations of anti-racists:

(11)   [Handsworth] Contrary to much doctrine, and acknowledging a small malevolent fascist fringe, this is a remarkably tolerant society. But tolerance would be stretched were it to be seen that enforcement of law adopted the principle of reverse discrimination.
(*Daily Telegraph*, editorial, 11 September)

(12)   [Racial attacks and policing] If the ordinary British taste for decency and tolerance is to come through, it will need positive and unmistakable action.
(*Daily Telegraph*, editorial, 13 August)

(13)   [Racial attacks against Asians] . . . Britain's record for absorbing people from different backgrounds, peacefully and with tolerance, is second to none. The descendants of Irish and Jewish immigrants will testify to that. It would be tragic to see that splendid reputation tarnished now.
(*Sun*, editorial, 14 August)

(14)   [Immigration] Our traditions of fairness and tolerance are being exploited by every terrorist, crook, screwball and scrounger who wants a free ride at our expense. . . . Then there are the criminals who sneak in as political refugees or as family members visiting a distant relative.
(*Mail*, 28 November)

(15)   We have racism too – and that is what is behind the plot. It is not white racism. It is black racism. . . . But who is there to protect the white majority? . . . Our tolerance is our strength, but we will not allow anyone to turn it into our weakness.
(*Sun*, 24 October)

These examples not only assert or presuppose white British 'tolerance' but at the same time define its boundaries. Tolerance might be interpreted as a position of weakness and, therefore, it should not be 'stretched' too far, lest 'every terrorist', 'criminal' or other immigrant, takes advantage of it. Affirmative action or liberal immigration laws, thus, can only be seen as a form of reverse discrimination, and hence as a form of self-destruction of white Britain. Ironically, therefore, these examples are self-defeating because of their internal contradictions. It is not tolerance *per se* that is aimed at, but rather the limitations preventing its 'excesses'. Note that in example (15) positive self-presentation is at the same time combined with the well-known move of reversal. 'They are the real racists', 'We are the real victims'. We shall come back to such reversal moves below.

Denial and counter-attack

Having constructed a positive self-image of white Britain, the conservative and tabloid press especially engages in attacks against those who hold a different view, at the same time defending those who agree with its position, as was the case during the notorious Honeyford affair (Honeyford was headmaster of a Bradford school who was suspended, then reinstated and finally let go with a golden handshake, after having written articles on multicultural education which most of the parents of his mostly Asian students found racist). The attacks on the anti-racists often embody denials of racism:

(16)   [Reaction of 'race lobby' against Honeyford] Why is it that this lobby have chosen to persecute this man. . . . It is not because he is a racist; it is precisely because he is not a racist, yet has dared to challenge the attitudes, behaviour and approach of the ethnic minority professionals.

(Daily Telegraph, 6 September)

(17)   [Honeyford and other cases] Nobody is less able to face the truth than the hysterical 'anti-racist' brigade. Their intolerance is such that they try to silence or sack anyone who doesn't toe their party-line.

(Sun, 13 October, column by John Vincent)

(18)   [Honeyford] For speaking commonsense he's been vilified; for being courageous he's been damned, for refusing to concede defeat his enemies can't forgive him. . . . I have interviewed him and I am utterly convinced that he hasn't an ounce of racism in his entire being.

(Mail, 18 September, column by Lynda Lee-Potter)

(19)   [Honeyford quits] Now we know who the true racists are.

(Sun editorial, 30 November)

These examples illustrate several strategic moves in the press campaign against anti-racists. First, as we have seen above, denial is closely linked to the presupposition of 'truth': Honeyford is presented as defending the 'truth', namely the failure and the anti-British nature of multiculturalism. Second, consequent denials often lead to the strategic move of reversal: *we* are not the racists, *they* are the 'true racists'. This reversal also implies, thirdly, a reversal of the charges: Honeyford, and those who sympathize with him, are the victims, not his Asian students and their parents. Consequently, the anti-racists are the enemy: *they* are the ones who persecute innocent, ordinary British citizens, *they* are the ones who are intolerant. Therefore, victims who resist their attackers may be defined as folk heroes, who 'dare' the 'anti-racist brigade'.

Note also, in example (17), that the 'truth', as the supporters of Honeyford see it, is self-evident, and based on common sense. Truth and common sense are closely related notions in such counter-attacks, and reflect the power of the consensus, as well as the mobilization of popular support by 'ordinary' (white) British people. Apart from marginalizing Asian parents and other anti-racists by locating them outside of the consensus, and beyond the community of ordinary people like 'us', such appeals to common sense also have powerful ideological implications: self-evident truth is seen as 'natural', and hence the position of the others as 'unnatural' or even as 'crazy'. The anti-racist left, therefore, is often called 'crazy' or 'loony' in the right-wing British press.

Moral blackmail

One element that was very prominent in the Honeyford affair, as well as in similar cases, was the pretence of censorship: the anti-racists not only ignore the 'truth' about multicultural society, they also prevent others (us) from telling the truth. Repeatedly, thus, journalists and columnists argue that this 'taboo' and this 'censorship' must be broken in order to be able to tell the 'truth', as was the case after the disturbances in Tottenham:

> (20)   [Tottenham] The time has come to state the truth without cant and without hypocrisy . . . the strength to face the facts without being silenced by the fear of being called racist.
> (*Mail*, 9 October, column by Lynda Lee-Potter)

Such examples also show that the authors feel morally blackmailed, while at the same time realizing that to 'state the truth', meaning 'to say negative things about minorities', may well be against the prevalent norms of tolerance and understanding. Clamouring for the 'truth', thus, expresses a dilemma, even if the dilemma is only apparent: the apparent dilemma is a rhetorical strategy to accuse the opponent of censorship or blackmail, not the result of moral soul-searching and a difficult decision. After all, the same newspapers extensively *do* write negative things about young blacks, and never hesitate to write what they see as the 'truth'. Nobody 'silences' them, and the taboo is only imaginary. On the contrary, the right-wing press in Britain reaches many millions of readers.

Thus, this strategic play of denial and reversal at the same time involves the construction of social roles in the world of ethnic strife, such as allies and enemies, victims, heroes and oppressors. In many respects, such discourse mimics the discourse of anti-racists by simply reversing the major roles: victims become oppressors, those who are in power become victims.

Subtle denials

Denials are not always explicit. There are many ways to express doubt, distance or non-acceptance of statements or accusations by others. When the official Commission for Racial Equality (CRE) in 1985 published a report on discrimination in the UK, outright denial of the facts would hardly be credible. Other discursive means, such as quotation marks, and the use of words like 'claim' or 'allege', presupposing doubt on the part of the writer, may be employed in accounting for the facts, as is the case in the following editorial from the *Daily Telegraph*:

> (21) In its report which follows a detailed review of the operation of the 1976 Race Relations Act, the Commission claims that ethnic minorities continue to suffer high levels of discrimination and disadvantage.
>
> (*Daily Telegraph*, 1 August)

Such linguistic tricks do not go unnoticed, as we may see in the following reaction to this passage in a letter from Peter Newsam, then Director of the CRE.

> (22) Of the Commission you say 'it claims that ethnic minorities continue to suffer high levels of discrimination and disadvantage'. This is like saying that someone 'claims' that July was wet. It was. And it is also a fact supported by the weight of independent research evidence that discrimination on racial grounds, in employment, housing and services, remains at a disconcertingly high level.
>
> (*Daily Telegraph*, 7 August)

Denials, thus, may be subtly conveyed by expressing doubt or distance. Therefore, the very notion of 'racism' usually appears between quotation marks, especially also in the headlines. Such scare quotes are not merely a journalistic device of reporting opinions or controversial points of view. If that were the case, also the opinions with which the newspaper happens to agree would have to be put between quotes, which is not always the case. Rather, apart from signalling journalistic doubt and distance, the quotes also connote 'unfounded accusation'. The use of quotes around the notion of 'racism' has become so much routine, that even in cases where the police or the courts themselves established that racism was involved in a particular case, the conservative press may maintain the quotes out of sheer habit.

Mitigation

Our conceptual analysis of denial already showed that denial may also be implied by various forms of mitigation, such as downtoning, using euphemisms or other circumlocutions that minimize the act itself or the responsibility of the accused. In the same editorial of the *Daily Telegraph* we quoted above, we find the following statement:

> (23) [CRE report] No one would deny the fragile nature of race relations in Britain today or that there is misunderstanding and distrust between parts of the community.
>
> (*Daily Telegraph*, editorial, 1 August)

Thus, instead of inequality or racism, race relations are assumed to be 'fragile', whereas 'misunderstanding and distrust' is also characteristic of these relations. Interestingly, this passage also explicitly denies the prevalence of denials and, therefore, might be read as a concession: there *are* problems. However, the way this concession is rhetorically presented by way of various forms of mitigation, suggests, in the context of the rest of the same editorial, that the concession is apparent. Such apparent concessions are another major form of disclaimer in discourse about ethnic relations, as we also have them in statements like: 'There are also intelligent blacks, but . . .', or 'I know that minorities sometimes have problems, but . . .'. Note also that in the example from the *Daily Telegraph* the mitigation not only appears in the use of euphemisms, but also in the *redistribution of responsibility*, and hence in the denial of blame. Not we (whites) are mainly responsible for the tensions between the communities, but everybody is, as is suggested by the use of the impersonal existential phrase: '*There is* misunderstanding . . .'. Apparently, one effective move of denial is to either dispute responsible agency, or to conceal agency.

Defence and offence

On the other hand, in its attacks against the anti-racists, the right-wing press is not always that subtle. On the contrary, they may engage precisely in the 'diatribes' they direct at their opponents:

> (24) [Anti-fascist rally] The evening combined emotive reminders of the rise of Nazism with diatribes against racial discrimination and prejudice today.
>
> (*Daily Telegraph*, 1 October)

> (25) [Black sections] In the more ideologically-blinkered sections of his [Kinnock's] party . . . they seem to gain pleasure from identifying all difficulties experienced by immigrant groups, particularly Afro-Caribbeans, as the result of racism . . .
>
> (*Daily Telegraph*, editorial, 14 September)

(26)   [Worker accused of racism] . . . The really alarming thing is that some of these pocket Hitlers of local government are moving into national politics. It's time we set about exposing their antics while we can. Forewarned is forearmed.

(*Mail*, editorial, 26 October)

These examples further illustrate that denial of discrimination, prejudice and racism is not merely a form of self-defence or positive self-presentation. Rather, it is at the same time an element of attack against what they define as 'ideologically blinkered' opponents, as we also have seen in the move of reversal in other examples. Anti-racism is associated with the 'loony left', and attacking it therefore also has important ideological and political implications, and not just moral ones.

'Difficulties' of the Afro-Caribbean community may be presupposed, though not spelled out forcefully and in detail, but such presuppositions rather take the form of an apparent concession. That is, whatever the causes of these 'difficulties', as they are euphemistically called, they can not be the result of racism. Implicitly, by attributing 'pleasure' to those who explain the situation of the blacks, the newspaper also suggests that the left has an interest in such explanations and, therefore, even welcomes racism. This strategy is familiar in many other attacks against anti-racists: 'If there were no racism, they would invent it'. It hardly needs to be spelled out that such a claim again implies a denial of racism.

The amalgamation of comparisons and metaphors used in these attacks is quite interesting. That is, in one example an ironic reference is made to the 'emotive reminders' of Nazism, and in another these same opponents of Nazism are qualified as 'pocket Hitlers'. Yet, this apparent inconsistency in sociopolitical labelling has a very precise function. By referring to their opponents in terms of 'pocket Hitlers' the newspapers obviously distance themselves from the fascist opinions and practices that are often part of the more radical accusations against the right. At the same time, by way of the usual reversal, they categorize their opponents precisely in terms of their own accusations, and thus put them in a role these opponents most clearly would abhor.

Thus, the anti-racist left is associated with fascist practices, ideological blinkers and antics. Apart from their anti-racist stance, it is, however, their (modest) political influence which particularly enrages the right-wing press – although virtually powerless at the national level, and even within their own (Labour) party, some of the anti-racists have made it into local councils, and therefore control (some) money, funding and other forms of political influence. That is, they have at least some counter-power, and it is this power and its underlying ideology that is challenged by a press which itself controls the news supply of millions of readers. What the denial of racism and the concomitant attacks against the anti-racists in education or politics is all about, therefore, is a struggle over the definition of the ethnic situation. Thus, their ideological and political opponents are seen as symbolic competitors in the realm of moral influence. Whether directed at a headmaster or against other ordinary white British or not, what the right-wing press is particularly concerned about is its own image: by attacking the anti-racists, it is in fact defending itself.

. . .

Conclusions

Whether in the streets of the inner city, in the press or in parliament, dominant group members are often engaged in discourse about 'them': ethnic minority groups, immigrants or refugees, who have come to live in the country. Such discourses, as well as the social cognitions underlying them, are complex and full of contradictions. They may be inspired by general norms of tolerance and acceptance, but also, and sometimes at the same time, by feelings of distrust, resentment or frustration about those 'others'.

Topics, stories and argumentation may thus construct a largely negative picture of minorities or immigrants, e.g., in terms of cultural differences, deviance or competition, as a problem or as a threat to 'our' country, territory, space, housing, employment, education, norms, values, habits or language. Such talk and text, therefore, is not a form of individual discourse, but social, group discourse, and expresses not only individual opinions, but rather socially shared representations.

However, negative talk about minority groups or immigrants may be heard as biased, prejudiced or racist, and as inconsistent with general values of tolerance. This means that such discourse needs to be hedged, mitigated, excused, explained or otherwise managed in such a way that it will not 'count' against the speaker or writer. Face-keeping, positive self-presentation and impression management are the usual strategies that language users have recourse to in such a situation of possible 'loss of face': they have to make sure that they are not misunderstood and that no unwanted inferences are made from what they say.

One of the major strategic ways white speakers and writers engage in such a form of impression management is the denial of racism. They may simply claim they did not say anything negative, or focus on their intentions: it may have sounded negative, but was not intended that way. Similarly, they may mitigate their negative characterization of the others by using euphemisms, implications or vague allusions. They may make apparent concessions, on the one hand, and on the other hand support their negative discourse by arguments, stories or other supporting 'facts'.

Also, speakers and writers may abandon their position of positive self-presentation and self-defence and take a more active, aggressive counter-attack: the ones who levelled the accusations of racism are the real problem, if not the real racists. They are the ones who are intolerant, and they are against 'our' own people. We are the victims of immigration, and we are discriminated against.

It is interesting to note that despite the differences in style for different social groups, such discourse may be found at any social level, and in any social context. That is, both the 'ordinary' white citizens as well as the white elites need to protect their social self-image, and at the same time they have to manage the interpretation and the practices in an increasingly variegated social and cultural world. For the dominant group, this means that dominance relations must be reproduced, at the macro- as well as at the microlevel, both in action as well as in mind.

Negative representations of the dominated group are essential in such a reproduction process. However, such attitudes and ideologies are inconsistent with dominant democratic and humanitarian norms and ideals. This means that the dominant group must protect itself, cognitively and discursively, against the damaging charge of intolerance and racism. Cognitive balance may be restored only by actually being or becoming anti-racist, by accepting minorities and immigrants as equals, or else by denying racism. It is this choice that white groups in Europe and North America are facing. So far they have largely chosen the latter option.

References

Billig, M. (1988) 'The notion of "prejudice": some rhetorical and ideological aspects', *Text* 8: 91–110.

Boskin, J. (1980) 'Denials: the media view of dark skins and the city', in Rubin, B. (ed.) *Small Voices and Great Trumpets: Minorities and the Media*, New York: Praeger, 141–7.

Hartmann, P. and Husband, C. (1974) *Racism and the Mass Media*, London: Davis-Poynter.

Phizacklea, A. and Miles, R. (1979) 'Working-class racist beliefs in the inner city', in Miles, R. and Phizacklea, A. (eds) *Racism and Political Action in Britain*, London: Routledge & Kegan Paul, 93–123.

Van Dijk, T.A. (1988a) *News Analysis: Case Studies of International and National News in the Press*, Hillsdale, NJ: Erlbaum.

Van Dijk, T.A. (1988b) *News as Discourse*, Hillsdale, NJ: Erlbaum.

Van Dijk, T.A. (1991) *Racism and the Press*, London: Routledge.

Chapter 28

Ian Hutchby

POWER IN DISCOURSE: THE CASE OF ARGUMENTS ON A BRITISH TALK RADIO SHOW

. . .

I N THIS ARTICLE, I show how an approach informed by conversation analysis (CA) can provide an account of power as an integral feature of talk-in-interaction. CA has placed great emphasis on examining how participants in interaction display their orientation to phenomena that analysts claim are relevant (Schegloff 1991). This has proved a highly successful platform for analysing talk in institutional settings (e.g., Drew and Heritage 1992). What I show is that this approach, through focusing on such issues as how participants orient to features of a setting by designing their turns in specialized ways (e.g., restricting themselves either to asking questions or to giving answers), can be used to address how power is produced through oriented-to features of talk. One way in which this might be shown is by looking for occasions when participants actually topicalize or *formulate* the power relations between themselves (in the sense intended in Garfinkel and Sacks 1970). However, this clearly does not happen very often. An alternative possibility is this: the very ways in which participants design their interaction can have the effect of placing them in a relationship where discourse strategies of greater or lesser power are differentially available to each of them. In this sense, power can be viewed as an 'emergent feature' of oriented-to discourse practices in given settings. It is that possibility that I want to explore in the case of calls to a British talk radio show.

The data come from a collection of approximately 100 recorded calls to a British talk radio show. I began to study interaction on talk radio out of an interest in analysing argument and conflictual talk, and a recognition that this was a common occurrence on open-line talk radio shows. Observing the data, my interests rapidly turned to the question of how participation in talk radio disputes can be asymmetrical. In

Source: Ian Hutchby, 'Power in discourse: the case of arguments on a British talk radio show', *Discourse & Society*, 1996, 7: 481–97.

institutionalized settings for dispute, one of the things that may be of interest is the relationship between verbal patterns and resources used and the asymmetric social identities associated with the setting. In this article, I go further and argue that some of the asymmetrics we identify can be conceptualized in terms of the power of certain participants to engage in communicative actions not available (or not available in the same way) to others. This argument is based on a CA account of the ways in which arguments on talk radio articulate with, and are shaped and constrained by, the organizational and interactional parameters of the talk radio setting itself.

. . .

Analysing power: 'first' and 'second' positions

Talk radio represents a public context in which private citizens can articulate their opinions on social issues. In different shows, the space allotted to callers to forward their views is mapped out in different ways. For instance, some shows expressly address themselves to one issue per broadcast and the caller's role is to have a say on that issue while the host acts as a moderator, relating contributions together and drawing out differences and similarities between them. But in other shows, known as open-line, callers select their own issue to talk about and are given the floor at the beginning of calls in order to introduce their issue and express an opinion on it. In this sense, open-line talk radio shows enable callers to set the agenda for a discussion with the host.

However, agendas are not fixed things, nor are they established from one perspective only. In fact, agendas can become the contested arena for disputes focusing on what can relevantly be said within their terms. This leads to a paradox in talk radio disputes. While it may seem that the caller is in a position to control what will count as an acceptable or relevant contribution to his or her topic, in fact it is the host who tends to end up in that position. The very fact that introducing an agenda is the caller's prerogative on talk radio leads to a situation in which the argumentative initiative can rest with the host and the caller can relatively easily be put on the defensive.

How does this situation emerge? I suggest that it is an outcome of two factors. First, the way that arguments are sequentially organized and second, the way in which calls on talk radio themselves are organized. The principal sequential unit in an argument is the 'action–opposition' sequence (Hutchby 1996: 22–4), in which actions that can be construed as arguable are opposed, with the opposition itself subsequently open to being construed as arguable (Eisenberg and Garvey 1981; Maynard 1985). Within the organization of calls on talk radio, callers are required to begin by setting out their position (Hutchby 1991). This in turn situates the caller's opening turn as a possible first action in a potential action–opposition sequence. To put it another way, it is the host who has the first opportunity for opposition within each call. This turns out to be a powerful argumentative resource, which is not only linked to a particular kind of asymmetry between hosts and callers, but also has consequences for the shape and trajectory of disputes in the talk radio setting.

The asymmetry between first and second positions in arguments was first remarked on by Sacks in one of his lectures on conversation (1992: 2: 348–53). Sacks proposed that those who go first are in a weaker position than those who get to go second, since the latter can argue with the former's position simply by taking it apart. Going first means having to set your opinion on the line, whereas going second means being able to argue merely by challenging your opponent to expand on or account for his or her claims.

In many situations, first and second positions are open to strategic competition between participants. In such situations we can find speakers using systematic means to try and avoid first position, or to try and prompt or manoeuvre another into taking first position. For instance, Sacks (1992: 2: 344–7) discusses the following fragment of data:

Extract (1) GTS [From a conversation among teenagers]

1   Jim: Isn't the New Pike depressing?
2   Mike: hhh The Pike?
3   Jim: Yeah. Oh the place is disgusting. Any day of
4   the week.

In line 1, Jim indicates a position on the 'New Pike', a local amusement park. The way he states this position is designed to invite Mike's agreement that the New Pike is in fact 'depressing'.

In the next turn, however, Mike neither agrees nor disagrees with Jim. Rather, he produces a turn which on one level looks like an 'understanding check': a turn in which he initiates repair on Jim's prior turn, perhaps because he isn't sure he properly heard what Jim said. But there are features of Mike's turn which militate against that interpretation. For instance, he doesn't say: 'The what?' – which would be a straightforward way of indicating a possible mishearing or misunderstanding (Schegloff et al 1977). Neither does he repeat Jim's naming of the place in full (i.e., 'The New Pike?'), which again might suggest a difficulty in locating the referent in his own stock of knowledge (Clark and Schaefer 1989). Rather, Mike 're-references' the amusement park, calling it 'The Pike' – an abbreviation which suggests he is in fact familiar with the place. Finally, Jim himself exhibits in his next turn that he does not take Mike's utterance to be initiating repair, by carrying on with and expanding his assessment (lines 3–4) instead of repairing his first turn by saying, for example: 'Yeah. You know, the amusement park?'.

Instead of an understanding check, Mike's turn can be treated as a move in an incipient argument: a manoeuvre by which the floor is thrown back to Jim with an invitation to go on and develop his position on the ways in which the New Pike is depressing. In other words, it is a manoeuvre which seeks to place Mike in second position with respect to Jim's opinion of the Pike. If he can succeed in manoeuvring Jim into first position, Mike would then be in a position to attack Jim's opinion by using what Jim said as a resource for disagreeing, rather than immediately focusing on building a defence for his own opinion.

In fact, this is precisely what happens as the conversation proceeds. Jim goes on to elaborate on his view of the Pike, which then places Mike in a position to attack that view merely by undermining its weaknesses rather than arguing for a particular counter-position:

Extract (2) GTS

```
1    Jim:     But you go down- dow- down to the New Pike
2             there's a buncha people, oh:: an' they're old,
3             an' they're pretending they're having fun, but
4             they're really not.
5    Mike:    How can you tell. Hm?
6    Jim:     They're- they're tryina make a living, but the
7             place is on the decline, 's like a degenerate
8             place . . .
```

In line 5 here, Mike takes up a critical stance *vis-à-vis* Jim's argument, not by putting forward a counter-position, but by undermining Jim's competence to make the claims he is making. This is done by using 'How can you tell' (line 5) to challenge Jim's grounds for the claim that people at the New Pike are 'really not' having fun. This turn does not give Jim much in the way of resources that will allow him to take up the offensive and challenge Mike. Rather, his options are either to account for how he can tell, or to attempt to change tack.

It is this situation which is at the root of the asymmetry between first and second positions in argument. While first-position arguers are required to build a defence for their stance, those in second position are able to choose if and when they will set out their own argument, as opposed to simply attacking the other's.

The point I want to make is that on talk radio, this asymmetry is one that is 'built into' the overall structure of calls. Callers are expected, and may be constrained, to go first with their line, while the host systematically gets to go second, and thus to contest the caller's line by picking at its weaknesses. The fact that hosts systematically have the first opportunity for opposition within calls opens to them a collection of argumentative resources which are not available in the same way to callers.

In the following sections, I explore some of the uses and consequences of these second-position resources. In order to do this, I concentrate on episodes in which the participants argue about the dispute's agenda itself.

Agenda contests

One of the things that argument may be about is the struggle between participants over what can and cannot legitimately be said in a dispute: in other words, defining the boundaries of the dispute's agenda. I have already remarked that on talk radio, callers' agendas have an interesting status. While it is the role of the caller to set up an agenda for discussion, the agenda is not something that the caller necessarily maintains subsequent control of. By being in second position, the host is able to challenge the 'agenda-relatedness' of the caller's remarks: to question whether what the caller says is actually relevant within the terms of his or her own agenda.

One way in which this may be done is through the use of a class of utterances, including 'So?' and 'What's that got to do with it?' which challenge a claim on the grounds of its validity or relevance to the matter in question. However, a significant aspect of such turns is that they need not make clear precisely on what terms the claim is being challenged. They may function purely as second position moves by which the first speaker is required to expand on or account for the challenged claim.

In the following extract the caller is complaining about the number of mailed requests for charitable donations she receives. Note that in line 7, the host responds simply by saying 'So?'

Extract (3) H:21.11.88:6:1

```
 1   Caller:   I: have got three appeals letters here this
 2             week.(0.4) All a:skin' for donations. (0.2) .hh
 3             Two: from tho:se that I: always contribute to
 4             anywa:y.
 5   Host:     Yes?
 6   Caller:   .hh But I expect to get a lot mo:re.
 7   Host:     So?
 8   Caller:   .h Now the point is there is a limi┌t to (    )
 9   Host:                                        └What's that
10             got to do- what's that got to do with telethons
11             though.
12   Caller:   hh Because telethons . . . ((Continues))
```

As an argumentative move, this 'So?' achieves two things. First, it challenges the validity or relevance of the caller's complaint within the terms of her own agenda, which in this case is that charities represent a form of 'psychological blackmail'. Second, because it stands alone as a complete turn, 'So?' requires the caller to take the floor again and account for the relevance of her remark.

. . .

Another way in which the host may attempt to establish control over the agenda is by selectively *formulating* the gist or upshot of the caller's remarks. Heritage (1985: 100) describes the practice of formulating as: 'summarising, glossing, or developing the gist of an informant's earlier statements'. He adds: 'Although it is relatively rare in conversation, it is common in institutionalised, audience-directed interaction', that is, settings such as courtrooms, classrooms and news interviews, as well as other forms of broadcast talk.

Heritage also notes that in these institutional settings, formulating 'is most commonly undertaken by questioners' (1985: 100). This accords with the common finding in studies of institutional discourse that '[i]nstitutional incumbents (doctors, teachers, interviewers, family social workers, etc.) may strategically direct the talk through such means as their capacity to change topics and their selective formulations, in their "next questions," of the salient points in the prior answers' (Drew and Heritage 1992: 49).

In Extract 4, we see a particular kind of strategic direction of talk, that is related to the argumentative uses of formulations in a setting such as talk radio. The host here uses two closely linked proposals of upshot to contentiously reconstruct the position being advanced by the caller. The caller has criticized the 'contradictions' of telethons, claiming that their rhetoric of concern in fact promotes a passive altruism which exacerbates the 'separateness' between donors and recipients. He goes on:

Extract (4) H:21.11.88:11:3

```
 1   Caller:  . . . but e:r, I- I think we should be working at
 2            breaking down that separateness I ⌈ think ⌉these
 3   Host:                                      ⌊ Ho:w?⌋
 4            (.)
 5   Caller:  these telethons actually increase it.
 6   Host:    Well, what you're saying is that charity does.
 7   Caller:  .h Charity do::es, ye⌈::s I mean-          ⌉
 8   Host:                         ⌊ Okay we- so you'⌋re (.) so
 9            you're going back to that original argument we
10            shouldn't have charity.
11   Caller:  Well, no I um: I wouldn't go that fa:r, what I
12            would like to ⌈ see is-
13   Host:                  ⌊ Well how far are you going then.
14   Caller:  Well I: would- What I would like to see is . . .
```

In line 6, the host proposes that the caller's argument in fact embraces charities in general and not just telethons as one sort of charitable endeavour. This is similar to the 'inferentially elaborative' formulations that Heritage (1985) discusses. Note that although the caller has not made any such generalization himself in his prior talk, he assents to this in the next turn (line 7).

However, it turns out that the caller, by agreeing, provides the host with a resource for *reformulating* the agenda in play here. By linking a second formulation to the first, this time describing the 'upshot' of the caller's position, it is proposed that the caller is going back to an argument which the host had with a previous caller ('that original argument'), whose view had been that 'we shouldn't have charity' (lines 8–10).

The caller in fact rejects this further formulation (line 11). But the point is that the host is able to use the fact that the call is based on what the caller thinks about an issue to construct an argument without having to defend his own view. By relying on his ability to formulate the gist or upshot of the caller's remarks, the host can argumentatively define – and challenge – an underlying agenda in the caller's remarks.

In this sense, the 'agenda contests' which occur within calls begin to reveal significant aspects of the play of power in talk radio disputes. The fact that callers must begin by setting out a topical agenda means that argumentative resources are distributed asymmetrically between host and callers. The host is able to build opposition using basic second-position resources. The characteristic feature of these resources is that they require callers to defend or account for their claims, while enabling hosts to argue without constructing a defence for an alternative view. At the same time, as long as the host refrains from setting out his own position, such second-position resources are not available to the caller. Distinctive interactional prerogatives are thereby available to the host, by which he can exert a degree of control over the boundaries of an agenda which is ostensibly set by the caller.

Strategies for resistance

The implication so far has been that the way calls are set up provides the host with a natural incumbency in second position. This does not mean, however, that callers are incapable of offering resistance to the host's challenges. One way of doing this is to adopt the use of second-position resources on their own part. But as I have suggested, particular sequential environments are necessary for this. In particular, the host must have moved or been manoeuvred into adopting first position (that is, indicating an opinion in his or her own right). On talk radio, the host is able to choose when, or if, to express a view on the caller's issue: technically, the host is able to conduct a whole call simply by challenging and demanding justifications for the caller's claims. This, however, is very rare. And once the host has abandoned second position, that position then becomes available for the caller.

Extract 5 shows how a caller may succeed in turning the tables in this way. In this case the tables are turned only briefly because the host subsequently adopts a strategy for re-establishing himself in second position:

Extract (5) H:2.2.89:3:3

```
 1   Caller: But I still think a thousand pounds a night at a
 2           hotel:, .hhh a:nd the fact that she's going on
 3           to visit homeless peop ┌ le,
 4   Host:                          └ Where should sh- Where
 5           should she be staying in New York.
 6           (0.2)
 7   Caller: We:ll u-th- at a cheaper place I don't think the
 8           money-=.h WE'RE paying that money for her to
 9           stay there and I think it's ob°scene.
10   Host:   Well we're not actually paying the ┌ -e the money,
11   Caller:                                     └ Well
12           who:'s paying for it.
13   Host:   Well thee:: e:rm I imagine the the:r the money
14           the Royal Family has .h er is paying for it, .h
15           or indeed it may be paid for by somebody else, .h
16           erm but .h y'know if the Princess of Wales lives
17           in: (.) a palace in this country, w-w-why do
18           you think she should not live in something which
19           is comparable, .hh when she's visiting New York?
```

```
20   Caller:  Well I should think that she could find
21            something comparable that- that- or- e-it could
22            be found for her that doesn't cost that money.
```

One thing to notice is the way the caller responds to the host's hostile questioning (which has been going on for some while) by suddenly attempting to shift the topical focus of her agenda (line 8). From the question of the price of the hotel suite, she shifts, by means of a self-interruption, to the more emotive issue of the ultimate responsibility of the tax-payer for footing the bill: '.h WE'RE paying that money for her to stay there' (lines 8–9).

The host's response to this, in line 10, is significant. By opposing the caller's assertion, he abandons his series of questioning challenges and instead asserts an opinion in his own right. It is this turn which allows the caller to move onto the offensive and produce a challenge of her own which, in a way characteristic of the second-position moves I have been discussing, requires the host to account for his assertion (lines 11–12).

At this stage, then, the local roles of challenger and defender of a position have been inverted. The host, from being in his customary challenger role, has suddenly been swung around into the role of defender. However, this inversion turns out to be only temporary. In the very next turn, the host manages to re-establish the prior state of affairs. He does this by not simply responding to the caller's challenge but also going on to produce a next challenge-bearing question of his own (lines 16–19). With this move, the host succeeds in doing two things. First, he re-establishes the agenda to which his earlier question, in the second turn of the extract, had been addressed and which the caller had attempted to shift away from. Second, he resituates the caller as the respondent to his challenging initiatives, rather than as the initiator of challenge-bearing moves herself.

The asymmetry between first and second positions is not, then, a straightforward, one-way feature of talk radio disputes. Although the organizational structure of calls situates callers in first position initially, they may subsequently find themselves with opportunities to move into the stronger second position. As the previous extract shows, the sequential space for this arises once the host has abandoned the second-position strategy of issuing challenges and made an assertion in his own right. However, the extract also shows that there are strategies available for turning the tables back again; and this suggests that the second position itself can become actively contested over a series of turns.

To illustrate this, finally, we can continue with this call and find that the caller subsequently adopts the host's strategy in order to retake the initiative in the argument. The following extract takes up towards the end of Extract 5:

Extract (6) H: 2.2.89:3:3

```
20   Caller:  Well I should think that she could find
21            something comparable that- that- or- e-it could
22            be found for her that doesn't cost that money.
23            A⌈nd ⌉you're only imagining that she's paying=
24   Host:     ⌊But⌋
```

```
25   Caller:  =for herself you don't know ei:ther do you.
26   Host:    E:rm, well . . .
```

The feature of interest here is in lines 22–5. In a similar way to the host in Extract 5, the caller moves from responding to a challenge to issuing a question. This requires the host in turn to respond and further account for his own position that 'she's paying for herself'. In part, the basis for this second challenge lies in the host's long turn in lines 13–19 of Extract 5, where he responded to the caller's first challenge. That is, the caller is not simply revisiting or revamping the earlier challenge, but developing a new line of attack which relies on the fact that the host's earlier response had been quite vague (see especially lines 13–15 of Extract 5).

To summarize: the call's initial stages situate the caller in first position and furnish the host with the power of second position. But that asymmetry is not an unchanging feature of the context. The more powerful argumentative resources attached to second position may also become available to the caller. Yet this is dependent upon the host expressing an opinion in his own right. Nonetheless, once the opportunity arises, determined and resourceful callers may challenge the host using second position tactics; although second position itself can then become the focus of a discursive struggle.

Discussion

In this article I have used the idea of a relationship between interactional activities and organizational structures as the basis for developing an account of the play of power in calls to a British talk radio show. In doing so, I have illustrated how power is a phenomenon brought into play through discourse. I focused on relatively small sequential details of arguments in order to show this. The upshot is that the sequential approach developed within CA has been applied to a question which has concerned critical linguists and discourse analysts – i.e., how power operates in and through language – by viewing power in terms of the relationships between turns (as actions) in sequences.

The analysis has detailed the relationship between the organization of activities within calls and the asymmetrical distribution of argument resources. On talk radio, the opening of the call is not only designed to set up an environment in w hich callers introduce the topic, but by virtue of that it also places the participants on significantly asymmetrical footings with respect to those topics. The fact that callers are required to go first by expressing a point of view on some issue means that hosts systematically get to go second. Going second, I have argued, represents a more powerful position in argumentative discourse than first position. Principally, the host is able to critique or attack the caller's line simply by exhibiting scepticism about its claims, challenging the agenda relevance of assertions, or taking the argument apart by identifying minor inaccuracies in its details (see also Hutchby 1992).

However, the fact that hosts may conduct arguments without expressing a counter-opinion or providing explanations and accounts for their own positions does not mean that they never do the latter. The asymmetry that I have noted is simply this: hosts are in a position to do this whereas callers, by virtue of the organization of the call, are not. At the same time, there are resources available for callers to resist the host's powerful strategies and sometimes to exercise powerful strategies themselves. Thus, power is not a monolithic feature of talk radio, with the corresponding simplistic claim that the host exercises power over the caller by virtue of his or her 'control of the mechanics of the radio program' (Moss and Higgins 1984: 373). Rather, in a detailed way, the power dynamics at work within calls are variable and shifting.

This argument results in a model of power which comes close to the theoretical conception outlined by Foucault (1977). Like Foucault, a CA approach seeks to view power not as a zero–sum game but as a set of potentials which, while always present, can be variably exercised, resisted, shifted around and struggled over by social agents. Foucault argued that power is not something that is possessed by one agent or collectivity and lacked by another, but a potential that has to be instantiated within a network equally including those who exercise power and those who accept or resist it. The network itself is viewed as a structure of possibilities and not as a concrete relationship between determinate social entities.

While Foucault's work is often pitched at the broadest theoretical level, the empirical analysis in this article goes some way towards demonstrating how two of his central ideas can be located in the analysis of power in the details of talk-in-interaction. These ideas are, first, that wherever there is power, there is resistance; and second, that power operates in the most mundane contexts of everyday life, not just at the macro-level of large processes (Foucault 1977).

On the first point, I have stressed that although hosts have a 'natural' incumbency in second position, and thereby have a set of powerful resources available for dealing sceptically with callers' contributions, there are ways in which callers may resist those strategies. They may do this by recognizing and attempting to forestall the effects of the powerful strategy being used by the host (as discussed, for example, by Hutchby 1992). Or they may resist by attempting to adopt the powerful strategies available to the host for themselves, by taking opportunities to move into second position.

The second point is perhaps the one with which this article resonates most strongly. There is a tendency in both mundane and social scientific discourse to conceive of power as a 'big' phenomenon, operating at the largest scale within social formations. Foucault, on the other hand, suggests that power is pervasive even at the smallest level of interpersonal relationships. The kind of power with which Foucault is mainly concerned exists in the form of the manifold 'discourses' by which we make sense of ourselves, others and the world in which we are situated. This tends to lead Foucault's analyses away from the detailed character of social interaction and towards the larger-scale historical trajectories of discursive formations that can be traced in archive documents. I have focused on a different kind of power, traced in a different level of discourse. By power, I have meant the interactional power that threads through the course and trajectory of an argument. But in line with the conversation analytic approach, I have located that form of power in some of the smallest details of social life: the relationship between turns at talk-in-interaction.

References

Clark, H. and Schaefer, E. (1989) 'Contributing to discourse', *Cognitive Science* 13: 259–94.

Drew, P. and Heritage, J. (1992) *Talk at Work: Interaction in Institutional Settings*, Cambridge: Cambridge University Press.

Eisenberg, A. and Garvey, C. (1981) 'Children's use of verbal strategies in resolving conflicts', *Discourse Processes* 4: 149–70.

Foucault, M. (1977) *Power/Knowledge*, Hemel Hempstead: Harvester.

Garfinkel, H. and Sacks, H. (1970) 'On formal structures of practical actions', in McKinney, J.C. and Tiryakian, E.A. (eds) *Theoretical Sociology*, New York: Appleton Century Croft, 338–66.

Heritage, J. (1985) 'Analysing news interviews: aspects of the production of talk for an overhearing audience', in Van Dijk, T. (ed.) *Handbook of Discourse Analysis*, vol. 3, London: Academic Press, 95–119.

Hutchby, I. (1991) 'The organisation of talk on talk radio', in Scannell, P. (ed.) *Broadcast Talk*, London: Sage, 119–37.

—— (1992) 'The pursuit of controversy: routine skepticism in talk on talk radio', *Sociology* 26: 673–94.

—— (1996) *Confrontation Talk: Arguments, Asymmetries and Power on Talk Radio*, Hillsdale, NJ: Erlbaum.

Maynard, D.W. (1985) 'How children start arguments', *Language in Society* 14: 1–30.

Moss, P. and Higgins, C. (1984) 'Radio voices', *Media, Culture & Society* 6: 353–75.

Sacks, H. (1992) *Lectures on Conversation*, vols 1 and 2, Oxford: Blackwell.

Schegloff, E.A. (1991) 'Reflections on talk and social structure', in Boden, D. and Zimmerman, D. (eds) *Talk and Social Structure*, Cambridge: Polity Press, 44–70.

Schegloff, E.A., Jefferson, G. and Sacks, H. (1977) 'The preference for self-correction in the organisation of repair in conversation', *Language* 53: 361–82.

Chapter 29

Hugh Mehan

ORACULAR REASONING IN A PSYCHIATRIC EXAM: THE RESOLUTION OF CONFLICT IN LANGUAGE

Men define situations as real and they are real in their consequences.

(W.I. Thomas[1])

THE TWO MAJOR PURPOSES of this chapter are (1) to show how competing definitions of the situation are constructed and revealed in ongoing interaction within an institutionalized setting (a mental hospital), and (2) to show how institutionalized power is displayed and used to resolve disputes over conflicting definitions of the situation. In so doing, I will be commenting on the famous "Thomas Theorem." Parts of what I say will provide support for Thomas's idea that people define situations as real in and through their interaction. Other parts will stretch the limits of the theorem. Not all definitions of situations have equal authority. Competing definitions are resolved by imposing institutional definitions on lay persons' definitions. This "ironicizing of experience" (Pollner 1975) requires a modification in Thomas's consensual world view, which I have reformulated as follows:

> All people define situations as real; but when powerful people define situations as real, then they are real *for everybody involved* in their consequences.

My presentation will take a circuitous route. Before showing how institutionalized power is used to impose a certain definition on the situation, I will place the discussion in the context of debates about the thinking of "primitive" and "advanced" peoples. After introducing the notion of "oracular reasoning" (a concept which is central to the understanding of the events which follow), I will examine closely the interaction between a board of examining psychiatrists and a mental patient.

Source: Hugh Mehan, 'Oracular reasoning in a psychiatric exam: the resolution of conflict in language', in Allen D. Grimshaw (ed.) *Conflict Talk: Sociolinguistic Investigations of Arguments in Conversation*, Cambridge: Cambridge University Press, 1990, 160–77.

The thinking of primitive and advanced peoples

. . .

Oracular reasoning in a "primitive" society

The quintessential example of oracular reasoning is found in Evans-Pritchard's (1937) account of the Azande of Africa. When the Azande are faced with important decisions – decisions about where to build their homes, or whom to marry, or whether the sick will live, for example – they consult an oracle. They prepare for these consultations by following a strictly prescribed ritual. First, a substance is gathered from the bark of a certain type of tree. Then this substance is prepared in a special way in a séance-like ceremony. The Azande then poses a question to the oracle in a way that permits a simple yes or no answer and feeds the substance to a small chicken. The person consulting the oracle decides beforehand whether the death of the chicken will signal an affirmative or negative response, and so they always receive an unequivocal answer to their questions.

For monumental decisions, the Azande add a second step. They feed the substance to a second chicken, asking the same question, but reversing the importance of the chicken's death. If in the first consultation sparing the chicken's life meant the oracle said "yes," in the second reading, the oracle must now kill the chicken to once more reply in the affirmative and be consistent with the first response.

Seemingly, insuperable difficulties accrue to people who hold such beliefs, because the oracle could contradict itself. What if, for example, the first consultation of the oracle produces a positive answer and then the second produces a negative reply? Or, suppose that someone else consults the oracle about the same question, and contradictory answers occur? What if the oracle is contradicted by later events – the house site approved by the oracle, for example, is promptly flooded; or the wife the oracle selected dies or turns out to be infertile? How is it possible for the Azande to continue to believe in their oracle in the face of so many evident contradictions of their faith?

The answers to these questions are both simple and complex. Simple, because the Azande do not see the events just listed as contradictions, as threats to the oracle. Complex, because of the reasoning practices that are invoked to keep the efficacy of the oracle intact. The Azande know that an oracle exists. That is their beginning premise. All that subsequently happens is interpreted in terms of that "incorrigible proposition" – a proposition that one never admits to be false whatever happens; one that is compatible with any and every conceivable state of affairs (Gasking 1955: 432 as quoted in Pollner 1975). The Azande employ what Evans-Pritchard (1937: 330) calls "secondary elaborations of belief," practices which explain the failure of the oracle by retaining the unquestioned faith in oracles.

The culture provides the Azande with a number of ready-made explanations of the oracle's seeming contradictions. The secondary elaborations of belief that explain the failure of the oracle attribute the failure to other circumstances, some of this world, some of the spirit world – the wrong variety of poison being gathered, breach of taboo, witchcraft, the anger of the owners of the place where the poison plants grow, the age of the poison, the anger of ghosts, or sorcery.

By explaining away contradictions through these secondary elaborations of the belief in oracles, the reality of a world in which oracles are a basic feature is re-affirmed. Failures do not challenge the oracle. They are elaborated in such a way that they provide evidence for the constant success, the marvel, of oracles. Beginning with the incorrigible belief in oracles, all events reflexively become evidence for that belief.

Recent research suggests that maintaining belief by denying or repelling contradictory evidence is not limited to so-called primitives. Well-educated "modern" people also give evidence of oracular reasoning.

Oracular reasoning in modern form

EVERYDAY REASONING

Wason (1977) reviewed a set of delightful experiments that he and Johnson-Laird have conducted, with the same problems presented to subjects alternatively in abstract and concrete form. Again and again, the subjects of these ingenious experiments seemed to be influenced by the context and the content of the problems. When information was presented in semantically coherent form, such as stories, or with real-life manifestations, subjects performed consistently better than when information was presented in algebraic or symbolic form. When the totality of these studies is considered, we find that people do not employ problem-solving procedures that would challenge or falsify the hypothesis being tested nearly as often as they employ problem-solving procedures that confirm the hypothesis under consideration.

Pollner and McDonald-Wikler (1985) examined the routine transactions of a family with their severely mentally retarded child. They reported that the family employed practices which sustained the family's belief in the competence of the child in the face of overwhelming evidence to the contrary, i.e., a team of medical practitioners had diagnosed the child as severely mentally retarded. The authors' observations of video-taped family interaction revealed that family members pre-structured the child's environment to maximize the likelihood that whatever the child did could be seen as meaningful, intentional activity. The child's family would estab-lish a definition of the situation and use it as a frame of reference for interpreting and describing any and all of the child's subsequent behavior. They also tracked the child's ongoing behavior and developed physical or verbal contexts that could render the behavior intelligent and interactionally responsive.

RELIGIOUS REASONING

Millennial groups are organized around the prediction of some future events, for example, the second coming of Christ and the beginning of Christ's reign on earth, the destruction of the earth through a cataclysm – usually with a select group, the believers, slated for rescue from the disaster.

. . .

No millennial group is more fascinating than the Millerites. William Miller was a New England farmer who believed in literal fulfillment of biblical prophecy. In 1818, after a two-year study of the Bible, Miller reached the conclusion that the end of the world would occur in 1843. He slowly developed a following. The faithful took all the necessary precautions including dissolving relationships, settling debts, selling possessions – and waited together for the second coming of Christ. When the fateful day came – and went – the faithful were confronted with a devastating contradiction to their belief (and lives which were in total disrepair). Their response to this devastation was amazing: instead of turning away from their religious beliefs and spiritual leaders, they used the failure of prophecy as further proof of the wonder and mystery of God. The leaders, far from doubting their basic belief in the second coming, elaborated their belief by citing errors in calculation and weakness in faith as reasons why God did not reveal Himself at the time they predicted. Group leaders retreated to their texts and emerged some time later with new calculations. The number of believers increased – as if conviction was deepened by evidence which contradicted their beliefs. Alas, after three more specific predictions failed, the group disbanded in disbelief.

SCIENTIFIC REASONING

Oracular reasoning appears among scientists as well as among religious zealots, as Gould's (1981) chronicle of a long history of research conducted in defense of Caucasian racial superiority shows. Morton's craniology, Lombroso's criminal anthropology and Burt's intelligence testing start from the premise that whites are superior to blacks, native Americans and other racial or ethnic groups. Gould describes the methodological errors and outright fraud which arose, often un-intentionally, when researchers held too dearly to that basic belief. For example, Gould's meticulous re-analysis of Morton's data uncovered a systematic pattern of distortion in the direction of the preferred hypothesis. Statistics were summed inappropriately across groups, and groups which seemed to counter the argument were excluded from statistical analysis. The overall effect of these practices was the production of data that confirmed the hypothesis of racial superiority, but did so by systematically manipulating or excluding potentially contradictory evidence.

Gould says that the recurrence of racist uses of IQ tests and other measurement techniques is aided by "unconscious bias." This concept liberates us from the suspicion that all racists are cynical plotters against the truth and it implies the existence of a coherent structure of expectations about the phenomena of the world which guides the thoughts of scientists and non-scientists alike. But "unconscious bias" is too limited an idea for such a pervasive intellectual practice (Greenwood 1984: 21). To the extent that unconscious biases are shared widely and perpetuated despite the use of empirical data and sound analytical procedures, they are not biases at all; they are collective conceptions about the structures and operation of the natural world.

Oracular reasoning in a psychiatric exam

These discussions have identified oracular reasoning in general terms. I want to show its practice concretely, in the detail of ongoing discourse. To do so, I will discuss a "gatekeeping encounter" (Erickson 1975) between a board of psychiatrists and a mental patient. Unlike most gatekeeping encounters (in which the gatekeeper is judging whether the applicant is worthy of *entering* an institution – a place of business, a college, a medical care center) in this encounter the gatekeepers are deciding whether the applicant can *leave* the institution (the mental hospital).

The materials used in this analysis come from an unusual source, which requires some comment. During the course of making his documentary film on a mental hospital in the State of Massachusetts, *Titicut Follies*, Frederick Wiseman filmed a "psychiatric out-take interview." The edited version of this interview appearing in the film is the one I use for the analysis which follows. The use of edited documentary film for discourse analysis, of course, places me at a disadvantage: I neither have the background knowledge of the setting normally available to ethnographers nor am I privy to the film-editing process. Nevertheless, the language in the interview is so provocative that I can not resist analyzing it. It is my hope that readers of the analysis will forgive problems associated with the data in exchange for the heuristics with the analysis.

I approached the analysis of this film as I have others: I have watched the film numerous times – both in private viewings and in courses I teach. I constructed a transcript of the interview. The transcript and my memory of the audio and visual record served as the basis of my interpretation. After I completed the analysis which follows, I watched the film again, and made minor modifications – mostly concerning seating arrangements and the physical movements of the participants.[2]

The basis of the conflict

The interview starts with the patient, Vladimir, being led into the examining room. He stands before a table, behind which are seated four members of the examining board. The head psychiatrist begins questioning the patient, but the interrogation quickly breaks down into an argument about the quantity and quality of the patient's treatment. After a number of exchanges, the head psychiatrist abruptly orders the patient to be taken away. At this point, the film is edited; we see the members of the examining board give their interpretation of the case, and reach a conclusion about the patient's status.

The status of a patient's "career" in a hospital (Goffman 1959), indeed, about the patient's life, was established during the course of this gatekeeping encounter. He will remain in the hospital, diagnosed as a paranoid schizophrenic, and receive increased dosages of medicine.

At the outset, it is important to comment on the *social* nature of the outcome. The state of the patient's mental health was not the automatic result of a machine or a meter reading; the patient's mental state was determined by people, who participated in the assembly of an outcome. Here then we have a quintessential example of social construction (Berger 1968; Garfinkel 1967; Scheff 1966; Cicourel 1973;

Mehan 1983a; 1983b): the medical fact of mental illness is constructed in social circumstances.

While this event is social in that a medical fact is assembled in interaction, it is not social in another sense. The event is not social in the sense that the participants failed to reach a mutually agreed-upon definition of the situation. Here we have a set of circumstances in which people, a group of doctors and a patient, have interacted with each other for a stretch of time; each has arrived at a definition of the situation, but the definitions are considerably different, indeed, in conflict with each other.

By looking at the interaction which takes place among the participants in this meeting closely, I will try to determine how it is that the doctors and the patient come to conflicting definitions of the situation. Putting the punch line up front, I will try to demonstrate that both the doctors and the patient were engaged in "oracular reasoning." Normally associated with the procedures used by so-called primitive, or poorly educated peoples when making decisions about life, both the psychiatrists (a presumably well-educated group of people in an "advanced" Western society) and a mental patient (not as well educated, nonetheless a member of an industrialized society) are engaged in this mode of discourse.

The practices of oracular reasoning which are visible in the out-take interview include the following:

> A basic premise or a fundamental proposition is presented which forms the basis of an argument.
>
> When confronted with evidence which is potentially contradictory to a basic position, the evidence is ignored, repelled or denied.
>
> The presence of evidence which opposes a basic position is used reflexively as further support of the efficacy of the basic position.

I will now go through the transcript of the out-patient interview and show the presence of these features in both the doctors' *and* the patient's discourse. Doing so will enable us to understand how multiple and conflicting definitions of the situation were arrived at. The location of these features in the doctors' and not just the patient's discourse will illustrate the further point that oracular reasoning practices are not limited or confined to primitives or the uneducated; they make their appearance in the reasoning of highly educated thinkers. The persistent presence of oracular reasoning in a wide variety of domains recommends that we consider the possibility that oracular reasoning is a more widespread practice than often acknowledged.

The basic propositions

The basic premise or proposition which underlies the psychiatrists' definition of the situation concerns the health or rather, ill-health of the patient. From the doctors' point of view, the patient is mentally ill. The conclusion about this particular case is founded in even a more basic premise about a physician's expertise: the psychiatrist has access to a body of knowledge which is inaccessible to lay people. This premise gains ready empirical support: the patient is, after all, in a mental hospital. People who are in mental hospitals are presumed to be mentally ill (Scheff 1966). The psychiatrists' commitment to this assumption is voiced by the head psychiatrist, who begins the hearing by saying:

> okay, now Vladimir, as I've promised you before, if I see enough improvement in you . . .

Although the patient, Vladimir, interrupts the psychiatrist before he finishes his introductory statement, the syntax of the psychiatrist's utterance enables us to infer the concluding phrase: (if you show improvement, then we will release you). The "need to show improvement" presupposes a prior mental state which is in need of improvement, i.e., mental illness. The fact of incarceration presupposes that same damaged mental state.

The psychiatrists' commitment to this assumption is reinforced throughout the hearing, especially as the head psychiatrist challenges the patient's arguments. He parries the patient's assertions of his mental health with questions about how he came to be a patient in the hospital ("what got you down here?") and his strange beliefs ("you felt the coffee was poison . . . you felt that people were mixing you up in your thinking").

The patient also has a basic premise from which he argues his definition of the situation. It is the exact opposite of the psychiatrists' definition: he is mentally healthy and does not deserve to be hospitalized. The patient's assertion of his mental health, argued in the face of underlying belief in psychiatric expertise, is to be found in virtually every one of his utterances during the hearing. Here are some quotes which give a sense of belief in his health and the depth of his commitment to this belief:

> my mind's perfect . . . I'm obviously logical, I know what I'm talk-ing about. . . . everytime I come in here you call me I am crazy. Now, what's, if, if it's something you don't like about my face, that's I mean, that's another story. But that has nothing to do with my mental stability.

The incorrigibility of the propositions

The reasoning of the psychiatrists and of the patient share another feature: they both retain their belief in their basic premises and do so despite evidence which is presented to the contrary. The psychiatrists and the patient maintain the incorrigibility of their propositions by deflecting, ignoring, or reinterpreting evidence which is contrary to their basic beliefs.

The incorrigibility feature of oracular reasoning is present in virtually every exchange between the psychiatrists and the patient. I include some of these exchanges here to show how each uses the evidence presented by the other to retain their commitment to their original belief.

The head psychiatrist asks the patient about his participation in hospital activities, including work, sports and therapy. The assumption underlying the doctor's line of questioning is that affirmative answers to these questions indicate a positive approach on the part of the patient – a patient who is making an effort to improve himself. The following exchanges indicate that the patient has a different attitude about these issues:

(1) HP: Are you working here Vladimir?
(2) Pt: No, there is no suitable work for me here. All I've got is, all I got is
(3)   the kitchen and all they do is throw cup cups around. In fact,
(4)   they got two television sets which are blaring, machines which
(5)   are going, everything which is against the mind. There is one
(6)   thing uh uh uh that a patient does need, and this is what I do
(7)   know, absolutely, is is quiet, if I have a mental problem or even
(8)   an emotional problem. I'm thrown in with over a hundred of
(9)   them and all they do is yell, walk around, televisions are blaring,
(10)   so that's doing my mind harm!
(11) HP: Are you involved in any sports here?
(12) Pt: There are no sports here. All I've got is a baseball and – and–a a
(13)   glove, and that's it! There's nothing else. Hum. There's nothing
(14)   else . . .
(15) HP: Are you in any group therapy here?
(16) Pt: No! There is no group, obviously I do not need group therapy, I
(17)   need peace and quiet. See me. This place is disturbing me! It's
(18)   harming me . . . I'm losing weight. Every, everything that's been
(19)   happening to me is bad. And all I got, all I get is: "well, why don't
(20)   you take medication?" Medication is disagreeable to me. There
(21)   are people to whom you may not give medication. Obviously,
(22)   and the medication that I got is hurting me, it's harming me!

The doctor has phrased his questions (1), (11), (15) in such a way that a "yes" or "no" is the expected reply. Instead of providing the canonical yes or no response to the doctor's questions about work, sports and therapy, the patient denies the premise underlying the doctor's questioning (and by extension his professional expertise). There *is no* work, there *are no* sports, there *is no* therapy:

> I was supposed to only come down here for observation. What observation did I get? You called me up a couple of times.

In denying the doctor's fundamental assumption, the patient articulates his commitment to his own belief – his health:

> I do not need group therapy, I need peace and quiet. . . . This place is disturbing me.

The doctors do not respond immediately to the patient. We must wait until the patient is removed from the room to hear them articulate their reaction to his position. In general, they do not accept the patient's assertion of his health; in fact, they maintain the opposite – that "he's now falling apart", "reverting". "So he's not looking ready to be able to make it back to prison". The patient's assertions on his behalf contribute to the doctors' conclusion. By his own admission, he doesn't participate in hospital activities, sports, work and therapy. These are the very activities which have been established to help to rehabilitate the patient. The patient's calculated avoidance of these rehabilitative activities becomes further proof of his recalcitrance and contribute to his regression to a prior, unhealthy state of mind.

The attitude that the doctors and patient adopt toward medicine is a particularly telling example of how the same evidence can be used to support diametrically opposed positions. For the patient, medicine is for sick people; since he is healthy, he doesn't need it. In fact, to take medicine would be to admit that he *is* sick. Since he is healthy, he doesn't need the medicine. For the doctors, medicine is a part of a rehabilitation process; the patient's admitted reticence to take medicine is taken as a sign that the patient is both sick and unwilling to help in his own rehabilitation:

> Well I think what we have to do with him is, uh, put him on a higher
> dose of tranquilizers and see if we can bring the paranoid element under
> a little bit better control and see if we can get him back on medication.
> If he's taking it now, and I'm not even sure that he is.

Coulter (1979: 101) discusses how psychiatrists may engage in "strategic contextualization" to make sense out of what is manifestly disorderly or contradictory. In this instance, we seem to have the opposite set of circumstances: a strategic contextualization which undermines the ostensive rationality or logic of the patient's presentation. The patient's very logic becomes an expression of disorder. This strategic decontextualization through the selective invocation of background knowledge and the demand for literal (yes/no) answers to questions, simultaneously frames and undercuts the speaker and the power of his discourse. From the psychiatrists' point of view, even the patient's expressed emotion is symptomatic of his disorder (cf. Rosenhan 1973):

> the louder he shouts about going back the more frightened he indicates
> that he probably is.

The patient has presented himself to the doctors as agitated and unreasonable, which is further proof that he is mentally ill.

Of course, there is another perspective on the patient's presentation of himself. He feels unjustly treated, confined against his will. Given this one, brief opportunity to present his case, he does so forcefully, energetically. Anticipating the prospect of leaving the hospital, he is excited, which is an understandable emotion for a person who sees himself languishing in a cell:

> I have a perfect right to be excited. I've been here for a year and a half,
> hum, and this place is doing me harm.

With the patient's presentation of himself, as with the medicine and hospital activities, then, we have an instance in which the same state of affairs is interpreted differently from different perspectives. This perspectivally induced perception contributes to the maintenance of belief on the part of the physicians and on the part of the patient. Both cling to their basic assertions, denying the information presented which has the potential of undermining those basic beliefs.

One member of the board of examiners makes this belief-validating process visible for us during her contribution to the board's interpretation of the case:

> Dr 2:   He argues in a perfectly paranoid pattern. If you accept his basic premise the rest of it is logical. But, the basic premise is not true.

She admits to the possibility of the patient's interpretation ("If you accept his basic premise"), entertains the viability of the patient's conclusions and the evidence he has presented in defense of his conclusions ("the rest is logical"), yet she does not change her opinion. She rejects the patient's line of reasoning and remains committed to her belief that the patient is mentally ill.

Competing languages of expression: the medical and the sociological

Two competing languages about the nature of mental illness have developed in the recent history of medicine. One, called the "medical model," treats the issue in biological terms. Because the body is an organism, its various parts are subject to pathologies. Mental illness has developed as an extension of this way of thinking. The mind is treated by analogy to an organ of the body; it, like the heart, liver or pancreas, is subject to disease. As an organ, it can be treated in the same way as disease to other organs, i.e., by medicine, confinement, operations to remove diseased tissues. The cause and the cure of mental illness, like physical illness, is to be found in the biological realm, a state or trait of the individual person.

The second, called the "sociological" or "deviance" model, treats the issue of mental illness in social and contextual terms. Denying the analogy between the mind and organs of the body, mental illness is talked about in terms of actions and rules. Mental illness is the label attached to people who break a certain set of society's rules. Its origins are to be found, therefore, not in biological pathologies, but in the social context of relationships between people, people who identify rule breakers, people who apply labels and in extreme cases, institutionalize the rule breakers (Scheff 1966; Kitsuse 1963; Becker 1963; Goffman 1959; Laing 1967; Szasz and Hollender 1956). Mental illness is eliminated by rearranging social contexts such that bizarre behavior is no longer necessary.

The participants in the meeting use these two languages during the course of their interaction. The medical language appears in most pronounced form during the discussion among the doctors after the patient was removed from the room. The cause of the patient's difficulties are talked about in terms of the patient's personal states. He is "paranoid," "schizophrenic", "depressed." That is, the cause of the problem is located within the patient. Increased doses of medicine are prescribed in order to gain better control of his paranoid state.

The patient voices the sociological model in virtually every one of his pronouncements. He blames the circumstances, focusing particular attention on the hospital and the treatment he has been getting (or rather, has not been getting) but *not* his mental state for his problems:

I've been trying to tell you. I can tell you, day by day, I'm getting worse, because of the circumstances, because of the situation.

So, it's obviously the treatment I'm getting or it's the situation or the place or or or the patients or the inmates or either of them. I don't know which.

His denial of the equation of mind to body, internal causes of illness, and the proposition that medicine can cure the mind, could have come from any of Thomas Szasz's or R.D. Laing's books:

You say "well, take some medication." Medication for the mind? I am supposed to take medication for, if I have some bodily injury. Not for the mind. My mind's perfect.

A crucial exchange between the head psychiatrist and the patient highlights the patient's articulation of the sociological theory of mental illness with its emphasis on contextual causes:

Pt: if you leave me here, that means that YOU want me to get harmed.
       Which is an absolute fact. That's plain logic. That goes without
       saying. Obviously.
HP: That's interesting logic.
Pt: Yes. It's absolutely perfect, because if I am, if I am at a point, it's
       as if I were in some kind of a hole or something, right, and if you
       keep me there, obviously you intend to do me harm.

By blaming the hospital and the doctors, the patient gives us a perfect rendition of the iatrogenic theory of illness; the locus of the patient's trouble is in the social context, not his own mental state.

Conclusions

We can draw the following conclusions from the doctor–patient exchange:

1   The psychiatrists and the patient differ in their definitions of the situation.
2   These differences are assembled because an array of behavioral particulars
     are bestowed with different meaning by participants operating from differ-
     ent theoretical perspectives and in different common sense systems of
     belief.
3   Within each system of belief, the participants marshal evidence to support a
     basic proposition and deflect evidence which has the potential to challenge the
     basic proposition.

If left here, the conclusion would be a (potentially interesting) demonstration of the Thomas theorem and would point to relativism played out in face-to-face interaction, i.e., that each perspective – that of doctor and patient – is equivalent.

While we can see that differences in perspective were visible in the interaction and maintained by a belief-validating process, there is another, important, dimension to the interaction that can not be overlooked. That dimension has to do with conflict and its resolution in language.

Conflict resolution in language: the politics of experience

While the physicians and the patient have conflicting definitions of the situation, these definitions are not equal. The patient's definition of his sanity is not on a par with the psychiatrists' definition of his insanity. The doctors' definition prevails. Despite the vehemence of his protestations and the admitted logic of his presentation, at the end of the meeting the patient is led from the examining room and returned to his lodgings, still convinced that he is healthy, there to await the decision and subsequent treatment recommended by the examining board.

So, although there is evidence of the socially negotiated construction of a medical fact here, the constituent negotiation is not evenly balanced. Instead, we have an example of what R.D. Laing (1967) has called "the politics of experience." Some persons, by virtue of their institutional authority, have the power to impose their definitions of the situation on others, thereby negating the others' experience. Speaking with the authority of the medical profession, in particular psychiatry, and, by extension, the legal institution, the definition voiced by members of the board is imposed on the definition voiced by the patient. The conflict between the patient and the psychiatrists is resolved by the imposition of an institutional definition of the situation on top of an everyday or lay definition of the situation. This imposition negates the patient's definition, relegating his experience to an inferior status.

The process by which the patient's experience is ironicized demonstrates how institutionalized power is manifested in language, making it necessary to fashion the corollary of the Thomas theorem that I proposed at the outset of this chapter.

> All people define situations as real; but when powerful people define situations as real, then they are real *for everybody involved* in their consequences.

The logical status of oracular reasoning

In closing, I'd like to make some final comments on the status of the logic of oracular reasoning. These comments are admittedly speculative, requiring further specification.

The parties in the conflict that I examined each operated within a certain frame of knowledge. They adhered to statements about the world whose validity could neither be confirmed nor disconfirmed (Shweder 1984: 39–40). The doctors maintained the absoluteness of their belief in the patient's mental illness by denying, repelling and transforming evidence which was contrary to their basic belief. The patient, too, used evidence presented in opposition to his argument as further support for the efficacy of his position. Thus, both a poorly educated, hospitalized patient and professionally educated physicians engaged in similar reasoning process. They admit to no universal standard (i.e., one that is outside both frames or in some frame acceptable by the people in the two frames) for judging the adequacy of ideas. As a result, no evidence or experience was allowed to count as disproof by either party.

. . .

The widespread appearance of belief-validating practices should lead us to realize that oracular reasoning is not limited to primitives, ancients, children or the uneducated, and to consider the possibility that it is a more extensive feature of reasoning. Since the appearance of oracular reasoning is not universal but variable, a productive next step would be to investigate how belief-validating practices operate in detail. If such practices can be found in any group, in any belief system, then it becomes important to determine when protection against discrediting evidence becomes so extensive that disconfirmation becomes virtually impossible and how potentially contradictory evidence is sufficient to change the structure and practice of belief.

Acknowledgements

This chapter was prepared for presentation at the Eleventh World Congress of the International Sociological Association, New Delhi, India, 18–24 August 1986.

A number of colleagues have commented on earlier drafts of the chapter. I wish to thank Dede Boden, Aaron Cicourel, Roy D'Andrade, Allen Grimshaw, Ed Hutchins, Jean Lave, Jim Levin, Tom Scheff, Ron Ryno, Alexandra Todd, Jim Wertsch – and especially Mell Pollner for penetrating criticisms and helpful suggestions.

Permission to quote from Frederick Wiseman's film, *Titicut Follies*, was kindly granted by *Zipporah Films*, Cambridge, Mass.

Notes

1   Thomas, W.I. and Thomas, D.S. (1928) *The Child In America*, New York: Alfred Knopf, 81.
2   [Excerpts from the transcript are used as examples in the text of the article. Pt is Patient (Vladimir), HP is head psychiatrist and Dr 2 is the Second doctor.]

References

Becker, H. (1963) *Outsiders*, New York: The Free Press.
Berger, P. (1968) *The Sacred Canopy*, Garden City, NY: Doubleday.
Cicourel, A.V. (1973) *Cognitive Sociology: Language and Meaning in Social Interaction*, New York: The Free Press.
Coulter, J. (1979) *Social Construction of Mind: Studies in Ethnomethodology and Linguistic Philosophy*, London: Macmillan.
Erickson, F. (1975) 'Gatekeeping and the melting pot: interaction in counseling encounters', *Harvard Educational Review* 45: 44–70.
Evans-Pritchard, E.E. (1973) *Witchcraft, Oracles and Magic Among the Azande*, Oxford: Clarendon Press.

Garfinkel, H. (1967) *Studies in Ethnomethodology*, Englewood Cliffs, NJ: Prentice-Hall.

Gasking, D. (1955) 'Mathematics: another world', in Flew, A. (ed.) *Logic and Language*, Garden City, NY: Anchor Books.

Goffman, E. (1959) 'The moral career of the mental patient', *Psychiatry* 22: 123–42.

Gould, S.J. (1981) *The Mismeasure of Man*, New York: W.W. Norton.

Greenwood, D.J. (1984) *The Taming of Evolution*, Ithaca: Cornell University Press.

Kitsuse, J. (1963) 'Societal reaction to deviant behavior', in Becker, H.S. (ed.) *The Other Side: Perspective on Deviance*, New York: Free Press.

Laing, R.D. (1967) *The Politics of Experience*, New York: Pantheon.

Mehan, H. (1983a) 'Le constructivism social en psychologie et sociologie', *Sociologie et Societés* XIV (2): 77–96.

—— (1983b) 'The role of language and the language of role in practical decision making', *Language in Society* 12: 1–39.

Pollner, M. (1975) '"The very coinage of your brain": the anatomy of reality disjunctures', *Philosophy of Social Science* 5: 411–30.

Pollner, M. and McDonald-Wikler, L. (1985) 'The social construction of unreality', *Family Process* 24: 241–54.

Rosenhan, D.L. (1973) 'On being sane in insane places', *Science* 179: 250–8.

Scheff, T.J. (1966) *Being Mentally Ill: A Sociological Theory*, Chicago: Aldine Publishing Company.

Shweder, R.A. (1984) 'Anthropology's romantic rebellion against the enlightenment, as there's more to thinking than reasoning and evidence', in Shweder, R.A. and LeVine, R.A. (eds) *Cultural Theory, Essays on Mind, Self and Emotion*, Cambridge: Cambridge University Press, 27–66.

Szasz, T. and Hollender, M.H. (1956) 'A contribution to the philosophy of medicine: the basic models of doctor–patient relationship', *AMA Archives of Internal Medicine* 97: 585–92.

Wason, P.C. (1977) 'The theory of formal operations: a critique', in Gerber, B.A. (ed.) *Piaget and Knowing*, London: Routledge & Kegan Paul, 119–35.

Chapter 30

Paul Baker and Tony McEnery

'FIND THE DOCTORS OF DEATH'[1]

Press representation of foreign doctors working in the NHS, a corpus-based approach

Introduction

THIS CHAPTER DESCRIBES HOW corpus linguistics methods can be applied to the field of critical discourse analysis (CDA). CDA can be described as 'a way of doing discourse analysis from a critical perspective, which often focuses on theoretical concepts such as power, ideology and domination' (Baker et al 2008: 273). CDA advocates that analyses of linguistic features in texts are carried out in concert with an analysis of social context, which is used to interpret, explain and evaluate findings (see for example Fairclough 1995; Reisigl and Wodak 2001). CDA practitioners might be interested in the conditions of production and reception that would have influenced how a text was created, for example. They may also want to take into account intertextuality (which other texts are referenced in the text under examination) and aspects of social context such as how laws and traditions in a society relate to aspects of the text. This expansion of analysis from the linguistic to the social can result in a complex of interconnected qualitative analyses, helping to provide an explanatory account of the subject under study. However, the qualitative and interdisciplinary nature of CDA can sometimes mean that it is difficult to adequately carry out a detailed analysis on large amounts of text. As a result, CDA needs to guard against making generalizations based on having chosen, by accident or design, to analyse unrepresentative texts. Additionally, as CDA aims to address social problems, including issues of the abuse of power or unequal social relations, the researchers undertaking CDA often hold a committed political stance. Thus their analyses would benefit from being backed up by rigorous methodological techniques that can help to stave off criticisms regarding researcher subjectivity resulting in a biased analysis.

Corpus linguistics has the potential to offer such a set of methodological techniques, as it is based on a number of premises that advocate a systematic and rigorous approach to data. Corpus linguistics involves the collection of large amounts of text in electronic form, which are usually sampled and balanced in order to be representative of a particular language or genre (such a set of texts is referred to as a *corpus*, plural *corpora*). Corpora are subjected to quantitative analytical procedures carried out by specialist computer software that aim to identify what is linguistically frequent or salient in them, using statistical tests of frequency and often involving comparisons of different corpora against each other. While analysts can use corpus approaches to explore an existing hypothesis (such as: to what extent is group x negatively represented by linguistic construction y in this corpus?), some analysts begin from a more 'naïve' position, allowing the analysis to be largely dictated by whatever linguistic features emerge through an initial quantitative investigation (for example, are any words or phrases in a corpus of one type of texts statistically more frequent when compared against a much larger corpus which represents general language?). Two principles of corpus linguistics are also of help in countering claims of analyst bias – total accountability and no prior selection of texts (see McEnery and Hardie 2012). Total accountability means that all data gathered must be accounted for, with no data being discarded. No prior selection of texts means that just as texts should not be disregarded as inconvenient during analysis, there should be no systematic bias evident that is designed to exclude texts that are inconvenient when the corpus itself is collected (in the case of new corpora) or selected (in the case of existing corpora).

The fusion of corpus linguistics and CDA has brought 'objective, quantitative CL approaches' to CDA 'as quantification can reveal the degree of generality of, or confidence in, the study findings and conclusions, thus guarding against over- or under-interpretation' (Baker et al 2008: 297). This chapter aims to contribute to a growing body of work, such as that of Hardt-Mautner (1995), Mautner (2007), Koller and Mautner (2004), O'Halloran and Coffin (2004), Baker (2005, 2006) Baker and McEnery (2005), Orpin (2005) and Baker et al (2008), which seeks to integrate CDA and corpus linguistics in a more balanced way.

A more specific aim of this chapter is to examine how foreign doctors are represented in the British press. This research thus relates to and expands on our previous work on the British press, which has examined how minority groups such as gay men (Baker 2005), refugees and asylum seekers (Baker and McEnery 2005; Baker et al 2008) and Muslims (Baker et al 2012) are 'othered' and often represented in negative ways. The social groups we examined in previous studies could be classed as vulnerable, either due to the existence of (past) criminalizing laws around them, negative societal attitudes or their relatively powerless social status. For this study, we wanted to continue our focus on immigration but look at a specific case involving one group of immigrants to the UK who were both highly educated, relatively well-paid and thus far from powerless – foreign doctors. We wondered if foreign doctors would also be represented negatively or whether such representations would be attenuated by the higher social status afforded to doctors.

Data and analysis

Using the online search engine Nexis UK, a search of all British national newspapers[2] for the term *foreign* followed by *doctor*, *doc*, *medic*, *GP*, *locum* or *physician* was carried out. Plurals of these terms were also searched for. The time period searched for was 1 January 2000 to 31 December 2010. The search elicited 782 articles, amounting to just over half a million words (533,750) in total. We chose to explore this term as it is the most frequent term used by the British press to identify doctors from overseas working in the UK. While other terms, such as *overseas doctor*, are used, they are not as frequent. For example, there are nearly three times as many articles using the phrase *foreign doctor* in the UK press in this period (649 articles) as there are using *overseas doctor* (255 articles).[3] In order to explore the dominant representation of such doctors in the UK press we chose to focus upon the search term outlined above.

Figure 30.1 suggests that the topic of foreign doctors has been of sustained interest to the British press, although there have been fluctuations in interest as attested by the changing number of articles on the topic, from year to year. There is also some evidence that interest in the topic grew over the time period examined (the years with the most stories are 2007, 2009 and 2010). To begin to explore if these fluctuations were random or whether they could be explained by shifts in the discourse around foreign doctors over time, we conducted an analysis of the representation of foreign doctors in the corpus. This analysis focuses upon their representation in the texts gathered, using corpus techniques to explore that representation. Our goal is to reveal the multifaceted, and at times contradictory, attitudes the UK press hold towards foreign doctors.

Rather than simply looking at what was frequent or salient in the corpus, we decided to take a more focused approach by looking directly at how foreign doctors were represented. Using the corpus analysis software WordSmith 5 (Scott 2008) we carried out a search of *foreign doctor/doc/medic/locum/physician/GP* (and their plurals), which elicited 1,180 citations. We then searched for collocates (which we define for this study as words that occurred five times or more within a span of five words

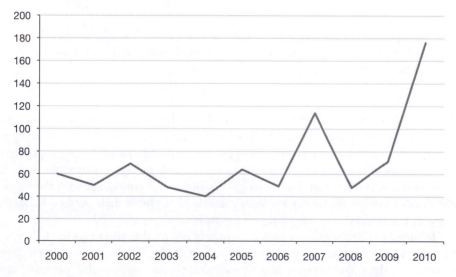

Figure 30.1 Total number of articles about foreign doctors in the UK press over time

to the left or the right of the search term). Durrant and Doherty (2010) have demonstrated that frequently paired words can prime each other, e.g., if we see one word we are primed to more quickly recognize the other. Psycholinguists have argued that such a 'speeded reaction to primed words is a result of neurological activation "spreading" from the context word to related words' (Durrant and Doherty 2010: 128).

Having obtained a list of collocates, we examined their usage in more detail, by looking at the newspaper articles that they occurred in. This allowed us to put the collocates into four (related) groups, which help to build up a typical picture of how foreign doctors are constructed in the British press. The first group of collocates were concerned with foreign doctors coming to the UK: *flown* (14 occurrences), *brought* (13), *cover* (14), *coming* (13), *fly* (12), *bring* (11), *bringing* (6). A second group consisted of words that described mistakes or incompetence: *killed* (23), *competence* (11), *poor* (8), *incompetent* (7), *accidentally* (6), *competent* (6). These were generally used in stories about foreign doctors who had made errors treating patients in the UK. The third group were terms to do with ability to speak English: *English* (56), *language* (35), *speak* (15), *understand* (5), *communication* (5), *grasp* (5) and were often used to describe or criticize foreign doctors as not being able to speak English well enough, leading to mistakes or a poorer quality of care for patients. Finally, a fourth group comprised of words related to regulation: *tests* (25), *test* (18), *training* (16), *checks* (14), *tougher* (9), *rules* (8), *system* (9), *tighter* (6), *quality* (6), *testing* (5), *trained* (5). These words were used in articles that described, called for or criticized increased regulation of foreign doctors, as in the following two cases.

> The initiative by the shadow Health Secretary, Liam Fox, calling for a tougher language test for foreign doctors working in the NHS, is deeply unpleasant. The cynicism of it is perhaps the most offensive aspect. Dr Fox protests that he did not think that his remarks would encourage racists.
>
> (*The Independent*, 28 August 2000)

> Background checks on foreign doctors and other health workers migrating to Britain are to be stepped up after the bomb scares in London and the Glasgow airport attack.
>
> (*The Telegraph*, 5 July 2007)

Upon reading articles containing collocates from the fourth group, an ideological split between newspapers was noticed, with liberal newspapers being more likely to view calls for such checks as racist, and the conservative newspapers being supportive of the checks. However, whatever the stance towards foreign doctors, the analysis of collocates identified that the 'majority' discourse was concerned with the representation of foreign doctors as an 'issue', unable to perform their duties adequately or speak English and requiring tougher regulation.

In order to further explore how newspapers oriented to this majority discourse, we next carried out a more detailed examination of the 1,180 references to foreign doctors and the related terms, first by examining other quantifiable patterns, and then by conducting more detailed qualitative analyses of individual articles (Figure 30.2 shows a screenshot that shows part of this concordance). For this we used the

File	Edit	View	Compute	Settings	Windows	Help

N	Concordance
220	WHO asks Britain to stop poaching foreign doctors BYLINE: By Jeremy Laurance Health
221	Health Organisation to stop poaching foreign doctors and nurses from the world's poorest
222	of this y ear alone more than 5,000 foreign doctors came to Britain to register with the
223	body show. In total, the number of foreign doctors who have come to Britain to work has
224	Committee, said: "The number of foreign doctors applying for jobs has pushed us over
225	Express August 21, 2005 FOREIGN DOCTORS PUT OUR MEDICS ON DOLE
226	697 words MORE than 40,000 foreign doctors have flooded into Britain in the past
227	they did not factor in the number of foreign doctors coming here to work. In addition,
228	rules to prevent the recruitment of foreign doctors and nurses by both the NHS and the
229	figures on the number of registered foreign doctors who had obtained employment in
230	"We should have a system where foreign doctors can only apply to register here from
231	they have a job. "There are a lot of foreign doctors coming to Britain in the expectation
232	founder of a company that recruits foreign doctors for the NHS is poised to net almost
233	a company specialising in recruiting foreign doctors for the NHS is poised to net almost
234	founder of a company that recruits foreign doctors for the National Health Service is
235	scheme, health trusts can fly in foreign doctors to relieve British GPs who do not
236	of a recruitment agency that hires foreign doctors for the NHS is set to make pounds

Figure 30.2 Screenshot of concordance of *foreign doctors* and related terms

concordance facility of WordSmith to explore the context in which the terms searched for were used. A concordance programme allows us to search through a corpus, showing the words or terms we have searched for and the context that surrounds them, as shown in Figure 30.2.

We began to group similar concordance lines together, based on whether they referenced similar topics or news stories or whether their representation of foreign doctors was similar in some way. We also carried out additional concordance searches of words that came to our attention via this analysis and we thought might be used elsewhere in the corpus, and would contribute towards discourses of foreign doctors. For example, the word *killer* was not a collocate of *foreign doctor*, but it was a related word to *killed*, which was a collocate, and we had noticed *killer* in the headline of some articles when we investigated expanded concordance lines in more detail. It was therefore decided to investigate the word *killer* in more detail.

Killer foreign doctors

Some of the categories we noted through an analysis of concordance lines related to the four groups of collocates we had previously identified. For example, 11 per cent of concordance lines of *foreign doctor* (and its related terms) referred to them as being brought to the UK to work, often describing how many such doctors were being employed by the UK or how much they were earning or could earn. An additional 41 per cent of the references to foreign doctors described them directly in terms of their incompetence, with a further 16 per cent indirectly implying that foreign doctors were incompetent by calling for tighter regulation of them or 'crackdowns' on them. Such doctors were variously described as *bungling*, *incompetent*, *poor*, *substandard*, *inept*, *underskilled* or *unsupervised*. Such articles include those about Daniel Ubani, a German doctor who accidentally administered a lethal injection to a patient:

> The death of David Gray at the hands of a German locum who could barely
> speak English showed the tragic consequences of not carrying out proper
> checks on overseas doctors. The reason Daniel Ubani, who administered
> his 70-year-old victim with a lethal drug overdose, was not prevented
> from working in the UK was the EU free movement directive.
>
> (*Daily Mail*, 12 July 2010)

In the above article, Gray's death is 'at the hands of a German locum', and Ubani 'administered his 70-year-old victim with a lethal drug overdose'. We do not question the accuracy of the article, although we find it interesting that the language used here seems more akin to an article about a serial killer than a doctor who made a terrible mistake – note the description of the patient as Ubani's 'victim' and the term 'at the hands of'.

The British National Corpus (Aston and Burnard 1998) allows us to gain a clearer view of how the term 'at the hands of' is used in English. The BNC is a large corpus containing many genres of English, which acts as a general reference for how language is normally used. The phrase 'at the hands of' occurs 375 times in the approximately 90,000,000-word written section of the BNC. Its collocates allow us to see that the phrase is associated with a detriment experienced by someone or something brought about by someone or something else. Yet the phrase *at the hands of* also attracts collocates in the L1 position (one word to the left of the word searched for) that are not simply detrimental to the patient – they also imply suffering on the behalf of the patient brought about by the actor. In the BNC, the most prominent collocation of the phrase is *defeat* – this is invariably a detriment and is closely linked into the L1 position, i.e., occurs typically one word to the left of the phrase *at the hands of*. Of the 58 examples of *defeat* collocated with *at the hands of*, 54 occur in the L1 position. The collocates *suffered* (38 of 57 examples in the L1 position), *death* (17 of 22 examples in the L1 position), *treatment* (15 of 17 examples), *suffer* (7 of 10 examples), *defeats* (7 of 7 examples) and *humiliation* (4 of 5 examples), similarly prefer the L1 position and show the type of detriment associated with the phrase in question. It is often a type of detriment that would seek one to evaluate the phrase, in a wider context, as not merely noting detriment and foregrounding the patient, but of evoking pity for the patient and condemnation of the actor also. It is certainly consistent with the use of the word *victim* in the discussion of the Gray case in the *Daily Mail*. However, the use of a nominalized form when discussing the detriment experienced by Gray, *death*, seems slightly unusual – the common L1 collocates of *at the hands of* in the BNC are verbs. A search of the BNC confirms that the construction *the death . . . at the hands of* is relatively rare – only four examples occur in the whole 100,000,000 words of the BNC. Yet they are similar to the examples in which *at the hands of* collocates with a verb. Consider the following examples of *the death of* followed by *at the hands of* from the BNC:

> It is exactly the equality before the law, which Ms Pith-Helmet invests
> with so much trust, that has betrayed blacks and Asians in the courts, in
> their treatment at the hands of vicious and prejudiced police (that has
> resulted in the death of 10 blacks at the hands of police during the course
> of arrest and interrogation in the last 15 years). . .[4]

>In Scaramouche the main character, intent on avenging the death of a friend at the hands of an unscrupulous marquis, joins a band of travelling players and becomes involved in the French revolution.[5]

In the both cases, opprobrium attaches to the agent of the adversity deliberately inflicted upon the people who have died. In one case it is racist police, in the other is it an unscrupulous marquis. In both cases, pity is also clearly evoked for the patients of the actions of the agents. Consequently, while talking about *the death of* Gray may appear to be neutral in tone, the use of the phrase *at the hands of* implies hostile intent on the behalf of the actor, an impression amplified by the later use of the word *victim* to refer to Gray. Ubani is implied to be an actor who has caused suffering and detriment to a patient in a non-accidental fashion.

The impression that a malign actor was at work is also reinforced by what is *not* present in this article — terms like *accidentally* or *mistakenly* are not used to suggest that the overdose was not purposefully administered. Is such a construction typical of the corpus though? We carried out another concordance search of the word *killed* in the foreign doctors corpus and examined only cases which referred to foreign doctors who had killed a patient by accident. Of the 111 such cases in the corpus, 21 contained the phrase *accidentally killed*, while a further three also referred to the death as an accident. Another eight cases referred to an error or blunder, but in 71 per cent of cases, the death was not directly referred to as an accident.

Another point of note is that in some of the conservative newspapers such doctors are labelled with the emotive term *killer* (there are 11 such cases in the corpus). For example, in another article the *Daily Mail* referred to Ubani as a 'killer German GP' (17 June 2010), *The Express* called him a 'killer German doctor' (3 June 2010), whereas *The Sun* referred to an unnamed East European doctor as a 'killer German locum' (14 April 2010). Such cases use *killer* as a modifier of another noun, although the *Daily Mail* (9 August 2010) also uses the word *killer* as a nominalization to stand for Ubani in the headline 'If this shameless killer is allowed to silence his victim's sons, it will be an outrage against common decency'. This case (and three others like it) are particularly salient because Ubani is identified by a single noun: *killer*, which acts as a form of functionalization (Van Leeuwen 1996: 55), the man's identity is reduced to an act.

It is also useful to consider the sorts of associations that the world *killer* more generally holds. In the British National Corpus the word *killer* tends to be used to refer to animals (such as whales or bees), or to refer to humans who kill people on purpose (such as *serial killer* or *psychopathic killer* as well as collocating with words referencing crime like *jailed*, *hunt*, *catch* and *find*). Due to readers' many previous encounters with the word *killer*, this term is therefore likely to prime a mental image of a dangerous psychopath 'at large', rather than a professional who made a mistake.

A German invasion?

German doctors seemed to be of particular interest to the *Daily Mail*. On 17 March 2010 the *Mail* published an article which began: 'A grandmother died because of appalling blunders by a German surgeon flown in by the NHS.' The article described the grandmother, 94-year old Ena Dickinson who died after contracting pneumonia, two months after a failed hip operation. Dickinson was described as a 'war veteran' who was a member of the Women's Auxiliary Air Force during the Second World War. She 'had the task of delivering top secret documents' and was a 'driver for Winston Churchill's colleagues'. This article did not make an explicit connection between Ena's war service and the fact that ultimately her death was caused by a German doctor, but allowed readers to draw their own conclusions regarding how German doctors treat elderly British patients who served in the Second World War.

This article led us to carry out additional searches on related terms, including *German* and *army*, and we found that an 'invasion' discourse was present in other articles, which used metaphors to refer to foreign doctors. *The Daily Star* (18 June 2005) wrote: 'A 2,600-strong army of German doctors are flying into Britain every weekend to cover for British GPs.' While the reference to the doctors as a collective army is highly suggestive of invasion, more subtly, the choice of the preposition *into*, which indicates penetration, rather than the preposition *to*, which merely suggests movement, further stresses the invasion metaphor. The newspaper raised a further sense of concern by the article's headline which warned 'Your life in their hans', punning on the near homophony of the word *hands* and the German name *Hans* to emphasize the foreign nature of the threat the article discussed. *The Express* (16 February 2005) also wrote about 'an army of foreign doctors' who are 'putting patients' health at risk by botching operations at the taxpayers' expense'. The invasion metaphor continued with *The People* (29 July 2007), which wrote that 'foreign docs parachuted in . . . will not have time to undergo crucial criminal record checks' while the *Daily Mail* (25 July 2002) noted that 'Surgeons have hit out at Government plans to use "medical flying squads" from Europe to cut NHS waiting lists'. The word *squad* (from *squadron*) is a term used in the military.

A related negative conceptualization of foreign doctors is that they are akin to the scout troops of a foreign invasion. *The Mail on Sunday* (9 February 2003) claimed that 'scores of foreign doctors are exploiting the system to illegally invite more distant relatives to Scotland for treatment ahead of native-born patients'. These sentiments were echoed by *The Express* (10 February 2003), which reported that 'scores of foreign doctors are said to be bringing cousins, uncles, aunts and distant relatives to Scotland for treatment ahead of patients already on lengthening waiting lists'. Such doctors were represented as not particularly caring about British patients, but instead using their status to give preferential treatment to other foreigners.

Terrorists and AIDS-carriers

While the competence of foreign doctors was the overwhelming concern of the newspaper articles, there were other reasons why foreign doctors were problematized in them. Some newspapers viewed them as potential disease carriers (and spreaders): 'Public health is threatened by failing to screen foreign doctors and nurses for deadly diseases, warn campaigners' (*Daily Mail*, 17 January 2005), 'HIV checks urged for foreign doctors' (*The Daily Telegraph*, 17 January 2005). *The People* (14 December 2003) reported that there were 'fears foreign doctors and nurses will infect patients unless they are screened'. On the same day, *The Sun* wrote 'AIDS and TB are soaring because of a "gaping hole" in checks on foreign medics, experts warned last night'. Such doctors were therefore implied to be irresponsible and likely to spread diseases rather than cure them.

Additionally, foreign doctors were sometimes viewed as terrorist threats, with a number of articles appearing in 2007 after five foreign doctors were held responsible for car bombs in London and Glasgow. On 3 July 2007, a *Mail* headline read 'NHS and an open door to terrorism: 6,000 Arab doctors at work in UK' (sic). The following day, an *Express* headline was 'Find the doctors of death: how many more terror cells in the NHS?' and the same article noted: 'More terrorist sleeper cells of foreign doctors are ready to strike in Britain, MI5 feared last night.' On 7 July, a former CIA case officer was quoted in *The Times* as saying that 'the existence of a terror plot involving foreign doctors should surprise no one'. The officer claimed that doctors are 'more active in their everyday lives, trying to do things . . . more action-oriented' than other professionals, such as lawyers, and that doctors 'experience a sense of dislocation from the society in which they live and work'. And by 16 July, suspicion of foreign doctors had escalated to the point where a letter in the *Daily Mail* unironically suggested: 'Perhaps the many foreign doctors in the NHS could also wear Muslims Against Terrorism badges on their white coats.'

Four contradictions

As we began to examine, categorize and group together hundreds of concordance lines that referred to foreign doctors, we observed a number of contradictions. Considering that the corpus spans almost ten years, and covers reporting of the entire world (although with a focus on the UK), this would perhaps be expected. But the contradictions are of interest because they are suggestive that multiple stances can be taken with regard to the same topic or issue.

The first contradiction concerned unemployment. We noted that some concordance lines contained words such as *job*, *dole* and *unemployed*, so we grouped them together. These lines tended to place blame on foreign doctors for putting British doctors out of work, or causing them to emigrate:

> Across the country up to 1,000 doctors fight over each training place. The job shortage is largely blamed on a huge rise in foreign doctors applying for work here.
>
> (*Daily Star*, 3 August 2005)

> Foreign doctors put our medics on dole.
>
> (*Sunday Express*, 21 August 2005)

> As foreign doctors are recruited from Third World countries, hundreds of the best-qualified British doctors have been left unemployed. Several have emigrated.
>
> (*The Sunday Times*, 7 October 2007)

However, at other points in the data, a different story emerges – one of staff shortages, and the NHS being unable to recruit doctors:

> Britain's top surgeon, Professor Sir Magdi Yacoub, is to travel the world recruiting foreign doctors at a cost of £200,000 each to ease the NHS's staffing crisis.
>
> *(The Express*, 28 February 2002)

> The shocking case once more highlights how foreign doctors brought in to cover staff shortages in the NHS can evade punishment if tragedy strikes.
>
> *(Daily Mail*, 17 June 2010)

> One in three primary care trusts is flying in foreign GPs because of a shortage of doctors in Britain willing to work in the evenings and weekends.
>
> *(Sunday Telegraph*, 6 September 2009)

A second contradiction involves the cost of foreign doctors. Some articles emphasized that large amounts of money had been spent on employing them, such as the *Daily Mail* (12 April 2010), which wrote of 'Incompetent foreign doctors flown in, at huge expense, to cover for local GPs', or the *Sunday Mirror* (22 May 2005), which echoed the sentiment: 'It's a scandal that foreign doctors are flown into our country, put up in hotels and then receive huge fees to cover the massive shortage of GPs.' However, other articles seemed to imply that the opposite is true, that it is actually a cost-cutting measure to employ them. For example, *The Sunday Times* (3 July 2005) writes of a 'Plan to use foreign doctors to reduce out-of-hours costs', whereas *The Mail on Sunday* (25 April 2004) says that 'the Government would rather train too few doctors and then just fill the gaps with doctors from overseas as a cheaper option'. A letter in the *Express* (4 July 2007) complained about out-of-work British doctors and mentioned the fact that the 'latest car bomb incidents were foreign doctors', conflating issues of unemployment and terrorism. The letter writer then asks 'Does this mean that you have to be foreign to get a job as an NHS doctor? Or is it just that foreign doctors are cheaper?'

The third contradiction involved whether foreign doctors are desperate to work in the UK, or not. Along with the army/invasion metaphor identified above, some articles referenced a 'water' metaphor to describe foreign doctors, with terms like *flood* or *influx*. Such a metaphor constructs foreign doctors as an out-of-control disaster:

> Fury as £1,000-per-day foreign GPs flood into Scotland.
>
> *(Daily Mail*, 20 January 2008)

> Flood of foreign doctors inquire about NHS jobs.
>
> *(The Guardian*, 28 August 2001)

> The influx of foreign doctors covering out-of-hours care can be traced back directly to the Government's flawed reforms of GP contracts.
>
> *(Daily Mail*, 5 May 2009)

> The influx of German doctors, they have dubbed it 'island hopping', is
> one of the most dramatic indications of the growing problems with the
> out-of-hours system, according to GPs.
>
> (*The Guardian*, 17 June 2005)

However, at other points, foreign doctors were viewed as *not* wanting to work in
the UK. *The Times*, for example, describes how such doctors 'ignore' vacancies. Such
doctors then are seen as problematic, either because they want to come to the UK,
or they refuse to come.

> Even a small number of early retirements would create problems, as the
> NHS has found it hard to attract foreign doctors despite an intense
> recruitment drive.
>
> (*The Times*, 28 October 2002)

> Doctors ignore A&E vacancies . . . Dr McGowan, of St James's University
> Hospital in Leeds, said that efforts to attract foreign doctors were failing
> because those countries that have specific A&E consultants – such as
> Canada, the United States and Australia – offered their doctors better
> working conditions. To date, fewer than ten A&E consultants from
> abroad had come to Britain, he said.
>
> (*The Times*, 18 October 2004)

Finally, as already noted, the corpus contained many stories about incompetent foreign
doctors 'Foreign doc mistakes leukaemia for wind' (*The Mirror*, 14 April 2010), 'A
bungling foreign doctor killed a baby by crushing her skull with forceps' (*The Sun*, 22
April 2008), 'Foreign doc drugs blunder killed Dad' (*The Mirror*, 5 May 2009).
However, another set of articles told a different story. Here, foreign doctors were
constructed as 'professionals' who are sorely needed in their own countries. *The Mail
on Sunday* (20 February 2005) asked 'Can we really justify stripping poorer countries
of professionals they have educated at great expense and who are badly needed at home?'
The Independent (7 April 2006) reported that 'Britain has been warned by the World
Health Organisation to stop poaching foreign doctors and nurses from the world's
poorest nations to shore up the NHS' while the *Daily Express* (4 July 2007) was also
critical of the UK's use of foreign doctors: 'Most absurdly of all, the NHS is employing
1,985 doctors who trained in Iraq. If ever there was a country which needed its
professionals – medics particularly – to stay and help rebuild it, it is Iraq.' This argument
is interesting because it presents the newspapers in question as concerned over the
plight of poorer countries, while at the same time constructing foreign doctors as greedy
and the government as amoral poachers of foreign talent. Yet if we are to believe the
many articles that characterize foreign doctors as bungling, incompetent and killers,
how should readers interpret the wish for such doctors to go to the 'poorest nations'?

These last two contradictions in particular, indicate that foreign doctors can be
represented negatively no matter what they do. Either they are incompetent (and
not wanted) or competent (and not wanted because they should be helping their own
countries). Similarly they either are flooding to the UK to earn large amounts of
money or 'ignoring' vacancies because they view other places as better.

Generalizing the situation?

The above analysis suggests that the British press (particularly the tabloids, but also some broadsheets) are engaging in a moral panic about foreign doctors. Goode and Ben-Yehuda (1994) present moral panics as having the following characteristics: concern, hostility, consensus, disproportionality and volatility. It is easy to demonstrate that the first three characteristics are present in these stories – while there may be a lack of consensus about the specifics of how foreign doctors are bad, as the section on the contradictions suggests, most of the stories generally agree that they are 'bad'. However, it is perhaps more difficult to tackle disproportionality, particularly because some of the stories examined are about a single doctor who has made a single mistake. One way of examining disproportionality would be to consider whether newspaper articles generalize these single cases as being representative of a wider problem.

An article by the *Daily Mail* (18 March 2010) entitled 'Terrifyingly inept foreign doctors are a symptom of a sickness in the NHS – not the cause' again refers to Ena Dickinson who died after a hip replacement when she was operated on by Dr Werner Kolb. The use of the plural term serves to generalize the incident beyond Kolb, potentially encompassing all foreign doctors, a generalization further encouraged by the article: 'The episode raises troubling questions about the NHS's increasing reliance on foreign doctors, both from the European Union and from further overseas, a practice that has been driven partly by the Government's fixation with meeting targets and partly by an inadequate supply in the number of domestic trained doctors.' Similarly, an article in *The Sunday Telegraph* (4 October 2009) describes the Dr Ubani case (also referred to above). No statistics are given with regard to how typical this case is. However, the headline of this article: 'The fatal cost of inaction over foreign doctors' is another case of generalizing from a single example. These examples reflect a larger pattern. The corpus contains 1,030 references to *foreign doctors* (and related words such as *medics*) in the plural, of which 68 per cent of such references implied that there were concerns over the competence of such doctors in general. Examples include 'New concern over use of foreign doctors', 'expensive and dangerous flying-in of foreign locums', 'Foreign doctors should face tough language tests', 'foreign doctors with little grasp of English', 'The case is the latest in a series to highlight the use of bungling foreign doctors under Britain's out-of-hours medical care system', 'At last our foreign doctors are told . . . SPEAK ENGLISH!' The overwhelming picture then, is of generalization – the single cases are not viewed as isolated incidents, but as typical of a general picture, a pattern that is in perfect keeping with the construction of a moral panic.

Is the panic about doctors, foreigners or foreign doctors?

A potential flaw in searching only for terms that relate to foreign doctors is that any discoveries may simply be due to all doctors (foreign or otherwise), or all foreigners (doctors or otherwise) being characterized in the same way. In order to determine whether the negative representations are restricted to foreign doctors, we built a second corpus of British newspaper articles, again using Nexis UK and searching on the term *doctor*. This time, the amount of available data was much larger, so in order to create a corpus of reasonably comparable size, we sampled 500 articles each from October 2000, June 2003, March 2006 and January 2009. The resulting 2,000 article corpus contained 1,362,201 words, of which there were 3,284 references to *doctor(s)* but only 3 references to *foreign doctor(s)*. Again, we carried out a search of *doctor/doc/medic/locum/physician/GP* (and their plurals), resulting in 3,989 citations, and then we identified words which frequently co-occurred within a span of five words either side of the search term. Words were then examined and grouped into categories that referred to similar semantic concepts.

Common sets of words included references to different types of doctors (*medical* 55, *junior* 43, *new* 45, *old* 27, *family* 42, *senior* 38), references to people or places where doctors worked (*nurses* 120, *patients* 52, *hospital* 102), verbs of speech and thought presentation (*called* 28, *warned* 21, *believe* 21, *said* 229, *told* 90) and 132 cases of the unrelated term *spin* (which referred to *spin doctors*). As these categories did not suggest negative representations of medical doctors, we decided to look for some of the words which had been found to frequently co-occur when we conducted the analysis of *foreign doctors*, focussing on those which referred to incompetence (*killed, poor, incompetent, competence, tired, blunder, bungling, competent, death*) and those that referred to calls for greater regulation of doctors (*test, checks, tougher, check, rules, quality, tighter, regulations*). Interestingly, we found that most of these words simply did not collocate with *doctors*. Those that did were *killed* (5), *poor* (5), *death* (14), *tests* (7) and *check* (18). However, further examination of these words in context found that only ten cases actually referred to incompetent doctors or requirements for tests. Instead, *tests* and *check* were generally used when referring to doctors who carried out tests, or in advising people to check something with their doctor. Some cases of *killed* and *death* referred to doctors being killed by other people or killing themselves.

As a second test, we examined 100 randomly chosen citations of *doctor* and identified those that referred to doctors who were described as incompetent, dangerous or neglectful in some way. Ten such cases were identified. On closer inspection, it was found that five of them referred to the same story, an anaesthetist, called John Evans-Appiah who was banned from practice after a patient suffered a heart attack. Evans-Appiah was described in *The Mirror* (24 October 2000) as a 'Ghanaian-born doctor, who trained in the Ukraine'. Of the remaining five cases, one involved a doctor from Texas who had hired a hitman to kill a patient, while the other four were cases of doctors in the UK who were described as making bad decisions or being neglectful. While doctors who make serious mistakes will always be seen as newsworthy, it seems that such stories tend to be exceptional, and doctors (non-foreign ones) are generally talked about in ways that represent them as respectable and competent (phrases like *see your doctor* were reasonably frequent in the doctors corpus). On the other hand, when foreign doctors were mentioned in the British press, more than half of the time, they were described as or implied to be incompetent, with that incompetence often ascribed to foreign doctors as a group.

Having established that doctors *per se* are not generally the subject of negative representation in the British media, but that foreign doctors are, we need now to explore further whether the negative representation of foreign doctors is a result of foreigners in general being represented negatively in the UK press. To pursue this question, a third corpus was built as described above, this time searching national

478 PAUL BAKER AND TONY MCENERY

newspapers in Nexis for the words *foreign* and *foreigner(s)*, and sampling 500 articles from the same four time periods. This corpus was 1,221,456 words in size, and contained 4,831 references to the search terms collectively. Common collocates (in a span of five words either side) of these terms included words relating to government and politics (*office* 485, *secretary* 310, *minister* 283, *policy* 212, *affairs* 145, *committee* 84, *ministry* 61, *spokesman* 59), finance and industry (*workers* 145, *investment* 96, *companies* 54) and sport (*players* 79, *coach* 66). A closer analysis of 100 citations of the search terms taken at random found that 21 of them referred to foreigners in a way that could be interpreted as constructing them as negative, either by describing them with stereotypes: e.g., 'a ship full of swarthy foreigners', 'Damned foreigner', implying that they are taking British jobs ('Olympic chiefs are fast-tracking foreign workers into construction jobs as Brit brickies join the dole queue'), using up British resources ('The number of foreigners entitled to healthcare in this country is increasing all the time') or controlling British interests ('I hope that Brown loses this battle and the Royal Mail is not allowed to slide into foreign ownership', 'Foreigner may deny my baby a life saver'). There were three cases where foreigners were described as having encountered racism, e.g., 'myths about foreigners receiving preferential treatment'. So while the majority of references to *foreign* tend to refer to political institutions like the *foreign office*, it is notable that there is a more general discourse around foreigners posing a threat to British society, which echoes the representations of foreign doctors in the press.

Conclusion

Our analysis indicates that foreign doctors appear to be viewed as foreigners first and doctors second, in that their representations appear to have more in common with stories about foreigners generally than with other doctors. In general, the British press showed an increasing focus on stories about foreign doctors in the period 2000 to 2010, with numerous stories linked to a small number of cases of 'bungling' foreign doctors who accidentally caused deaths. Our analysis of collocates found that the language abilities of such doctors were often remarked upon, triggering a debate regarding the amount of regulation that such doctors are subject to. We also found evidence that these individual stories of negligence were generalized and seen as representative of a larger problem, indicating evidence for a moral panic surrounding foreign doctors working in the UK. The analysis of concordance lines found further problematic constructions relating to terrorism, AIDS and an 'invasion' metaphor, while the presence of contradictory statements indicated that foreign doctors could be constructed negatively, no matter whether they were competent or not.

Hopefully, our analysis has shown that corpus linguistics techniques have the potential to identify larger-scale linguistic patterns across many thousands of words. We should note that such analyses give one type of perspective, but they do not constitute a 'full' critical discourse analysis unless further consideration of social context and methods of text production and reception are also taken into account. Additionally, these techniques are better at identifying what is *present* in a text rather than what is not, and they remove texts from their original context (viewing concordance lines is a very different matter to reading a newspaper article in its original form with pictures and text formatting present). With that said, no method is able to achieve everything and it is reasonable to view a corpus approach as an additional tool that can be combined with other CDA approaches in order to reach a set of more wide-reaching, representative and objective conclusions. A good example of that from this paper is, we believe, the analysis of the article on Ena Dickinson (see the section 'A German invasion?'). The rhetorical strategy employed by the *Mail*, to lay out the facts to draw the reader to a conclusion without expressly stating that conclusion, illustrates well a circumstance where interfacing between large-scale corpus methods and smaller-scale qualitative research is necessary. It would be difficult to imagine a corpus search strategy that would allow one to search for all articles in which this was used as a rhetorical strategy. However, by the use of corpus analyses to approach the data, qualitative investigation of examples such as this may be focussed and contextualized in such a way that both qualitative and quantitative analyses become mutually reinforcing and enriching.

References

Aston, G. and Burnard, L. (1998) *The BNC Handbook*, Edinburgh: Edinburgh University Press.

Baker, P. (2005) *Public Discourses of Gay Men*, London: Routledge.

—— (2006) *Using Corpora in Discourse Analysis*, London: Continuum.

Baker, P. and McEnery, A. (2005) 'A corpus-based approach to discourses of refugees and asylum seekers in UN and newspaper texts', *Journal of Language and Politics* 4(2): 197–226.

Baker, P., Gabrielatos, C., KhosraviNik, M., Krzyzanowski, M., Wodak, R. and McEnery, T. (2008) 'A useful methodological synergy? Combining critical discourse analysis and corpus linguistics to examine discourses of refugees and asylum seekers in the UK press', *Discourse and Society* 19(3): 273–306.

Baker, P., Gabrielatos, C. and McEnery, A. (2012) *Discourse Analysis and Media Bias: The Representation of Islam in the British Press,* Cambridge: Cambridge University Press.

Durrant, P. and Doherty, A. (2010) 'Are high frequency collocations psychologically real? Investigating the thesis of collocational priming', *Corpus Linguistics and Linguistic Theory* 6(2): 125–55.

Fairclough, N. (1995) *Critical Discourse Analysis: The Critical Study of Language*, London: Longman.

Goode, E. and Ben-Yehuda, N. (1994) *Moral Panics: The Social Construction of Deviance*, Oxford: Blackwell.

Hardt-Mautner, G. (1995) *Only Connect: Critical Discourse Analysis and Corpus Linguistics*, UCREL Technical paper 5, Lancaster University.

Koller, V. and Mautner, G. (2004) 'Computer applications in critical discourse analysis', in C. Coffin, A. Hewings and K. O'Halloran (eds.) *Applying English Grammar: Functional and Corpus Approaches*, London: Hodder & Stoughton, 216–28.

Mautner, G. (2007) 'Mining large corpora for social information: the case of *elderly*', *Language in Society* 36: 51–72.

McEnery, T. and Hardy, A. (2012) *Corpus Linguistics: Method, Theory and Practice*, Cambridge: Cambridge University Press.

O'Halloran, K. and Coffin, C. (2004) 'Checking over-interpretation and under-interpretation: help from corpora in critical linguistics', in C. Coffin, A. Hewings and K. O'Halloran (eds.) *Applying English Grammar: Functional and Corpus Approaches*, London: Hodder & Stoughton, 275–97.

Orpin, D. (2005) 'Corpus linguistics and critical discourse analysis: examining the ideology of sleaze', *International Journal of Corpus Linguistics* 10(1): 37–61.

Reisigl, M. and Wodak, R. (2001) *Discourse and Discrimination: Rhetorics of Racism and Antisemitism*, London: Routledge.

Scott, M. (2008) *WordSmith Tools version 5*, Liverpool: Lexical Analysis Software.

Van Leeuwen, T. (1996) 'The representation of social actors', in C.R. Caldas-Coulthard and M. Coulthard (eds.) *Texts and Practices: Readings in Critical Discourse Analysis*, London: Routledge, 32–70.

Notes

The research in this chapter was supported by the ESRC Centre for Corpus Approaches to Social Science, ESRC grant reference ES/K002155/1.

1   *Daily Express*, 4 July 2007
2   *The Daily Express*, *The Guardian*, *The Independent*, *Daily Mail*, *The Mirror*, *The Observer*, *The People*, *The Star*, *The Sun*, *The Daily Telegraph*, *The Times*, *The Express*, *The Business*, *The Morning Star* and all Sunday editions.
3   The expression *foreign doctor* retrieves more articles than *overseas doctor* in all of the newspapers looked at with the exception of *The Morning Star* where the terms retrieve equal numbers of articles. However, in the case of *The Morning Star* the topic seems barely discussed, with each term retrieving only eight articles in the decade studied. By way of contrast, *The Daily Express* and *Sunday Express* have seven articles mentioning *overseas doctor* in the period, yet have 47 articles mentioning *foreign doctor*.
4   Sentence A4U 341 in the BNC.
5   Sentence GTB 394 in the BNC.

Chapter 31

Crispin Thurlow

DISCIPLINING YOUTH

Language ideologies and new technologies

Texting more popular than face-to-face conversation

Daily Telegraph, UK

Too much phone texting reduces moral, spiritual goals

Vanguard, Nigeria

OMG! Texting ruins kids' grammar

Los Angeles Times, USA

GIVEN HOW WELL ESTABLISHED mobile phones are in the lives of many people around the world, it might seem surprising that journalists are *still* so preoccupied with the idea that a digital technology such as text messaging poses a threat to human communication and, specifically, to language. Although selected at random, the three newspaper headlines quoted above are actually very typical of the way 'new' media are talked about in the 'old' media.[1] Seen from the light of New Media Studies and Discourse Studies, however, it is not surprising at all that the combination of technology and language is such a newsworthy topic. Journalists and their editors are simply feeding off (and feeding) widespread, persistent anxieties about the impact of technology on social life and about changing standards in the use of language, be it English or any other established way of speaking. When you add young people into the mix, what ensues is a kind of triple-whammy moral panic about the unwinding of the social and moral fabric of society. All of which makes popular representations of digital discourse an ideal site for the study of *folk linguistics* (Niedzielski and Preston 1999) and *language ideology* (e.g., Irvine and Gal 2000; Woolard and Schieffelin 1994). These closely related strands of research are chiefly concerned with metalanguage, the explicit thematizing of language in everyday speech or writing, and the way this language-about-language or talk-about-talk expresses people's personal attitudes, cultural beliefs and social prejudices.[2] When people complain about grammar, spelling and punctuation, for example, we can learn a lot about how they think language works, why they feel it matters (or not), and what they think about other people's ways of speaking or writing. While metalanguage is surely central in policing different ways of communicating, it is also – and often primarily – the *speakers* of different language/s who are being disciplined (cf. Foucault 1977). Whether or not this policing appears to be done on linguistic grounds and for the sake of communicative transparency, these judgements inevitably reproduce hierarchies of symbolic and material inequality (Bourdieu 1991; Irvine 1989). It is precisely this slippage between the policing of language and the disciplining of certain groups of people that I want to examine in this chapter.

Policing language, disciplining youth

The socially constructed period of the lifespan known as 'adolescence' is often represented as different, strange and exotic. The otherwise ordinary, uneventful lives of most young people usually end up being eclipsed by the youthful 'storm and stress' images of most popular and much professional discourse (Lesko 2003). A key topic in this homogenizing mythology of adolescence is the notion of the non-communicative or communicatively inept young person, often coupled with adult complaints about young people's deleterious impact on received standards of language and communication. Regularly, one hears adults characterizing their interactions with young people as a kind of distinctive intercultural communication in much the same way that men and women's exchanges are sometimes exaggerated as being a form of cross-cultural (or inter-planetary!) communication.

   Just as recurrent cultural anxieties exist about youth and adolescence, new or emerging technologies are regularly accompanied by societal concerns regarding their psychological and cultural impact. Public discourse about these technologies is also typically polarized by judgements of their being either 'all good' or 'all bad'. Once again, a common thread in people's concerns is the way social interaction, communication and language are being negatively affected (Baron 2000). This particular set of social anxieties coalesce around much the same kind of verbal hygiene (Cameron 1995) or linguistic puritanism (i.e., 'all change is bad') that characterize most discussions of language change. Added to popular discourses about young people and about new technologies, therefore, one finds a wide range of folk-linguistic concerns about conventional or established standards of speech and writing. That young people (as in 'teen-talk') and new technologies (as in 'netlingo') might be to blame merely compounds matters. This seems to have been particularly true of young people's text messaging, where, as in the newspaper extracts below, we find young people being framed as 'dumbed down' and accused of reinventing or destroying not only (English) language but also the entire social order.[3]

   •   As a dialect, text ('textese'?) is thin and unimaginative. It is bleak, bald, sad shorthand. Drab shrinktalk. The dialect has a few hiero-glyphs (codes comprehensible only to initiates) and a range of face symbols. . . . Linguistically it's all pig's ear. . . . Texting is pen-manship for illiterates.

- Text messaging . . . is posing a threat to social progress.
- The English language is being beaten up, civilization is in danger of crumbling.

In a much earlier study, I started to challenge these kinds of folk-linguistic beliefs about young people's digital discourse by examining their *actual* text messaging practices (Thurlow 2003; see also Thurlow and Poff 2013). In this modest study, based on a convenience sample of text messages from my students at Cardiff University, I was able to show how adult complaints about the oddity and impene-trability (hence 'hieroglyphs' in the extract on p. 482) of this particular genre of digital discourse were greatly exaggerated and largely unfounded.[4] Since then, a number of scholars have gone on to produce studies based on much larger, more comprehensive corpora (see, for example, Dürscheid and Stark 2011). In the meantime, I have been extending the scope of my initial critique with more systematic, focused analyses of the metalanguage produced in newspaper reports (e.g., Thurlow 2006, 2007, 2011). As one reasonable basis for this kind of metalinguistic study, I started by searching two major newspaper databases (ProQuest and LexisNexis) for any English-language articles covering issues related to young people, language and new technology. (Search terms included, in order of priority, *language*, *teenagers*, *adolescents*, *adolescence*, *youth*, *young people*, *technology*, *email*, *text messaging* and *instant messaging*.) An initial sample of more than 150 different news stories was eventually condensed to form a dataset of about 100 articles specifically addressing young people's language practices in new media contexts such as the internet and mobile phones. While the majority of these articles were from national and regional British and US newspapers, the rest came from Australia, Canada, Hong Kong, Indonesia, Ireland, Malaysia, New Zealand, the Philippines and Singapore. As is typical industry practice, a handful of news stories in the corpus were based on syndicated reports or had picked up on stories reported by other papers.

Few people read the same newspaper more than once; even fewer people regularly read more than one newspaper. It is really only people like academics and media analysts who make a point of reading and rereading dozens – perhaps even hundreds – of different papers. The advantage of doing this kind of research is that it affords an otherwise unusual opportunity to track how a single issue is reported (a) in many different papers, (b) from many different locations, and (c) over a decent period of time. This in turn puts researchers in a far better position to identify the consistency and ubiquity of folk-linguistic beliefs and language ideologies by which (some) people's communicative practices come to be organized and understood – or misunderstood. In taking a more Critical Discourse approach to media texts (e.g., Fairclough 2003), my intention is always to eschew a strictly quantitative content analysis in favour of a more interpretative review, highlighting repetitive or dominant themes rather than strictly statistical patterns. As such, my analyses do not make claims to 'representativeness' but rather appeal to an informed judgement of *typicality*, supported by the inclusion of multiple examples selected from a range of different data sources (i.e., newspapers).

For this chapter, I have chosen to reorganize and extend some of my original 'findings' into three distinct but related sections. In Part 1, my concern is with the explicitly folk-linguistic framing of young people's text messaging, paying attention to a series of rhetorical strategies used by journalists to present digital discourse as a 'linguistic revolution' that is 'taking over' standard language practices. This apparently linguistic commentary is loaded with cultural judgement. Indeed, the material presented in Part 1 directs us nicely to one of the common semiotic processes Judith Irvine and Susan Gal (2000) identify in most language-ideological discussions: namely, *erasure*. In order to sustain their particular characterizations (or gross generalizations) of young people's digital discourse, journalists consistently obscure or obliterate a world of alternative sociolinguistic insights and evidence. Against this backdrop, Part 2 focuses on the framing of young people through the semiotic process of *iconization*. In this regard, and still following Irvine and Gal (2000), we see how certain linguistic features of texting style are selectively presented as if they somehow depicted young people's 'inherent nature or essence'. Finally, in Part 3, I return to the newspaper articles whose headlines are quoted at the start of this chapter. Potted critiques of these three pieces not only reiterate the semiotic processes of erasure and iconization but also demonstrate how *fractal recursivity* is always at work in journalistic accounts of digital discourse: specific (and specifically linguistic) phenomena are extrapolated onto broader aspects of communicative practice and social life. It is here, too, that the cultural politics and disciplinary force of metalanguage really come to the fore.

Part 1: The *erasure* of digital discourse

- A language all of its own {*headline*}
- A new language of the airwaves has been born.
- Not since man uttered his first word and clumsily held a primitive pencil nearly 10,000 years ago has there been such a revolution in language. . . . today's technology is changing the way in which we communicate at an alarming rate.

One way new media language is often framed in popular discourse is through the coining of labels such as 'netlingo', 'weblish', 'netspeak', 'textese', 'webbish', and so on. As a rhetorical strategy these neologisms encourage people to think of digital discourse as being somehow a unique variety, as being a fully-fledged, *new* language. In keeping with this, a number of the articles I looked at explicitly depicted digital discourse as a form of linguistic 'revolution' to imply a decisive, dramatic break with conventional practice. (The added use of the indefinite article in phrases such as 'a new language' as opposed to 'new language' further reiterates the implication of a distinctive variety.) Regardless of whether digital discourse is explicitly being labelled 'revolutionary', a similar rhetoric of distinction is evident in many other ways; for example in descriptive phrases such as these (all taken from different articles):

> a text messaging movement; a shorthand language; a nouveau form of communication; a lexicon for electronic communication; a virtual new written language; a new language; a language of its own; a hybrid language; a whole new language; a separate, private language; new truncated language; a new dialect; hottest new language; electronic lingo; a language

all of its own; a lingua franca; the lingo of generation text; a second language; new idiom; a truncated language; new language of smileys and abbreviations; new shorthand language; a new language called 'globespeak'; a new written language; a new abbreviated language; slanguage; a sub-language

Claims about the distinctiveness of digital discourse can also be made by more subtle rhetorical means; in particular, by establishing relations of equivalence (Fairclough 2003: 87) between new media language and 'proper' or standard language/s. For example, references to bilingualism or the idea of translation and/or fluency are not uncommon in the way journalists write about new media language. By the same token, talk about the diffusion of digital discourse into mainstream usage, its codification into dictionaries and other forms of official recognition all serve to create the image of digital discourse as a clearly bounded variety with the status and material substance of *a* language.

- Most texters are, in essence, bilingual.

- Thousands of teens . . . are fluent in another language.

- Hallelujah for the world's first text-messaging dictionary.

- Words from text messaging . . . find their way into the highest authority on the English language, the Oxford English Dictionary.

Together with the broader theme of 'revolution', these relations of equivalence ultimately serve to exaggerate both the nature *and* extent of digital discourse. Such dramatic – and sometimes alarmist – framings of digital discourse can, of course, be passed off as poetic/journalistic licence (see below); however, a single-mindedly negative tone is usually established, especially when combined with other repetitive strategies such as the use of superlatives and a rhetoric of degeneration.

Superlatives and/as narrative detail

By 2004, a projected 10.5 billion will be sent in the United States alone. Worldwide, the number of messages is projected to increase from 20 billion last year to 82 billion by 2004. This works out to a rise from $1.73 billion in worldwide text-messaging revenue to $6.6 billion in 2004.

In the light of more recent markers (e.g., Facebook's 1.2 billion profiles at the time of writing), these figures may seem a little less than impressive; nonetheless, the folk-linguistic principle remains. A key rhetorical resource by which the prevalence of digital discourse – the extent of the 'revolution' – can be made vivid is through the use of superlative numerical citations. Statistical displays such as this typically make one of four rhetorical claims:

QUANTITY

- More than 1 billion text messages are sent every month in the UK.
- Billions of text messages are already being sent daily in this country.

GROWTH

- Text messaging is expanding at the rate of 1,800% a year.
- In New Zealand texting has grown from fewer than 60,000 a day in 1999 to more than 10 million a day this year.

MONETARY VALUE

- An estimated 20 billion text messages sent worldwide last month – worth almost £4 billion to Europe's phone operators.
- US carriers are starting to tap into this market, estimated at $20 billion worldwide.

USER DEMOGRAPHICS

- Nearly three quarters of online teens use instant messaging.
- Text totals of 2000 to 3000 a month are common for older teenagers.

Just as digital discourse was elsewhere in my corpus depicted as creating a whole new culture ('cr8ts a hul nu cltur') or, indeed, as a cultural revolution, the assumption that underpins this kind of 'statistical panic' (Woodward 1999) is that digital discourse is not only ubiquitous but also far-reaching in its impact. Sometimes these figures are patently inaccurate or contradictory (e.g., compare the two extracts under 'Quantity'), at other times they are nonsensical (e.g., it is hard to make sense of the 1,800% in the extract under 'Growth'). Nonetheless, accuracy and transparency are not where their real persuasive function lies. With seldom any specific source cited for these sorts of figures, their credibility is less important than their dramatic, narrative effect. Most obviously, there is the straightforward display of quantity: the larger the numbers, the greater the escalation and ubiquity of digital discourse. An added claim to the validity or veracity of these news reports is also created through the scientific and/or objectivist connotations of statistics themselves; in other words, we are persuaded that the rise and spread of digital discourse is fact. The persuasion may, however, be even more subtle than this. Just as detail in everyday conversational narratives fosters the perception of authenticity (Tannen 1989), the repetitive use of numeric detail in these articles also works to legitimate the representation of digital discourse as a whole. In other words, if journalists have these 'facts' and are concerned about this level of specificity, then everything they are saying must be true.

Degenerating language

Media stories about young people's digital discourse are arguably at their most pejorative when framed as an attack against conventional or 'correct' orthography, that is 'proper' spelling. Indeed, for well over half of the articles I looked at the impact of young people's new-media language on conventional standards of literacy was not simply a topic of discussion but the primary focus. It is, quite literally, headline news:

- Texting shortcuts worry examiners {*headline*}
- Is text messaging threatening literacy? {*headline*}
- Phone txt chat 'harms literacy' {*headline*}
- A Langwidge going from bad 2 worse {*headline*}
- 1 dA wil Nglsh B ritN li this? {*headline*}

Without wanting to rehearse the all too familiar complaints of what Deborah Cameron calls the 'great grammar crusade' (Cameron 1995: 78), the issue of young people's literacy (or lack thereof) was a topic covered extensively in my corpus. And this is where the *erasure* of digital discourse is most apparent and where underlying language ideologies rise to the surface. (I will indicate below how *fractal recursivity* is simultaneously at work, too.) Instant messaging, emailing and especially text messaging were, for example, described throughout as 'destroying', 'impacting', 'harming', 'limiting', 'damaging', 'ruining', 'threatening', 'massacring', 'corrupting' or 'eroding' standard English. Concern about falling standards of literacy centred specifically on standards of grammar, spelling, punctuation, capitalization and sentence structure that were usually reported as being 'sloppy', 'atrocious', 'inferior', 'errant', 'improper', 'undisciplined' or simply 'ugly'. In true Puritan form, new media language is almost always positioned in opposition to standard language, and change framed as a bad thing. Almost never does one find a sustained discussion about the sociolinguistic creativity and poetry in many young people's new-media language practices (Shortis 2007; Thurlow 2011). Nor, of course, is there ever an acknowledgement that Standard English is itself a construction, that non-mediated forms of language are far from standardized, or that new ways of using language never simply replace old ways.

As one might expect, young people's supposed attack on English is sometimes epitomized with reference to official markers of received practice and canonical literary texts, as with these examples:

- Text messaging is hardly the Queen's English.
- SMS . . . has little resemblance to Oxford English.
- And to think this happened in the land of Shakespeare. If the bard were alive today, he'd probably write, '2B or not 2B'.

This type of claim is clearly underpinned by the assumption that newer forms and styles of communication are necessarily inferior to older, more established ones. Ironically, the ideological preference for uniformity, transparency and accessibility that usually promotes 'plain English' as the most desired style seems not to apply to practices such as text and instant messaging, whose economic and succinct styles receive no credit. For the most part, the different generic and stylistic features of instant messaging, text messaging and email are usually conflated and almost always characterized in terms of, for example, excessive abbreviation, the use of lower-case lettering (or the 'loss' of capitalization), and the absence of punctuation. That literacy is thereby apparently rendered in the print media as equivalent to formal aspects of written language is itself of interest; however, it also reflects the common tendency to 'de-discourse' new-media language altogether, isolating linguistic forms from communicative functions and both from their cultural contexts of use. What is also left out of the picture is the simple fact that texting is not a uniquely youth practice; whole communities of texters are effectively erased.

What is perhaps more troubling – more ideologically problematic – about this type of framing of digital discourse is less the fact that dismissing it as 'meaningless messages', 'staccato statements', 'unimaginative' or 'shallow' fails to acknowledge its sociolinguistic complexity and diversity, but that this one-sided folk-linguistic framing devalues a mode of communicating that clearly has great interpersonal and symbolic value for many young people. Ultimately, young people are left to feel that their ways of speaking/communicating are bad because theirs are not standard or appropriate ways – just as researchers suggest is the case with ethnic-minority dialects and other non-standard speakers (see Collins 1999). It is very much in this way also that adolescence, like other marginalized or minoritized groups, becomes a site for policing the social order, for preserving the status quo, and for preventing moral decay/decline (see Lesko 2003). Herein lies some of the core language-ideological work being done: it is not only young people's language that is a problem but young people themselves.

Part 2: The *iconization* of digital discourse

- Across the land, every night . . . teenagers and their ilk are yakking online in chat rooms.

- Fears are growing that today's teenagers are becoming 'Generation Grunt', a section of society that has effectively lost the ability to talk or express itself.

- We may well be raising the thickest, most incoherent and sub-literate generation for centuries.

As I have already suggested, the overriding stance of newspaper reports towards digital discourse is critical, consistently painting young people (and 'their ilk') in a less than favourable light. From my own sample of articles, these are some of the labelling practices journalists seem to favour: 'idiot student', 'fickle teenagers', 'rapid-fire lifestyle of youth', 'impressionable youth', 'dull and spotty', 'yoof market', 'trend-setting teens', 'garrulous youngsters', 'typical teenager chatter' and 'seemingly [sic] sophisticated'. Young people nowadays certainly appear to be characterized as a generation defined uniformly and almost solely in terms of their communication technologies, hence homogenizing references to the 'keyboard generation', 'Generation IM', 'the gen-txt community', 'Generation Text', 'mobile generation', 'the thumb generation', 'gen.txtrs' and 'GNR8N TXT'. With their use of communication technologies often depicted as a 'craze', 'mania', 'youth obsession' or of 'having cult status', young people are also frequently caricatured as 'hooked', 'addicted', 'text addicts', 'feverishly punching in text on cell phones', 'fervent practitioners of text messaging', 'dependent and compulsive users'. These kinds of sweeping characterization have the added rhetorical value of supporting otherwise unsubstantiated, anecdotal claims regarding the nature and extent of digital discourse as well. By the same token, digital discourse is taken up as an iconic (i.e., a defining or quintessential) feature of young people as a social group. This happens everywhere but particularly in the case of 'mock texting' and exaggerated claims about the unintelligibility of new media language.

Mock texting

- Mst f d tym dey usd ds knd f lng'ge 2 tlk 2 1 anthr nt 1ly n txt bt evn n wrtng ltrs 2
- lfYaMthWozNEBiGrUWdntHavNEFAcLft2Wsh

In their generally dismissive framing of young people's digital discourse, and as a quintessential example of *iconization*, journalists are prone to use humorous, tokenistic displays of putative texting style. Exemplified clearly in some of the extracts already shown, headlines abound with these and in-text examples often appear with 'translations' or a glossary or 'do-it-yourself' listing at the end of articles. For the most part, the depiction of texting style relies on a fairly restricted repertoire of hackneyed features or items (e.g., IMHO, CU, L8R, BRB, LOL, GR8, ASL), usually concealing their origins (e.g., letter-number homophones have a history that predates texting by centuries; Shortis 2007), and conflating different technologies (i.e., assuming instant messaging, text-messaging and email are stylistically equivalent). These 'examples' are invariably very simplified caricatures and bear little resemblance to the kinds of messages most young people actually send (see Thurlow 2003 and Poff 2013). Not only are they improbable, these displays are often also counterintuitive, requiring precisely the kind of effort or space that digital discourse almost always seeks to avoid. While stylistic forms such as the use of capitalization to indicate elongated vowels are promoted in commercial publications such as the *Ltl bk of Txt Msgs*, my own students do not recognize them and are left flummoxed by 'messages' such as the ones shown above.

The oppositional rhetoric already alluded to is also evidenced by newspapers constantly setting digital discourse in contrast with 'proper' language and received, canonical markers of acceptability (e.g., the poetry of Shakespeare or the novels of Jane Austen, see below). However tongue-in-cheek, the intention behind these parodic exemplifications is always to tell a story about the subversion of acceptable, educated language use, and, by implication, digital discourse is rendered uneducated and unacceptable.

- Shall I compare U 2 a 0's day? U R mo luvlE & mo temperate. Rough winds do shAk d darling buds of mA, & 0's lease hz all 2 sht a D8.
- It Is A TrOth UniverslE Aknowledgd, Tht a SngI Man In PoSeSn Of A GOd 4tun, Mst B In 1 nt Of A Wit

That these and many other 'examples' are fabricated exaggerations of real digital discourse is clearly irrelevant. In fact, contrary to the usual journalist standard of reporting the facts, many examples appear to have been created by 'translating' otherwise unlikely phrases into 'textese' using commercially available resources like transl8it.com. Seldom do journalists furnish ethnographic or other empirical evidence to validate examples (save for a few choice quotes from scholars and other 'experts'); examples are almost always based on popular, anecdotal hearsay. Nor at any point in my original corpus did a journalist allow for changing fashions in text messaging style, or in subcultural and age-related variations, or in differences in personal style. Following the lead of Jane Hill (2001), there seems to be a strong parallel here between journalists' ultimately condescending use of 'mock texting' and the use of mock Spanish (as in 'hola, amigo!') by Anglo Americans. In this case, apparently playful but ignorant crossings into digital discourse elevate and promote the superiority of adults; young people's own communication capital (see Bourdieu 1991), meanwhile, is devalued even further.

Exaggerating unintelligibility

- The evolving language of online chat is leaving parents – as well as grammar and punctuation – behind.

- The page was riddled with hieroglyphics, many of which I simply could not translate.

- They have created their own words to foil teachers and other adults.

One of the main conceits in mock texting – and central to the iconization of digital discourse – is the performance of unintelligibility (to adults) and inaccessibility (to adults). On behalf of their peers, journalists constantly complain about text messaging style being 'opaque', 'baffling', 'impenetrable' or 'exclusive'; it also 'causes confusion' and leaves parents and others 'stumped'. Accordingly, digital discourse can only be understood by those in the know – the initiated, those who understand. It is simply incomprehensible to the untrained reader. For the uninitiated, the 'text-illiterate', digital discourse remains a 'mysterious lexicon', 'technobabble', 'cryptic chat', 'a bizarre activity', 'hodgepodge communication', 'secret code', 'language soup', 'jumble', 'ramblings', 'cryptic symbols', 'word jumble', 'quirky, cryptograms', 'garbled', 'encoded messages', 'gobbledegook', 'gibberish', 'argle-bargle', 'a cipher' and 'a secret language'. Once again, this artful hieroglyphic code must be cracked. There is, however, something almost narcissistic in the persistent implication that young people are somehow deliberately texting or messaging in order to exclude (or 'foil') adults. The primary symbolic value of young people's digital discourse lies precisely in the fact that it is not meant to be for, or necessarily about, adults in the first place.

This rendering of digital discourse as being somehow unintelligible not only serves to promote the validity of 'distinctive variety' claims (see Part 1), but also plays up its supposed exoticity and otherness. All of which, points to a clear set of reinscribed assumptions about young people and the nature of youth. This, as Kathryn Woolard and Bambi Schieffelin (1994: 55–6) explain, is precisely the work of language ideologies: 'Ideologies of language . . . envision and enact links of language to group and personal identity, to aesthetics, to morality, and to epistemology.' Particularly with comments such as 'leaving parents . . . behind', one might speculate that what is really at issue is adults' underlying frustration (or fascination) with their own lack of technical competence in contrast to the technical capacity of many young people. This possible sense of disempowerment is no doubt also disruptive of the usual power relations that characterize adolescence more generally. Regardless, young people's digital discourse appears to be a key resource for adults (journalists are almost always adults) to exaggerate and fetishize the 'teen-ness' of digital discourse. What is more, just as Rosina Lippi-Green (1997) sees the 'burden of communication' usually being imposed on ethnic minorities, young people are apparently obliged to make themselves understandable to adults. If they do not, they become the object of ridicule, critique and, sometimes, outright condemnation.

Part 3: The *fractal recursivity* of digital discourse

I now want to return to the three newspaper articles whose headlines were quoted at the start of this chapter. A closer look at extended extracts from these stories reveals at least two important things: most notably, how persistent (and consistently pejorative) the old media's coverage of digital discourse is; also, how this metalanguage (or *metadiscourse*) continues to be organized around so many of the same pet themes and rhetorical strategies detailed above. In addition to the semiotic processes of erasure and iconization, the three extracts here point nicely to the third of Irvine and Gal's language-ideological processes: *fractal recursivity*. Following each extract, I offer a few brief interpretive remarks to show the kinds of critical analysis that can (and should) be applied to these types of popular, high-profile representations of digital discourse.

> More than half (58 per cent) of adults now say they use text messages at least once a day to communicate with family and friends, while only 49 per cent meet people face-to-face on such a regular basis. . . . Despite the figures, British adults say that they would prefer to meet (67 per cent) or speak on the phone (10 per cent) than communicate with people by text (5 per cent). But the trend looks set to continue, with text messaging also the most commonly used method of communication among the younger generation. Some 90 per cent of 16 to 24-year-olds exchange texts with friends and family at least once a day, followed by social networking (74 per cent), mobile phone calls (67 per cent) and face-to-face contact (63 per cent). James Thickett, Ofcom's director of research, said: 'Our research reveals that in just a few short years, new technology has fundamentally changed the way that we communicate . . . new forms of communications are emerging which don't require us to talk to each other – especially among younger age groups.'
>
> *Daily Telegraph*, UK

Two persistent but mistaken assumptions made by this article are that face-to-face communication is necessarily a better mode of communication, and that one mode necessarily replaces other modes. By claiming that texting is *not* talking, the article also misrecognizes the ways computer-mediated communication often blurs the usual distinctions drawn between speech and writing. Contrary to the explicit claim ('texting more popular') made in the headline, the survey cited makes clear that adults actually prefer to meet face-to-face even if they *report* texting more often. The article offers no equivalent survey data or any other comment about young people's communicative preferences, thereby implying that reported frequency of use equates to preferred communicative mode. The article then ends by reframing itself (and the cited survey) as being ultimately and exclusively a youth issue.

> The latest communication craze among teens worldwide is SMS text messaging. Although a useful form of technology, texting can be abused or even dangerous. . . . Apart from developing sore thumbs, heavy texters could be exhibiting evidence of weakness in goals and attitudes that indicate low interest and engagement in reflective thought. . . . findings presented in San Diego at the 13th Annual Meeting of the Society for Personality and Social Psychology, show there could be 100 different reasons why these associations exist. . . . It suggests that very brief media social interaction such as texting encourages rapid, relatively shallow thought.
>
> *Vanguard*, Nigeria

True to form, this second article centres on the deleterious effects of texting through a charged language of abuse (as in drugs) and danger (as in health risks) – regardless of the creative, positive uses to which texting is often put. As with the previous example, the article explicitly cites research evidence that contradicts the article's key premise; in this case, texting is blamed even though 'there could be 100 different reasons'. Probably inaccurately, the article introduces text messaging as a recent phenomenon (not in Nigeria at least); it also frames texting as a distinctively youth phenomenon or rather 'craze', hinting at the non-normative and possibly passing nature of this communicative practice.

> If you have teens, you've probably grown accustomed to seeing them lighted by the glow of a phone screen. . . . Good news: The hours your kids spend face-to-phone are paying off. They have become fluent in a second language. Bad news: That language is texting. . . . A new study confirms what many parents suspect. The more kids send and receive texts, the worse their grammar skills become. . . . With 'the culture of mobile communication – quick back and forth – inevitably, there are compromises on traditional, cultural writing,' said S. Shyam Sundar, professor of communications and co-director of Pennsylvania State University's Media Effects Research Laboratory, which conducted the study. 'Techspeak,' as Sundar and his research partner Drew P. Cingel call it, has become so routine and prevalent among young users that it's eroding their foundation of basic grammar. 'Routine use of textual adaptations by current and future generations of 13–17-year-olds may serve to create the impression that this is normal and accepted use of the language and rob this age group of a fundamental understanding of standard English grammar,' they said in their published findings.
>
> *LA Times*, USA

Once again, we have an article explicitly framing the practice of texting as a somehow exclusively 'teen' phenomenon, also in sweeping generational terms. Texting is explicitly presented as a bad thing (i.e., the 'bad news'). Text-messaging style is framed here, however playfully, as a fully-fledged language ('fluent in a second language'). Later, the expert's reference to 'techspeak' further promotes the idea that texting style is a distinctive variety. (This neologism inherently frames texting as speech, which is precisely what the *Telegraph* article above refutes.)

In each of these three articles we have clear evidence of the ways ostensibly linguistic phenomena/judgements are extrapolated to broader communicative 'issues' and social domains. This seems to be what Irvine and Gal (2000: 38) have in mind when they speak of *fractal recursivity*. In the first article, for example, an explicit claim (presented as reported expert speech) is made for the way communication (or conversation) has been 'fundamentally' changed and how this change can be attributed to technology. The first is a matter of debate, the second is a deterministic assumption. In the next article, we find a twofold recursive extrapolation of text messaging to issues of public health (i.e., the physiology of repetitive strain injuries), which itself slips readily into a psychological-cum-moralizing concern for 'weakness in goals' and reduced 'reflective thought'. A highly improbable and, once again, patently deterministic relationship is fabricated between even 'very brief' mediated interaction and 'shallow thought'. Arguably the grossest – but not atypical – instance of fractal recursivity is to be found in the last article where we find text messaging being mapped directly and emphatically onto matters of literacy (see also my earlier discussion about 'degenerating language'). With no reference to well-established research offering contradictory findings, the article hinges on a single media-effects study published by a 'Stanford-trained', 'Distinguished Professor' of Communication. Although the explanatory link between texting and 'standard English' is modalized and fleetingly mitigated, the overriding sense of 'inevitability' and causality is clearly a deterministic exaggeration.

This last newspaper article is an important reminder that it is not only journalists who are in the business of (mis)representing digital discourse or, at least, singlehandedly fuelling major language ideological debates. As self-proclaimed experts in their own right, scholars too are heavily invested in language and especially the linguists among us. In a posting on the *Language Log*, University of Pennsylvania professor Mark Liberman (2012) offers a trenchant critique of the Cingel and Sundar (2012) study cited in the *LA Times*. For all its flaws (e.g., a striking lack of key research literature), Cingel and Sundar's scholarly take on digital discourse has spawned a predictably enthusiastic response from various national and international newspapers, together with the usual mock-text headlines and hyperbolic certainties (e.g., 'absolutely', 'destroying', 'leading to a generation' from the extracts below).

- Text-speak and tweens: Notso gr8 4 riting skillz {*headline*}
- Duz Txting Hurt Yr Kidz Gramr? Absolutely, a new study says {*headline*}
- Texting iz destroying student grammar {*headline*}
- Texting tweens lack 'gr8' grammar {*headline*}
- OMG: Researchers say text messaging really is leading to a generation with poor grammar skills {*headline*}

To suggest that this one academic study appropriately assesses the cultural significance and impact of texting is to misinterpret the evidence (there can be no absolutes); it also misconstrues the realities of young people's actual, everyday, usual practices. To further suggest (as in the last extract above) that texting might also epitomize the lives and literacies of an entire generation is simply nonsense. That adults get away with *mis*representing young people on such a scale and in such a questionable manner says a great deal about the relations of power that structure youth. Print-media metalanguage about young people and their new-media language is, it seems, more than a harmless and otherwise understandable 'mis-recognition' of language, of technology, and of young people; this news-making reveals itself as being somewhat more intentionally and effectively irresponsible. Young people are unquestionably disempowered by adults' almost total control of the print media and the surprisingly persistent absence of 'youth voices' in reports about new media language. This is not an equal playing field and media representations have significant influence.

Conclusion: language workers at work (and play)

There are, of course, always a number of institutional conditions that need to be taken into consideration when unravelling the ideological basis of any folk-linguistic commentary. In this case, one must recognize the particular status of journalists as a community of professional *language workers* who, like academics, teachers and lexicographers, are especially dependent on the crafting of language for their livelihoods. It is also widely known that news-making disproportionately and consistently values negativity (McGregor 2002). Not surprisingly, therefore, the print media predictably generates more than its fair share of language mavens and grammar crusaders invested in upholding/preserving received orthographic or other linguistic standards. It is understandable too if news-makers are especially prone to worrying and writing about perceived threats to language. In which case, the endless schooling of the style manual and the disciplining of editors are just too easily redirected to the broader community of language users. To be fair, the writing of newspaper articles – as with the writing of scholarly chapters – is also an act of linguistic creativity in its own terms. Many of the journalists whose articles I have quoted here were no doubt also having fun playing with words. That this all comes at the expense of young people – and with such blind antagonism – is less pardonable.

Verbal hygiene and morality are always recursively interconnected, just as commerce and profit are always closely implicated in the reproduction and maintenance of standard varieties (Bourdieu 1991; Irvine 1989). In these terms, text messaging style not only poses a threat to the authority and expertise of professional language workers such as newspaper journalists; it is also a commodity by which those who make a living from wordsmithery are able to establish their authority and perform their expertise, their craft. No less is true of other language workers such as academic linguists or discourse analysts who are also wedded to their own institutional practices and expert performances. It is certainly not the place of academics necessarily to evaluate the merits or accuracy of everyday metalanguage against our own scholarly standards – simply substituting one set of metalinguistic judgements for another. We are, however, duty-bound to critique those metalinguistic claims to authority by which prejudice is normalized and power relations are exercised. This is, of course, why folk linguistics is also always a matter of language ideology. All talk about language, regardless of its apparent linguistic validity, is a site of constant interpersonal, bureaucratic and cultural struggle. Invariably, the promotion or denigration of certain styles and ways of speaking – the devaluing of some people's communication capital – serves as a means of rehearsing or reproducing the social order. It is also a way for researchers to better understand the place and meaning of language in people's lives.

References

Baron, N.S. (2000) *Alphabet to Email: How Written English Evolved and Where It's Heading*, New York: Routledge.

Bourdieu, P. (1991) *Language and Symbolic Power*, Cambridge: Polity Press.

Cameron, D. (1995) *Verbal Hygiene*, London: Routledge.

Cingel, D.P. and Sundar, S.S. (2012) 'Texting, techspeak, and tweens: the relationship between text messaging and English grammar skills', *New Media & Society* 14(8): 1304–20.

Collins, J. (1999) 'The Ebonics controversy in context: literacies, subjectivities and language ideologies in the United States', in J. Blommaert (ed.) *Language Ideological Debates*, New York: Mouton de Gruyter, 201–34.

Coupland, N. and Jaworski, A. (2004) 'Sociolinguistic perspectives on metalanguage: reflexivity, evaluation and ideology', in A. Jaworski, N. Coupland and D. Galasiński (eds.) *Metalanguage: Social and Ideological Perspectives*, Berlin: Mouton de Gruyter, 15–51.

Dürscheid, C. and Stark, E. (2011) '*sms4science*: An international corpus-based texting project and the specific challenges for multilingual Switzerland', in C. Thurlow and K. Mroczek (eds.) *Digital Discourse: Language in the New Media*, New York: Oxford University Press, 299–320.

Fairclough, N. (2003) *Analysing Discourse: Textual Analysis for Social Research*, London: Routledge.

Foucault, M. (1977) *Discipline and Punish: the Birth of the Prison*, New York: Pantheon.

Herring, S.C. (2001) 'Computer-mediated discourse', in D. Schiffrin, D. Tannen and H. Hamilton (eds.) *The Handbook of Discourse Analysis*, Oxford: Blackwell, 612–34.

Hill, J.H. (2001) 'Language, race, and white public space', in A. Duranti (ed.) *Linguistic Anthropology: A Reader*, Malden, MA: Blackwell, 450–64.

Irvine, J. (1989) 'When talk isn't cheap: language and political economy', *American Ethnologist* 16(2): 248–67.

Irvine, J. and Gal, S. (2000) 'Language ideology and linguistic differentiation', in P.V. Kroskity (ed.) *Regimes of Language: Ideologies, Polities, and Identities*, Santa Fe, NM: School of American Research Press, 35–84.

Lesko, N. (2003) *Act Your Age! A Cultural Construction of Adolescence*, New York: Routledge Falmer.

Liberman, M. (2012) 'Texting and language skills', posted 2 August 2012 on *Language Log*, http://languagelog.ldc.upenn.edu/nll/?p=4099.

Lippi-Green, R. (1997) *English with an Accent: Language, Ideology, and Discrimination in the United States*, New York: Routledge.

McGregor, J. (2002) *Restating News Values: Contemporary Criteria for Selecting the News*, Proceedings of the Australian & New Zealand Communication Association, www.anzca.net/conferences/conference-papers/41-adam.html

Niedzielski, N.A. and Preston, D.R. (1999) *Folk Linguistics*, Berlin: Mouton de Gruyter.

Shortis, T. (2007) 'Gr8 txtpectations: the creativity of text spelling', *English Drama Media* 8.

Tannen, D. (1989) *Talking Voices: Repetition, Dialogue, and Imagery in Conversational Discourse*, Cambridge: Cambridge University Press.

Thurlow, C. (2003) 'Generation Txt? The sociolinguistics of young people's text-messaging', *Discourse Analysis Online* 1(1), http://extra.shu.ac.uk/daol/articles/v1/n1/a3/thurlow2002003-paper.html.

—— (2006) 'From statistical panic to moral panic: the metadiscursive construction and popular exaggeration of new media language in the print media', *Journal of Computer Mediated Communication* 11(3): 667–701.

—— (2007) 'Fabricating youth: new-media discourse and the technologization of young people', in S. Johnson and A. Ensslin (eds.) *Language in the Media: Representations, Identities, Ideologies*, London: Continuum, 213–33.

—— (2011) 'Determined creativity: language play in new media discourse', in R. Jones (ed.) *Discourse and Creativity*, London: Pearson, 169–90.

Thurlow, C. and Mroczek, K. (2011) 'Fresh perspectives on new media sociolinguistics', in C. Thurlow and K. Mroczek (eds.) *Digital Discourse: Language in the New Media*, New York: Oxford University Press, xix–xliv.

Thurlow, C. and Poff, M. (2013) 'The language of text messaging', in S.C. Herring, D. Stein and T. Virtanen (eds.) *Handbook of the Pragmatics of Computer Mediated Communication*, Berlin and New York: Mouton de Gruyter, 151–81.

Woodward, K. (1999) 'Statistical panic', *differences* 11: 177–203.

Woolard, K.A. and Schieffelin, B.B. (1994) 'Language ideology', *Annual Reviews in Anthropology* 23: 55–82.

Notes

1   These three newspaper headlines were from 2012 (July, February and August, respectively).

2   In their overview of sociolinguistic perspectives on metalanguage, Nikolas Coupland and Adam Jaworski (2004) offer useful snapshots of a range of approaches in addition to folk linguistics and language ideology.

3   In countries where English is not a recognized/official language, folk-linguistic discourse usually also concerns the deleterious impact of young people's use of English on the local language.

4   The study of new media language sometimes falls under the title Computer-Mediated Discourse (CMD), a term established by Susan Herring (e.g., 2001), a leading scholar in the field. In the introduction to my edited volume *Digital Discourse*, I offer a review of the field of new media sociolinguistics and briefly discuss these different labelling conventions (Thurlow and Mroczek 2011).

Chapter 32

Jan Blommaert

ORDERS OF INDEXICALITY AND POLYCENTRICITY

Introduction

IT IS ONE OF SOCIOLINGUISTICS' main accomplishments to have demonstrated that 'language' is, in the practice of its occurrence in real situations of use, a repertoire: a culturally sensitive ordered complex of genres, styles and registers, with lots of hybrid forms, occurring in a wide variety of ways both big and small. We have also learned that due to this fragmentation of 'language', the spectre of variation is tremendously wide – from variation between 'languages' (codeswitching in the traditional sense) to variation playing out small phonetic variables, microscopic style shifts and shifts in register. The spectre of sociolinguistic variation now covers macro-variation as well as micro-variation, and such forms of variation matter in social life (Gumperz 2003; Hymes 1996; Maryns and Blommaert 2001; Rampton 1995). They function as powerful sources of indexical meanings – meanings that connect discourses to contexts and induce categories, similarities and differences within frames, and thus suggest identities, tones, styles and genres that appear to belong or to deviate from expected types (Agha 2005; Silverstein 2003). Indexicality connects language to cultural patterns, and considerations of multilingualism thus also become considerations of multiculturalism.

Mainstream discourse analysis, however, often starts from a sociolinguistically and culturally unproblematized object: a text, document or fragment of spoken discourse usually sensed to 'be in a language X' (e.g., 'the text is in English'), which is then analysed as to its intradiscursive characteristics. Such intradiscursive characteristics are, then, often 'intra-language X' characteristics – discourse markers, forms of lexical, syntactic or semantic coherence, metrical or other 'poetic' structuring

Source: Jan Blommaert, Orders of Indexicality and Polycentricity. Extracted from J. Blommaert. 2007. Sociolinguistics and discourse analysis: Orders of indexicality and polycentricity. *Journal of Multicultural Discourse* 2: 115–130.

devices – belonging to language X. Sociolinguistic features such as language variety/varieties and shifts therein, accent, register or other are rarely drawn into the analytic exercise. The only exception is when such varieties become overtly visible (or audible) and are easy to recognize as essential in structuring the text. Codeswitching is a case in point – a sociolinguistic feature of variation recognized as an important discourse-structuring device (Auer 1998; Gumperz 1982). But by and large, discourse analysis displays a marked preference for 'monolingual' discourse, and if sociolinguistic variation is addressed, the preference is for 'big', visible, abundantly flagged variation.

The argument in this paper is that whenever we say that 'this text is in English', we should address that text through the sociolinguistic spectre of variation: what do we mean by 'in French'? Do we see sociolinguistic variation discursively deployed in the text? And if so, what does it mean? The drive behind this argument is general as well as practical. In general, we should all strive towards a better discourse analysis, one that keeps abreast of developments in related branches of language studies. In this case, drawing attention to the possibilities of incorporating sociolinguistic micro-variation into discourse analysis looks to me to be a worthwhile goal in itself. The practical motive has to do with the simple fact that globalization compels us to take multilingualism and multiculturalism as a rule rather than as an exception, and address the phenomenology of non-nativeness in language usage as something that crucially connects with social, political and ideological processes characterizing Late Modernity (Blommaert 2005; Chouliaraki and Fairclough 1999; Collins and Slembrouck 2005; Coupland 2003; Heller 1999).

In sum, developments in the structure of societies compel us to devote more attention to issues of sociolinguistic variation in discourse, because features of such variation become ever more important to users. We are no longer at ease when it comes to the monolingual default in discourse analysis. Consequently, our discourse analytic toolkit needs to be complemented with some seriously useful sociolinguistic tools. I will present two such tools in this paper: orders of indexicality and polycentricity. Both concepts are designed to observe forms of variation that characterize Late Modern diasporic environments (Blommaert 2005; Blommaert et al 2005a, 2005b).

Orders of indexicality

The point of departure is quite simple: indexicality, even though largely operating at the implicit level of linguistic/semiotic structuring, is not unstructured but *ordered*. It is ordered in two ways, and these forms of indexical order account for 'normativity' in semiosis. The first kind of order is what Silverstein (2003) called 'indexical order': the fact that indexical meanings occur in patterns offering perceptions of similarity and stability that can be perceived as 'types' of semiotic practice with predictable (presupposable/entailing) directions (see also Agha 2003, 2005). 'Register' is a case in point: clustered and patterned language forms that index specific social personae and roles, can be invoked to organize interactional practices (e.g., turns at talk, narrative), and have a *prima facie* stability that can sometimes be used for typifying or stereotyping (e.g., 'posh' accents – see Rampton 2003). Speaking or writing through such registers involves insertion in recognizable (normative) repertoires of 'voices': one then speaks *as* a man, a lawyer, a middle-aged European, an asylum seeker and so forth, and if done appropriately, one will be perceived as speaking *as such* (Agha 2005). Indexical order, thus, is the metapragmatic organizing principle behind what is widely understood as the 'pragmatics' of language.

Such forms of indexical order sometimes have long and complex histories of becoming (Agha 2003 and Silverstein 2003 offer excellent illustrations) often connected to the histories of becoming of nation-states and their cultural and sociolinguistic paraphernalia – the notion of a 'standard language' and its derivative, a particular 'national' ethnolinguistic identity (Errington 2001; Silverstein 1996, 1998). Yet, they also display a significant degree of variability and change, and they can erupt and fade under pressure of macro-developments such as capitalist consumer fashions (as e.g., Silverstein's *oenologia* – the register of contemporary wine connoisseurs, Silverstein 2003; also Agha 2005). Indexical order of this sort is a positive force, it produces social categories, recognizable semiotic emblems for groups and individuals, a more or less coherent semiotic habitat.

It does so, however, within the confines of a stratified general repertoire, in which particular indexical orders relate to others in relations of mutual valuation – higher/lower, better/worse. This is where we meet another kind of order to indexicalities, one that operates on a higher plane of social structuring: an order in the general systems of meaningful semiosis valid in groups at any given time. This kind of ordering results in what I call orders of indexicality – a term obviously inspired by Foucault's 'order of discourse'. Recall that Foucault was interested in the general rules for the production of discourses: their positive emergence as well as their erasure and exclusion. He started from the hypothesis

> that in every society the production of discourse is at once controlled, selected, organized and redistributed by a certain number of procedures whose role is to ward off its powers and dangers, to gain mastery over its chance events, to evade its ponderous, formidable materiality.
> (Foucault 1984 [1971]: 109; see also his notion of 'archive', Foucault 2002 [1969]: Chapter 5)

If we now paraphrase Foucault's hypothesis we see that ordered indexicalities operate within large stratified complexes in which some forms of semiosis are systemically perceived as valuable, others as less valuable, and some are not taken into account at all, while all are subject to rules of access and regulations as to circulation. That means that such systemic patterns of indexicality are also systemic patterns of authority, of control and evaluation, and hence of inclusion and exclusion *by real or perceived others*. That also means that every register is susceptible to a politics of access. And it also means that there is an economy of exchange, in which the values attached by some to one form of semiosis may not be granted by others: the English spoken by a middle-class person in Nairobi may not be (and is unlikely to be) perceived as a middle-class attribute in London or New York.

Orders of indexicality is a sensitizing concept that should point a finger to (index!) important aspects of power and inequality in the field of semiosis. If forms of semiosis are socially and culturally valued, these valuation processes should display traces of power and authority, of struggles in which there were winners as well as losers, and in which, in general, the group of winners is smaller than the group of losers. The concept invites different questions – sociolinguistic questions on indexicality – and should open empirical analyses of indexicality to higher-level considerations about relations within sociolinguistic repertoires, the (non-)exchangeability of particular linguistic or semiotic resources across places, situations and groups, and so forth. It invites, in sum, different questions of authority, access and power in this field.

Polycentricity

One such question is: how do we imagine such patterns of authority and power? Rather than to fall back on notions such as 'habitus' (with its suggestions of incorporated automatisms) or on images of perpetual reinvention in interaction I would suggest that authority emanates from real or perceived 'centres', to which people orient when they produce an indexical trajectory in semiosis. That is, I suggest that whenever we communicate, apart from our real and immediate addressees, we orient towards what Bakhtin called a 'superaddressee': complexes of norms and perceived appropriateness criteria, in effect the larger social and cultural body of authority into which we insert our immediate practices vis-à-vis our immediate addressees. And very often, such authorities have names, faces, a reality of their own: they can be individuals (teachers, parents, role models, the coolest guy in class), collectives (peer groups, subcultural groups, group images such as 'punk', 'gothic', etc.), abstract entities or ideals (the church, the nation-state, the middle-class, consumer culture and its many fashions, freedom, democracy), and so on: the macro- and micro-structures of our everyday world. The point is: we often project the presence of an evaluating authority through our interactions with immediate addressees, we behave *with reference to* such an evaluative authority, and I suggest we call such an evaluating authority a 'centre'.

The authority of centres is evaluative, and it often occurs as an authority over clusters of semiotic features, including *thematic domains*, *places*, *people* (roles, identities, relationships) and *semiotic styles* (including linguistic varieties, modes of performance, etc.). Thus, broaching a particular topic will trigger a particular semiotic style and suggest particular roles and relationships between participants, and certain types of communicative events require appropriate places – *Not here! Not now! Not while the children are listening!* (Scollon and Scollon 2003; also Blommaert et al 2005a). One speaks differently and as a different person about cars or music than about the economy or about sex – in one instance, one can speak as an expert using a particular register indexing membership of expert groups, in other instances one can speak as a novice; one can shift from a very masculine voice on a particular topic (e.g., sex or cars) to a gender-neutral voice (e.g., when discussing the war in Iraq), each time also shifting registers, often even accents, pace, tone and rhythm (a declarative tone on one topic, a hesitant one on another). And topics, styles and identities belong to places and are excluded from other places (a thing that becomes apparent during after-hours escapades at scientific conferences). Each time one orients towards other centres of authority offering ideal-types of norms or appropriateness criteria, as it is called in pragmatics: the places where 'good' discourse about these topics is made.

It is the packaging of topic, place, style and people that makes up the indexical direction of communication: the fact that certain topics require specific semiotic modes and environments, and so organize identities and roles (Agha 2005). Goffman (1981) called such patterns shifts in 'footing': delicate changes in speaker position that were accompanied by shifts in linguistic and semiotic mode and redefined the participant roles in the interaction. We are now in a position to empirically 'dissect' footing and bring it in line with larger organizational features of life in society.

It is obvious that even though places impose rules and restrictions on what can happen in communication there, every environment in which humans convene and communicate is almost by definition polycentric, in the sense that more than one possible centre can be distinguished: one can follow norms or violate them at any step of the process, and sometimes this is wilfully done while at other occasions it comes about by accident or because of the impossibility to behave in a particular way. Again, Goffman's descriptions of the multiple layers that characterize mundane interaction scenes are informative. Goffman, for instance, distinguished between 'focal' and 'non-focal' activities occurring in the same event – as when a pupil in class produces an offensive reaction to a teacher's question, giving off negative impressions (focal, for the teacher) as well as positive ones (non-focal, towards his peer group who studiously try to avoid being qualified as 'nerds'). In our own research on asylum seekers' narratives, we often found that 'truthful' accounts by the applicant were interpreted as 'implausible' (i.e., untruthful) accounts by the interviewers, because describing the chaotic and often paradoxical realities truthfully, often iconically, resulted in a chaotic and paradoxical story, and whereas interviewees oriented towards 'the truth' as defined by situated, densely contextualized realities in, for example, Africa, interviewers oriented towards a particular textual (bureau-cratic) ideal of decontextualizable coherence, linearity and factuality (Blommaert 2001). Both centres were always present in such a polycentric interview situation, although the interviewers' centre was often 'non-focal', kept in the background during the interview itself. In telling 'the truth', thus, the applicants were often 'wrong-footed' by the interviewers, and in the real world, the dominant order of indexicality is that of the interviewer and his/her bureaucratic apparatus.

Polycentricity is a key feature of interactional regimes in human environments: even though many interaction events look 'stable' and monocentric (e.g., exams, wedding ceremonies), there are as a rule multiple – although never unlimited – batteries of norms to which one can orient and according to which one can behave (as when the bride winks at the groom when she says 'I do'), and this multiplicity has been previously captured under terms such as 'polyphony' or 'multivocality'. A term such as 'polycentricity' moves the issue from the descriptive to the interpretive level, and again, my attempt is towards sensitizing others about the fact that behind terms such as 'polyphony', social structures of power and inequality are at work, and that such structures – orders of indexicality – account for the fact that certain forms of polyphony never occur while other forms of polyphony miraculously seem to assume similar shapes and directions. The bride can wink to her groom, but baring her breasts would be highly unusual. Certain voices, like the bureaucratic one in the asylum system, *systemically* prevail over others, because the impact of certain centres of authority is bigger than that of others. The multiplicity of available batteries of norms does not mean that these batteries are equivalent, equally accessible or equally open to negotiation. Orders of indexicality are stratified and impose differences in value onto the different modes of semiosis, systematically give preference to some over others and exclude or disqualify particular modes.

Both concepts, orders of indexicality and polycentricity, thus suggest a less innocent world of linguistic, social and cultural variation and diversity, one in which difference is quickly turned into inequality, and in which complex patterns of potential-versus-actual behaviour occur. They also enable us to move beyond the usual sociolinguistic units – homogeneous speech communities – and consider situations in which various 'big' sociolinguistic systems enter the picture, as when people migrate in the context of globalization, or when in the same context messages start moving across large spaces. In both cases, people do not just move across space: given what has been said above we also realize that they move across different orders of indexicality, and that, consequently, what happens to them in communication becomes less predictable than what would happen in 'their own' environment. Sociolinguistics in the age of globalization needs to look way beyond the speech community, to sociolinguistic systems and how they connect and relate to one another. Big things matter if we want to understand the small things of discourse.

On the move: playful polycentricity

Let us now turn to an example. The following fragment was recorded in Cape Town in December 2000. It was recorded from Radio UCT, the campus radio station of the University of Cape Town (an affluent, majority-white 'Ivy League' university), and the fragment is taken from a Reggae programme deejayed by a man – a UCT student – who calls himself Ras Pakaay. The programme is a call-in programme, and listeners can call to tell stories and/or to request particular songs. In the fragment below, Ras Pakaay first concludes a song, then tells a small story about a listener who called just now, and then goes on to take the call of a girl from the Khayelitsha township.

{music}
Part 1

R. definite he is.

I'm a noossssssmoke [smo:k]
No chronic to bother no one [no kronik. tu bo:də nowaɲ]..
but = I man [maɲ]. . .

Yes: my brethren.
you must {laughin voice} ha = ( ) with a smoke ̩smoᵃk] you know =
I had a smoke [smo:k]
I tell you my brethren {end laughin voice}.

{style shift}
While it = am. time is = has goneh twelve minutes pas the hour of five
    o'clock on UCT radio wonderful point five fm studio.

Part 2

{style shift}
I just had a brethren right **now [noːʷ]**.
he's actually calling **all the way [oːl də weːᵃ]** from (Heideveld **[hiᵃːdəfeld]**)
    I say
        yo Ras Pakaai gone to heave' .
        *Bush *Band
   an=I say
        my brethren I do have **Budj Band**
   and I say   yo.
        Why do wanna come live on air
    I said allright allright allright
and then az' I was preparing to pu' the man [man] 'pon line.
the man [maɲ] got *cut [kot] off with Ras Pakaai.

but then on that very same **note [noᵃt]**
beautiful listeners of this=e show
we have. a caller on the line {technical sound}
..

Part 3

cottin edge hoi

F. hello?
R. hello yo live on air [ɛ:]
F. OK
R. yea who'm I speaking to everythin is all right thanks and how 'bout you?
F. yeah I'm fine
R. yeah. an=
F. (=   NAME)
R. hehehe (NAME). everythin is all right. I know you're calling from **all the
way [oːI də weːᵃ]**. what am calling now **all the way [oᵃːl də weːᵃ]** from
Khayelitsha [koyəlisha] is that right
F. yeah
R. allright..how may I help you
F. yeah OK I would like to uhm if you just wanted(ed) to play mh. this song
for *me please
R. What song you'd like me to play for you
F.   [= by Luciano
R. by? Luciano
F.   [=yeah
R. well. I don know what's happenin' with Luciano today..Ehm what a song
you'd like me to play for you
F. = Kiss me again = ja
R. **Kiss me again olmos' I gat Jah**. I'm definitely gonna play that song for
you my sisterene allright?. And who'd you like me to play the song for
F. for   my*se:lf

R. for yourself?.   Oh really. hahahahha an you =
F.   yeah   = what you *laughin {laughing
voice} at me (about)?
R. ehhr?

Part 4

F. why you laughing at me?
R. no I'm not laughin'
my sisterene *otherwise* [a:dawais] I thaught you would ehm actually want to
play the song..or want me to play the song for somebody else or:. for some
people **dem** seen?
F. = just for myself
R. = just for yourself. .so you just sitting at home?
F.   yeah
R. = listenin' to reggae music, with Ras Pakaai on UCT radio
F. yeah
R. ([kom tru yu]) my sisterene sha me do dat (   ) all right?
F. okay
R. yeah give thanks [tʃanks]
F. (   )
**R. {laughing} thanks for callin my sisterene all right?. and = e
keep dem things under control [kɔntroˀl].** I don know
{jingle}

The text is an instance of discourse-in-globalization: it originates in an event celebrating
Reggae (one of the best known and most widely spread forms of 'World Music'), a
Caribbean popular cultural icon performed at the southern tip of Africa. The DJ is
a local black man, as we shall be able to demonstrate in a moment, but he poses as
a 'Rasta', that is – he poses as a Jamaican adept of Ras Tafari, and he makes every
effort to produce semiotic tokens that articulate that impersonation: Jamaican
Creole imitations, Rasta slang, references to Rasta emblems such as smoking weed,
knowledge of Reggae artists, song titles and lyrics. In that sense, we have already
one orientation towards a particular centre: Ras Pakaay orients towards the transnational world of Reggae and Rastafarism, he 'climbs into' an identity that he suggests
belongs to that world. But let us go a bit deeper into this example and return to
some of the things mentioned earlier.

In this short fragment, Ras Pakaay shifts frequently, and he deploys at least four
different varieties of English. All of them are recognizably South African: Ras Pakaay
has a local, 'black' accent whenever he speaks; notwithstanding that, he has a
remarkable competence in different varieties of English. We can distinguish:

(1)   'Standard' English, i.e., a variety that within the local economy of linguistic
       resources would qualify as 'good', despite the 'black' accent; this variety has
       been reproduced in Roman in the transcript.
(2)   'Black Englishes': varieties that remind us of African-American 'tough'
       varieties, of Hip-Hop slang and 'talking black'; reproduced in underlined in
       the transcript.

(3)   Rasta slang and varieties reminiscent of Jamaican Creole, reproduced in bold in the transcript.

(4)   'Township English' – a one-word switch ('otherwise') betrays a lower-class accent, widespread in subaltern 'black' varieties of English in the townships; this is reproduced in italics.

The shifts are minuscule – we are not talking about codeswitching in the traditional sense here but about small changes within a continuum of 'English'. The linguistic shifts, however, co-occur with a number of other shifts, and together they produce the sort of dense feature packages mentioned earlier, and they structure the discourse.

(1)   Standard English seems to belong to a place: UCT. Being a black student at UCT means being in a prestigious and previously inaccessible place – an elite place where elite status is articulated, amongst other things, by high-quality Standard English. Ras Pakaay uses Standard English as his 'neutral' mode of interaction on UCT Radio, and he also shifts into it whenever he thematizes UCT Radio itself, as in the time announcements. Standard English, in contrast to some of the other varieties, does not seem to flag gender roles or specific topics – it is a class variety tied to a particular physical and social space.

(2)   Black English occurs in Part 2 of the fragment – the part in which Ras Pakaay narrates an incident with a caller who got cut off just as he was going to put him on air. It is a variety that correlates with narrative style, but it also occurs here and there in his conversation with the female caller. It is a high-performance variety: its use is accompanied by creaky voice, a slow and truncated pace of talk, heavy stress on some syllables, etc. Black English is also gender-marked: it organizes an outspokenly masculine voice producing 'tough', black-male-peer-group talk. Black English is not tied to any particular place, it belongs to a transnational network of male, black, urban and lower-class, disenfranchised youngsters.

(3)   Rasta Slang co-occurs with a clearly marked thematic domain: Reggae and the Rastafari ways of life. Whenever Ras Pakaay refers to songs or to his radio show, for instance, he shifts into Rasta slang and inhabits a Rasta persona. Rasta slang connects Ras Pakaay to transnational networks of Reggae fans and Rastas. Like Black English, Rasta slang is a high-performance variety, and whenever Ras Pakaay shifts into it, we notice singing, heavy stress on some words or syllables, dragged out vowels, rhythmic production of song titles, etc.

(4)   Township English occurs only once, in a repair strategy which Ras Pakaay develops after being challenged by the girl ('why you laughing at me?'). The girl's challenge breaks the interactional routine in which Ras Pakaay normally asks the questions, and the repair work involves a dramatic shift in footing by Ras Pakaay, away from the high-performance, bragging and self-assured verbal display towards a serious, flat, apologetic utterance in which he lapses into the only egalitarian code used in this fragment: Township English. Township English situates talk in the poor black townships – it indexes place and class – and in that sense it is similar to Standard English, both being recognizable accents occupying opposite ranks on the prestige hierarchies within a real social geography in the Cape Town area. Its use defines Ras Pakaay as a member of

the communities living in these townships, and its use is triggered by egalitarian male–female interaction – it is gender-sensitive, but in a very different way than Black English was.

The four varieties also seem to organize particular participation frameworks (in the sense of Goffman 1981). Ras Pakaay, of course, goes public: as a DJ, whatever he says is audible for a large and undifferentiated audience. But his radio show also offers slots for dialogue with individual members of that audience, and so we get a complex and layered pattern of participation, in which the four varieties again seem to play an organizing role.

(1) The 'high-performance' varieties Black English and Rasta slang, one could argue, are *audience-directed,* they target the wider community of listeners rather than individual callers, and they design Ras Pakaay's public persona during the show.

(2) Standard English is also audience-directed (it is the 'neutral' code of UCT Radio), but it is used as well in conversational involvement with callers. The contrast with Township English allows us to infer that Standard English allows Ras Pakaay a speaking position that Goffman called that of a 'principal': 'someone whose position is established by the words that are spoken' (Goffman 1981: 144) – an institutional persona related to a place and a social class.

(3) Township English, finally, here represents a brief moment of *strictly one-on-one* conversational engagement: this is an intimate, egalitarian code that does not allow any 'principal' speaking position for Ras Pakaay, is thus not made to be heard by overhearers, and compels Ras Pakaay to get out of it as fast as he can, back into the audience-directed varieties.

So Ras Pakaay speaks as four different personae: as a member of a privileged elite associated to a prestige place – UCT; as a tough black male, member of a transnational tough black male community; as a Rasta and expert on Reggae music; and as a black township boy trying to appease a black township girl. Each time, the shift in variety and identity also triggers shifts in the kind of relationships Ras Pakaay entertains with his interlocutors:

(1) Standard English, Black English and Rasta slang are all asymmetrical codes, codes over which Ras Pakaay has superior control – specialized registers with restrictions on access, one could say.

(2) Township English is an egalitarian code over which the girl has equal control.

Ras Pakaay's preference for asymmetrical codes becomes clear towards the end of the fragment, when after having produced the flat, prudent Township English apology to the girl, he gradually shifts back into full performance – shifting topics towards 'Reggae' and thus reintroducing the code he can dominate, Rasta slang, and moving back out of the Township sphere in which the girl had dragged him, and into the transnational, nonlocal sphere of Reggae and Rastafarism. For each of the shifts, there appear to be 'ideal-types' – centres – and Ras Pakaay moves in a polycentric environment with at least four such centres. The complexity of the polycentric orientations (another term, one could argue, for 'codeswitching') thus performed can be summarized as in Table 32.1.

Note that in all of this, Ras Pakaay deploys semiotic resources that make sense *locally*. We have seen that the labels I used for the varieties must be understood as referring to relative distinctions within the local repertoires of speakers, and make sense in terms of a local, real, social geography in which accents betray social belonging, trajectories and ambitions. In the transcript, I added phonetic notes, enough to show that Ras Pakaay does not produce any 'stable' variety – South African English shines through in some of his Black English talk, alongside faint traces of his mock Jamaican Creole. However, he brilliantly moves along a continuum of variation that indexically produces relevant distinctions in the specific environment in which he operates: he plays into the orders of indexicality that are locally valid and recognizable.

To put it in simple terms: his Jamaican Creole may be oriented towards an ideal-type – 'real' Jamaican Creole, as it transpires through Reggae lyrics and the speech of prominent Rastas – but its realization is something *recognized as Jamaican Creole in Cape Town*. The same goes for Standard English: what counts is that Ras Pakaay is capable of producing a variety *recognized as Standard in Cape Town* – and so on. The variation he displays is simultaneously oriented towards centres that impose ideal forms and fashions of speaking *and* inserted in a locally salient stratigraphy of variation, and apart from an awareness of 'quality' and where it comes from, we see that Ras Pakaay and his listeners operate on the basis of a real, local political sociology of semiosis. In that particular sociology, Standard English is 'high': in a society where 'good' English is a rare commodity, tied to particular social strata and places such as UCT, it is a linguistic variety which unambiguously qualifies people – especially if they are non-white people – as elite members. Township English, conversely, is a 'low' linguistic commodity, one that identifies speakers as members of a struggling, suffering class and as ethnically–racially marked: black. But within this black world, as well as within part of the wider world of transnational popular culture, linguistic varieties such as Black English, and even more so Rasta slang, are hip, they are linguistic and semiotic emblems of racial pride, solidarity and accomplishment-against-all-odds, of *black cool*. Thus, even partial realizations of these varieties trigger the indexicalities of category and personality that operate within this stratified system – *a little bit* of Rasta slang qualifies one as 'Rasta' in Cape Town and offers one all the indexical benefits of that category.

Conclusion

I hope to have shown in the discussion above how concepts such as orders of indexicality and polycentricity offer us possibilities to connect microscopic instances of communicative practice to larger-scale political and sociological patterns and structures. I consider this an interpretive step in which the detection of what we used to call 'norms' and 'polyphony' is followed by an interpretation of such phenomena as *praxis,* as politically and sociologically 'determined' action – action that *systemically* displays particular, explicable structures and directions, not just incidentally or as by miracle. It forces us to reflect on the fact that every emblem of distinction in societies is subject to dynamics of availability and accessibility, of inclusion and exclusion, and

Table 32.1 Summary of orientations

	Thematic domain	Scope	Performance	Indexes	Gender sensitive	Participation framework	Access
SE	Place: UCT	Local	Low	'High' place & class	No	Audience + conversational (principal)	Exclusive
BE	Black–black male groupness	Global	High	Masculinity, toughness	Yes	Audience	Exclusive
RS	Reggae, Rastafarism	Global	High	Expertise, Rasta identity	No	Audience	Exclusive
TE	Gender roles, conflict	Local	Low	'Low' place & class	Yes	Conversational (intimate)	Egalitarian

that consequently the delicate play of voices in polyphonic discourse tells us a story of that kind – of availability and accessibility, inclusion and exclusion. This, then, offers us a view of variation which is less bucolic than the current ones: difference, we have seen, goes hand in hand with inequality, because every difference can become distinction – valued, hierarchized emblematicity of categories and identities.

The polycentric orientations we have seen organize the discourse produced. They provide its patterns, its 'order' and thus account for its recognizability, value and effect. They provide multiple 'frames', in Goffman's sense, through which, on which and with which people can make sense, and they do so in a socially sensitive way, a way which enables some frames to be played out, organizes relations between frames – some are foregrounded and others (like the interpersonal conversational township frame) remain in the background. Sociolinguistic micro-shifting of this kind thus illuminates sociological substrate processes at work in a particular discursive environment.

Concepts such as these have no *descriptive* advantage over the existing ones, and they should not be seen as substitutes for such terms. They offer an additional *analytic* dimension to established concepts: a dimension of system and structure that allows us to investigate the 'macro' in the 'micro', rather than just posit or presuppose it. Discourse analysis has a long way to go before it will get there; but it needs to start from a sociolinguistics that theorizes the conditions under which discourse comes about or fails to do so.

Bibliography

Agha, A. (2003) 'The social life of cultural value', *Language & Communication* 23: 231–73.
—— (2005) 'Voice, footing, enregisterment', in A. Agha and S. Wortham (eds.) *Discourse Across Speech Events: Intertextuality and Interdiscursivity in Social Life*, special issue of *Journal of Linguistic Anthropology* 15(1): 38–59.

Agha, A. and Wortham, S. (eds.) (2005) *Discourse Across Speech Events: Intertextuality and Interdiscursivity in Social Life*, special issue of *Journal of Linguistic Anthropology* 15(1): 1–150.

Auer, P. (1998) 'Bilingual conversation revisited', in P. Auer (ed.) *Code-switching in Conversation*, London: Routledge, 1–24.

Blommaert, J. (2001) 'Investigating narrative inequality: African asylum seekers' stories in Belgium', *Discourse & Society* 12(4): 413–49.
—— (2005) *Discourse: A Critical Introduction*, Cambridge: Cambridge University Press.

Blommaert, J., Collins, J. and Slembrouck, S. (2005a) 'Spaces of multilingualism', in J. Collins and S. Slembrouck (eds.) *Multilingualism and Diasporic Populations: Spatializing Practices, Institutional Processes, and Social Hierarchies*, special issue of *Language & Communication* 25(3): 197–216.
—— (2005b) 'Polycentricity and interactional regimes in "global neighborhoods"', *Ethnography* 6(2): 205–35.

Brown, G. and Yule, G. (1983) *Discourse Analysis*, Cambridge: Cambridge University Press.

Chouliaraki, L. and Fairclough, N. (1999) *Discourse in Late Modernity: Rethinking Critical Discourse Analysis*, Edinburgh: Edinburgh University Press.

Collins, J. and Slembrouck, S. (eds.) (2005) *Multilingualism and Diasporic Populations: Spatializing Practices, Institutional Processes, and Social Hierarchies*, special issue of *Language & Communication* 25(3): 189–333.

Coupland, N. (ed.) (2003) *Sociolinguistics and Globalisation*, special issue of *Journal of Sociolinguistics* 7(4): 465–623.

Errington, J. (2001) 'State speech for peripheral publics in Java', in S. Gal and K. Woolard (eds.) *Languages and Publics: The Making of Authority*, Manchester: St Jerome, 103–18.

Fairclough, N. (2003) *Analysing Discourse: Textual Analysis for Social Research*, London: Routledge.

Foucault, M. (1984 [1971]) 'The order of discourse', in M. Shapiro (ed.) *Language and Politics*, London: Basil Blackwell, 108–38.

—— (2002 [1969]) *The Archaeology of Knowledge*, London: Routledge.

Goffman, E. (1981) *Forms of Talk*, Philadelphia: University of Pennsylvania Press.

Gumperz, J. (1982) *Discourse Strategies*, Cambridge: Cambridge University Press.

—— (2003) 'Response essay', in S.L. Eerdmans, C.L. Prevignano and P.J. Thibault (eds.) *Language and Interaction: Discussions with John J. Gumperz*, Amsterdam: John Benjamins, 105–26.

Heller, M. (1999) *Linguistic Minorities and Modernity: A Sociolinguistic Ethnography*, London: Longman.

Hill, J. (2001) 'Mock Spanish, covert racism, and the (leaky) boundary between public and private spheres', in S. Gal and K. Woolard (eds) *Languages and Publics: The Making of Authority*, Manchester: St Jerome, 83–102.

—— (2005) 'Intertextuality as source and evidence for indirect indexical meanings', in A. Agha and S. Wortham (eds.) *Discourse Across Speech Events: Intertextuality and Interdiscursivity in Social Life*, special issue of *Journal of Linguistic Anthropology* 15(1): 113–24.

Hymes, D. (1996) *Ethnography, Linguistics, Narrative Inequality: Toward an Understanding of Voice*, London: Taylor & Francis.

Maryns, K. and Blommaert, J. (2001) 'Stylistic and thematic shifting as a narrative resource: Assessing asylum seekers' repertoires', *Multilingua* 20: 61–84.

Rampton, B. (1995) *Crossing: Language and Ethnicity among Adolescents*, London: Longman.

—— (2003) 'Hegemony, social class, and stylisation', *Pragmatics* 13(1): 49–83.

Scollon, R. and Scollon, S.W. (2003) *Discourse in Place: Language in the Material World*, London: Routledge.

Silverstein, M. (1996) 'Monoglot "standard" in America: standardization and metaphors of linguistic hegemony', in D. Brenneis and R. Macaulay (eds.) *The Matrix of Language: Contemporary Linguistic Anthropology*, Boulder, CO: Westview Press, 284–306.

—— (1998) 'Contemporary transformations of local linguistic communities', *Annual Review of Anthropology* 27: 401–26.

—— (2003) 'Indexical order and the dialectics of sociolinguistic life', *Language & Communication* 23: 193–229.

INDEX